Rock Climbing
Joshua Tree

Formerly Joshua Tree Rock Climbing Guide, Second Edition

Randy Vogel

FALCON®
GUILFORD, CONNECTICUT
AN IMPRINT OF THE GLOBE PEQUOT PRESS

A FALCON GUIDE®

Rock Climbing Joshua Tree
Formerly Joshua Tree Rock Climbing Guide, Second Edition

Copyright © 1992 by Randy Vogel
Published by The Globe Pequot Press
Previously published by Falcon Publishing, Inc.

Falcon and FalconGuide are registered trademarks of The Globe Pequot Press.

ISBN 0-934641-30-7

Manufactured in Canada
Revised edition/Fourth printing

WARNING: CLIMBING IS A SPORT WHERE YOU MAY BE SERIOUSLY INJURED OR DIE. READ THIS BEFORE YOU USE THIS BOOK.

This guidebook is a compilation of unverified information gathered from many different climbers. The author cannot assure the accuracy of any of the information in this book, including the topos and route descriptions, the difficulty ratings, and the protection ratings. These may be incorrect or misleading and it is impossible for any one author to climb all the routes to confirm the information about each route. Also, ratings of climbing difficulty and danger are always subjective and depend on the physical characteristics (for example, height), experience, technical ability, confidence and physical fitness of the climber who supplied the rating. Additionally, climbers who achieve first ascents sometimes underrate the difficulty or danger of the climbing route out of fear of being ridiculed if a climb is later down-rated by subsequent ascents. Therefore, be warned that you must exercise your own judgment on where a climbing route goes, its difficulty and your ability to safely protect yourself from the risks of rock climbing. Examples of some of these risks are: falling due to technical difficulty or due to natural hazards such as holds breaking, falling rock, climbing equipment dropped by other climbers, hazards of weather and lightning, your own equipment failure, and failure of fixed protection.

You should not depend on any information gleaned from this book for your personal safety; your safety depends on your own good judgment, based on experience and a realistic assessment of your climbing ability. If you have any doubt as to your ability to safely climb a route described in this book, do not attempt it.

The following are some ways to make your use of this book safer:

1. **CONSULTATION:** You should consult with other climbers about the difficulty and danger of a particular climb prior to attempting it. Most local climbers are glad to give advice on routes in their area and we suggest that you contact locals to confirm ratings and safety of particular routes and to obtain first-hand information about a route chosen from this book.

2. **INSTRUCTION:** Most climbing areas have local climbing instructors and guides available. We recommend that you engage an instructor or guide to learn safety techniques and to become familiar with the routes and hazards of the areas described in this book. Even after you are proficient in climbing safely, occasional use of a guide is a safe way to raise your climbing standard and learn advanced techniques.

3. **FIXED PROTECTION:** Many of the routes in this book use bolts and pitons which are permanently placed in the rock. Because of variances in the manner of placement, weathering, metal fatigue, the quality of the metal used, and many other factors, these fixed protection pieces should always be considered suspect and should always be backed up by equipment that you place yourself. Never depend for your safety on a single piece of fixed protection because you never can tell whether it will hold weight.

Be aware of the following specific potential hazards which could arise in using this book:

1. **MISDESCRIPTIONS OF ROUTES:** If you climb a route and you have a doubt as to where the route may go, you should not go on unless you are sure that you can go that way safely. Route descriptions and topos in this book may be inaccurate or misleading.

2. **INCORRECT DIFFICULTY RATING:** A route may, in fact be more difficult than the rating indicates. Do not be lulled into a false sense of security by the difficulty rating.

3. **INCORRECT PROTECTION RATING:** If you climb a route and you are unable to arrange adequate protection from the risk of falling through the use of fixed pitons or bolts and by placing your own protection devices, do not assume that there is adequate protection available higher just because the route protection rating indicates the route is not an "X" or an "R" rating. Every route is potentially an "X" (a fall may be deadly), due to the inherent hazards of climbing, including, for example, failure of fixed protection, your own equipment's failure, or improper use of climbing equipment.

THERE ARE NO WARRANTIES, WHETHER EXPRESS OR IMPLIED, THAT THIS GUIDEBOOK IS ACCURATE OR THAT THE INFORMATION CONTAINED IN IT IS RELIABLE. THERE ARE NO WARRANTIES OF FITNESS FOR A PARTICULAR PURPOSE OR THAT THIS GUIDE IS MERCHANTABLE. YOUR USE OF THIS BOOK INDICATES YOUR ASSUMPTION OF THE RISK THAT IT MAY CONTAIN ERRORS AND IS AN ACKNOWLEDGEMENT OF YOUR OWN SOLE RESPONSIBILITY FOR YOUR CLIMBING SAFETY.

PREFACE

Climbing at Joshua Tree and in general, has changed a lot in the five-and-a-half years since the 1986 edition of this guide was published. The most obvious changes: a whole lot more climbs, and a whole lot more climbers. Most of these climbers are climbing at higher and higher difficulty levels.

Yet the changes at Joshua Tree have been more than an mere increase in numbers. For most climbers, personal style and so-called climbing "ethics" have become a less divisive issue. Instead, the rapidly-growing threat to climbing access nationwide has brought most climbers together.

Climbers have come to realize (myself included) that environmentally-sound climbing practices are the only "ethics" that really matter. How a bolt was placed often is less important than whether it is in the right place (and solid). Most importantly, bolt hangers should be camouflaged to blend with the rock. Placements should be thought out, and most importantly, they should be **discreet.**

Twenty years ago, Joshua Tree seem a limitless climbing resource, untouched and likely to remain that way. In the intervening years, exploration of the monument by climbers has grown at a pace few could have foreseen. Not only does this mean that guide books go out of date a lot faster, but also that climbers can have a real impact on the fragile desert ecology.

Climbers are, on the whole, much better stewards of the land than most visitors. In the past several years, climbers have organized trash clean-ups, removed routes from sensitive areas (Soviet Block and Schwarzenegger Wall), built bathrooms and paid for trail markers. Yet much more can and should be done to mitigate impacts. In the introduction, there is detailed information on what each one of us can do to minimize our impacts and ensure continued access.

It is my hope that this guide reflects the changes that have happened at Joshua Tree in a positive and thoughtful manner. I also hope that all climbers will work together (not against each other) to ensure a long future for climbing at Joshua Tree. I also strongly urge **every** climber to join The Access Fund and support local organizations such as Friends of Joshua Tree.

A guidebook is mostly a compilation of the collective knowledge of the climbing community. Without the contribution of many individuals, this guide would never have been possible. I would like to thank all those people who helped or provided information for the 1986 edition. I also am particularly indebted to: Todd Swain, who helped me tromp around and locate innumerable routes; Alan Bartlett, who shared much information from his vast personal knowledge and his guidebook manuscript; the ever-present Todd Gordon, whose information and was tremendously helpful; Don Wilson, who helped straighten out information; Dave Mayville, whose tours of several new areas was greatly appreciated; and Jonny Woodward, whose comments and suggestions were always right on the mark.

Other people who went out of their way to provide information and were generally a tremendous help include: Louie Anderson, Geoff Archer, Todd Battey, Bill Cramer, Dave Evans, Craig Fry, Geoff Fullerton, Bob Gaines, Mari Gingery, Warren Hughes, Randy Leavitt, Mike Lechlinski, Roger Linfield, Troy Mayr, John Mireles, Al Peery, Rex Pieper, Jeff Rhoads, Kelly Rhoads, Aleida Weger and James Weger.

Other individuals deserve mention for providing route information, suggestions or corrections: such stuff is grist of a guidebook editor. They include: Agust Agustsson, Robert Alexander, Rich Baerwold, Jeff Ball, Scott Batie, Steve Bour, Larry Braten, Chris Breemer, Andy Brown, Dana Brown, Manfred Buchroithuer, Cam Burns, Randall English, Randy Faulk, Stan Horn, Peter Hunt, Robert Hynes, Eric Jackson, Craig Kain, Joe Kelsey, Eric Knuth, Larry Kuechlin, Mark Niles, Mark Pfundt, Allen Sanderson, Mike Shacklett, Steve Shearer, Alois Smrz, Kris Solem, Mark Spencer, Mike Stewart, Allison Stocks, Roy Suggett, Kevin Thaw, Mark Uphus, Mike Van Volkom, Lavon Weighall, Mike Witteried, Todd Worsfold, Kevin Zimlinghaus, and Mike Zinsley.

I would also like to thank Bill Freeman, John Mireles, Kevin Powell and Troy Mayr for providing the excellent action shots that grace the covers and interior of this guide. Lastly, I would like to acknowledge the patience and tireless assistance of Sarah Tringali, who helped in many important ways.

To the other individuals who provided information, help or encouragement whom I may have inadvertently failed to specifically mention, Thank You.

TABLE OF CONTENTS ——————————

INTRODUCTION
    Getting There...1
    Being Square..2
    Beware 3
    Climbing Season...4
    About The Rock..5
    Equipment 5
    Staying at the Monument 6
    Off Road Travel 8
    Ratings..8
    About Trash 11
    About Chipping, Gluing and Bolting 13
    New Route Information 14
    How to Use This Guide 15

QUAIL SPRINGS 23

WONDERLAND OF ROCKS – NORTH 43

LOST HORSE 81

ROADSIDE ROCKS...................................135

REAL HIDDEN VALLEY 148

HIDDEN VALLEY CAMPGROUND 183

THE OUTBACK...208

ECHO ROCK AREA 229

COMIC BOOK AREA...258

BARKER DAME AREA...267

WONDERLAND OF ROCKS 279

QUEEN MOUNTAIN...333

SHEEP PASS 357

GEOLOGY TOUR ROAD...397

DESERT QUEEN MINE AREA 423

JUMBO ROCKS 434

LIVE OAK AREA...448

SPLIT ROCKS 452

LOVELAND...467

BELLE CAMPGROUND..473

WHITE TANK CAMPGROUND 476

STIRRUP TANK..479

OZ AREA 488

INDIAN COVE..504

ROUTES BY RATING...552

INDEX...584

INTRODUCTION ─────────────────────

Joshua Tree National Monument is one of the most popular climbing areas in the world. Climbers from all over the United States, as well as Europe, Japan, Australia and elsewhere have visited (and enjoyed) this truly unique climbing area. Joshua Tree also has a very large population of "local" climbers, including a large number of individuals who actually live in the Joshua Tree area, as well as climbers throughout southern California who call Joshua Tree "home."

This introduction is intended to help both the seasoned regular and the first-time visitor understand how to use the book and how to minimize environmental impacts. There is also information about how to get to Joshua Tree, weather, camping, park regulations and, of course, some thoughts on ratings and equipment.

MINIMIZE YOUR IMPACT

Rock climbers constitute a significant percentage of all visitors to this beautiful and often wild part of southern California's high desert. For this reason, climbers must take particular care to ensure their visit to the monument has as minimal an environmental impact as possible. Although climbers, as a group, tend to be among the most environmentally-conscientious users, carelessness has resulted in officials taking a intense and often critical look climbing activities in the monument and elsewhere in the United States.

As a result, considerable space in the introduction is devoted to what you, the individual climber, can do (or not do) to ensure minimal climbing restrictions and continued access for all climbers. I believe it is critically important that all climbers familiarize themselves with how to use the monument in an environmentally-sound manner. In this regard, every climber should support groups dedicated to preserving access and the environment for climbers, such as The Access Fund and The Friends of Joshua Tree.

Be responsible; unfortunately, the thoughtless act of one individual can affect the rights of everyone.

HOW TO GET TO JOSHUA TREE

Joshua Tree National Monument is located in the high desert of eastern southern California, approximately 140 miles east of Los Angeles and 35 miles northeast of Palm Springs.

FROM SOUTHERN CALIFORNIA

Most climbers "approach" the monument from metropolitan southern California:

From the Los Angeles area, plan on a 2.5- to 3-hour drive. Take either Interstate 10 or U.S. 60 east to Beaumont/Banning, and continue on Interstate 10.

From the Orange County area, plan on a 2- to 2.5-hour drive. Take U.S. 91 east to Riverside, then take U.S. 60 east to Beaumont/Banning where it merges into Interstate 10.

From the San Diego area, plan on a 2.5- to 3.5-hour drive. Take Interstate 15 eastbound north to U.S. 60, then head east to Beaumont/Banning, and continue on I-10.

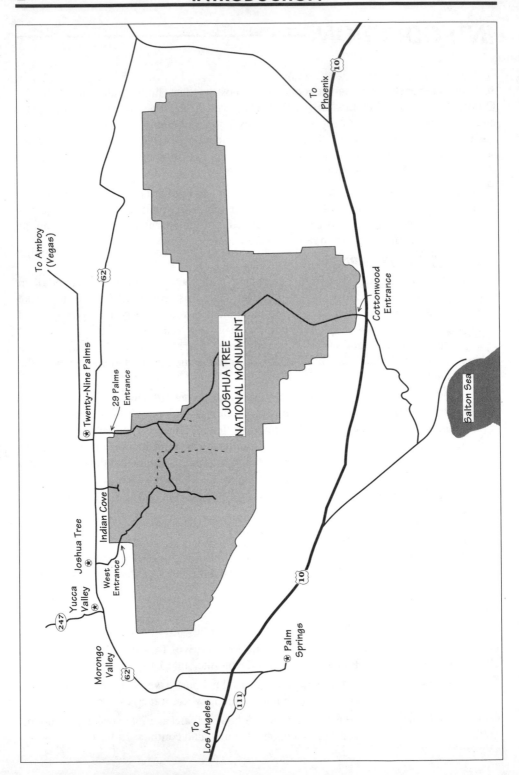

From Beaumont/Banning, continue east on Interstate 10 past the Palm Springs/Highway 111 exit to the U.S. 62 exit north (to 29 Palms). Several uphill grades take you through Morongo Valley to Yucca Valley. The town of Joshua Tree is several miles past Yucca Valley. From Joshua Tree, turn right (south) on Quail Springs Road, and follow it directly to the monument entrance some 5 miles up the road.

FROM POINTS NORTH AND EAST

If headed towards Joshua Tree from the north or east, you can take many routes and shortcuts to the monument. Here are a few suggested routes.

FROM THE LAS VEGAS AREA

A particularly good shortcut directly to 29 Palms begins approximately 55 miles west of Los Vegas (on Interstate 15). Travel through the railroad towns of Cima and Kelso, past the Granite Mountains, then cross Interstate 40 and head through Amboy to 29 Palms. This road is extremely desolate, and a few miles follow a well-graded dirt road. The alternative (normal) route is to take I-15 to Barstow, then take Highway 247 south until it terminates in Yucca Valley.

FROM THE BAY AREA AND PACIFIC NORTHWEST

From the San Francisco Bay Area and Pacific Northwest, head south via either Interstate 5 or Highway 99 to Bakersfield. From Bakersfield, take Highway 58 east to Barstow (Highway 58 turns into I-40). From Barstow, take Highway 247 south to Lucerne Valley, and continue to Yucca Valley.

Highway 247 becomes Old Woman Springs Road where it intersects Highway 62 (29 Palms Highway) in Yucca Valley.

FROM THE SOUTHWEST

From the southwestern part of the United States (Arizona, New Mexico, etc.), one can take U.S. 10 west directly to the monument entrance near the City of Indio (through the southern Cottonwood entrance). Alternatively, one can take I-40 west, then head south to Amboy and eventually to 29 Palms.

The above are only suggested routes; climbers will undoubtedly find their own shortcuts. A good road map is suggested.

VIA AIRLINE OR BUS

Other climbers may, for practical reasons, make their initial "approach" via commercial airlines to either the Los Angeles Area or Palm Springs. Although a rental car is helpful to get around the monument, it is, by no means, a necessity. Bus transportation is available from Palm Springs (about 35 miles southwest of the monument) to the towns of Yucca Valley, Joshua Tree and 29 Palms via Desert Stageline, (619) 367-3581. The Desert Stageline Bus leaves both Palm Springs Airport and the Palm Springs Greyhound Bus Terminal three times daily.

ENTRANCE FEES

Prior to 1987, entrance to Joshua Tree National Monument was free. These days, the National Parks Service imposes an entrance (user) fee. As of the date of this writing, the fees are as follows:

$2 per walk-in/rider or bus or motorcycle (good for seven days).

$5 per vehicle (no limit on occupants and good for seven days).

$15 for the Joshua Tree yearly pass (good for one calendar year, Jan. 1 to Dec. 31, only at Joshua Tree National Monument).

$25 for the Golden Eagle Pass, which may be used at all National Parks and monuments (good for one calendar year, Jan. 1 to Dec. 31).

There is no charge for camping in the monument, with the exception of the Black Rock and Cottonwood Campgrounds. However, since neither Black Rock or Cottonwood are frequented by climbers, camping is essentially free.

CLIMBING SEASON

The single most important factor for Joshua Tree's popularity with climbers lies in its climbing season. When most other areas are covered in snow or rained out, Joshua Tree is often sunny and warm. The season starts in early to mid-October and extends to late April or early May.

The best periods for climbing run from late October to early December and early March through April. However, there is no such thing as a sure bet with the weather, and some seasons have wonderful Januarys and Februarys and terrible springs. The monument receives approximately 7.5 inches of precipitation per year, with nearly 40% falling (oddly enough) during the months of July, August and September. Because of the large number of local climbers living near the monument, it is not unusual to see climbers in

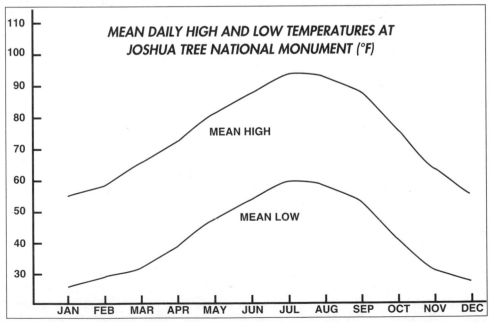

Joshua Tree during the summer months. Additionally, it is quite possible (but certainly not a sure bet) that temperatures may be quite reasonable even during July, August and September. The following mean high and low temperatures by month help illustrate the variance in temperature at Joshua Tree during the year.

ABOUT THE ROCK

The rock formations at Joshua Tree tend to be dome-like, and in most cases are surrounded by flat sandy washes and open plains. Some of the rock formations, in fact, are no more than a huge pile of stacked boulders. Other formations lie on hillsides, but still tend to be dome-like. Many formations have a number of boulders around their bases. These boulders offer numerous, excellent problems at the most severe level. While there are many established bouldering spots and problems, there remains a tremendous untapped potential for bouldering.

Joshua Tree rock is granitic in origin, of a type called quartz monzonite. The rock in the monument is part of a huge underground sea of granite (a batholith) that has pushed its way to the surface throughout this area of southern California. Due to the particular way the rock has cooled and was subsequently weathered, it is generally quite rough in texture. This means there is a high friction coefficient and a need to use care to avoid cuts and scrapes.

Fortunately, for climbers, this translates into a rock surface that is very climbable. Sections of formations that look unclimbable or hideously hard may be only moderately difficult. Steep faces also often have "plates," which provide large hand holds.

The cracks at Joshua Tree are plentiful, and vary from shallow and flared to clean and split. Generally, areas with coarser rock (e.g.: Jumbo Rocks) sport flaring cracks, whereas rock of a more compact structure tend to have cleaner, deeper cracks (Queen Mountain, etc.). Camming devices are extremely helpful (and often necessary), and provide protection in flared or horizontal cracks that are commonly seen in the monument.

Generally, the western faces of the rock formations are lower-angled and rougher in texture. The eastern faces are steeper, often overhanging, and the rock usually is much smoother, even polished. These different textures have resulted from the way the rock has faulted and weathered.

Crystallin and other dikes crisscross many of the formations. In fact, it is possible to trace a single intrusion as it crosses various different formations. Such dikes have provide numerous excellent traversing and vertical face climbs.

It is not uncommon for the rock at Joshua Tree to vary considerably in quality. It can range from quite grainy and loose to extremly high in quality and smooth. Certain areas are known for poor rock; other areas have mostly excellent rock. However, as a general rule, the rock tends to be sound, and if the rock of a certain climb is loose or granular, it tends to become solid after several ascents.

EQUIPMENT

Unlike some climbing areas, Joshua Tree is a relatively "traditional" climbing area, although there are a large number of "sport" routes. Usually, it is necessary to place some protection and anchors, even at the tops of bolted face routes. Many of the bolted face routes also require use of natural protection.

If you are used to climbing exclusively on sport routes, remember that even fully bolted face climbs at Joshua Tree may not have "sport"-type protection. It may be possible to take long falls. Additionally, because of the shortness of many climbs and a sensitivity about placing too many bolts, many face climbs remain are "toprope" problems and should be left that way.

For the purposes of discussion, a "standard Joshua Tree rack" (if there is such a thing) should consist of camming devices (.5 through 3 inches), small to medium wired nuts (.25 inch to .75 inch), micro-nuts (brass-aluminum) and an assortment of quickdraws and runners.

There has been an attempt in this guide to list general protection requirements for routes when this information was readily available. Many climbs listed do not have any recommended protection sizes, and it would be best to take a good selection.

STAYING AT THE MONUMENT

CAMPING

There are many campgrounds in the monument, but only five campgrounds at which climbers will be interested in staying. On many weekends, all of these are congested. The weekend climber should plan on getting a site early or having a friend hold one. Since there is no fee for most of the camping, there is no means of reserving a campsite (except for group camping in Sheep Pass, which is reserved through the national monument). However, there is no compelling reason to reserve campsites in the monument, as most visitors make day trips from the Los Angeles srea. To contact the visitor's center, call (619) 367-7511. To contact the monument headquarters, call (619) 367-6376.

Generally, climbers stay in Hidden Valley Campground. Not only is this campground near many fine climbs (often right outside one's "front door"), it is very close to most other major climbing areas. Climbers who plan extended stays in Joshua Tree should know that there is a 14-day per year camping limit in the monument. Because of the popularity of Hidden Valley Campground with climbers (and all other campers), this campground is where most camping limit problems arise. For this reason, it is probably best, if planning a long stay, to make alternative arrangements.

Other campgrounds frequented by climbers are, in preferential order: Ryan, Jumbo, Belle and Indian Cove. However, due to its remote location, Indian Cove is a practical alternative only for climbers who intend to climb exclusively in Indian Cove and Rattlesnake Canyon.

There are virtually no formal car camping areas outside the monument. The sole exception is Knott's Sky Park in 29 Palms (which is primarily a RV park). Rates are approximately $7.50 per day.

EATING

There is no water or food available in the monument. For this reason, either stock up before entering the monument or have a car at your disposal. For many climbers who cook meals over campstoves, the nearby town of Yucca Valley has several well-stocked, modern supermarkets. Additionally, in recent years, the towns of Yucca Valley, Joshua Tree and 29 Palms have sprouted a virtual swarm of reasonably-priced restaurants, as well as "fast food" places.

SHOWERS

Although you won't get as dirty climbing in Joshua Tree as you might in Yosemite and other mountain areas, climbers in the monument have been known to need occasional showers. This necessitates a trip into town. The most popular place to shower is Lee's Health Club in Yucca Valley. Hours are: Monday-Wednesday-Friday from 6 a.m. to 9 p.m.; Tuesday and Thursday from 9 a.m. to 9 p.m.; Saturday from 8 a.m. to 5 p.m.; and Sunday from 8 a.m. to 1 p.m. For $4, climbers can work out and shower, or for $2.50 ($3 with towel), just shower. Lee's is very friendly towards climbers, and welcomes your business. Lee's is about 5 blocks west of Denny's at 56460 29 Palms Highway, Yucca Valley. The telephone number is 619-365-9402.

CAMPFIRES

If you want an evening campfire, bring wood with you (it can be purchased in town). No natural vegetation (dead or not) may be gathered for burning or any other purpose in the monument. The desert ecology depends on natural decay of plant life; the removal of this decaying matter by visitors is damaging to the delicate balance of life. Aside from being an environmentally-unsound practice, it is illegal; you can be cited by a ranger and fined.

MOTEL ACCOMMODATIONS

Climbers who travel long distances to the monument for short visits may find all the campgrounds full, or may not have brought camping gear with them. These climbers may want to stay in one of the many reasonably priced motels in the Yucca Valley and 29 Palms area. All the following motels are recommended and welcome climbers' business:

OASIS OF EDEN MOTEL (60 rooms, unique "theme" rooms, pool, continental breakfast)
56377 29 Palms Highway
Yucca Valley, CA 92284
(619) 365-6321
Rates: $34.75 to $49.75

YUCCA SUPER 8 MOTEL (48 rooms, pool, HBO, group discounts)
57096 29 Palms Highway
Yucca Valley, CA 92284
(619) 228-1773 (800) 800-8000
Rates: $34.88 to $42.88

DESERT VIEW MOTEL (14 rooms, pool, in-room coffee, HBO)
57471 Primrose Drive
Yucca Valley, CA 92284
(619) 365-9706
Rates $34.50 to $42.50

YUCCA INN (55 rooms, 17 with kitchens, workout room, climber discounts, pool)
7500 Camino Del Cielo
Yucca Valley, CA 92284
(619) 365-3311
Rates: $36.00 to $57.98

OFF ROAD TRAVEL

Mountain bikes frequently are used by climbers as a quick and easy way to get from one climb to another. However, climbers should be aware that the use of mountain bikes (or any vehicles) off established roads is prohibited. Bicycles can cause accelerated damage to the fragile desert environment. Violation of this monument rule is grounds for both citation and imposition of a fine. To encourage compliance with this policy, the monument has placed several bike racks at convenient locations.

Because of the number of climbers visiting the monument, literally hundreds of informal trails have been created by repeated foot traffic. Many of these paths run next to, across and duplicate others. These approaches must be consolidated to minimize impact of walking from the car to the crags. In an effort to help consolidate these "braided" trails, The Access Fund and the monument have installed, at several popular climbing areas, trail marker signs. Please follow the trails indicated by the signs, and use only consolidated and established footpaths where possible. Try to follow the footpaths of others so consolidated trails can form. Climbers also can minimize their impact by walking in sandy wash areas whenever possible.

RATINGS

All the climbs in this guide have been given a difficulty rating, and where applicable, a quality and/or protection rating.

DIFFICULTY RATINGS

The difficulty rating system used in this guidebook is the Tahquitz Decimal System, (also known erroneously as the Yosemite Decimal System – YDS). This system is used throughout the United States, and most climbers are familiar with its idiosyncracies.

Climbing routes are rated on an ascending scale from 5.0 (the easiest climbs requiring ropes and belays) to 5.14 (currently, the most difficult climbs). Within the 5.10, 5.11, 5.12, 5.13 and 5.14 categories, the subgrades of a, b, c and d are used to denote finer distinctions in difficulty.

Climbers may find the ratings at Joshua Tree harder or easier than what they are accustomed to. Although the ratings given to routes in the monument generally are consistent, **the ratings given some routes may be wrong.** Inconsistent ratings stem from many different things. Many climbs in the monument have seen few ascents, so no consensus rating has formed. Some first ascensionists chronically over-rate or under-rate difficulty. Other climbers have different opinions based upon their own strengths and weaknesses. Keep this in mind, take the ratings with a grain of salt (or granite) and use your own judgment.

A rating comparison chart is included on the next page to help foreign climbers determine the relative difficulty of the climbs listed.

QUALITY RATINGS

The "star" or "quality" rating used in the first edition of the Joshua Tree guide, and Joshua Tree Select, is again used here. This system is designed to let climbers know which are better climbs.

Climbs are given no stars if they are considered average or less-than-average in terms of overall quality. If routes are thought to be of above average quality, they are given one to

INTERNATIONAL RATING SYSTEMS COMPARED

West German	YDS	British	Australian	East German	French
	5.0				
	5.1				
	5.2				
	5.3				
	5.4				
	5.5				
	5.6				
5+	5.7			VIIa	5a
6-	5.8		15	VIIb	5b
6	5.9		16 / 17	VIIb	5c
6+	5.10a		18	VIIc	6a
7-	5.10b		19	VIIIa	6a+
7	5.10c		20	VIIIb	6b
7+	5.10d		21	VIIIc	6b+
8-	5.11a			IXa	6c
8	5.11b		22		6c
8	5.11c		23	IXb	6c+
8+	5.11d		24	IXc	7a
9-	5.12a		25	Xa	7a+
9	5.12b		26	Xb	7b
9	5.12c		27	Xb	7b+
9+	5.12d		28	Xc	7c
10-	5.13a				7c+
10	5.13b		29		8a
10	5.13c		30		8a+
10+	5.13d		31		8b
11-	5.14a		32		8b+

five stars (the more stars, the better the route). Five star routes are acknowledged classics. This system is highly subjective. Since quality ratings are still a new phenomenon in the United States and most climbers are unfamiliar with them, this rating system is far more unreliable than a difficulty rating. Additionally, there may be no consensus formed about certain climbs that deserve stars; they may not have recieved their due in this guide. Consequently, use it as an indication only, and remember that many "unstarred" routes may, in fact, be worthy of your attention (and vice versa).

PROTECTION RATINGS

Most climbs at Joshua Tree tend to be either reasonably well-protected or topropeable. For this reason, systematic use of protection ratings has not been used in previous guidebooks. However, some climbs in this guide have less than "perfect" protection (whatever that is).

In other climbing areas in the United States, protection ratings are a popular way to warn climbers of poorly-protected climbs. This guide attempts to give tentative protection ratings for such routes. However, what constitutes good protection for one climber may be poor protection to another. This is especially true for climbers trained on well-protected, bolted "sport climbs." If your protection skills are rusty or undeveloped, you may find some routes very difficult to adequately protect. Also, little consensus exists for protection ratings. Do not rely on the absence of a protection rating to indicate good protection. Use common sense.

In this guidebook, "R" and "X" ratings are given. The definition of "R" and "X" ratings here may be slightly different than those used by other guidebook authors. To understand the use of these protection ratings, please read this section carefully.

This guide does not use either the G or PG protection ratings. The protection ratings in this guide are **not** intended to tell you that a climb is well protected; you should **never** presume that a route not given a R or X rating is well-protected.

"R" Rating. If a route is poorly-protected **at its difficult sections,** but not without some protection, it is given a "R" rating. A fall on a "R"-rated route, at the wrong place, could result in very long or serious fall, and could cause injury or worse. (Technically, a long or even deadly fall could occur on almost any route).

"X" Rating. If a climb that is so poorly protected **at the difficult sections,** that a severe fall, (e.g. hitting a deck) is possible, it is given an "X" rating. A fall from the wrong place on a route with an "X" rating could result in severe injury or death.

The "R" and "X" ratings in this guide are intended as a guideline only. Only you can be the judge of whether a route is adequately enough protected for you. Please note, many easier routes that deserve a protection rating may not have them. **Never assume a route without a protection rating is safe.** You, alone, are responsible for your own safe climbing. Comments are welcome, so this tentative rating system can be improved.

ABOUT TRASH, POOT SLINGS
AND OTHER FORMS OF POLLUTION

Climbers have become one of the larger users of Joshua Tree National Monument. There are certain areas of the monument that once were rarely visited by humans, but are now heavily used, almost entirely by climbers. Climbers can have a very real (and negative) impact on the delicate desert environment of Joshua Tree. The responsibility for lessening this impact rests with each and every climber. However, climbers tend to cause less impact than some visitors. Major resource impacts are identical to those of hikers, sightseers, etc.

One of the most tangible forms of environmental impact inflicted by climbers on the monument is the refuse they leave behind. This trash takes many forms, however, the most common and serious forms of trash pollution are discarded (used) tape, improperly disposed of human waste (including toilet paper), and "poot" slings (runners left on fixed protection or anchors).

While there is absolutely no excuse for ever leaving used tape behind (this will easily fit into your pack or pocket), the proper disposal of human waste is a bit trickier. Unfortunately, convenient restroom facilities are not available in most areas in the monument. For this reason, The Access Fund has installed restrooms near several popular climbing areas. Use these restrooms. Where restrooms are not available, climbers must use common sense and care when using the "facilities a la natural." A few rules should be observed. Don't ever leave human waste near waterways (i.e., dry stream beds). When it rains in the monument, this waste will pollute the valuable and scarce rain water that is relied upon by many animals in the monument. Human waste also should never be left on or near the many informal trails that climbers use. Although many climbers make a habit of burying their waste, the fact remains that in desert areas human waste decomposes the quickest when not buried. Soiled paper should be carried out in a small, plastic zip-lock bag; this is the only way to ensure that the dry desert environment does not have to struggle for years to decompose it on its own.

"Poot" slings are often an unsightly and unnecessary form of pollution. There is now available, at almost every climbing shop, natural (rock-colored) webbing. Every climber should carry some of this webbing, so should it be necessary to leave webbing behind, it will not clash with the rock. Additionally, when climbers, for some unknown reason, tie slings directly into bolts, it may be impossible for subsequent climbers to clip into the hangers. There is very little reason to tie directly into a bolt with a runner (except at anchors). Looping a sling through a bolt works just as effectively, and means that subsequent parties can remove the sling easily. Furthermore, climbers should familiarize themselves with ways of retrieving slings after rapping off fixed protection (this is almost always possible in Joshua Tree).

Brightly-colored bolt hangers (as opposed to natural-colored bolt hangers) contribute to visual pollution (they have been banned in the monument since June of 1989). The continued use of bright hanger invites the banning of all bolting. Colored bolts serve no functional purpose on the relatively short climbs of Joshua Tree. Climbers installing bolts (or replacing bolt hangers) **should only buy bolt hangers that blend with the natural rock color.** "Rock colored" bolt hangers currently are available at a very modest premium over regular bolt hangers. Buy only natural-colored bolt hangers. Encourage your retailer to carry only rock-colored hangers.

What makes colored bolt hangers (and even regular bolt hangers that clash with rock surface) objectionable is that they have actually precipitated numerous access problems and resulted in restrictive regulation throughout the United States. You can do something about brightly-colored webbing or colored bolt hangers. Buy only natural-colored slings (or only leave these slings behind), and refuse to buy or install colored bolt hangers or bolt hangers that are not natural-colored.

Climbing in the United States is, for the most part, very different than in Europe and elsewhere. Europe has **no** wilderness areas at all. Joshua Tree is largely wilderness. Climbers should adopt at Joshua Tree (and elsewhere in the United States) only those "trends" that make sense in such a wilderness setting.

THE ACCESS FUND

The Access Fund is a national, non-profit climbers organization, and is at the forefront of efforts to preserve climbing areas throughout the United States. In support of climbers' interest, The Access Fund provides financing for land acquisitions and support facilities, funds scientific research, publishes educational materials promoting low-impact climbing and environmental awareness, and provides start-up money, free legal counsel and organizational resources to local climbers' groups.

In Joshua Tree National Monument, The Access Fund has provided financing for the Climber Information brochures handed out by the monument, put up trail signs in popular areas (to cut down on braided trails) and paid for installation of restroom facilities near popular climbing areas (Echo Rock, Hall of Horrors and Wonderland Ranch).

The funding of these projects are just a few of the many projects undertaken by The Access Fund. The Access Fund has provided financing to purchase climbing areas or provide important resource improvements (parking lots, bathrooms, trails, signs, etc.) in areas from California to Connecticut, City of Rocks to Hueco Tanks and Boulder Mountain Parks to Mississippi Palisades, Illinois.

Every climber should contribute generously to The Access Fund; access affects everyone. Climbers must realize that unlike participants in other sports, climbers traditionally have not contributed toward the real cost of climbing. By acting together through The Access Fund, climbers can directly participate in saving the rich diversity of climbing in the United States. No one can afford to stand on the sidelines on this issue.

The Access Fund is also the only national organization dedicated on a daily basis to the prevention of unreasonable and overly-restrictive regulation of climbing, and the promotion of environmentally-sound climbing practices. You can help The Access Fund by sending a tax-deductible donation to: The Access Fund, P. O. Box 67A25, Los Angeles, California, 90067.

ABOUT CHIPPING, GLUING AND BOLTING

Currently, it is illegal in the monument to use motorized (electric) drills to place bolts. It also is illegal throughout the National Park System to chip holds or use glue to add or reinforce a hold.

BOLTS

If anything is to be said about bolts at all, it is that climbers should:

1. Install (and buy) **only** camouflaged hangers.

2. Use only ⅜ or ½-inch diameter bolts (¼-inch bolts are not secure in Josh rock).

3. Be discreet as to **where** and **how** you place bolts. Avoid bolting next to public trails/parking areas or where visually intrusive.

The monument banned electric bolt drills in 1989. This development is regrettable, as electric drills made feasible the traditional-style bolting of even the most difficult climbs, as well as the near-universal use of three-eighth-inch and half-inch bolts. Banning power drills will not stop the explosion of new routes, but it has and will make climbing more dangerous, and thwart a "traditional" climbing ethic at Joshua Tree.

Adding bolts to an established route is so seldom justified that it should be rarely considered. However, it may be necessary when: (1) belay bolts are inadequate or need reinforcing (belays should always be bomb-proof); (2) an existing bolt has come out or is in such poor shape that is needs replacing; or (3) when replacing older quarter-inch bolts with more reliable three-eights-inch or half-inch bolts. When replacing an old bolt, it should be pulled directly out, not "chopped." The old hole can either be drilled out to a larger size, or filled with epoxy and the mouth covered with granite dust.

Additional protection bolts generally should not be placed on existing routes. Routes are being given protection ratings to warn of some of the more runout climbs. Because different people establish routes in different styles, some routes will be perceived "under-protected" by some people, and other routes will be considered "over-protected" by others. The boldness (or lack of boldness) used by the first-ascent party when establishing a particular route should be respected.

There appears to be a movement among some climbers to turn many toprope problems at Joshua Tree into leadable "sport" climbs. Because of the fact that bolting is such an explosive issue with the National Park Service, U.S. Forest Service and other land managers, the practice of bolting established toprope routes is discouraged. If local consensus is that a climb should be bolted, only rock-colored bolt hangers should be used.

CHIPPING

The "chipping" or "improving" of holds is never acceptable. It also is illegal, and robs future climbers of the ability to establish harder and harder routes. Chipping or adding holds to a route (or potential route) presumes no one will ever be able to climb at a higher standard; therefore it is ok to alter the rock. History (including recent history) has proven the falsity of such thinking. In the early 1970s, climbers were chipping on routes such as Outer Limits (5.10c) in Yosemite.

In fact, in recent years, climbers in France chipped and improved holds on routes that were then considered to be at the limit of difficulty. However, in looking for more difficult climbs to develop, climbers realized the routes they had previously chipped were in fact the routes they were seeking.

If the reasons given above are not in any way compelling to you, also consider that the National Park Service and other public land managers have placed climbing activities under microscopic scrutiny. While the use of bolts for protection currently is acceptable and defensible, there is no defense for the impacts caused by chipping holds. The National Park Service has made it a crime to chip or manufacture holds on rocks. Consider also that if the very small minority of climbers who chip holds continue such practices, the overly-restrictive regulation of all climbing could result. Unfortunately, one climber's actions affect every other climber, not only at Joshua Tree, but throughout the United States.

GLUING

Although the use of epoxy glue on rock at Joshua Tree is extremely uncommon, certain individuals and the National Park Service have made this a major issue. In the past, a small number of climbs at Joshua Tree have had epoxy placed behind certain loose holds in order to "reinforce" them and keep the hold from coming off after repeated use. It is an understatement to say that there is severe and divisive disagreement among climbers about the use of glue for reinforcement of holds.

Nevertheless, it currently is illegal in Joshua Tree National Monument (and the entire National Park System) to use epoxy glues for the purpose of attaching or reinforcing natural or artificial holds. Since this regulation has come into effect, the use of glue at Joshua Tree has ceased for all practical purposes. Unfortunately, certain climbers wishing to hammer the point home and be "proven right" have made much more of this issue with Park Service officials than was warranted. The obvious consequence of this has been the disparagement of all climbers (the overwhelming majority of which have never used or thought of using glue). This also has created exaggerated bad press as to climbers' actions.

To avoid such situations in the future, it is urged that climbers not use epoxy anywhere in the monument. Not only is it illegal, but it inevitably affects the rights of all climbers.

NEW ROUTE INFORMATION

Now that this comprehensive guidebook is completed, I do not wish face the nightmare of accumulating more route information to revise this book in several years. Instead, regular supplements to this guide will be issued. To accomplish this, all route information, as received, will be put into a data base, and will, periodically (every 6 months or so), be compiled and printed in the form of inexpensive supplements.

However, to ensure that new route information is received, all new route information should be mailed directly to: Randy Vogel, P. O. Box 4554, Laguna Beach, CA 92652.

The quality (and sufficiency) of new route information varies wildly. Some individuals provide wonderfully detailed information with photographs (even photo overlays), while some provide descriptions that are totally worthless or confusing at best. To ensure that new route information is useable (and included in updates), here are a few tips on how to submit new route information:

1. Provide the **name** of the route, the **rating** (try to use a, b, c or d rather than plus or minus), the approximate **date** of the first ascent, and the **full names** of the first ascent party.

JOSHUA TREE NEW ROUTE CORRECTION/SUBMISSION FORM

NAME OF ROUTE _____

RATING (Please use a, b, c or d for all 5.10, 5.11, 5.12 or 5.13s) _____

FIRST ASCENT (FFA) PARTY _____

DATE OF FIRST ASCENT OR FFA _____

TYPE OF PROTECTION (List # bolts, size in inches of nuts, fixed pins, fixed anchors, etc.)

PROTECTION RATING (R or X, if warranted) _____

QUALITY RATING (0 to 5 stars) _____

LOCATION (Reference to photos in guide, route number of nearby routes, maps in guide appreciated. A photo is always helpful. A xerox of photo/map in guide with route/formation marked is great.)

_____
_____
_____
_____
_____

ATTACHMENTS: ☐ MAPS(S) ☐ PHOTO(S) ☐ OTHER

☐ CHECK HERE IF THE ABOVE/BELOW IS A CORRECTION TO THE GUIDE

OTHER RELEVANT INFORMATION

_____
_____
_____
_____
_____
_____

HOW TO CONTACT YOU IF MORE INFORMATION IS NEEDED
(Your address and phone number)

_____
_____

TO SUBMIT THIS INFORMATION: Copy this page and send in an envelope addressed to: RANDY K. VOGEL, P.O. Box 4554, LAGUNA BEACH, CA 92652.

2. If the route lies adjacent to an existing route, give directions or reference in relation to an existing route, including the route number used in this guide. You should also give approximate distances (right or left) in feet or yards.

3. Enclose a photograph of the climb (snapshots are fine) – this is extremely helpful in locating the route so that it can be described for publication. You may wish to mark directly on the photograph with a pen the line taken by the route, including the location of any bolts or fixed pins.

4. A map is extremely helpful. If a route (or a formation) that you are describing is located somewhere in an area covered by a map in the guide (even if the formation is not specifically shown), xerox the map from the guide (you are given permission for the sole purpose of submitting route information) and show on the map where the route or formation lies. Similarly, if a photograph in the book shows the route, xerox the photograph out of the guide and mark the route right on the xerox copy.

Remember, just because a climb is reported in a climbing magazine or is written down somewhere does not mean it necessarily finds it ways into my hands. The best approach is to send the route information directly. Your assistance in this regard is greatly appreciated. I would like to again thank all of the many individuals who have submitted route information in the past – in essence, this has become "their" guidebook.

HOW TO USE THIS GUIDE
ORGANIZATION
Generally, this guide is arranged in the order that you would encounter rock formations as you drive into the monument from the Joshua Tree (west) entrance. Obviously, since the monument is an incredibly complex area, the guide makes "side trips" into various areas, depending on where the best approach route is located as you drive into the monument. Believe it or not, there is some logic to the order of description.

MAPS, PHOTOS AND DESCRIPTIONS
For nearly every area in this book, there is an overview map showing the various rock formations. The rough geographical area of each new section, as defined by the header at the top of the page and monument map on pages 18 and 19, is shown at the start of each section as a shaded area on a minature overview map of the monument. On all other maps, the rock formations are simplified into single line closed figures. For the most part, these maps have been taken from information obtained from the United States Geological Survey, and tends to be fairly accurate. I have used overview maps liberally, as well as more detailed locator maps for specific formations/climbs. These maps usually are located adjacent to the pertinent route information, and there should always be a reference in the guide to the closest map that covers the area in question. In addition, most maps have references to other maps that may be adjacent.

There also is liberal use of photographs for the identification of formations as well as specific routes. Usually, the line of the route is drawn in on the photo, and often this is in the form of a "topo." Maps, verbal descriptions and photographs should be used together to locate routes.

In some cases, (to keep the size and cost of this book down), no photographs are used of particular areas or formations. In this case, verbal descriptions and maps are used.

Generally, climbs are described on a cliff from left to right. Exceptions usually are noted and (it is hoped) obvious.

Often, directions are given in the description of routes. If "right" or "left" is used, this refers to direction assuming you are facing the cliff. Additionally, north, south, east and west (and combinations thereof) are used. Often, these are only approximations. Likewise, distances between formations and climbs may only be approximate as well. Directions and distances should be used in conjunction with maps, photographs and other verbal descriptions to locate climbs and formations.

Topo and map symbols used in this book are as follows:

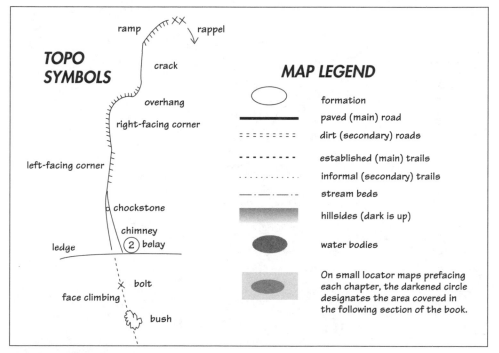

CORRECTIONS

Sometimes, the information provided in ths guidebook may not be entirely clear or may have inaccuracies. Please send any corrections to this information to the author at P.O. Box 4554, Laguna Beach, CA 92652. All corrections and suggestions are welcome.

INDEXES

This guide also contains several indexes. There is a general alphabetical index to all climbs and formations. This will direct you to a particular climb or area. This index also lists the difficulty, protection and quality ratings, as well as the route name and page numbers. Additionally, there is Routes by Rating Index, which compiles all climbs in the monument by their ratings. This index also lists page and route numbers, and quality and protection ratings. If you are looking for climbs of a particular difficulty, merely look in the Routes by Rating Index, then refer to the page number indicated.

You will also notice that in the Routes by Rating Index, a small box is located in front of

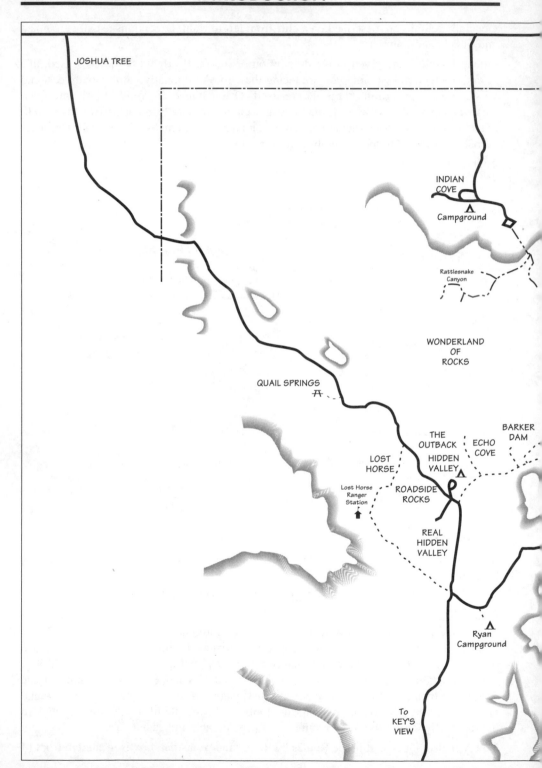

JOSHUA TREE

INDIAN COVE

Campground

Rattlesnake Canyon

WONDERLAND OF ROCKS

QUAIL SPRINGS

THE OUTBACK

ECHO COVE

BARKER DAM

LOST HORSE

HIDDEN VALLEY

Lost Horse Ranger Station

ROADSIDE ROCKS

REAL HIDDEN VALLEY

Ryan Campground

To KEY'S VIEW

29 PALMS

QUEEN
MOUNTAIN

OZ

DESERT QUEEN
MINE

SPLIT
ROCKS

SHEEP PASS

yan
untain

JUMBO ROCKS

Belle
Campground

White
Tank
Campground

Pinto Basin

To
COTTONWOOD

GEOLOGY TOUR
ROAD AREA

STIRRUP TANK

Hexie Mountains

the name of every route. As with prior Joshua Tree Guides, this is indeed a "check-off" box, which can be used as a check list of all the climbs that you have done (or wish to do) in the monument.

HISTORY

Joshua Tree has a relatively long and interesting climbing history. Many top climbers climb regularly or have visited Joshua Tree and left their mark in the many fine climbs that exist. As you will see, no first-ascent information is provided in this guidebook. This was not a easy decision to make, as I feel first-ascent information often is very helpful, as well as one of the principal resources for historical information about climbing. However,to fit the huge number of climbs into one volume, first-ascent information was removed and will, along with a more detailed history of climbing the monument, be available in a separate volume. The removal of first-ascent information reduces the size of this book by nearly 80 pages! This also resulted in a considerable saving in cost.

Joshua Tree's early climbing days are shrouded in mystery. Little is known about the period from 1940 to the early 1960s, when climbing in the monument was in its infancy. What is known is that local hardmen such as Royal Robbins, T.M. Herbert, Mark Powell, Eric Beck, Tom Frost and others frequented the monument during this time framealong with other climbers who found respite in the area's temperate winter climate.

For the most part, activity took place when poor weather closed more alpine areas, like Tahquitz and Yosemite. Climbers simply bided their time at Joshua Tree until some "real" climbing was in condition. It was commonly felt that Joshua Tree was merely a "practice area," and for the most part this feeling prevailed throughout the 1960s and into the early 1970s.

Unfortunately, no one took JT climbing seriously enough to record route names or first-ascent parties. It is known, however, that many of the obvious cracks in the Hidden Valley Campground area were free climbed in the late 50s and early 60s.

From the mid 60s to the beginning of the 70s, several new groups of climbers "discovered" Joshua Tree. The predominant group, "The Desert Rats," included Woody Stark, Dick Webster, John Wolfe, Bill Briggs, Dick James, Al Ruiz, Howard Weamer and others. There also was a group of Los Angeles area climbers who regularly climbed Joshua Tree during this period of time. These climbers were generally unaware of their predecessors' (and contemporaries') accomplishments. Generally, free climbing standards were years (if not decades) behind what was being done in Yosemite, Tahquitz, Colorado and the Shawangunks.

In 1970, the first "official" guidebook was published (although rumor of an earlier underground guidebook remains unconfirmed). None of the routes listed were more difficult than 5.9; most routes were 5.7 or under, and aid was common. The appearance of this guidebook focused more attention on the monument and climbing experienced a boom.

In the early 70s, climbers such as Richard Harrison, Rick Accomazzo, John Long, Tobin Sorenson, Jim Wilson and John Bachar brought high free-climbing standards to the monument. In two short years (1970 to 1972), the most difficult routes went from 5.9 to 5.11.

Development also began to intensify outside the campground, and areas like Saddle Rocks, Hall of Horrors and the Rusty Wall saw development.

Classics of the early 70s include **Illusion Dweller** (5.10b, 1973), **The Exorcist** (5.10a, 1974), **Hyperion Arch** (5.11c, 1974), **O'Kelley's Crack** (5.10c) and **Wanger Banger** (5.11c). Other climbers active in the early 70s were Matt Cox, Spencer Lennard, David Evans, Randy Vogel and Dean Fidelman.

By the mid and late 70s, exploration of the monument began in earnest. People began to look at the vast route potential in the Wonderland of Rocks. Climbers "discovered" the Astrodomes, and within a few short years established classics such as **Solid Gold** (5.10a), **Such A Savage** (5.11a) and **Figures on a Landscape** (5.10b).

For the most part, the majority of climbs established in the monument in the late 70s and the early 80s were established by a few groups of individuals, including Dave Evans, Randy Vogel, Charles Cole, Herb Lager, Craig Fry, Kevin Powell, Gib Lewis, John Bachar, Tony Yaniro, Mike Lechlinski, Randy Leavitt, Vaino Kodas and Alan Nelson.

Since about the mid 80s, an increasing number of climbers have established new routes at the monument. Difficulty standards also began to take a big leap in the mid to late 80s and early 90s. Many extremely difficult "sport" routes have been established in the Wonderland of Rocks and elsewhere. Amazingly enough, a tremendous number of new areas were discovered and developed. Prolific climbers of recent years include Geoff Archer, Scott Cosgrove, Mike Lechlinski, Mari Gingery, David Evans, Todd Gordon, Alan Bartlett, Don and Karen Wilson, Todd Swain, Craig Fry, Bob Gaines, Todd Battey, Louie Anderson, Walt Shipley, David Bengston, Troy Mayr, Todd Swain, Jonny Woodward and many others. Development of new routes at Joshua Tree continued at an unending pace (please slow down!).

TRIVIA QUIZ

The following trivia quiz is intended to provide entertainment on cold, rainy or rest days. Due to the fact that all first-ascent information is being published in a separate volume, much of this trivia relates to the cultural history of the monument (with a few climbing-related questions as well). All the answers can be found in this book, although the questions may presume knowledge of other generally known events or historical facts. Bonus point questions require information or knowledge outside the purview of this guide.

1. How many "poodle" routes are there in the monument?

2. What was the first "poodle" route? (Bonus: What was the name of the poodle who inspired the route name?)

3. What was the first 5.12 in the monument? (Bonus: Who was the first person to lead this route and who first free soloed it?)

4. What route was named after a 1973 science fiction movie staring Sean Connery? (Bonus: Name the director.)

5. Who was Worth Bagley and what rock formation bears his name?

6. What route names where inspired by a Sir Arthur Conan Doyle novel? (Bonus: When was this book written?)

7. What route was named for an Oscar Wilde play? (Bonus: What was the subtitle of this play and when was it first staged?)

8. What routes were named for two runners involved in a racing "mishap," and where did this mishap occur?

9. What route is named after a song in the musical *West Side Story?*

10. What route is named after former annual event in the town of Joshua tree?

11. What route has increased in difficulty the most since it was put up, and what was its original rating? (Bonus: What other name has been attributed to this route?)

12. When was the first Joshua Tree Guidebook published? (Bonus: Who wrote this guide, how many routes were described and what significant erroneous rating was in the guide?)

13. What route is named after a Lina Wertmuller film? (Bonus: What is the film's full title, when was it released and which actors staring in the movie?)

14. What route's original name was taken from the title of a Ken Kesey book, and what was that original name?

15. When was the Desert Queen Mine discovered, and by whom? (Bonus: How old was this person when he discovered the mine?)

16. What happened to the Desert Queen Mine prospector and where is he buried? (Bonus: Who is buried next to him, and where did this other person work?)

17. Who built the "original" Barker Dam?

18. When did Jim McHaney move to the Joshua Tree area, and where did he first live?

19. Where did Bill McHaney spend his last years, and what is his relation to Jim McHaney?

20. Name 4 members of the McHaney Gang.

ANSWERS:

1. 31

2. Poodles Are People Too. (Bonus: Gus)

3. Just Slightly Ahead of Our Time

4. Zardoz. (Bonus: John Boorman)

5. An ex-LA County Sheriff who was shot by Bill Keys in 1943 near the Wall Street Stamp Mill; Worth Bagley Memorial Dome.

6. The Baskerville Cracks (Hound Rocks). (Bonus: 1902)

7. The Importance of Being Ernest [sic]. (Bonus: The Importance of Being Earnest was subtitled "A Trivial Comedy For Serious People"; first staged February 14, 1895.)

8. Zola Budd and Mary Decker, 1984 Olympic games.

9. When You're a Jet.

10. Turtle Days.

11. Pinched Rib, 5.7. (Bonus: Snake Dike.)

12. 1970 [2nd printing, 1973]. (Bonus: John Wolfe, 76 routes, The Damper was rated 5.5 in the first printing [it is 5.9]).

13. Swept Away (Bonus: Swept Away By An Unusual Destination In The Blue Sea of August: 1975; Biancario Giannini and Marangela Melato).

14. Illusion Dweller: Original name: Candy Colored Tangerine Flake Streamlined Baby.

15. In 1894, by Frank James. (Bonus: 35 years old)

16. He was shot/murdered; he is buried near Ryan Ranch (near Ryan Campground.) (Bonus: Lopes, Mexican miner who worked at the Lost Horse Mine.)

17. George Myers.

18. 1879, Desert Queen Ranch (Keys Ranch).

19. At a cabin near the Indian Wave Boulders; they were brothers.

20. George Myers, Charles Martin, Willie Button and Charley Button.

LIZARD'S LANDING

This area lies .75 mile northeast of the main road into the Joshua Tree National Monument (Quail Springs Road). You'll find Lizard's Landing at a point about 1.8 miles (2.9 km) towards Hidden Valley Campground from the Joshua Tree entrance to the monument. A small pullout is on the left side of the road just where the road makes a sharp right (southerly) turn. Several approaches are possible. From the parking area, you can hike northeast along a old road (100 yards) to a gravel pit. The easiest approach is to head east-northeast about .5 mile up the low hillside, skirting to the east of the hill ahead. From here, head roughly north (and slightly west) .4 mile over low ridges to the Central Formation. An alternative approach (longer and rougher) begins at the gravel pit and

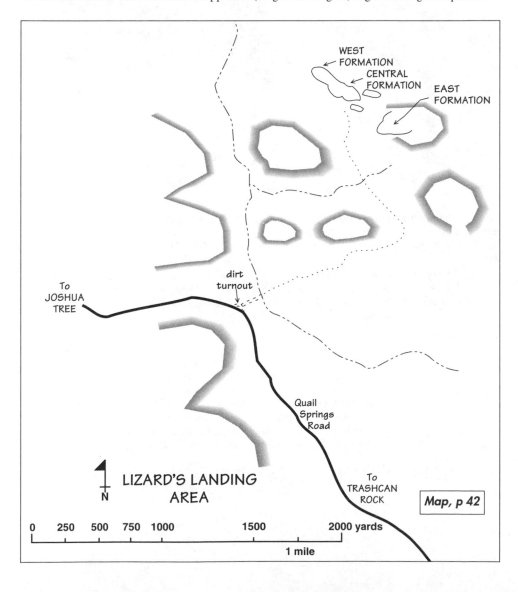

WEST FORMATION

CENTRAL FORMATION

EAST FORMATION

To JOSHUA TREE

dirt turnout

Quail Springs Road

To TRASHCAN ROCK

LIZARD'S LANDING AREA

N

Map, p 42

0   250   500   750   1000   1500   2000 yards

1 mile

heads to the north along an obvious wash for about .4 miles, until you can make a sharp right up a steep side wash (which levels out); follow this for .2 mile east, then head roughly .3 mile north to the Central Formation (joining the other approach at this point). Plan on 20 to 30 minutes for the approach.

The Central (westernmost) Formation sits lower down and to the north of the point where the approach ends. The East Formation lies on the western edge of a higher hill about 300 yards to the east. The Western Formation, which lies immediately adjacent to and west of the Central Formation, has no recorded routes (it appears somewhat loose).

CENTRAL FORMATION
See map on page 23.

1 **MARK OF ZORRO 5.11b ★★** This overhanging thin crack lies on the backside of a small formation in front (south) of the main Central Formation. The crack has a "Z" shape to it.

2 **LAST TICKET TO OBSCURITIVILLE 5.9 ★** This is located on the central rock formation. The climb follows a giant flake that starts out of an alcove located half way up the south face of the rock. Climb up to the alcove, and then up the flake to the summit.

3 **MAXWELL GRUNSTER 5.10a** The crack/corner about 10 feet right of **Last Ticket To Obscuritiville.**

4 **TWO AGAINST EVEREST (AKA: ON THE BACK) 5.11c ★** This steep, quarter-inch crack is on the north face of the summit block of the Central Formation.

EAST FORMATION

See map on page 23.

5   **LIZARD'S LANDING 5.7** ★   This route follows the west buttress of the formation to the east of the Central Formation. Climb ledges and cracks to a chimney that leads to the summit.

6   **JET STREAM (AKA: MOMENTARY LAPSE OF REASON) 5.10b R** ★★   This route lies on the right-hand arête of the second terrace of the East Formation; the upper face has two protection bolts. Pro: Small to 3 inches, two bolts.

7   **BIGHORN BIVVY 5.8+** ★   Start 40 feet right of **Jet Stream,** climb up to and over a roof, then continue up thin cracks above.

8   **CANINE CRACK 5.9+**   This right-leaning crack is 150 yards right of **Jet Stream,** on south face the of rock.

9   **THE BONE CLUB 5.10a R** ★★   This left-facing corner is 30 feet to the right of **Canine Crack,** and on the east face. Climb past three bolts just to the left of the corner.

10   **LITTLE CRIMINALS 5.10b** ★★   This also is a left-facing corner about 30 feet right of **Canine Crack** on the east face.

11   **TEETER TOTTER 5.9**   Climb the thin, left-facing flake about 10 feet to the right of **Little Criminals.**

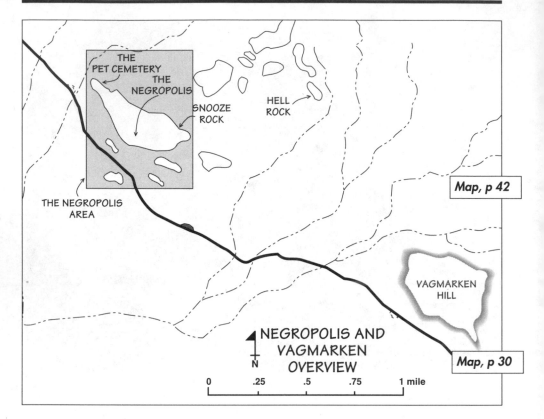

THE NEGROPOLIS AREA

This area encompasses several varied formations that lie about a large hill on the left (east) side of Quail Springs Road, approximately 3.3 miles past the Joshua Tree entrance to the monument and 2.4 miles before you get to Trashcan Rock.

THE NEGROPOLIS

This series of brown buttresses lies high on the west side of the large hill described above.

12　**SLAP PRANCING　5.8+**　A one-bolt route on the pillar to the left of **Dance on Fire.**

13　**DANCE ON FIRE　5.11a R　★★★**　This is the three-bolt face climb on the left side of the buttress.

14　**TAP DANCING　5.11a R ★★★**　Start just right of **Dance On Fire**. Climb a face and thin crack past two fixed pins.

15　**RAP DANCING　5.10a or c**　(depending on start)　This two-bolt face route is around the corner and to the right of **Tap Dancing** on the same block.

16　**I FALL THEREFORE I AM　5.10c**　This route is on the next pillar to the right of the pillar containing **Tap Dancing**. Start out of gully, climb past three bolts, then use the wide crack above, avoiding bolts on arête to the left.

17　**ATROPHY　5.9 ★**　The clean, overhanging crack on the left of the upper block of **I Fall Therefore I Am.**

18　**B FOR BEERS　5.10b R ★★**　This is approximately 100 feet right of **Tap Dancing**. Climb a dike system past three bolts.

19　**GIRLS IN THE MIST　5.10d ★★★**　BIG black block on the far right side of the Negropolis area. Four bolts.

THE NEGROPOLIS

THE PET CEMETERY

This area is actually on the back (east) side of The Negropolis, near the northern end of the formation. Park at the pullout on the east side of Quail Springs Road near the north end of the Negropolis hillside. There are actually two small formations; the left one is the largest. The routes are described left to right.

20 **PET CEMETERY 5.11b ★★★** This route follows overhanging rock past five bolts to a lower-angled crack on the left side of the larger formation.

21 **BONECRUSHER ARETE 5.8 ★** Start in a gully system at the right end of the large formation, step left, and follow the dark arête to the top. Pro: Small to 2 inches.

22 **SKIN AND BONES 5.4 R** Follow the featured face just left of the crack system on the left side of the smaller (right) formation.

23 **NO BONES ABOUT IT 5.5** This is the prominent crack in the center of the smaller formation.

SNOOZE ROCK

Snooze Rock lies on the southernmost part of the east side (away from the road) of The Negropolis hill. The best approach is to park as for The Pet Cemetery and walk about .25 mile to the south. Snooze Rock is a small formation with excellent rock and a prominent arête.

24 **NAPTIME FOR MEGGLES 5.9 ★** Follow the left side of the arête past an overhanging start, passing one bolt up higher.

HELL ROCK

This formation faces south and is located to the east of The Negropolis Area. It is best approached by parking in the paved turnout (on the east side of Quail Springs Road) about .5 mile past The Negropolis. Hike northeast to the first (southernmost) hillside with rock formations. This formation has a large boulder perched on its top.

25 **ROUTE OF ALL EVIL 5.11d ★★** The route on the left. Pro: To 2 inches, four bolts.

26 **NO REST FOR THE WICKED 5.12a ★★** Just right of **Route Of All Evil.** Pro: To 2 inches, four bolts.

27 **BOLTERS ARE WEAK 5.8 R** Climb up the dike, over the roof and right up the crack on the face. This is to the right of the above routes.

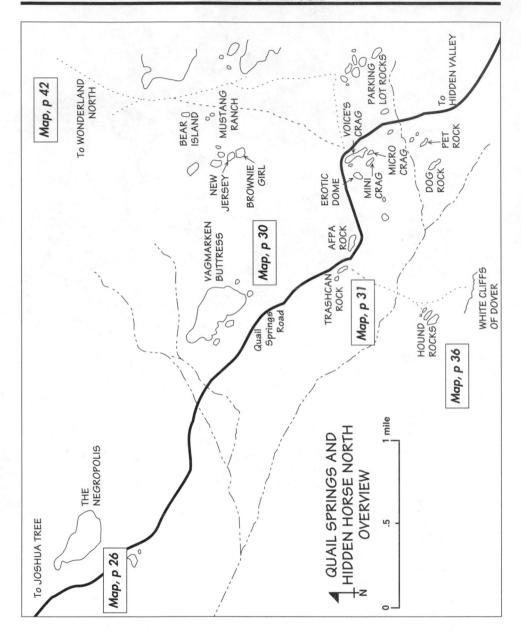

QUAIL SPRINGS AND HIDDEN HORSE NORTH OVERVIEW

VAGMARKEN HILL

Vagmarken is the large hill that comes into view approximately 5.5 miles past the Joshua Tree Entrance to the monument and 1.2 miles before you reach Trashcan Rock. It is on the left (east) side of the road. The known routes lie either on small brown formations on the lower left-hand (northwest) portion of the hillside (The Intimidator Rocks), or on the larger buttresses (Vagmarken Buttresses) to the right and higher on the hillside.

THE INTIMIDATOR ROCKS

28 **JUST STOP IT 5.10b** Climb up and right along a dike past two bolts, then straight up to the top. Pro: Small to 2 inches.

29 **BOLD IS A FOUR LETTER WORD 5.10a ★** Start near the toe of the buttress; climb past four bolts. Pro: Anchors, four bolts.

VAGMARKEN BUTTRESSES

There are several "buttresses" high on the hillside. The known routes are on either the left buttress (up and right from The Intimidator Rocks) or the right buttress (which is characterized by two long white dike systems). Map, page 30.

VAGMARKEN – LEFT BUTTRESS

30 **THE PODIUM OF INDECISION 5.10b (5.7 var)** This is the bolted face route up the varnished rock left of the **Vagmarken Buttress** route. If you traverse to larger holds in the gully on the left, the route is 5.7. Pro: Small to 2 inches.

31 **VAGMARKEN BUTTRESS 5.7** Climb the middle of the buttress past one bolt.

32 **VAGABONDS 5.8 R** A red dihedral rises 50 feet right of the **Vagmarken Buttress** route. Climb up into the dihedral, then exit (bolt) to the lower-angled face above. Pro: Small to 2 inches.

VAGMARKEN – RIGHT BUTTRESS

This formation is characterized by two long white dikes.

33 **THIN SPIN 5.8** To the left of the Right Buttress is yet another formation. On the left side of this formation is a thin, low-angled crack that ends at a two-bolt belay/rappel anchor.

34 **THE GEAR THIEF 5.6** This is on the left side of the Right Buttress, to the right of **James Brown's**. Start high in the gully in a crack that slants to the right, then heads back left. Pro: To 3 inches.

35 **JAMES BROWN'S CELEBRITY HOT TUB PARTY 5.10b** This route climbs the right white dike. Pro: To 2 inches, two bolts.

36 **THE RIGHT HAND DIKE 5.10a** This route ascends thin cracks and lieback flakes on the right white dike.

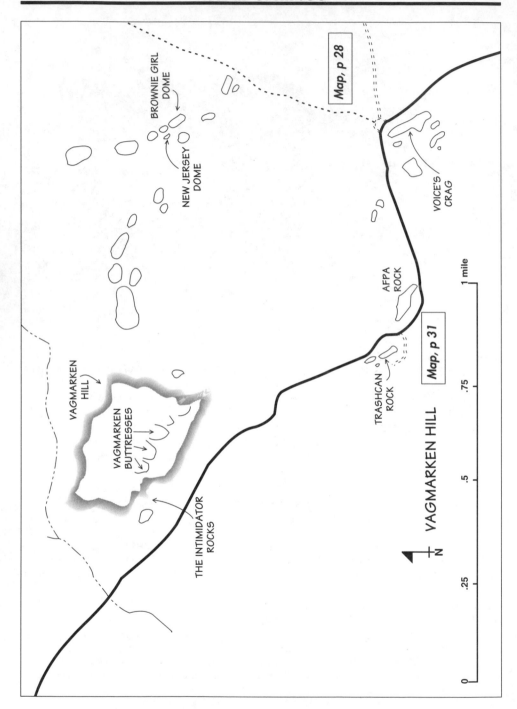

BROWNIE GIRL DOME

NEW JERSEY DOME

Map, p 28

VOICE'S CRAG

AFPA ROCK

Map, p 31

TRASHCAN ROCK

VAGMARKEN HILL

VAGMARKEN BUTTRESSES

THE INTIMIDATOR ROCKS

N

VAGMARKEN HILL

0   .25   .5   .75   1 mile

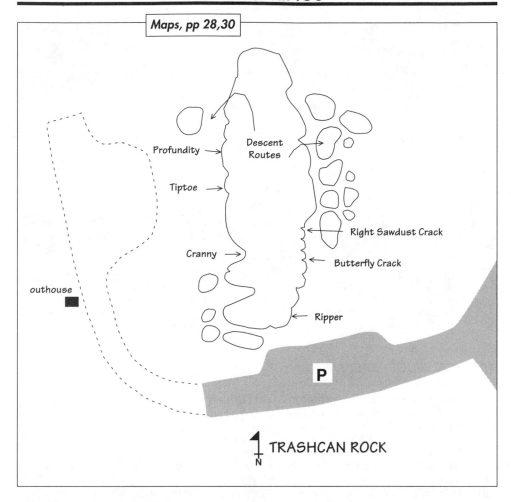

Maps, pp 28,30

Profundity →

Descent Routes

→

Tiptoe →

→ Right Sawdust Crack

Cranny →

← Butterfly Crack

outhouse

← Ripper

P

↑ TRASHCAN ROCK
N

TRASHCAN ROCK (Quail Springs Picnic Area)

Trashcan Rock is the first formation of major importance encountered on the drive into the Monument from the town of Joshua Tree. A paved parking area, picnic table and bathroom are found here, but no camping is allowed. The Park Service has designated this area for day-use only. This is a fine beginners' area. Trashcan Rock is located on the right (west) side of the road, approximately 6 miles from the park entrance. This area also serves as parking for Hound Rocks and The White Cliffs of Dover, located to the southwest.

TRASHCAN ROCK – EAST FACE

Easiest descent is off the north end of the formation. Map, page 31.

37   **FILTH**   **5.8 R**   Start atop a boulder left of **Filch;** climb short cracks past a horizontal.

38   **FILCH**   **5.5**   Wide and forgettable.

B1   **RIPPER**   **5.11**   Boulder problem.

B2   **GRIPPER TRAVERSE**   **5.10**   Boulder problem traverse.

39   **WALLABY CRACK 5.8 ★**   Pro: To 3 inches.

40   **HERMANUTIC**   **5.10c R ★★**   Thin and hard to protect at crux. Pro: Mostly small to 2 inches.

41   **BUTTERFLY CRACK**   **5.11c ★★★**   The classic on the formation. Start with a boulder problem-like crux at the bottom, which leads to easier (5.9) climbing. Pro: Small wired nuts to 3 inches.

42   **LEFT SAWDUST CRACK**   **5.10c ★**   Usually toproped; crux at the top. Pro: Small to 2 inches.

43   **RIGHT SAWDUST CRACK**   **5.8 ★★**   Hand crack. Pro: Med. to 2.5 inches.

TRASHCAN ROCK
WEST FACE

TRASHCAN ROCK – WEST FACE

Many of the face routes (with exception of **Tiptoe** and **Profundity**) are unprotected and usually toproped. Descend off the north end of the rock. Map, page 31.

44   **EYESTRAIN 5.2**   Easy rib right of **Eyesore.**
45   **EYESORE 5.4**   Not worth any stars.
46   **SIMPATICO 5.1**
47   **BLACK EYE 5.9 R**   Pro: A bolt and thin nuts to 2 inches.
48   **BLOODYMIR 5.9**
49   **CRANNY 5.8 ★★**   A fun route up double cracks. Pro: To 2 inches.
50   **HISTORY 5.11a (TR)**   Climb the face between **Cranny** and **Eschar.**
51   **ESCHAR 5.4 ★**   Pro: Medium to 2.5 inches.
52   **BIMBO 5.10a R/X**   Crux at the bottom. Pro: Either toprope or climb with no pro.
53   **TULIP 5.6 R/X**   Runout with little pro.
54   **BABY-POINT-FIVE 5.8 R/X**   Hard entry moves (unprotected) to easy crack-ramp.
55   **WALKWAY 5.4 R**   Unprotected crux at bottom.
56   **B-1 5.1 ★**   Pro: To 3 inches.
57   **TIPTOE 5.7+ ★★**   Fun route past three bolts.
58   **B-2 5.3 ★**   Pro: To 3 inches.
59   **PROFUNDITY 5.10a (or 5.10c)**   Two bolts. Going straight up past the bolt is more difficult than going slightly right, then up.
60   **B-3 5.3**   Pro: To 3 inches.
61   **KARPKWITZ 5.6**
62   **THE TROUGH 5.0**

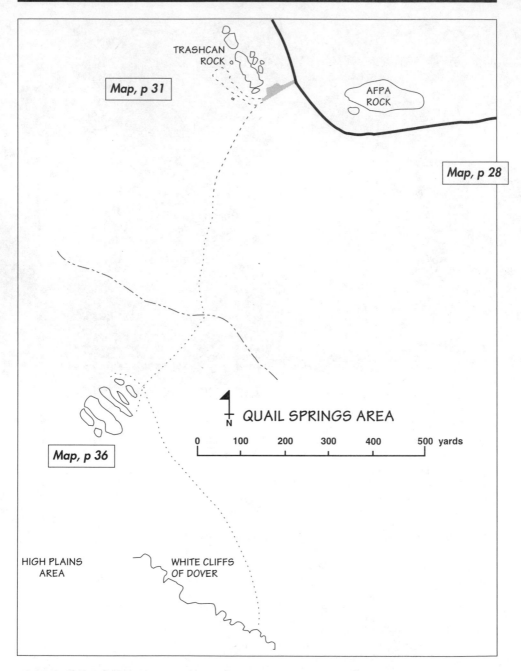

TRASHCAN ROCK

Map, p 31

AFPA ROCK

Map, p 28

QUAIL SPRINGS AREA

N

0   100   200   300   400   500 yards

Map, p 36

HIGH PLAINS AREA

WHITE CLIFFS OF DOVER

HOUND ROCKS

These rocks are located approximately .5 mile (.8 km) southwest of Trashcan Rock. Park at the Trashcan Rock parking area and follow a rough trail to this area. Many fine crack routes are found here. Most of the routes lie on the eastern faces of two principal rock formations.

BASKERVILLE ROCK

The first (and smaller) of the Hound Rocks is Baskerville Rock. The following routes all lie on the east face. Descend off back (west) side, behind **Right Baskerville Crack.** Map, page 36.

63   **WEATHERING FRIGHTS   5.9**

64   **STEMULATION   5.9 R ★**

65   **SOUND ASLEEP   5.10b**

66   **LEFT BASKERVILLE CRACK   5.10b R**   An awkward start and wide, hard-to-protect portions above do not make this a popular choice. Pro: To 5 inches

67   **TALKING ABOUT MY VARIATION   5.9**   Pro: Thin to 2 inches.

68   **A GREAT TR, BUT DON'T BOLT ME   5.11b (TR) ★★**

69   **RIGHT BASKERVILLE CRACK   5.10a ★★★**   THE classic climb in this area, on good rock. Pro: Small to 2 inches.

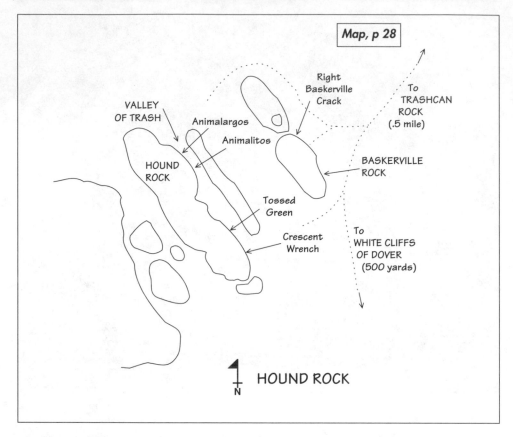

Map, p 28

Right
Baskerville
Crack

To
TRASHCAN
ROCK
(.5 mile)

VALLEY
OF TRASH

Animalargos

Animalitos

HOUND
ROCK

BASKERVILLE
ROCK

Tossed
Green

Crescent
Wrench

To
WHITE CLIFFS
OF DOVER
(500 yards)

HOUND ROCK

N

HOUND ROCK

This is the larger of the two main formations. Several good crack routes lie on the east face and are described below. The small gully along the base of the east face is dubbed "The Valley of Trash" because it is littered with old cans and bottles from early homestead/mining days (Please do not remove these). The west face has a number of crack routes that vary from 5.6 to 5.9 in difficulty; these are not described. Easiest descent is down the south end of the formation.

70   **DIRECT WRENCH 5.11a (TR)**
71   **CRESCENT WRENCH 5.10d ★★**   Pro: Many small to 1.5 inches.
72   **AN EYE TO THE WEST 5.9 ★**   Pro: Medium to 2.5 inches.
73   **TOSSED GREEN 5.10a ★★★**   Pro: Many to 2.5 inches.
74   **WHITE POWDER 5.7**   Pro: To 3.5 inches.
75   **OVER THE HILL 5.9**   Pro: To 3 inches.
76   **ANIMALITOS 5.11b ★★**   Pro: Many small to 2.5 inches.
77   **ANIMALARGOS 5.11c R ★★★**   Pro: Good variety of small to 3 inches.

WHITE CLIFFS OF DOVER

WHITE CLIFFS OF DOVER

This band of cliffs is approximately .75 mile (1.2 km) south of Trashcan Rock, and approximately .33 mile south-southeast of Hound Rocks. It sits high on the hillside. The rock tends to be quite excellent, and although a bit of a hoof, well worth it. The approach to the White Cliffs of Dover is essentially the same as that for Hound Rocks. Most routes are located near the left end of the outcrop; however, a number of fine routes have been established all along the cliff. Map, page 34.

78 **MAKE OR BREAK FLAKE 5.10b** ★ This route ascends a flake/crack on a small face on the far left side of the cliff. A bolt protects the entry move. Pro: To 4 inches.

79 **QUEST FOR FIRE 5.11c** ★ This thin crack is just right of **Make or Break Flake.** Pro: To 4 inches.

80 **SOLAR FLARE 5.9** ★ This is just across the gully from **Make or Break Flake.** Climb an obvious flake, then face climb past a bolt. Pro: To 2.5 inches.

81 **NOLINA CRACK 5.10a** ★ Start 30 feet right of **Solar Flare** on a block above and left of **Digital Watch.** Climb a crack past a huge nolina plant, joining **Solar Flare** at the bolt. Pro: To 2.5 inches.

82 **DIGITAL WATCH 5.10d R** ★★ This short, thin finger crack is just left of **Jack of Hearts.** Start out of an ant-covered tree. Pro: Small to 1.5 inches.

83 **SEN BLEN 5.10c** ★ This route lies on the pillar between **Digital Watch** and **Jack Of Hearts.** Approach the route from the high ledges to the left, or climb **Digital Watch** to start. Climb past two bolts and a fixed (hopefully) rurp. Tricky descent.

84 **JACK OF HEARTS 5.9** ★ This route follows a hand crack on the left side of the tiered pinnacle left of **Popular Mechanics.** Pro: To 3 inches.

85 **SCIENTIFIC AMERICANS 5.8 R** ★★ Climb the arête right of **Jack Of Hearts** past two bolts.

86 **CARD CHIMNEY 5.5** (descent route) The obvious clean chimney right of **Jack of Hearts.**

87 **POPULAR MECHANICS 5.9** ★★★ This ascends the attractive white dihedral to the right of **Jack of Hearts.** Descend via a two-bolt rappel station at belay. Pro: Small to 2 inches.

88 **ACE OF SPADES 5.9** ★★★ Follows the leftmost of two parallel hand cracks that are located on the left wall of the **Popular Mechanics** dihedral. Pro: Medium to 2.5 inches.

89 **WILTED FLOWER CHILDREN 5.9** Climb the chimney and hand crack in a small right-facing corner 40 feet right of **Popular Mechanics.**

90 **HIGH ANXIETY 5.10d ★** This large, light-colored buttress is 100 feet right of **Popular Mechanics.** It is the largest buttress on the cliff. Scramble up ledges on the left side of the buttress. Climb a thin crack on the left edge of the buttress, face climb past two bolts, then follow the left-hand crack up a steep left-facing corner to the top. Pro: Many small to 2.5 inches.

91 **HIGH TENSION 5.11d** Start atop stacked boulders at the toe of the large light-colored buttress (about 100 feet right of **Popular Mechanics**). Climb up a thin seam past three bolts, traverse up and right past a large (loose) flake, up past two more bolts, left and up to a sixth bolt, and then left to the seventh bolt. Climb the thin crack above over the headwall to the top. Pro: Thin to 2 inches.

92 **AN OFFICER AND A POODLE 5.9 R** On the right side of the large light-colored buttress mentioned above, climb a crack, then up the face past one bolt.

93 **SEARCH FOR CHINESE MORSELS 5.10b ★** This brown wall is 100 feet to the right of the large light-colored buttress mentioned above. Climb past two bolts, then up cracks to top.

94 **WOKKING THE DOG 5.11c (TR) ★** Climb the overhanging face just right of **Search For Chinese Morsels.**

95 **MISFORTUNE COOKIES 5.8** On the left face directly across the wide gully from **Search For Chinese Morsels** rises a left-facing dihedral with a left-facing flake. Climb the flake and the corner.

96 **WANTON SOUP 5.10a (TR)** Climb the steep, rounded arête just left of **Misfortune Cookies,** on the right edge of the wide gully.

97 **SHIBUMI 5.10d ★** This thin, straight-in crack that steepens at the top is to the right of **Misfortune Cookies** (across the wide gully from **Search For Chinese Morsels**).

98 **DOVER SOLE 5.6** Approximately in the middle of the White Cliffs band of rocks is a large face with a roof near its bottom. It is easily distinguished by the thin seam splitting the roof and face above. Climb a right-facing corner system to the right of the face.

99 **RED SNAPPER 5.11a ★★★** This ascends a nice piece of rock about 120 feet right of **Dover Sole.** In the middle of the face is a nice crack system. A difficult entry move/overhanging crack leads to a right-facing corner. Pro: Fingers to 2.5 inches.

100 **RED TIDE 5.10d R ★★★** This climb is just around the corner and right of **Red Snapper** (about 20 feet). Climb past a bolt and follow shallow discontinuous cracks to top. Pro: Many thin to 1 inch.

101 **SOVIET UNION 5.11c ★★** The crescent crack on the steep face 100 feet right of **Red Snapper.** Pro: Many very thin to 1 inch.

HIGH PLAINS AREA

Above and to the northwest of The White Cliffs of Dover is a high plateau. This plateau and the hillsides to the south hold a number of rock formations. Apparently, there has been new route activity up here, but no detailed information was available at the time this guide went to press. Check the supplements to this guide for route information. Map, page 34.

AFPA ROCK

This nondescript formation faces Quail Springs Road and lies about 200 yards east of Trashcan Rock. Maps, pages 30,34.

102　**BOULDER CRACK　5.8**　The boulder to the left of the main face has a crack on its west side.

103　**BOULDER FACE　5.7**　Climb a face and short crack just right of **Boulder Crack.**

104　**ZSA ZSA GOES TO JAIL　5.7 R**　Start up and left of **Bitch, Bitch;** follow knobs to where an overlap and corner meet; follow the crack above.

105　**BITCH, BITCH　5.7**　This is the leftmost obvious line on the main face of AFPA Rock. Follow cracks and grooves up and slightly left, then straight up.

106　**SAND WITCH　5.10a**　Directly above **Bitch, Bitch** is a large, varnished boulder with a short dihedral. It faces the road. Climb past a bolt into the corner, then up the slab and thin crack above.

107　**WHICH BITCH　5.9 ★**　Climb cracks right of **Bitch, Bitch.**

108　**MCDONALD-WILSON　5.10c R**　Poorly protected.

109　**ANDROMEDA STRAIN　5.7 ★**

110　**RIP OFF　5.6**

111　**WHICH WITCH　5.8**

112　**SPAGHETTI SAUCE SUNSET　5.10c**　Pro: Thin to 2 inches, one bolt.

113　**TWO OUR SURPRISE　5.9**

114　**HURRICANE HUGO　5.10b**　Climb two finger cracks separated by a ledge 15 feet left of **Sheltered.** Above, climb past two bolts on the slab next to a small left-facing corner.

115　**SHELTERED　5.8**　This route is on the back side of AFPA Rock, near its right side. It is a crack that starts fingers and progressively widens.

EROTIC DOME

This formation is 50 yards south of Quail Springs Road approximately .3 miles past AFPA Rock. All of the routes listed face the road on the northeast side of the rock. Map, page 42.

116 **EROTIC CITY 5.11b ★★★** Climb a thin crack until it's possible (necessary) to traverse right to a crack that leads to the top. Pro: Very thin to 2.5 inches.

117 **VULGAR BOOT MEN 5.8** Climb the wide crack between **Erotic City** and **Volga Boat Men.**

118 **THE LEG LIFTER 5.11a ★** Climb "zig-zag" thin cracks around the corner about 20 feet to the right of **Erotic City.** Pro: Two bolts, two manky fixed pins, a poor fixed nut; .5 to 2.5 inches.

119 **VOLGA BOAT MEN 5.8** This less-than-quality route climbs the hand crack on the narrow rib to the right of **Erotic City.**

120 **THE AWFULWIDTH 5.8 R** This nasty, grainy, right-leaning offwidth on the west face of Erotic Dome is 200 feet to the right of **The Leg Lifter.**

121 **WAKE ME WHEN IT'S OVER 5.8 X** Climb the thin right-leaning seam just right of **Awfulwidth**.

122 **ORGASMATRON 5?** This four-bolt face route on the west face of Erotic Dome may not have free climbed as of yet.

123 **BALD WOMEN WITH POWER TOOLS 5.10b** This climb is on the buttress to the right of the chimney on the west face. Climb a crack to a face with three bolts.

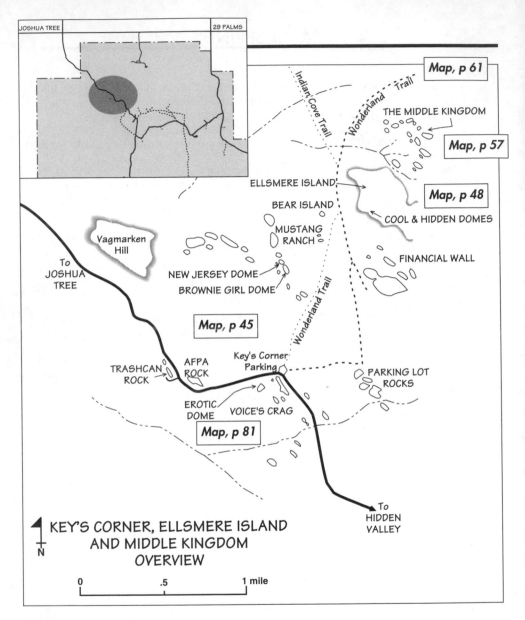

JOSHUA TREE

29 PALMS

Map, p 61

Indian Cove Trail

Wonderland Trail

THE MIDDLE KINGDOM

Map, p 57

ELLSMERE ISLAND

Map, p 48

BEAR ISLAND

COOL & HIDDEN DOMES

MUSTANG
RANCH

Vagmarken
Hill

FINANCIAL WALL

To
JOSHUA
TREE

NEW JERSEY DOME

BROWNIE GIRL DOME

Wonderland Trail

Map, p 45

Key's Corner
Parking

TRASHCAN
ROCK

AFPA
ROCK

PARKING LOT
ROCKS

EROTIC
DOME

VOICE'S CRAG

Map, p 81

To
HIDDEN
VALLEY

KEY'S CORNER, ELLSMERE ISLAND
AND MIDDLE KINGDOM
OVERVIEW

N

0   .5   1 mile

WONDERLAND OF ROCKS – NORTH

The Wonderland of Rocks constitutes the largest concentration of rock formations in the entire monument. This area (in excess of nine square miles) is bounded by Indian Cove to the north, Barker Dam to the south, Key's Ranch to the west and Queen Mountain to the east. Due to its vast size, exploration has been divided by two separate points of entry. For this reason, the Wonderland is treated in two different sections. The northern section (Wonderland North) and areas within the vicinity of the approach trail are described in the following section (see map for coverage). The southern section (Wonderland South) is described near the Barker Dam section of this guide.

At Key's Corner (a sharp right turn in the road .7 mile (1.1 km) east of Trashcan Rock), there is a parking area (Key's Corner Parking) that serves as the trailhead for the northern portion of Wonderland of Rocks. This also serves as trailhead for the journey to Indian Cove. Access to Parking Lot Rocks also is from the Key's Corner Parking area. See map above.

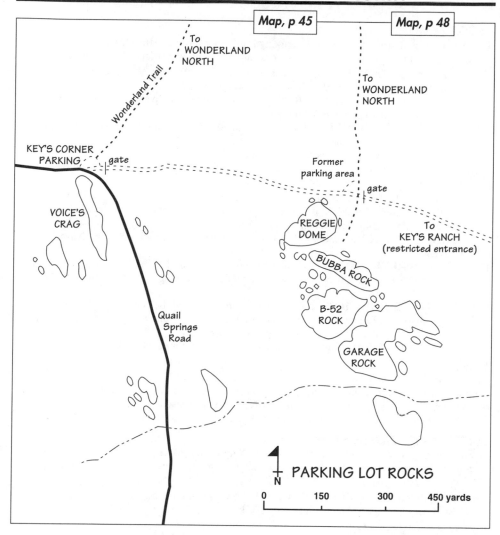

Map, p 45   Map, p 48

To
WONDERLAND
NORTH

To
WONDERLAND
NORTH

Wonderland Trail

KEY'S CORNER
PARKING   gate

Former
parking area

gate

VOICE'S
CRAG

REGGIE
DOME

To
KEY'S RANCH
(restricted entrance)

BUBBA ROCK

Quail
Springs
Road

B-52
ROCK

GARAGE
ROCK

N

PARKING LOT ROCKS

0   150   300   450 yards

Wonderland North and all other areas in this vicinity (with the exception of Parking Lot Rocks) are approached via a trail (the Wonderland Trail) that heads northeast from the Key's Corner parking lot. Parking Lot Rocks are approached via a closed dirt road that continues straight east from Key's Corner.

PARKING LOT ROCKS

If you walk east from the Key's Corner Parking area along the now-closed dirt road for about .5 mile (.8 km.), you'll soon encounter several formations just to the south (right). These are the Parking Lot Rocks. A gated fence blocks further progress east; this is the "parking area" for Parking Lot Rocks. From this point, a road/trail heads straight north; it eventually joins the Wonderland Trail, which heads northeast from Key's Corner Parking area. If you are climbing at Parking Lot Rocks, you can walk straight north to reach the other Wonderland North areas listed in this section.

REGGIE DOME

This is the westernmost formation of the Parking Lot Rocks, closest to the closed dirt road/former parking lot. The first three of the following routes are on the northeast face. Map, page 43

124 **THOMSON ROOF 5.9 ★** This climb is 30 feet right of a large dark roof. Climb up and right, then step left and climb a finger crack over a small roof.

125 **REGGIE'S PIMPLE 5.10c (TR)** Climb a very thin crack up and right of **Thomson Roof** (just left of **Reggie On A Poodle**).

126 **REGGIE ON A POODLE 5.10a** Climb shallow cracks to a bolt up and to the right of **Thomson Roof.** Loose face climbing leads to the top.

Routes from **Tender Flakes of Wrath** through **The Chief** lie on the northwest face of Reggie Dome, to the right of a low-angled slab that is plainly visible when walking down the dirt road from Key's Corner Parking area.

127 **TENDER FLAKES OF WRATH 5.7 ★** This route lies on the low-angled slab facing northwest, about 15 feet left of a deep chimney/gully. Start behind a large pine tree, climb to a bolt, go left to a thin crack, then wander past a second bolt to top.

128 **THOMSON'S ACNE 5.10b (TR)** Climb the face between **Unknown** and **Ninny's Revenge.**

129 **NINNY'S REVENGE 5.9** This climb begins just left of the deep chimney/gully on the right-hand part of the low-angled slab. Climb a flared crack up to face climbing. Walk off left.

130 **POPS GOES HAWAIIAN 5.7 ★★** This climb is around the corner and 30 feet to the right of **Ninny's Revenge,** on the left side of a wide gully. Follow a steep dike in brown rock past a bolt to a flake, then move right to rejoin the dike.

131 **THE CHIEF 5.5 ★★** Climb the crack up and to the right of **Pops Goes Hawaiian.**

BUBBA ROCK

Bubba Rock is 100 yards south of what used to be the parking lot. The only recorded route lies on the north face, which rises directly to the south of the parking area. What seems to be the west face of Bubba Rock is actually the west face of B52 Rock, which is reached by walking around the west face of Reggie Dome, or by scrambling between Reggie Dome and Bubba Rock.

BUBBA ROCK – NORTH FACE

A faint dirt road running south from the former parking area leads to the north face. On the north side of the formation (facing the dirt road), the rock has a mottled brown appearance. Map, page 43.

132 **BUBBA TAKES A SIESTA 5.10a ★** Follow huecos on good rock on the north face of Bubba Rock past one bolt to an arching crack.

B52 ROCK – WEST FACE

To reach the west face of B52 Rock, either hike around the west face of Reggie Dome and head south, or scramble between Reggie Dome and Bubba Rock. A short walk south will bring you to the base of a thin crack in shallow corner, which is **Private Idaho.**

133 **PRIVATE IDAHO 5.11b ★★★** Pro: Many thin to 2 inches.

134 **ROMPER ROOM 5.11a ★** Climb the face with four bolts just right of **Private Idaho.**

135 **TOXIC AVENGER 5.10d ★★** This route lies on the face 50 feet right and around the corner from **Private Idaho.** Follow a fixed head and two bolts to a ledge, then continue up the finger-and-hand crack above.

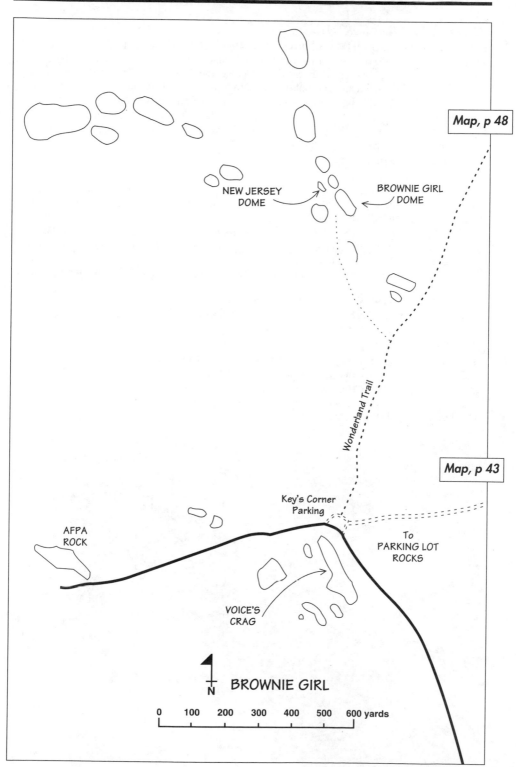

Map, p 48

Map, p 43

BROWNIE GIRL
DOME

NEW JERSEY
DOME

Wonderland Trail

Key's Corner
Parking

To
PARKING LOT
ROCKS

AFPA
ROCK

VOICE'S
CRAG

BROWNIE GIRL
N

0 100 200 300 400 500 600 yards

WONDERLAND NORTH

To approach to Willow Hole, Financial Wall, Cool Dome, Hidden Dome, Mustang Ranch and other formations in the northern portion of the Wonderland of Rocks, follow a trail that heads northeast from the large parking area near Key's Corner (the Wonderland Trail). After about 1 mile, this trail joins up with a larger trail (that used to be a dirt road) heading directly north.

As you walk northeast along the Wonderland Trail, you pass to the south of (in order) Brownie Girl/New Jersey Domes, The Mustang Ranch and Bear Island. These formations are best approached by following the Wonderland Trail until direct approaches can be made. The direct approaches are described below. Maps, pages 42, 45.

THE BROWNIE GIRL DOME

This formation is about .6 mile north of Key's Corner Parking area. It is best approached by taking the Wonderland Trail northeast for about .4 mile to a point just before some low rocks to the south of the trail are passed. Head straight north from here (.2 mile) to the west faces of Brownie Girl and New Jersey Domes. Map, page 45.

136   **WHERE BROWNIES DARE 5.10a** This route is on the north face of Brownie Girl Dome, 10 feet left of the main crack system (**James Brown**). Lieback a crack up to a patina face, then follow a crack to the top.

137   **JAMES BROWN 5.6** This is the wide crack/corner around and left of **Buster Brown** on the north face.

138   **BUSTER BROWN 5.9 ★★** Pro: One bolt, small to medium nuts.

139   **BROWNIE POINTS 5.9+** Pro: Small to 2 inches.

140   **TIGE 5.8** Pro: One bolt, small to 2 inches.

NEW JERSEY DOME

This formation lies immediately northwest of Brownie Girl Dome; it is the lower (westernmost) of two formations. Prominent black roofs on the southwest side distinguish it. Map, page 45.

141   **JERSEY GIRL 5.10a** The route is on the southwest corner of the dome, below the dark roof. Climb easy but loose rock up and left of the roofs to an overhanging face. Small brass/steel nuts are mandatory.

MUSTANG RANCH

The Mustang Ranch consist of two rocks 100 yards northwest of the Wonderland Trail, about .75 mile from Key's Corner Parking area. The first three routes are on the north face of the larger southern formation. Map, page 48.

142   **PAHRUMP 5.4** Climb the chimney just left of **Blue Velvet.**

143   **BLUE VELVET 5.11d (TR)** ★ This route follows a right-slanting crack/seam that rises 25 feet left of the large crack/chimney (**The Chicken Ranch**) near the middle of the north side of the formation.

144   **WHIPS AND GRAINS 5.10b** Climb the brown, bucketed face 20 feet right of **Blue Velvet** past one bolt.

145   **THE CHICKEN RANCH 5.6** This is the crack/chimney that forms a break in the center of the north face.

146   **PRETTY IN PINK 5.11b (TR)** ★★ Follow the leftmost of two thin crack/seams that lie 15 feet to the right of **The Chicken Ranch.**

147   **WOMEN IN CAGES 5.11c (TR)** ★ This route is the right-hand crack/seam in the system mentioned above.

148   **PADDED HANDCUFFS 5.9** This route climbs the dike at the very right end of the north face.

The next three routes are located on the right end of the north face of the smaller, northernmost formation. They are about 25 feet long, and you can boulder as well as toprope them.

149   **STABLE GIRL 5.11 (TR)** This is the leftmost of two thin cracks/seams.

150   **VIVA LAS VEGAS 5.11 (TR)** The right thin crack/seam.

151   **MUSTANG RANCH 5.10 (TR)** Climb protruding dike to the right of **Viva Las Vegas.**

BEAR ISLAND

This fairly worthless formation lies 100 yards northwest of the Wonderland Trail (just before it joins the larger trail/road running north-south). It is about .9 mile from Key's Corner Parking area and about 125 yards north of Mustang Ranch. Map, page 48.

152   **SHARDIK 5.3** Climb the crack on the arête at the north end of the formation.

153   **POLAR BEARS IN BONDAGE 5.7** Climb a short crack through a bulge, then head up the casy gray face 15 feet left of **Kodiak.**

154   **KODIAK 5.5** Climb the face and varnished crack on the right side of the west face.

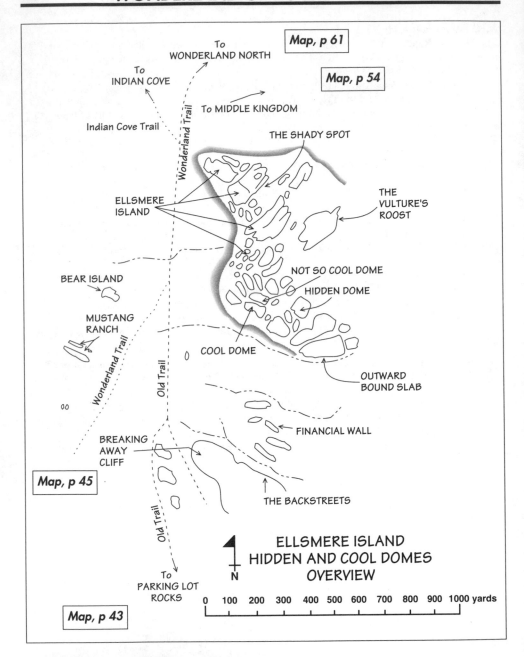

To
WONDERLAND NORTH

Map, p 61

Map, p 54

To
INDIAN COVE

To MIDDLE KINGDOM

Indian Cove Trail

Wonderland Trail

THE SHADY SPOT

THE
VULTURE'S
ROOST

ELLSMERE
ISLAND

BEAR ISLAND

NOT SO COOL DOME

HIDDEN DOME

MUSTANG
RANCH

Wonderland Trail

Old Trail

COOL DOME

OUTWARD
BOUND SLAB

oo

FINANCIAL WALL

BREAKING
AWAY
CLIFF

Map, p 45

Old Trail

THE BACKSTREETS

ELLSMERE ISLAND
HIDDEN AND COOL DOMES
OVERVIEW

N

To
PARKING LOT
ROCKS

Map, p 43

0   100   200   300   400   500   600   700   800   900 1000 yards

SOUTHERN (OLD) TRAIL AREAS

About 1 mile from the Key's Corner Parking area, the Wonderland Trail joins up with a larger trail (that used to be a dirt road) heading straight north. An unused road/trail (the Old Trail) heads straight south from here. Outward Bound Slab, Financial Wall and Breaking Away Cliff all are approached by taking the Old Trail straight south (Parking Lot Rocks also lie in that direction). Outward Bound Slab, etc. are described roughly in the order in which they are encountered when walking south along the Old Trail.

OUTWARD BOUND SLAB

Just south of where the Wonderland Trail joins the Old Trail, a broad valley opens to your left (east). At the northern end of the valley, and on the southern side of the hillside holding Cool and Hidden Domes, you will see an obvious south-facing slab. This is Outward Bound Slab.

155   **OH PINYON CRACK   5.10a**   This is the steep 40-foot hand crack on the left side of Outward Bound Slab. It starts behind a pinyon pine.

156   **PAINT ME GIGI   5.7 X**   Ascend the leftmost crack on the face (no pro); slants left.

157   **OUTWARD BOUND SLAB ROUTE   5.8**   Climb past three bolts to the right of **Paint Me Gigi.**

158   **MASTERING   5.2**   Easy gully right of **Outward Bound Slab Route.**

159   **LOOK MOM, NO HANDS   5.7**   Follows crack to face right of **Mastering 5.2.**

160   **MOM FOR THE ROAD   5.7**   Climbs the corner to the left of **One For The Road.**

161   **ONE FOR THE ROAD   5.10a**   This route is located on the far right side of Outward Bound Slab, 200 feet right of **Look Mom, No Hands.** Climb a finger crack just right of a left-facing book capped by a roof.

162   **TRES FUN   5.10a**   This the flared hand crack above **One For The Road.**

THE HILLSIDE

On The Hillside are formations that lie up and behind (north) of Outward Bound Slab and south of Hidden Dome. Two routes are known. Map, page 48.

163   **EXPERIENTIAL ED.   5.9**   A prominent crack approximately two pitches in length lies to the left and above Outward Bound Slab. Start below the dark, left-facing corner below the small roof. The second pitch follows a 70-foot hand crack.

164   **OMNIA EXTERES   5.10c**   This is short, varnished crack starts out thin and widens to an offwidth, then to an oddly-shaped corner

FINANCIAL WALL

The best way to find Financial Wall is to follow the Old Trail south from its juncture with the Wonderland Trail for about .25 mile, to the point where it bears right. From here, walk east into the southern part of a broad valley. Go east until you can turn south to a formation with an overhanging east face. This is Financial Wall. Map, page 48.

165   **TAXED TO THE LIMIT   5.12a ★**   This is the left-slanting crack on the left side of the wall.

166   **HIGH INTEREST   5.11a ★★**   An obvious hand crack rises slightly left of center on the wall. Climb this, but take the jog right at the top.

167   **THE SPECULATOR   5.11d ★**   This route follows the obvious central crack that leads up into a body slot.

168   **THE CRASH   5.12c ★**   The Crash follows the left-leaning corner and leads to a finger crack just right of **The Speculator.**

169   **HIGHER YIELD   5.10d**   Climbs the obvious line on the right side of the wall.

THE BACKSTREETS

The Backstreets lies about 100 yards south of Financial Wall. The only known route is on the east face. Map, page 48.

170   **JUST A SKOSH   5.9**   This route is the left of a break in the east face. Climb over a small roof, then continue up a more moderate crack.

BREAKING AWAY CLIFF

The best way to find Breaking Away Cliff is to follow the Old Trail south from its juncture with the Wonderland Trail for about .25 mile, to the point where the Old Trail bears right. From here, continue straight south (along another road/trail) for about 150 feet to a cliff with a thin crack going over a roof; this is **Breaking Away.** Map, page 48.

171   **BREAKING AWAY   5.11a (TR) ★**

COOL DOME, HIDDEN DOME AND ELLSMERE ISLAND

After taking the Wonderland Trail northeast from Key's Corner Parking area for about 1 mile, you join up with a old road/trail that heads straight north (the Old Trail). At this point, you are below a large hillside with many rock formations. The gully that leads up to Cool Dome and Hidden Dome lies roughly due east. Ellsmere Island also is on this hillside, about 200 yards further north. Map, page 48.

COOL DOME

Cool Dome is on your left about one-third of the way up the approach gully to Hidden Dome.

172 **BANK NOTE BLUES 5.9** This route follows the obvious offwidth crack on the west side of Cool Dome, and starts in a right-facing dihedral.

173 **BEDTIME FOR DEMOCRACY 5.10b ★** This route follows a right-slanting crack on the southwest face of Cool Dome. It is reached via a traverse left from the top of a small dihedral on the southwest arête. Pro: Two bolts, two fixed pins, small to 2.5 inches.

174 **STARDUST MEMORIES 5.9+** Climb past 5 bolts on the left side of Cool Dome's east face.

175 **TOO SILLY TO CLIMB 5.5** Ascend the left-facing book just right of **Stardust Memories.**

176 **FINGER STACKS OR PLASTIC SACKS 5.10b** This route follows the double thin cracks on the east face of Cool Dome to the left of a tree. Start in a "pit."

177 **RICKETS AND SCURVY 5.10b** Climb a thin crack leading to twin hand cracks right of **Finger Stacks or Plastic Sacks.**

NOT SO COOL DOME

This formation lies on the northern (left-hand) side of the gully that leads to Hidden Dome, just east (across from the east face) of Cool Dome.

178 **CLAMMING AT THE BEACH 5.9** This 3-inch crack rises across the canyon from the east face of Cool Dome (roughly opposite **Stardust Memories**).

HIDDEN DOME

This formation lies high up and on the right side (facing north) of the gully you ascend to reach Cool Dome. Routes are described right to left.

179 **CALGARY STAMPEDE 5.9 ★★**

180   **TUCSON BOUND   5.8** ★   Climb cracks just right of **Calgary Stampede.**
181   **THE SCREAMING WOMAN   5.10a** ★★   Pro: Thin to 2 inches, one bolt.
182   **THE SCREAMING POODLE   5.10c (TR)** ★★
183   **TOO SECRET TO FIND   5.10d** ★★★★   Pro: .5 to 3 inches.

184   **BALANCE DUE 5.10c ★★★**   Pro: Many thin to 2 inches, two bolts.
185   **MAJOR CREATIVE EFFORT 5.10a**

ELLSMERE ISLAND

This area lies several hundred yards north of Cool and Hidden Domes. Walk north from the point where the Wonderland Trail meets the Old Trail for about 200 yards; at this point you'll see a left-facing red dihedral (**The Great Escape**) low on the hillside. This is the Ellsmere Island area. Map, page 48.

186   **GO WITH THE FLOE 5.9+**   This route is located in the gully right (south) of the Ellsmere Island routes. It is a vertical crack on a steep wall that leads to a left-slanting traverse crack.
187   **MADE IN THE SHADE 5.9**
188   **FUN IN THE SUN 5.9+ (TR)**
189   **FRIGHT NIGHT 5.4**
190   **ABLE WAS I ERE I SAW ELLSMERE 5.7**
190a   **ARMS ARE FOR HUGGING 5.11b ★★★**   Pro: 4 bolts
191   **THE GREAT ESCAPE 5.11d ★**   Pro: Many very thin to 1.5 inches.
192   **THE HOUDINI ARETE 5.11c (TR)**
193   **FOREIGN LEGION 5.10d ★★★**
194   **MATH 5.10b**
195   **AFTERMATH 5.10a ★★★**
196   **GEOMETRY 5.11a**   Climb this left-facing roof/crack system that lies to the left of **Aftermath**.
197   **BABY FACE 5.7**   This route is located 50 feet right of **Baby Roof** and just right of the descent. Face climb past two bolts.

198 **GAIL WINDS 5.9 ★** Pro: Three bolts.
199 **BABY ROOF 5.8 ★★★**
200 **LEFT OVERS 5.7 (TR)**
201 **EL SMEAR OR LAND 5.10b ★** Climb face left of **Baby Roof** past two bolts.
202 **THE LINDEN-FROST EFFECT 5.12a** This thin finger crack lies on the overhanging block above **Baby Roof.**
203 **HIT IT ETHEL 5.8 ★** Pro: To 3 inches, three bolts.
204 **ROUTE 66 5.4 ★**
205 **WHALE OF A TIME 5.8+** Climb past one bolt to a flake/crack on the formation below **Route 66.**
206 **APE MAN HOP 5.10a ★** Pro: To 3 inches, two bolts.
207 **NORTHWEST PASSAGE 5.10a ★** Climb past four bolts on an arête 50 feet left of **Route 66.**
208 **GJOA 5.9** Start on the first 20 feet of **Northwest Passage,** then climb a flake to a crack and past a roof formed by a huge block.
209 **CHOCOLATE DECADENCE 5.7** This is the dogleg dihedral 150 feet left of **Ape Man Hop.**

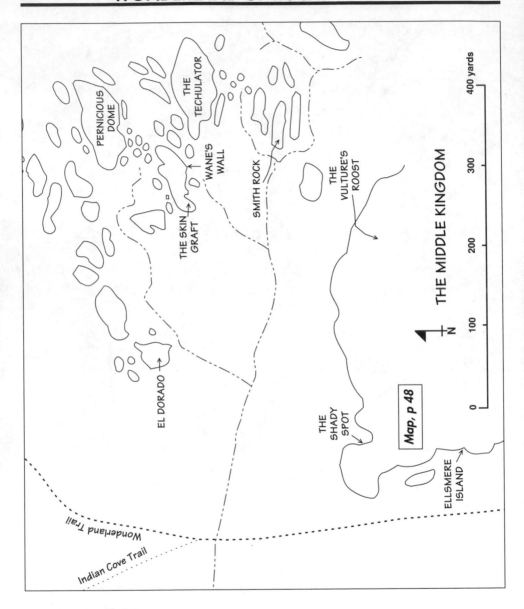

THE MIDDLE KINGDOM

Map, p 48

N

400 yards

PERNICIOUS DOME

THE TECHULATOR

WANE'S WALL

THE SKIN GRAFT

SMITH ROCK

THE VULTURE'S ROOST

EL DORADO

THE SHADY SPOT

ELLSMERE ISLAND

Wonderland Trail

Indian Cove Trail

GILLIGAN'S ISLAND

This small formation is located below and right of the **Ape Man Hop** slab. It contains good moderate routes. Photo, page52.

210   **LOVEY   5.9 ★**   This is the curving crack on the left side of the formation, which starts out very thin.

211   **TEDDY   5.9 ★★**   This route goes over a roof on excellent rock, then up the face past two bolts.

212   **AS THE WIND BLOWS   5.7**

213   **GUN FOR THE SUN   5.10a ★★**   Pro: Nuts to 2 inches, two bolts.

THE SHADY SPOT

Just around the corner (from Gilligan's Island?), on the northern end of the hillside hosting Cool and Hidden Domes and Ellsmere Island, is a rock-filled canyon/gully. The east side of this gully has a nice-looking, steep brown face with many discontinuous cracks. Two routes lie on this face.

214   **UNNAMED 5.11b (TR)** ★★   This route is to the left. Climb solution pockets up the face.

215   **UNNAMED 5.11d** ★★   Climb the discontinuous "curving" cracks up the right part of the steep brown face. Pro: Many small to 2.5 inches.

THE VULTURE'S ROOST

This formation is high on a hillside on the east side of the Ellsmere Island clump, about 150 yards up and left of The Shady Spot.

216   **VULTURE'S ROOST 5.9**   The route is northfacing, and climbs a crack above a large flake.

THE MIDDLE KINGDOM

About one mile northeast of Key's Corner parking area, the Wonderland Trail joins a larger north-south trail (the Old Trail). Several hundred yards further north, the Indian Cove hiking trail continues in a northerly direction. Don't take this trail! Instead, it marks almost exactly the northern end of the hillside holding Ellsmere Island, Cool and Hidden Domes (where The Shady Spot is located). Follow the Old Trail as it slowly curves to the northeast. Map, page 42.

As you walk, you'll see various formations rising to the east (right); this is the Middle Kingdom area. The rest of the northern Wonderland of Rocks is reached by following the Wonderland/Old Trail to where it ends in a stream bed/wash. The northernmost obvious formation in The Middle Kingdom is called El Dorado. It is a brown, square-shaped crag. The other formations are located in reference to El Dorado. Pernicious Dome is the large, rounded, brown dome southeast and back in a wash from El Dorado. The Techulator is a large, complex formation that lies south of Pernicious Dome. Several other formations are located nearby. Map, page 57.

EL DORADO

The northernmost obvious formation in the Middle Kingdom is El Dorado. It is a brown, square-shaped crag. Maps, pages 42, 54, and 57.

217　**YET ANOTHER CILLEY TOPROPE　5.11c (TR)**　This is the thin crack left of **Mary Decker.**

218　**MARY DECKER　5.11 (TR)**　This ascends the smooth left side of the north face.

219　**ZOLA BUDD　5.10d (TR)**　Zola is to the right of **Mary Decker.** Climb up and right to a seam that leads to the top.

220　**ROB'N THE CRADLE　5.10c**　This left-leaning offwidth is just right of **Zola Budd.** Start to the left of this crack, then climb up and right into it, following the crack to a horizontal break (meeting **Zola Budd** briefly). Go right, then up a crack.

221　**WIDE WORLD OF SPORTS　5.10c**

222　**AGONY OF DEFEET　5.8 R**

CLEAN CRACK FORMATION

This is an obvious dome east of El Dorado, reached by continuing past that formation on the approach to Willow Hole.

223　**CLEAN CRACK　5.10b**　This route faces north (toward the Wonderland Trail) and is a thin crack in flawless rock.

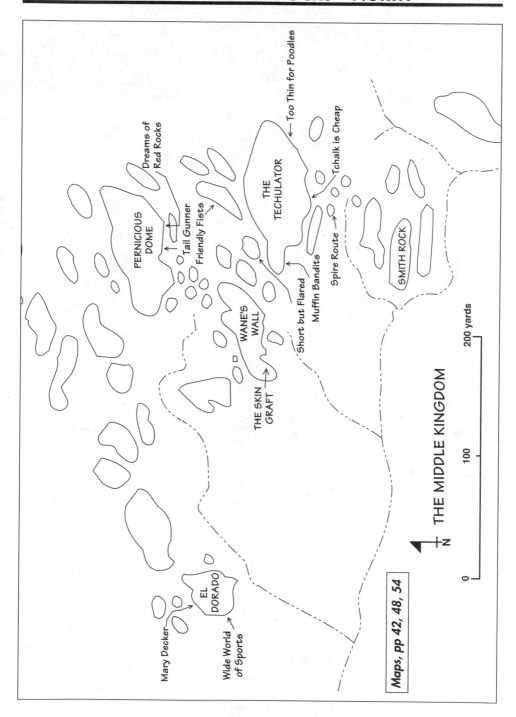

Too Thin for Poodles

Dreams of
Red Rocks

Tchalk is Cheap

THE
TECHULATOR

PERNICIOUS
DOME

Tail Gunner

Friendly Fists

Muffin Bandits

Spire Route

SMITH ROCK

WANE'S
WALL

Short but Flared

THE SKIN
GRAFT

EL
DORADO

Mary Decker

Wide World
of Sports

THE MIDDLE KINGDOM

N

Maps, pp 42, 48, 54

0   100   200 yards

PERNICIOUS DOME
The following routes are located on the west face of Pernicious Dome. Pernicious Dome is the large, rounded, brown dome that lies southeast and across a wash from El Dorado. Maps, pp 54,57.

224   **UNDERCLING BYPASS 5.8**
225   **TAIL GUNNER 5.11b ★★★★**   Pro: Five bolts, two fixed pins, nuts to 2 inches.
226   **A LITTLE BIT OF MAGIC 5.10c**   Pro: Thin to 2 inches.
227   **DREAMS OF RED ROCKS 5.7**
228   **FRIENDLY FISTS 5.9**   This short, left-arching corner with a fist crack rises opposite the west face of Pernicious Dome on the northeast side of The Techulator.

THE SKIN GRAFT
This formation lies approximately 100 yards north of the Techulator, and west-northwest of Pernicious Dome. Its dark brown south face has a large ledge/ramp running along the bottom.

229   **TANNING SALON 5.6**   This route lies to the right and around the corner from the main south (brown) face. It is a right-facing corner in dark rock.

WANE'S WALL
Wane's Wall is an 80-foot north-facing wall in a very narrow corridor with vertical and overhanging cracks. The corridor looks across to a mushroom-shaped boulder, and lies roughly southwest of Pernicious Dome and left (north) of the Techulator; it is to the right (southeast) of The Skin Graft. A large boulder is wedged in the corridor. Maps, pages 54, 57.

230   **NOW WE KNOW 5.4**   A vertical, solution-pocketed face on the left side of the wall.
231   **RED EYE 5.9 (TR)**   The steep, "huecoed" face to the right of **Now We Know.**

232 **JAH LOO 5.10c** Start in the "Pit," take the overhanging face left of the left-facing corner, then climb up a right-arching crack to a hueco that resembles a "human mold."

233 **WREN'S NEST 5.11a** This overhanging face/corner/crack is to the right of the "human mold."

234 **ALEXANDER'S SALAMANDER 5.10d** An overhanging finger crack at the right end of the face.

THE TECHULATOR

The Techulator is the large massif south of Pernicious Dome. Maps, pages 54, 57.

235 **SHORT BUT FLARED 5.10b**

236 **MUFFIN BANDITS 5.10b ★★**

237 **SLOW MUTANTS 5.11a ★★** Pro: One fixed pin, four bolts.

238 **SPIRE ROUTE 5.5 ★** This route climbs the northwest face of the obvious pinnacle 150 feet south of **Muffin Bandits.** Pro: One bolt; one rap bolt.

239 **TCHALK IS CHEAP 5.10d** This lies around the corner and uphill from **Spire Route.** Avoid easy cracks to either side, and climb past one bolt, then follow cracks above a Gothic arch.

240 **GARDEN PATH 5.10a** Climb a gully behind an oak tree 70 feet right of **Tchalk Is Cheap**.

241 **CHUTE TO KILL 5.11a ★★** This route is right of **Garden Path.** Lieback a large flake, then follow three bolts up a loose water chute.

242 **UNDER A RAGING MOON 5.10b** This is the short, right-facing corner above **Garden Path.**

243 **TOO THIN FOR POODLES 5.10c** This line lies 150 feet right of **Under a Raging Moon** and **Chute to Kill.** Climb a thin crack until it forks. Take the left fork, then head up past two bolts.

244 **PILLAR OF DAWN 5.10a** A large pillar rises several hundred feet right and around the corner from the previous routes. This route follows a dihedral on the south face of the pillar.

SMITH ROCK

Smith Rock lies 100 yards southwest of **Too Thin For Poodles.** This formation is oriented in an east-west manner. Maps, pages 54, 57.

245   **THE NUTS AND BOLTS OF CLIMBING   5.10c**   This route is on the northeast corner of Smith Rock. Climb an overhanging hand crack to a flake, then up a face past two bolts.

246   **BIGHORN HAND CRACK   5.7**   This is the straight-in hand crack on the south face of Smith Rock.

247   **RIDERS ON THE STORM   5.10a**   Above and east of **Bihorn Hand Crack** are a pair of clean, slightly overhanging offwidths facing west. This is the rightmost crack.

THE NORTHERN WONDERLAND

About one mile from Key's Corner parking area, the Wonderland Trail, which heads northeast, joins a larger north-south trail (the Old Trail). Pass the junction of the Wonderland/Old Trail with the Indian Cove hiking trail (don't take this trail), continuing past the hillside on which lies Ellesmere Island, Cool and Hidden Domes. Follow the Wonderland/Old Trail as it slowly curves to the northeast, to the point where it ends in a sandy wash. Maps, pages 42, 61.

THE ATOM SMASHERS

This area lies about 3 miles (4.8 km) from Key's Corner Parking area. Hike along the Wonderland Trail to where it ends in a sandy wash. Straight ahead (east by northeast) a group of angular-shaped boulders and formations can be seen. Although the main wash now heads south, follow a narrow streambed east until you reach an open basin. The main Atom Smashers area lies directly ahead.

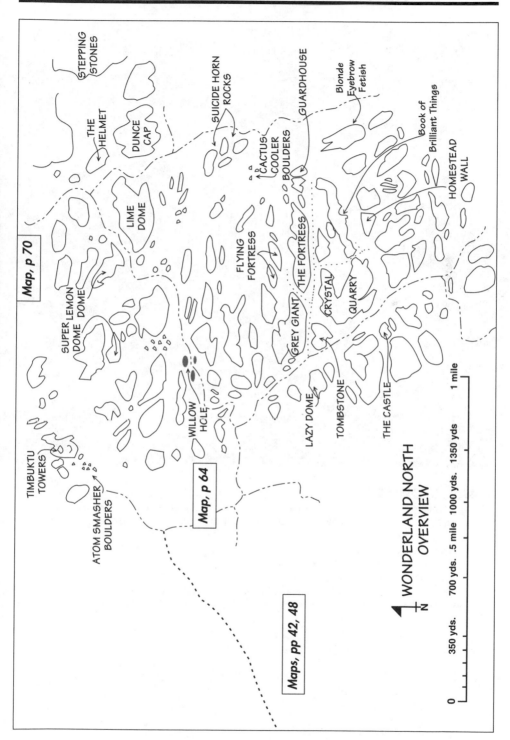

STEPPING STONES

THE HELMET

DUNCE CAP

SUICIDE HORN ROCKS

GUARDHOUSE

Blonde Eyebrow Fetish

Book of Brilliant Things

CACTUS COOLER BOULDERS

HOMESTEAD WALL

LIME DOME

Map, p 70

FLYING FORTRESS

THE FORTRESS

SUPER LEMON DOME DOME

GREY GIANT

CRYSTAL QUARRY

WILLOW HOLE

Map, p 64

LAZY DOME

TOMBSTONE

THE CASTLE

TIMBUKTU TOWERS

ATOM SMASHER BOULDERS

Maps, pp 42, 48

WONDERLAND NORTH OVERVIEW

N

0   350 yds.   700 yds. .5 mile 1000 yds. 1350 yds.   1 mile

JUMBO ROCKS   EAST VIRGIN ISLES   VIRGIN ISLES   LOST PENCIL   SADDLE ROCKS   COMIC BOOK   HALL OF HORRORS

ASTRO DOMES

ECHO ROCK

WONDERLAND OF ROCKS
LOOKING SOUTHEAST

WILLOW HOLE

TO PARKING LO

TO ATOM SMASHERS

Photo: Dave Houser

TIMBUKTU TOWERS

The large (main) formations on the hillside are referred to as the Timbuktu Towers. The largest formation has may routes on the west and south faces. The large, leaning pillar high on the north side of the Timbuktu Towers is the Ivory Tower. Maps, pages 61, 64.

248   **SINE WAVE   5.9** (1 bolt)
249   **GRAVITY WAVES   5.11a ★★★★★**
250   **GRAVITY WORKS   5.11c ★★★**
251   **OFFSHOOT   5.10b**   This is the obvious, wide, offwidth crack in the middle of the face.
252   **THE BATES MOTEL   5.12b ★★★**   This route follows the long, obvious arête to the right of **Offshoot;** climb past six bolts.

TIMBUKTU TOWERS

THE IVORY TOWER
261-265

256

250

255

248

252

249

251

253 **POLYTECHNICS 5.10c ★★** Three bolts on the wall to the left of **Psychokenesis.**

254 **NUCLEAR WASTE 5.9+** This route is the offwidth crack about 50 feet left of **Psychokenesis.**

255 **PSYCHOKENESIS (aka MISSING IN ACTION) 5.11b ★★** Climb an overhanging thin crack/ramp to the upper dihedral.

256 **PSYCHOTECHNICS 5.11b ★★** This route allows for a better second-pitch alternative to **Psychokenesis.** Climb that route, and belay where the upper dihedral eases in difficulty. Climb right, out of the dihedral, then up the exposed arête past a bolt to the top.

257 **PSYCHO 5.10d** This and the following route lie on the east face of the Timbuktu Towers, directly below the east side of the Ivory Tower. Climb the face on the left, past three bolts, to the top of a left-leaning arch.

258 **SHOWER SCENE 5.10c** This is the two-bolt face route leading to the base of the left-leaning arch; belay as for the above route.

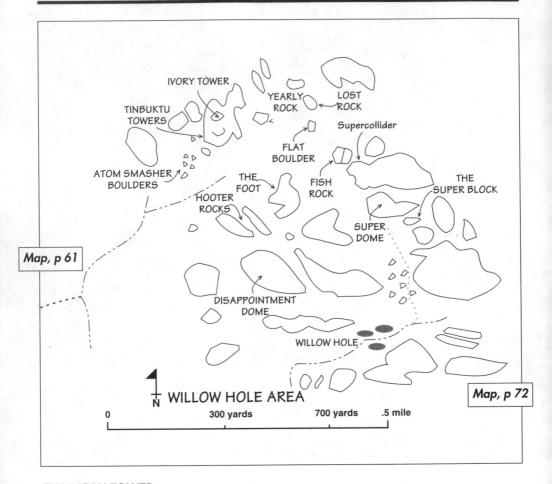

WILLOW HOLE AREA

0   300 yards   700 yards   .5 mile

THE IVORY TOWER

This is the obvious, leaning pillar above and right (northeast) of the west face of Timbuktu Towers. **Famous Potatoes** is on its east face. Four difficult routes have been done on its overhanging north face.

IVORY TOWER – EAST FACE

259   **FAMOUS POTATOES 5.11c ★**   This follows two bolts on the east face of the Ivory Tower.

260   **THIS SPUD'S FOR YOU 5.10c**   This six-bolt face route is left of **Famous Potatoes.**

IVORY TOWER – NORTH FACE

261   **THE POWERS THAT BE 5.13a ★★★★★**   This route has five bolts and is near the left edge of the face.

262   **CHAIN OF ADDICTION 5.13c ★★★★★**   Climb the center of the face past nine bolts.

263   **OCEAN OF DOUBT 5.13b/c ★★★★★**   This route is just right of **Chain of Addiction.**

264   **LA MACHINE 5.13d ★★★★**   This route is near the right edge and has six bolts.

265   **TELEKINESIS 5.11c or 5.10a**   The best approach for this route appears to be boulder-hopping up the gully left of **Sine Wave,** then proceeding north (left) in a gully between the two formations north of the main Timbuktu Towers. A large, scoop-shaped boulder is perched at the top of the northwest end of the formation on your right (east). **Telekinesis** climbs the crack(s) directly below the scoop.

WONDERLAND OF ROCKS
Looking southeast from near The Atom Smashers

DISNEYLAND DOME

FREAK BROS. DOM

THE INAUGURON

ONE MOVE

POODLE SMASHER

LOST IN THE WONDERLAND

THE FORTRESS

THE TOMBSTONE

FLYING FORTRESS

BACK OF GREY GIANT

RATTLESNAKE CANYON

TO WILLOW HOLE PARKING LO

TO SUPER DOME

THE FOOT

WILLOW HOLE

DISAPPOINTMENT DOME

HOOTER ROCKS

Photo: Dave Houser

(Var.1) **5.10a** Undercling the flake up and right to a thin crack.
(Var.2) **5.11c** Start down and right of the above variation; climb up and left along double arching cracks to reach the top thin crack.
266   **PUMPING HATE 5.13a ★★★** This route follows five-bolts on the east face of the first rock southeast of the main Timbuktu Towers formation.

ATOM SMASHER BOULDERS

These boulders lie about 125 yards south-southeast and down the hill from the main area. The boulders are generally about 50 feet high. Many face climbs are found on the sharp arêtes. Map page 64.

267   **NUCLEAR ARMS   5.12a ★★★**   Climb west face of Boulder I, starting above the overhanging bottom via either **Atom Ant** or **Gumshoe.**

268   **ATOM ANT   5.11b ★★**   Start left of the northwest arête of Boulder II, and continue up and left past bolts to top.

269   **GUMSHOE   5.10d ★★**   Start as for **Atom Ant.** Traverse up and right around the arête from the first bolt to summit.

270   **IONIC STRENGTH   5.12a ★★★★**   This climbs the steep arête on the southwest corner of Boulder II.

271   **SHIN BASHERS   5.11c ★**   Climb just right of the northeast arête of Boulder III.

272   **QUANTUM MECHANICS   5.11b ★★**   Climbs the center of the north face of Boulder III.

273   **ISOTOPE   5.9 ★★**   Climbs the northwest arête of Boulder III.

YEARLY ROCK

Yearly Rock is a small formation just east of The Timbuktu Towers. Map, page 64.

274   **YEAR AFTER YEAR   5.9**   This route lies on the east face of Yearly Rock. It is a finger crack to a hand/fist crack that leads to a flake.

HOOTER ROCKS

The best approach is to head for the Atom Smashers area, but stay to the south (right) in the open basin. Hooter Rocks lie just past the Atom Smashers on the right (south). Map, page 64.

275   **THE CROW'S NEST   5.11c**   This route is the overhanging face/crack that leads to a crack going through a roof near the summit of the middle formation's north face.

276   **HOOTERVILLE TROLLEY   5.10c**   This route lies on the north face of the leftmost (eastern) formation. Climb a clean crack to a face, then past two bolts.

277   **KP CORNER   5.10a**   This is to the left of **Hooterville Trolley** and slightly around the corner. Climb a face up to a brown, right-facing corner.

THE FOOT

The Foot is an aptly-named formation that lies approximately .25 mile southeast of the Atom Smashers area. The best approach is to hike toward Hooter Rocks, but continue east past this formation and head southeast in the canyon. The Foot is on your left. Map, page 64.

278   **DR. SCHOLL'S WILD RIDE   5.10a**   This is the long, "glassy clean" offwidth on The Foot formation; two pitches.

279   **THE NEW SHOE REVIEW   5.10d**   This is a six-bolt face route to the left of **Dr. Scholl's Wild Ride.**

DISAPPOINTMENT DOME

This formation is the large southwest-facing face/dome that lies adjacent to and south of The Foot. It is on the left side of a gully that starts between Hooter Rocks and The Foot. Several routes have been done on the large face of Disappointment Dome, but information for all these is incomplete. Map, page 64.

280   **THE FIASCO   5.10a**   Bolted face route on the right hand part of the southwest face.

281   **THE LETDOWN   5.9**   Climb thin cracks to the right of a brown, left-leaning dihedral. This route is also right of the unknown bolted face route.

282   **ROLLER COASTER   5.9**   This is the short finger crack to the right of **The Letdown.**

283   **WHAT A SHAME   5.10a**   Face route to the right of **Roller Coaster** on a face separated from the southwest face.

284   **LET'S EAT ORGAN MEAT   5.10a**   This route ascends the left center of the south face, past two bolts to a crack.

LOST ROCK

This formation lies just northeast of a large flat boulder that lies east of Timbuktu Towers and north of Supercollider Rock. The flat boulder is a good vantage point from which to find Lost Rock as well as Fish Rock and Supercollider Rock. Map, page 64.

285   **TWO LOST SOLES   5.8**   Located on the west face of Lost Rock. Climb a semi-chute with a crack to a flake; above climb the fist crack to top.

FISH ROCK

This is the formation just northest of Supercollider Rock.

286   **LIVING IN A FISHBOWL   5.10b**   This is the thin crack in a distinct right-facing dihedral on the north face of Fish Rock.

SUPERCOLLIDER ROCK

The Supercollider Rock is a small formation north of the Super Dome. The known routes lie on the west face. Map, page 64.

287   **SUPERCOLLIDER   5.8**   This is a 150-foot finger crack on the west face.

288   **SPANKING   5.11c (TR)**   This route is left of **Supercollider,** near the northwest corner of the rock. It is a finger crack out a roof that leads to a rounded arête.

THE SUPER DOME

From Willow Hole proper, walk east along Rattlesnake Canyon about 200 yards. A narrow canyon heading north can be seen from here. Follow talus up this canyon to the base of the obvious and beautiful Super Dome. Map, page 64.

289   **STONE HINGE   5.11b**   This route lies on the north side of The Super Dome, where several "terraces" can be seen. A large block rests against the lower terrace, which sports a finger to thin hand crack in its right side.

290   **THE COLE-LEWIS   5.10b ★★**

291   **THE GREAT UNKNOWN   5.10b ★★★**
      5.10a Var. ★★★   Take the crack in the left corner up to the face.

292   **WARPATH   5.12c ★★★★★**

293   **THE LAST UNICORN   5.11a ★★★★★**

294   **BLEED PROOF   5.7**

295   **THE MOHAWK   5.12c ★★★**   Runout at top.

296   **CHIEF CRAZY HORSE   5.12a ★★★**   First pitch runout (5.10b).

297   **SITTING BULL   5.10b ★★★**   This is a classic finger-to-fist crack in a corner on the southeast side of the dome.

THE SUPER BLOCK

This formation lies immediately to the right of The Super Dome. To approach the routes, start at the base of **Chief Crazy Horse.** "Third class" (5.6) up the slab to the right (you actually can use this to avoid the first pitch of **Chief Crazy Horse**) until a bolt anchor is reached. Stem out right and traverse around to the south face of the rock. The following routes lie on the south face. Map, page 64.

298   **SIDEBURN   5.12a ★★**   Climb over the roof and continue up the southwest arête. This is the leftmost route on the formation.

299   **HYDRA   5.13c ★★★★★**   This bolt-protected route leads up to the crest of the "wave-like" face to the right of **Sideburn.**

300   **LION'S SHARE   5.10b ★★★**   This route climbs the arête to the right of **Hydra.**

Linh Nguyen on Ionic Strength, 5.12, Atom Smasher Boulders

Photo: Kevin Powell

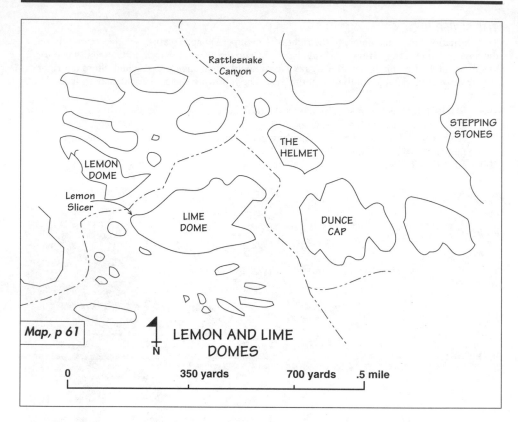

Rattlesnake
Canyon

STEPPING
STONES

THE
HELMET

LEMON
DOME

Lemon
Slicer

LIME
DOME

DUNCE
CAP

Map, p 61

N

LEMON AND LIME
DOMES

0   350 yards   700 yards   .5 mile

LEMON DOME

Lemon Dome is approx. .25 mile east of The Super Dome. From Willow Hole proper, continue east, then northeast, following Rattlesnake Canyon for about 450 yards. The canyon narrows, and becomes filled with large boulders. At this point, two large formations form the sides of the canyon. The dome on the left (north) is Lemon Dome.

301   **THE LEMON HEAD   5.10b** ★   This route lies on the large south face of Lemon Dome. Start on the left side of the face, climbing past four bolts up to the middle of the face. Above, slung plates and knobs protect the climbing to the top.

LIME DOME

Lime Dome is the huge, complex formation south of Lemon Dome and across the canyon.

302   **THE LEMON SLICER   5.11a** ★★   This perfect, split crack lies directly across from **The Lemon Head.** It's low on Lime Dome and to the right.

303   **LEMON LEMON   5.10a** ★   This two-pitch route lies about 150 feet to the left (east) of **The Lemon Slicer.** It is on the north face of Lime Dome.

THE DUNCE CAP

The Dunce Cap lies a third of a mile east of Lime Dome, and is reached by continuing past Lemon and Lime Domes down Rattlesnake Canyon to an open area. The formation in the middle of the open area (on your right) is The Helmet. Continue right of The Helmet until you see an imposing face/formation to your right (south). This is the north face of The Dunce Cap.

304   **THE DUNCE CAP   5.10c** ★★   From the highest pillar on the north face, climb past a bolt to a crack that leads to the top.

SUICIDE HORN ROCK

This dome lies about .25 mile south of The Dunce Cap. It can be reached either by continuing south along the west side of The Dunce Cap, or more easily from Willow Hole by walking east toward Lemon Dome, then continuing east (south of Lime Dome) to a large north-south wash (.5 mile from Willow Hole). Go south along the wash to Suicide Horn Rock. Map, page 61.

305   **BIGHORN DIHEDRAL 5.10b ★** This route follows a classic steep flake to a thin corner on the west face of Suicide Horn Rock.

306   **COMPACT PHYSICAL 5.11c ★** This is the 40-foot finger crack splitting the summit block above **Bighorn Dihedral.** It could be climbed as a second pitch to that route.

307   **ROCK LYPSO 5.10a** This route is on the east face of Suicide Horn Rock. Climb a wide undercling protected by a bolt and large friends.

THE STEPPING STONES

This band of cliffs lies about 350 yards east and slightly north of The Dunce Cap. Approach as for The Dunce Cap, but after passing The Helmet on the north (left) side, head east to the cliffs on the hillside. Routes are described from left to right. Maps, pages 61, 70.

308   **STEPPING OUT OF BABYLON 5.9** This route lies just left of **Stepping Razor.**

309   **STEPPING RAZOR 5.10b** This is the perfect two-pitch wide-hand crack leading to a slightly overhanging corner near the left side of the cliff band.

310   **STEPS AHEAD 5.10c, A1** Two pitches of mixed aid and free climbing to the right of **Stepping Razor.**

311   **FIRST STEPS 5.8** This crack climb lies to the right of **Steps Ahead.**

CACTUS COOLER ARETES

This formation lies south of Suicide Horn Rock, and roughly east of the Fortress area. If you are at the Fortress, head east out the valley, then go somewhat south to this "split" formation. If you are near The Dunce Cap/Suicide Horn Rock area, head south. The "arêtes" are formed by the north-south split of the formation. All of the routes are toprope problems. Map page 61.

312   **ARETE #1 5.10a (TR)** This is the northwest arête of the eastern formation.

313   **ARETE #2 5.11b (TR)** This is the west side of the southwest arête of the eastern formation.

314   **ARETE #3 5.11a (TR)** This is on the south side of the southwest arête of the eastern formation.

315   **ARETE #4 5.11a (TR)** This is the southeast arête of the western formation.

316   **HONORABLE HERSHEYS 5.11a (TR)** This route lies on the northeast arête. It climbs the brown-spotted rock of a formation 300 yards north of the Grey Giant. There are two bolts on top. See map on page 999.

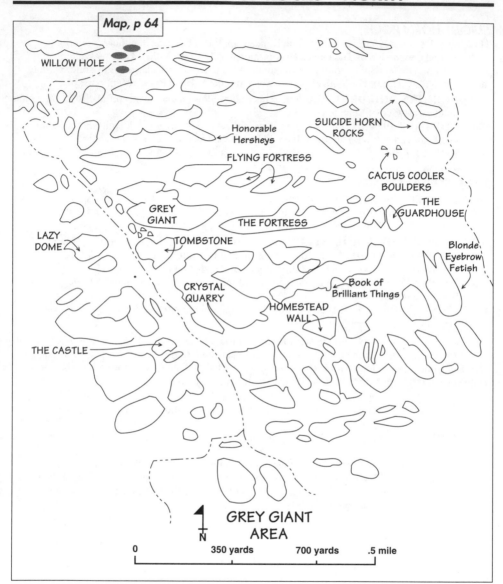

Map, p 64

WILLOW HOLE

Honorable
Hersheys

SUICIDE HORN
ROCKS

FLYING FORTRESS

CACTUS COOLER
BOULDERS

THE
GUARDHOUSE

GREY
GIANT

THE FORTRESS

LAZY
DOME

TOMBSTONE

Blonde
Eyebrow
Fetish

CRYSTAL
QUARRY

Book of
Brilliant Things

HOMESTEAD
WALL

THE CASTLE

GREY GIANT
AREA

N

| 0 | 350 yards | 700 yards | .5 mile |

GREY GIANT, TOMBSTONE, FORTRESS AREAS

From the major wash that leads to Willow Hole from the west, take the second side wash (compass direction) to the right (the Grey Giant can just be seen). Follow this wash in a southeasterly direction until rock scrambling leads to the west end of the Grey Giant. On the right is the large face of Lazy Dome. To the left, a rock-filled side canyon separates the Grey Giant and the Tombstone (the formation to the south) The Castle is further southeast down the major wash.

LAZY DOME

This formation lies west of the Grey Giant and Tombstone, just across the canyon. It is to your right as you approach the Grey Giant. Maps, pages 61,72.

317 **COMMON LAW MARRIAGE 5.10c** This route climbs the northeast arête of the formation.

GREY GIANT – SOUTH FACE

See map on page 72.

318 **ILLUSION 5.7** Pro: To 3 inches..

319 **TRANSFUSION 5.12a ★★★** Pro: Mostly thin to 3 inches.

320 **LITHOPHILIAC 5.11a ★★★** Pro: Mostly thin to 3 inches.

321 **HYPERION 5.11c ★★★★** Pro: Thin and many .5 to 4 inches.

322 **(Var.) JANUS 5.10d**

323 **(Var.) VORTEX 5.10a**

324 **THE DMB 5.9 ★★** Pro: Three bolts.

325 **TWO LEFT FEET 5.9+ ★** Pro: Med. nuts, two bolts.

326 **DIMORPHISM 5.7** Pro: Medium to 2 inches, one bolt.

327 **THE JEWEL OF DENIAL 5.9** Pro: Three bolts.

328 **DAWN YAWN 5.11d ★★★**

THE TOMBSTONE
NORTH FACE

331

330

THE TOMBSTONE

GREY GIANT

THE TOMBSTONE AND GREY GIANT
LOOKING WEST

333   332

To PARKING AREA

THE TOMBSTONE

329   **TURTLE DAYS   5.8**   This is a three-bolt face climb on a slab/buttress across from the
      Grey Giant.
330   **CINNAMON GIRL   5.10d ★★**
331   **THE TOMBSTONE   5.11c ★★**
332   **THE S CRACKER   5.10c ★★★**
333   **HEAVEN CAN WAIT   5.10c ★★★**
334   **THE FUGITIVE   5.10d ★★**   This is a five-bolt climb on the west face, 200 feet down and
      left from **Heaven Can Wait.**

THE FORTRESS AREA

To reach The Fortress, continue east in the rock-filled gully between the Grey Giant and Tombstone. Head straight east to the righthand canyon that leads to the back (south) face of The Fortress proper. **Rope Drag** is located in, and **Book of Brilliant Things** is approached from, this canyon. If you head slightly left and around the west buttress of The Fortress, you will find yourself in a wide flat valley. The north face of The Fortress is located on the south side of this valley. The north side of the valley is bounded by The Flying Fortress. The north side of the Grey Giant is reached easily by walking west from this valley. Map, page 72.

335   **ROPE DRAG**   **5.10b**   This route lies on the south side of the right-hand canyon.

To get to **Book of Brilliant Things, B.A.S.E Arrest** and **Bailey's Foster,** walk east in the rock-filled gully on the back (south) side of The Fortress. **Book of Brilliant Things** is on the southeast face of a formation on the right side of this canyon. Near the east end of this formation, tunnel through (south) to the south face. See map page 72.

336   **BOOK OF BRILLIANT THINGS**   **5.12d** ★★★★★
337   **B.A.S.E. ARREST**   **5.10c**   This is a thin hand crack on the northwest face of a small formation 100 yards south of **Book of Brilliant Things.**
338   **BAILEY'S FOSTER**   **5.10b**   This is on the north face of the formation left (east) of **B.A.S.E. Arrest.** Climb an offwidth leading to a hand crack in a corner.
339   **THE THRILL OF DESIRE**   **5.12c** ★★★★   This route is about 100 yards right of **B.A.S.E. Arrest,** on a separate formation. It is a steep, left-facing corner with a very thin crack and some bolts in its lower section.

THE HOMESTEAD WALL

This is the north face of the formation to the right (west) of The Thrill of Desire. Map on page 72.

340   **MERCY ROAD**   **5.11a**   This is a steep, bolted route on the left.
341   **LOOKING FOR MERCY**   **5.11a**   Climb the face right of **Mercy Road.** The routes join for the last 15 feet.
342   **EMPTY STREET**   **5.10c**   The face right of **Looking for Mercy.**
343   **MOONSTRUCK**   **5.10b**   The rightmost route, this climbs a face and a hairline fracture.

THE GUARDHOUSE

This is a formation on the east end of The Fortress. The following four routes can be approached from the Cactus Cooler/Suicide Horn area, but an easier approach can be made from Wonderland Valley by walking about 600 yards north along the Wonderland Wash from The Cornerstone. If you're approaching that way, The Guardhouse will be on the left side of a broad valley after the wash has opened up. See map, page 72.

344   **DIHEDRALMAN**   **5.13a** ★★★   Climb a left-facing dihedral with a thin crack on the south face of The Guardhouse.
345   **AVANTE GUARD-DOG**   **5.11d** ★★   This is a double roof right of **Dihedralman.**
The next two routes are on the east face of a formation south of The Guardhouse.
346   **LUSTING CLH**   **5.8**   Climb a flake/crack on the left side of the face.
347   **BLONDE EYEBROW FETISH**   **5.10c**   This is a 1.5-inch crack right of **Lusting CLH.**

THE FORTRESS – NORTH FACE

348   IT'S EASY TO BE BRAVE FROM A SAFE DISTANCE   5.12a ★★
349   IT'S EASY TO BE DISTANT WHEN YOU'RE BRAVE   5.11c ★★
350   TOAD WARRIOR   5.10b (Var) ★
351   WEEKEND WARRIOR   5.11a ★
352   SUBLIMINATION   5.10a
353   NATURAL SELECTION   5.11a ★★★★
354   PEAR-GRAPE ROUTE   5.10a
355   GRUNGY   5.10d
356   TOWER OF GODLINESS   5.10a ★
357   TOWER OF CLEANLINESS   5.10b ★★★
358   CATAPULT   5.11b ★★★★
359   WHERESABOLT?   5.11c (TR)
360   ARMS CONTROL   5.11d ***
361   ROARK   5.10c .
362   NEW HAMPSHIRE, NATURALLY   5.10b
363   THE OLD MAN DOWN THE ROAD   5.10a
364   JULIUS SEIZURE   5.10a
365   GANADO   5.10b

THE FORTRESS – NORTH FACE

THE FLYING FORTRESS – SOUTH FACE

366   **NO SAN FRANCISCO   5.11a (TR)**
367   **BOOGS' ROUTE   5.10b**
368   **NO SELF CONTROL   5.12c ★★★★**   Pro: Many small to 2 inches.
369   **NO SELF RESPECT   5.10c ★★★**
370   **NO SELF CONFIDENCE   5.10b ★★**
371   **42N8 ONE   5.10a**

FLYING FORTRESS – RIGHT SIDE

372 **HYPERVENTILATION 5.10d**
373 **NEW DAY YESTERDAY 5.10a**
374 **THUMBS UP 5.10a**
375 **TROGLODYTE CRACK 5.8**

GREY GIANT – NORTH FACE

376 **THE COLISEUM 5.10b ★** Climb the obvious corner left of **5 Crying Cowboys.**
377 **DROP YOUR DRAWERS 5.9** Offwidth/chimney between **The Coliseum** and **Drop a Frog.**
378 **DROP A FROG 5.9 ★** This squeezes up the offwidth chimney that closes to a finger crack on a slab. It is immediately left of **5 Crying Cowboys.**
379 **5 CRYING COWBOYS 5.12b ★★★★** Climb this thin finger crack for 50 feet to rappel bolts (rock deteriorates above this point).

THE CASTLE

This formation lies to the south of the Grey Giant. Walk about 250 yards south along the main canyon between Lazy Dome and the Grey Giant. The Castle lies to the east from here and contains two short routes. A left-facing dihedral is on the left, a widening crack to the right. Map, page 72.

380 **WARRIOR EAGLE 5.12b ★★★** This is the left-facing corner.
381 **THE KNIGHT IN SHINING ARMOR 5.11b ★★★★** Finger crack widening to 2 inches.

CRYSTAL QUARRY

This formation lies northeast of The Castle, roughly opposite and across the gully/valley from it. Approach as for The Castle routes. See map, page 72.

382 **SACK IN THE WASH 5.10b** Approach this and the following route by third-classing up slabs. This is a right-facing dihedral on the left side of the formation.
383 **HANDS OF FIRE 5.11c (TR)** The overhanging "wave-shaped" crack right of **Sack in the Wash.**
384 **CRYSTAL DEVA 5.10c** This route climbs discontinuous cracks and faces. It starts down low and right of the two previous routes.

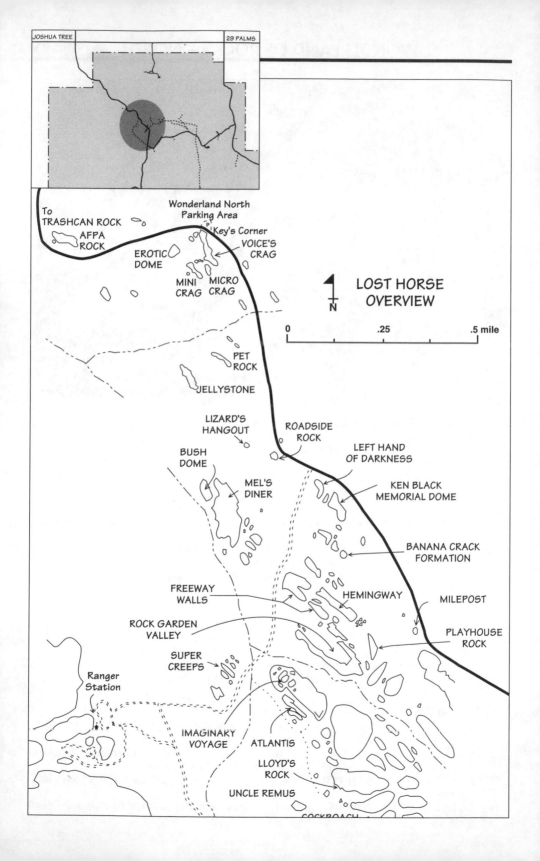

JOSHUA TREE | 29 PALMS

To
TRASHCAN ROCK
AFPA
ROCK
EROTIC
DOME
MINI
CRAG
MICRO
CRAG

Wonderland North
Parking Area
Key's Corner
VOICE'S
CRAG

LOST HORSE
OVERVIEW

N

0   .25   .5 mile

PET
ROCK
JELLYSTONE

LIZARD'S
HANGOUT
ROADSIDE
ROCK
LEFT HAND
OF DARKNESS
BUSH
DOME
MEL'S
DINER
KEN BLACK
MEMORIAL DOME

BANANA CRACK
FORMATION

FREEWAY
WALLS
HEMINGWAY
MILEPOST

ROCK GARDEN
VALLEY
PLAYHOUSE
ROCK

SUPER
CREEPS

Ranger
Station

IMAGINARY
VOYAGE
ATLANTIS
LLOYD'S
ROCK
UNCLE REMUS
COCKROACH

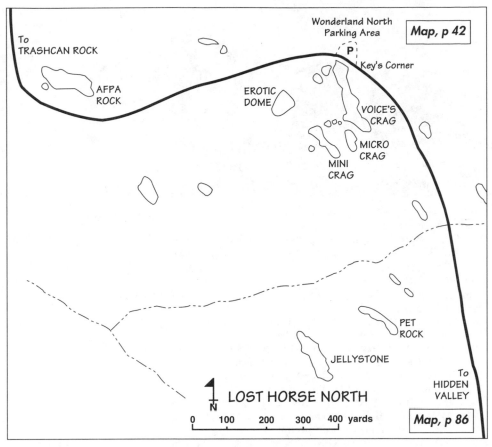

To TRASHCAN ROCK

AFPA ROCK

EROTIC DOME

Wonderland North Parking Area

Map, p 42

P

Key's Corner

VOICE'S CRAG

MICRO CRAG

MINI CRAG

PET ROCK

JELLYSTONE

To HIDDEN VALLEY

LOST HORSE NORTH

0   100   200   300   400 yards

Map, p 86

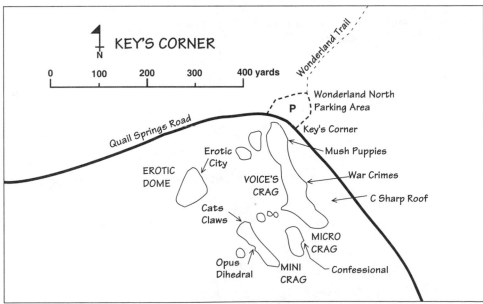

KEY'S CORNER

0   100   200   300   400 yards

Wonderland Trail

Wonderland North Parking Area

P

Quail Springs Road

Key's Corner

Mush Puppies

War Crimes

C Sharp Roof

Erotic City

EROTIC DOME

VOICE'S CRAG

Cats Claws

MICRO CRAG

Opus Dihedral

MINI CRAG

Confessional

VOICE'S CRAG

This long, low, reddish-colored crag lies .2 mile (.3 km) south of Key's Corner on the west side of the road. All the routes are located on the east face. Map, page 81.

385   **B FLAT   5.7+**   Pro: To 2 inches. This is the right-leaning crack system 30 feet left of **C Sharp Roof.**

386   **B SHARP   5.7+**   Pro: To 2.5 inches. Start 20 feet left of **C Sharp Roof.** Climb up a black flake, then right and up.

387   **C SHARP ROOF   5.10c**   Pro: Thin to 2 inches.

388   **IRONSIDES   5.9**   Pro: To 2 inches.

389   **BLONDE BOMBSHELL BABYLON   5.8+**   Pro: To 2.5 inches.

390   **HOT CROSS BUNS   5.7**   Pro: To 2.5 inches.

391   **LIFE IN THE FAT LANE   5.9**   Pro: To 3 inches.

392   **WAR CRIMES   5.10a**   Pro: To 4 inches.

393   **DWINDLING GREENBACKS   5.11a R ★★**   Pro: Many thin to 1inch.

394   **MUSH PUPPIES   5.8+**   This route lies on a tower on the right end of Voice's Crag, facing the road. This route connects several right-slanting cracks.

395   **ADAMS' HAPPY ACRES   5.5**   Steep flakes and cracks rise to the right of **Mush Puppies.**

396   **GIBBERISH   5.10c (TR)**   Climb the brown streak on the short, steep west face up and right from **Mush Puppies.**

MICRO CRAG
This small crag lies about 75 yards off the road, just south and slightly behind Voice's Crag.

397   **THE TODD COUPLE   5.10c ★**   Pro: To 2.5 inches.
398   **CONFESSIONAL   5.10b R ★**   Pro: Very thin to 2 inches.
399   **WIRED   5.10b ★★**   Pro: Many very small to 2 inches.
400   **SNICKER BISCUIT   5.11b ★**   Pro: Thin to 2 inches.
401   **O.W.   5.10d**   Pro: To 4 inches.

MINI CRAG
Another little outcrop rises just west of Micro Crag. Several routes lie on the east face at the northern and southern sections (the middle section is fairly nondistinct). **Opus Dihedral** lies on the west face. Map, page 81.

MINI CRAG – EAST FACE, LEFT END
402   **STEEPED T   5.8**   This route climbs twin cracks, just right of a gully.
403   **MODEL T   5.7**   The two cracks 10 feet to the right of **Steeped T.** Start up left crack, finish up the right; tunnel under block at top.
404   **CATS CLAWS   5.11a ★★**   Follow two bolts next to steep crack at north end of the east face.
405   **ARETE BUSTER   5.11a R ★**   This arête split by a diagonal crack is just right of **Cats Claws.** Start on the leftmost of two possible bouldery starts, then follows the crack around the arête and up.
406   **PIDDLE PUG   5.7 R**   Start just right of Arête Buster in a flare, then head straight up.

MINI CRAG – WEST FACE
407   **OPUS DIHEDRAL   5.9 ★**   Pro: To 3 inches. High on the west face (near the middle of the formation) is a 35-foot right-facing dihedral. This is **Opus Dihedral.**
408   **BLOOM COUNTY   5.6**   The crack/corner just right of **Opus Dihedral.**

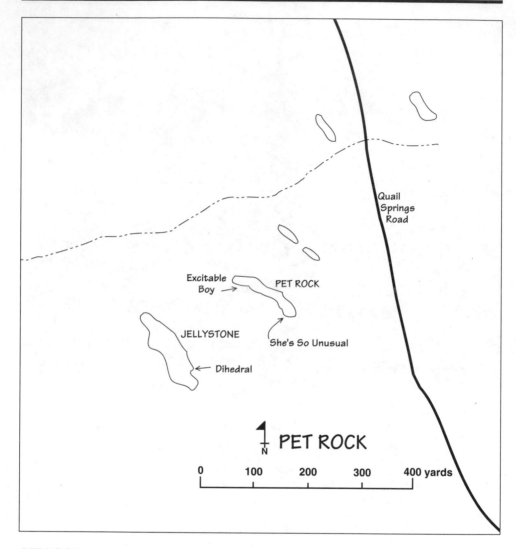

PET ROCK

This is the small (and fairly forgettable) formation midway between Voice's Crag and Lizard's Hangout, about 150 yards west of the road. The routes listed are on the west face, away from the road. Maps, pages 81 and above.

409   **EXCITABLE BOY 5.9**   Climb the short, shallow left-facing corner on the far left side of the face.

410   **PET PROJECT 5.4**   Flakes and face just left of **She's So Unusual.**

411   **SHE'S SO UNUSUAL 5.7**   A seam in brown rock on the south end of the cliff (150 feet right of **Excitable Boy**).

JELLYSTONE

This so-so formation lies about 90 yards to the southwest of Pet Rock (in fact, this obvious formation is often mistaken for the rather unimpressive Pet Rock). Several routes are located on the east face (facing the road), and a number of moderate possiblities exist on the west face. Map, page 84.

412   **YOGI 5.10c (TR)**   Could be led if you wanted to bother; very loose.

413   **BOO BOO 5.9 R**

414   **MR RANGER SIR 5.7**

415   **SMARTER THAN THE AVERAGE RANGER 5.11a ★**   Pro: Very thin to 3 inches.

416   **PICK-A-NICK BASKETS 5.9 R**

417   **THE BEAR NECESSITIES 5.7**

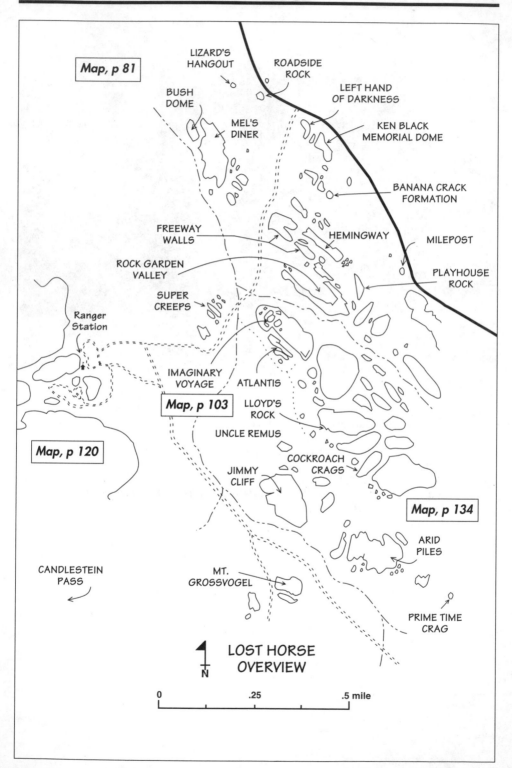

Map, p 81

LIZARD'S
HANGOUT

ROADSIDE
ROCK

LEFT HAND
OF DARKNESS

BUSH
DOME

MEL'S
DINER

KEN BLACK
MEMORIAL DOME

BANANA CRACK
FORMATION

FREEWAY
WALLS

HEMINGWAY

MILEPOST

ROCK GARDEN
VALLEY

PLAYHOUSE
ROCK

SUPER
CREEPS

Ranger
Station

IMAGINARY
VOYAGE

ATLANTIS

Map, p 103

LLOYD'S
ROCK

Map, p 120

UNCLE REMUS

COCKROACH
CRAGS

JIMMY
CLIFF

Map, p 134

ARID
PILES

CANDLESTEIN
PASS

MT.
GROSSVOGEL

PRIME TIME
CRAG

**LOST HORSE
OVERVIEW**

N

0   .25   .5 mile

ROADSIDE ROCK

Roadside Rock lies just west of Quail Springs Road, at a sharp left hand corner .75 mile (1.2 km) south of Key's Corner. Map, page 86.

418   **JUST ANOTHER ROADSIDE ATTRACTION   5.9 ★**

419   **CHEAP THRILLS   5.11a (TR)**

420   **RESTAURANT AT THE END OF THE UNIVERSE   5.10d ★**   Start on the upper tier of rock around the corner from the above routes. Climb a thin arch to a roof, then past two bolts.

421   **STAINS OF THE STARS   5.10a**   This right-slanting undercling leading to a offwidth crack is to the right of the above route.

422   **ROY'S SOLO   5.7**   This short diagonaling crack is right of the preceding route, on the backside of Roadside Rock.

LIZARD'S HANGOUT

This small rock is approximately 100 yards northwest (to the right) of Roadside Rock and about 50 yards from the road. The routes are located on the back, west side of the rock. Map, page 86.

423 **POODLE LIZARD 5.7**
424 **ALLIGATOR LIZARD 5.9**   Pro: To 2.5 inches.
425 **LIZARD SKIN 5.8**   Pro: To 2 inches.
B3   **WALLY GATOR 5.11**
426 **RIGHT LIZARD CRACK 5.9 ★**   Pro: To 2 inches.
427 **LEFT LIZARD CRACK 5.10d R ★**   Pro: Thin to 1.5 inches.
428 **LIZARD IN BONDAGE 5.10a R**   Pro: Thin to 1.5 inches.
429 **PROGRESSIVE LIZARD 5.9 ★**   Pro: To 2 inches.
430 **CHICKEN LIZARD 5.10b ★**   Pro: Very thin to 2 inches.
431 **LIZARD ROBBINS 5.5**   Chimney.
432 **LIZARD TAYLOR 5.5 R**   Climb the face left of **Lizard Robbins.**
433 **KOMODO DRAGON 5.6 R**   Climb the steep face 15 feet left of **Lizard Taylor.**
434 **INTO YOU LIKE A TRAIN 5.11c (TR)**   The bottomless groove 40 feet right of **Lizard Taylor.**

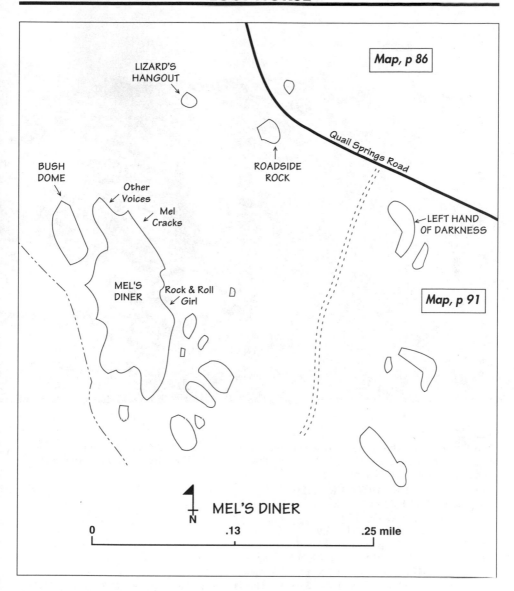

LIZARD'S
HANGOUT

Map, p 86

Quail Springs Road

ROADSIDE
ROCK

BUSH
DOME

Other
Voices

Mel
Cracks

LEFT HAND
OF DARKNESS

MEL'S
DINER

Rock & Roll
Girl

Map, p 91

MEL'S DINER

N

0   .13   .25 mile

MEL'S DINER

MEL'S DINER

This formation lies about 250 yards west of the Quail Springs Road, at about the point Roadside Rock adjoins the road, and about 350 yards northwest of of the Lost Horse dirt road. All of the routes face to the east. Map on page 89.

435   **SHAMROCK SHOOTER   5.11c**
436   **ROMAN PRETZEL   5.8+**
437   **MODERN JAZZ   5.10b**
438   **ROCK & ROLL GIRL   5.9**
439   **KICKIN' BACH   5.10a ★**
440   **RIGHT MEL CRACK   5.10c ★★**   The left crack.
441   **LEFT MEL CRACK   5.10c ★★**   The right crack.
442   **I LOVE BRIAN PICCOLO   5.8+ ★**   This is a steep crack high on the formation, above and right of the **Mel Cracks.**
443   **OTHER VOICES   5.7 ★**   This separate face is about 125 yards to the right and west of the main face of Mel's Diner.

BUSH DOME

This dome is located behind and to the right of Mel's Diner and is seen easily from the Quail Springs Road. Map, page 89.

444   **CHESTWIG   5.10a**   An improbable-looking thin crack left of the center of the crag.
445   **LEAN ON ME   5.10a ★**   Crack right of **Chestwig.** Pass asmall bush, then a large, helpful bush.
446   **KATE'S BUSH   5.8**   A long, obvious crack on the right side of the face that goes past a bush, then follows another crack up to the top.

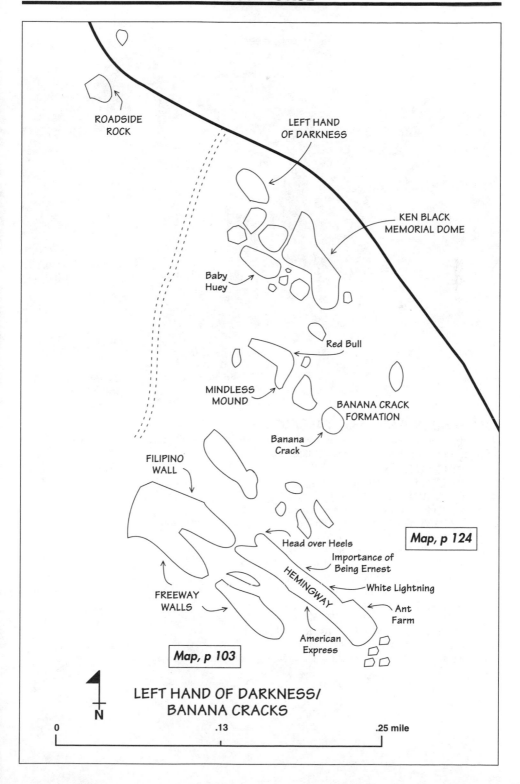

ROADSIDE
ROCK

LEFT HAND
OF DARKNESS

KEN BLACK
MEMORIAL DOME

Baby
Huey

Red Bull

MINDLESS
MOUND

BANANA CRACK
FORMATION

Banana
Crack

FILIPINO
WALL

Head over Heels

Importance of
Being Ernest

HEMINGWAY

White Lightning

FREEWAY
WALLS

Ant
Farm

Map, p 124

Map, p 103

American
Express

LEFT HAND OF DARKNESS/
BANANA CRACKS

N

0   .13   .25 mile

LEFT HAND OF DARKNESS – EAST FACE

This formation is located at the southwest corner of the junction of Quail Springs Road and the Lost Horse Ranger Station dirt road. Maps, pages 89, 91.

447 **BREW 102 5.8**
448 **ROUTE 152 5.10a R** Poor rock.
449 **LEFT ROUTE 5.10a R ★**
450 **RIGHT ROUTE 5.10c ★★** Direct start is 5.11.
     VARIATION 5.11c ★★ Climbs straight up the crack via toprope.
451 **THE UH CULT 5.10a (TR)**
452 **UNCLE FESTER 5.10d ★**
453 **TO AIR IS HUMAN 5.10d R ★★** Three bolts.
454 **WHISTLING SPHINCTER 5.11c (TR) ★**
455 **JANE PAULEY 5.8**
456 **BRYANT GUMBEL 5.8**
457 **PUMP UP THE VOLUME 5.11a ★** Three bolts.
458 **GRANDPA GANDER 5.10c R ★** Three bolts.
459 **GRANNY GOOSE 5.7**
460 **MOTHER GOOSE 5.4 X** The arête right of **Granny Goose.**

LEFT HAND OF DARKNESS – WEST FACE

The west side of the Left Hand of Darkness has a steep orange-colored face about 100 yards south of the Ranger Station Road. A large pillar lies about five feet away from the center of the face. Map, page 91.

461 **BABY HUEY SMOKES AN ANTI-PIPELOAD 5.11d ★★** The left-hand route. Pro: One bolt, thin to 2 inches.
462 **ANTI-GRAVITY BOOTS 5.11c R ★**
463 **GOMMA COCIDA 5.11b ★** Discontinuous crack just right of **Anti-Gravity Boots.**
464 **POTATO MASHER 5.12b ★** Seam with one bolt right of **Gomma Cocida.**
465 **MANO NEGRA (AKA: THE NOSE IN A DAY) 5.9** Pro: To 4 inches.

KEN BLACK MEMORIAL DOME

472 – 473
(ON FACE AROUND CORNER)

466

467

468

469 470 471

CRACK
AROU
CORN

KEN BLACK MEMORIAL DOME
This is the first formation southeast of Left Hand of Darkness. Map, page 91.

466 **BLACKOUT 5.11a R ★** Pro: Two bolts and thin camming units.
467 **PITCH BLACK 5.9 ★** Pro: To 3 inches.
468 **HOLIDAY IN THE SUN 5.10a R ★★** Pro: One bolt, small camming units.
469 **CHICKEN MECHANICS 5.9 ★**
470 **POULTRY PILOTS 5.7**
471 **FRYER FLYERS 5.5**
472 **PACIFIC AVE. DORM 5.7 ★** Three bolts. Face.
473 **UNKNOWN 5.8 X** Climb the face to the right of **Pacific Ave. Dorm.**

THE FREEWAY WALL
(LOWER)
WEST FACE

THE FREEWAY WALL – WEST FACE

This formation lies parallel and to the west of Hemingway Buttress. The upper (right-hand) portion ends just north of Copenhagen Wall, and it is possible to walk through a narrow corridor behind (west) of the Copenhagen Wall to the IRS Wall. Map, page 91.

474 **PLANETARY MOTION 5.8** Left and around the corner from **False Smooth As Silk.** Climb a hand crack to a bulge/headwall, go right, then head back left to an upper thin crack. This route is about 150 feet right of **Marcos/Exiled.**

475 **FALSE SMOOTH AS SILK 5.4 ★★** This is about 100 feet left of **Smooth as Silk.** A crack in a knobby buttress starts with a short headwall.

476 **SILKWORM 5.6** This is the left-facing corner with a thin crack on the right wall, between **Smooth as Silk** and **False Smooth As Silk.**

477 **SMOOTH AS SILK 5.7 ★** This is the smooth, low-angled slab with finger crack that faces the road. Pro: Small to 2 inches.

478 **ROLLING ROCK 5.9 (TR)**

479 **STOP TRUNDLING 5.10a** Pro: To 2.5 inches.

480 **STOP MAKING SENSE 5.11a** Pro: Very thin, one bolt.

481 **START TRUNDLING 5.10a ★** Pro: To 2.5 inches.

482 **START FUMBLING 5.10d R**

483 **STOP GRUMBLING 5.8** Pro: To 3 inches.

484 **BARNEY RUBBLE 5.1** Climb the loose blocks.

485 **WILMA RUBBLE 5.7** Rap off with one rope over the horn. Pro: To 3 inches.

THE FREEWAY WALL

486   **S'NOSE OF WINTER 5.8**   Start on above route, but traverse left under the roof to a steep face. Rap off previous route. Pro: To 3 inches.

487   **SWEET TRANSVESTITE 5.8 R**

488   **FREEWAY 5.7 R**

489   **PASSING ZONE 5.8 R/X** Pro: To 2.5 inches, 3 bolts.

490   **(Variation) SIGALERT 5.11a (TR)**

491   **TOTALLY NUTS 5.9 R**

492   **CAST UP A HIGHWAY 5.11a (TR)**

493   **NOBODY WALKS IN L.A. 5.9 ★★**

494   **PRETTY GRITTY 5.10a**

495   **ANACRAM 5.10c ★★★**

496   **CAKE WALK 5.9 ★★★**

497   **THE TALKING FISH 5.10d ★**

498   **JUNKYARD GOD 5.9**

TINY TOTS ROCK – EAST FACE

This pillar of rock lies opposite the upper Freeway Wall. Map, page 124.

499   **DATE RAPE**   **5.9** ★
500   **TINKER TOYS**   **5.10b** ★★
501   **DINKEY DOINKS**   **5.8** ★★
502   **WHO'DA THOUGHT**   **5.11c (TR)** ★
503   **COLE-LEWIS**   **5.8** ★
504   **SPONTANEOUS HUMAN COMBUSTION**   **5.11c** ★   Four bolts.
505   **FATAL FLAW**   **5.9** ★   Climbs the crack in the corner, going over a small overhang.

ROCK GARDEN VALLEY – EAST FACE

Rock Garden Valley is formed by the back (west) side of the IRS Wall on the left, and the back (east) side of the Lost Horse Wall on the right. All recorded routes lie on the right-hand side (East Face of Lost Horse Wall). Maps, pages 103, 124.

506   **POP ROCKS 5.10b ★★**   This is near the upper end of the Rock Garden Valley. Climb straight up a face (one bolt) to a nice crack, then head left, then climb straight up and over a roof to the top.

507   **TOP OF THE POPS 5.10 ★★★**   This six-bolt face route is 20 feet right of **Pop Rocks.**

508   **SILENT BUT DEADLY 5.9 R**   This climbs the right arête of the **Pop Rocks** formation, starting in a low-angled wide crack.

SHORTER WALL

A short wall with four distinct cracks rises to the right of **Pop Rocks.** A broken area at the base serves as a reference point.

509   **HOLLY DEVICE 5.10c ★**   Ascend the center of the buttress left of **Spitwad** past four bolts.

510   **THE GRIFFIN 5.10a R**   Ascend a double crack right of **Holly Device,** then angle right and climb past two bolts.

511   **FORTUNE COOKIE 5.10a**   Climb a short vertical crack right of Griffin, then climb the face above past three bolts.

512   **SPITWAD 5.10a ★★**   Start at the lower left-hand part of the broken area. A crack that goes left and up is followed until you can stem back right into a lieback crack near the top.

513   **EUTHYPHRO 5.9 ★**   This is a hand crack that goes up and left from the top of the broken section.

514   **YOUNG LUST 5.9 ★★★**   This is 10 feet right of the broken area. Follow another thin crack to the top.

515   **LEWD AND LASCIVIOUS CONDUCT 5.10c R ★**   This is the thin seam on the varnished face between **Young Lust** and **Smithereens.** Pro: Very small nuts to 2 inches.

516   **SMITHEREENS 5.9 ★★★**   Follow a thin crack located at the extreme right-hand section of the wall to the top.

517   **ROCK-A-LOT 5.7 ★**   Climb the somewhat wide crack left of **Rock Candy.**

518   **ROCK CANDY 5.9 ★★★**   Climb the steep face just left of **Double Dogleg.** Pro: Four bolts, thin nuts.

520   **ROCK DOG CANDY LEG 5.11c (TR) ★★**   Face between **Double Dogleg** and **Rock Candy.**

521   **DOUBLE DOGLEG 5.7 ★★★**   Located in the middle of a brown-and-white pocketed face, this crack heads up, doglegs left, then jogs back right.

522   **SPLIT PERSONALITY 5.9 ★★★**   Start up **Double Dogleg,** but stem out right to a very thin crack.

523   **PERSONAL SPACE 5.10c (TR) ★★**   The face to the right of **Split Personality.**

524   **BECK'S BET 5.8 ★**   This crack lies about 30 feet right of **Double Dogleg** and is fairly obvious.

525   **WHY DOES IT HURT WHEN I PEE? 5.10b ★**   Thin cracks just left of **What's Hannen.**

526   **WHAT'S HANNEN 5.10a**   Starts in a chimney/alcove. Pro: To 4 inches.

527   **SWISS CHEESE   5.6**   Climb solution pockets to the right of **What's Hannan.**
528   **MR. MICHAEL GOES TO WASHINGTON   5.8**
529   **BLUE SKY, BLACK DEATH   5.5**
530   **BARN DOOR, LEFT   5.9 (TR)**
531   **BARN DOOR, RIGHT   5.10a (TR)**
532   **BOLIVIAN FREEZE JOB   5.9 ★**
533   **CHILE WILLIE   5.7**
The next three routes lie on a small crag down (towards the road/north) of **Chile Willie**.

534   **TRAINING FOR PATAGONIA   5.10b R**   The left crack, past 2 ceilings.
535   **COLD COLUMBIAN   5.9**   The right-hand crack/arête.
536   **PERUVIAN POWER LAYBACK   5.9**   The clean, right-facing corner 20 feet right of **Cold Columbian.**

LOST HORSE WALL

A valley with a large, west-facing formation (which doubles as the backside of Rock Garden Valley), is located about .5 mile southwest along the Ranger Station Road from Quail Springs Road. The streambed in the middle of this valley can be followed south to The Land That Time Forgot and eventually to the Real Hidden Valley. Maps, pages 103,124.

537   **ENOS MILLS GLACIER   5.11a R**
538   **CRETIN BULL DANCER   5.11a R ★★**
539   **ARE YOU EXPERIENCED?   5.11a ★**
540   **TERROR IN DE SKIES   5.10a R**   Pro: To 3 inches, two bolts.
541   **MOVEABLE FEAST (AKA: MEAT WAGON)   5.9**
542   **HESITATION BLUES   5.10b ★**   Rappel 75 feet from the stance.
543   **HAPPY LANDINGS, LINDA   5.11b**   Pro: Thin to 2.5 inches.
544   **JUST ANOTHER CRACK FROM L.A.   5.9 ★**

LOST HORSE WALL – SOUTH END

545   **GOSSAMER WINGS 5.10a** Pro: To 3 inches.
546   **WILSON REGULAR ROUTE 5.5 ★**
547   **ALTITUDE SICKNESS 5.9** Pro: To 3 inches.
548   **THE SWIFT 5.7 ★★**
549   **BIRD ON A WIRE 5.10a ★★★** Pro: Thin to 2.5 inches.
550   **DAPPLED MARE 5.8 ★★★**
551   **EDGAR RICE BURROS 5.10c**
552   **HEADBANGERS' BALL 5.11c ★★**
553   **ROAN WAY 5.8 ★★**
554   **HAIRLINE FRACTURE 5.10a R ★★**
555   **MARE'S TAIL 5.9 ★★**
556   **LOST IN SPACE 5.8 ★★**

LOOKING SOUTH FROM SUPER CREEPS WALL

IMAGINARY VOYAGE FORMATION

LOST HORSE WALL (south)

559

560   561

562

WILD GRAVITY FORMATION

This formation lies opposite the south end of the Lost Horse Wall and faces east. The cliff is characterized by numerous vertical crack systems and many large roofs. Several routes have been done on this wall. Maps, pages 103,124.

557   **TOP FLIGHT   5.10a** This route takes the second crack to the left of **Wild Gravity**.
558   **WILD GRAVITY   5.9** This takes the crack directly under the left side of the largest, highest roof on the wall. An incipient crack marks the start, which leads to a right-facing corner just below the roof.

Several other cracks and roofs have been climbed further to the right of **Wild Gravity,** and range in grade from 5.9 to 5.10b.

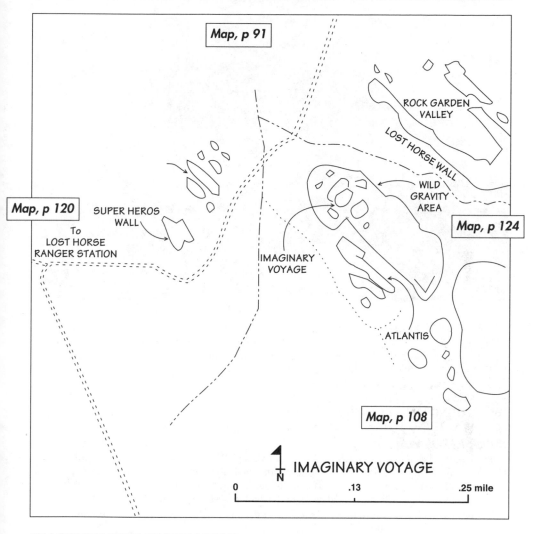

IMAGINARY VOYAGE

IMAGINARY VOYAGE FORMATION

This formation consists of a 50-foot summit block lying atop the **Wild Gravity** face. A large cave/crack is located on its west side. See maps above and page124.

559   **DEAD MAN'S PARTY   5.10b R**   Pro: Thin nuts, three bolts.
560   **BLACK PLASTIC STREETWALKER   5.10c R ★★★**   Pro: Many thin to 1 inch.
561   **IMAGINARY VOYAGE   5.10d ★★★★**   Pro: 1 to 5 inches.
562   **GRAVEL SHOWER   5.10b (TR)**

SUPER CREEPS WALL – EAST WALL

This small formation lies just north of the Ranger Station Road, approximately two-thirds of a mile from the junction with the Quail Springs Road. From this point on, the road to Lost Horse Ranger Station is closed to the public. Map, page 103.

563   **TALES OF POWDER   5.10b** ★
564   **SCARY MONSTERS   5.11d** ★★★
565   **YOUNG FRANKENSTEIN   5.11a** ★★
566   **WALTZING WORM   5.12a** ★★★

SUPER HEROS WALL

This formation lies about 100 yards west of Super Creeps Wall and faces west. Park as for Super Creeps Wall (off the Lost Horse Ranger Station dirt road, about two-thirds of a mile from its junction with Quail Springs Road). The center of the west face has two cracks next to each other in desert-varnished rock. The right-hand crack in the center is **Mr. Magoo.** Map, page 103.

567   **ELMER FUDD   5.11b (TR)**   This is the left-hand crack/shallow dihedral system near the center of the face, just left of **Mr. Magoo.**
568   **MR. MAGOO   5.9**   The right-hand crack near the center of the face.
569   **YOSEMITE SAM   5.4**   Loose crack/corner right of **Mr. Magoo.**

ATLANTIS WALL
LEFT END

577
578   579
580
583
582
581
571 573 575 576
572
584

ATLANTIS AREA

This area is located on an east-facing wall in a hidden canyon southwest and below **Imaginary Voyage**. It is best approached by parking approximately two-thirds of a mile from the Lost Horse junction with Quail Springs Road (the same place as for the Super Creeps Wall). The road beyond, which leads to Lost Horse Ranger Station (and to Jimmy Cliff, Arid Piles and Mt. Grossvogel), is closed to the public. Walk south, skirting along the base of the rocks below Imaginary Voyage, until you can turn left (east) and enter the canyon from the south. The routes are all on the west side of the canyon, facing east. It also is reasonable to approach Jimmy Cliff and Arid Piles from this spot (although the usual approach is from the Real Hidden Valley Area). Maps, pages 86, 103, 124.

570   **NEPTUNE   5.8**   Climb the left-leaning pillar 75 feet left of **Vorpal Sword.**
571   **TRIDENT   5.10c ★**
572   **VORPAL SWORD   5.9 ★**
573   **GRAIN SURPLUS   5.8**
574   **GRAIN FOR RUSSIA   5.7**   Crack right of **Grain Surplus.**
575   **MINOTAUR   5.7 ★**
576   **FANTASY OF LIGHT   5.10a ★**
577   **SELF ABUSE   5.6**
578   **HOT CRYSTALS   5.9 ★**
579   **POCKET PUSSY   5.11a (TR)**   Located between **Hot Crystals** and **Annointed Seagull.**
580   **ANNOINTED SEAGULL   5.8**   Starts off a block.
581   **CEREMONY   5.10c ★**   One bolt.
582   **SOLAR TECHNOLOGY   5.6**
583   **MEN WITH COW'S HEADS   5.5**
584   **WET PIGEON   5.8 ★**
585   **TAURUS   5.6**
586   **THE LABYRINTH   5.7**
584   **WET PIGEON   5.8 ★**
587   **UNWIPED BUTT   5.6**

TIRE TREAD WALL
This steep wall, with a weird black tread-like stain on it, is located up and right from the main Atlantis wall. Not shown on a map.

588   **MENTAL RETREAD   5.9**
589   **DON'T TREAD ON ME   5.10b (TR) ★**
590   **TREADMARK LEFT   5.8**
591   **TREADMARK RIGHT   5.8**
592   **FLAT TIRE   5.8**

LLOYD'S ROCK

Lloyd's Rock is located about .25 mile southeast of the Atlantis area; just northeast of Uncle Remus. It is part of the toe of the hillside and faces west. See maps, pages 86,108.

593　**FLAWLESS FISSURE　5.9 ★★**
594　**FRIEND EATER　5.8**
595　**RR DOES IT AGAIN　5.10d (TR)**
596　**MICRONESIA　5.10d**
597　**BORNEO　5.4**　The short crack uphill from **Micronesia.**

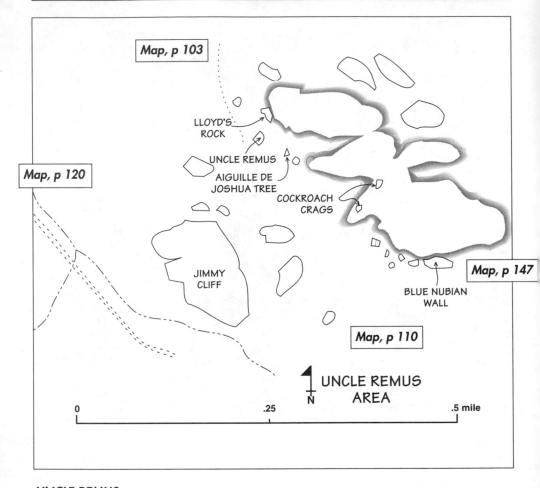

UNCLE REMUS

This is a small boulder/pillar 100 yards southwest of Lloyd's Rock and 100 yards north of a finger of rock known as Aiguille de Joshua Tree. See map, above.

598   **UNCLE REMUS 5.11b ★★★**   Follows three bolts on south face and arête. A tie-off sling is useful.

599   **UP THE ANTE 5.11d (TR) ★★**   Start up the crack to face climbing. This is to the right of **Uncle Remus.**

AIGUILLE DE JOSHUA TREE

This 30-foot, ultra-thin finger of rock is a must-do, if for the photo oportunities alone. It is located amongst boulders about 100 yards south of Uncle Remus and 350 yards northeast of Jimmy Cliff.

B4   **AIGUILLE DE JOSHUA TREE 5.6 X ★★★**

BEETLE BUTTRESS

This area lies about 100 yards south of Lloyd's Rock and directly east from a point about halfway between Uncle Remus and Aiguille De Joshua Tree. The rock is good, but the routes are rather short.

600   **THE BEATLES 5.4** The leftmost right-facing chimney.

601   **BEATLE BAILY 5.4** Blocky ramp/corner just right of **The Beatles.**

602   **LEFT BEETLE CRACK 5.10b** Short, overhanging hand crack that rises just left of **Beetle Corner.**

603   **BEETLE CORNER 5.11a** Obvious short corner near the right edge of cliff.

604   **RIGHT BEETLE CRACK 5.10b** Finger crack just right of **Beetle Corner.**

COCKROACH CRAG

This squat brown rock is 250 yards right (southeast) of Lloyd's Rock (about 100 yards southeast of Aiguille De Joshua Tree), and high up on the talus. **Classic Corner** and **Arms For Hostages** lie on faces up and right of the main Cockroach Crag. **The Dungeon** lies on the northwest face of a small crag 100 yards right and behind Cockroach Crag. Maps, pages 108, 110.

605   **CLASSIC CORNER 5.7 ★** This is a hand crack in a clean grey dihedral located behind and left of the main Cockroach Crag.

606   **ARMS FOR HOSTAGES 5.11b (TR) ★** A severely-overhanging brown wall about 50 yards up and right of **Classic Corner.**

607   **THE DUNGEON 5.9+ ★** This dogleg thin crack starts deep in a pit about 100 yards right and up from Cockroach Crag.

608   **R.S. CHICKEN CHOKER 5.11b ★★** This finger crack over a roof lies on the southwest (left) side of Cockroach Crag.

609   **THE FABULOUS T. GORDEX CRACKS 5.8** Double cracks to the right of **R.S. Chicken Choker.**

610   **ROACH MOTEL 5.10a R** Located around the corner to the right of the two previous routes on the left end of the southeast face. This route ascends thin cracks and passes several horizontals.

611   **CLIMB OF THE COCKROACHES 5.8 R** Ascend a big flake leading to face moves 15 feet right of **Roach Motel.**

612   **ROACH ROOF 5.6** Climb the short, right-facing corner leading to a roof. This is to the right of **Climb of the Cockroaches.**

About 250 yards right of and facing Cockroach Crag is a steep wall with two bolted face routes. Maps, pages 108, 110.

613   **GREEN VISITOR 5.11d ★★★** The left bolted route.

614   **THIRD BOLT FROM THE SUN 5.11a ★** The right bolted route.

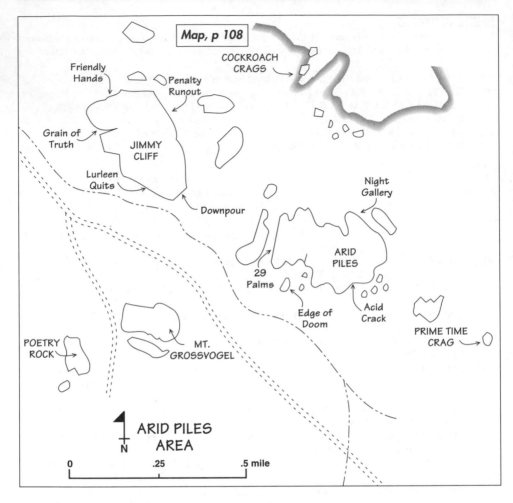

JIMMY CLIFF AREA

This area is about two-thirds of a mile south of the parking area for Super Creeps Wall/Atlantis Area (two-thirds of a mile from the junction of Lost Horse Ranger Station road and Quail Springs Road). The road to Lost Horse Ranger Station is closed to the public from this point on. This is unfortunate because the closed dirt road passes just west of the two largest formations (Jimmy Cliff to the north and Arid Piles to the south) and just east of the smaller Mt. Grossvogel. However, this area's close proximity to the Real Hidden Valley makes it possible to walk here by way of the trail leading past Houser Buttress. In fact, it is probably closer to approach Arid Piles and Mt. Grossvogel from the Real Hidden Valley area.

JIMMY CLIFF

This is the northernmost of three large formations rising from the otherwise level desert floor. It is west of the Uncle Remus and Coackroach Crag areas.

615　**BAD BOY CLUB　5.9 R**　A wall with several horizontal cracks is located about 150 feet down and left from **I Forgot**. Climb the central seam/flake past the horizontals.

616　**I FORGOT　5.10a**

617　**LAST MINUTE ADDITIONS　5.6**

JIMMY CLIFF – EAST FACE
618   **CHILLY WILLY 5.10c, A1**
619   **FREE Variation 5.11a**   Traverse left (6 feet off the deck) from **Penalty Runout.**
620   **PENALTY RUNOUT   5.9 R ★★**
621   **SUDDEN DEATH   5.10a ★**
622   **THIRD WORLD   5.9 ★**

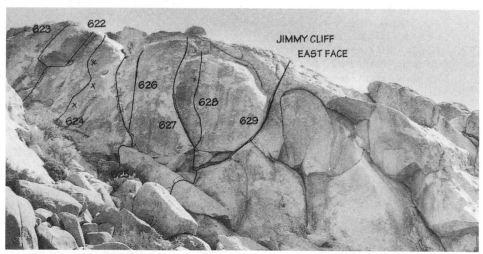

JIMMY CLIFF – EAST FACE
623   **THE HARDER THEY FALL   5.10a ★★**
624   **THE BRONTO'S OR US   5.11a ★★** Pro: To 2 inches, three bolts.
625   **THE DIKE   5.10c R ★★**
626   **DICK VANDIKE   5.10b (TR)**
627   **FRIENDLY HANDS   5.10b ★★★** Pro: To 2.5 inches.
628   **CLIFF HANGER   5.10b R ★★** One bolt.
629   **FIENDISH FISTS   5.9 ★**

JIMMY CLIFF – WEST FACE
See map on page 110.

630   **GRAIN OF TRUTH   5.10d** ★
631   **GS-5   5.9 (TR)**
632   **THE LONE RANGER   5.9** ★★
633   **TASGRAINIAN DEVIL   5.9**   Start 100 feet left of **Live from Tasmania** in an alcove below a chimney. Climb a hidden finger crack to varnished lieback flakes. This climb is only visible from **Live from Tasmania.**
633a   **LIVE FROM TASGRAINIA**
634   **LIVE FROM TASMANIA   5.9** ★
635   **BAD CZECH GIRL   5.11a**   Three bolts.
636   **LURLEEN QUITS   5.8**
637   **QUIT DOING CZECH GIRLS   5.9 (TR)**
638   **A PEANUT GALLERY   5.11a** ★★★   This is a steep, bolted climb on the backside of the large block right of **Lurleen Quits.** It is not visible from the road or the approach.
639   **THE VELVEETA RABBIT   5.7**   This climb is located about midway between **Lurleen Quits** and **Downpour,** at the closest point of Jimmy Cliff to the road. It is a crack in a slab that goes over a small roof.

JIMMY CLIFF – SOUTH FACE

See map on page 110.
640 **THEY FOUND HITLER'S BRAIN 5.12b** ★ Located on the southwest face. Climb past three bolts on small face near the road.
641 **SHORT STOP 5.10a**
642 **DOWNPOUR 5.8** ★
643 **THIN FLAKES 5.9** ★ Pro: Thin.
644 **RATRACE 5.10d** ★★ Pro: Three bolts.

ARID PILES

This formation lies just south of Jimmy Cliff and consists of a complex series of faces and corridors. Map, page 110.

ARID PILES – NORTH FACE

645 **NICE AND STEEP AND ELBOW DEEP   5.10b** This is a north-facing, overhanging fist crack on a ridge of rock 100 yards north of **The Outsiders.**

646 **THE OUTSIDERS   5.11a R ★** Pro: Two bolts, thin to 2 inches.

647 **QUARTER MOON CRACK 5.10a**

648 **NAPKIN OF SHAME   5.10b ★** Pro: To 3 inches.

These routes lie in a narrow corridor to the right of **Napkin of Shame.** Some routes are located on the north side of the corridor.

649 **QUICKSTONE   5.12c R ★★★** A bolted face left of **29 Palms.**

650 **29 PALMS   5.11d ★★★★** This route takes the beautiful dihedral on the left side of the corridor, 100 feet right of **The Outsiders.** Pro: Many thin to 1.5 inches.

651 **THE 39 SLAPS   5.11c R ★★** Climb the bolted outside arête right of **29 Palms.**

652 **TOWER OF BABEL   5.10d** This route lies on the face of one of the rocks forming the right side of the corridor. Three bolts.

653 **MR. BUNNY QUITS   5.10a ★** This takes the thin finger crack opposite **29 Palms.** Pro: Thin to 2 inches.

654 **U.B. KOOL   5.10d** Follows an undercling flake start, up and left to overhanging hand crack, then up and left to the top of **29 Palms.**

ARID PILES
NORTHWEST FACE

The next two routes lie on the outer (west) faces of the crags/boulders that form the west side of the **29 Palms** corridor.

655   **JACKALOPE 5.11b**   This route is more or less in front of **29 Palms,** and climbs an undercling leading to face past one bolt.

656   **SECRET SAUCE 5.11b**   This is an undercling/lieback about 100 yards left of **Jackalope** and also west-facing. Pro: One bolt.

657   **SPINNER 5.7 R**   This route climbs the west face of a small boulder/spire 100 yards southwest of **29 Palms.**

658   **EDGE OF DOOM 5.10c ★★**   The start is height-dependent. Pro: Bolts.

ARID PILES – SOUTHWEST FACE

See map on page 110.

659   **SWIFT   5.11a ★**

660   **THE ACID CRACK   5.12d ★★★★**

661   **JUST ANOTHER NEW WAVE ROUTE   5.9**

662   **I'D SLAP YOU BUT SHIT SPLATTERS   5.9+**

663   **POPEYE   5.11a ★★**   This route climbs the left side of the hourglass formation opposite **The Taming of the Shoe.** Pro: To 3 inches.

664   **THE TAMING OF THE SHOE   5.10d R ★★★**   Pro: Very thin to 1 inch.

665   **BARLEY, WHEAT OR RYE (ITS ALL GRAIN)   5.10a**   Climb a right-leaning groove to a bolt about 50 feet left of **Generic Route.** Above, climb past horizontals, move left 15 feet, then up an easy crack.

666   **GENERIC ROUTE   5.8**   This in on a smaller wall, separated from the main formation by a boulder-filled corridor and front of the east face. This climb is a right-slanting crack that starts wide and peters out into face climbing; it is just right of a chimney system with a tree in it.

667   **ELBOW ROOM   5.10d**   The right-hand offwidth/fist crack 60 feet right and around the corner from **Generic Route.**

ARID PILES – EAST FACE

See map on page 110.

668 **HIP, HIP BELAY 5.7+ R** Either start up an unnamed 5.7 fingercrack left of **Night Gallery,** or traverse up and right on a chimney/ramp to a belay ledge above the 5.7 crack. Climb up and left from the belay, then climb discontinuous cracks to a short corner and to the top.

669 **NIGHT GALLERY 5.8+**

670 **SHOOTING GALLERY 5.10b ★★**

671 **SHOOTING GALLERY DIRECT 5.10a**

PRIME TIME CRAG

This small rock lies about 100 yards south of Arid Piles. The only known route is on the west side. Map, page 110.

672 **THE MING DALLAS 5.10b**

MT. GROSSVOGEL – EAST FACE

This formation lies just west of Arid Piles and across the dirt road. A branch in the dirt road heads to the right (southwest) and behind this rock. Map, page 110.

673   **BLIND ME WITH SCIENCE   5.10b**
674   **RANGER DANGER   5.8**
675   **DR. SEUSS VOGEL   5.6**
676   **IRON MANTEL   5.10c R ★**
677   **BIG BIRD   5.7+**
678   **ROBORANGER   5.5**
679   **ROBAXOL   5.6**

MT. GROSSVOGEL – WEST FACE

680   **OHM ON THE RANGE   5.4**   Start in the chasm between the east and west faces of Mt. Grossvogel, on the back (east) side of the **Chaffe N' Up** summit block. Climb a short, right-leaning finger crack, then move left and follow a vertical hand crack to the top.
681   **KILLER BEES   5.10a**
682   **CHAFFE N' UP   5.8 R**
682A **THE MARITIMER   5.10d (TR)**
683   **LAZY RHYMER   5.10c (TR)**
684   **CRAZY CLIMBER   5.11a ★★★**   Two bolts and fixed pin.
685   **BERSERK   5.10a ★**

POETRY ROCK

This small formation rises across the branch in the road on the west side of M.t Grossvogel (to the west). Map, page 110.

686   **POETRY IN MOTION   5.9 ★**   This route lies on a small pinnacle. Two bolts, without hangers, protect the west face of the pinnacle. Start at a left-diagonaling crack.

MT. GROSSVOGEL – WEST FACE

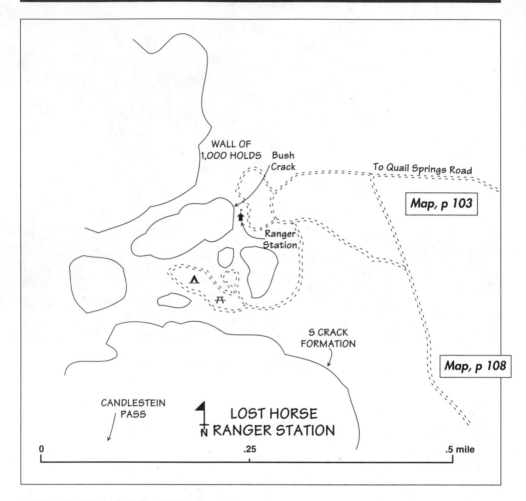

LOST HORSE RANGER STATION WALL

This formation lies behind the ranger station, which is located about .25 mile beyond the point where the Lost Horse Ranger Station road is closed to public. This is the parking spot for the Atlantis/Jimmy Cliff areas as well as for the Super Creeps Wall.

687 **BARBARA BUSH 5.10b ★** Two bolts.
688 **BUSH CRACK 5.7 ★**
689 **OPEN CASKET FUNERAL 5.11a (TR)**
690 **HERCULES 5.11c ★★★**
691 **SWAIN IN THE BREEZE 5.6 ★★** Climbs the face above the left side of the sunken garden. (Numerous bolts, without hangers, were placed on the second ascent.)
692 **4U2DO2 5.5 X** Climb the face between **Swain In The Breeze** and **Owatafooliam,** starting in the sunken garden.
693 **OWATAFOOLIAM 5.8** Climb a flake/crack to the sunken garden. Above, follow a left-facing flake to a yucca, then follow the face to the top.
694 **SWAIN LAKE 5.5 R** The finger crack just left of **Ranger Rendezvous.**
695 **RANGER RENDEZVOUS 5.7** Start as for **Swain Song,** but climb a thin crack in a slab to the left.
696 **SWAIN SONG 5.11a ★★** This is 100 feet right of **Swain In The Breeze.** Follow flakes and cracks to a steepening face with four bolts; traverse up and right at the top.

LOST HORSE RANGER STATION WALL

697   **WALL OF 10,000 HOLDS**   **5.4 R**   Friends in pockets are helpful. Approach by
       scrambling the groove and chimney on the right of the sunken garden to a 20-by-100-foot
       ledge. Above, the climb follows a "swiss cheese" wall above a block that is just right of the
       approach chimney.

The following two routes are on a wall in front and slightly right of from **Wall of 10,000 Holds.**
Rap from a bolt anchor on top.

698   **PEGLEG**   **5.7**   Face climb "diagonal" holds left of **Polly Wants A Crack** to ledge. Follow
       a crack to the top.

699   **POLLY WANTS A CRACK**   **5.10a**   ★   Start off a pointed boulder and climb past three
       bolts to a left leaning crack.

700   **SCARIED TREASURE**   **5.10b**   ★★   Located between **Polly ...** and **Pirates...** Climb a
       right-leaning crack, then up past horizontals to a bolt. Follow a rib/arête to a giant
       chockstone which is passed on the left, then past one more bolt.

701   **PIRATES OF THE CARABINER**   **5.10b**   ★   Climb past a bolt to a flake to the right of
       the preceding route. From the top of the flake, go past two more bolts to a right-leaning
       offwidth.

702   **SWATCHBUCKLER**   **5.8**   This is the crack/corner right of **Pirates of the Carabiner.**

The following routes are in the ranger campground/picnic area at the end of the service road
behind Lost Horse Ranger Station.

703   **WHEN TWO BECOME THREE**   **5.8**   This is the obvious south-facing dike near the end
       of the service road.

704   **JOSAR CRACK**   **5.8+**   This north-facing wall is located in the upper part of the
       campground; the route climbs the central handcrack.

705   **MOSAR**   **5.9+**   A bouldering start leads from discontinuous cracks to horizontal slashes.
       This is just right of **Josar Crack.**

706   **HOW SPOILERS BLEED**   **5.10d**   This right-leaning ramp is directly opposite **Josar** and
       Mosar in the ranger campground. It is actually the back side of the **Wall of 10,000 Holds.**
       Pro: Very thin to 2 inches.

This rather small, dark rock is located about 300 yards south of the ranger station and about 100
yards west of the dirt road. It sits at the base of the hillside.

THE S CRACK FORMATION

HILL STREET BLUES

719

S CRACK FORMATION

721

716 717 718

720

708

707 709

710 711 712

713

S CRACK FORMATION
See map on page 120.
707   **VOGELS ARE POODLES TOO   5.11b (TR)**
708   **ANDROID LUST   5.11a R ★★**
709   **ROBOTICS   5.8**
710   **LEFT S CRACK   5.8 ★**
711   **MIDDLE S CRACK   5.11c R ★★★**
712   **RIGHT S CRACK   5.9 ★**
713   **JINGUS CON   5.11c ★★**

HILL STREET BLUES

This formation lies uphill and left of the S Crack Formation. Map, page 120.

714 **ONCE IN A BLUE MOON 5.4 R** Climb the low-angled face around and left of **Blue Nun.**

715 **BLUE NUN 5.8** Climb the zigzag crack 20 feet left of the obvious corner and just left of the offwidth crack.

716 **BLUE BAYOU 5.4** Climb the right-facing, exfoliated corner system.

717 **BLUES BROTHERS 5.10a ★★★** Climb the obvious thin crack that runs up the center of the slab.

718 **BLUE MONDAY 5.10b ★** This is a thin crack just right of **Blues Brothers.**

719 **RHYTHM & BLUES 5.10b ★★** Very short. Climb a thin crack/flake system to a ledge uphill and right of **Blue Monday.**

720 **BLACK & BLUE 5.6** This starts atop a boulder 100 feet right of **Rythm & Blues,** and follows a thin crack that leads to boulders at the top.

721 **BABY BLUE EYES 5.10b R** To the right of **Black and Blue.**

CANDLESTEIN PASS

This is the gateway to the canyon south of the Hill Street Blues area. It is best approached from the Jimmy Cliff parking area. Stay left of a small formation as you walk into the canyon. The main formation, The Amoeba, splits the canyon in two. Two of the following routes are on The Protozoan, a formation on the left side of the left canyon. The remaining seven routes are on The Amoeba. See maps, pages 103, 120.

THE PROTOZOAN

722 **13-YEAR-OLD DEATH TRAP 5.7** This climb faces north and ascends cracks in a right-facing book.

723 **THE TOOTHPICK 5.11c (TR)** A thin seam 100 feet right of the previous route.

THE AMOEBA

724 **HOLLOW DREAMS 5.11d (TR)** This ascends a difficult, friable flake on the south side of the formation (facing The Protozoan).

725 **THE AMOEBA 5.10** This climb has two bolts and ascends a thin flake right of **Hollow Dreams.** It faces southeast.

726 **SMALL BUSINESS 5.11a** This is left of **Chamber of Commerce.** Climb a crack past a bush into shallow, left-facing corner.

727 **CHAMBER OF COMMERCE 5.10c** This straight-in thin crack is right of **The Amoeba.**

728 **CITY COUNCIL 5.9** Start at the same place as **Illicit Operations**. Climb a thin crack/ramp out left and around the corner; continue up a fist crack to chimney.

729 **ILLICIT OPERATIONS 5.11c** Located to the right of the previous route, this is a thin crack in a rust-colored wall. It starts with a wide lieback.

730 **THE SKEPTIC 5.10c** This is the leftmost of two arching cracks located on the north face of The Amoeba.

731 **PERUVIAN PRINCESS 5.10b** The right-arching crack.

732 **LOWER LIFE FORMS 5.10b ★★** This is a finger-and-hand crack right of the previous routes.

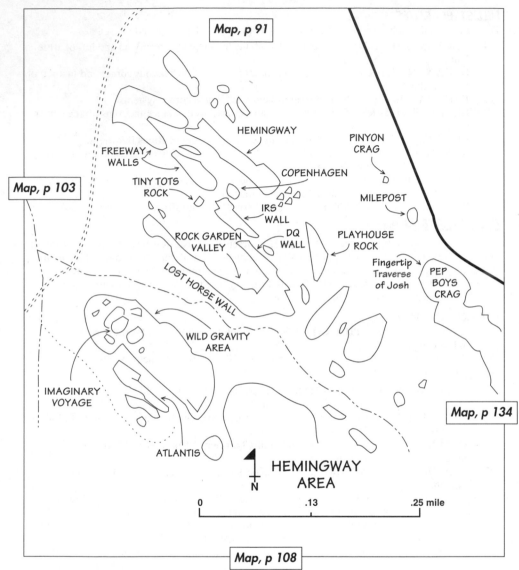

Map, p 91

Map, p 103

Map, p 134

Map, p 108

HEMINGWAY
AREA

0   .13   .25 mile

BANANA CRACKS

This formation lies between the Quail Springs Road (near Left Hand of Darkness) and Hemingway Buttress. The Banana Cracks lie on the west side of the summit block. Map, page 91.

733 **PAPAYA CRACK 5.11b ★★**
734 **LEFT BANANA CRACK   5.10c ★★**
735 **RIGHT BANANA CRACK   5.11a ★★★**
736 **BANANA PEAL 5.11b ★★** Climb the steep face right of **Right Banana Crack.** Pro: To 2 inches, two bolts.
737 **TAILS OF POODLES   5.10a**
738 **BABY BANANA 5.+** This left-slanting crack is on the northeast side of the Banana Cracks formation (facing Quail Springs Road). Start behind a tree and climb up into a left-facing book, then traverse right to reach the upper part of the left-slanting crack.

739 **ROTTEN BANANA 5.6 R** Climb from a flake to a grainy face between **Baby Banana** and **Barfing At Zeldas.**

740 **BARFING AT ZELDAS 5.10d** Start to the right of **Baby Banana.** Climb past two fixed pins.

741 **RED BULL 5.11b R ★★** About 200 feet right of **Baby Banana,** climb a thin crack past one bolt and fixed pin.

MINDLESS MOUND

This rock (really a continuation of the Banana Cracks formation) lieas about 175 feet left (north) of the Banana Cracks and slightly farther back (east). It can be recognized by a dihedral leading to a roof (**Don't Think Twice**). Map, page 91.

742 **SHAKE THE MONSTER 5.10d** A three-bolt face route just right of **Don't Think Twice.**

743 **DON'T THINK TWICE 5.9** This is the dihedral leading to a roof.

744 **RAINY DAY WOMEN 5.7** This hand crack is 75 feet left of **Don't Think Twice.** It is in a brown flare.

745 **MAGGIES FARM 5.7** This is the crack left of **Rainy Day Women,** but not the offwidth, which lies in between.

HEMINGWAY BUTTRESS – EAST FACE

See map on page 91.

746   **SEA MONKEYS   5.10c R**   Start at **Ant Farm,** undercling left, over roof, then up the left-slanting crack.

747   **ANT FARM   5.8** ★   This climb lies about 150 feet left (south) and slightly below **More Funky Than Junky.** Climb flakes up to ledge, then up a brown left-facing corner. Rap from a tree 20 feet right of finish.

748   **HORN DOG   5.10C** ★   The face right of **Ant Farm.** Pro: Fixed pin, three bolts.

749   **MORE FUNKY THAN JUNKY   5.10a**

750   **SMOKE-A-BOWL   5.9** ★   One bolt.

751   **FUNKY DUNG   5.8**

752   **OVERSEER   5.9** ★★★

753   **DIRECT START   5.10a** ★

754   **DUNG FU   5.7** ★

755   **PIG IN HEAT   5.9 R**

756   **DIRECT START   5.10b**

757   **WHITE LIGHTNING   5.7** ★★★

758   **POODLES ARE PEOPLE TOO   5.10b** ★★★   This is the original "Poodle" route.

759   **MAN'S BEST FRIEND   5.9 (TR)**   The arête left of **Poodlesby.**

HEMINGWAY BUTTRESS
EAST FACE

760   **POODLESBY   5.6**
761   **COYOTE BAIT   5.7+**
762   **SUCH A POODLE   5.8+**
763   **GOLDEN YEARS VARIATION   5.9+ ★**   Pro: To 2 inches, one fixed pin, one bolt.
764   **FELTONEON PHYSICS   5.8 ★**   Pro: Thin to 2 inches.
765   **PREPACKAGED 5.10a ★★★**   Pro: To 2.5 inches.
766   **SPOODLE   5.9 ★**
767   **THE IMPORTANCE OF BEING ERNEST 5.10c R ★★★**   Pro: Very thin to 2 inches.
768   **FRANK AND ERNEST   5.11a (TR)**
769   **POODLE JIVE   5.9**
770   **SCARY POODLES 5.11b ★★★**   Pro: Thin to 1inch.
771   **POODLE IN SHINING ARMOR   5.8**   Pro: To 2 inches.
772   **POODLE-OIDS FROM THE DEEP   5.10b**
773   **MOVEABLE FEAST   5.10c ★**
774   **ON THE NOB   5.10b**
775   **976 5.9+ R**   Pro: To 3 inches.

HEMINGWAY BUTTRESS – EAST FACE
See map on page 91.
774   **ON THE NOB   5.10b**
775   **976   5.9+ R**   Pro: To 3 inches.
776   **THE OLD MAN AND THE POODLE   5.8**
777   **FOR WHOM THE POODLE TOLLS   5.9 ★**
778   **A FAREWELL TO POODLES   5.9**
779   **HEAD OVER HEALS   5.10a ★★★**
780   **ASTROPOODLE   5.10c ★**   Do the **Head Over Heels** roof, then continue straight up to a bolt at the next roof. Work right past another bolt to meet **Space Walk.**
781   **SPACE WALK   5.8 ★**   Start 15 to 20 feet right of **Head Over Heels** and climb a hand crack that leads left around a corner to a large ledge.
782   **MIND OVER SPLATTER   5.10a**   This lies about 40 feet right of **Space Walk.** Climb a thin flake/crack to the obvious clean dihedral that is followed to the top.
783   **PUZZLIN' EVIDENCE   5.11B**   This climb is just left of **Fusion Without Integrity** and has several bolts and a fixed pin.
784   **FUSION WITHOUT INTEGRITY   5.10b**
785   **ROUTE 182 5.9**
786   **RAVENS DO NASTY THINGS TO MY BOTTOM   5.9**   The crack left of **Easy as Pi.**
787   **EASY AS PI   5.7**   This follows the 2-inch, left-leaning crack located about 80 feet right of **Fusion Without Integrity.** A small pine marks the start.

FILIPINO WALL

The following routes are on the extreme right side of Hemingway Buttress, several hundred feet right of **Easy as Pi.** They are best approached from the Lost Horse Road, starting around and left of **Smooth As Silk** (route 477). The best approach is from a small turnout along the ranger station road about 350 yards from the Quail Springs Road intersection. Map, page 91.

788   **IMELDA'S NEW SHOES 5.10a**   Pro: Thin to 3 inches. This is the leftmost route. climb the leftmost of twin thin cracks that eventually join.

789   **THE ORGASMATRON 5.10b**   This is located 12 feet right of **Imelda's New Shoes.** Climb a flared crack up and left to a small, right-facing corner. Continue up a hand crack above. Pro: Thin to 3 inches.

790   **SUMMER SCHOOL 5.10a**   Start as for **The Orgasmatron,** but take thin cracks just to the right.

791   **THE GRANULATOR 5.10c**   Located roughly halfway between **Summer School** and **Aquino**. Climb the right-hand crack over a small roof, then up discontinous cracks and the face to top.

792   **AQUINO 5.8**   This is a hand crack 35 feet right of **The Granulator** on the right-hand buttress. It is best approached up ledges.

793   **EXILED 5.10a**   This is located directly under **Marcos,** and 25 feet down and right from **Aquino.** Climb past two bolts to a thin crack ending on the ledge where **Marcos** starts.

794   **MARCOS 5.10a**   As seen from the ranger station road, this is the high, right-facing dihedral. It starts on the ledge where **Exiled** ends Pro: Thin to 2.5 inches.

HEMINGWAY BUTTRESS – WEST FACE

See map on page 91.

795   **AMERICAN EXPRESS 5.9 ★**

796   **LAYAWAY PLAN 5.11a (TR) ★★**

IRS AND COPENHAGEN WALLS

THE IRS WALL – EAST FACE

797 **SQUATTER'S RIGHT** **5.10d** ★★
798 **ALF'S ARETE** **5.11a** ★★★★ Seven bolts.
799 **NUCLEAR WASTE** **5.10b**
800 **ATOMIC PILE** **5.9**
801 **COMMANDER CODY** **5.7** Climb cracks and the plated face midway between **Atomic Pile** and **Tax Free.**
802 **THE THING** **5.10a** Pro: To 3 inches.
803 **TAX FREE** **5.10d R** Pro: To 2.5 inches.
804 **BULLET HEAD** **5.11a** Pro: To 2 inches, two bolts.
805 **TAX MAN** **5.10a** ★★★★
806 **TAX EVASION (var)** **5.7** The traverse from **Tax Man** to **Tax Free.**
807 **BLOODY TAX BREAK** **5.10b** ★
808 **MR. BUNNY'S TAX SHELTER** **5.5**
809 **H & R BLOCK** **5.7** ★ Pro: Two bolts.
810 **MR. BUNNY vrs. SIX UNKNOWN AGENTS** **5.8**
811 **MR. BUNNY'S REFUND CHECK** **5.10a** ★
812 **HIDDEN TAXES** **5.6** This short finger crack is just to the right of the descent route for the preceding routes.

COPENHAGEN WALL

This wall can be reached from the south end of Hemingway Buttress or via the "pass" just south of the Freeway Formation. Map, page 124.

813 **IT SATISFIES** **5.7**
814 **QUANTUM JUMP** **5.10c** ★★★
815 **THE SCHRODINGER EQUATION** **5.10b R** ★★★
816 **HEAVY METTLE** **5.10d** ★★ Pro: Thin to 2 inches, three bolts.
817 **HEAVY WATER** **5.10a R**
818 **PERHAPS THE SURGEON GENERAL** **5.8** This face climb with one bolt is on the backside of Copenhagen Wall, up and right through the tunnel from **Heavy Water.**
819 **DIAL-A-PILE** **5.5** Located on the small formation right (north) of the Copenhagen Wall. Climb a crack right of a tree, then traverse right to another crack leading to the top.

DAIRY QUEEN WALL

This formation lies to the left of the IRS Wall. Its right section is very knobby and has several cracks of varying widths. At the left end of the formation is the severely overhanging, right-facing Pat Adams Dihedral. Map, page 124.

820   **BROTHER FROM ANOTHER PLANET 5.11a R ★★** Three bolts.
821   **ELECTRIC TREE GORDON 5.12a R ★★** Three bolts.
822   **PAT ADAMS DIHEDRAL 5.11b ★★★★** Pro: Thin to 2 inches.
823   **TOXIC WALTZ 5.12a ★★★** Five bolts.
824   **BLIZZARD 5.9** Loose.
825   **LEAP ERICKSON 5.10b (TR)**
826   **LEAP YEAR FLAKE 5.7**
       Variation Instead of following **Leap Year Flake** as it moves left out the flake, climb straight up arête.
827   **DOUBLE DELIGHT 5.7**
828   **CHILI DOG 5.6**
829   **SLUSHIE 5.10b ★**
830   **ADDAMS FAMILY 5.9 ★**
831   **GOMEZ 5.10a (TR)**
832   **LURCH 5.8**
833   **I FORGOT TO HAVE BABIES 5.10b (TR) ★**
834   **AIRY SCENE 5.11b ★★★** Pro: To 2.5 inches, one fixed pin, four bolts.
835   **SCRUMDILLYISHUS 5.7 ★**
836   **FROSTY CONE 5.7 ★★★**
837   **A HOT FUDGE 5.9 R ★**
838   **B CHILI DOG 5.10a ★** Pro: Small wires to 2 inches.
839   **DILLY BAR 5.5**
840   **MR. MISTY KISS 5.7 ★★★**
841   **DOUBLE DECKER 5.6 ★**
842   **NUTS AND CHERRIES 5.6**
843   **DATE SHAKE 5.6**
844   **BIOLOGICAL CLOCK 5.9+ ★** This route is on the small wall right of Dairy Queen Wall, facing south. Climb a hand crack, then go over a roof and up plates past one bolt.

PLAYHOUSE ROCK

This nondescript formation lies approximately .6 mile past the ranger station road turnoff and along Quail Springs Road. It is just past a 50-pillar next to the road. Map, page 124.

845   **FINAL ACT 5.4**
846   **BREAK A LEG   5.9 R**
847   **CURTAIN CALL 5.6**
848   **PSYCHO GROOVE   5.9** One bolt.
849   **FIGHTING THE SLIME 5.9**
850   **I'M SO EMBARRASSED FOR YOU   5.7**
851   **LEADING LADY 5.9 R**
852   **BECK's BEAR   5.7**
853   **STUCCA BY A YUCCA 5.7**
854   **PRACTICE REHEARSAL 5.7**

THE COHN PROPERTY

The area marked off on the map on page 80, located across the road from the Hemingway Buttress Area, is privately owned. The owners are very unfriendly, and climbers have been actually shot at for trespassing here. Unless or until this situation changes, all climbers are advised to stay off this property.

THE MILEPOST

This formation lies approximately .6 miles south of the Lost Horse Ranger Station/Quail Springs road junction. It is a large pinnacle of rock no more than 50 feet west of Quail Springs road. Map, page 124.

855   **SCRAMBBLED LEGGS 5.10c ★★**   Climb a crack on the southwest corner of the formation to its end. A bolt protects face moves up and right to another small crack. Pro: Thin to 2 inches.

856   **THE GETTYSBURGER 5.10b ★★**   Start right of **Scrambbled Leggs,** near the center of the southwest face. Climb a leaning crack up and right to reach a bolt. A thin flake above leads to the top. Pro: Thin to 2 inches, one fixed head and pin, one bolt.

857   **FRENCH FLIES 5.7** This is located on the north face of The Milepost. Climb up to a halfway ledge, then up the left crack to the top.

858   **CHOCOLATE SNAKE 5.6** Start as for the previous route, but take the right crack to the top.

PINYON CRAG

This small, broken rock lies about 150 feet northwest of The Milepost (about 200 feet west of the road). Map, page 124.

859   **PINYON CRACK 5.10b**   This short (25 foot) climb is on the east side of Pinyon Crag near a pinyon pine. It is a short finger crack to a horizontal, then up the widening hand crack. Pro: Thin to 2.5 inches.

860   **THE SATCHMO 5.9+ ★**   Another very short route is located left of **Pinyon Crack** (on the south face). Climb a left-leaning crack to a face with one bolt. Pro: Small to .5 inch.

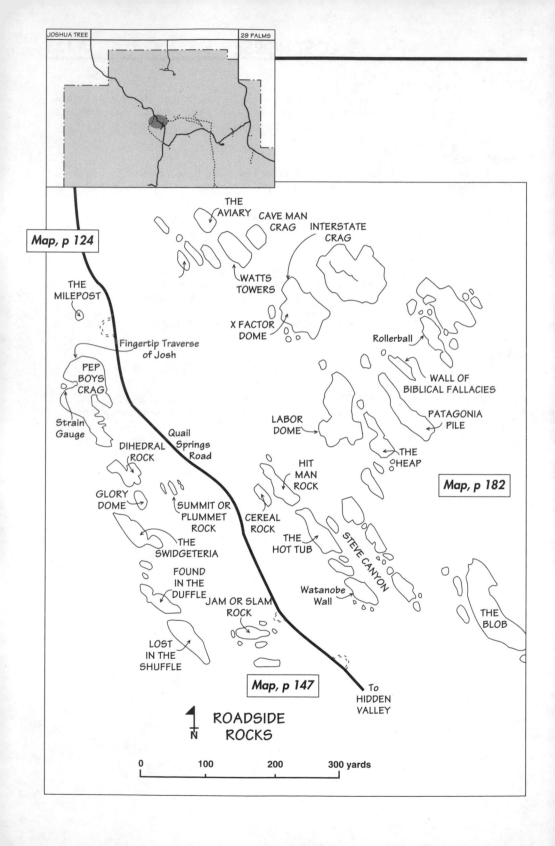

Map, p 124

THE AVIARY

CAVE MAN CRAG

INTERSTATE CRAG

THE MILEPOST

WATTS TOWERS

X FACTOR DOME

Rollerball

Fingertip Traverse of Josh

PEP BOYS CRAG

WALL OF BIBLICAL FALLACIES

Strain Gauge

LABOR DOME

PATAGONIA PILE

Quail Springs Road

DIHEDRAL ROCK

THE HEAP

Map, p 182

HIT MAN ROCK

GLORY DOME

SUMMIT OR PLUMMET ROCK

CEREAL ROCK

THE SWIDGETERIA

THE HOT TUB

STEVE CANYON

FOUND IN THE DUFFLE

JAM OR SLAM ROCK

Watanobe Wall

THE BLOB

LOST IN THE SHUFFLE

Map, p 147

To HIDDEN VALLEY

ROADSIDE ROCKS

N

0   100   200   300 yards

NORTH END PEP BOYS CRAG

UPPER COW

866

865

4

TO THE LAND THAT TIME FORGOT

THE PEP BOYS CRAG
This formation lies .75 mile past the Lost Horse Ranger Station Road turn off, and just west of the Quail Springs Road. Maps, pages 124,134.

861   **YABO PHONE HOME   5.10c**

862   **MANNY, MOE & JACK   5.9 ★**

863   **THE THREE BEST FRIENDS YOU EVER HAD   5.10c ★★**

864   **FINGERTIP TRAVERSE OF JOSH   5.8 ★★**   This route is down low and on the right side of the Pep Boys Crag massif. It is close to the road and faces The Milepost. Climb up to and follow the left side of a short Gothic arch. Traverse right from its top, then go up.

865   **STRAIN GAUGE   5.10c ★**   This is several hundred feet around and right from the previous route, facing away from the road. Climb out of an alcove via a finger crack that widens to thin hands.

866   **WE MUST, WE MUST, WE MUST IMPROVE OUR BUST   5.11b ★★**   This bolted face route lies on the northeast corner of the block up and left (south) of **Strain Gauge.** Pro: One fixed pin, 2 bolts.

DIHEDRAL ROCK

This formation lies about 100 yards further south of the Pep Boys Crag. The large, left-facing dihedral on its left side can be seen easily from the road. Map, page 134.

867   **COARSE AND BUGGY 5.11b** ★★★★ Pro: thin to 2 inches.

868   **ROTS O' ROCK 5.12c**

869   **TONS OF JUNK A3**

870   **SOW SICKLE 5.11d** ★★★ Pro: Bolts, fixed pins and small to medium nuts.

871   **LIMP WRISTED FAGGOT 5.11c** ★★ This route follows a very thin diagonalling crack that faces the road (west), but lies in the descent gully. Pro: Two bolts and small to medium nuts.

The next five routes are on north face of Dihedral Rock, which is referred to as the Road Block.

872   **MIDNIGHT OIL 5.11c** The leftmost line, with two bolts.

873   **RAMMING SPEED 5.11d** The next line right, also with two bolts.

874   **VANISHING POINT 5.12b** The next route right, with four bolts.

875   **IMMACULATE CONCEPTION 5.9** Right of **Vanishing Point,** this climbs a dihedral to a roof.

876   **FAR SIDE OF CRAZY 5.10b R** The farthest right route, this ascends a low-angled face with seams and one bolt.

GLORY DOME

This little slabby rock lies about 150 feet left of Dihedral Rock. Map, page 134.

877   **GLORY ROAD 5.12a** Climbs the right center face of Slab Rock. Pro: Five bolts.

878   **HOPE AND GLORY 5.8** This is the finger crack/flake 25 feet right of **Glory Road.**

SUMMIT OR PLUMMET ROCK

THE SWIDGETERIA

THE SWIDGETERIA

This formation lies about 150 left (southwest) and behind (further away from the road) Glory Dome. Map, page 134.

879   **GORDO STARTED IT   5.10c R/X**   Located on the very left side of the formation climb a crack to a bolt, then ascend a poorly-protected face up and right (crux) to a small corner.

880   **THREE SWIDGETEERS   5.2**   The easy right-angling ramp starting at **Gordo Started It.**

881   **FOR A FEW SWIDGETS MORE   5.9**   Located 30 feet right of **Gordo Started It.** Climb up a crack, then go left on dike.

882   **CALLING ALL SWIDGETS   5.10b**   Located 10 feet right of **For A Few...** Start on ledge, climb up a crack, then up a face.

883   **THE SWIDGETERIA   5.9**   This is a crack to arête climb located 50 right of **Gordo Started It.**

884   **SWIDGETS REQUIRED   5.10b**   A straight crack 15 feet right of **The Swidgeteria.**

885   **FIDGET WITH SWIDGETS   5.8+**   Climb up an obvious crack/flake 10 feet right of **Swidgets Required.** Climb the face to reach the crack.

SUMMIT OR PLUMMET ROCK

This rock is about 150 yards southeast of (left and closer to the road) Dihedral Rock. It has a steep east face with several cracks/face routes that face the road. Map, page 134.

886   **UNKNOWN   5.12a ★★**   The leftmost route. Pro: Thin, two bolts.

887   **KODAS SILENCE   5.11c ★★★**   The middle route. Pro: Thin to 1 inch, two bolts.

888   **LAEGAR DOMAIN   5.10d ★★★**   The right route. Pro: Thin to 1 inch, one bolt.

THE AVIARY

This formation (and the next several formations) are on the east side of Quail Springs Road (the opposite side from Dihedral Rock). It is about 150 yards east of the Quail Springs Road and roughly opposite the Playhouse Rock/Pep Boys Crag areas. The property to the north, as shown on the map, is private. Avoid crossing this private land in approaching the Aviary. Map, page 134.

889   **BIRDMAN FROM ALCATRAZ   5.10a**   Climbs a finger crack over a small roof.
890   **STUDEBAKER HAWK   5.10c ★**
891   **SOUL RESEARCH   5.9**   This is a straight crack directly opposite The Aviary.

KNOCKOUT ROCK

This small formation faces the road and lies 100 yards west of Watts Towers. Map, page 134.

892   **TKO   5.10c ★**   Straight in hand crack.

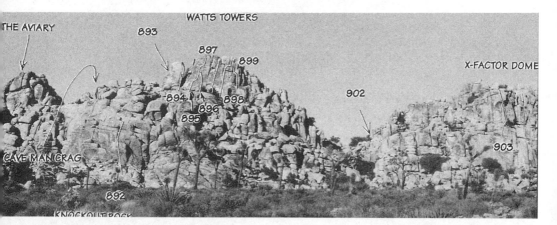

WATTS TOWERS   See map on page 134.

893   **INFECTIOUS SMILE   5.9** This climbs a narrow, north-facing arête with one bolt near the bottom.

894   **JEMIOMAGINA   5.10b ★★** This is the left-most crack on the west face, and it goes over a roof formed by a huge block.

895   **SOLE FOOD   5.10a ★★** Left of the center of the west face is an extremely thin RP crack that disappears after 40 feet, then reappears higher up and 10 feet to the right.

896   **URBAN REDEVELOPMENT   5.8 ★** This is a direct start to **Sole Food,** right of the regular start.

897   **TALUS PHALLUS   5.6 ★** There are two cracks right of Sole Food. This is the rightmost one.

898   **BANDERSNATCH   5.10b ★** This is a steep, tricky climb right of **Talus Phallus,** with the crux near the bottom.

899   **ADULT BOOKS   5.11a ★★** On the right end of the west face are disconnected right-facing dihedrals; climb the lower book, then move left and climb the upper (crux) book.

CAVE MAN CRAG

This small cliff is to the east of **Infectious Smile** and faces to the south and east. Many short cracks are located on the south face and are all 5.9 or 5.10. The arching crack on the right end is **Cave Man Crack 5.11a.** Map, page 134.

900   **PTERODACTYDL CRACK   5.9** This is just left of **Monster Mash,** on the east face.

901   **MONSTER MASH   5.10a** This takes the 80-foot overhanging crack on the east face.

INTERSTATE CRAG

This short cliff lies 100 yards southeast of Watts Towers and faces north. Several cracks are located on this crag, but all are short. Map, page 134.

902   **FREEWAY JAM   5.10d ★★** This is the longest crack (approx. 35 feet) on the right-hand side and is between on and one-and-a-quarter inches in width.

X FACTOR DOME

This formation is very complex and has several crack systems that lead through roofs on its upper west face. Several toprope problems have been done on the south end of the rock. Map, page 134.

903   **FALSE T.K.O.   5.10d**

904   **WHOVILLE   5.8** Crack to the left (20 feet) of **Charles Who.**

905   **CHARLES WHO?   5.11c ★★** At the extreme south corner of the dome (50 yards north of Labor Dome) climb a thin flake leading to face climbing past three bolts.

906   **5.10 WHO   5.11c (TR)** Climb a very thin seam 10 feet to the right of **Charles Who.**

907   **CHARLES CHIPS   5.9** This is the very thin, right-facing flake 20 feet right of **Charles Who.**

908   **CHARLES IN CHARGE   5.9** This is the thicker, left-facing flake 8 feet further right of **Charles Chips.**

LOST IN THE SHUFFLE CRAG   FOUND IN THE DUFFLE CRAG

LOST IN THE SHUFFLE CRAG
This formation is on the west side of Quail Springs Road and is almost directly across from Watanobe Wall and Steve Canyon. Best parking is the same as that for Jam Or Slam Rock. It is about one-quarter mile south along the road from Dihedral Rock. Map, page 134.

909   **IMPULSE POWER   5.11a** ★
910   **DADDY LONG LEGS   5.11a** ★
911   **BLACK HOLE   5.11c** ★★
912   **WARP FACTOR   5.11c R**   It is possible to reach over to **Sugar Daddy** higher up, diminishing the difficulty significantly.
913   **SUGAR DADDY   5.7**

FOUND IN THE DUFFLE CRAG
This is the crag immediately right of Lost in the Shuffle Crag. Map, page 134.

914   **TWINS   5.7** The grainy fist crack on the left edge of the cliff.
915   **SEPARATED AT MIRTH   5.9+**
916   **UNKNOWN   5.10a**
917   **THE MAGIC TOUCH   5.9**
918   **THE GAUNTLET   5.12a** ★★ Climb past bolts to thin crack. Pro: Thin to 2 inches, four bolts.
919   **HEAVY HANDED   5.10c**
920   **BOOMERANG   5.7** This ascends a large, right-slanting ramp on the west (back) side of the crag.
921   **LIFE WITHOUT T.V.   5.9**   This is a grainy, right-slanting fist crack on the small formation right (north) of Found in the Duffle Crag. It is visible from the road.

JAM OR SLAM ROCK

This small rock is just west of a small parking lot on the west side of the road, across from Steve Canyon. Map, page 134.

922   **CRANKING SKILLS OR HOSPITAL BILLS**   **5.10d ★**

923   **FIRE OR RETIRE**   **5.10c ★**

924   **FIRE OR RETIRE, DIRECT FINISH**   **5.10b R**

925   **CRIMP OR WIMP**   **5.10d (TR)**

926   **FREE BUBBA JOHN**   **5.10d**   Pro: One fixed pin, one bolt.

927   **GRIP OR WHIP**   **5.11b (TR)**   Located 8 feet right **Free Bubba John.** Climb up a right-leaning seam.

928   **NO PERCH IS NECESSARY**   **5.10d ★**   This climb is on the front side of Jam or Slam Rock, facing the road. Climb past two bolts, then up a thin crack.

WALL STREET

This large, low-angled dome (as seen from Quail Springs Road) is actually the back side of Elephant Dome. Map, page 147.

929   **BUYER BEWARE**   **5.10a R**   Climb the upper left-hand arête, using steep buckets and one bolt.

930   **WALL STREET**   **5.9**   The left route, with a fixed knifeblade near the start.

931   **INSIDER INFORMATION**   **5.7**   The center route, which goes over a small roof.

932   **POWER LUNCH**   **5.10b (TR)**   The face and overhang between **Insider Information** and **Lunch Is For Wimps.**

933   **LUNCH IS FOR WIMPS**   **5.9**   The right route, with a bolt at the start.

934   **WALRUS-LIKE AND WIMPY 5.8 R**   The face and right-facing corner right of **Lunch Is For Wimps.**

THE RED BURRITO
This is a short, steep, brown wall left and slightly in front of Wall Street. Map, page 147.

935   **TUNA AND CHEESE   5.8**   Climb a short crack to a left-leaning crack, then to an arête at the left side of the formation.

936   **SPAM & BEAN   5.11a (TR)**   This follows vertical cracks just right of **Tuna and Cheese.**

937   **RED CHILE   5.10d (TR)**   Climb the face eight feet left of **Beef and Bean.**

938   **BEEF AND BEAN   5.10a**   Climb the obvious central crack.

939   **GREEN CHILE   5.11a (TR)**   This is the face four feet right of **Beef and Bean.**

940   **CHEESE   5.11a (TR)**   This is eight feet right of **Beef and Bean.**

941   **JALAPENO   5.10b (TR)**   Climb the thin, vertical crack 20 feet right of **Beef and Bean.**

942   **CHICKEN   5.10a (TR)**   Climb the short crack on the right, finishing by a small pine tree.

SLUMP ROCK
This rock lies .75 mile south of the Jam or Slam parking area, on the west side of the road, just where the road takes a turn to the left. Map, page 143.

943   **NIP AND TUCK   5.10a**   Two bolts.

944   **NIP IN THE AIR   5.10a**   All but the top bolt was added later. This was previously protected by nuts.

945   **THE PILE   5.7**

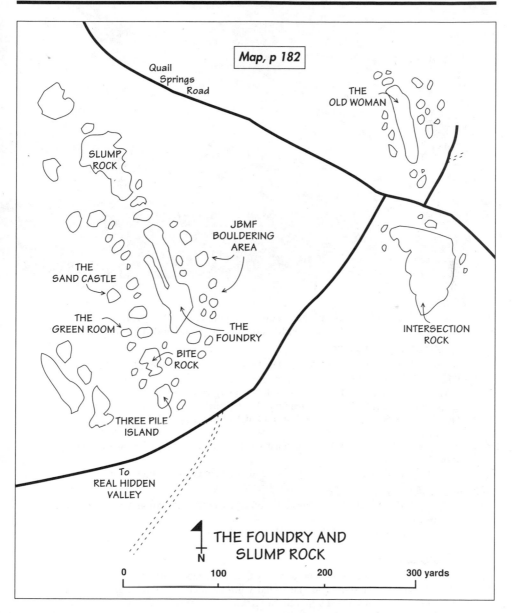

Map, p 182

Quail
Springs
Road

THE
OLD WOMAN

SLUMP
ROCK

JBMF
BOULDERING
AREA

THE
SAND CASTLE

THE
GREEN ROOM

THE
FOUNDRY

BITE
ROCK

INTERSECTION
ROCK

THREE PILE
ISLAND

To
REAL HIDDEN
VALLEY

N

THE FOUNDRY AND
SLUMP ROCK

0   100   200   300 yards

JBMF AREA AND THE FOUNDRY

THE FOUNDRY

948A
949
946
950
947
948
B11
B13
B12
JBMF BOULDER
ALSE UP 20
BOULDER

THE FOUNDRY
This is the complex "broken rock" formation directly behind the JBMF bouldering area. There are also two routes on its southwest (backside) face, facing into Real Hidden Valley. Map, page 143.

THE FOUNDRY – EAST FACE
946   **STAINLESS STEEL RAT   5.10b**   The leftmost crack on the northeast face.
947   **STEEP PULSE   5.12 (TR)**   The center route.
948   **VAINO'S CRACK   5.10c**   This is the left-leaning crack on the right.
948a **UNKNOWN   5.11a   ★**   Pro: One bolt, thin to 2 inches.
949   **IRONWORKS   5.7**   The crack just right of **Vaino's Crack;** tunnel beneath a block at the top. Pro: To 3 inches.
950   **MOLTEN METTLE   5.11a**   The face and flake/crack right of **Ironworks.** Two bolts. Pro: Thin to 1 inch.
951   **LITTLE LIEBACK   5.10a**   This is a wide lieback crack leading to a roof.

THE FOUNDRY – WEST FACE
952   **JUMAR OF FLESH   5.9+**   This is the left of two offwidth/chimney routes on the southwest face.
953   **SIX-PACK CRACK   5.10b**   The right route.

JBMF BOULDERS
In the roughly triangular shaped area bordered by Quail Springs Road on the northeast, the Real Hidden Valley Road on the south and The Foundry immediately to the west, is an area of several excellent boulders. This lies just south of Slump Rock. A distinctive lieback flake on a boulder is the **Up 20.** Steep face problems lie on the east face of the boulder to its north; this is the JBMF (John Bachar Memorial Face). Maps, pages 143, 145.

TERMINATOR BOULDER
The boulder just northwest of JBMF Boulder. Map, page 145.
B5   **ORANGE CURTAIN   5.11**   The east face.
B6   **THE TERMINATOR   B1**   The southeast corner.

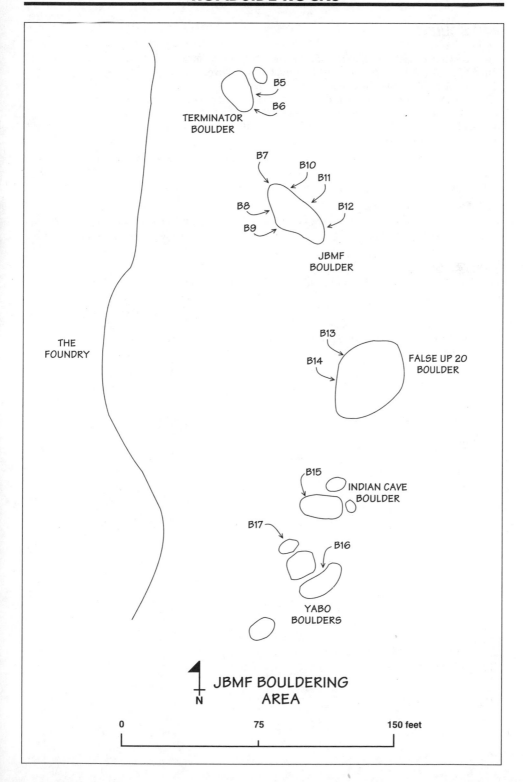

B5
B6
TERMINATOR
BOULDER

B7
B10
B11
B8
B12
B9
JBMF
BOULDER

THE
FOUNDRY

B13
B14
FALSE UP 20
BOULDER

B15
INDIAN CAVE
BOULDER

B17
B16
YABO
BOULDERS

N
JBMF BOULDERING
AREA

0   75   150 feet

JBMF BOULDER

See map on page 145.

B7   **LECHLINSKI'S CORNER   5.11+** The northwest arête.

B8   **HENSEL FACE   5.11+** West face right of the above.

B9   **UNAMED   5.10**   Face right of **Hensel Face.**

B10   **EASY JBMFP   B1** This is the right-hand start of **JBMFP,** on northeast face.

B11   **JBMFP   B1+** Very steep thin face on northeast face.

B12   **TRUE GRIT   5.11+**   The traversing arête left of **JBMFP.**

FALSE UP 20 BOULDER

This large boulder has a large curving flake on the northwest face (**False Up 20**). Map, page 145.

B13   **FALSE UP 20   5.9+**

B14   **SPLATTER PROOF   5.10 R** On the west face.

INDIAN CAVE BOULDER

This is the boulder just southwest of the False Up 20 Boulder; it has an small cave. Map, page 145.

B15   **SHINDIG 5.11** This lies on the north face of the boulder, above the cave mouth. Climb the face to a curving crack.

YABO BOULDERS

These are the group of boulders just south of the Indian Cave Boulder. A cave/roof (the Yabo Roof) is formed by the juncture of two boulders on the northeast side of this group. Map, page 145.

B16   **YABO ROOF   5.11+**   Start on the ground.

B17   **FALSE BLOCKHEAD   5.11+**   Located on the northwest face of boulder to left (west) of Yabo Roof.

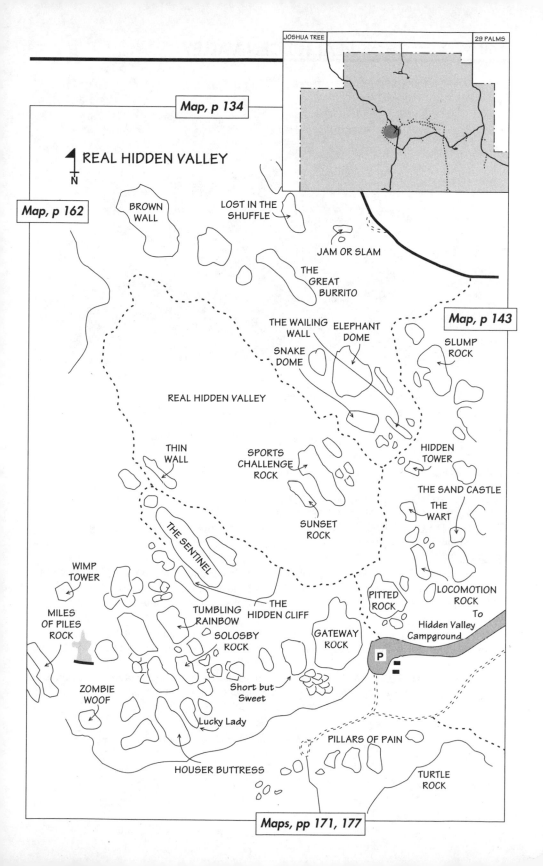

Map, p 134

Map, p 162

REAL HIDDEN VALLEY
N

BROWN
WALL

LOST IN THE
SHUFFLE

JAM OR SLAM

THE
GREAT
BURRITO

THE WAILING   ELEPHANT
WALL   DOME

SNAKE
DOME

Map, p 143

SLUMP
ROCK

REAL HIDDEN VALLEY

THIN
WALL

SPORTS
CHALLENGE
ROCK

HIDDEN
TOWER

THE SAND CASTLE

THE
WART

SUNSET
ROCK

THE SENTINEL

WIMP
TOWER

MILES
OF PILES
ROCK

TUMBLING
RAINBOW

SOLOSBY
ROCK

THE
HIDDEN CLIFF

PITTED
ROCK

LOCOMOTION
ROCK

To
Hidden Valley
Campground

GATEWAY
ROCK

P

ZOMBIE
WOOF

Short but
Sweet

Lucky Lady

PILLARS OF PAIN

HOUSER BUTTRESS

TURTLE
ROCK

Maps, pp 171, 177

JOSHUA TREE   29 PALMS

THREE PILE ISLAND

THE REAL HIDDEN VALLEY AREA

Just before the Hidden Valley Campground (just before!), is a road that heads southwest from the Quail Springs Road. This road leads to the Real Hidden Valley. A blocky crag known as Three Pile Island is on the right (north) approximately one-tenth of a mile southwest from the junction of Real Hidden Valley and Quail Springs Road. Map, page 143.

THREE PILE ISLAND
See map on page 143.
954   **RHOID WARRIOR   5.10c**   Pro: To 3 inches, two bolts.
955   **THE COLOSSUS OF RHOIDS   5.11a**
956   **HOLD YOUR FIRE   5.13a**   This is a bolted face route just right of **The Colossus of Rhoids.**

BITE ROCK
This small tower-like formation lies northeast of Three Pile Island about 40 yards. Map, page 143.
957   **ACUPUNCTURE   5.8**   This is an obvious hand crack facing the road.
958   **THE WOLFMAN   5.10d ★★**   Follows four bolts right of **Acupuncture.**

THE GREEN ROOM
This rock is located a short distance up the canyon to the left of Three Pile Island; it is roughly southeast of Hidden Tower and The Sand Castle, and can be approached easily from Hidden Tower.
959   **VICKI THE VISITOR   5.10b**   Climb thin cracks on the right side of the formation, with several traverses to the right. The route leads up into a cleft near the top.

THE REAL HIDDEN VALLEY

At the end of the paved section of the Real Hidden Valley Road is a parking area. The entrance to the Real Hidden Valley is to the north: a sign and trail marker make this obvious.

It is reputed that during the 1880s and 90s, the Real Hidden Valley was used by the McHaney Gang to hide stolen horses and cattle until they could be rebranded. Jim McHaney ran a large-scale "rustling" operation, and was generally involved in various unsavory activities during this period of time. Willie Button generally is credited with discovering the present day entrance to Hidden Valley. Gang members, Button and his brother Charley met their end in a barroom fight. Maps, pages 147,171.

BOULDERING
ENTRANCE BOULDER
This is the boulder just behind the entrance sign, to the right of the start of the trail.

B18   **UNNAMED   5.10**   On the left side of the east face.
B19   **UNNAMED   B1**   The southeast arête.
B20   **UNNAMED   5.7**   The west face.
B21   **STAND UP FOR YOU RIGHTS   5.10+**   On the left side of the north face.

YABLONSKI BOULDER
See map on page 171.

B22   **BETTY JO YABLONSKI   5.10+ R**   A high-off-the-deck problem (crux at top) just left of the trail near the entrance.

GATEWAY ROCK

PARKING AREA BOULDERS

Several boulders lie west of the southern part of the main parking area (near the southeast base of Gateway Rock). **Saturday Night Live** lies on the south side of one of these boulders. Maps, pages 147, 171.

B23   **UNNAMED   5.10**   A traverse on the east face of boulder (around corner from below).

B24   **SATURDAY NIGHT LIVE   B1**   A dyno problem on the south face.

PITTED ROCK

This large formation is to the right of the trail into the Real Hidden Valley, is northwest of the parking area. Maps, pages 147, 171.

960   **PITFALL   5.11c ★★**   This is a four-bolt face climb on the steep (brown) south face of Pitted Rock, facing the parking area.

The next routes are on the south face (facing the parking lot) of a large block to the right of **Pitfall.**

961   **OVER-POWERED BY HOOTCH   5.12a (TR)**   Up the block, traversing left and up corner near top.

        REEFER MADNESS   5.12c var. (TR)   Same as above, but go straight up at the top.

962   **PIT SLUT   5.12a ★★**   This is around the corner (east face of Pitted Rock), about 60 right of **Pitfall.** A thin crack leads to a slightly overhanging face. It may be more easily approached from the vicinity of Locomotion Rock. Pro: Three bolts, thin to 3 inches. No fixed anchors.

963   **THE GASH   5.10a**   This is the left-leaning crack that meets the top of **Pit Slut.**

GATEWAY ROCK

This is the east side of the large formation on your right as you walk into the Real Hidden Valley. Maps, pages 147, 171.

964   **FALSE TUMBLING RAINBOW   5.8**   Approach is best made up hidden crevice (tunnel) by **In the Pit.**

965   **HANDS AWAY   5.10a**

966   **LAY BACK AND DO IT   5.11a (TR)**

Just as you enter the Real Hidden Valley (where the trail splits to the right and left), two obvious cracks can be seen on the northeast corner of Gateway Rock.

967 **SOLO 5.8**
968 **BROKEN GLASS 5.10a**
Broken Glass lies on the east side of a buttress. To the right of this buttress is a narrow crevice/gully/tunnel. **In The Pit** lies in the lower end of this crevice system. The crevice system is the easiest approach to **False Tumbling Rainbow.**

969 **IN THE PIT 5.10a ★**
970 **PIT BULL ATTACK 5.10d** Pro: Thin to 2 inches, one bolt.
971 **SEMI TOUGH 5.10d ★★★** Pro: Several thin to 1.5 inches.
972 **MARTIN QUITS 5.10c ★★★** Pro: Thin to 2 inches. This thin crack lies on a small east-facing rock 50 yards west of route **Semi Tough.**

PITTED ROCK – EAST FACE
This part of Pitted Rock faces Locomotion Rock and is best approached by walking to Locomotion Rock and looking to the right. Maps, pages 147, 171.

973 **BETTY GRAVEL 5.9** This is the left-leaning dogleg crack directly west and facing Locomotion Rock.

LOCOMOTION ROCK

979 – 982

974   975 976 977   978

LOCOMOTION ROCK

This small crag lies in the extreme southeast corner of the Real Hidden Valley. Map, page 147.

974   **JUMPING JEHOSAPHAT 5.7** ★

975   **GRAIN DANCE   5.10b (TR)** The crack/seam right of **Jumping Jehosaphat.**

976   **LEAPING LEANA 5.6** ★★

977   **SLIP AND SLIDE   5.11c (TR)** ★ Climb a face to a groove. Located just right of **Leaping Leana.**

978   **LUMPING FAT JENNIE 5.7**

979   **SNNFCHTT 5.8**   Starts in the pit on the right.

980   **GUNKS WEST   5.10b** This route is just right of **Snnfchtt.** A hangerless bolt marks its start.

981   **HHECHT 5.6**

982   **JUMP BACK LORETTA   5.5**   Climb a hand crack in a right-facing corner at the far right end of Locomotion Rock.

THE WART – WEST FACE

This small formation is just east of the trail, right after it passes over the bridge. Map, page 147.

984   **SYMBOLIC OF LIFE   5.11a ★** Four bolts.
985   **PREPARATION H   5.11a (TR)**
986   **COMPOUND W   5.11b (TR)**
987   **TOAD WARRIORS   5.12b R ★** Four bolts.
988   **THE GOOD, THE BAD AND THE UGLY   5.10a**

SUNSET ROCK

This small formation is located in front (just west) of the west face of Sports Challenge Rock. Map, page 147.

989   **SUNSET STRIP   5.9** Located on the west face of Sunset Rock. Climb a flake to enter a left-slanting crack, then go up and right on easy face to the top.

SPORTS CHALLENGE ROCK WEST FACE

SPORTS CHALLENGE ROCK
This excellent formation lies roughly in the central part of the Real Hidden Valley, and is one of the best (and most popular) rock formations in this area. Most routes on Sports Challenge Rock are easily (and commonly) toproped. Nevertheless, almost all the routes may be led. Map, page 147.

SPORTS CHALLENGE ROCK – WEST FACE
The west face sports mostly vertical crack and face routes on solid dark-brown rock. A good assortment of thin to medium protection is helpful in protecting most of these climbs.

990   **ALLIGATOR TEARS 5.9** Located directly below the start of **Ride A Wild Bago** on rocks facing west. Start in a 10-foot dihedral, go over a roof, then up to top.

991   **SPHINCTER QUITS 5.9 ★★** Pro: To 2+ inches.

992   **WHAT'S IT TO YOU 5.10d ★★★** Use the first bolt of **Rap Bolters Are Weak** to protect the initial traverse. Pro: Thin to 1+ inches.

993   **RAP BOLTERS ARE WEAK 5.12a ★★★** Pro: To 3 inches for anchors.

994   **RIDE A WILD BAGO 5.10a ★★** Pro: To 3 inches.

995   **DON'T BE NOSEY 5.10d (TR) ★**

996   **NONE OF YOUR BUSINESS 5.10c R ★★** Pro: To 2 inches.

997   **I JUST TOLD YOU 5.10b ★** Pro: Small to 2 inches.

998   **RANGER J.D. 5.6** Pro: To 2+ inches.

999   **RANGER J.B. 5.8** Pro: To 2+ inches.

1000 **EDDIE HASKEL TAKES MANHATTAN 5.10b ★** Pro: Two bolts; nuts to 2 inches.

1001 **MORTAL THOUGHTS 5.11b R ★** Use the third bolt on **Rap Bolters.** Pro: To 3 inches.

SPORTS CHALLENGE ROCK – EAST FACE

The east face is continuously overhanging and has many excellent crack and face climbs. Excellent boulder problems are located on the face just below **Leave It To Beaver.** Map, page 147.

1002 **TRIATHLON 5.11c (TR)**
1003 **CLEAN AND JERK 5.10c ★★★★** Pro: To 3 inches.
1004 **COOL BUT NOT TOO CONCERNED 5.12c (TR)**
1005 **DICK ENBERG 5.11c ★★** (with tree) Pro: To 2 inches.
1006 **THE LOBSTER (Var.) 5.12a (TR)★★★** (no tree)

BOULDERING

The following two boulder problems lie below **Leave It To Beaver.**

B25 **UNNAMED B1+** This is the lieback up curvy, right-facing flakes just right of the **Dick Enberg** Tree.
B26 **KIRKATRON B1** This is the traverse starting just right of the above and leading to the offwidth of **Championship Wrestling.**
1007 **LEAVE IT TO BEAVER 5.12a ★★★★★** Pro: To 4 inches. This is generally thought to be the first 5.12 in the monument.
1008 **CHAMPIONSHIP WRESTLING 5.10a ★** Pro: To 5 inches.
1009 **COOL BUT CONCERNED 5.11d ★★★** Pro: Many small to 1+ inches.
1010 **DISCOY DECOY 5.11a ★★** Pro: To 2+ inches.
1011 **HANG AND SWING 5.10d ★** Pro: To 3 inches.

SPORTS CHALLENGE ROCK – EAST FACE, RIGHT END

HIDDEN TOWER
This small tower is to the east of Sports Challenge Rock and just east of the Nature Trail. The formation also can be reached easily from Quail Springs Road by walking southwest from the vicinity of Slump Rock. Map, page 147.

1012 **NOT FORGOTTEN 5.10a** ★   Climb a thin crack/lieback on the west face until you can reach left to another crack which leads to the top. Pro: Thin to 2 inches.

1013 **WILD WIND 5.9** ★★   Pro: Thin to 2 inches.

1014 **SAIL AWAY 5.8-** ★★★★   Pro: To 2 inches.

1015 **SPLIT 5.6** This route lies in a deep groove 25 feet left of **Wild Wind.**

1016 **SPLOTCH 5.6**   This route lies in the chimney system that splits the summit. Face moves at the bottom (crux) lead to the chimney. This also serves as a downclimb route.

THE SAND CASTLE
This tower is located just east of Hidden Tower. Map, page 147.

1017 **MY FIRST FIRST 5.9**   A smooth face with one bolt leads to a short crack near the top.

1018 **BIVY AT GORDON'S 5.4**   Rotten flakes and cracks right of **My First First.**

1019 **UNDER 6'2", DON'T KNOW WHAT YOU'LL DO 5.11a to 5.12a (TR)** (height dependent) This is located 25 feet right of **Bivy at Gordon's.** Climb the crack on the arête; above the ledge, climb a crack to the top.

1020 **FINGERSTACK OR PLASTIC SACK 5.9+**   Overhanging cracks on the east face.

HIDDEN TOWER
NORTH EAST FACE

1015+ 1016

1013

1014

HIDDEN TOWER

THE WAILING WALL   WEST FACE

THE WAILING WALL – WEST FACE
This extremely narrow wall with several large summit blocks is approximately 65 yards north of Hidden Tower. The east face has a ramp system that provides the easiest descent. Map, page 147.

1021 **DECENT BUCKETS 5.2**   This may be used for descent, although it's a bit loose.
1022 **BURN OUT 5.10b ★**
1023 **GOOD GRIEF   5.10c (TR)**
1024 **COMIC RELIEF   5.11a ★**
1025 **PUSSY GALORE   5.10d ★**
1026 **LEGAL BRIEFS   5.9**
1027 **BRIEF CASE   5.10c (TR)**
1028 **LIQUID CONFIDENCE   5.10d**   Pro: Bolts.

ELEPHANT DOME

Elephant Dome, a rock with an elephant-shaped flake on the southwest face, is located 200 yards north of Sports Challenge Rock. Map, page 147.

1029 **PACHYDERMS TO PARADISE 5.9**

SNAKE DOME

This is the small formation south of Elephant Dome. Three routes have been done, all on the southwest face. Map, page 147.

1030 **HANDLIN' SNAKESKIN 5.10c** Follow thin RP cracks on the far left side of the face.

1031 **I LOVE SNAKES 5.9+** The central crack system leads up into a break in the summit.

1032 **BLACK TODD 5.10b** The rightmost route, which has one bolt midway up. Poor rock.

THE GREAT BURRITO

This light-colored face lies about 200 yards north of Elephant Dome. Although a bit loose, it promises to clean up in time, providing good, moderate routes. Map, page 147.

1033 **STOOD UP   5.8**   Climb a flated crack to the horizontal break/roof near the left end of the cliff. Go left a few feet, then up a crack.

1034 **DESPERADO   5.10a**   Located 20 feet right of **Stood Up.** Face climb past a bolt to parallel cracks, then up and right to the horizontal break/roof. Continue straight up.

1035 **KEMOSABE AND TONTO   5.9**   Located near the center of the face by a clump of large nolinas. Climb straight up to the top, following a crack system.

1036 **TONTO AND THE GREAT WHITE LEADER 5.9**   Start as for **Kemosabe and Tonto.** Climb to a large depression a third of the way up that route, then traverse out left to a crack system that can be followed to the top.

1037 **NON-DECUMBENT DESTINY   5.8**   Located 40 feet right of **Kemosabe and Tonto,** below some precariously perched boulders. Climb up and slightly left until you reach the horizontal break/roof. You can continue straight up (5.10a R), or traverse right 15 feet, then up the finish of **Three Burner Stove** (5.8).

1038 **THREE BURNER STOVE   5.10b**   Start as for **Non-Decumbent Destiny.** Ascend that climb for 25 feet, then head up and to the right slightly. Climb past a bolt and continue straight up cracks.

1039 **EARN QUICK OR DIE   5.9**   This is near the right-hand part of the west face, about 40 feet left of the previous climb (80 feet left of **Kemosabe and Tonto**). Climb a crack wth a goldenbush up past two bolts to cracks that lead to the top.

THE BROWN WALL

1042
1045
1044
1043
1040 1041

THE BROWN WALL
This formation is approximately 500 yards north of Sports Challenge Rock and just east of the terminus of the Nature Trail. Map, page 147.

1040 **CAPTAIN KRONOS 5.7** ★
1041 **BROWNIAN MOTION 5.10c**
1042 **JERRY BROWN 5.10b** ★★
1043 **JAMES BROWN 5.11b (TR)**
1044 **BROWN 25 5.11a R** ★★
1045 **IF IT'S BROWN, FLUSH IT 5.11b (TR)** ★

FINGERTIP ROCK
This formation lies up and left of The Brown Wall, across from a face with a large yucca.

1046 **FINGERTIP PLEASURE 5.10c (TR)**   This route is on the left of Fingertip Rock.
1047 **COUGH UP PHLEM 5.7**   This loose crack system in the middle of the face is located around the corner and right of **Fingertip Pleasure**.

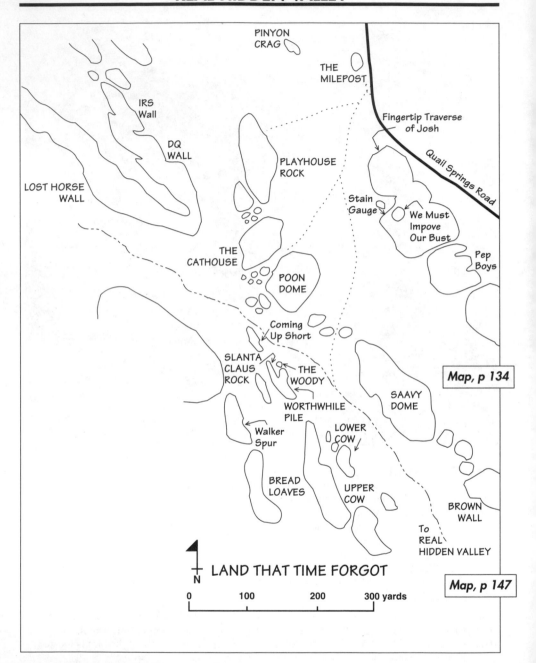

PINYON CRAG

THE MILEPOST

IRS Wall

DQ WALL

LOST HORSE WALL

PLAYHOUSE ROCK

Fingertip Traverse of Josh

Quail Springs Road

Stain Gauge

We Must Impove Our Bust

Pep Boys

THE CATHOUSE

POON DOME

Coming Up Short

SLANTA CLAUS ROCK

THE WOODY

SAAVY DOME

WORTHWHILE PILE

Walker Spur

LOWER COW

BREAD LOAVES

UPPER COW

BROWN WALL

To REAL HIDDEN VALLEY

Map, p 134

Map, p 147

N

LAND THAT TIME FORGOT

0   100   200   300 yards

THE LAND THAT TIME FORGOT

This canyon runs northwest from the Brown Wall and eventually takes one to the Lost Horse Wall.
The following routes/formations are described as though one is coming from Real Hidden Valley,
but they could be approached as easily from the Lost Horse Wall, or from Quail Springs Road by
walking between Dihedral Rock and Pep Boys Crag. Map, page 134.

UPPER AND LOWER COW ROCKS

SAAVY DOME

This formation lies about 100 yards left of the Brown Wall on a buttress that falls almost straight into the east side of the wash. Map, page 162.

1048 **SAVWAFARE IST EVERYWHERE 5.9** A Mojave cactus marks the route's start. The route takes a direct line up a discontinuous crack system on desert-varnished rock.

1049 **CHIMNEY 5.8** Climb the chimney just right of **Shame.**

1050 **SHAME 5.10c** Thin cracks just right of **Savwafare Ist Everywhere,** with one fixed pin.

1051 **FLARE 5.7** Climb the flare 10 feet left of **Tube Steak.**

1052 **TUBE STEAK 5.10c** This is 40 feet left of **Savwafare...** It is a left-leaning tube with a finger-and-hand crack in its back.

1053 **7 5.10a** Located 30 feet left of **Tube Steak.** Climb the seam to the **"7"** crack.

LOWER COW ROCK

This formation is on the west side of the wash, a little farther down and across from Saavy Rock and part way up the hillside. The Upper Cow is the larger, longer formation above. It has a summit feature that, from some angles, resembles a cow. Map, page 162.

1054 **SACRED COW 5.10a** The route climbs a crack leading to the "cow" formation.

UPPER COW ROCK

This is the long, east-facing rock directly above the Lower Cow formation. Map, page 162.

1055 **UPPER COW 5.10a** This is an obvious crack on the highest formation.

1056 **REACH FOR A PEACH 5.10b (TR)** Climb the face right of **Upper Cow.**

1057 **COW PIE CORNER 5.6** This is the corner right of **Reach for a Peach.**

1058 **ONE BOLT JOLT 5.10d** Located on the right portion of the **Upper Cow.** Climb past an eye bolt to reach a hand crack.

1059 **SUPER QUICKIE 5.12b** Located 20 feet right of **One Bolt Jolt.** Follow a thin crack/flair past three bolts. There is a two-bolt anchor.

1060 **DON'T HAVE A COW 5.9+** This route is on the back (west) side of the Upper Cow, facing the wall with many cracks (The Bread Loaves). Climb past a fixed knifeblade near the left side of the face, then up thin cracks and over a small roof.

WORTHWHILE PILE AND SLANTA CLAUS ROCK

THE ALPS ROCK
Right of the formation hosting **Sacred Cow** is a wall with many cracks (The Bread Loaves), which bears some resemblance to a loaf of sliced bread. The following routes are on a wall about 100 feet right of The Bread Loaves. Map, page 999.

1061 **NORTH FACE OF THE EIGER 5.10a** This is the leftmost of two cracks on the formation, and starts behind a pine tree.

1062 **FORMIC ACIDHEAD 5.10b** This is the face between **North Face of The Eiger** and **Walker Spur.** Stem off an ant-infested tree, then up face past two bolts.

1063 **WALKER SPUR 5.10a** This is the rightmost of the two cracks.

SLANTA CLAUS ROCK AND WORTHWHILE PILE
Worthwhile Pile is set further down the wash from Saavy Dome and Lower Cow Rock. It is a small formation with many cracks on the lower east face, and several converging cracks on the upper right face (Slanta Claus Rock). It is identifiable by a phallic-shaped spire (The Woody) on its right side. Map, page 162.

WORTHWHILE PILE
1064 **HOLDEN ON 5.10A**
1065 **HOLDEN BACK 5.7**
1066 **WORTHWHILE PILE 5.10a R**
1067 **HOLDEN UP 5.8**

SLANTA CLAUS ROCK
1068 **SLANTA CLAUS, LEFT 5.7** The left crack.
1069 **SLANTA CLAUS, CENTER 5.10a** The center crack.
1070 **SLANTA CLAUS, RIGHT 5.8** The right crack.

SHORT ROCK

This small formation lies about 50 yards north of Worthwhile Pile/Slanta Claus Rock, on the west side of the wash (facing east). It has a roof on the east face. Map, page 162.

1071 **COMING UP SHORT   5.10a**   Climb over a roof to a hand crack above.

POON DOME

This formation is on the right side of the canyon as one approaches from the Real Hidden Valley, 300 yards north of The Brown Wall. It is much more easily approached from the vicinity of Playhouse Rock. It is a large, low-angle gray slab which faces west.

1072 **POON   5.10a**   This is the left route and has a difficult start. There is no protection.
1073 **TANG   5.5**   The right route in the middle of the formation.

CZECH DOME

This is the whitish/grey face to the north of The Thin Wall. Map, page 147.

1074 **AHOY   5.10c**   This route follows a thin seam/crack up the middle of the Czech Dome.
   Pro: Thin to 2 inches, one fixed pin, two bolts.

THIN WALL EAST FACE

THE THIN WALL – EAST FACE

This formation lies northwest of Sports Challenge Rock and just east of the Nature Trail. Map, page 147.

1075 **CHILD'S PLAY 5.10d (TR)** ★★
1076 **CONGRATULATIONS 5.11a R ★★**
1077 **NO CALCULATORS ALLOWED 5.10a ★★**
1078 **COUNT ON YOUR FINGERS 5.9**
1079 **CONSERVATIVE POLICIES 5.8**
1080 **BUTTERFINGERS MAKE ME HORNY 5.8/9**
1081 **CHOCOLATE IS BETTER THAN SEX 5.9+**
1082 **ALMOST VERTICAL 5.7** The left crack.
1083 **THE FACE OF TAMMY FAYE 5.8**
1084 **AIN'T NOTHING BUT A J-TREE THING 5.6** The right crack.

THE THIN WALL – WEST FACE

1085 **SANDBAG 5.10c (TR)** This is a thin crack near the middle of the fac ethat leads to the summit block.
1086 **KEITH'S WORK 5.11a (TR)** These thin diagonally cracks lead to a "V" crack.

THE WIMP TOWER

This formation is about .25 mile northwest of The Sentinel and is notable for a thin crack on the east face that leads to a large crystal dike. Map, page 147.

1087 **MAGNETIC WOOSE 5.10b ★** This route follows the crack that diagonals left after passing the dike.
1088 **THE BAT CAVE 5.11c ★★** This is on a big, steep wall behind and left of The Wimp Tower. Four bolts and a two-bolt anchor.
1089 **THE JOKER 5.12c ★★** This steep, three-bolt route is high up on a west-facing wall 200 yards across from **The Bat Cave.**

THE OTTER CLIFFS

These indistinct, east-facing rocks are the northern extension of the Tumbling Rainbow Formation. The following route is located on the northeast corner of these rocks. Map, page 147.

1090 **ROBERTS CRACK 5.10d** This is the overhanging finger-to-hand crack on the north end of the Otter Cliffs, around and right of the northern entrance to the west face of The Sentinel.

THE SENTINEL – EAST FACE

This large formation lies on the west side of the Real Hidden Valley and sports two large faces. The east face is next to the Nature Trail, and the west face lies in a canyon and is approximately 200 feet high at its tallest point. Map, page 147.

1091 **CLIMB OF THE SENTRY 5.5**
1092 **SENTINEL BEACH 5.8**
1093 **UNKNOWN 5.7** Start 30 feet right of **Sentinel Beach.** Climb thin seams to a right-facing flake; an old bolt is on top.
1094 **BEAUTY AND THE BEACH 5.9** Start at a big flake 40 feet right of **Sentinel Beach.** Climb past a bolt to an obvious crack system.
1095 **BE GOOD OR BE GONE 5.10d**
1096 **BALL BEARING 5.10a ★★**
1097 **FOTE HOG 5.6 ★★**
1098 **WESTERN SAGA 5.9 ★**
1098A **UNKNOWN 5.8**

THE SENTINEL – WEST FACE

See map on page 147.

1099 **THE BUTT BUTTRESS 5.10b** This is a four-bolt climb on the far left side of the face, starting from ledges about 50 feet off the ground.

1100 **FLARED BEAR 5.8** This route takes the right-arching chimney at the extreme left side of the west face. Rappel from a horn, below a cubbyhole.

1101 **WHERE JANITORS DARE 5.7**

1102 **WHERE EAGLES DARE 5.11d ★★**

1103 **CRYSTAL KEYHOLE 5.9**

1104 **NOT FOR LOAN 5.10b ★★** (5.10c if you join **Where Eagles Dare** to the top)

1105 **SOME LIKE IT HOT 5.12c ★★★★** The first pitch is 5.12b; the second pitch is 5.12c.
Pro: To 3 inches, many bolts.

1106 **DESERT SONG 5.11b R ★★★** Pro: to 4 inches.

1107 **SCARED BARE (Variation) 5.10d** Loose.

1108 **NAMELESS A3 (var)**

1109 **THE SCORPION 5.13b ★★★** Pro: Bolts, nuts to 3 inches.

1110 **THE TARANTULA 5.12c ★★★** Pro: Eight bolts, nuts to 2 inches.

1111 **ILLUSION DWELLER** (AKA **Candy-Colored Tangerine Flake Streamlined Baby**)
5.10b ★★★★★ Pro: to 3 inches.

1112 **THE CHAMELEON 5.12b ★★★★** Pro: Five bolts, nuts to 3 inches.

1113 **THE RUBBERFAT SYNDROME 5.11a (TR)**

THE HIDDEN CLIFF

This cliff lies directly opposite **Illusion Dweller** and **The Rubberfat Syndrome** and in the canyon/gully area. It is an overhanging featured face. Map, page 147.

1114 **BIKINI WHALE   5.12a** ★★★   Climbs knobs and horizontal bands straight up. Pro: Thin to 2 inches, five bolts.

1115 **RAILER   5.12c** ★   Climb **Bikini Whale** until it is possible to work out left in a horizontal crack, then up to the top. Pro: To 2.5 inches.

1116 **BIKINI BEACH   5.12b (TR)** ★   Climb **Bikini Whale** to where **Railer** splits off left, move right in the horizontal crack, then up to the top.

1117 **G STRING   5.13d** ★★★   Climb **Bikini Whale** to a horizontal crack (**Railer**), go left a short distance, then up a thin flake/corner and face. Pro: Eight bolts.

1118 **AGAINST THE GRAIN   5.10a (TR)**   This climb is located to the right of all the above. Climb knobs up to a crack, thin at first, that gradually widens.

TUMBLING RAINBOW FORMATION

See map on page 147.

1119 **RUN FROM YOUR MOTHER-IN-LAW   5.10a**   This is a hand to offwidth that starts in a cave.

1120 **TWO STAGE   5.10a**

1121 **RUN FROM YOUR WIFE   5.10c**   Pro: Small nuts, fixed pin, two bolts.

1122 **RUN FOR YOUR LIFE   5.10b** ★★★★

1123 **TUMBLING RAINBOW   5.9 R** ★★   Pro: To 4 inches.

1124 **TONIC BOOM   5.12d** ★★★   Five bolts.

1125 **TIC TIC BOOM   5.12a** ★★★   Five bolts.

1126 **RAINY DAY, DREAM AWAY   5.11b R** ★★★   Pro: Thin to 2.5 inches.

1127 **DON'T LOOK A GIFT FROG IN THE MOUTH   5.9**   Follows the right-facing corner (hidden). Pro: To 3 inches.

1128 **TALES OF BRAVE ULYSSES   5.9**   This is a finger crack. Pro: To 4 inches.

1129 **FISTICUFFS   5.10b** ★★   Pro: To 4 inches.

SOLOSBY FACE

This overhanging, knobby, orange-colored face lies to the left (south) of the Tumbling Rainbow Formation and behind a series of blocks that face the trail. The descent from Tumbling Rainbow leads past this face. To reach it from below, scramble up between huge blocks to the left of the Tumbling Rainbow Face. Map, page 147.

1130 **SOLOSBY 5.10b** Take the crack on the left side of the face.

1131 **LATIN SWING 5.11b ★★** This route ascends the center of the face before traversing right to a thin crack. Pro: Thin to 2 inches, bolts.

1132 **BEBOP TANGO 5.11a ★★★** Climb buckets and holds on the right side of the face. Pro:

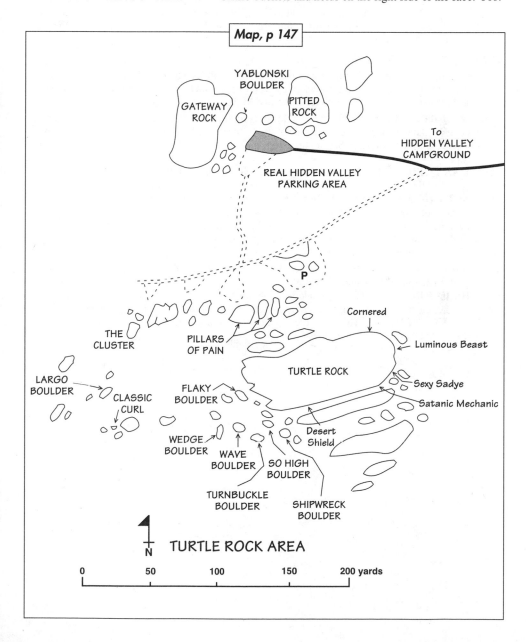

Map, p 147

YABLONSKI
BOULDER

GATEWAY
ROCK

PITTED
ROCK

To
HIDDEN VALLEY
CAMPGROUND

REAL HIDDEN VALLEY
PARKING AREA

P

Cornered

THE
CLUSTER

PILLARS
OF PAIN

Luminous Beast

LARGO
BOULDER

CLASSIC
CURL

FLAKY
BOULDER

TURTLE ROCK

Sexy Sadye

Satanic Mechanic

WEDGE
BOULDER

WAVE
BOULDER

SO HIGH
BOULDER

Desert
Shield

TURNBUCKLE
BOULDER

SHIPWRECK
BOULDER

N

TURTLE ROCK AREA

0   50   100   150   200 yards

TURTLE ROCK

This large formation lies 150 yards south of the main parking area for the Real Hidden Valley. Routes are listed from the south face (left) to the north face (right). This formation provides very diverse climbing. The far (west) end of the south face has several overhanging, difficult sport routes; the east face is more broken and contains multi-pitch, easy to moderate routes.

Descend via the west end of the rock. The descent is not straightforward and several possibilities exist. You may want to scope the descent route ahead of time if your descent skills are not well developed.

The area to the southwest of Turtle Rock sports some of the best bouldering in Joshua Tree. Many fine (and high off-the-deck) problems are found here. This is the site of the famous So High Boulder. The principal boulder problems in this area are listed and locations are shown on the overview map. Map, page 171.

TURTLE ROCK – SOUTH FACE

The following three routes lie on the western end of the south face in a small corridor formed by rocks to the south. They are best approached by walking around the western end of the rock and entering the corridor near the So High Boulder. See Map, page 171.

1133 **DESERT SHIELD 5.12d** ★★★★ This excellent climb is the first route encountered upon entering the corridor on the south side of the rock. Seven bolts lead to cold-shut hooks; one rope reaches on lowering. Setting up a toprope requires medium to 3-inch pro and a second rope.

1134 **UNNAMED 5.12c** This route and **Satanic Mechanic** both lie at the far eastern end of the corridor. Both routes start roughly in the same place; this route climbs up and left past bolts.

1135 **SATANIC MECHANIC 5.12b** ★★★ This fine sport route climbs up and right to a crack/roof, then heads out left and up to hook anchors. One rope lowers. A belay may be necessary to set up a toprope off the hooks. Pro: Bolts; some may want a nut down low.

The next three routes, although on the south face, are best approached by walking around the east face and up the boulders lying agaist the face.

1136 **KIPPY KORNER 5.9** This route takes the crack system on the south face up to a small roof, then up the crack and face above.

1137 **BISKERING 5.9** This route takes the obvious crack system that diagonals up and left and lies to the right of **Kippy Korner** and left of the corner crack of **OK Korner.**

1138 **OK KORNER 5.9** This takes the obvious steep corner/crack system on the right edge of the south face.

TURTLE ROCK – EAST FACE

The east face is accessed easily from the picnic/day use area that lies along the north side of the rock. Routes are described from left to right.

1139 **LIEBACK AND LINGERIE 5.10d R ★★** A lieback 30 feet left of **Sexy Sadye.**

1140 **SEXY SADYE 5.10d ★★★** This follows bolts up the face to the right of **OK Korner.**

1141 **SHUT UP AND CLIMB 5.10a** Chimney up a large flake to the right of **Sexy Sadye**. Climb up and right past one bolt to a right-leaning crack. Pro: To 2.5 inches.

The following routes are two pitches in length. A good selection of small to 2.5 inch pieces should be sufficient for most of these climbs.

1142 **BISK 5.4**

1143 **RIPPLES 5.7**

1144 **LUMINOUS BREAST 5.8 R**

1145 **REHAB 5.9** One bolt.

1146 **WANDERING TORTOISE 5.3**

1147 **BLISTERING 5.5**

1148 **EASY DAY 5.4**

1149 **TURTLE SOUP 5.3**

TURTLE ROCK NORTH FACE

PILLARS OF PAIN

TOWER 2

TOWER 1

TOWE

TURTLE ROCK – NORTH FACE
See map on page 171.
1150 **CORNERED 5.4**
1151 **TOUCHE AWAY 5.9** ★
1152 **PILE IN THE SKY 5.10c**

THE PILLARS OF PAIN
These rocks lie just to the north of the western end of Turtle Rock and next to the road/picnic area. Three pillars or towers can be seen. The eastern-most tower is Tower 1, the middle, Tower 2, and the western, Tower 3. Map, page 171.

TOWER 1 – EAST FACE
1153 **SUPER SPY 5.11d (TR)** ★ This is the left-hand of the "V" cracks.
1154 **SECRET AGENT MAN 5.11c (TR)** ★ The right-hand route.

TOWER 2 – EAST FACE
1155 **ACID ROCK 5.11a** ★ Takes the right-diagonalling hand crack on the left side of the east face of Tower 2. Pro: to 2.5 inches.
1156 **DANNY GORE 5.10d** This is the first crack on the right side of the east face of Tower 2. Pro: to 2.5 inches.

TOWER 3
1157 **WHATCHASAY DUDE 5.11a** This route takes the very short, overhanging finger crack on the upper east side of the the summit block of Tower 3. Pro: thin to 2 inches.

THE CLUSTER

From the Pillars of Pain, the road continues west about 150 yards. At the terminus of the road, walk between the boulders to the south into an open area where you'll find very large boulders and singular, small formations. To the east is a steep face with several solution holes on the east face. Maps, pages 171, 177.

1158 **GRIPPED UP THE HOLE 5.10a** ★   Pro: Two bolts. No anchors exist on top (tricky descent).

1159 **DIGITALIS DESTRUCTI 5.11c** ★   Pro: thin to 1.5 inches, most people TR or solo.

TURTLE ROCK BOULDERING

See map on page 171, 177.

B27   **CLASSIC CURL 5.10+**

LARGO BOULDER

B28   **JUMP CHUMP B1**   Run and jump.
B29   **UNNAMED 5.11+**

FLAKY BOULDER

B30   **LEFT 5.11**
B31   **MIDDLE 5.10+**
B32   **RIGHT 5.10**

WEDGE BOULDER

B33   **UNNAMED 5.10**
B34   **ARETE 5.8**
B35   **LEFT 5.10**
B36   **TURTLE CLASSIC 5.11+**
B37   **TURTLE KNOB B1-**

WAVE BOULDER

B38   **ACCOMAZZO FACE 5.11+**
B39   **SOUTH FACE 5.11 R**
B40   **SOUTHWEST ARETE 5.11**
B41   **NORTHWEST ARETE 5.8**
B42   **NORTH FACE 5.4**
B43   **NORTHEAST ARETE 5.10+**

TURNBUCKLE BOULDER

B44   **TURNBUCKLE 5.11+** (undercling to mantle)

SO HIGH BOULDER

B45   **SORTA HIGH 5.11+ R**
B46   **BUTTON HIGH B1 R**
B47   **BOILER PLATES**   (overhanging plates, doesn't go to top)
B48   **SO HIGH B1- X**
B49   **CRANK CITY B1 X** (right hand start to So High)

SHIPWRECK BOULDER

B50   **SHIPWRECK B1 R**
B51   **FIST FULL OF WALNUTS 5.11+**
B52   **UNNAMED 5.11**
B53   **UNNAMED 5.11**
B54   **UNNAMED 5.11+**

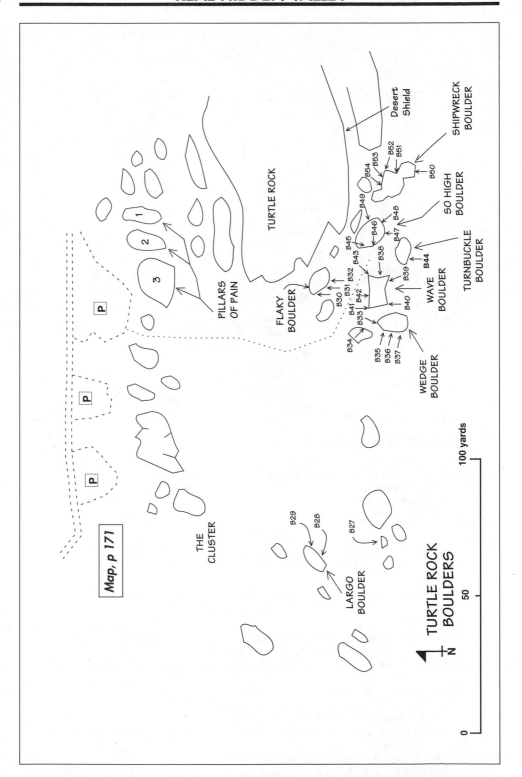

Map, p 171

THE CLUSTER

PILLARS OF PAIN

TURTLE ROCK

FLAKY BOULDER

Desert Shield

SHIPWRECK BOULDER

SO HIGH BOULDER

TURNBUCKLE BOULDER

WAVE BOULDER

WEDGE BOULDER

LARGO BOULDER

TURTLE ROCK BOULDERS

100 yards

50

HOUSER BUTTRESS AREA

A dirt trail leads west along the outside perimeter of the Real Hidden Valley from the western end of the Real Hidden Valley parking area. This ridge of rocks and buttresses can be seen easily from the Pillars of Pain/Cluster area. A prominent buttress of rock (Houser Buttress) is approximately 225 yards to the west. Map, page 147.

LITTLE STUFF CRAGS

Several small formations rise high above the boulder fields/talus on your right (north approximately midway between the parking area at Real Hidden Valley and Houser Buttress.

1160   **SMALL BUT SHORT**   **5.8**   This is a thin crack leading to a small, right-facing corner. Pro: to 2 inches.

1161   **SHORT BUT SWEET**   **5.9 ★★**   Located 70 feet right of **Small But Short.** This is a straight-in thin crack. It has a slight "S" shape to it. Pro: to 2 inches.

HOUSER BUTTRESS

1162   **ARMAGEDEN TIRED**   **5.10d**   Three bolts lead up the east face/arête.

1163   **SNAP ON DEMAND**   **5.11d ★**   Pro: Three bolts.

1164   **HIDDEN ARCH**   **5.11d ★★**   Face climb up into a leaning flared dihedral. Pro: Many thin to 2 inches, two bolts.

1165   **LOOSE LADY**   **5.9+ ★★★★**   Pro: Bolts, 2 bolt anchor/rap.

1166   **PUSS N' BOOTS**   **5.11c ★★**   Pro: Bolts, 2 bolt anchor/rap.

1167   **DUMMY'S DELIGHT**   **5.9 ★★★**   Pro: To 3 inches.

1168   **DELIGHTFUL LADY**   **5.10b (TR) ★**   Climbs the crack/face starting out of the "pit" high on the east side.

1169   **LUCKY LADY**   **5.8 ★★**   Pro: Bolts, to 2 inches.

1170   **DODO'S DELIGHT**   **5.10a ★**   This climbs the right of two cracks. Pro: To 3 inches.

1171 **HERBIE'S HIDEAWAY 5.10d** This thin finger crack is in a canyon to the right of **Dodo's Delight.** It heads up to the same belay as that route. Pro: Thin to 2.5 inches.

The next two routes are located on a north-facing wall more or less directly behind the Solosby face. They are approached by going up the rocky gully right of Houser Buttress. This gully soon becomes a corridor, and the wall is on your left. There are a couple of roof boulder problems on the right wall, opposite these routes.

1172 **THE ALBATROSS 5.10c** This is a thin crack above an alcove that widens to hands.

1173 **ALL BOOKED UP 5.7** This nice hand crack in a right-facing corner to the right of **The Albatross.**

1174 **SUNDAY PAPERS 5.10b** Located about 200 feet uphill from **All Booked Up.** Start in a "pit", climb a short flake to a slab, then up and left to a fist crack.

1175 **TODD'S HARDCOVER 5.10b (TR)** Goes up just right of **Sunday Papers.**

ZOMBIE WOOF ROCK

ZOMBIE WOOF ROCK

From Houser Buttress, continue west for about 50 yards to a point where it is possible to turn north in a wash. Follow this wash for another 50 yards. Look back south and slightly east and you can see this small formation, facing a small clearing. Map, page 147.

1176 **POODLE WOOF 5.10b** ★

1177 **ZOMBIE WOOF 5.12b** ★★

1178 **WOOF WOOF 5.10b** Pro: 2 bolts.

MILES OF PILES WEST FACE

MILES OF PILES ROCK – WEST FACE

This excellent rock lies approximately 150 yards northwest of Zombie Woof, in a narrow canyon. From Zombie Woof, stay just right of the open plains to the west, in a small valley. This narrows, and after a bit of scrambling leads to this west-facing rock. Map, page 147.

1179 **MAKING WIND 5.9 (TR)**
1180 **FLARING RHOID 5.10b ★** Pro: to 2.5 inches.
1181 **WINDS OF CHANGE 5.10c (TR)**
1182 **WINDS OF WHOOPEE 5.11a ★★★** Pro: to 3 inches.

MILES OF PILES ROCK – EAST FACE

The following three routes are on the east face of Miles of Piles Rock, reached by walking around its south side, right of **Winds of Whoopee.** Map, page 147.

1183 **CRUELTY TO ANIMALS 5.10a** This is a hand crack in a left-facing book on the left side of the face.

1184 **RAT BOY 5.10c** Start at the same place as **Cruelty to Animals.** Climb a right-slanting crack, pass a yucca bush, and continue up a thin crack in a small corner.

1185 **CRIPPLE CRACK 5.10b** This two-pitch route in the center of the wall starts with an overhanging thin crack and belays on a large ledge. The second pitch goes up over a small roof, then moves left into a chimney.

1186 **LIQUID RATS 5.10d** This double overhanging lieback crack system leads to a thin, slightly right-slanting crack above. It is to the right of **Cripple Creek.**

1187 **FEEDING THE RAT 5.11b** This thin, thin crack is located on the right side of the east face.

1188 **LONG-NECKED GOOSE 5.9** This route is across the canyon (east) and faces on its west side the east face of Miles of Piles Rock. It follows a left-slanting, inverting corner and passes two bolts near the top. Poor rock.

1189 **FASCIST GROOVE THING 5.11a** (TR) This is on a west-facing wall behind and left of **Long-Necked Goose.** It also could be approached easily from The Wimp Tower. The climb is a long, right-slanting groove that starts with a small roof. Head left near the top.

SOUVENIR ROCK

This formation lies in a narrow corridor between Miles of Piles Rock and the Blue Nubian Wall.

1190 **SOUVENIR 5.10d** This is two-bolt crack-and-face route.

BLUE NUBIAN WALL

This formation is about 250 yards northwest of Zombie Woof Rocks, on the east margin of the open plains to the west. This rock faces west and has several vertical crack systems and horizontal bands. Map, page 108.

1191 **BLUE NUBIAN 5.10a ★** The crack on the left.

1192 **CONCEPTUAL CONTINUITY 5.11c (TR)** The crack on the right.

1193 **MOMENTO MORI 5.11a** This is a thin crack on the buttress right of **Conceptual Continuity.** There is a fixed pin at the start, and the route stays in the left-hand crack midway up.

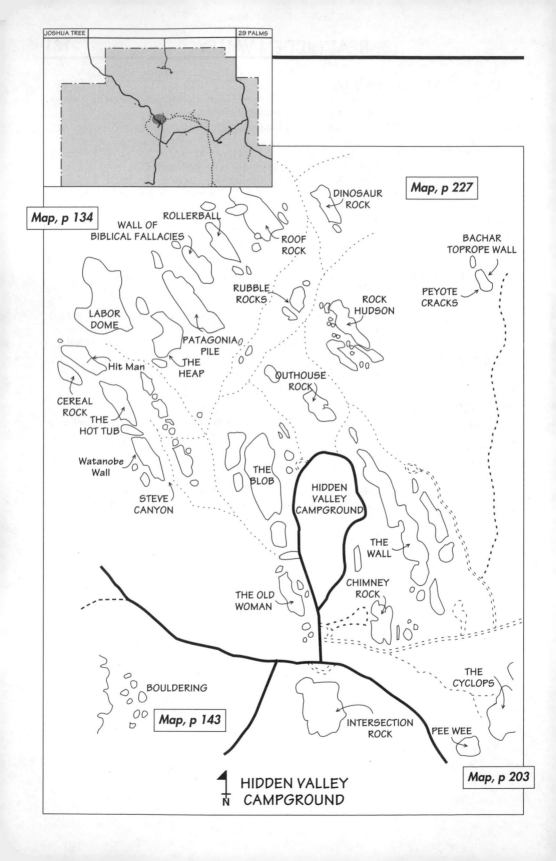

JOSHUA TREE   29 PALMS

Map, p 134

Map, p 227

DINOSAUR ROCK

ROLLERBALL

WALL OF BIBLICAL FALLACIES

ROOF ROCK

BACHAR TOPROPE WALL

PEYOTE CRACKS

RUBBLE ROCKS

ROCK HUDSON

LABOR DOME

PATAGONIA PILE

THE HEAP

Hit Man

CEREAL ROCK

THE HOT TUB

OUTHOUSE ROCK

Watanobe Wall

THE BLOB

STEVE CANYON

HIDDEN VALLEY CAMPGROUND

THE WALL

THE OLD WOMAN

CHIMNEY ROCK

BOULDERING

Map, p 143

THE CYCLOPS

INTERSECTION ROCK

PEE WEE

Map, p 203

HIDDEN VALLEY CAMPGROUND

N

INTERSECTION ROCK NORTH FACE

HIDDEN VALLEY CAMPGROUND

This campground is the true center of the Joshua Tree scene. Most climbers camp here, although a 14-day limit can be enforced. The rocks surrounding the campground offer many good to excellent routes. There is a parking lot on the south side of the road at the intersection of Quail Springs Road and the entrance to the campground. The rock on the south side of the parking area is Intersection Rock. There is good bouldering along the base and around Intersection Rock. It is described after the route descriptions.

INTERSECTION ROCK – NORTH FACE (facing road)

1194A HUEVOS **5.11d** ★★ Pro: bolts
1194 **UPPER RIGHT SKI TRACK** **5.3** ★
1195 **LOWER RIGHT SKI TRACK** **5.10b** ★★★ Pro: to 2 inches, 1 bolt.
1196 **TRAPEZE** **5.11d** ★★
Variation: **TRAPEZE LEFT** **5.12c** Climb up to a long roof, move left and go over the roof's left side.
Variation: **TRAPEZE CENTER** **5.12a** Climb over the center of the roof.
1197 **LEFT SKI TRACK** **5.11a** ★★★
1198 **KOOL AID** **5.10d A4** ★
1199 **IGNORANT PHOTONS FROM PLUTO** **5.11a (TR)** ★
1200 **HALF TRACK** **5.10a** ★
1201 **ZIGZAG** **5.7**

INTERSECTION ROCK EAST FACE

INTERSECTION ROCK – EAST FACE

1202   **GAZ GIZ   5.6**   Start just left of **Zigzag** and climb up to double horizontal cracks. Follow these cracks left to meet **Goldenbush Corner** above its roof.

1203   **COLE SLAW 5.10c**

1204   **GOLDENBUSH CORNER   5.11a**

1205   **SOUTHEAST CORNER   5.3**

1206   **JUNGLE   5.7**

1207   **SECOVAR   5.5**

INTERSECTION ROCK BOULDERING

The following are a few of the more-popular boulder problems around Intersection Rock.

The following lie to the right of **Right Ski Track. Intersection Traverse** goes from **Right Ski Track** to the right for about 35 feet (or vice versa). Several vertical problems – a crack and face problems – are to the right of the traverse. See photo on page 183.

B55   **INTERSECTION TRAVERSE   5.10**

B56   **AUGIE PROBLEM   5.11-**   Left of the crack.

B57   **KNUCKLE CRACKER   5.9+**   The crack.

B58   **RIEDER PROBLEM   B1-**   Right of the crack.

INTERSECTION BOULDER

This boulder lies below the northeast corner of Intersection Rock (see photo, page 184).

B59 **INTERSECTION MANTEL 5.9**
B60 **INTERSECTION BOULDER LEFT 5.10**
B61 **INTERSECTION BOULDER MIDDLE 5.11**
B62 **INTERSECTION BOULDER RIGHT B1-**
B63 **MEDITERRANEAN SUNDANCE B1+** Around corner to right of B62.
B64 **SWEETSPOT B1** Just left of **Anglo Saxophone.**
B65 **ANGLO SAXOPHONE B1** (cheatstone, W/O B1+) On northwest face.

INTERSECTION ROCK – SOUTH FACE

1208 **THE WATERCHUTE 5.10b**
1209 **ELIJAH'S COMING 5.10b R** One bolt.
1210 **MIKE'S BOOKS 5.6 ★★**
1211 **BONGLEDESH 5.10c**

INTERSECTION ROCK – WEST FACE

1212 **TRAVERSE OF NO RETURN 5.11a**
1213 **DRAWSTRING 5.7**
1214 **SOUTHWEST PASSAGE 5.8**
1215 **PINNACLE STAND 5.7**
1216 **LET IT ALL HANG OUT 5.10b**
1217 **BAT CRACK 5.5**
1218 **A QUESTION OF MASCULINITY 5.12c (TR)**
1219 **SYMPATHY TO THE DEVIL 5.10b**
1220 **BILLABONG 5.10c ★★**
1221 **DEATH BY MISADVENTURE 5.10c X** .
1222 **SHOVLING-COLE 5.10b**

INTERSECTION ROCK – NORTHWEST FACE

1223 **OUTER LIMIT 5.6 A3**
1224 **WEST CHIMNEY 5.6**
1225 **THE FLAKE 5.8 ★★**
1226 **WHEN SHEEP RAN SCARED 5.10c ★★**
1227 **OVERHANG BYPASS 5.7 ★★★** Various variations exist to the first pitch, ranging in grade from 5.6 to 5.8.
1228 **NORTH OVERHANG 5.9 ★★★** This route starts off the ledge that leads up to **Upper Ski Track.** Climb a flake/crack to a ledge, just below the summit overhang. Climb out and left around the overhang, along a crack to the top.
1229 **BEGINNER'S THREE 5.3**

THE OLD WOMAN – EAST FACE

This is the first formation on the left (west) as you enter the campground.

1230 **TOE JAM 5.7 ★★** Pro: To 2.5 inches.
1231 **SPIDER 5.8** Pro: To 3 inches.
1232 **JUDAS 5.10b ★** Pro: To 2.5 inches, two bolts.
1233 **CHONGO BOLT ROUTE 5.11b**
1234 **BEARDED CABBAGE 5.10c ★★★** Pro: To 3 inches, one bolt.
1235 **SPIDER LINE 5.11c ★★★★** Pro: Thin to 2.5 inches.
1236 **DEVIATE 5.10a**
1237 **GERONIMO 5.7 ★★★**
1238 **JOINT EFFORT A4**
1239 **DYNAMIC PANIC 5.11d**
1240 **CHURCH BAZAAR 5.10c**
1241 **THE HINTERTOISER TRAVERSE 5.10c**
1242 **TABBY LITTER 5.8**

THE OLD WOMAN WEST FACE

THE OLD WOMAN – WEST FACE

1243 **NORTHWEST CHIMNEY 5.2** The chimney 50 feet left of **Dogleg.**
1244 **DOGLEG 5.8 ★★★** Pro: To 2.5 inches.
1245 **THE FANG 5.11b R**
1246 **DOUBLE CROSS 5.7+ ★★★★** Pro: To 3 inches.
1247 **ROUTE 499 5.11b (TR) ★★**
1248 **LOWER BAND 5.10b ★★ R** Pro: To 2.5 inches.
1249 **DOUBLE START 5.7**
1250 **BAND SAW 5.10c ★** Pro: To 2 inches, three bolts.
1251 **MIDDLE BAND 5.10d R** Pro: To 3 inches.
1252 **TREINTE ANOS 5.10b (TR)**
1253 **ORPHAN 5.9 ★★★** Pro: To 3 inches.
1254 **IRON MAN TRAVERSE 5.10c** Pro: To 3 inches.
1255 **DANDELION 5.10a ★★** Pro: To 2 inches. Located on the south end. Climb the arching crack above the ledge to the vertical crack that rises up the face past a bolt.

OLD WOMAN BOULDERING

See the photo on page 188 and the map on page 191.

CAVEMAN BOULDER

This boulder lies near the southeast corner of The Old Woman. See map, page 999.

B66   **CAVEMAN B2**   (Easier if entire problem isn't done) This climb starts in the far end (south) of the cave; traverse left, then under and out the overhang.

B67   **MANTEL 5.10-**

TRIANGLE BOULDER

This is the boulder below the west face, between two campsites. See photo on page 999.

B68   **DYNAMO HUM 5.10+**   Climb up plates on the northwest face/edge.

B69   **WEST FACE CENTER B1**   Climb up the center of the face.

B70   **OLD TRIANGLE CLASSIC 5.10**   Head up the right edge of the west face.

B71   **DESCENT 5.5**

B72   **EAST FACE 5.9**

B73   **SOUTH FACE 5.10**

SCHOOL BOULDER

This lies on the south side of the gap between The Old Woman and The Blob. See photo on page 999.

B74   **JUNIOR VARSITY PROBLEM 5.10+**   Located on the right end of the north face.

B75   **VARSITY CRANK PROBLEM 5.11**   On the right side of the north face.

B76   **NORTH FACE CENTER 5.8**   Located in the center of north face.

B77   **NORTHEAST CORNER 5.6**   On the left corner of the north face.

B78   **CHEESE GRATER B1**

B79   **LARGONAUT B1-**

B80   **MUMBLES MUMBLEPHONE B1**

STEM GEM BOULDER

The classic boulder on the north side of the gap between The Old Woman and The Blob.

B81   **SLAM DUNK 5.11+**   Located to the left of **Stem Gem.** Jump for a scoop, then mantel.

B82   **STEM GEM 5.11+**

B83   **STEM GEM MANTEL B1**

B84   **RURP SEAM B1**   Around to the right of **Stem Gem.**

B85   **PISS CRACK 5.9+**   This is the overhanging crack in a corner 40 feet right of **Stem Gem.**

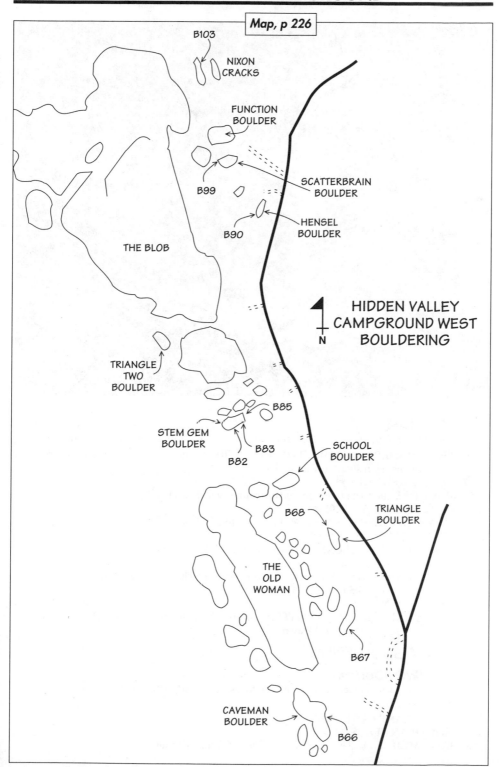

Map, p 226

B103

NIXON
CRACKS

FUNCTION
BOULDER

SCATTERBRAIN
BOULDER

B99

HENSEL
BOULDER

B90

THE BLOB

HIDDEN VALLEY
CAMPGROUND WEST
BOULDERING
N

TRIANGLE
TWO
BOULDER

B85

STEM GEM
BOULDER

B83

B82

SCHOOL
BOULDER

B68

TRIANGLE
BOULDER

THE
OLD
WOMAN

B67

CAVEMAN
BOULDER

B66

THE BLOB — EAST FACE — LEFT END

1256

1261

1257   1258

1260

1259

THE BLOB – EAST FACE

This aptly-named formation lies on the left (west) side of the campground, near its north end.

1256   **THE WONDERFUL WORLD OF ART   5.10+**   Climb a thin crack to an awkward bombay chimney just left of **Buissonier.**

1257   **BUISSONIER   5.7 ★★**

1258   **JUNIOR   5.10c**   The face right of **Buissonier,** which has two bolts.

1259   **PAPA WOOLSEY   5.10b ★★**

1260   **MAMA WOOLSEY   5.10a R ★**   Pro: Thin to 2 inches.

1261   **PETE'S HANDFUL   5.9 ★★**

1262   **SURREALISTIC PILLAR   5.10b ★**   Loose blocks rest near the top. Pro: To 3 inches.

1263   **DISCO SUCKS   5.10c**   Pro: To 2.5 inches.

1264   **I'M NOT AFRAID ANYMORE   5.11b ★★★**   Pro: Three bolts, medium to 2 inches.

1265   **PERFIDIOUS   A4 5.6**

1266   **ZULU DAWN   5.10d**

1267   **THE PERSIAN ROOM   5.13a (TR)**   This overhanging thin crack, which starts down low, is 100 feet right of **Zulu Dawn.**

BLOB AREA BOULDERING

TRIANGLE TWO BOULDER

This triangular-shaped boulder lies near the southwest corner of The Blob. See photo on page 194 and map on page 191.

B86   **NORTHEAST FACE   5.10**

B87   **NORTH ARETE   5.8**

B88   **UNNAMED   5.11**   This takes the arête across from face route.

HENSEL BOULDER

This popular boulder lies adjacent to the paved campground loop road, below the east side of The Blob. Map, page 191.

B90 **SOUTHWEST PROBLEM 5.10+**
B91 **HENSEL ARETE 5.10+** The southeast arête (facing the road).
B92 **HENSEL FACE 5.11** On the center of the east face.
B93 **FACE 5.10** Located just right of the center.
B94 **CARVED SCOOP 5.6** Carved holds lead up the left side of the east face.
B95 **NORTHEAST ARETE 5.9**
B96 **SCOOP PROBLEM 5.10**

SCATTERBRAIN BOULDER

This boulder lies just south of and facing the huge square boulder in the campsite near the northwest part of the campground loop (below the east face of The Blob). Map, page 191.

B97 **BARD'S ANKLE 5.11+**
B98 **SCATTERBRAIN B1+**
B99 **LAPSE OF LOGIC 5.10+**

FUNCTION BOULDER

This is the huge, square boulder mentioned above. Map, page 191.

B100 **THE FUNCTION 5.11+ R** Located on the south face (crux to start).

NIXON CRACKS

These crack boulder problems lie north of the Function Boulder about 100 yards, on the left side of the wash (facing east) that leads out from Function Boulder toward The Outback. Map, page 191.

B101 **RIGHT NIXON CRACK 5.10**
B102 **LEFT NIXON CRACK 5.9+**
B103 **CENTRAL SCRUTINIZER B1 X** This very difficult off-the-deck problem lies west of the Nixon Cracks and faces east. It can be toproped.

THE BLOB — WEST FACE

THE BLOB – WEST FACE

1268 **BALLBURY** **5.7** Lieback a right-facing flake 45 feet left of **The Bong.**
1269 **USE IT OR LOOSE IT** **5.10c** Face climb 15 feet left of **The Bong.** Pro: Two bolts.
1270 **THE BONG** **5.4** ★★
1271 **THE BONGLETT** **5.10a** One bolt.
1272 **HOBLETT** **5.7**
1273 **BEGINNER'S TWO** **5.2**
1274 **DIALING FOR DUCATS** **5.10b** Two bolts.
1275 **SAFETY IN NUMBERS** **5.10a R** Pro: To 2.5 inches, two bolts.
1276 **SAFETY IN SOLITUDE** **5.9**
1277 **SMEAR TACTICS** **5.10c**
1278 **FRISCO KNIGHT** **5.10b (TR)**
1279 **BERKELEY DYKE** **5.9 R**
1280 **BEGINNER'S LUCK** **5.9**
1281 **BEGINNER'S ONE** **5.3**
1282 **REALITY CHECK** **5.9**
1283 **BEGINNER'S TWENTY-SIX** **5.10d**
1284 **HOBBIT ROOF** **5.10d** ★★ The crux is the face below the 5.10b roof. Pro: To 2 inches.

OUTHOUSE ROCK – WEST FACE

This formation lies in the Hidden Valley Campground, just right (north) of the apex of the campground loop. Map, page 182.

1285 **NORTHWEST CHIMNEY 5.4**
1286 **PICKING UP THE PIECES 5.10a**
1287 **FIVE-FOUR-PLUS 5.8**
1288 **FROSTLINE 5.10a**
1289 **OUTHOUSE FLAKE 5.4**

OUTHOUSE ROCK — EAST FACE

OUTHOUSE ROCK – EAST FACE
1290 **OUT FOR A BITE 5.10d (TR)** ★
1291 **CREAMY PEANUT BUTTER 5.11c (TR)** ★
1292 **STRAWBERRY JAM 5.9** ★★ Pro: To 3 inches.
1293 **DIAGONAL CHIMNEY 5.6**
1294 **MT WITNESS 5.10a** Pro: To 3 inches, three bolts.
1295 **STRAIGHT FLUSH 5.8**
1296 **WISE CRACK 5.9**

THE WALL – NORTH END

This formation is a very long wall that starts just south of Outhouse Rock and extends to a point just east of Chimney Rock. Maps, pages 182, 202.

1297 **HANDS TO YOURSELF 5.11a (TR)**
1298 **HANDS DOWN 5.11b (TR)**
1299 **TWO SCOOPS PLEASE 5.10c R ★★** Pro: Two bolts.
1300 **HANDS OFF 5.8 ★★★**
1301 **HANDS UP 5.10d** Pro: To 2.5 inches, one bolt.

THE WALL – NORTH END (EAST FACE)

The following routes are on the east side of the Wall, on the backside of the North End.

1302 **TYRANNOSAURUS REX 5.9** This wide, low-angled dike with two bolts is located 40 yards northeast of the end of the campground loop.
1303 **TIGHTS CAMERA ACTION 5.11a (TR)** This is the face 15 feet right of **Tyrannosaurus Rex.**
1304 **PYRANNOSAURUS NEXT 5.10a** This is the two-bolt route 75 feet right of **Tyrannosaurus Rex.**

THE WALL – MIDDLE SECTION
1305 **WALLFLOWER 5.10a**   Pro: One bolt.
1306 **SOLO-ARIUM 5.7 X**
1307 **C.F.M.F. 5.8 R/X**
1308 **LASERATOR 5.11b (TR)**
1309 **LAID BACK 5.8** ★

THE WALL AREA BOULDERING
These boulder problems lie near the east side of the campground loop, roughly below and slightly north of the routes on the Middle Section of The Wall. Map, page 202.

B104 **THE BLANK 5.10**
B105 **LUNAR LIEBACK 5.11-**

THE WALL — SOUTH END

1315

DESCENT OFF BACK

1312

1311

1313

1310

1314

1317

1316

THE WALL – SOUTH END

1310 **BROWN SQUEEZE** **5.10b** Pro: Two bolts.
1311 **GOOD TO THE LAST DROP** **5.10a R** ★★
1312 **FATTY WINDS HIS NECK OUT** **5.10d R**
1313 **DON'T DICK WITH WALT** **5.10c**
1314 **DON'T WALTZ WITH DICK** **5.10d (TR)**
1315 **DAMN JAM** **5.6**
1316 **CHALK UP ANOTHER ONE** **5.10a** ★★★ Pro: To 2.5 inches, five bolts.
1317 **PUMPING EGO** **5.10b** ★ Pro: Four bolts.

CHIMNEY ROCK – WEST FACE

This rock is located at the east side of the campground, just east of where the dirt road to Echo Cove and Barker Dam heads off the paved loop road. Maps, pages 182 ,202.

1318 **DYNO IN THE DARK 5.10b** ★

1319 **LOOSE LIPS 5.11a** ★★★ Pro: Many to 3 inches.

B106 **COPPER PENNY 5.11+ R** This boulder problem lies 25 feet right of the "chimney," and rises off the desert floor.

1320 **WEST FACE OVERHANG 5.7** ★

1321 **BALLET 5.10a R/X** ★

1322 **FEAR OF FLYING 5.10d** Pro: To 2 inches, two bolts.

1323 **HOWARD'S HORROR 5.7** (Direct 5.10b)

1324 **BREAK DANCING 5.11a** Pro: To 2 inches, three bolts.

1325 **DIRTY DANCING 5.10a** Pro: To 3 inches, one drilled angle.

1326 **TWISTED CRYSTALS 5.11a** Pro: Three bolts.

1327 **DAMPER 5.9** ★ Pro: To 4 inches.

1328 **PINCHED RIB 5.10b** ★★★ (originally only 5.7!) Pro: Two bolts.

CHIMNEY ROCK – EAST FACE

1329 **CAMOUFLAGE 5.12c** Pro: Four bolts.

1330 **THE FLUE 5.8 ★★★** Pro: To 3 inches.

1331 **FLUE RIGHT 5.10b R/X ★★** Pro: To 2.5 inches.

1332 **RAVEN'S REACH 5.10a**

B107 **RATS WITH WINGS 5.11** This problem lies on the east face of the corridor just east of the east side of Chimney Rock.

B108 **PHALLUS 5.7** This is the "obvious" pinnacle located below the south end of The Wall

HVCG BACK SIDE

The following climbs are located west of the back loop of the campground. Most are on the back (east) side of The Wall.

B109 **THE UPSIDEDOWN PINEAPPLE 5.11+** This roof with a slanting crack is to the left of **Moonlight Crack.**

The following three toprope routes are on a steep wall behind campsite #42.

1333 **MOONLIGHT CRACK 5.10+ (TR)** This is a shallow offwidth that doesn't quite reach the ground; it starts with mantel moves.

1334 **MAJOR THREAT 5.12a (TR)** Climb the face 12 feet left of **Moonlight Crack.**

1335 **MINOR THREAT 5.11d (TR)** Climb the face six feet right of **Moonlight Crack.**

The following routes lie on the small formation east of the back side of The Wall (north of campsite #42). It has an "obvious" corner/crack on its south end.

1336 **CAMPCRAFT 5.9** This is the crack in the right-facing corner.

1337 **FACE OF MUSIC 5.10c (TR) ★** This is the face/arête to the left of the above route.

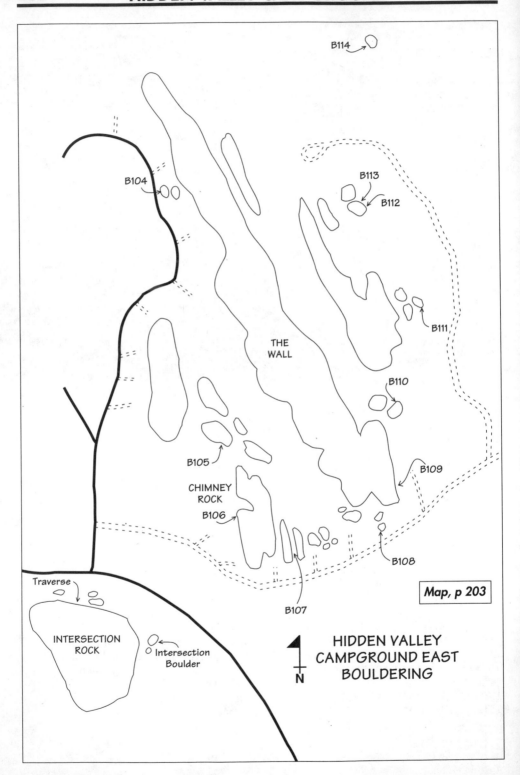

B114

B104

B113

B112

B111

THE
WALL

B110

B105

B109

CHIMNEY
ROCK

B106

B108

Map, p 203

Traverse

B107

INTERSECTION
ROCK

Intersection
Boulder

HIDDEN VALLEY
CAMPGROUND EAST
BOULDERING

N

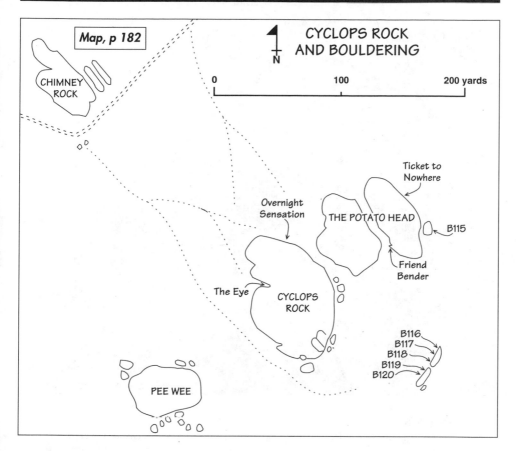

BACK LOOP BOULDERING

The following problems have been done in the vicinity of the back loop of the campground. Brief descriptions/locations are given.

B110 **HAVING FUN YET 5.12- X** This problem lies on the northeast face of a boulder south and below **Campcraft.**

B111 **FIRE'E OR RETIRE'E B1** This is an extreme friction problem on the south side of a boulder below the east face of the small pile of rocks containing **Campcraft.**

B112 **ORANGE JULIUS B1+** This problem is on an orangish dike near the northern end of the loop.

B113 **SCOOP PROBLEM 5.11-** This is the scoop to the right of **Orange Julius.**

B114 **PINHEAD 5.11-** This thin seam is on the west face of a boulder that lies about 75 yards north-northeast of the end of the back loop.

CYCLOPS BOULDERING

B115 **PIG PEN (AKA Bachar Cracker of the Desert) B1** (cave start) A 15-foot-high boulder with a cave on the southeast side rests about 50 yards south of **Spud Patrol.** A hand crack in the roof of the cave leads to a thin crack above the lip.

THE CYCLOPS BOULDERS

B116 **OFF CAMBER B1-** (mantel or dyno)

B117 **UNNAMED 5.11**

B118 **UNNAMED 5.10**

B119 **UNNAMED 5.11**

B120 **UNDERTOW 5.11**

A clump of boulders lies about 200 yards east of the Cyclops boulders; there are several good problems here.

CYCLOPS ROCK — NORTHEAST FACE

1338

1339   1340

CYCLOPS ROCK

This formation lies outside Hidden Valley Campground, about 300 yards east of the entrance. Map, page 203.

CYCLOPS ROCK – NORTHEAST FACE

1338   **OVERNIGHT SENSATION   5.11b** ★★   Pro: Four bolts, small to 2 inches.

1339   **FOUL FOWL   5.6**

1340   **CAROLYN'S RUMP   5.4**

CYCLOPS — NORTHWEST FACE

CYCLOPS ROCK – NORTHWEST FACE
1341 **ULYSSES' BIVOUAC 5.8** .
1342 **BUSINESS TRIP 5.4**
1343 **OVERSIGHT 5.10a**
1344 **THIN RED LINE 5.12b R** ★★ Pro: Two bolts, nuts to 2 inches.
1345 **SURFACE TENSION 5.10d** ★★★ Scary to the first bolt. Pro: Four bolts, nuts to 2.5 inches (anchors).
1346 **THE EYE 5.1** ★★★ Pro: To 3 inches.
1347 **CIRCE 5.6** ★
1348 **FRACTURED FISSURE 5.10d (TR)**
1349 **TELEGRAM FOR MONGO 5.10c R** ★★ Pro: Two bolts, nuts to 2.5 inches.
1350 **STAIRWAY TO HEAVEN 5.12a (TR)** ★
1351 **LEADER'S FRIGHT 5.8 R** ★★★ Pro: To 2 inches.

CYCLOPS ROCK — WEST FACE

CYCLOPS ROCK – SOUTHWEST FACE
1352 **THE OFFICIAL ROUTE OF THE 1984 OLYMPICS** **5.10c** ★★ Pro: To 2.5 inches.
1353 **ESCAPE (Var.)** **5.10c**
1354 **ARE WE OURSELVES** **5.8**
1355 **SPAGHETTI & CHILI** **5.7**
1356 **PENELOPE'S WALK** **5.4**
1357 **GOLDILOCKS** **5.7**

THE POTATO HEAD
Two smaller formations lie immediately northeast of Cyclops Rock. The northeast face of the second rock contains the following routes (from left to right). Map, page 203.

1359 **SPUD PATROL** **5.7** On the left of the face is a left-arching corner. Start 20 feet right of the corner, where a horizontal crack curves down. Climb to the crack, traverse left to the corner, then up it and left to the top.

1360 **TICKET TO NOWHERE** **5.8** Climb a left-leaning crack in the center of the face to its end. Rappel off or downclimb the route.

1361 **MR. DNA** **5.11 (TR)** Start at a flake six feet left of a patch of yellow lichen and continue straight up to the top.

1362 **KIDNEY STONE** **5.10d (TR)** Start five feet right of the lichen patch and climb straight to the summit.

1363 **FRIEND BENDER** **5.11b** This climb is located on the south wall, at the northwest end of the central corridor of The Potato Head. Climb a finger crack up and right to overhanging face moves. Escape right above this.

1364 **TUBERS IN SPACE** **5.4** This route ascends a slab to a hand crack. It is located directly opposite **Overnight Sensation** on Cyclops Rock.

1365 **COMITMENTS ARE FOR ME** **5.8** To right of **Tubers In Space.**

PEEWEE ROCK
This rather pathetic formation lies just southwest of Cyclops Rock. Map, page 203.

1366 **BELLY SCRAPER 5.4**
1367 **THE WEE-WEE 5.10c** Pro: Four bolts.

PEEWEE ROCK – SOUTH FACE
A large boulder at the south corner of the rock has a large depression on its side. Route 1368 is to the left, 1369 to the right.

1368 **SPAN-NISH FLY 5.8** Climb a large water chute to a cave.
1369 **TRI-STEP 5.8** Climb a shallow water chute to a ledge just left of the orange-colored face. Above, take the middle chute past a bolt to the top.

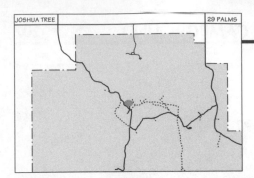

THE OUTBACK

This area covers territory starting northwest of Hidden Valley Campground and continuing east in an arc to just west of the Echo Rock/Echo Cove area. Maps, pages 134, 182.

STEVE CANYON

This group of rocks lies 200 yards northwest of the gap between The Old Woman and the Blob. They can be approached easily from either the campground or from pullouts along Quail Springs Road located about a quarter-mile northwest of the campground. The formations form a canyon that runs in a north/south direction. Routes lie both within the canyon as well as on the east and west faces "outside" the canyon. The area north of Steve Canyon (and north and east of Hidden Valley Campground) is called The Outback, and is covered in the section of the guide immediately after Hidden Valley Campground.

STEVE CANYON – OUTSIDE, WEST

The following routes lie on the west face of the west side of the Steve Canyon, and face Quail Springs Road. Also, the northern extension of the outside of Steve Canyon (which also faces the road) is described here. This is called The Hot Tub.

1370 **WATANOBE WALL 5.10a ★★** Pro: To 3 inches.
1371 **WATASILLYWALL 5.11b (TR)**
1372 **YEI-BEI-CHEI CRACK 5.9 ★** Pro: To 3 inches.
1373 **OPEN SEASON 5.9+** Pro: To 3 inches, two bolts, one fixed pin.
1374 **SEASON OPENER 5.8 ★★**
1375 **COME-N-DO-ME 5.10b ★** Pro: To 2.5 inches, three bolts.
1376 **WITHOUT A TRACE 5.8 X**

THE HOT TUB

This is the jumble/formation that lies north (left) of **Watanobe Wall** and faces the road. Map, page 182.

1377 **HOT TUB OF DEATH 5.10a** Climb the right- slanting crack through the roof 100 feet left of **Watanobe Wall.**

1378 **JACUZZI OF NO RETURN 5.10b** Start as for the above route. At the roof, take a flake and thin crack left.

1379 **HOT TUBS FROM HELL 5.8** Climb a right-facing corner/groove to a ledge 20 feet left of **Hot Tub Of Death,** then up a right-facing corner left of a chimney.

1380 **FROM HERE TO INFIRMARY 5.8** Climb the fist crack out of a roof. This is located directly behind a pine tree left of **Hot Tubs From Hell.**

1381 **CYNDIE'S BRAIN 5.10a** Climb disjointed cracks up desert varnish 40 feet left of **From Here To Infirmary.**

CEREAL ROCK

This is the nondiscript jumble adjacent to (left/north) of The Hot Tub. It is separated (barely) from The Hot Tub by a small gap. It is the northernmost extension of the west-facing rocks constituting Steve Canyon/Hit Man Rock. Hit Man Rock lies around the corner (east and south) of Cereal Rock. Map, page 182.

1382 **BUCKWHEAT 5.10a R** This is on the west-facing brown buttress near the extreme right end of Cereal Rock (40 feet right of **Raising Bran**). Start on the left edge, go up to an alcove, then right, then up past bolt.

1383 **RAISING BRAN 5.8** Climb up ledges to a short dihedral capped by a roof, then up cracks. This is near the left end of the west face, very low to the ground.

1384 **THE OAT ROUTE 5.8** Climb past horizontals 20 feet left of **Raising Bran.** Move right and up the crack.

1385 **BRAN NEW 5.5** Start at a right-facing flake/chimney on the north end of Cereal Rock. Climb up the flake, then up knobby face.

1386 **CEREAL KILLER 5.6** Climb up and right to a chimney left of **Bran New.**

1387 **OAT CUISINE 5.10c** Climb a left-leaning flake on the back of Cereal Rock (facing **Acuity**). Continue up the face and left-leaning crack above.

STEVE CANYON — EAST FACE OF WEST WALL

STEVE CANYON – EAST FACE OF THE WEST WALL
1388 **GRAND THEFT AVOCADO 5.7**
1389 **CANDELABRA 5.10a R (X, if entire flake comes off!)** ★   Pro: To 3 inches.
1390 **THE ORC 5.10a** ★★ Pro: Thin to 2.5 inches.
1391 **ORC SIGHS 5.10c** (var) Pro: To 3 inches.
1392 **UNKNOWN 5.11c** ★★ Pro: To 2.5 inches, two bolts.
1393 **WINGTIPS 5.11b (TR)** Climb up past a horizontal to a flake just left of **Tennis Shoe Crack.**
1394 **TENNIS SHOE CRACK 5.8** ★ This sits up off a ledge to the right of The Orc about 100 feet. A hand crack curves up and left above a shelf halfway up the rock.

STEVE CANYON – UPPER WEST SIDE (East Face)
The west side of Steve Canyon is broken into two parts. The upper formation is distinguished by large roofs located about halfway up.
1395 **LET'S GET HORIZONTAL 5.11a (TR)** ★★ Located just left of **Super Roof,** past horizontals.
1396 **SUPER ROOF 5.9** ★★★ This is the left-hand crack splitting the roof. Pro: To 3 inches.
1397 **COMFORTABLY NUMB 5.11** ★★ This is an offwidth roof 20 feet right of **Super Roof.** Pro: To 5 inches.

STEVE CANYON – UPPER EAST SIDE (West Face)

1398 **FEMALE MUD MASSACRE 5.10a** A wide, light-colored, overhanging groove rises across from **Super Roof.** Stem and chimney up the groove, then follow overhanging hand jams to the left. First lead: Todd Gordon and Brian Polvony, May, 1989.

1399 **FRIGID DARE 5.11c (TR)** This strenuous route takes the overhanging and leaning lieback/groove across from **Super Roof**; to the right of Female Mud Massacre.

1400 **GRAIN SURGERY 5.10b R ★★★** Pro: To 2 inches.

1401 **SUPER MONSTER KILLER 5.11a ★** Pro: Three bolts, thin to 2 inches.

1402 **FIST FULL OF CRYSTALS 5.10d ★★** Pro: .5 to 2 inches.

1403 **HOOPHARKZ 5.4**

1404 **DEFLOWERED 5.6 ★★** Pro: To 3 inches.

1405 **THE DECOMPENSATOR OF LHASA 5.10d ★★★** Pro: Several .5 to 2 inches.

1406 **PHINEAS P. PHART 5.10a**

1407 **LOV'IN KOHLER 5.9** Below and left of **Phineas P. Phart.**

STEVE CANYON — LOWER EAST SIDE (West Face)

STEVE CANYON – LOWER EAST SIDE (West Face)

1408 **SKINNY DIP 5.7 R ★★** Follow a hand crack to a tunnel-through, then go up the chimney to the top.
1409 **INVISIBLE TOUCH 5.10d ★★**
1410 **KING PIN 5.11b ★** A bolt is missing (pulled?).
1411 **SKINNY PIN 5.4**
1412 **JUMPING JACK CRACK 5.11a ★★★** Pro: To 2 inches.
1413 **VENUCIAN FECE 5.11a (TR)**
1414 **SIDEWINDER 5.10b ★★★★** Pro: Medium to 2.5 inches.
1415 **DIAMONDBACK 5.10d ★**
1416 **KINGSNAKE 5.12b ★**
1417 **RATTLE AND HUM 5.11d ★** This is a three-bolt friction route left of **Rockwell 41C.**
1418 **MUNCHKIN LAND 5.10d** Crack-to-face climb with one bolt on the west face of the small formation just right of the Sidewinder formation.

STEVE CANYON – EAST SIDE (East Face)
1419 **ROCKWELL 41C** **5.11a** ★   Pro: Two bolts.
1420 **JACK GRIT** **5.10a**
1421 **LAND OF THE LONG WHITE CLOUD** **5.10b**   Pro: to 2.5 inches.
1422 **KIWI ROUTE** **5.10d**   Pro Thin to 2 inches.
1423 **ICE CLIMBING** **5.10a**
1424 **FREE CLIMBING** **5.10a**
1425 **SLIPPERY WHEN WET** **5.7**

HIT MAN ROCK

This rock is actually a northern continuation of the west side of Steve Canyon. Hit Man Rock lies about 150 yards north of **Super Roof.** It can be reached easily via a trail that passes just east of the east side of Steve Canyon (**Slippery When Wet,** etc.). Hit Man Rock is the far north end of the formation, and the routes are on the east face. Map, page 182.

1426 **THE HIT 5.9**
1427 **THE ENFORCER 5.9** ★
1428 **BISCUIT EATER 5.10a**
1429 **SKINWALKER 5.10c**
1430 **THE BRUISER 5.10C ★★★**
1431 **THE MECHANIC 5.10c (TR)**
1432 **ACUITY 5.7** This is a large V-slot/corner on the northwest corner of Hit Man Rock. It is visible from the Quail Springs Road.

LABOR DOME

This small, dark-colored formation lies directly opposite Hit Man Rock. Map, page 182.

1433 **WORKING OVERTIME 5.9 ★★**
1434 **WOMAN'S WORK IS NEVER DONE 5.10c ★★**
1435 **TIME AND A HALF 5.10d**

THE HEAP
This blocky, squarish rock lies to the right of Labor Dome about 75 yards. Map, page 182.

1436 **PINCH A SMELLY SCRUTINIZER   5.10c**   Pro: To 2.5 inches, three bolts.
1437 **CHICAGO NIPPLE SLUMP   5.11c (TR)** ★
1438 **BAD FUN   5.11a**

LOOKING NORTH FROM HIDDEN VALLEY CAMPGROUND

THE HEAP

PATAGONIA PILE

WALL OF
BIBLICAL FALLACIES

ROLLERBALL

PATAGONIA PILE – WEST FACE

Patagonia Pile is approximately 450 yards north-northwest of the apex of the Hidden Valley Campground loop. A trail leads from the deep campsite just east of The Blob (containing a large, squarish boulder) out to an open area, then to the north of the campground. Patagonia Pile is the square-looking formation with an overhanging east face. Maps, pages 134, 182.

1439   **KING OF THE MOUNTAIN   5.8**   A small separate formation lies uphill and left (north) of the west face of Patagonia Pile. This route climbs a curving thin crack.

1440   **STUDENT UNREST   5.6**   This crack lies left of an obvious chimney that is left of **Patagucci.**

1441   **PATAGUCCI   5.5**   The crack left of **Peabody's Peril.**

1442   **PEABODY'S PERIL   5.9** ★★   Two prominent cracks rise near the right half of the south face. The route climbs the left crack, which has a fixed pin about 30 feet up.

1443   **NOBODY'S RIGHT MIND   5.9**   This is the right crack. It is a bit loose and has a bolt 30 feet up.

1444   **FILET OF ROCK SHARK   5.10b**   Located just right of **Noboby's Right Mind.** Climb a crack to a roof to bulging double cracks above.

1445   **SITTING AROUND THE CAMPFIRE TELLING FISH STORIES   5.10a (TR)**   The crack/seam 20 feet right of **Filet of Rock Shark.**

PATAGONIA PILE – EAST FACE

1446 **WET ROCK DAY 5.10d (TR)** ★
1447 **MALE EXOTIC DANCERS (AKA SHIRT HEADS) 5.11d** ★★ Pro: Thin to 2 inches, one bolt.
1448 **NO SHIRT NEEDED 5.10d** ★★
1449 **HOT LEGS CONTEST (AKA: JUGLINE) 5.11c** Pro: Thin to 2 inches, five bolts.
1450 **WET T-SHIRT NIGHT 5.11c** ★★★ Pro: Thin to 2 inches, two bolts.
1451 **SHIP OF FOOLS 5.11a** Pro: Thin to 2.5 inches, one bolt.
1452 **DEAD MAN'S EYES 5.11b**
1453 **THE FLYING DUTCHMAN 5.12** This starts on a stack of rocks and climbs straight up on pin scars.
1454 **THE YARDARM 5.11** This is the leftmost of two bolted routes right of **The Flying Dutchman.**
1455 **WALK THE PLANK 5.11** The rightmost bolted route.
1456 **THE POOPDECK 5.10a** Climb the groove/cracks right of **Walk The Plank.**

WALL OF BIBLICAL FALLACIES

WALL OF BIBLICAL FALLACIES
This is the overhanging northeast face of the formation northeast of Patagonia Pile. It faces the Rollerball formation; approach as for that formation. Map, page 182.

1457 **FISSURE OF MEN 5.1** This is the easy chimney on the left side of the wall.

1458 **NAILED TO THE CROSS 5.13a** Climb the thin crack 15 feet left of **Resurrection.** Start from a block; finish as for **Resurrection.** Pro: Very small nuts to 2.5 inches.

1459 **RESURRECTION 5.11d/12a ★★★** Climb a steep crack past three pins to the right of **Fissure of Men.** Take the left crack in the upper headwall.

1460 **MEDUSA 5.12c** Climb the lower section of **Resurrection** and take the right crack in the upper headwall.

1461 **NEW TESTAMENT 5.9** The large, left-facing book right of **Resurrection.**

1462 **WALK ON WATER 5.12b/c ★★★** Climb a seam right of **New Testament** past a pin and two fixed copperheads.

1463 **BLOOD OF CHRIST 5.11d/12a ★★★** This is the three-bolt climb right of **Walk on Water.**

1464 **BURNING BUSH 5.12c/13a ★** This is the two-bolt climb right of **Blood of Christ.**

1465 **MANNA FROM HEAVEN 5.9** Climb short, inverting corners at the far right side of the wall.

ROLLERBALL FORMATION

ROLLERBALL FORMATION
This formation lies about 150 yards northeast of Patagonia Pile. Scramble up the valley located 100 yards east of Patagonia Pile. Map, page 182.
1466 **ROLLER COASTER 5.11c (TR)**
1467 **ROLLERBALL 5.10b ★★★★**
1468 **KEEP THE BALL ROLLING 5.9** Pro: Thin to 2.5 inches.
1469 **BAM BOOZLER 5.10d ★★★** This steep face route is about 40 feet left of Rollerball. Pro: Thin cams, three bolts, two-bolt anchor.

RUBBLE ROCKS
This "formation" lies just northwest of Rock Hudson, midway between that formation and the Rollerball formation. Two routes are known. Map, page 182.
1470 **CARY GRANITE 5.3** Climb a water groove and finger crack on the northwest face of the formation.
1471 **TOPROPE CONVERSION 5.11+** This is on the east face of a narrow corridor splitting Rubble Rocks. Bolts and other fixed pro mark this 40-foot route.

DINOSAUR ROCK – WEST FACE
This small rock lies 500 yards directly north of the campground loop and Outhouse Rock. Map, page 182.
1472 **GO 'GANE 5.8**
1473 **TOO LOOSE TO TREK 5.10b ★**

DINOSAUR ROCK – NORTH FACE
1474 **GORGASAURUS 5.7** Pro: To 2.5 inches.
1475 **DYNO-SOAR 5.10c A1** Pro: To 2 inches, two bolts.
1476 **NEGASAURUS 5.9** Pro: To 2.5 inches.
1477 **GOOLABUNGA 5.10b** Pro: To 2 inches, four bolts.

ROOF ROCK
Roof Rock 150 yards to the west-northwest of Dinosaur Rock, and is marked by a very large roof, not very high above its floor. It extends inside for about 30 feet. Map, page 182.
1478 **THE LIVING CONJUNCTION 5.11d (TR) ★★** Climb the roof.

ANTHRAX ROCK
This formation lies to the right (north) of Roof Rock.
1479 **MOUTHFULL OF GANK 5.10a** This is a two-bolt face, on Anthrax Rock's southeast corner.
1480 **FISTFULL OF BUSH 5.4** The crack to the left of **Mouthfull of Gank.**

DUTZI ROCK

Dutzi Rock lies about 350 yards north of Dinosaur Rock. The hillside to the left (west) of Dutzi Rock is Mt. Dutzi. Map, page 227.

1481 **SUZIE'S CREAM SQUEEZE 5.6**
1482 **SUZIE'S LIP CHEEZE 5.9** Three bolts.
1483 **PRETZEL LOGIC 5.10c** Pro: To 2.5 inches.
1484 **PINHEAD 5.10a ★** Pro: Thin to 2 inches.
1485 **ELUSIVE BUTTERFLY 5.6 ★★**
1486 **ELUSIVE BUTTERFLY ARETE 5.6 (TR)**
1487 **PAPILLON 5.10c R** Pro: Thin to 2 inches.
1488 **FINGERS ON A LANDSCAPE 5.11b ★** Pro: Thin to 2 inches.
1489 **TEQUILA 5.10d (TR)**
1490 **SHAKIN' THE SHIRTS 5.10a** Pro: To 2.5 inches.

ROCK HUDSON

Rock Hudson is located about 150 yards north of Outhouse Rock. Map, page 182.

1491 **DOING THAT SCRAPYARD THING 5.10d ★★** This route is on the north end of the rock and follows a left-leaning crack just left of a crack beneath a right-facing corner.

1492 **NERELTNE 5.7 ★★**

1493 **ABSOLUTE ZERO 5.10c ★**

1494 **LOONEY TUNES 5.9 ★★★**

1495 **STAND AND DELIVER 5.12a ★★★** Pro: Eight bolts, .5 to 1.5-inch camming units for horizontals.

1496 **HOT ROCKS 5.11c ★★★★★** Pro: Several thin to 3 inches.

1497 **BOLT, A BASHIE AND A BOLD MANTEL A4 5.8 ★★★**

1498 **WHERE EES DE SANTA CLAUS? 5.10a** a small face with a right-slanting dike rises on the left side of the northeast face of Rock Hudson. Climb this to a steep flake/crack leading to a bolt. Traverse left from the bolt to the top.

PEYOTE CRACKS — WEST FACE

THE PEYOTE CRACKS

This small but oft-climbed formation is about 250 yards northeast of Rock Hudson; roughly between Hidden Valley Campground and Echo Cove. Its west face is less vertical and has three prominent cracks. The east face is overhanging and contains a number of excellent and difficult routes. The formation is an easy walk from Hidden Valley Campground. A small parking area near Echo Cove Rocks also provides good access. Map, page 182.

PEYOTE CRACKS – WEST FACE

1499 **BUTTON SOUP   5.2**
1500 **MATT'S PROBLEM   5.10b**
1501 **LEFT PEYOTE CRACK   5.10 ★★**   Pro: To 2 inches.
1502 **STAND BY ME   5.10a (TR)**
1503 **MIDDLE PEYOTE CRACK   5.9 ★★**   Pro: To 2 inches.
1504 **RIGHT PEYOTE CRACK   5.8 ★★**   Pro: To 2.5 inches.
1505 **FACE IT   5.10a R ★★**   (1 bolt)
1506 **WHEN YOU'RE A POODLE   5.11c R**   Pro: 2 bolts. Climb around corner and right of the above.
1507 **ZYGOTE   5.11a**   There is a weird hole in the rock about 40 feet right of **Right Peyote Crack.** Climb past one bolt.

PEYOTE CRACKS — EAST FACE

PEYOTE CRACKS – EAST FACE (aka BACHAR TOPROPE WALL)

This overhanging face contains many difficult and excellent routes. Many of these routes were toperope problems that have since been lead; in some cases, bolts have been added to protect these leads. Most of these routes are good sport climbs. Map, page 182.

1508 **DIMP FOR A CHIMP 5.11b** Pro: To 3 inches or toprope.

1509 **THE MOONBEAM CRACK 5.13a ★★** This route has been lead, but most prefer a toprope. Pro: From .25 to 2 inches.

1510 **BABY APES 5.12c ★★★** Pro: Thin to 2 inches. Most will toprope.

1511 **RASTAFARIAN 5.13b** Pro: Thin to 2 inches, four bolts.

1512 **THE WATUSI 5.12c ★★** Pro: To 2 inches, three bolts.

1513 **DIAL AFRICA 5.12c ★★★** Pro: Very thin to 2 inches, four bolts (poorly located).

1514 **APARTHEID 5.12a ★★★** Pro: To 1.5 inches, four bolts.

1515 **BUFFALO SOLDIER 5.12b ★** Pro: To 2 inches, four bolts.

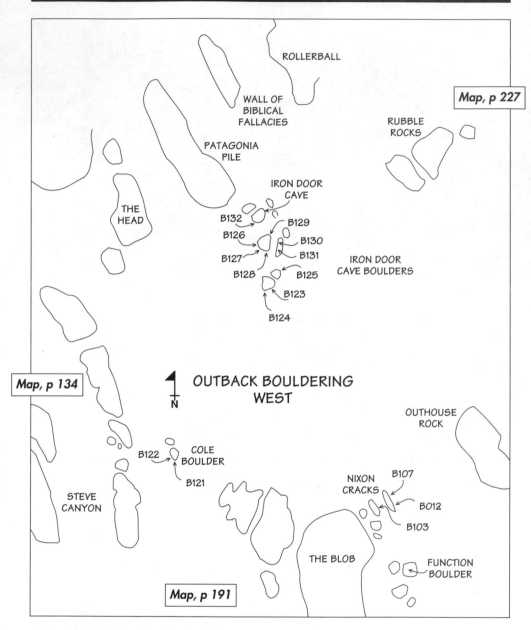

ROLLERBALL

WALL OF
BIBLICAL
FALLACIES

Map, p 227

RUBBLE
ROCKS

PATAGONIA
PILE

IRON DOOR
CAVE

THE
HEAD

B132

B126

B129

B130

B127

B131

B128

B125

IRON DOOR
CAVE BOULDERS

B123

B124

Map, p 134

OUTBACK BOULDERING
WEST

N

OUTHOUSE
ROCK

B122

COLE
BOULDER

B121

NIXON
CRACKS

B107

B012

STEVE
CANYON

B103

THE BLOB

FUNCTION
BOULDER

Map, p 191

THE OUTBACK BOULDERING

COLE BOULDER

B121 **COLE ARETE** 5.11+
B122 **COLE FACE** 5.11+

IRON DOOR CAVE BOULDERS (AKA FLINTSONE BOULDERS)

DINO'S EGG BOULDER

B123 **DINO'S EGG** 5.10
B124 **WEST ARETE** 5.9
B125 **NORTH FACE** 5.10+

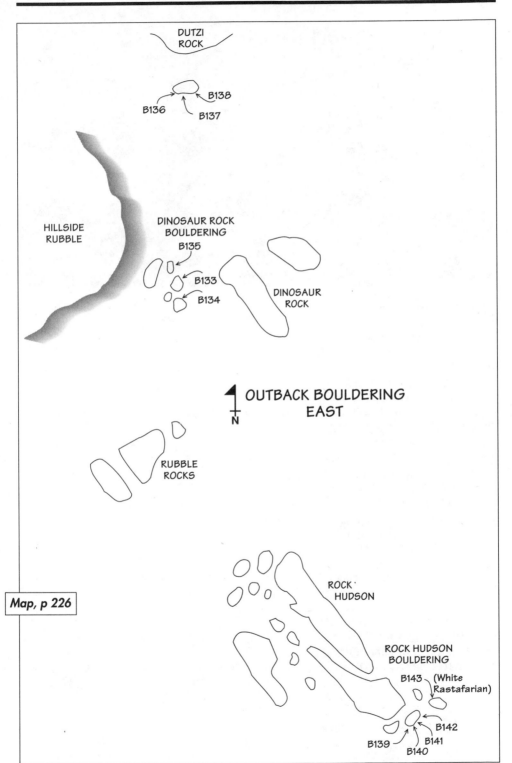

DUTZI
ROCK

B138
B136
B137

HILLSIDE
RUBBLE

DINOSAUR ROCK
BOULDERING
B135

B133
B134

DINOSAUR
ROCK

OUTBACK BOULDERING
EAST
N

RUBBLE
ROCKS

ROCK
HUDSON

ROCK HUDSON
BOULDERING

B143 (White
Rastafarian)

B142
B139
B141
B140

Map, p 226

BEDROCK BOULDER
B126　**BEDROCK ARETE　5.10**
B127　**BAM BAM　5.10+**
B128　**YABBA-DABBA-DOO　5.11+**
B129　**TIDAL WAVE　B1+**

CHUCKAWALLA BOULDER
B130　**CHUCKAWALLA　5.10**　Lieback start.
B131　**FLINTLOCK DYNO　5.9**　Many variations.

IRON DOOR CAVE BOULDER
B132　**CAVE MAN 5.11**

DINOSAUR ROCK BOULDERING
B133　**HOBBIT HOLE OFFWIDTH　5.10-**
B134　**THE ANIMAL　B1-**
B135　**UNNAMED　5.10**

POWELL BOULDER (see photo on page 222)
B136　**POWELL FACE　5.11**
B137　**LARGO DYNO　B1**
B138　**LARGOTOT　5.9**

ROCK HUDSON BOULDERING
B139　**FAMILY ROCK HOW'S YOUR PAPA　B1**
B140　**FAMILY FUED　5.11+**
B141　**HOW'S YOUR MAMA　5.11+**
B142　**HOW'S YOUR GRANNY　5.10+**

WHITE RASTAFARIAN BOULDER
B143　**WHITE RASTAFARIAN　5.11+ R**

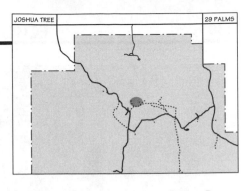

ECHO ROCK AREA

This area lies about .7 mile to the northeast of Hidden Valley Campground. The dirt road leading to Echo Rock begins just south of Chimney Rock. A large parking area marks the spot where the road "tees" (Echo Tee). The road is called Big Horn Pass Road. The road to the northwest leads to Keys Ranch, an old ranch site that is off limits to all but guided tours. If you head right (east) from Echo Tee, you'll pass parking areas for the Comic Book Area, Barker Dam and Wonderland of Rocks, and eventually get back to the main, paved monument road (Queen Valley Road).

The following route is found by following the dirt road northwest from Echo Tee towards Keys Ranch. After about a third of a mile, you'll see an offwidth through a roof down low on the hillside to the left.

1516 **THE MANEATER 5.10d** Climb the offwidth.

RUSTY WALL

From Echo Cove (.25 mile north of Echo Tee), follow the dirt road (closed) for about .75 mile to a gate/fence for Keys Ranch. A short hike west (of about 400 yards) leads to the base of this orange-tinted, overhanging wall. Two cracks are located on the wall.

1517 **WANGERBANGER 5.11c ★★★★**   This is the left crack.
1518 **O'KELLEY'S CRACK 5.10c ★★★★**   This is the right crack. The start is 5.11.
1519 **RIDDLES IN THE DARK 5.11c ★★★**   This route takes a right-facing corner (one-inch flake) past two bolts on an arête to top.

AUSSIE SNAKE FOODS

This short wall lies to the south of Rusty Wall in a small canyon, and is on the west-facing side of the canyon. Further south the canyon becomes private property; please **do not trespass.**

1520 **CHEEZELS 5.9+ R** This is the second crack from the north, which disappears after 10 feet.
1521 **FANTAILS 5.8** This crack is just (3 feet) right of **Cheezels.**
1522 **TWISTIES 5.9 R** This crack lies about 30 feet right of **Cheezels.**
1523 **LOLLYGOBBLEBLISSBOMBS 5.10d R/X** This three-bolt face route lies to the right of **Twisties.**
1524 **ICED VO-VO'S 5.11d** This five-bolt face route lies on the far right end of the cliff.

COMIC BOOK AREA

ECHO COVE

TO RUSTY WALL

TO BARKER DAM

ECHO ROCK

LITTLE ROCK CANDY MTN.

SNICKERS

MOUNDS

LITTLE HUNK

BIG HUNK

HUNK ROCK

GUNSMOKE

Photo: Dave Houser

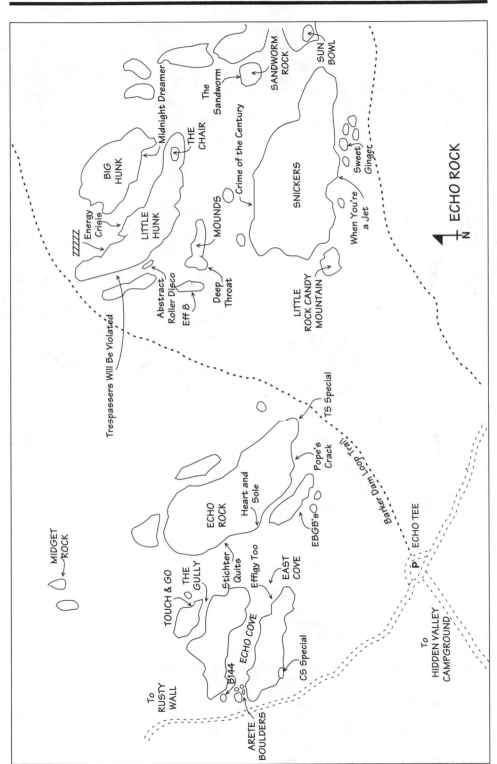

MIDGET ROCK

SANDWORM ROCK

SUN BOWL

The Sandworm

Midnight Dreamer

THE CHAIR

Crime of the Century

BIG HUNK

Energy Crisis

ZZZZZ

LITTLE HUNK

MOUNDS

SNICKERS

Sweet Ginger

When You're a Jet

Abstract Roller Disco

Eff 8

Deep Throat

LITTLE ROCK CANDY MOUNTAIN

Trespassers Will Be Violated

TS Special

Pope's Crack

Heart and Sole

ECHO ROCK

EBGB's

TOUCH & GO

THE GULLY

Stichter Quits

Effigy Too

EAST COVE

ECHO COVE

B144

CS Special

To RUSTY WALL

ARETE BOULDERS

Barker Dam Loop Trail

P ECHO TEE

To HIDDEN VALLEY CAMPGROUND

ECHO ROCK

N

ECHO COVE — LEFT (NORTH) SIDE

KEYS RANCH

Keys Ranch is approximately .75 mile north of Echo Tee. This area is closed to the general public (and climbing activities), although the park service does conduct tours of this high desert homestead area. The presence of water in the area has made it culturally rich; it is dotted with ancient Indian artifacts, including many pictographs and petroglyphs. The first modern inhabitants were the infamous McHaney brothers, who settled here in 1879. It has been asserted that the "Hidden Valley" used by McHaney's cattle rustling operation was in fact near Keys Ranch (and is now the site of a reservoir). By 1910, the ranch was occupied by Bill Keys (who called it Desert Queen Ranch). Keys lived on the ranch until his death in 1969 (although he served a five-year prison term for the shooting death of Worth Bagley). Keys ranched (cattle), prospected (he worked many mines in the area) and scavanged tools and machinery abandoned by others. The Keys Ranch Tour is well worth a visit during rest days or when the weather is less than optimal.

GADGET DOME

This formation faces east, and lies in a canyon about .6 mile north of Echo Cove. Approach from about 275 yards down the Keys Ranch Road (north from Echo Cove), then head roughly north-northeast for about .5 mile until you can go north into a canyon. The formation is on your left a ways into the canyon.

1525 **GILA MONSTER 5.9** Climb the lefthand crack that heads straight up (just left of a right-slanting crack with a bush part way up). This leads to a ledge (belay). The second pitch goes left around the corner, then up to the top.

1526 **ROBERTS-DAVIS 5.10a** This route lies to the right of of **Gila Monster.** Face climb up to a small roof, then up a crack above, leading to the righthand end of the same ledge where you belay for **Gila Monster.** Climb up a left-facing corner over a small roof to the top.

ECHO COVE

This little "cove" lies about .25 mile northwest of Echo Tee, on the right (east) side of the road. Routes are described in sequence as they lie on either wall of the cove. Right and left is used in reference to how you would view the walls if you were facing east into the cove. Map, page 231.

1527 **RUBIK'S REVENGE 5.12b (TR)** This climb is on The Toy Block, a large boulder on the southeast side of the clump of rocks 100 yards northeast of the Echo Cove parking area. Climb the overhanging south face with a roof crack start. There is a two-bolt anchor on top.

ECHO COVE – LEFT (north) SIDE

1528 **FUN STUFF 5.8**
1529 **ECHO BUTTRESS 5.10b (TR)**
1530 **RAGING INTENSITY 5.8** Crack right of **Fun Stuff.**
1531 **CHUTE UP 5.2**
1532 **THE SOUND OF ONE SHOE TAPPING 5.8** Three bolts.
1533 **W.A.C. 5.8 ★**
1534 **HELIX 5.2**
1535 **PEPASON 5.9+**
1536 **R.A.F. 5.9 ★★**
1537 **PENELOPE STREET 5.10a (TR)**
1538 **PINKY LEE 5.10d ★**
1539 **PORKY PIG 5.11b (TR) ★**
1540 **HOT KNIFE 5.10a**
1541 **TOFU THE DWARF 5.9**
1542 **PALM-U-GRANITE 5.7**
1543 **HANG TEN 5.8**
1544 **SANTA'S LITTLE HELPERS 5.11a ★★**
1545 **THE ALIEN LIFE FORM ARETE 5.11a R** This one-bolt arête route is just right of **Santa's Little Helpers.**
1546 **YANKEE POODLE 5.7** Climb the obvious crack up and right from previous route.
1547 **UNNAMED 5.10b** On back side of **Tofu The Dwarf**, et al. Two bolts above a roof/crack.

ECHO COVE BOULDERING

Several good, moderate boulder problems are at the western entrance to Echo Cove. A boulder facing south with a thin crack lies on the north side of the cove, about 100 feet left of **Fun Stuff;** this is the **Classic Thin Crack** (B144). Several boulders, called the Arête Boulders, lie to the right (northwest) of **Out To Lunge** (on the opposite side of the cove from B144) have excellent moderate problems. Map, page 231.

B144 **CLASSIC THIN CRACK 5.11**

THE ARETE BOULDERS

B145 **LEFT ARETE 5.10**
B146 **CRACK 5.9**
B147 **MIDDLE ARETE/FACE 5.10+**
B148 **RIGHT ARETE 5.10–**

ECHO COVE – RIGHT (South) SIDE

1548 **OUT TO LUNGE** **5.10d R/X** ★
1549 **OUT FOR LUNCH** **5.11a** ★★   Two variations. Pro: Medium to 3 inches, no fixed anchors.
1550 **BIG MOE** **5.11a R** ★★★★   Usually toproped (bolts on top).
1551 **BOULDER DASH** **5.9** ★★   Variations on the start rate from 5.10 to 5.11+.
1553 **DECEPTIVE CORNER** **5.7** ★★
1554 **DEATH ON THE NILE** **5.10a** ★   Pro: To 2 inches, one bolt.
1555 **OCEAN OF NIGHT** **5.10c**
1556 **BUCKET BRIGADE** **5.7** ★

ECHO COVE — SOUTH SIDE (RIGHT END)

ECHO COVE ROCKS — SOUTH FACE (LEFT END)

1557   1558   1559   1560   1561   1562   1563

ECHO COVE ROCKS — SOUTH FACE (MIDDLE SECTION)

WALK OFF

RAP

1563   1564   1565   1566   1567   1568   1569   1570   1573

ECHO COVE ROCKS — SOUTH FACE (RIGHT END)

ECHO COVE ROCKS – SOUTH FACE

The Echo Cove Rocks form the cove itself, and the outer faces of these rocks contain many fine routes. The south face faces the Big Horn Pass Road. Map, page 231.

1557 **THE RIDDLER 5.12a ★★** Pro: Thin to 2 inches, one bolt.
1558 **TM'S TERROR 5.10b**
1559 **UNKNOWN 5.11a** Pro: To 2.5 inches, four bolts.
1560 **ATARI 5.10c R ★★** Pro: To 3 inches, two bolts.
1561 **BONZO DOG BAND 5.7 ★** Pro: To 2.5 inches.
1562 **ASS OF DOG 5.9** Pro: Thin to 2 inches.
1563 **AXE OF DOG 5.10a ★** Pro: Thin to 2 inches.
1564 **SABRETOOTH 5.7** Pro: To 2.5 inches.
1565 **POODLE SKIRT 5.11c** Pro: To 2 inches, one bolt.
1566 **SICKER THAN JEZOUIN 5.10d ★** Pro: Two bolts.
1567 **CHIPS AHOY 5.7**
1568 **WILD EAST 5.9 R**
1569 **HORNY CORNER 5.9** Climb the crack and corner immediately left of **R.M.L.** until you can clip a bolt and step right onto the arête leading to the top.
1570 **R.M.L. 5.9 ★★**
1571 **JB'S VARIATION (TR)**
1572 **F.U.N. 5.10c (TR)**
1573 **C.S. SPECIAL 5.10b ★★★**
1574 **HIGH WIRE 5.12a**
1575 **POCKET VETO 5.10a**
1576 **POSSESSED BY ELVIS 5.10d ★★** This is the water groove left of **Bacon Flake.** Start left of the pit. Three bolts.
1577 **BACON FLAKE 5.9**
1578 **FLAKE AND BAKE 5.8 ★★**
1579 **SITTING HERE IN LIMBO 5.9 ★★** Pro: Five bolts.
1580 **OUT ON A LIMB 5.10b ★★★** Pro: Five bolts. The start may be more difficult if you're under 5'11'' or so.

ECHO ROCK

THE CHONGO BOULDER

This boulder lies down low and below **Out On A Limb.** Several good (short) toprope problems (bolt anchors on top) are to be found.

1581 **SOUTH ARETE   5.12a (TR)**   The southern arête.
1582 **RIGHT SIDE   5.10d (TR)**   The northeast arête.
1583 **FACE   5.11a (TR)**   The face on the north side.

EAST COVE — RIGHT SIDE

EAST COVE/ECHO COVE ROCKS

This small cove actually is a continuation of Echo Cove itself; a pile of boulders separates the two areas. A trail connects the two.

EAST COVE – LEFT SIDE
1584 **THE REAL MCCOY 5.12b (TR)** ★★
1585 **HALFWAY TO PARADISE 5.10a R** ★★★
1586 **EFFIGY TOO 5.10a/b** ★★★
1587 **CROSSROADS 5.10d** ★ The direct start past the pin is 5.11+.
1588 **MISFITS 5.11b** ★★ Climb up the cracks and face past several bolts about 50 feet right of **Effigy Too.** Pro: Small to 2 inches, with several 1 to 1.5 inches.

EAST COVE – RIGHT SIDE
1589 **UNKNOWN 5.10a R** Pro: One bolt.
1590 **MAKE THAT MOVE OR SIX FOOT GROOVE 5.10c** ★
1591 **NO MISTAKE OR BIG PANCAKE 5.10d- 5.11b** ★★ Difficulty varies with the climber's height; the taller, the easier.
1592 **SOLO DOG 5.11b** ★★★ Pro: Very thin to 1 inch, three bolts.
1593 **THE ROBBINS ROUTE 5.10+** On the corner/arête right of Solo Dog climb a thin crack up and over a small roof.

ECHO COVE FORMATIONS – EAST SIDE

A very narrow side canyon/gully is about 100 yards to the right of East Cove. Several routes lie on the left side of this fissure. This gully also serves as the descent for routes 1600 – 1605.

1594 **QUARANTINE 5.10a**
1595 **SOLITARY CONFINEMENT 5.11b** Climb past bolts (may not have hangers to belay). Pro: Small to medium nuts.

THE GULLY

1596 **THE D.E. CHIMNEY 5.6 ★★**
1597 **THE SNATCH 5.10a ★**
1598 **THE ASHTRAY 5.6**
1599 **JUGHEAD 5.10a** Climb past three bolts up a knobby face.

TOUCH AND GO FACE

An east-facing part of the Echo Cove Rock is to the right of the gully. The excellent-looking left-facing corner is **Touch and Go.** Map, page 231.

1600 **THE CORNERSTONE 5.10a**
1601 **TOUCH AND GO 5.9 ★★★★**
1602 **BROWN OUT 5.12b/c (TR)**
1603 **THE GOLD HUNK 5.11a (TR)**
1604 **GILDED LUMP 5.11a**
1605 **CREDIBILITY GAP 5.9**
1606 **THRASH OR CRASH 5.9**

ECHO ROCK

This rock lies nearly straight ahead (northeast) of the parking area at Echo Tee. The North (left) End is directly across from the east side of the Echo Cove formation. The South (right) End is best reached via an excellent trail (a continuation of an old road) that starts at the Echo Tee parking lot. This trail (Barker Dam Loop Trail) also provides easy access to the Candy Bar Area. Climber trail markers have been placed to reduce the proliferation of "braided" trails through this area. **Please** reduce your impact on the desert by following these marked paths. Also, a bathroom (paid for by The Access Fund) is located at the Echo Tee parking area. If you are climbing anywhere in the vicinity, please use this facility rather than leaving your waste in the desert. Map, page 231.

ECHO ROCK – NORTH END, WEST FACE

The west face of Echo Rock, due to its good rock and moderate angle, is ideally suited to face climbing. Theoretically, face climbs can be done almost anywhere, and the following list of routes clearly demonstrates this point. The addition of new bolted climbs only detracts from the existing routes. There are many excellent faces awaiting first ascents elsewhere in the monument; new route attention should be directed to those projects.

1607 **THE TROUGH 5.0** This takes the easy gully near the very left side of the face.
1608 **TEAM SLUG 5.10b** This is a three-bolt face climb just right of **The Trough.**
1609 **TOO OLD TO BOLT 5.10b (TR)** Face climb midway between **Team Slug** and **Too Bold To Bolt.**
1610 **TOO BOLD TO BOLT 5.8** Climb loose flakes past one bolt a short distance right of **Team Slug.** The bolt was added after the first ascent.
1611 **PENNY LANE 5.8** Climb the face between **Too Bold to Bolt** and **Double Dip.** No protection.
1612 **DOUBLE DIP 5.6 ★★**
1613 **BATTLE OF THE BULGE 5.11c/d ★★**
1614 **UNZIPPER 5.10+ (TR)**
1615 **TRY AGAIN 5.10c ★★**
1616 **MINUTE MAN 5.10d**
1617 **GONE IN 60 SECONDS 5.10a R ★**
1618 **CHERRY BOMB 5.10c ★**
1619 **STICHTER QUITS 5.7 ★★★**
1620 **DAVE'S SOLO 5.9** Some climbers have since bolted this route (three bolts), claiming a "first ascent."
1621 **LEGOLAS 5.10c**
1622 **STICK TO WHAT 5.9 ★★★**
1623 **FORBIDDEN PARADISE 5.10b ★★★**
1624 **TEN CONVERSATIONS AT ONCE 5.10a** The bolt has no hanger.
1625 **FALL FROM GRACE 5.10c ★**
1626 **APRIL FOOLS 5.10c R ★**
1627 **QUICK DRAW MCGRAW 5.10a ★★**
1628 **THE FALCON AND THE SNOWMAN 5.10b ★★**
1629 **HEART AND SOLE 5.10A ★★★★**
1630 **LOVE & ROCKETS (var) 5.10b**
1631 **EFF FOUR 5.6**
1632 **A DREAM OF WHITE POODLES 5.8** This is a three-bolt climb just right of **Eff Four.**
1633 **COLE-EVANS 5.10a ★**

ECHO ROCK — WEST FACE (LEFT SIDE)

WALK OFF

WALK OFF

1612 1613 1614 1615 1616 1617 1618 1619 1620 1621 1622

ECHO ROCK — WEST FACE (RIGHT SIDE)

RAP

1630

1633

1623 1624 1625 1626 1627 1628 1629 1631 1632

1621 1622

EBGB AREA

A large block (the EBGB'S Block) sits high on a pile of rocks to the right and west of the West Face of Echo Rock. A narrow corridor runs between the block and Echo Rock. The large block has several high-angled face routes on it. Descend off the block down a chimney on the back (east) side. Map, page 231.

1634   **CONTROL   5.10a**   A large boulder on a slab is left of EBGB'S block. This ascends a finger-and-hand crack that turns into a right-facing corner behind the boulder.

1635   **CHAOS   5.11b**   From the ledge where **Control** ends, climb this is a crack over a 12-15-foot roof.

1636   **JANE'S GETTING SERIOUS 5.12b ★★★**   This is a six-bolt climb 40 feet left of **EBGB'S**. The first bolt was used for aid on the first ascent.

1637   **EBGB'S   5.10d ★★★★**

1638   **CHEETAH   5.12b ★★**   Face left of **Tarzan** (bolts? or TR?).

1639   **TARZAN   5.11b**

1640   **ZONDO'S PERKS   5.10a ★**   This route is just left of the descent chimney.

1641   **FAST LANE   5.11a ★★**

1642   **SINNER'S SWING   5.10b (TR) ★**   This takes the first dike system to the right of route 1640.

1643   **SUN CITY   5.11a**   This is the next dike right of **Sinner's Swing,** with one bolt.

1644   **THE TURD   5.11c**   A round boulder sits in front of **Sinner's Swing** and **Sun City.** This climbs the south side of the boulder past one bolt.

1645   **SIN CITY   5.10c**   A slanting dike rising out of the boulders is on the backside of the **Sun City** formation (facing the **Pope's Crack** area).

ECHO ROCK – SOUTH END

1646 **FEATS DON'T FAIL ME NOW 5.9 R ★** Located on the brown face left of the descent route. Climb past two bolts, but the route is runout at top.

1647 **MOMENT'S NOTICE 5.6 R ★** Pro: Thin, one bolt.

1648 **GRAIN PILE 5.11c** Four bolts.

1649 **POPE'S CRACK 5.9 ★★★**

1650 **BRITISH AIRWAYS 5.11d R ★★**

1651 **RULE BRITANNIA 5.11c R ★★★**

1652 **RAKED OVER THE COLES 5.10d ★★** Pro: Thin cams to 3 inches.

1653 **NUTS ARE FOR MEN WITHOUT BALLS 5.8**

1654 **PRIMAL SCREAM 5.10c** Pro: To 3 inches.

1655 **THE ROOF 5.10a**

1656 **SOLE FUSION 5.12a ★★★**

1657 **STREET SWEEPER 5.12a ★★★**

1658 **SWEPT AWAY 5.11a ★★★★**

1659 **T.S. SPECIAL 5.9 R ★★★** Start at the base of the buttress, then traverse out left below roof. This scary route goes straight up the buttress over the roof.

ECHO ROCK – EAST FACE

1660 **SECOND THOUGHTS** **5.10a** ★
1661 **AMAZING GRACE** **5.11c** ★
1662 **FINGER FOOD** **5.10a**
1663 **IGOR PRINCE OF POODLES** **5.11c** Pro: Three bolts.
1664 **DANCES WITH POODLES** **5.12a** Pro: Three bolts.
1665 **BEADWAGON** **5.11a** Two left-slanting dikes are on the face right of **Second Thoughts.** This ascends the lower dike past two bolts and a pin.
1666 **GUT FULL OF SUDS** **5.9** This route climbs the higher left-slanting dike.
1667 **THE STINKBUG** **5.10b** This climb is on the smallish tower left of **Closed on Mondays.** Climb a gritty hand crack, then traverse right and go up a thin crack to the top.
1668 **CLOSED ON MONDAYS** **5.10a** Pro: to 3 inches, two bolts.
1669 **BAMBI MEETS GODZILLA** **5.8+** ★★ Pro: To 4 inches.
1670 **GUMBY SAVES BAMBI** **5.10d** Climb the face right of **Bambi Meets Godzilla** past five bolts. Best done in two pitches.

THE CANDY BAR

A group of formations is to the east of Echo Rock; this is the Candy Bar. The main trail proceeds northeast just south of Echo Rock, passing just north of a large dome with a right-diagonalling dike system on the west face. This is Little Hunk. Map, page 231.

LITTLE HUNK — WEST FACE
1683
1682
1685
1684
MOUNDS
1672 1673
1671

MOUNDS

1671 **DEEP THROAT 5.9**

1672 **BEHIND THE GREEN DOOR 5.10d** ★ Pro: Three bolts.

1673 **CALIGULA 5.9** Pro: Two bolts.

1674 **EFF EIGHT 5.8** This is on the small formation located just north of Mounds. It climbs the short crack that faces west.

LITTLE HUNK – WEST FACE

1675 **TOP 40 TO MIDDLE TOILET 5.9** This route lies on the left end of the west face. Climb a face/flake past a bolt; easy climbing leads to a bolt at the top.

1676 **GO FOR BROKE 5.8** Climb to the right of route 1675. Climb from the top of a triangular-shaped block past three bolts to the top of the face.

1677 **TRESPASSERS WILL BE VIOLATED 5.10c** ★★ This is the right-diagonalling dike system.

1678 **CRASH COURSE 5.10b** This is the first bolted route right of (and crossing) **Trespassers.**

1679 **TORTURERS APPRENTICE 5.10b** The next route right of **Crash Course.**

1680 **GUNSHY 5.11b** This is the third bolted face route right of **Trespassers** (or the second left of **The Compassion of the Elephants**).

1681 **OFFICIAL RUBBER TESTER 5.12a** The first route left of **The Compassion of the Elephants.**

1682 **THE COMPASSION OF THE ELEPHANTS 5.10c** ★★★ Located 80 feet right of route 1677, this route climbs off a 10-foot boulder past four bolts to grey flakes. Two more bolts protect face climbing to the summit.

1683 **PERVERTS IN POWER 5.9** This is a two-bolt face leading to a corner/arête. It is behind and left of **Abstract Roller Disco.**

1684 **ABSTRACT ROLLER DISCO 5.11a** ★★ This climbs past four bolts on the large slab 100 feet right of route 1682.

1685 **TIN GOD 5.10d** This starts just right of **Abstract Roller Disco.** Climb up and right past four bolts.

1686 **FEELING GROOVY 5.10a** Climb a water groove 30 feet right of the flake containing route 1682.

1687 **EXHIBIT A 5.10a** This crescent-shaped arch is approximately 75 yards right of **Feeling Groovy.** Climb up and right on a ramp to above the middle of the ramp. Climb straight up on mantels past a bolt to the top.

LITTLE HUNK — EAST FACE

LITTLE HUNK – EAST FACE
1688 **DISRYTHMIA   5.12a ★★**   Pro: Five bolts.
1689 **NEW DEAL   5.13d ★**   Pro: Nine bolts, two-bolt anchor.
1690 **WHITE MISCHIEF   5.12b ★★**   Pro: Three bolts, two-bolt anchor.
1691 **CASHEWS WILL BE EATEN   5.8**
1692 **UNSOLVED MYSTERY   5.10d**
1693 **ENERGY CRISIS**   This route has been closed to climbing due to the discovery of Indian
     petroglyphs at the base of the route.
1694 **POLICE & THIEVES   5.11c**
1695 **TVC15   5.9 R**   No bolts.
1696 **TEAM SCUMBAG   5.10b**   Pro: Three bolts.
1697 **ZZZZZ   5.9 R ★★★**
1698 **ELECTRIC BLUE   5.11c ★★★**   Pro: To 2 inches, five bolts.
1699 **POWER LINE   5.7**
1700 **POWER LICHEN   5.10b**
1701 **FLOWER POWER   5.9**
1702 **POWER DROP   5.10b ★**
1703 **FUNCTIONAL ANALYSIS   5.11d (TR)**

LITTLE HUNK — EAST FACE

1699

1700

1697

1698

1699

1700

1701

1702

1705

1706

1704

1692

1693
CLOSED

1694

BIG HUNK
This formation parallels and is east of Little Hunk. Map, page 231.

1704 **TOBIN BIAS 5.6**
1705 **WISH YOU WERE HERE 5.10c** Pro: To 2 inches, one bolt.
1706 **ELECTRIC EYE 5.11b** Pro: To 2 inches, three bolts.
The next two routes are on the west face of the summit block of Big Hunk, above and left of the finish of **Tobin Bias.** They can be approached by scrambling up easy rock a few hundred feet left of that route.

1707 **RAILROAD 5.11a** This is a thin crack in a small left-facing, left-leaning book. After the initial crack, hand traverse along a flake to the top.
1708 **FINGER FOOD 5.10b** This climbs the crack right of **Railroad,** starting in its right branch. The two routes end at the same point.
1709 **TRY IT, YOU'LL LIKE IT 5.10a** This is 30 yards left of **Midnight Dreamer,** to the right of the above routes. Climb past a bolt to a crack, then over a boulder to ledge. Take a crack to another ledge, then up the face to acrack (three pitches).

LITTLE HUNK – NORTHEAST FACE
The following routes are on the northeast face of Little Hunk, several hundred feet left of **Cashews Will Be Eaten.** They are approached by ascending the boulder- filled gully between Big Hunk and Little Hunk (the same approach as for **Midnight Dreamer**). All are bolted face climbs.

1710 **REVENGE OF THE CHUCKWALLA 5.11c ★** This four-bolt route goes up the groove and headwall. It is 20 feet left of **Return of the Chuckwalla.**
1711 **RETURN OF THE CHUCKWALLA ★ 5.10c** The farthest left line, with two bolts.
1712 **SWAIN-BUCKEY 5.10d ★★** The next route right, with four bolts.
1713 **PLAYING HOOKEY 5.10a ★★** This three-bolt climb starts off a block.
1714 **SHADY GROVE 5.10c ★★** The farthest right route, with four bolts.
The next routes are a few hundred feet left of the previous routes, just left of the descent from those routes and almost directly below the northwest corner of The Chair.

1715 **THE CHEEZ-IT 5.10d** Two bolts. Located 25 feet left of **Move to the Groove.**
1716 **MOVE TO THE GROOVE 5.10c (TR)** Climb directly up to, then follow, a steep groove.
1717 **GROOVE AVOIDANCE SYSTEM 5.10a (TR)** This is a jug problem right of the groove.
1718 **MIDNIGHT DREAMER 5.9** Located about 150 yards right of **Tobin Bias** and up the talus gully. This is a 100-foot high black buttress on the left. Climb up to a small roof, around to the left, and up a crack to the top.
1719 **MIDNIGHT RAMBLER 5.9 R** Start just right of **Midnight Dreamer** and climb thin seams and flakes.
1720 **CRYOGENICS 5.11c** Located just left of **Gentlemen Adventure** (100 feet right of **Midnight Dreamer,** almost directly across from The Chair). Pro: Three bolts.
1721 **GENTLEMEN ADVENTURE 5.9 X** This is on an east-facing brown wall up and right form **Midnight Dreamer.** Climb the huecoed face left of a thin crack.
1722 **GENTLEMEN BUMBLIES 5.9** Climb the thin crack mentioned in the description for **Gentlemen Adventure.**

LITTLE HUNK – RIGHT SIDE (Southwest End)
The right (southwest) end of Little Hunk has several prominent roofs. Directly above this is a large boulder (The Chair), which sits atop the rock. Map, page 231.

THE CHAIR
The following routes lie on The Chair boulder.

1723 **ORDINARY ROUTE 5.11a R ★★** This is on the west corner of The Chair. Pro: One poor bolt.
1724 **LADDER BACK 5.10b R ★** This route lies about 25 feet left of **Ordinary Route.**
1725 **TAKE A SEAT 5.10b** Located on the south face of The Chair. Pro: One bolt, small camming devices.

LITTLE HUNK

The following lie on the right (southwest) end of Little Hunk.

1726 **ROAST LEG OF CHAIR 5.7**

1727 **RIGHT BETWEEN THE EYES 5.7 ★★**   Rap from a two-bolt anchor. Pro: Many .5 to 3 inches.

1728 **WHITE LINE FEVER 5.9**

1729 **ROOFING COMPANY 5.10a ★★**

1730 **MONKEY BUSINESS 5.8 ★★**

1731 **WAGE AND PRICE CEILING 5.10d (TR) ★**

1732 **SPACE SLOT 5.10a**

1733 **POINT OF NO RETURN 5.10c ★**   An offwidth crack in a chimney, topped with a roof, is 100 feet around the corner and to the right of **Wage and Price Ceiling.** The crux is underclinging the roof.

SNICKERS – NORTH FACE
This formation lies directly east of Echo Rock and south of Little Hunk. The north face of Snickers faces the right end of Little Hunk. Map, page 231.

1734 **NORWEGIAN WOOD 5.9**
1735 **FRANKENWOOD 5.7**
1736 **FUNNY BONE 5.8**
1737 **DON'T THINK JUST JUMP 5.10a** ★
1738 **KNIGHT SHIFT 5.10d (TR)**
1739 **CRIME OF THE CENTURY 5.11a** ★★★
1740 **TWO FLEW THE COOP 5.11a (TR)**
1741 **ALPINE DIVERSIONS 5.11b** ★★ Start at a pine tree 100 feet right of **Crime of The Century.** Climb over a roof and up a thin seam to a ledge; walk off right. Pro: Many thin to 2 inches, one bolt.
1742 **DEATH BY CHOCOLATE 5.11b** This route lies on a large dark brown block (above the desert floor) about 175 feet right of **Crime of the Century**. Climb an overhanging crack/seam. Pro: To 3 inches, one bolt.
1743 **SOULS OF BLACK 5.11d** This is on the north face of Snickers, across from Mounds, and up on a large, overhanging brown block next to a large dead tree. Pro: To 2 inches, two bolts, two-bolt anchor.

SANDWORM ROCK
This small formation lies to the east of Snickers and at the southeast end of Little Hunk. Map, page 231.

1744 **SANDWORM 5.10c R** ★ An overhanging dike/crack on the north side.
1745 **MASTER & SERVANT 5.11d (TR)** This is the 1.5-inch crack to flare to the right of **Sandworm.** Two-bolt anchor.

Dave Griffith on When You're Erect   Photo: John Mireles

DWEEB SPIRE

Dweeb Spire is a large, white, detatched pillar high on the northwest side of Snickers, and directly across from **Deep Throat.** One route is known.

1746 **DISOBEDIENCE SCHOOL   5.10c**   Climb up and left across the north face (with tricky pro), then up a thin crack to an arête finish. One bolt.

LITTLE ROCK CANDY MOUNTAIN

This small, roundish formation is located at the southwest end of Snickers. Map, page 231.

1747 **KENDALL MINT CAKE 5.6** This climbs the easy crack on the left side of the north end of Little Rock Candy Mountain. Face climb up to the crack. (This can also be used as a downclimb.)

1748 **SQUIRREL ROAST 5.8** This is a one-bolt face climb right of **Kendall Mint Cake.**

1749 **SUGAR DADDY 5.9** ★

1750 **NESTLE CRUNCH 5.10c** ★

1751 **CHICKEN BONES 5.4**

1752 **JOLLY RANCHER FIRESTIX 5.10d** The direct start is 5.11a.

1753 **CHICK FLAKEY 5.11b** ★

1754 **LIPS LIKE SUGAR 5.10b**

1755 **FLAKE HICKY 5.7**

1756 **M & M'S PEANUT 5.10a**

1757 **M & M'S PLAIN 5.9** ★★

1758 **CREME EGG 5.9 (TR)**

1759 **LITTLE ROCK CANDY CRACK 5.7** ★

1760 **McSTUMPY SANDWICH 5.9**

1761 **THE THREE MUSKETEERS 5.7+** Pro: To 2 inches, two bolts.

LITTLE ROCK CANDY MOUNTAIN — EAST FACE

SNICKERS – SOUTH FACE

A small canyon is about 100 yards east of Little Rock Candy Mountain and on the south face of Snickers. The right wall has a couple routes. Map, page 231.

1762 **WHEN YOU'RE NOT A JET 5.10b**

1763 **IRON MAIDEN 5.11d ★★★** This two-pitch route starts in the extreme recesses of the narrow corridor below **Rock Shark** et al. Climb a corner system, then face climb up and right to a hanging belay. Proceed up steep rock to the top. Pro: To 2.5 inches, eight bolts.

1764 **WHEN YOU'RE ERECT 5.12a ★★** This route lies on the left (west) side of the narrow corridor below **Rock Shark,** et al. Pro: Four bolts.

1765 **FUNNY MONEY 5.8+** Pro: Thin to 2 inches.

1766 **ROCK SHARK 5.11a** Pro: Thin to 2 inches.

1767 **HENNY PENNY 5.10d ★** RPs are useful.

1768 **WHEN YOU'RE A JET 5.11c (TR) ★★★**

1769 **TOXIC WASTELAND 5.10d** This is a rotten seam with one bolt that leads to a hand crack. It is about 50 yards right of **When You're a Jet.** Very poor rock.

1770 **GRAIN DEATH 5.9** The handcrack left of **Toxic Wasteland.**

1771 **EXTRA CHUNKY 5.10b** This is the two-bolt face route to the left of **Grain Death.**

1772 **CAYENNE 5.11c** A large boulder sits a short distance right of **Toxic Wasteland.** This climbs the west arête past one bolt.

1773 **SWEET GINGER 5.11b ★★★** This six-bolt climb is to the right of **Cayenne,** on the south face of the boulder. If you are shorter than 6'0'', the first bolt may be difficult to clip.

1774 **SWEET ETERNITY 5.11c R ★** This route is on the rock just right of **Sweet Ginger.** Start up a shallow corner 35 feet right of **Sweet Ginger.** Move past three bolts and a fixed pin, then traverse right and up on runout and difficult ground past one more bolt.

1775 **FOOLING MYSELF 5.8** Climb the dihedral just left of **Swimming In A Sea Of Deception.**

1776 **SWIMMING IN A SEA OF DECEPTION 5.10b** A lower-angled face that faces west is to the right of **Sweet Ginger** about 75 feet. This route climbs somewhat loose rock past three bolts on the left. (This is an easy escape to **Fooling Myself**).

SNICKERS — SOUTH FACE

1777 **ART OF DECEPTION 5.11b** Climb past four bolts up the center of the face mentioned above. Rock is a little loose.

1778 **SUN BOWL 5.13a** Climb a steep brown corner past three bolts.

MORE MONKEY THAN FUNKY

MORE FUNKY THAN MONKEY

This small formation lies about 200 yards west of the Barker Dam road and about 200 yards north of Big Horn Pass Road. The low formation is marked by a 20-foot roof about 30 feet off the ground. Map, page 268.

1779 **MORE MONKEY THAN FUNKY 5.11c ★★★★** This route can be led (using 2 ropes), but is usually toproped. Pro: Several 1 to 3 inches.

1780 **MONSEY 5.11d R Climb More Monkey...** to the lip, then traverse right 12 feet to a crack. Pro: To 3 inches.

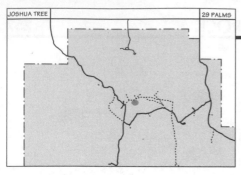

THE COMIC BOOK AREA

The Comic Book Area lies to the south of Big Horn Pass Road and is most easily approached from a point about 600 yards west of the Barker Dam turnoff. Two small parking areas on the south side of the road are located about 100 yards apart. The main climbing area consists of several distinct formations located on the hillside about 1/2 mile from the road.

THE DAKOTA DOMES
These two small rocks sit in the desert west of the Herman Rocks. Just to make things confusing, north rock is South Dakota Dome and the south rock is North Dakota Dome.

SOUTH DAKOTA DOME
1781 **NOT WORTH YOUR WHILE 5.5** This is a dogleg crack containing a bush on the south face.
1782 **BLACK HILLS GOLD 5.10b (TR)** Climb thin cracks and a dike in black, varnished rock on the north face.

NORTH DAKOTA DOME
1783 **NORTH DAKOTA BIG WALL PROBLEM 5.10** This is the overhanging left crack in the corridor on the north side of the formation.
1784 **CUSTER WAS HERE 5.4** This is across the corridor from **North Dakota Big Wall Problem.** Climb a left-leaning crack to a bush, move right then up a flake/crack to top.
1785 **MAYBE BABY 5.5** Climb the center crack on the south face.
1786 **SOUTH END OF A NORTHBOUND POODLE 5.8** This climb is to the right of **Maybe Baby.**

HERMAN ROCKS
This small group of rocks lies about 500 yards south of Big Horn Pass Road and sits against the hillside north of the Comic Book area, (east of the trail leading to the Comic Book area, if one is coming from the Bighorn Pass Road).

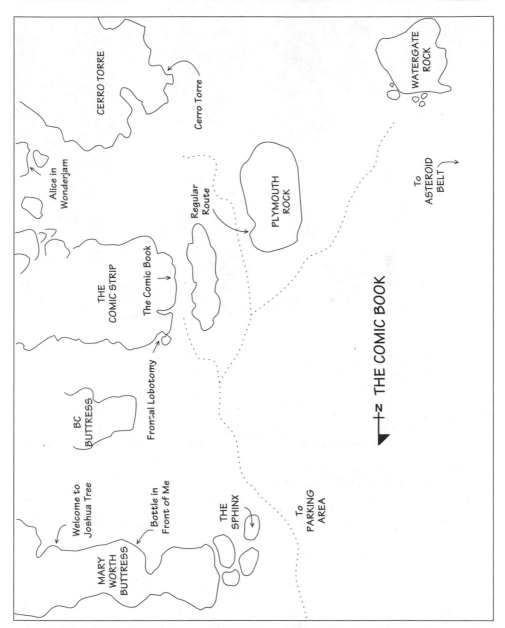

1787 **HERMAN 5.9** This route lies on a large boulder on the left. Two bolts protect steep face
climbing up the northeast face.

1788 **CONTROVERSIAL 5.9** This lies to the left of **Herman.**

MAIN COMIC BOOK AREA

The main Comic Book area is about .5 mile south of Big Horn Pass Road. The area consists of
several distinct buttresses/ridges of rock against the hillside. The northernmost formation is called
The Mary Worth Buttress; the main formation (containing **Comic Book,** 5.10a) is The Comic
Strip; up and right from **Comic Book** is the Alice In Wonderland Area, and to the right (southwest)
is Cerro Torre (named for the main tower's strong resemblance to . . . what else).

THE SPHINX
This small, round formation/boulder lies below and just west of the Mary Worth Buttress.
1789   **CLEOPATRA   5.11a ★★**   This is a five-bolt face route on the north side of The Sphinx.

THE MARY WORTH BUTTRESS
This ridge of rock lies to the left (north) of the main Comic Book formation (The Comic Strip).
Map, page 259.
1790   **CHERRY BLOSSOM   5.9**   The three-bolt route on the toe of the Mary Worth Buttress.
1791   **DON'T TOUCH THAT FLAKE   5.9**   The two-bolt route 15 feet to the right of **Cherry Blossom.**
1792   **DISTANT EPISODE   5.10c ★★**   Four bolts.
1793   **BOTTLE IN FRONT OF ME   5.10a ★★**
1794   **CEREBRAL DYSFUNCTION   5.10a ★**   Three bolts.
1795   **STARGAZER   5.10b ★★**   Three-bolt arête.
1796   **WELCOME TO JOSHUA TREE   5.10c ★★**   This is a two-pitch face climb; belay on the dike.
1797   **OOBY DOOBY   5.10a**   Three bolts.

BC BUTTRESS
This is the nondescript jumble of rocks between Mary Worth Buttress and the Comic Strip. Map, page 259.
1798   **FRONTAL LOGRANITY   5.10a**
1799   **RUSSIAN GRAIN CRISIS   5.10c**   This is a crack on a small dome above **Frontal Logranity.** Climb an easy slab, traverse left 15 feet to gain a crack in a left-facing corner, then go to the top.

THE COMIC STRIP

The Comic Strip is the main formation/buttress of rock in the Comic Book area. The middle west face of the Comic Strip has an obvious crack leading to a "hole;" this is the **Comic Book** (5.10a). Map, page 259.

1800 **STOLI DRIVER 5.10d** Near the top of the formation.

1801 **TAKE IT FOR GRANITE 5.10c ★★★**

1802 **TUBULAR BALLS 5.10b ★**

1803 **FRONTAL LOBOTOMY 5.10a ★★★**

1804 **CIRCUS ACT 5.10c** Pro: To 2.5 inches, slings (for tying off horns), five bolts.

1805 **CRUISING FOR BURGERS 5.10d ★** This is a two-pitch face climb; belay on a dike.

1806 **FULL FRONTAL NUDITY 5.10a ★★★** This is a two-pitch face climb. Start up the crack of **Comic Book,** traverse left on a dike to a belay, and climb straight up to the top.

1807 **COMIC BOOK 5.10a ★★★** This follows an obvious crack for two pitches. Belay in the "hole." The crux is starting the second pitch.

1808 **CHARLIE BROWN 5.9** This is to the right of the previous route. Climb left and up a ramp until you reach a crack that parallels **Comic Book.** Follow the straight up and over a small roof to the top.

THE COMIC STRIP

ALICE IN WONDERLAND AREA

This is the jumble of large boulders and rocks up and right (southeast) of The Comic Strip. Map, page 259.

1809 **COMBINATION LOCKS** **5.11c** ★★ Climb the thin crack just left of **Alice in Wonderjam.** There is one bolt at the start.

1810 **ALICE IN WONDERJAM** **5.9** ★★★

1811 **WHITE RABBIT** **5.10a** ★★

CERRO TORRE AREA

The Cerro Torre area is the complex of formations and buttresses down and to the right of the Alice In Wonderland Area and directly right (south-southwest) of The Comic Strip. Map, page 259.

1812 **EDCHADA** **5.7** This is a thin crack just left of **Urine Trouble.**

1813 **URINE TROUBLE** **5.8**

There are five cracks on the right (west) side of a small box canyon that lie just right of **Urine Trouble.**

1814 **JAMBURGER** **5.10a** The left-most crack.

1815 **HAM & SWISS** **5.10b** The crack that is second from left.

1816 **B.L.T.** **5.10b** Third crack from the right.

1817 **BRAIN DEATH** **5.12a R** ★★ Second crack from right. Start off a small pinnacle.

1818 **BRAIN DAMAGE** **5.12a** This is the rightmost crack-and-face climb to the right of **Brain Death.** One bolt.

1819 **DRANO** **5.10a** ★

CERRO TORRE TOWER

This tower is up and right (southwest) of **Drano.** Map, page 259.

1820 **FITZROY WAS HERE** **5.10b** ★★★ This is to the left of the chimney route on the southwest face. Climb a finger crack to a ledge (optional belay here); then climb up and right past four bolts. Traverse the crack under the summit block, then follow the arête to summit. Pro: Small to 2 inches.

1821 **SW FACE** **5.8** ★ Climb a chimney on the southwest face. Rappel to descend.

1822 **80 PROOF ROOF** **5.10b** ★★★ Face climb just right of **SW Face** chimney route. Climb over an improbable roof. Pro: .5 to 2 inches, four bolts.

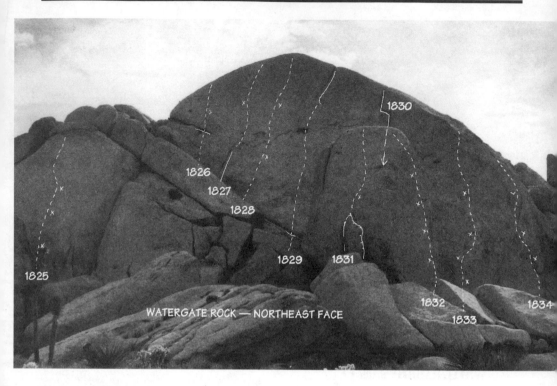

WATERGATE ROCK — NORTHEAST FACE

PLYMOUTH ROCK

This small rock is southwest of the **Comic Strip**, and west of the area with **Drano** and **Urine Trouble.** One route has been recorded on the northeast face. Map, page 259.

1823 **THE REGULAR ROUTE 5.10c** Climb up a crack to the right end of a roof, then up another crack.

WATERGATE ROCK

This lies about 300 yards southwest of the main Comic Book Area. Map, page 259.

1824 **I AM NOT A CROOK 5.8** This route is about 75 feet left of **H.R. Hardman,** on a perched pinnacle of rock. Climb the pinnacle up to a smooth face with two bolts.

1825 **THE BIG LIE 5.8**

1826 **POLITICAL REHABILITATION 5.8**

1827 **PARDON ME 5.9** Climb the face left of **White Collar Crime** past one bolt.

1828 **WHITE COLLAR CRIME 5.8**

1829 **H.R. HARDMAN 5.8 ★**

1830 **FIFTEEN MINUTE GAP 5.6**

1831 **POLITICAL ASYLUM 5.7** This route climbs the outer face of the boulder right of **H.R. Hardman. Fifteen Minute Gap** chimneys behind this boulder. Starting off a block, climb past one bolt to the top.

1832 **T-N-T 5.10c** This four-bolt face climb is right of **Political Asylum,** on the right side of the boulder.

1833 **DIRTY TRICKS 5.11d**

1834 **T. GORDON LIDDY 5.11a** This is a three-bolt face route to the right of **Dirty Tricks.**

1835 **PARANETIEUM 5.8** Climb the disjointed cracks on the left side.

1836 **SHIRLEY MaCLAINE MEETS EDLINGER 5.9** Climb past a bolt to a short, varnished dihedral that is just right of the previous route.

1837 **DAZE OF WHO 5.10a** This is down and right from the preceding route. Climb to a bolt 25 feet up. Move right over a bulge, then back up left to the top.

1838 **DEJA VU 5.10a ★**

WATERGATE ROCK — NORTH FACE

1835 1836 1837

1839

ASTEROID BELT

This small formation lies about .5 mile west of the main Comic Book area. It also is about .5 mile east of Cyclops Rock, in Hidden Valley Campground. Much bouldering lies around and to the right of **Asteroid Crack.**

1839 **ASTEROID CRACK 5.12d**

Three short cracks are left of **Asteroid Crack**.

1840 **KILOBYTE 5.11a** The left crack – steep fingers.

1841 **MEGABYTE 5.11a (TR)** The center crack – also steep fingers.

1842 **COSMIC BOOK 5.10c** The right crack – an overhanging corner.

BARKER DAM AREA

WONDERLAND VALLEY

ASTRO DOMES

RAT ROCK

LAKESIDE ROCK

BARKER DAM

HUNK ROCK

INDIAN WAVE BOULDERS

GUNSMOKE

MORE MONKEY THAN FUNKY

EXCAPE ROCK

BED ROCK

ROCKWORK ROCK

PIANO ROCK

BIG HUNK

Photo: Dave Houser

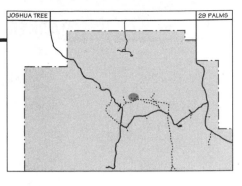

BARKER DAM AREA

To reach Barker Dam from Echo Tee, turn right and follow the Big Horn Pass Road as it heads east. After about one mile, turn on a side road that heads north. This road ends after about 300 yards at a large parking area. A trail (which connects with the Barker Dam Loop Trail) heads straight north to Barker Dam, about 600 yards away. Barker Dam was first built in the late 1800s a little ways upstream of the present dam – when water levels are particularly low, this old dam is sometimes visible. George Myers was responsible for the first dam (Myers was an accomplice of Charles Martin, who killed miner Frank James). Later, C.O. Barker built a stone dam at the dam's current location. This structure was improved and heightened by Bill Keys in the 1950s. The Keys family's names are inscribed near the southern part of the dam.

BARKER DAM PARKING AREA

Concrete slabs just west of the parking lot are remnants of cages where wild animals were kept during the filming of a so-called "nature" movie in the 1950s. The Disney film crew also painted over several Indian petroglyphs so they could be more easily photographed for the film.

These"movie" petroglyphs can still be seen near the trail junction west of Piano Rock.

HUNK ROCK WEST FACE

A formation with light-colored faces can be seen about 100 yards to the east of the parking lot. This is Hunk Rock. Map, page 268.

1843 **GUT REACTION 5.6**
1844 **PAINT AND BODY 5.4**
1845 **ON THE AIR 5.8**
1846 **THE MAD MEN 5.10a ★** Four bolts.

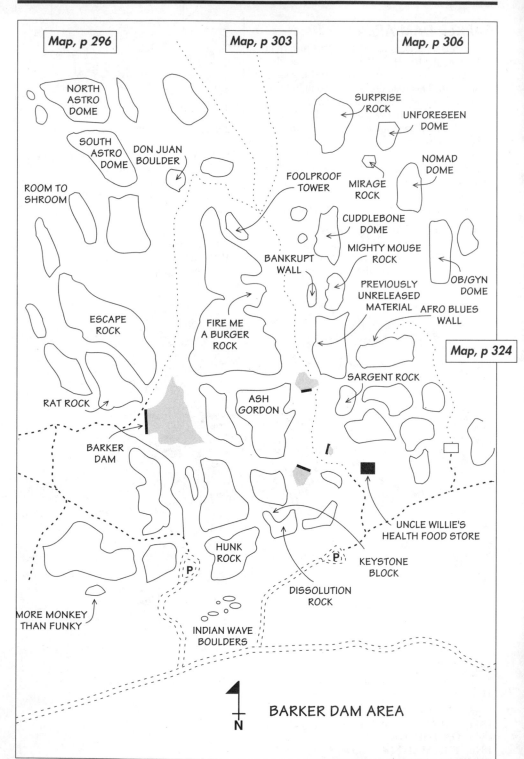

Map, p 296

Map, p 303

Map, p 306

NORTH ASTRO DOME

SURPRISE ROCK

UNFORESEEN DOME

SOUTH ASTRO DOME

DON JUAN BOULDER

NOMAD DOME

ROOM TO SHROOM

FOOLPROOF TOWER

MIRAGE ROCK

CUDDLEBONE DOME

MIGHTY MOUSE ROCK

BANKRUPT WALL

PREVIOUSLY UNRELEASED MATERIAL

OB/GYN DOME

ESCAPE ROCK

FIRE ME A BURGER ROCK

AFRO BLUES WALL

Map, p 324

RAT ROCK

SARGENT ROCK

ASH GORDON

BARKER DAM

UNCLE WILLIE'S HEALTH FOOD STORE

HUNK ROCK

P

KEYSTONE BLOCK

MORE MONKEY THAN FUNKY

DISSOLUTION ROCK

INDIAN WAVE BOULDERS

BARKER DAM AREA

N

HUNK ROCK – EAST FACE

See maps on pages 268, 270.

1848 **HEAT WAVE 5.9 ★** One bolt.

1849 **HUNKLOADS TO HERMOSA 5.9 ★** Three bolts.

1850 **SOFT CELL 5.11a** Five bolts.

1851 **DEATH OF A DECADE 5.10a ★★** Climb the dihedral past one bolt.

1852 **TEN YEARS AFTER** Offwidth/chimney right of **Death of A Decade.**

1853 **BREATH OF DEATH 5.11a** This is a left-leaning, overhanging 1-inch crack rising out of the boulders 50 yards right of **Death of a Decade.**

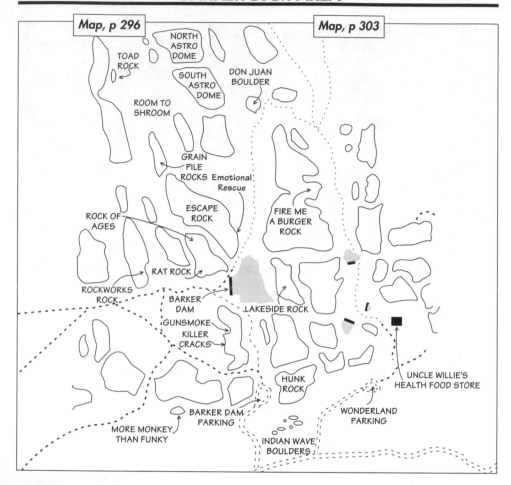

INDIAN WAVE BOULDERS

These large, angular-shaped boulders are south of Hunk Rock and just southeast of the Barker Dam parking area. They lie between the turnoff for Barker Dam and the Wonderland Ranch parking area turnoff. The concrete slab adjacent to the boulders marks the site of Bill McHaney's cabin. Bill's infamous brother (cattle rustler, murderer and prospector) was behind the murder of Frank James, the prospector who discovered the Desert Queen Mine. Bill McHaney spent his last years in this cabin. Map, above and page 268.

B149 **SURF'S UP 5.10**
B150 **OLD WAVE 5.11**
B151 **NEW WAVE B1**
B152 **BIG KAHUNA 5.10+ (TR)**
B153 **LIQUID WRENCH 5.10+** A traversing flake.
B154 **CHICKEN WING 5.9**
B155 **McHANEY CRACK 5.10+ (TR)** A "boost" is needed to start/reach crack.

GUNSMOKE AREA

To reach the Gunsmoke area from the Barker Dam parking area, head north for about 25 yards to a point where a trail heads west through some small boulders. This leads to a large, open basin extending to the west and north. The trail continues in a northwest direction and joins up with the Barker Dam Loop Trail. A large boulder, Piano Rock, can be seen in the middle of the basin, west of Gunsmoke. In times past, a piano was installed on top of the boulder to entertain horse groups.

THE KILLER CRACKS

The Killer Cracks can be found by heading straight north about 150 yards from a point where the trail enters the basin. Directly east is a small formation with several wide cracks. These are the Killer Cracks. Map, page 270.

1854 **DIE-HEDRAL 5.7**
1855 **FISTS OF FURY 5.10a**
1856 **ENTER THE DRAGON 5.9**
1857 **JACK THE RIPPER 5.8**

GUNSMOKE AREA

This excellent bouldering spot lies about 175 yards north of where the Barker Dam Loop Trail enters the open basin (30 yards past The Killer Cracks). Another trail branches straight north from here (approach to The Killer Cracks). Map, page 270.

B156 **GUNSMOKE 5.11+** An excellent boulder traverse.
B157 **HIGH NOON B1 R** The thin crack/seam above the left end of **Gunsmoke.**
B158 **CORNER 5.10** Straight up the corner at left end of **Gunsmoke.**
B159 **STREETCAR NAMED DESIRE B1+** This blank stemming corner is just south (and west) of **The Killer Cracks** (just east of the trail). Mantel on northwest side of boulder.

RICH AND FAMOUS CLIFF

This cliff is about 200 yards west of and facing the **Gunsmoke** traverse.

1858 **RICH BITCH 5.9+** Climb a small clean brown dihedral on the far left side of the cliff.

1859 **FILTHY RICH 5.8** This ascends cracks going over a roof. It is right of **Rich Bitch.**

1860 **RICH AND FAMOUS 5.9** This prominent, clean dihedral rises up high and right of **Filthy Rich.**

1861 **FOUR CAR GARAGE 5.9** The farthest right crack, which goes up and right to a steep finish.

ROCKWORKS ROCK

This long, narrow formation lies about 650 yards northwest of the Gunsmoke area (350 yards west of Barker Dam). A flared, overhanging, orange colored dihedral at the south end of the rock distinguishes this crag. Map, page 270.

1862 **ROCKWORK ORANGE 5.11d ★★★**
1863 **ROCKY VS. RAMBO 5.11c**
1864 **SNOW FALLS 5.9**
1865 **AGUILITY 5.10a**
1866 **EASY LOOKER 5.6**
1867 **UNKNOWN 5.9**
1868 **FLAMING ARROW 5.10b R ★**
1869 **RAIN DANCE 5.11a R ★**
1870 **KICKOFF 5.8**
1871 **UNKNOWN 5.7**
1872 **UNKNOWN 5.11a**
1873 **UNKNOWN 5.10b**

The righthand portion (north end) of **Rockwork Rock** (known as The Schwarzenegger Wall) **is closed to all climbing.** Native American rock art exists in this area, and **climbers** have voluntarily removed all routes from this area. **Please respect this closure.**

Routes listed in the 1986 Guide and 1989 Supplement as 786 El Brujo, 787 El Blowhole, 787A The Predator and 787B Pepo Mover, together with several newer routes have been removed and/or closed. Monument regulations forbid climbing within 50 feet of Native American rock art.

The next three routes are on the wall across from Rockwork Rock.

1874 **HOLE IN ONE 5.10b (TR)** This route is directly opposite **Flaming Arrow.** It starts by a hole and hand traverses left to a vertical flake.

1875 **A SCAR IS BORN 5.11c** This finger crack, which curves up and right, is 20 feet right of the preceding route.

1876 **WHEN YOU'RE A SANCHO 5.11 (TR)** This climbs a prominent face via a diagonal dike. It is right of the previous routes, and across the canyon from **Rockwork Orange.**

BED ROCK

This crag lies about 200 yards up the canyon from **Rockwork Orange** and is on the righthand (east) side.

1877 **HARD SCIENCE 5.8 ★**
1878 **SOFT CORE 5.9 ★★**
1879 **BARNIE RUBBLE 5.10b ★★**
1880 **MOONDANCE 5.13a/b** Three bolts.
1881 **PEBBLES AND BAM BAM 5.7**
1882 **EVOLUTIONARY THROWBACK 5.10c** Three bolts, one fixed pin.
1883 **MEANDERTHAL 5.8 (TR)**
1884 **SATIN FINISH 5.9** This is a straight-in crack on the back side of Bed Rock.

ESCAPE ROCK

This face lies about 500 yards northwest of Barker Dam. It can be reached easily from Bed Rock, which lies directly west of Escape Rock. Map, page 270.

1885 **EXIT STAGE RIGHT 5.9 ★★**
1886 **PSORIASIS 5.9 ★**
1887 **ESCAPE FROM THE PLANET EARTH   5.10a ★★** This route climbs a left-facing dihedral with a bush at its top. It is about 150 feet right of **Psoriasis.**
1888 **BALLBEARINGS UNDER FOOT 5.10a**

TOAD ROCK

This formation is located 300 yards north of Escape Rock and on the west (east-facing) side of the next valley. To the east is a large flake/block with a wide crack on its left side. This wide crack is **Toad Crack.** Map, page 270.

1889 **TOAD CRACK 5.9**
1890 **FISSURE TODD 5.10b** A right-facing corner, that leads to a hand crack on the left wall is around and right 30 feet from **Toad Crack.**

ROCK OF AGES

This formation is about 225 yards south of Escape Rock. Map, page 270.

1891 **HALLOW FRICTION 5.10c**

1892 **GODZILLA EATS HUMAN SUSHI 5.10d** This is a steep hand-and-finger crack across the canyon fron **Hallow Friction.**

1893 **BED OF NAILS 5.10d** This route is about 100 feet left of **Godzilla Eats Human Sushi.** Climb past a bolt into a crack that doesn't quite reach the top.

1894 **MULLIGAN STEW 5.11b (TR)** This steep thin crack starts from a horizontal crack on a north-facing wall. It is in the narrow corridor right of **Hallow Friction.**

BARKER DAM

This reservoir was constructed in the 1930s to supply much-needed water for nearby Keys Ranch. There is almost always water standing behind this concrete dam. However, drinking from or swimming in this lake is very hazardous. Maps, pages 268, 270.

1895 **NO FALLS 5.10d** This obscure route lies on a small, northeast-facing wall, which contains several overhangs on its left. It is on the left (west) side of the Barker Dam Trail, just before the lake. A thin crack on the right leads up and over this roof.

1896 **DENTAL HYGIENE 5.8** Climb a crack and jugs over a small roof 20 feet right of **No Falls.**

1897 **R.D. MEMORIAL 5.10a** Climb a right-facing corner to the left of **No Fallsm** then step left and up straight in crack.

1898 **THREE MEN AND A BABY 5.12b** This is located on the right side of the trail to Barker Dam, about two corridors up, on an overhanging face.

HARDLY ROCK

This is a small, long face on the opposite side of the trail from **No Falls.** A large dike system ascends the wall. Several very short routes (5.0 to 5.7) have been done on this face.

LAKESIDE ROCK

Just as you get to Barker Dam, a large, low-angled dome can be seen to the right (east). This is Lakeside Rock. Map, page 270.

1899 **FAT MAN'S FOLLY 5.8**
1900 **SHIT SANDWICH 5.9** Loose.
1901 **THIN MAN'S NIGHTMARE 5.9**
1902 **COYOTE EGGS 5.10d** Six bolts.
1903 **AN EYE FOR AN EYE AND A ROUTE FOR A ROUTE 5.10b ★★★**
1904 **X-RATED TITS 5.9 ★**
1905 **PARENTAL GUIDANCE SUGGESTED 5.8 ★**
1906 **LAURA SCUDDERS 5.10b** Three bolts.

LAKESIDE ROCK – EAST SIDE

The following routes are approached by walking right (south and then east) around the southern end of the formation.

1907 **FATHER FIGURE 5.12d ★★★★** An overhanging face with four bolts.
1908 **PATRICIDE 5.11b** Two bolts on an arête left of **Father Figure.** Pro: Small to 2 inches.

RAT ROCK

This formation lies at the north end of the dam wall. To get across the dam, walk across the top of the wall. From here you can scramble northeast to where the trail starts again. The dam ends right at the start of **Rat Ledge.** Maps, pages 268, 270.

1909 **THE FORSAKEN MEIN-KEY 5.10c**
1910 **SPRING OR FALL 5.11b** This is up and left of **Bad Lizards** and right of **The Forsaken Mein-Key.** Climb past a bolt to a thin crack and a ledge, then up a dike past another bolt.
1911 **DAMM DIKE 5.7** This is a one-bolt face climb on the wall behind **Spring or Fall.**
1912 **WINNING TIME 5.10a**
1913 **BAD LIZARDS 5.10a ★★**
1914 **THE ARRAIGNMENT 5.10a** Very contrived.
1915 **RAT LEDGE 5.8 ★**
1916 **GRADUATE AND DON'T LOOK BACK 5.10c**
1917 **OASIS OF EDEN 5.10d R ★★★** Pro: Four bolts.
1918 **THE WAY IT SHOULD BE 5.10a ★★** Start to the right of **Oasis of Eden.** Face climb up to reach that route's belay. Pro: Four bolts.

Emotional Rescue lies about 200 yards northeast of the dam. It is under a roof on the left (west) side of the valley.

1919 **EMOTIONAL RESCUE 5.12a ★** This route is a finger-to-offwidth crack in a 15-foot roof.
1920 **MAKITA'S RESCUE 5.6** This is the offwidth, right-facing corner below and left of **Emotional Rescue.** It leads up to that route.
1921 **COURIER'S TRAGEDY, ACT IV, SCENE 8 5.8** This and the following route lie approximately 100 yards northwest of **Emotional Rescue,** on the left side of the east face of a somewhat low-angled and grainy wall. Start at a tree above a deep hole. See map, page
1922 **VIVALDI KAZOO CONCERTS, BOYD BEAVER, SOLOIST 5.9** Climb the crack to the right of the above route, right of the tree.

ROOM TO SHROOM

This formation is about 700 yards north of Barker Dam. As you walk north from the dam you will see very large formations. These are the Astro Domes. The righthand part of the valley takes you to the east face of the Astro Domes.

A left (northwest) turn into a narrow gully leads to the Room to Shroom rock. Maps, pages 268, 270.

1923 **ROOM TO SHROOM 5.9 ★★★★**
1924 **CHEMICAL WAREFARE 5.10b ★★★**   This is a variation to **Room To Shroom.**
1925 **MUD DOG 5.10a**

GRAIN PILE ROCKS

This formation lies opposite of the Room to Shroom formation, and is characterized by numerous cracks. Map, page 270.

1926 **FRANKIE LEE 5.7**   This climb is on an east-facing wall opposite **Room to Shroom,** and slightly farther south. It follows a hand crack that is left of a smooth wall and just right of a wide crack.
1927 **QUEST FOR THE GOLDEN HUBRIS 5.9**   This climb is on the east-facing wall behind **Frankie Lee.** It is a thin crack that peters out near the top, and is left of center in a smooth wall, in the midst of several wider cracks.

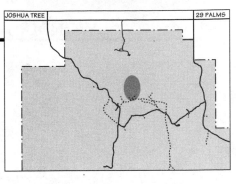

WONDERLAND OF ROCKS SOUTH

The southern part of the Wonderland of Rocks lies to the north and east of Barker Dam. Although the Wonderland is one contiguous area from Willow Hole to Barker Dam, its vast size dictates entry be made from divergent locations to provide reasonable access. Although you can also approach the southern Wonderland from Barker Dam, the most common (easiest) way to get into this enormous area is from the Wonderland Ranch Trailhead.

Drive 200 yards on the Big Horn Pass Road past the Barker Dam turnoff; here, you'll find another turn off to the north. Follow this until it ends at a parking area. A bathroom (the only one in the area; paid for by The Access Fund), and a trashcan are found here. Keep your impact to a minimum; use these facilities.

From the parking area, you can choose one of two approaches. The first takes you north into the main central part of the southern Wonderland via the Wonderland Wash and Wonderland Valley. The other heads northeast to access The Near East areas.

WONDERLAND PARKING AREA

A few routes and good bouldering are located near the parking area. These include Hunk Rock and Indian Wave Boulders (described in Barker Dam parking area descriptions), and Dissolution Rock.

DISSOLUTION ROCK

This formation is on the lefthand (western) end of the jumbled rocks lying north and northwest of the parking area. Dissolution Rock is about 175 yards west of the parking area. It is a brown formation with two cracks and a sharp arête.

1928 **TILL DEATH DO US PART 5.9 (TR)** ★★ This climbs the arête on the left side of the formation. Start up a dihedral off a large ledge, and continue up the arête.

1929 **LIFE'S A BITCH AND THEN YOU MARRY ONE 5.7** ★★ This is the hand crack in the middle of the face. It is to the right of **Till Death...**

1930 **MARITAL SIN 5.10c** ★★★ Climb up a face to a finger crack on the right side of the face. Pro: Thin to 2 inches, two bolts.

KEYSTONE BLOCK

This formation lies about 75 yards north of Dissolution Rock. It can be approached either by hiking between Dissolution Rock and Hunk Rock, or from Barker Dam (if you are already at the dam) by walking south and slightly east from the vicinity of **Father Figure.** From Dissolution Rock, Keystone Block looks like a blunt arête.

1931 **JILL AND JERRY 5.7** This is the flaring and grainy crack in the center of the west face.

1932 **KEYSTONE CRACK 5.6** ★★ The obvious dogleg crack on the left side of the north face.

1933 **KEYSTONE ARETE 5.10b (TR)** ★★ This is the arête to the right of **Keystone Crack.**

SUPER DOME

DIARRHEA DOME

PUNK ROCK

LENTICULAR DOME

GUMBY ROCK

DISNEY LAND DOME

RED BLUFFS

BIGHORN DOME

LOST IN THE WONDERLAND TRAIL

NOMAD DOME

SOUTH ASTRO DOME

FREAK BROS.

THE SHOULDER

SURPRISE ROCK

WONDERLAND VALLEY TRAIL

LAKESIDE ROCK

N. ASTRO DOME

ROOM TO SCHROOM

BARKER DAM TRAIL

RAT ROCK

BARKER DAM

Photo: Dave Houser

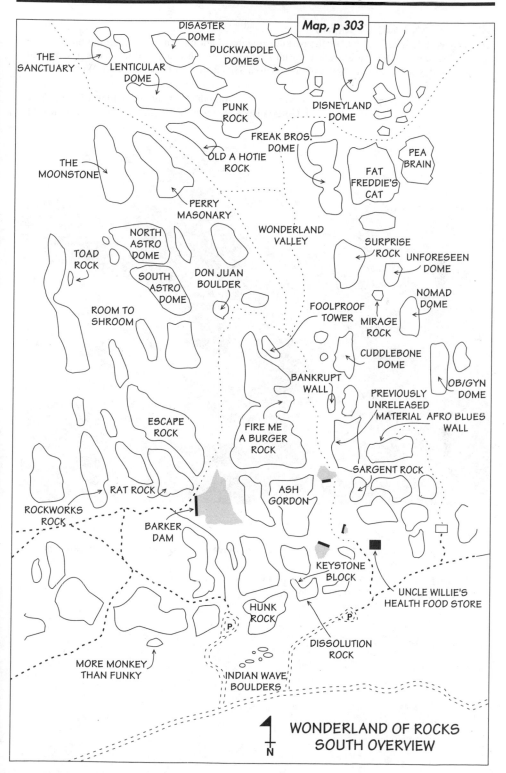

Map, p 303

THE SANCTUARY

DISASTER DOME

DUCKWADDLE DOMES

LENTICULAR DOME

PUNK ROCK

DISNEYLAND DOME

FREAK BROS. DOME

OLD A HOTIE ROCK

PEA BRAIN

FAT FREDDIE'S CAT

THE MOONSTONE

PERRY MASONARY

WONDERLAND VALLEY

SURPRISE ROCK

UNFORESEEN DOME

NORTH ASTRO DOME

TOAD ROCK

SOUTH ASTRO DOME

DON JUAN BOULDER

FOOLPROOF TOWER

MIRAGE ROCK

NOMAD DOME

ROOM TO SHROOM

CUDDLEBONE DOME

BANKRUPT WALL

PREVIOUSLY UNRELEASED MATERIAL

OB/GYN DOME

AFRO BLUES WALL

ESCAPE ROCK

FIRE ME A BURGER ROCK

SARGENT ROCK

RAT ROCK

ASH GORDON

ROCKWORKS ROCK

BARKER DAM

KEYSTONE BLOCK

UNCLE WILLIE'S HEALTH FOOD STORE

MORE MONKEY THAN FUNKY

HUNK ROCK

P

P

DISSOLUTION ROCK

INDIAN WAVE BOULDERS

WONDERLAND OF ROCKS SOUTH OVERVIEW

N

WONDERLAND VALLEY AREAS

To reach Wonderland Valley from the parking area, head north to an old, burned-out building (Uncle Willie's Health Food Store). A wash to the left (west) of Uncle Willie's leads past a small dam to a valley that runs in a north-south direction. This is the southern end of the Wonderland Valley.

Another small dam is approximately 400 yards north along the Wonderland Valley wash. This is an important landmark for locating Ash Gordon Rock, Sergeant Rock and Previously Unreleased Material.

ASH GORDON ROCK

ASH GORDON ROCK

This rock lies just southwest of the dam mentioned above and across the wash from Sergeant Rock. Map, page 281.

1934 **ASH GORDON 5.10a** This crack lies to the southwest of the dam.
1935 **GARDENING AT NIGHT 5.9 A1+**

SERGEANT ROCK

SARGEANT ROCK

This lies directly east of the dam mentioned, and across (east of) Ash Gordon Rock. Map, page 281.

1936 **WAR GAMES 5.10a ★★**
1937 **ROCK STAR 5.10d R ★★** Pro: Three bolts.
1938 **SCHOOL DAZE 5.10a** Pro: To 2 inches, one bolt.
1939 **SUFFERING CATFISH 5.10b** Pro: Two bolts.
1940 **39 STEPS 5.4 ★★**

PREVIOUSLY UNRELEASED MATERIAL

PREVIOUSLY UNRELEASED MATERIAL

This large formation is northeast of the flat sandy area north of the dam. Map, page 281.

1941 **HOUR OF DARKNESS 5.9+** Pro: Thin to 2 inches, two bolts.
1942 **KNIGHT MARE 5.7**
1943 **ROCKY HORROR 5.7**

FIRE ME A BURGER ROCK
This rock lies almost directly opposite Previously Unreleased Material. It is distinguished by the roof cracks on the upper righthand side. Maps, pages 268, 281.

1944 **RED HEADED STRANGER 5.11a ★★**
1945 **HO MAN! 5.11b**
1946 **IT DON'T MEAN A THING IF IT AIN'T GOT THAT SWING 5.12b ★★★**
1947 **SOLSTICE 5.10c ★**

BANKRUPT WALL

This small crag is on the right side of the wash, just a little north of Previously Unreleased Material, and nearly opposite Fire Me A Burger Rock. Map, page 281.

1948 **INSOLVENT   5.10b ★★**
1949 **OVERDRAFT   5.8 (TR)**
1950 **CHAPTER 7   5.6**
1951 **CREDITOR'S CLAIM   5.7**
1952 **WASTING ASSETS   5.6**

MIGHTY MOUSE ROCK

This formation is identified as a buttress of rock 100 yards past (north of) Bankrupt Wall, on the right (east) side of the wash.

1953 **MIGHTY MOUSE   5.9** This route climbs a crack and jugs halfway up the face, then past two bolts to the top.
1954 **MINOR DETOUR   5.10a** Ascend a finger crack in a small corner on the block above **Mighty Mouse.**

THE CUDDLEBONE DOME

This white face is best found by walking past (north of) Bankrupt Wall until a large boulder that looks like a walrus or whale (from the north it resembles a large open mouth) is seen on the right (east) side of the wash. The white slab face of Cuddlebone Dome is to the east of this boulder. Map, page 281.

1955 **CUDDLEBONE   5.7** The lefthand, three-bolt route.
1956 **TEXAS BIG HAIR   5.9+** The two-bolt route to the right of **Cuddlebone.**

FOOLPROOF TOWER

FOOLPROOF TOWER

The Wonderland Valley widens out about 450 yards north of Bankrupt Wall. Foolproof Tower, an outcrop with a large flake/block, capped by a roof, lying against its face can be seen from here. Map, page 281.

1957　**BUFORD'S HOUSE OF LIVER　5.11a**　Six bolts.

1958　**HIGH STRUNG　5.9 ★★**

1959　**RICE CAKE ROOF　5.10c ★**

1960　**ANIMAL MAGNETISM　5.11a ★**

1961　**YOGI THE OVERBEAR　5.10a**　The direct start is 5.10c.

NOMAD DOME – WEST FACE

Nomad Dome is approximately 600 yards northeast of Foolproof Tower and 300 yards east of the nearest approach from the Wonderland Valley. Several approaches are possible; the easiest follows a wash just south of Surprise Rock to the southeast, then east. Map, page 281.

1962 **BEN 5.10a ★★**
1963 **LAST ANGRY ARAB 5.6**
1964 **WILLARD 5.7 ★**
1965 **RICOCHET 5.5 ★**

MESOPOTAMIA DOME

Walk east along the south end of Nomad Dome, then head north along a canyon. A white slab facing east is on the left side of the canyon.

1966 **MESOPOTAMIA 5.10b ★★★** This route starts behind several large boulders. Climb the face past four bolts up a faint water streak.

OB/GYN DOME

This formation is just southeast of Nomad Dome. Routes are on the northeast face and in a boulder-choked corridor running north-south. Map, page 281.

1967 **BURN BUSH 5.10a** Several bolts lead up this line near the entrance to the corridor on east side.
1968 **NEW DECAYED 5.7** Ascend an obvious pillar farther in the corridor (right of **Burn Bush**) past three bolts.
1969 **SPECULUM SCRAPINGS 5.11b** Start atop a pedestal on the northeast face of the formation. Climb up and right into a left-facing book. From the book's top, go up and left to the summit.
1970 **MR. BUNNY'S PETRI DISH 5.9** Climb a left-facing book to the right of the preceding route. From its top, an unprotected face leads to a left-leaning crack and to the top.

THE ASTRO DOMES

These two domes offer some of Joshua Tree's finest face climbing routes. The rock on the northeast faces of both the North and South Astro Domes is uncharacteristically smooth. Most routes climb sharp edges or flakes on excellent rock.

The Astro Domes are about 350 yards to the northwest from the point where the Wonderland Valley widens (near Foolproof Tower). Maps, pages 281, 296.

DON JUAN BOULDER

This very large boulder overhangs on all sides. It is about halfway between Foolproof Tower and the South Astro Dome. Maps, pages 281, 296.

1971 **AID ROUTE A2** This bolt ladder is on the southeast corner. It was established in 1972.

1972 **THE DUKE 5.9 A1** Located on the northwest corner of the boulder. Lasso a horn about 12 feet off the ground, then climb the rope to get on the horn. Continue past two bolts to the top.

Mari Gingery on Mamunia, 5.12, Astro Domes   Photo: Kevin Powell

RODEO ROCK

This rock is really the southern end of the chain of domes of which the North and South Astro Domes are a part. It lies about 100 yards south of the South Astro Dome.

1973 **SERIOUS FASHION 5.10c ★** This route is on the southeast corner of Rodeo Rock. Climb up the corner past five bolts.

1974 **BEVERLY DRIVE 5.10c (TR)** This route climbs the face left of **Serious Fashion,** and starts on a small flake.

SOUTH ASTRO DOME – EAST FACE

The easiest descent from South Astro Dome is down the northwest shoulder. This is Class 3.

1975 **PRIMAL FLAKE 5.9+** Climb a 60-foot 5.9 face past two bolts on the southeast shoulder of the South Astro Dome. Above, hand traverse the "Primal Flake" to a bolt. Climb right and up to an overhang/corner, then continue to the summit.

1976 **IF YOU REALLY LOVED ME, YOU'D BUY ME A TURKEY 5.10b** Three bolts.

1977 **HEX MARKS THE POOT (aka Lightning Bolt Crack) 5.7 ★★★** A second pitch can be added (5.8); climb up an obvious lieback flake.

1978 **STRIKE IT RICH 5.10a ★**

SOUTH ASTRO DOME — EAST FACE
(MIDDLE SECTION)

SOUTH ASTRO DOME – NORTHEAST FACE

1979 **MAMUNIA 5.13a ★★★**
1980 **STONE IDOL 5.11d R ★★★★** Six bolts.
1981 **BOLT HEAVEN 5.10 A1**
1982 **MY LAUNDRY 5.9 ★★★**
1983 **CRIMPING LESSONS 5.11b ★★★**
1984 **SOLID GOLD 5.10a ★★★★** Pro: Thin to 1.5 inches, bolts.
1985 **MIDDLE AGE CRAZY 5.11b ★★★** Pro: To 2 inches.
1986 **SHOOTING STAR 5.11a ★★**
1987 **SUCH A SAVAGE 5.11a ★★★★★** Runout to the first and second bolts. Pro: To 1.5 inches, bolts. The direct start is 5.10.
1988 **WALKING PNEUMONIA 5.11b R/X ★** Pro: To 2 inches, bolts.
1989 **BREAKFAST OF CHAMPIONS 5.8+ ★★** Pro: To 3 inches, one bolt.
1990 **PIGGLE PUGG 5.10c ★★★** Climb a lieback flake to right of **Breakfast of Champions** and join that route. Pro: Many thin to 2 inches.
1991 **THE BOOGIE WOOGIE BLUES 5.11c** Pro: Three bolts, to 2 inches.

SOUTH ASTRO DOME — NORTHEAST FACE

NORTH ASTRO DOME – EAST FACE

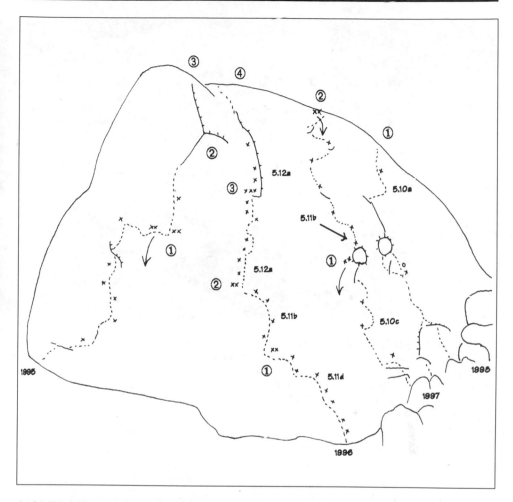

NORTH ASTRO DOME – NORTHEAST FACE

The easiest descent off the North Astro Dome is down the northwest shoulder (5.4). It is possible to rappel from the belay bolts of a west-face route, but two ropes are required. Maps, pages 281, 296.

1991A **IN SEARCH OF HUSH PUPPIES 5.8 R/X**
1992 **THROAT WARBLER MANGROVE 5.9 R** Dirty.
1993 **ZION TRAIN 5.10d ★★**
1994 **REPO MAN 5.12a R ★★★**
1995 **FIGURES ON A LANDSCAPE 5.10b ★★★★★** Pro: To 3 inches, bolts.
1996 **THE GUNSLINGER 5.12a ★★★★** Four pitches. Pro: 21 bolts, belay anchors, nuts to 2.5 inches.
1997 **UNKNOWN SOLDIER 5.11b ★★★★** Pro: Bolts, thin, and slings for flakes.
1998 **THE UNKNOWN ROUTE 5.10a R ★★**

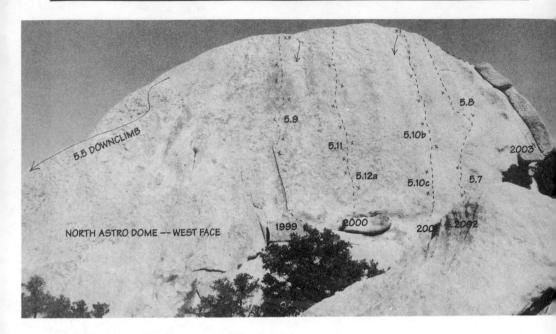

5.5 DOWNCLIMB

5.9

5.11

5.12a

5.10b

5.10c

5.8

5.7

2003

NORTH ASTRO DOME — WEST FACE

1999   2000   2001   2002

NORTH ASTRO DOME – WEST FACE
1999 **LEAD US NOT INTO TEMPTATION 5.9** ★★★
2000 **LIFE'S A PITCH 5.12a** ★★ Eight bolts.
2001 **CHUTE TO KILL 5.10c** ★ Six bolts.
2002 **DELIVER US FROM EVIL 5.8 R** ★
2003 **HUSH PUPPIES 5.6**

DESCENT

EASY SCABS

SOUTH ASTRO DOME — WEST FACE

06

006

2007

2008

2008A

2009

2010

SOUTH ASTRO DOME – WEST FACE

2004 **BOZO BUTTRESS 5.1** This route lies just left of the descent route, across from **Deliver Us From Evil.** It climbs the low-angled face and buttress past two bolts.

2005 **MR. LIZARD MEETS FLINTSTONE 5.6** This is a five-bolt climb right of **Bozo Buttress.**

2006 **DIDN'T YOUR MAMA EVER TELL YOU ABOUT A STRANGER'S BOLTS 5.9** This is to the right of the preceding climb. The route has three bolts.

2007 **AIR VOYAGER 5.11b** There are two bolts at the start.

2008 **IT SEAMS POSSIBLE 5.10c** The right groove, with no bolts.

2008A **RED LINE 5.8**

2009 **AQUA TARKUS 5.9+ ★**

2010 **BOZO'S RAINDANCE 5.11c** This is a five-bolt climb (the second bolt is doubled).

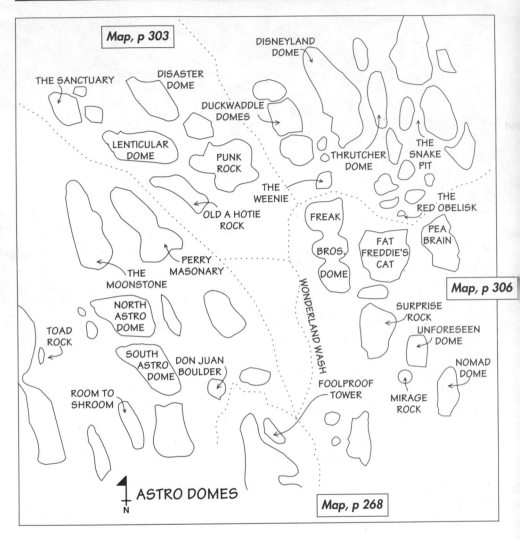

Map, p 303

DISNEYLAND DOME

THE SANCTUARY

DISASTER DOME

DUCKWADDLE DOMES

LENTICULAR DOME

PUNK ROCK

THRUTCHER DOME

THE SNAKE PIT

THE WEENIE

OLD A HOTIE ROCK

FREAK

THE RED OBELISK

PEA BRAIN

FAT FREDDIE'S CAT

BROS. DOME

PERRY MASONARY

THE MOONSTONE

Map, p 306

NORTH ASTRO DOME

TOAD ROCK

SURPRISE ROCK

UNFORESEEN DOME

NOMAD DOME

SOUTH ASTRO DOME

DON JUAN BOULDER

WONDERLAND WASH

ROOM TO SHROOM

FOOLPROOF TOWER

MIRAGE ROCK

↑ ASTRO DOMES
N

Map, p 268

GET IT TOGETHER ROCK

This north-facing wall lies west of the north face of the North Astro Dome and across from the south end of The Moonstone. Map, page

2011 **I GOT IT 5.9** An obvious left arching flake/crack is to the left of several large, rust-colored roofs. Climb an easy chimney up to this crack, and continue to the top.

THE MOONSTONE – NORTHEAST FACE (as seen from Lenticular Dome)

This dome lies northwest of the North Astro Dome and across a small gully that runs east-west. The best approach is via Lenticular Dome. Head southwest 300 yards from that dome. Maps, pages 281, 296.

2012 **ANTY MATTER 5.10a** Climb the obvious ramp 30 feet left of **Cosmic Debris,** then up the face past two bolts.

2013 **COSMIC DEBRIS 5.10a ★** Climb up a corner and discontinuous cracks to a bolt; face climb to the summit.

2014 **ONE SMALL STEP 5.6** This is the big crack 10 feet right of **Cosmic Debris.**

2015 **THE MOONWALK 5.6** Climb the short crack 30 feet right of **Cosmic Debris.**

LOOKING NORTH FROM THE ASTRO DOME

LENTICULAR DOME

PUNK ROCK

DISNEYLAND DOME

THRUTCHER DOME

FREAK BROS. DOME

2012   2013

2014

2015

THE MOONSTONE — NORTHEAST FACE

PERRY MASONARY

This formation is directly south of Old A Hotie Rock, and on the left side of the wash as one approaches Lenticular Dome from Wonderland Valley. The routes are all on the northeast face. Maps, pages 281, 296.

2016 **TROWEL AND ERROR 5.9** This is the obvious curving flake/crack in the left center of the face.

2017 **SAKRETELIGIOUS 5.8** Climb the leftmost of three cracks right of **Trowel and Error.**

2018 **MORTARFIED 5.10b** Climb the rightmost of the three cracks, then continue past three bolts.

2019 **CEMENTARY 5.8** This is the right-facing, right-leaning crack/corner right of **Mortarfied.** It starts behind a tree.

2020 **ANOTHER BRICK IN THE WALL 5.9 (TR)** Climb the very thin flake just right of **Cementary,** then up the face.

LENTICULAR DOME

This attractive rock lies about 450 yards north of the North Astro Dome. However, it is best approached via the main trail through the Wonderland Valley. Eventually, you must cut into a wash that heads northwest and passes directly below the southwest face of Lenticular Dome. A trail that heads north from near Don Juan Boulder leads directly into this wash and offers an alternative route. Descend to the right, then down slabs into a gully. Map, page 296.

2021 **UNCONSCIOUS OBSCENITY 5.9** This follows five bolts on the face left of **Hand Wobler Delight.**

2022 **HAND WOBLER DELIGHT 5.9**

2022A **UNKNOWN 5.10a**

2023 **DAZED AND CONFUSED 5.9 ★★★**

2024 **MENTAL PHYSICS 5.7+ ★★★★**

THE SANCTUARY

This is a well-hidden but worthwhile corridor north of Lenticular Dome. Follow the approach to that formation, and continue past the dome for about five minutes. Turn right (northeast) and enter a small wash/gully. The top of the gully is the back of The Sanctuary. Walk right to get around the formation, and drop down into the corridor. Just before descending into the corridor, look right and you'll see a formation peppered with jugs. This is called The Brain Box. Maps, pages 281, 296.

2025 **POP TART 5.8** Climb a hand-and-fist crack on the left side of The Sanctuary.

2026 **HOLY HAND 5.10a** This is the next crack right of **Pop Tart.**

2027 **LITURGY 5.11a** This is a finger crack is the next crack right.

2028 **BLACK SLACKS 5.10a** This is an offwidth farther right.

2029 **TOP HAT 5.11+ (TR)** This is a crack-to-face climb right of **Black Slacks.**

2030 **SANCTUARY MUCH 5.11a** This is the farthest crack on the right, finishing with a left-slanting crack.

2031 **THE BRAIN 5.7** This goes straight up the middle of The Brain Box, as viewed from the approach.

LENTICULAR DOME

OLD A HOTIE ROCK

This rock forms the small ridge of the gully along the southern end of Lenticular Dome. The following routes lie on the north side. This formation also may be reached using the Punk Rock approach. Map, page 296.

2032 **LAID BACK AND DOING IT 5.10c** This route lies directly across from the descent route for Lenticular Dome. A large, arching roof is located on the right side of a straight, two-inch crack. Lieback up a right-arching fingertip crack to the hand crack, which is followed more or less straight up to the top.

2033 **EXISTENTIAL DECAY 5.12d R ★★** This route climbs a thin lieback right of **Nihilistic Pillar.** Pro: To 2 inches, bolts.

2034 **NIHILISTIC PILLAR 5.11c R ★★** Pro: Small to 3.5 inches.

2035 **ENDLESS SUMMER 5.9** This route is on the southwest face of the rock, directly opposite the Perry Masonary routes. Climb double left-slanting cracks which pass a ledge with a yucca bush on it.

PUNK ROCK (aka Beagle Rocks) – SOUTHWEST FACE

This prominent pile of rocks lies squarely in the middle of the northern part of the Wonderland Valley. It is easily approached via the main trail. Just before the Freak Brothers Domes, head northwest. **Punked Out Porpoise** is easily seen from the approach. Map, page 296.

2036 **PUNKED OUT PORPOISE 5.8+** ★★ Loose and poor pro.

2037 **BOMBS OVER LIBYA 5.12a** ★★★★ This is a three-bolt climb on the steep right side of the south face of the rock. It is somewhat above and left of **Scar Wars.**

2038 **TOP GUNS 5.11a** ★ This route lies opposite **Bombs Over Libya.**

2039 **SLAVES OF FASHION 5.12b** ★ This is the obvious finger crack left of **Scar Wars,** which starts by ascending a face past one bolt.

2040 **SCAR WARS 5.11a** This route ascends a finger crack to a very obvious offwidth crack on the east end of Punk Rock. It is best seen and approached from Freak Brothers Domes.

2041 **COLE-GORDON OFFWIDTH 5.10c** Climb an obvious left-curving chimney to an offwidth around the corner and to the right of **Scar Wars.**

DISASTER DOME

Although this formation lies to the north of Lenticular Dome, it probably is best approached by turning west from the main Wonderland Wash just past The Freak Brothers Dome. It is approximately 100 feet high, and the vertical north face can be seen in profile from here. Two cracks are located on the right side of the north face; both cracks start about 30 feet off the ground. Descent is via rappel from top of **Towering Inferno.** See map page 296.

2042 **THE TOWERING INFERNO 5.11c** ★★ Start up a flake on the far right side of the north face, traverse left at a horizontal, and climb the rightmost crack.

2043 **THE POSEIDON ADVENTURE 5.11b** ★★ Start as for **Towering Inferno,** but traverse further left past a bolt to reach the left crack. Two ropes are helpful to reduce drag.

2044 **PLANTISMAL 5.9** This obvious hand crack lies across the corridor from the above two routes.

2045 **THE PANTY SHIELD 5.10c** This thin-hands crack is on a 40-foot, shield-shaped formation. It is approximately 100 yards northwest of **Plantismal** and faces northwest.

JUMBO ROCKS

ROOM TO SCHROOM

LAKESIDE ROCK

ASTRO DOMES

BAR
DA

MOONSTONE

LENTICULAR DOME

WONDERLAND LOOKING SOUTHEAST

Photo: Dave Houser

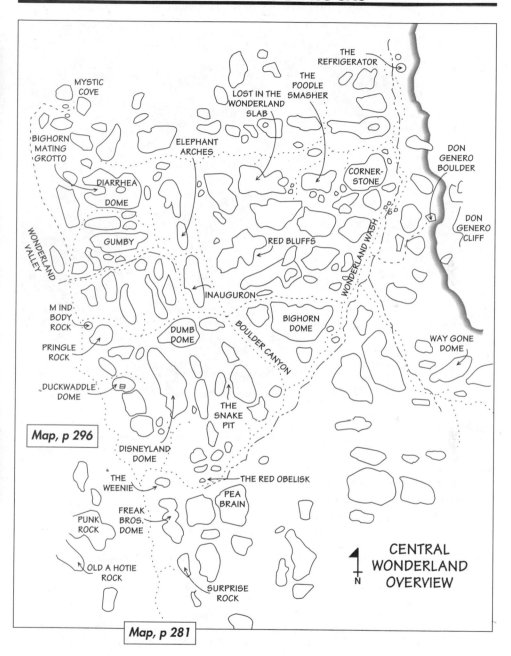

MYSTIC
COVE

THE REFRIGERATOR

THE
POODLE
SMASHER

LOST IN THE
WONDERLAND
SLAB

BIGHORN
MATING
GROTTO

ELEPHANT
ARCHES

DON
GENERO
BOULDER

CORNER-
STONE

DIARRHEA
DOME

DON
GENERO
CLIFF

WONDERLAND VALLEY

GUMBY

RED BLUFFS

WONDERLAND WASH

M IND
BODY
ROCK

INAUGURON

BIGHORN
DOME

WAY GONE
DOME

PRINGLE
ROCK

DUMB
DOME

BOULDER CANYON

DUCKWADDLE
DOME

THE
SNAKE
PIT

Map, p 296

DISNEYLAND
DOME

THE RED OBELISK

THE
WEENIE

PEA
BRAIN

PUNK
ROCK

FREAK
BROS.
DOME

CENTRAL
WONDERLAND
OVERVIEW

OLD A HOTIE
ROCK

SURPRISE
ROCK

N

Map, p 281

SURPRISE ROCK — WEST FACE

SURPRISE ROCK – WEST FACE
This small dome lies on the eastern side of Wonderland Valley, to the northeast of the Astro Domes. If you hike out on the main Wonderland Valley trail, you will pass just west of it. Maps, pages 296, 303.

2046 **TREMBLING TOES 5.9 ★** This can be done in one pitch.

2047 **DIRTY SURPRISE 5.9 ★**

UNFORSEEN DOME – WEST FACE
This formation lies almost directly behind (east) of Suprise Rock. The west face has several crack systems. Map, page 303.

2048 **ONE WHOLE CHICKEN IN A CAN 5.10d** This is the groove/chimney on the left end of the west face.

2049 **EAT WHAT YOU SECRETE 5.7** The obvious hand crack in a groove 20 feet right of **One Whole . . .**

2050 **RED HOT CHILI PEPPERS 5.11a** Climb seams/grooves, then face climb past five bolts. This is 40 feet right of **Eat What You Secrete** and 15 feet left of **Fissure of Fish.**

2051 **FISSURE OF FISH 5.9** This is the crack/chimney system on the righthand section of the cliff.

MIRAGE ROCK
This small formation lies approximately 50 yards south of Unforseen Dome (and northwest of Nomad Dome). Map, page 303.

2052 **TELL ME I'M NOT DREAMING 5.9** Face climb up to a left-facing corner with a bolt.

FREAK BROTHERS DOME — WEST FACE

FREAK BROTHERS DOMES – WEST FACE

This distinctive trio of domes is just north of Surprise Rock, and is recognizable by the three roofs that run through the domes. Maps, pages 303, 306.

2053 **I CAN'T BELIEVE IT'S A GIRDLE   5.10a ★★★★ (R** for follower)

2054 **THE SOUND OF ONE HAND SLAPPING   5.11c ★★**

2055 **SAFE MUFFINS   5.8 R**

2056 **GIRDLE CROSSING   5.10d ★★★**

2057 **FAT FREDDIE'S ESCAPE   5.8**   The upper part is "the escape," 5.6.

2058 **ZAP #4   5.6**

2059 **I CAN BELIEVE IT'S A SANDBAG   5.8**   This is on the far right (south) end of the domes. Climb a left-leaning ramp to its top, then right past a bolt to the top.

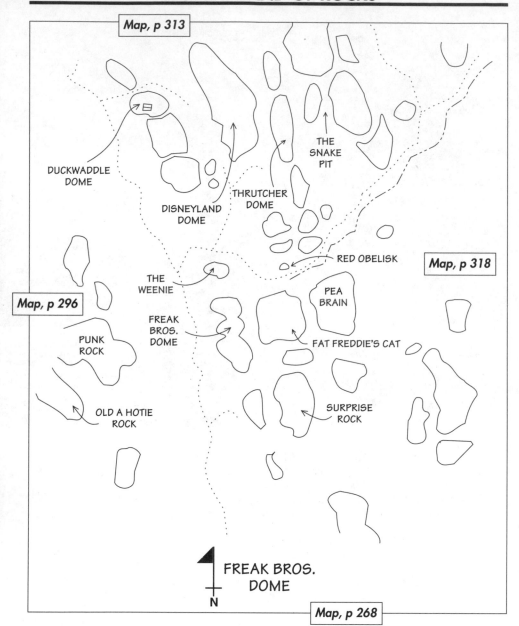

Map, p 313

THE
SNAKE
PIT

DUCKWADDLE
DOME

THRUTCHER
DOME

DISNEYLAND
DOME

RED OBELISK

Map, p 318

THE
WEENIE

Map, p 296

PEA
BRAIN

FREAK
BROS.
DOME

FAT FREDDIE'S CAT

PUNK
ROCK

OLD A HOTIE
ROCK

SURPRISE
ROCK

FREAK BROS.
DOME

N

Map, p 268

THE WEENIE

This is the pinnacle just north of the Freak Brothers Domes. See map above.

2060　**WEENIE ROAST　5.11a**　This overhanging crack to an offwidth finish is on the north face of The Weenie. Pro: To 3.5 inches.

FAT FREDDIE'S CAT

This long dome lies parallel to and immediately east of Freak Brothers Domes. A very narrow canyon separates these formations. See map above.

2061　**THE NORTH FACE　5.2 X ★★**

Several routes lie on the east and northeast faces of Fat Freddie's Cat.

2062 **BOOKMAN PITMAN 5.6** Climb the left-facing corner 25 feet right of **The North Face.**

2063 **FIELDS OF LAUGHTER 5.6 X ★★** This climbs the low-angled northeast face. No pro.

2064 **TIME AVENGER 5.11b ★★** This is a seven-bolt climb just left of **Early Bird.**

2065 **BROKEN BITS 5.9 ★★** This route follows **Time Avenger** to that route's second bolt, then traverses right on a dike, and climbs past three more bolts.

2066 **EARLY BIRD 5.9+ ★★** This is a two-pitch crack route opposite **Joan Jetson.**

2067 **LUST IN THE WONDERLAND 5.9 ★** This follows discontinuous cracks 100 feet left of **Early Bird.**

PEA BRAIN
This dome is just east and parallel to Fat Freddie's Cat. Map, page 306.

2068 **CACTUS DOG 5.9 ★**

2069 **JOAN JETSON 5.9 ★**

2070 **SPACELY SPROCKETS 5.8** Four bolts.

THE RED OBELISK
This is the red pillar of rock just north of Fat Freddie's Cat and Pea Brain. It sits in the wash running east-to-west that serves as the main trail to the Lost in the Wonderland Valley. Map, page 306.

2071 **THE RED OBELISK 5.10a ★** Pro: One fixed pin, one bolt.

THE SNAKE PIT
This is a popular name for areas in Joshua Tree. This obscure alcove is best reached by walking north from The Red Obelisk to an "open area," then turning right (east) into the alcove. Map, page 306.

2072 **SMOKE AND MIRRORS 5.11d ★★** This overhanging face is in a recess at the southeast end of The Snake Pit. Pro: Four bolts, thin nuts.

2073 **APPETITE FOR DESTRUCTION 5.10b** This is the striking hand crack on the north end of The Snake Pit.

2074 **THE VIPER 5.10c** This crack is 30 feet left of **Appetite for Destruction.**

THRUTCHER DOME
This lies southeast of Disneyland Dome. Map, page 306.

2075 **SCUD MISSILE 5.11a** Three bolts. This is just left of **Thrutcher.**
2076 **THRUTCHER 5.7**
2077 **INVASION ON MY FANTASY 5.7**
2078 **DESERT STORM 5.10c** Pro: Three bolts. This follows the arête just right of **Invasion . .**
2079 **LIFE WITHOUT PRINCIPLE 5.11b** This route climbs the obvious white trough on the formation just south of Thrutcher Dome. Nine bolts.
2080 **WHALES ON ICE 5.10a** On the west face of the formation that lies 150 south of **Life Without . . .**

DISNEYLAND DOME
This formation lies northeast of Freak Brothers Dome. Map, page 306.

2081 **STEREO IN B FLAT 5.10d (TR)** Climb a thin crack about 100 feet right of **Walt's Frozen Head.**
2082 **WALT'S FROZEN HEAD 5.10b** This is on the right side of the large brown buttress right of **Tragic Kingdom.** The route starts by traversing in from a ledge on the right. Two pitches, some bolts.
2083 **BRASS MONKEY 5.12a** Pro: Six bolts.
2084 **TRAGIC KINGDOM 5.8 A1**
2085 **ENCHANTED STAIRWAY 5.9 ★★** Pro: Thin to 2.5 inches, one bolt.
2086 **JUNGLE CRUISE 5.10b ★★★**
2087 **THE MAD HATTER 5.10b** Two pitches. Follow the rounded arête just right of **Fantasia** (four bolts) to the ledge; then climb the arête to the chimney above.
2088 **FANTASIA 5.10b** This route starts in the chimney left of **Jungle Cruise.** Climb right out of the chimney and into a corner leading to an arête. Go up the arête to a dike, and traverse left to a belay with a bolt. Continue left and go up an overhanging crack to the top. Three pitches, one bolt.
2089 **MENTAL BANKRUPTCY 5.10b ★★** This route climbs the left-diagonalling dike on the main face of Disneyland Dome. Three pitches.
2090 **SPACED MOUNTAIN 5.8** Start right of the first bolt on **Mental Bankruptcy.** Climb up the plated face to crack system.

2091 **AUTOPIA 5.9** This route starts with the first 20 feet of **Mental Bankruptcy,** and continues straight up the chimney. The second pitch traverses left out of the chimney before it narrows, and goes up a rotten face to the top of a pillar. The third pitch continues up thin cracks past one bolt.

2092 **THE ROUNDUP 5.11b** This thin crack leads to a face and brown patina plates. It is on a formation east of Disneyland Domes, and faces **Pea Brain**.

2093 **CRACK OF DARK 5.10b** This prominent offwidth right of **The Roundup** has a bouldering start.

DUCKWADDLE DOMES

This long formation has three distinct summits and parallels Disneyland Dome, but just to the west. The last summit has a summit block that is split in four sections. On the east side of the formation, facing **Mental Bankruptcy,** is **Innervisions.** Map, page 306.

2094 **INNERVISIONS 5.9** Climb a crack up to the base of the summit block. Follow the wide crack in the block to the summit.

2094A **SQUEEZE PLAY 5.8**

2094B **ARTIFICIAL INGREDIENTS 5.8** This steep, grainy crack with chickenheads lies directly across (west) of **Mental Bankruptcy.**

PRINGLE ROCK

This is the large, prominent rock about 150 yards northwest of the north end of Duckwaddle Domes. The one known route is on the southwest face, and is best approached via a rocky gully from the west. Map, page 313.

2095 **TIGERS ON VASELINE 5.9** Climb past a horizontal crack and a bolt to a right-facing flake. From the flake's top, continue past two more bolts to the top.

MIND BODY ROCK

This large round boulder is about 75 yards west of Pringle Rock. Map, page 313.

2096 **MIND BODY PROBLEM 5.12c (TR)** This ascends the concave east face of the boulder, starting with thin fingers and ending in an offwidth. To toprope the problem, gain the summit via aid off a bolt on the south side of the boulder.

2097 **ANECDOTES OF POWER 5.11c** This short, overhanging thin hands crack lies on the east side of a low rock wall about 75 yards north of Mind Body Rock.

DISNEYLAND DOME – NORTH FACE

Hike along the Wonderland Valley past Duckwaddle Domes and head right (east) into an open area that lies north of Disneyland Dome. This also can be used as an approach to the Inauguron Formation. Map, page 306.

2098 **THE WEAK FORCE 5.10a** ★ This route climbs the northeast face of Disneyland Dome via a series of ramps and cracks.

2099 **GRAIN AND BEAR IT 5.9** This climbs the left (east) side of a detached flake near the summit of the north face. This starts where **The Weak Force** ends.

2100 **WHEEL OF FORTUNE 5.11b** ★★ This is about 70 feet right of **The Weak Force** on the prow of the north face of Disneyland Dome. Climb a left-leaning crack to its end, then up past bolts. Pro: Thin to 3 inches.

2101 **BRIDGE-IT BARDOT 5.10d** ★ This is a groove/chimney with three bolts located around the corner and to the right of **Wheel of Fortune.** It is near the northwest end of Disneyland Dome and faces the main approach gully for the north face routes.

THRUTCHER DOME – NORTH FACE

See map on page 306.

2102 **GROUND RON 5.10c** This is the leftmost of two obvious parallel cracks that face north.

2103 **FEEDING FRENZY 5.10b** The rightmost of the two cracks on the north face.

THE TRAINING GROUND

This formation is 75 yards north of Disneyland Dome's north face. The one known route is on the south end of the formation.

2104 **THE UNDERWEAR BANDIT 5.10a** Follow cracks and ramps up and right to a vertical shallow crack that leads to the top.

DUMB DOME

This rock lies just northeast of Disneyland Dome. Several good lines remain to be climbed. Map, page 313.

2105 **MONUMENT MANOR 5.8** ★

2106 **SOUTH FACE DIRECT 5.7** Start in a chimney on the right, then face climb into cracks right of **Monument Manor,** and join that route near the top.

BUTLER CORRIDOR

The following two routes are on the west wall of the corridor west of Boulder Canyon. They probably are best approached from the south, from the vicinity of Pea Brain.

2107 **MOTHER BUTLER 5.10a** This is a finger crack near the south end of the corridor.

2108 **THE SECRET OF MOTHER BUTLER 5.10c** A right-leaning finger crack at the north end of the corridor.

GUMBY DOME

This formation is about 500 yards north of Disneyland Dome. It lies on the north side of an east-west canyon that leads to Secret Valley. Secret Valley contains the Inauguron, Elephant Arches and Hard Rock. The Inauguron Dome also may be reached via the boulder-choked gully just left (north) of Dumb Dome. Map, page 313.

2109 **GUMBY GOES TO WASHINGTON 5.8**

2110 **POKIE'S BIG CHANCE 5.4** This route is the easiest way down Gumby Dome.

GUMBY DOME

SECRET VALLEY

This canyon runs in a north-south direction, parallel to the Wonderland Valley but about 450 yards to the east. Several large west-facing rocks lie on the east side of Secret Valley. From south to north, they are the Inauguron, Elephant Arches and Hard Rock. Map, page 313.

INAUGURON DOME

This lies just south of the junction of Secret Valley and the canyon holding Gumby Dome. The best approach is from the Dumb Dome area. Map, page 313.

2111 **THE INAUGURON 5.11b ★★** Pro: Thin to 2 inches, bolts.
2112 **MORALITY TEST 5.11b ★★★** Pro: To 2 inches, fourbolts.
2113 **YARDY-HOO AND AWAY 5.10a ★★★** Pro: Bolts, to 2 inches.
2114 **BEAFCAKE 5.10a** Pro: To 3 inches.
2115 **WHEAT BERI-BERI 5.11c R ★** Pro: To 5 inches, two bolts.
2116 **WHITE BREAD FEVER 5.11c ★★** Pro: To 3 inches, two bolts.

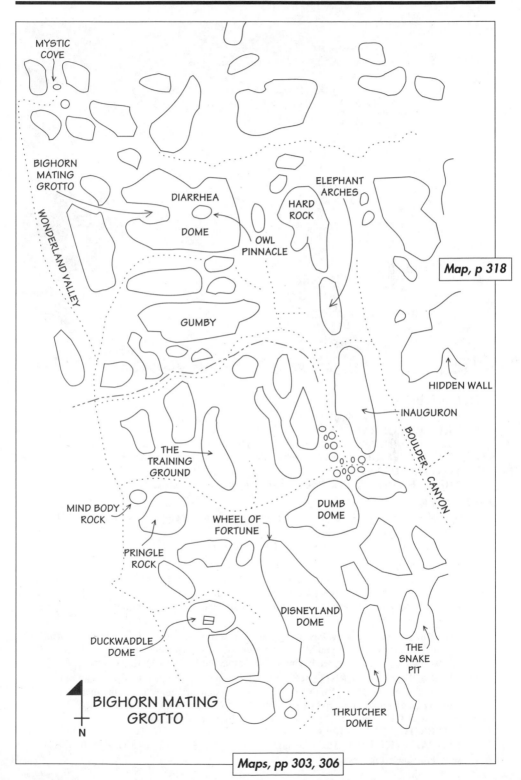

MYSTIC
COVE

BIGHORN
MATING
GROTTO

WONDERLAND VALLEY

DIARRHEA

DOME

OWL
PINNACLE

HARD
ROCK

ELEPHANT
ARCHES

Map, p 318

GUMBY

HIDDEN WALL

INAUGURON

BOULDER CANYON

THE
TRAINING
GROUND

DUMB
DOME

MIND BODY
ROCK

WHEEL OF
FORTUNE

PRINGLE
ROCK

DUCKWADDLE
DOME

DISNEYLAND
DOME

THE
SNAKE
PIT

BIGHORN MATING
GROTTO

N

THRUTCHER
DOME

Maps, pp 303, 306

ELEPHANT ARCHES

This formation is north of Inauguron Dome. Map, page 313.

2117 **TRUE DEMOCRACY 5.9 ★** Pro: To 3.5 inches.
2118 **VICE PRESIDENT 5.10b R ★★★** Pro: Thin to 3 inches.
2119 **BLACK PRESIDENT 5.11a ★★★★** Pro: Thin to 2 inches, two bolts.
2120 **POM POM DANCER 5.9**
2121 **MILK THE DOG 5.10a** Pro: Many to 3 inches.

HARD ROCK

This "layered" rock lies to the north of Elephant Arches in the Secret Valley. Map, page 313.

2122 **SOLAR WIND 5.8 ★★** Pro: To 2.5 inches.
2123 **HAWK WIND 5.10c R ★★★** Pro: Thin to 2 inches.

DIARRHEA DOME

This very large dome lies about 300 yards north of Gumby Dome. The best approach is to walk north along The Wonderland Valley past the canyon holding Gumby Dome. Follow the next canyon on the right (east) a short distance until you can head north (by scrambling) to the base of Diarrhea Dome. Map, page 313.

The main (south) face of the dome has several steep face routes; it also has a large boulder/pillar on its summit (Owl Pinnacle). If you head north along the western (right) end of the dome, a narrow canyon on the right (east) leads you into the amazing Bighorn Mating Grotto.

2124 **TRULY SNOOTY FURNITURE 5.10a** This route actually lies on the formation left (west) of Diarrhea Dome. You walk past it on the standard approach to the main south face. Climb past a bolt and up a right-traversing dike to a hand crack to a anchor/rap.
2125 **THE MANLY DIKE 5.12a ★★★★** Pro: 11 bolts, medium nuts.
2126 **BIG BROWN EYE 5.10d ★★★**
2127 **SVAPADA 5.11b ★★** This is an eight-bolt climb right of **Big Brown Eye.** It ends at a two-bolt stance/rap.

OWL PINNACLE

This pillar of rock lies on the top of Diarrhea Dome. Map, page 313.

2128 **OWL 5.9** ★

2129 **BROKEN WING 5.10c** ★   A three-bolt route on north face of the pinnacle.

2130 **THE TALON 5.12c** ★★★   A five-bolt arête on north side of the pinnacle.

BIGHORN MATING GROTTO

Routes are described from left to right. Map, page 313.

2131   **TAKE TWO, THEY'RE SMALL**   **5.9**   This is a fist crack/offwidth on the left.

2132   **EUPHRATES**   **5.11c** ★★   Climb the improbable thin cracks and face right of **Take Two, They're Small;** join **Dangling Woo Li Master** after about 60 feet.

2133   **DANGLING WOO LI MASTER**   **5.10a** ★★★★   This is the second crack on the left, and climbs red colored rock before exiting up a hand/fist crack on the left.

2134   **BOOK OF CHANGES**   **5.10b** ★★★★   The direct start is 5.10d. This is the third crack on the left. Climb up and left to a 5.10b crack, or straight up (5.10d). Two fixed pins and one bolt are at the top.

2135   **MORNING THUNDER**   **5.10d** ★★★   This route is the longest route in the grotto, and climbs an overhanging chimney system. It is hard to protect; angles are helpful.

2136   **CAUGHT INSIDE ON A BIG SET**   **5.10b** ★★★★★   This lies on the right wall of the grotto. Climb up discontinuous crack systems.

BIGHORN TERRACE

This area is above and northeast of the Bighorn Mating Grotto.

2137   **DOMINATRIX**   **5.10d**   This is the leftmost of three west-facing cracks.

2138   **WHIPS AND GRAINS**   **5.9**   This is a hand-and-fist crack on the corner right of **Dominatrix.**

MYSTIC COVE

This "cove" of rock lies directly north of the Bighorn Mating Grotto/Diarrhea Dome area. It is best approached by walking north through the Wonderland Valley, past the normal approach for Diarrhea Dome and continuing north for about 900 yards. At this point, it is possible to head east for a short distance, then southeast into the "mouth" of Mystic Cove. Near the entrance of the cove stand two towers of rock, one on the north side and one on the south. The established routes are on these towers. Map, page 313.

NORTH TOWER

2139   **THE PODIUM**   **5.10b** ★★★   This route climbs the southeast arête of the northern tower past four bolts.

2140   **NORTH SIDE**   **5.11a (TR)** ★★   This toprope route is to the right of **Zen.**

2141   **ZEN**   **5.12b** ★★★   Climb past four bolts on the north face of the northern tower.

SOUTH TOWER

2142   **KARMA**   **5.12d** ★★★★   This route lies on the north side of the southern tower. Climb past seven bolts.

THE FAR EAST

The Far East is an area of the Wonderland of Rocks that lies northeast of the Freak Brothers Domes and the Secret Valley. It is best reached via the wash just north of the Freak Brothers complex (passing near The Red Obelisk). A wash (Wonderland Wash) heads northeast from the obelisk. A canyon that heads northwest from the open area past the Freak Brothers complex can be used to get to Secret Valley Domes (Boulder Canyon). Map, page 318.

BIGHORN DOME – NORTH FACE

This rock forms the southern border of a canyon that runs east-to-west. The east entrance lies about 650 yards northeast along the Wonderland Wash from the Freak Brothers complex. The south face of Bighorn Dome actually faces out into the open area past the Freak Brothers complex.

2143 **THE TUBE 5.10b** This takes the obvious tube-shaped chimney. Map, page 318.

2144 **POACHING BIGHORN 5.11b ★★★★**

2145 **THE LOVE GOAT 5.10a ★★**

2146 **ALIENS ATE MY BUICK 5.10b** Three bolts and a fixed pin.

2147 **GREENHORN DIHEDRAL 5.10c ★★★**

2148 **ZORBA 5.11a R**

2149 **CUT TO THE BONE 5.10c**

2150 **TIME TO TAKE THE GARBAGE OUT 5.10a** Located on the far right side of the north face. Climb a perfect hand crack through a small overhang, then head up and left to the top.

2151 **HARD ROCK CAFE 5.10d** This is a doubly overhanging brown corner on the northwest end of Bighorn Dome.

2152 **AUTOMATIC TIGER 5.10d** Climb past a bolt into a thin crack. This climb is right of **Hard Rock Cafe** and faces north.

2153 **JACK IN THE CRACK 5.10d** This ascends the steep, arching crack on the east side of the summit block of Bighorn Dome.

2154 **GET THE BOOT 5.10b** This is a three-bolt face climb on a boot-shaped block north of Bighorn Dome.

2155 **RUSTY PIPES 5.2 ★** This crack lies northeast of the north face of Bighorn Dome. Take a reddish crack up a small face.

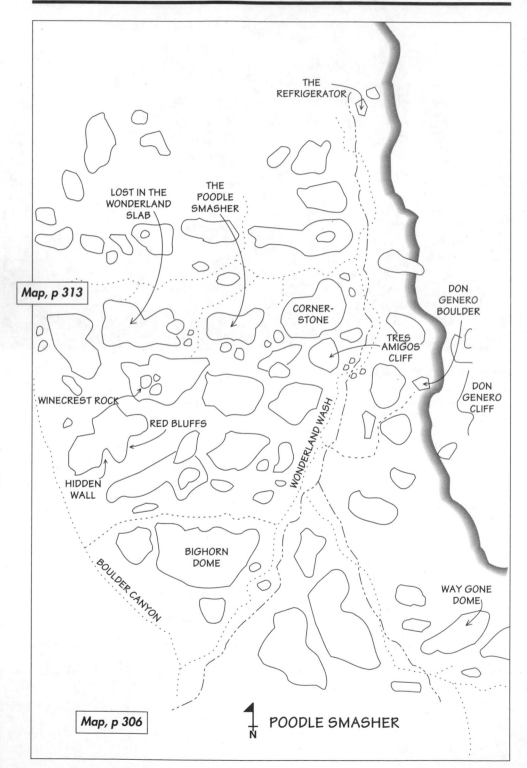

THE
REFRIGERATOR

LOST IN THE
WONDERLAND
SLAB

THE
POODLE
SMASHER

Map, p 313

CORNER-
STONE

DON
GENERO
BOULDER

TRES
AMIGOS
CLIFF

DON
GENERO
CLIFF

WINECREST ROCK

RED BLUFFS

WONDERLAND WASH

HIDDEN
WALL

BIGHORN
DOME

BOULDER CANYON

WAY GONE
DOME

Map, p 306

N

POODLE SMASHER

HIDDEN WALL AND RED BLUFFS

These obscure cliffs lie in a canyon that is north of the western end of Bighorn Dome. From the Bighorn Canyon, hike west to Boulder Canyon. Follow this for about 150 yards to another small canyon (Choke Canyon), which heads east. It is easiest to hike straight northwest up Boulder Canyon to Choke Canyon. Hidden Wall lies on the north side of Choke Canyon, and is a narrow north-south running corridor. Red Bluffs also lie on the north side of Choke Canyon, further east of Hidden Wall. Map, page 318.

HIIDDEN WALL

The following bolt-protected routes are described form left to right (as you encounter themupon entering the corridor on the north side of Choke Canyon). Several route "link-ups" are possible, and are given separate route names.

2156 **SKINTIGHT MOUSEHOUSE 5.11d ★★** Left-most route.
2157 **ADDER DANCE 5.12c ★★★**
2158 **PUFF ADDER 5.13a ★★★★**
2159 **COPPERHEAD 5.11b ★** Pro: To 3 inches.
2160 **MOJAVE GREEN 5.12d ★★★**
2161 **CROWDED MENTAL HOSPITAL 5.13b ★★★** **Mojave Green** to **Viper** link-up.
2162 **MONGOOSE 5.13a ★★★★**
2163 **AUTOMATIC VENOM SPRINKLER 5.13b ★★★** **Viper** to **Mojave Green** link-up.
2164 **PIT VIPER 5.13b ★★★★** **Mongoose** to **Viper** link-up.
2165 **VIPER 5.13b ★★★**
2166 **RUBBER BOA 5.13c ★★★** Start up the project on the right, and finish on **Viper.**
2167 **GARTER SNAKE 5.10b ★** The far righthand route.

RED BLUFFS

The Red Bluffs (obvious red-colored rock) lie further east of the Hidden Wall corridor, and face east. Map, page 318.

2168 **SLIP SKRIG 5.10c ★★★** This route lies on the far side of Red Bluffs.
2169 **RED RED 5.10d** This is the first crack right of **Slip Skrig.**
2170 **RED RAIN 5.13a ★★★** This bolt-protected route lies just right of **Red Rain.**

DON GENERO CLIFFS

This outcrop lies on the hillside about 500 yards northeast of Bighorn Dome and about 250 yards east of the Wonderland Wash. The outcrop has several unclimbed crack routes. Don Genero Boulder is a very large, rectangular boulder below the cliffs. Map, page 318.

2171 **WHAT IS THE QUESTION? 5.10d ★** This route is on the east face of Don Genero Boulder.
2172 **HOTPANTS (AKA: MEXICAN HAT OF JOSH) 5.13b ★★★★★** This is on the overhanging west face of Don Genero Boulder.

TRES AMIGOS CLIFF

This formation lies on the west side of the Wonderland Wash, and is the last formation before the Cornerstone. Map, page 318.

2173 **THE THREE AMIGOS 5.8** This 50-foot climb goes up a ramp and right to a 50-foot crack. It ends at a ledge with an oak tree; rap off tree.

LOST IN THE WONDERLAND VALLEY

This valley lies about 600 yards past Bighorn Dome along the Wonderland Wash. You must hike up a small rise to enter Lost In The Wonderland Valley. The east face of the Cornerstone, which is visible from Wonderland Wash, has two thin flakes on it. Map, page 318.

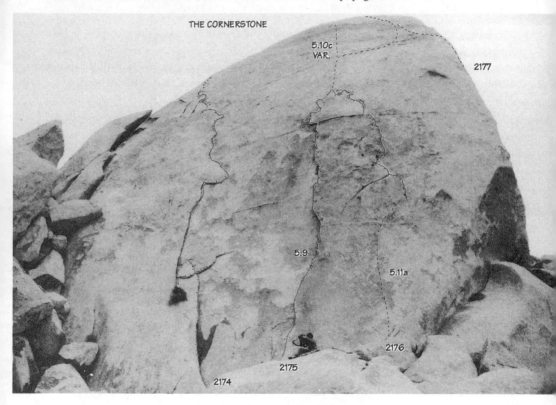

THE CORNERSTONE

5.10c VAR.

2177

5.9

5.11a

2176

2175

2174

THE CORNERSTONE

THE CORNERSTONE — NORTH FACE

THE CORNERSTONE

See map on page 318.

2174 **AS THE CRAGS TURN 5.7 ★★**   A little loose.

2175 **GENERAL HOSPITAL 5.9 ★★**   The 5.10c variation at the top has no pro.

2176 **ROPE OPERA 5.11a**   This route climbs the right side of the **General Hospital** flake with a two-bolt start.

2177 **ONE MOVE LEADS TO ANOTHER 5.10c ★★**

2178 **ALL MY CHILDREN 5.9**   This is a right-arching crack right of **One Move Leads to Another.**

2179 **TOMATO AMNESIA 5.10b ★**   Climb the crack right of **All My Children.**

POODLE SMASHER AREA

2181

2180

2182

2183

POODLE SMASHER AREA

This lies 100 yards west of the Cornerstone. Map, page 318.

2180 **THE POODLE SMASHER 5.11a ★★★**

2181 **IN ELKE'S ABSENCE 5.10a ★**   Located 50 feet left of **Mental Siege Tactics.** This goes
up a lieback crack/flake to a wide crack, then out the face to the left and the top.

2182 **MENTAL SIEGE TACTICS 5.10c ★**

2183 **DEFOLIATION 5.9 ★**

WAVECREST ROCK

This large "block" of rock lies about 75 yards southwest of **Mental Siege Tactics.** Some
scrambling leads to the following three routes, which are on the south face. Map, page 318.

2184 **SOUTH SWELL 5.9**   This is an obvious hand crack on the left side of the face.

2185 **THE SOUND OF WAVES 5.11b (TR)**   This is the arête right of **South Swell.**

2186 **WAVECREST 5.12a ★★★★**   Climb the left-arching dihedral right of **The Sound of
Waves.** Many small nuts are needed.

LOST IN THE WONDERLAND SLAB

LOST IN THE WONDERLAND SLAB
This large slab lies about 175 yards west of the Poodle Smasher. Map, page 318.

2187   **EYES WITHOUT A FACE   5.10b** ★

2188   **DESERT DELIRIUM (aka Lost In The Wonderland)   5.10a** ★★★

THE REFRIGERATOR
This brown, "refrigerator"-shaped formation lies 600 yards farther along the Wonderland Wash (north) from the Cornerstone. At this point, the wash opens into a broad valley; the formation is on your left (west).

2189   **THE REFRIGERATOR – LEFT SIDE   5.10b** ★★★   This route climbs the left-hand arête past bolts.

2190   **THE REFRIGERATOR – RIGHT SIDE   5.11a (TR)**   The forgettable right arête.

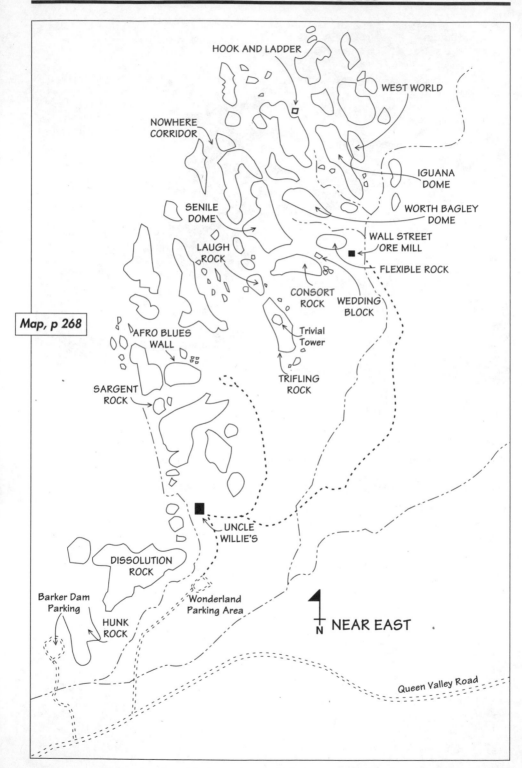

HOOK AND LADDER

WEST WORLD

NOWHERE
CORRIDOR

IGUANA
DOME

SENILE
DOME

WORTH BAGLEY
DOME

LAUGH
ROCK

WALL STREET
ORE MILL

FLEXIBLE ROCK

Map, p 268

CONSORT
ROCK

WEDDING
BLOCK

AFRO BLUES
WALL

Trivial
Tower

SARGENT
ROCK

TRIFLING
ROCK

UNCLE
WILLIE'S

DISSOLUTION
ROCK

Barker Dam
Parking

Wonderland
Parking Area

NEAR EAST

HUNK
ROCK

N

Queen Valley Road

THE NEAR EAST AREA (WALL STREET MILL AREA)

Drive 200 yards past the Barker Dam turnoff on the Big Horn Pass Road, where you'll find another turn off to the north. Follow this road until it ends at a parking area (The Wonderland parking area). A bathroom (the only one in the area; paid for by The Access Fund), and a trashcan are provided. Keep your impact to a minimum; use these facilities.

This area lies east of the Wonderland Ranch parking area. Do not head north toward Uncle Willie's from the parking area; instead, head straight (northeast) along the southern end of the Wonderland. If you head north into the Wonderland wash, you'll end up in the central part of the southern Wonderland and the Wonderland Valley. Map, page 324.

SLAB CANYON

From the Uncle Willie's/Wonderland parking area, an old dirt road heads into the first open area on the north. This is Slab Canyon. A cement slab marks an old homesite at the end of this road. Map, page 324.

AFRO BLUES WALL

The Afro Blues Wall is the dome on the left (northwest) of the cement slab. Map, page 324.

2191 **MY FAVORITE THINGS 5.10c ★★** Start climbing below a conspicuous crack in the middle of the north face, which starts some 60 feet above the ground. Face climb past two overhangs to the crack. Pro: Nuts to 3 inches, one bolt.

2192 **BLUE RIBBON 5.11a R** This line is right of **My Favorite Things.** Pro: To 3 inches.

2193 **FOUNDATION CRACK 5.10b** This route is on the wall across from Afro Blues Wall, and climbs a corner behind the old cement foundation slab.

LAUGH ROCK

Laugh Rock is on the west side of Slab Canyon, near the north end. Five routes are on the southwest face. Either rap off top of **What a Joke** or descend down and right over the southeast corner (4th class). Map, page 324.

2194 **WHAT A JOKE 5.8** Pro: To 2 inches, two-bolt anchor/rap.
2195 **SCHWEE 5.9** Pro: Three bolts, bolt anchor.
2196 **EVENING AT THE IMPROV 5.11a** Pro: To 3 inches, three bolts.
2197 **NEED TO HAVE A WORD WITH MYSELF 5.11a** ★ Pro: To 3 inches, three bolts.
2198 **SOMETIMES WE CRACK OURSELVES UP 5.7+** ★
2199 **CRACK WORTHY 5.6** ★

TRIFLING ROCK
This is the rather large and complex formation that forms the southern and eastern side of Slab Canyon. A small "pass" separates it from Laugh Rock just to the north. A large boulder is perched on top near the middle of the formation. Map, page 324.

TRIFLING ROCK – WEST FACE
2200 **BALD AMBITION 5.11a** This is a small right-facing dihedral/roof in the gully around and to the left of the **Trivial Pursuit** face. Pro: Two bolts, one fixed pin.

2201 **WHERE'S BALDO? 5.9** This is the arête/face left of **Trivial Pursuit.** Pro: Thin, bolt and fixed pin.

2202 **TRIVIAL PURSUIT 5.7** This face route is near the center of Trifling Rock. It climbs past a bolt down low, then up a diagonal crack to steeper face/trough past a second bolt.

2203 **TRIVIAL TOWER 5.9** This is a one-bolt route on the northwest shoulder of a large boulder that sits directly above the top of **Trivial Pursuit.**

2204 **SUPERFLUOUS BOLT 5.6** This is about 100 feet north of the southern edge of Trifling Rock (about 150 feet right of **Trivial Pursuit**), on the west face. Climb the leftmost of several short water troughs past one bolt.

2205 **SOUTHWEST OF NOWHERE 5.4 or 5.8** Located on the southwest shoulder of the formation (about 60 feet to the right of **Superfluous Bolt**). Climb either the unprotected ridge (5.4) or an unprotected trough (5.8) to the right of the ridge.

TRIFLING ROCK – EAST FACE
2206 **FAX MAN 5.9** This two-bolt face climb is near the southeastern edge of Trifling Rock, behind a large boulder.

2207 **MOTOR CITY COMIX 5.10a R** The low-angled crack leads up to the headwall, then up a thin crack that curves up and right, then peters out. It is just left of **Radio Free Utah.**

2208 **RADIO FREE UTAH 5.10b** This three-bolt face route is 125 feet right of **Fax Man.** Start behind some large boulders at the base.

2209 **UNKNOWN 5.10b** This is a five-bolt face route 70 feet right of **Radio Free Utah.** Start behind boulders about midway on the east face.

THE MILL AREA
An old gold mining mill, consisting of an ore-crushing facility (The Wall Street Mill), is about .5 mile northeast of the parking area. A bunkhouse was torn down by the park service a few years ago, but the mill is pretty interesting. This ore-crushing mill is one of many such mills throughout the monument. This area also is near the site where long time rancher/etc. Bill Keys (see history set forth in Echo Rock introduction) shot Worth Bagley on May 11, 1943. Bagley, an ex-L.A. County Deputy Sheriff, had a penchant for violence, and reportedly tried to ambush Keys. Keys' trial apparently was rigged and Keys was sentenced to 12 years at San Quentin penitentiary in San Francisco. Erle Stanley Gardner (who wrote Perry Mason stories) undertook to prove Keys' side of the story, and eventually got Keys' case reexamined. Keys spent 5 years in prison before he was paroled and eventually pardoned. Map, page 324.

SENILE CANYON

This canyon lies just west of the mill. A large block in the middle of the canyon is the Wedding Block; the formation on the northeast side of the canyon (facing the mill) is Flexible Rock; the formation on the south is Consort Rock; and the formation to the west of Flexible Rock is Senile Dome. See below for approaches to these formations. Map, page 324.

SENILE DOME

This formation lies directly north of Consort Rock and west of Flexible Rock. It is best approached by walking north up the open canyon on the east side of Trifling Rock. It faces south and has a crack/ramp on the left side. It can also be approached from the Mill by walking west up Senile Canyon. Map, page 324.

2210 **WAYWARD HAYWARD 5.10b**

2211 **NAKED REAGAN 5.11a ★★★** Pro: to 2.5 inches.

SENILE DOME – NANCY REAGAN'S FACE

This short (very featured) block faces east and sits atop Senile Dome, above **Naked Reagan.**

2212 **NAKED NANCY 5.10b (TR)** Ascend the left side of the block up an arête.

2213 **RONNIE'S RUMP 5.7 (TR)** Climb the center of the face.

SENILE DOME – NORTHEAST FACE

2214 **BIVO SHAM 5.8** This route lies on the northeast face of Senile Dome, (down from Nancy Reagan's Face) near the right side of a solution-pocketed face. It is easily approached by walking through the narrow gap between Senile Dome and Flexible Rock.

CONSORT ROCK

This formation makes up the southern side of Senile Canyon and faces Senile Dome and Flexible Rock. The only known route is best approached as for Senile Rock and Wedding Block. Map, page 324.

2215 **HAND OF THE BRIDE 5.10a, A1** Use a bolt for aid to reach a very short crack near the center of the north face.

THE WEDDING BLOCK

This is the large block/formation that lies in the middle of Senile Canyon. Map, page 324.

2216 **HERE COMES THE BRIDE 5.11a ★★** The four-bolt route on the north face.

2217 **THERE GOES THE BRIDE 5.10a** The three-bolt route on the west face.

2218 **MY BRIDE, MY HILTI & MY SHOULDERS 5.10d** The three-bolt route on southeast arête.

FLEXIBLE ROCK

This formation lies just east (right) Senile Dome and just west of the mill. A tricky descent goes down the north face, then west through the tunnel. Rap anchors are on top of south face. Map, page 324.

2219 **FLEXIBLE HUEYS 5.10d (TR)**

2220 **WHY DID WE DO THIS 5.9** A very short crack on the upper block of the north face, near the descent.

WORTH BAGLEY MEMORIAL DOME (WBMD)

This formation lies north of Flexible Rock and northeast of Senile Dome. It can be approached from the gap between those two formations, or from the first wash heading northwest behind the mill. Map, page 324.

2221 **WORTH BAGLEY DIHEDRAL 5.10b ★★** There are two obvious cracks/corners above a horizontal break in the rock on the south face of WBMD. This is the left crack. Hand traverse up and right to gain the "S"-shaped crack/dihedral.

2222 **SQUID OF MY DESIRE 5.10a** This is the left-facing dihedral to the right of the preceding route. Climb a thin diagonal crack to a ledge, then lieback the dihedral.

IGUANA DOME

This is the large dome directly north of the mill, and is reached by taking the wash 100 yards north of the mill into a canyon heading straight north. The dome is on the right (east) as one is walking up the wash. This is also the approach for the Hook and Ladder Area which lies further north and on the left (west) side. The back side of Iguana Dome is called West World. Map, page 324.

2223 **IGUANA MASTERS 5.10b ★★** Climb a crack/ramp leading to a loose and flaky face near the south end of the west face of the dome. Pro: To 2.5 inches, five bolts.

2224 **DHIP 5.10d** This is the straight crack/seam 10 feet right of the start of **Iguana Masters.** Pro: To 2.5 inches, two bolts, two-bolt anchor/rap.

2225 **ANGIONE CRACK 5.6** This is a steep dogleg hand crack on the northwest side of Iguana Dome.

2226 **MOHAVE GREEN 5.8 (5.10a var.) ★★** Climb the obvious, thin "tip-toe"-like dike past two bolts on the recessed north end of Iguana Dome, to the left of **Angione Crack.** Climb around the left end of the roof above. Var: Go straight up over the roof (5.10a). Descend down to the left.

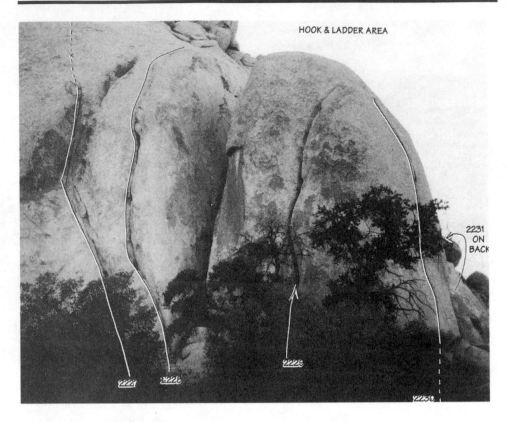

HOOK & LADDER AREA

HOOK AND LADDER AREA

Approach as for Iguana Dome, then follow the wash past the dome until you are at the north end of Iguana Dome (near **Angione Crack**). A large rock split by an offwidth crack is at the northern end of the large formation west of Iguana Dome. Map, page 324.

2227 **PINK THING 5.10a** Pro: Thin to 2 inches, one bolt.
2228 **CITY H 5.8** ★
2229 **POODLE BOY 5.10b**
2230 **HOOK AND LADDER 5.11a** (with ladder), **5.12b** (w/o ladder) ★★ Pro: Thin to 3 inches.
2231 **FISHING TRIP 5.9** Climb the offwidth on the back of **Poodle Boy.**

WEST WORLD

This area is the east face of Iguana Dome. From the mill, continue northeast along a wash, then north along the east side of Iguana Dome. This area also can be approached by walking east from the Hook and Ladder Area. The identifying landmark is a striking, overhanging, thin crack called **Stingray.** The other routes all are to the left of this crack. Map, page 324.

2232 **SOUL KITCHEN 5.11a** This is a two-bolt face climb that comes in from the left and ends at a bolted belay.

The following three routes can be approached by climbing a 5.10 crack left of **Stingray,** or by climbing up easy terrain left of the crack.

2233 **BOOT HILL 5.10a** A two-bolt climb on the left, ending at a bolt belay.
2234 **PALE RIDER 5.11a** Climb the crack right of **Boot Hill.** There is one fixed pin.
2235 **FEAR IS NEVER BORING 5.12a** This four-bolt climb slants up and right, ending at the belay bolts atop **Stingray.**
2236 **STINGRAY 5.13d** Pro: Many thin to 1.5 inches.

WAY GONE DOME

This formation lies about 500 yards northeast of Hook and Ladder. Consult the photo for reference. Map, page 324.

2237 **AIR CRACK 5.6**
2238 **BETA ZOID 5.11a, A2.** Aid climb the roof to the loose 5.11 crack above.
2239 **CRYSTAL VOYAGER 5.10d ★**

LOW MOTIVATION DOME

This is a large formation on the eastern edge of the Wonderland of Rocks, sitting near the hillside that rises up towards the summit of Queen Mountain. It is seen easily from many of the summits in the central Wonderland, as well as from the base of the east faces of the Astro Domes. It can be approached by walking up the canyon right (south) of Nomad Dome, or from the Hook and Ladder Area. It is distinguished by several cracks that slant up and left across its large, light-colored west face. One route is known. Map, page 332.

2240 **HEAD, ABDOMEN, THORAX 5.9 A2** This mixed two-pitch route goes up somewhere near the middle of the west face. Look for bolts (two of them mark the route).

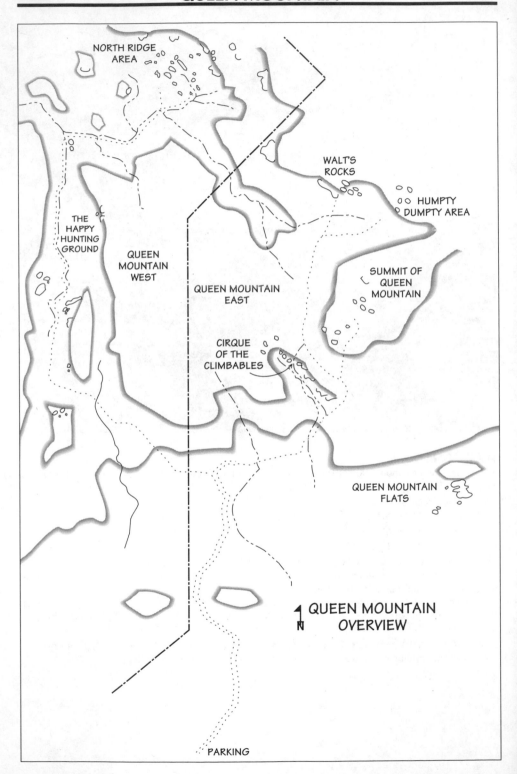

NORTH RIDGE
AREA

WALT'S
ROCKS

HUMPTY
DUMPTY AREA

THE
HAPPY
HUNTING
GROUND

QUEEN
MOUNTAIN
WEST

QUEEN MOUNTAIN
EAST

SUMMIT OF
QUEEN
MOUNTAIN

CIRQUE
OF THE
CLIMBABLES

QUEEN MOUNTAIN
FLATS

QUEEN MOUNTAIN
OVERVIEW

N

PARKING

QUEEN MOUNTAIN

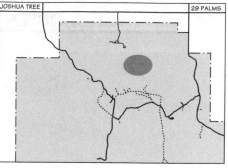

THE BLACK ROCKS

These very dark-colored cliffs lie on the west side of a small hillside .5 mile east-southeast of the Wonderland Ranch parking area. They lie just to the north of Bighorn Pass Road, about .6 miles after you pass the turnoff for the Wonderland Ranch parking area. The three separate "black" cliffs are fairly obvious.

2241 **UNNAMED 5.10c ★★** Climb up a seam to a bolt on the lefthand cliff, near the right side. Continue up until a hand traverse right leads to a crack heading up.

2242 **THE OPPORTUNIST 5.10b ★** Climb up and right on flakes, then straight up past a bolt to a crack. This is on the middle cliff, at the left end.

2243 **1BRP 5.10b ★** Climb straight up past a bolt into a chute above a ledge to the right of **The Opportunist.**

2244 **PREYING MANTELS 5.10a** Located near the right end of the middle cliff. Climb up a seam to a bolt, mantel, then face climb up a chute to the top.

QUEEN MOUNTAIN AREA

Queen Mountain is the large, mountainous area east of the Wonderland of Rocks and north of Queen Valley. Most of the climbing on Queen Mountain involves long approaches by Joshua Tree standards (usually more than 1 hour), most of which head uphill. Nevertheless, the climbing tends to be good, the rock superior and the scenery incredible.

This extensive area is composed of several distinct climbing areas, each consisting of many formations and domes. Prior to 1988 there were no routes on Queen Mountain whatsoever. In the last three years, an incredible number of excellent routes have been climbed. The routes described in the next few pages is an incomplete listing of what has been climbed; for many of the new routes, no information was available at the time this guide was prepared.

Climbers visiting Queen Mountain should take special care to leave the area as pristine as they found it. This is Joshua Tree wilderness; respect for the natural environment should be particularly stringent. This is no place for leaving litter (of any sort). The recommendations about low impact climbing in the introduction to this guide should be observed particularly closely here.

For ease of description and use, Queen Mountain has been divided into two areas: Queen Mountain East and Queen Mountain West. The western area of Queen Mountain (Happy Hunting Ground to the North Ridge of Queen Mountain) usually is approached differently than the summit and areas to the east (Spy Tower, Walt's Rocks, etc.). For this reason, theses area are broken up by the principal approach route used.

If approaching Queen Mountain from the Barker Dam area, head east on the Bighorn Pass Road for about .8 miles, past the Wonderland Ranch parking turnoff, to where the road splits. Take the left fork, head east for nearly a mile, then turn north (left) at the intersection of another dirt road. Continue north for about a mile to a parking area.

If approaching from the paved Sheep Pass Road, take the dirt road that heads northwest (Bighorn Pass Road) from a point about .75 mile west of Geology Tour Road. Follow Bighorn Pass Road northwest for about a .25 mile to where a dirt road branches off to the north. Follow this road roughly north for 1.25 miles to a parking area.

Vehicle travel on the road is not permitted past this point. Walk up the road and over a saddle between some small hills to where the road ends at the base of Queen Mountain; this is about a .75-mile walk. Approach descriptions for Queen Mountain West and Queen Mountain East from this point are different, and each is described at the beginning of the corresponding section.

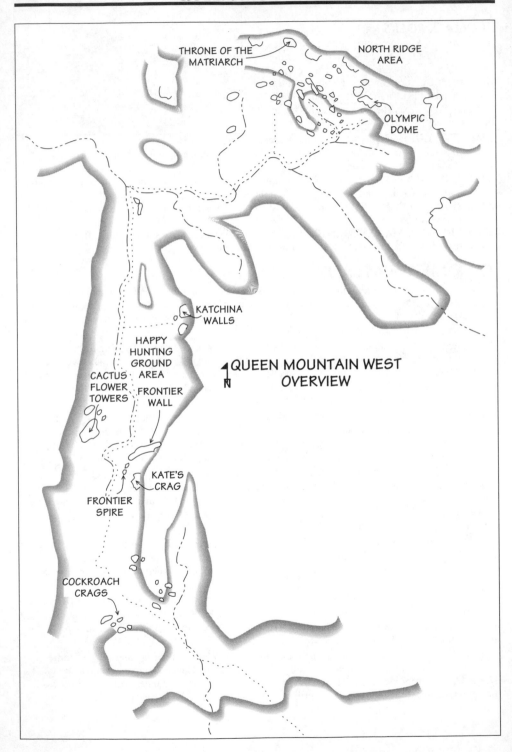

THRONE OF THE
MATRIARCH

NORTH RIDGE
AREA

OLYMPIC
DOME

KATCHINA
WALLS

HAPPY
HUNTING
GROUND
AREA

CACTUS
FLOWER
TOWERS

FRONTIER
WALL

N

QUEEN MOUNTAIN WEST
OVERVIEW

KATE'S
CRAG

FRONTIER
SPIRE

COCKROACH
CRAGS

QUEEN MOUNTAIN WEST

This area lies about one mile west of the summit of Queen Mountain, and appears from the Hidden Valley vicinity as a series of dark-colored crags in the saddle down and left from the summit.

From where the dirt road (foot traffic only) takes a sharp turn east and slightly uphill (about 200 yards after passing a pile of "black rocks"), walk about .5-mile west-northwest up a very small valley/drainage, then up the hillside and over an obvious saddle to a flat and open wash area. A few small formations lie straight ahead (north). Follow the wash for about a 100 yards, then head up the rocky hillside to the left (west), hike over another small saddle and enter a broad, north-south running valley (the Nile Valley). All of the following routes/formations are approached via the Nile Valley. A rather large (and relatively flat) sandy wash runs down the Nile Valley (to the north) from here.

COCKROACH CRAGS

As you hike over the last saddle and enter the Nile Valley, a pinnacle-like formation rises on the hillside directly to the south (to your left). The pinnacle is split in the middle by wide crack. The following routes lie on the pinnacle. Another small crag lies at the base of the hillside and 50 yards to the west of the pinnacle; no routes on this formation are known. Map, page 334.

2245 **THE FLY 5.11c** This is the three-bolt face climb to the left of the wide crack.

2246 **THE OFFROACH 5.11c** This rather difficult wide crack goes up the middle of the formation.

2247 **THE COCKROACH 5.12d/13a** This is the four-bolt route to the right of the wide crack.

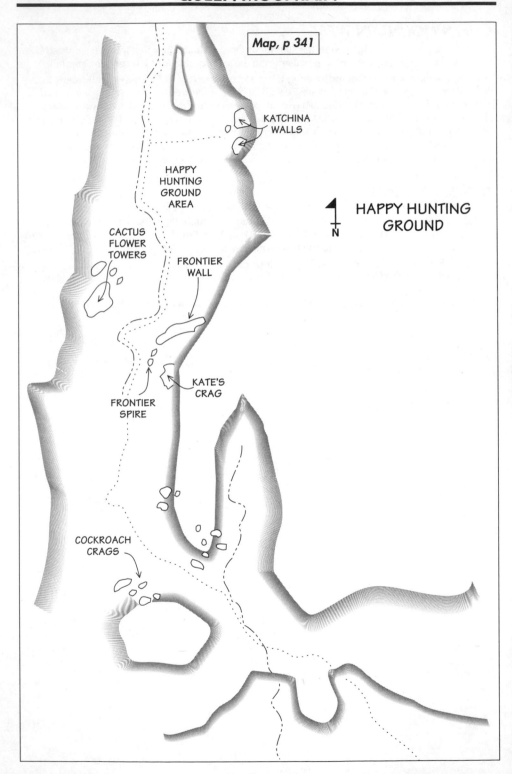

Map, p 341

KATCHINA
WALLS

HAPPY
HUNTING
GROUND
AREA

HAPPY HUNTING
GROUND
N

CACTUS
FLOWER
TOWERS

FRONTIER
WALL

KATE'S
CRAG

FRONTIER
SPIRE

COCKROACH
CRAGS

THE HAPPY HUNTING GROUND

To reach the Happy Hunting Ground from where you hike over the last saddle and enter the Nile Valley, head to the right (north) down the valley, following washes, for about .25 mile. At this point, you will see a large formation with a distinctive pinnacle on its west side on the lefthand (west) side of the valley. These are the Cactus Flower Towers.

Before you reach The Cactus Flower Towers, you'll see some brown, west-facing rocks with some clean looking cracks and faces on the righthand (east) side of the valley. This is Kate's Crag.

Two rock pinnacles lie about 75 yards north of Kate's Crag, still on the east side of the valley. These are the Frontier Spires. The Frontier Wall lies just north and around the corner from the Frontier Spires, and immediately opposite The Cactus Flower Towers. The Frontier Wall, which faces north, has many high-quality crack routes. Map, page 334, 336.

KATE'S CRAG

This is the brown, west-facing crag with two prominent cracks. It is on the east side of the valley. Map, page 336.

2248 **QUEEN BEE 5.6** The left crack.
2249 **IT'S NEVER ROBOT CITY 5.10d (TR)** The arête left of **Tar Face.**
2250 **TAR FACE 5.10b (TR)** The face just left of **Lady in Waiting.**
2251 **LADY IN WAITING 5.5** The right crack.
2252 **QUEEN FOR A DAY 5.7** Climb the buttress right of the cracks. Start off a boulder.
2253 **GOOD GOD Y'ALL 5.10c** Climbs the face in the grotto at the far right end.

FRONTIER SPIRES

These are two pointed formations about 75 yards northwest of Kate's Crag. Map, page 336.

2254 **ROCKET MAN 5.5** Climb a crack on the backside of the lower spire.
2255 **LITTLE BIG MAN 5.9** Climb the crack on the southwest face. Pro: To 2 inches.
2256 **HOMO ERECTUS 5.6** Climb the upper spire from the notch.
2257 **THE SCHLONG 5.11a** Four bolts.

FRONTIER WALL

This long, northwest-facing wall is just north of the Frontier Spires, and lies across the Nile Valley east of Cactus Flower Towers. The routes are generally of high quality. Map, page 336.

2258 **PROM QUEEN   5.9** Climb a right-facing book with a wide crack on the far right side of the wall.

2259 **THE CONUNDRUM   5.11c**

2260 **THE INTRUDERS   5.9, A1**

2261 **UNKNOWN   5.10d, A1**

2262 **JUST DRIVE, SHE SAID   5.10b**

2263 **THE TODD SQUAD (aka METTLE DETECTOR)   5.11a**   This starts from a tree.

2264 **FORBIDDEN ZONE   5.11b**

2265 **MEATLOCKER 5.11b**
2266 **SNAKE BITE 5.11c**
2267 **RITES OF PASSAGE 5.11a** ★★
2268 **DELUSIONS 5.10c**
2269 **GORDOBA 5.10d**
2270 **KISS ME WHERE I PEE 5.9**
2271 **GNATTY DREAD 5.9**
2272 **LAND OF WONDER 5.10c**
2273 **QUEEN MOTHER'S ROUTE 5.2**
2274 **MAN FROM GLAD 5.10d** Three-bolt variation.
2275 **GLAD HANDER 5.9** ★★

CACTUS FLOWER TOWERS

These two large formations are on the west side of the Nile Valley. As you approach them from the south, you will see a distinctive pinnacle on the west side of the formations. The existing routes all are on the steep west sides of the towers. The formations have several faces and other good route possibilities. Map, page 336.

2276 **THE ORGAN GRINDER 5.10b** This and the following route are on the larger, southwest tower. This route climbs a wildly overhanging crack system.
2277 **THE PILGRIM 5.11a** Climb a prominent overhanging dihedral left of **The Organ Grinder.**
2278 **THE FLANGE 5.11a (TR)** This goes up a steep face on the northwest tower, finishing left of a crack.
2279 **GYPSY QUEEN 5.9** This route lies on a small, west-facing wall to the northwest of the Cactus Flower Towers. Climb a zig-zag crack leading up into a right-facing book.
2280 **ANTS IN MY PANTS 5.9** A finger crack in a right-facing dihedral 20 feet left of **Gypsy Queen.**

The following route lies on the east face of the Cactus Flower Towers, facing the Frontier Wall.

2281 **OUTLAND 5.12a** Climb the right-slanting crack with four bolts for protection (bring other gear).

KATCHINA WALLS

These two formations lie on the east (right-hand) side of the Nile Valley, about .5 mile up the valley from its entrance, and nearly .25 mile past the Frontier Wall. The northern formation is slabby and light-colored (Kachina North), the southern steeper and brown-colored (Kachina South). Map, page 336.

2282 **THE RIGHT STUFF 5.10c** Rap anchors are on ledge. Pro: Many medium to 3 inches.
2283 **STEPPIN' OUT 5.10a** Pro: Thin to 2.5 inches.
2284 **KATCHINA 5.10a** Pro: Thin to 2.5 inches.

NORTH RIDGE OF QUEEN MOUNTAIN AREA

The remaining routes in the Queen Mountain West section are on crags on the southwest side of the ridge running northwest from the summit area. This area is approached by walking north through the Nile Valley for about seven-eighths of a mile to where the wash narrows. Head west at a point about .5 mile past Frontier Wall. Here, another wash joins in from the right; take this wash east for about .25 mile to where it opens into a large valley. From the car, plan on at least an hour to reach this area/formations. The formations and routes are listed from left to right throughout this section. Map, page 336, 341.

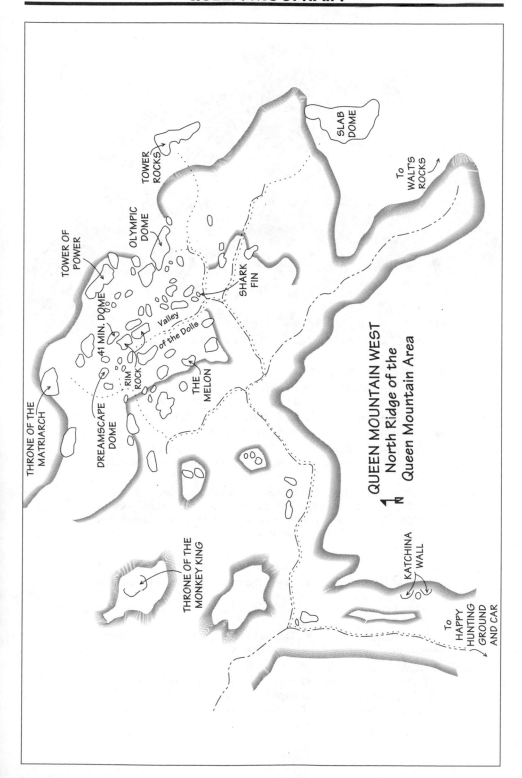

SLAB DOME

TOWER ROCKS

To WALT'S ROCKS

OLYMPIC DOME

SHARK FIN

TOWER OF POWER

41 MIN. DOME

Valley of the Dolls

THRONE OF THE MATRIARCH

DREAMSCAPE DOME

RIM ROCK

THE MELON

QUEEN MOUNTAIN WEST
North Ridge of the
Queen Mountain Area

N

THRONE OF THE MONKEY KING

KATCHINA WALL

To HAPPY HUNTING GROUND AND CAR

THRONE OF THE MONKEY KING
This is the farthest northwest (left) of the crags. It is reached by turning left from the main approach valley a short distance before reaching 41-Minute Dome. Map, page 341.

2285 **MONKEY KING 5.10a** Ascend the left branch of the jam crack to the right of the prominent corner. This is on the south face of the crag.

THRONE OF THE MATRIARCH
This is the northernmost of several closely-spaced crags, plainly visible on the approach. Map, page 341.

2286 **CROWN JEWELS 5.10a** Two pitches. Pro: Thin to 3 inches.

2287 **LEPER MESSIAH 5.12c (TR)** ★★★ The steep face with unique pockets.

2288 **RED SONJA 5.10c** A finger-and-hand crack leads to a ledge. Continue up thin cracks and face on an arête. Pro: Thin to 3 inches.

DREAMSCAPE DOME
The larger, easternmost of the previously-mentioned crags. Map, page 341.

2289 **SPIRITWORLD 5.10c** Climb a finger crack just left of the south arête, and continue up a left-slanting hand crack.

2290 **THE GEM 5.10b** Climb a short face past two bolts. Lies between 41 Minute Dome and Rim Rock.

2291 **PERFECT WORLD 5.10b** ★★ This two-bolt route lies on the north side of a 45 foot formation to the northeast of Dreamscape Dome.

41-MINUTE DOME
This very-inappropriately-named formation lies slightly "behind" and to the west of Rim Rock, somewhat behind and northeast of Dreamscape Dome. Map, page 341.

2292 **RAVING SKINHEAD 5.10c** Face climb up to the crack on the south arête of the formation.

RIM ROCK

This crag is east of Dreamscape Dome, and is hidden for most of the approach by a ridge to its southwest. It can be approached either from the vicinity of Dreamscape Dome by scrambling northeast between 41-Minute Dome and formations to the southwest, or more easily by heading up the wash towards Olympic Dome, then heading northwest into the Valley of the Dolls, near the Shark Fin. Map, page 341.

2293 **ICE STATION ZEBRA 5.9+** This route climbs a quality arête up from Rim Rock and just left of an offwidth. Diagonal dihedral.

2294 **30 SECONDS OVER BAGHDAD 5.11c** Climb up and left along a horizontal crack starting out of a deep chimney, past a bolt, then up a thin crack that ends on a headwall. Continue up and left past two more bolts to top. Pro: Thin cams to 2.5 inches, three bolts.

2295 **BROKEN CHINA 5.10b** A 140-foot jam crack on the west face.

THE MELON

This is a round dome with several vertical cracks southeast of Rim Rock and low on the hillside. Map, page 341.

2296 **UNNAMED 5.11a (TR)** Located left of **Fruits of Labor.** Climb a thin crack to its end, then up and left to the top.

2297 **FRUITS OF LABOR 5.11 (TR)** Overhanging thin cracks lead to a right-slanting hand crack on the south face.

2298 **FRUIT FLY 5.10b** A tree start leads to a hand crack on the southeast face.

THRONE OF THE MATRIARCH

41 MIN DOME

RIM ROCK

OLYMPIC DOME

DREAMSCAPE DOME

TOWER OF POWER

2288
2287
2286
THE MELON
2294
2305
2304
2307
2308
2313
2314
2302 2303 2301
2300
2299

NORTH RIDGE OF QUEEN MOUNTAIN FROM THE EAST

THE SHARK FIN

As you approach Olympic Dome, you'll see a spire on the left (northwest). This, called the Shark Fin, is about 80 yards southwest of Olympic Dome. Map, page 341.

2299 **THE SHARK FIN 5.10c ★★★** Climb the face of the formation past three bolts.

VALLEY OF THE DOLLS

When you reach the Shark Fin, turn left (northwest) into a canyon. Head about 100 yards into this canyon, which will take you into to a small round valley surrounded by dark formations. Map, page 341.

2300 **CHATTY BABY 5.7** Climb the dihedral to a bolt.

2301 **TEST TUBE BABY 5.8+ ★** This is to the left of **Chatty Baby**, on a separate rock. Climb a steep crack in a flare.

2302 **MY LIFE AS A DOG 5.11c ★★★** This is on the left side of the southeast face of Rim Rock, which sits at the northwest end of the Valley of the Dolls. Climb an overhanging crack to an overhanging face. The upper face is protected by one bolt.

2303 **THE BALL MONITOR 5.10a R ★★★** Located to the right of **My Life As A Dog.** Climb the clean, parallel thin cracks that end below the top.

TOWER OF POWER

This is the large formation high on the hillside; it lies roughly midway between Throne of the Matriarch and Olympic Dome. Three "towers" on the southwest side of the rock are formed by two large chimneys. Two routes are known. Map, page 341.

2304 **POWER TO THE PEOPLE 5.10b** The middle "tower" has a left-leaning crack on its face. Start to the left of this crack and climb the arête past one bolt to reach thin cracks that lead up near top of the left-leaning crack. Continue on discontinuous cracks up the arête. Pro: Many small to 2 inches.

2305 **THE NAVIGATOR 5.10d R** This route climbs the right-hand tower face. Climb past one bolt to a left-leaning crack, then continue straight up past a second bolt to top. Pro: Small to 2 inches.

OLYMPIC DOME

This formation lies northeast of The Melon, and has a prominent, left-slanting crack on its southwest face (**Bloodline**, 5.12). It is best approached by taking the right-hand wash from the valley just below the north ridge area. Easy slabs and boulders lead to the righthand part of the formation. Map, page 341.

2306 **RETURN OF LARGE MARGE** **5.7**   This route climbs the hand rack on the left side of Olympic Dome. It is left of **Bloodline** about 75 feet.

2307 **THE BLOODLINE** **5.12a ★★★★★**   Pro: Many small to 2 inches, bolts.

2308 **RED CROSS** **5.12a/b ★★★★**   Pro: Small camming units, bolts, bolt rap/anchor.

2309 **MATT BIONDI CHIMNEY** **5.5**   This is an obvious, parallel-sided chimney (passing just right of a large roof), just left of **Jamaican Bobsled.**

2310 **JAMAICAN BOBSLED** **5.11a ★★★**   Pro: Small to medium camming, bolts, bolt anchor/rap.

2311 **DON'T BOSCH ME AROUND** **5.10d ★★★**   Pro: To 2 inches, three bolts, a fixed pin.

2312 **BODY SHAVING FOR COMPETITION** **5.9**   A bit loose.

2313 **BLACK DIAMOND** **5.12b R ★★★★★**   Pro: Seven bolts.

2314 **ICON** **5.10c ★★★**   This is a beautiful hand crack just right of **Black Diamond.** Start on the same block.

2315 **ELVIS LIVES** **5.11d**   Climb up and left past four bolts 20 feet right of **Icon.**

2316 **JOHNNIE COME LATELY** **5.10d**

TOWER ROCKS

This formation lies up and right (northeast) of Olympic Dome about 100 yards. It faces southwest and is a very obvious blocky formation. Map, page 341.

2317 **STRAIGHT OUT OF COMPTON** **5.11d**   This route climbs the left hand margin of the southwest face on obvious, orange-colored rock. Climb a thin crack that ends at a horizontal. Climb up and right past four bolts and several horizontals to a thin crack leading to the top. Pro: Brass nuts to 2.5 inches, four bolts.

SLAB DOME

This large dome lies to the east of Olympic Dome and Tower Rocks. It is distinguished by a clean dihedral near the left side of the northwest face. Map, page 341.

2318 **SLAB HAPPY** **5.9 ★★★**   This is a clean, four-bolt face route just left of the clean dihedral on Slab Dome.

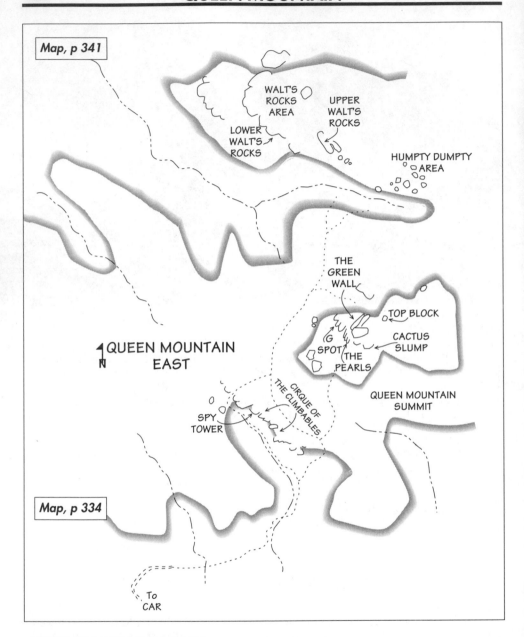

Map, p 341

WALT'S
ROCKS
AREA

UPPER
WALT'S
ROCKS

LOWER
WALT'S
ROCKS

HUMPTY DUMPTY
AREA

THE
GREEN
WALL

TOP BLOCK

CACTUS
SLUMP

G
SPOT

THE
PEARLS

QUEEN MOUNTAIN
EAST

N

QUEEN MOUNTAIN
SUMMIT

CIRQUE OF
THE CLIMBABLES

SPY
TOWER

Map, p 334

To
CAR

QUEEN MOUNTAIN EAST

The following routes are on the eastern part of Queen Mountain, some near or on the summit. They are approached differently than routes in the western area. There are innumerable routes in this area that are not described in this guide. Insufficient information was available to include all the routes.

Follow the dirt road/trail from where you park the car to its very end (past where you head off for the western area). From here, head eastward along a faint trail, angling up the hillside to a hidden gully/wash heading north. A band of cliffs lie along the eastern side of the gully (these are visible from where you park on the south side of Queen Mountain). These are the Cirque of the Climbables. Head up the gully (north) to below these formations and to Spy Tower at the top of the wash.

CIRQUE OF THE CLIMBABLES

This band of cliffs is the first encountered on the approach to the east side of Queen Mountain. It lies on the right (northeast) side of the gully that opens on your left (northwest) as you diagonal up the hillside. The first cliff encountered is Cirque of the Climbables-Right End; the prominent "pillar"-shaped formations further up (northwest) the gully on the left are the Left End of the Cirque. At the top of the gully rises the steep Spy Tower. Map, page 346.

CIRQUE OF THE CLIMBABLES – RIGHT END

2319 FUN FOR THE WHOLE FAMILY 5.4
2320 THE RED CRACK 5.10b ★
2321 CHRISTMAS TREE ARETE 5.10c ★★★

CIRQUE OF THE CLIMBABLES — MIDDLE SECTION

CIRQUE OF THE CLIMBABLES – LEFT END

2322 **GLUE RHYMES WITH POO 5.10a** S-shaped crack. Pro: Thin to 2 inches.

2323 **SOUP RHYMES WITH POOP 5.8+** Pro: Thin to 2 inches.

2324 **MOMMY DEAREST 5.9** Pro: To 3 inches.

2325 **REMAIN IN LIGHT 5.10a ★★** Two bolts.

2326 **PAGAN HOLIDAY 5.9** Pro: To 2.5 inches.

2327 **TREASURE OF THE SIERRA MADRE 5.10d ★★★★★** Four bolts and a fixed pin on lefthand face.

2328 **LABYRINTH 5.10a** Face route on right side of the corridor. Two bolts.

2329 **HORNS A'PLENTY 5.7 R** Pro: Tie offs for knobs.

2330 **THAT'S POWELL NOT ROWELL 5.10a**

2331 **PLEASURE PRINCIPAL 5.8+** Follow the obvious crack up to the easier face.

2332 **SLAP AND TICKLE 5.10b ★★** Face climb past two bolts, then up the face past a small roof. This is on the buttress right of **Pleasure Principal.**

2333 **REI MOMO 5.10b ★** Two bolts to the left of the roof.

2334 **THE MACHO COMBO 5.11c ★★★** Climb the lip of the large roof right of **Rei Momo.** Pro: Bolts, thin to 2 inches.

SPY TOWER

This steep formation lies at the top of the gully and faces west. Map, page 346.

2335 **COLD WAR 5.10b**
2336 **SPY HOLE 5.11a** Pro: To 3 inches.
2337 **SPY VS SPY 5.11c ★★** The ypper part is a bit loose. Pro: To 2.5 inches.
2338 **MIKE AND TOM'S EXCELLENT ADVENTURE 5.11d R** Pro: Thin to 1 inch.
2339 **SPY EYE 5.10a** Pro: Thin to 2.5 inches.

THE BIG LIE ROCK

This is the small formation to the left of Spy Tower. It is possible to walk up the gully to the left of the formation to reach The Pearls, etc., and to approach Walt's Area.

2340 **THE PRESS CONFERENCE 5.8+ ★**

THE PEARLS

This formation faces southwest and sits east of the Cirque of the Climbables, farther up the hillside. Approach as for the Cirque of the Climbables, but continue straight up the hillside, staying right of those cliffs. Continue up and right (east) until The Pearls are encountered. The formation is distinguished by two wide cracks on the left side and two bolted face routes on the right. Map, page 346.

2341　**GARNET 5.11b ★★**　Located on the left side of the formation. Face climb past a bolt to reach a widening crack ending on the left-hand summit.

2342　**ZIRCON 5.9+ ★★★**　This route face climbs up to a thin crack that widens. It is to the right of **Garnet.** Pro: Thin to 4 inches.

2343　**PEARL NECKLACE 5.11c ★★★★**　Start near the center of the formation, to the left of some sharp flakes/boulders. Climb discontinuous thin cracks to a ledge, then up past six bolts to a two-bolt anchor/rap. Pro: Many thin, six bolts.

2344　**PEARL DROPS 5.11a ★★★★**　Start at the sharp flake to the right of **Pearl Necklace.** Climb up to a ledge, then face climb past horizontals and five bolts to share the bolt anchor/rap of **Pearl Necklace.** Pro: Thin cams, five bolts.

2345　**BLACK PEARL 5.10d ★★★★**　Start atop boulders to the right of the start of **Pearl Drops.** Join that route at the third bolt. Pro: Thin cams, three bolts, two-bolt anchor/rap.

G-SPOT

This formation is the little brown wall to the left and slightly uphill from The Pearls. Down and right (southwest) is the Wizz Site. Map, page 346.

2346　**G-SPOT 5.11c**　Climb up the face past a single bolt to a crack heading straight to the top. Pro: Many to 2.5 inches.

2347　**G-WIZZ 5.7 X**　This is the rounded, varnished arête to the right of **G-Spot.**

2348　**MUY SWAINO 5.10a R**　Start off a boulder 20 feet right of the previous climb. Climb a short, overhanging face to a jug, then continue up a slab.

2349　**GREAT CAESAR'S GHOST 5.8**　Climb a steep face to an obvious flake/crack 20 feet right of the previous climb.

WIZZ SITE

This formation lies down and right (southwest) of the G-Spot. Map, page 346.

2350　**SWAINO VISTA 5.8+ R**　This is the left crack and arête on the lowest south block of this formation.

2351　**WIZZ SOUP 5.11a (TR)**　This is the overhanging face leading to a crack/corner just right of **Swaino Vista.**

WATCHA CALL IT PILLAR

This formation lies uphill and right (east) of G-Spot; two diverging cracks ("V"-shaped) distinguish the formation.

2352　**I DON'T KNOW 5.10a ★**　This is the left wide crack.

2353　**WHO CARES 5.11a ★★**　This is the right crack. The bottom is the crux.

2354　**SOMETHING OR OTHER 5.11b (TR)**　This is the steep face to the right of **Who Cares.**

THE CACTUS SLUMP

This formation lies almost directly east and uphill from The Pearls and southeast from the Watcha Call It Pillar. Map, page 346.

2355　**BARREL RACE 5.7 ★**　This is the crack on the left that leads to a ledge, then widens above.

2356　**PRICKLY PARE 5.10c ★★★**　Located to the right of **Barrel Race.** Climb a hand crack (crux) to a ledge, then up and left on the easier face above.

2357　**BEAVER TAIL 5.10b ★**　This is the short, discontinuous crack on the left, which ends on the right side of the ledge mentioned in the previous two routes.

THE TOP BLOCK

This 30-foot high block sits on the ridge, below and west of the true summit of Queen Mountain. It can be seen from the Queen Mountain Flats and Queen Valley as a square block of rock. Crack routes are located on all sides; the following are some of the known routes. Map, page 346.

2358 **THE DRUIDS 5.8** The hand crack on the right side of the south face.

2359 **CEROOTS OF THE GODS 5.10b** The steep finger crack near the southwest arête.

2360 **MY FAVORITE MARTIAN 5.9** The finger crack on the west face.

THE PASTRY PILE

This is the last cliff on the west side of the mountain below the true summit of Queen Mountain.

2361 **CREAM PUFF 5.8 ★** This is the right-leaning hand crack on the left side of the west face.

2362 **TOOTSIE POP 5.9+ ★★★** This is the wide hand crack in the center of the face. It leads from steep thin cracks to face climbing.

THE GREEN WALL

The Green Wall lies on the north face of the summit blocks of Queen Mountain. The wall is broken into three sections by ledge systems that run across the face. The lower section of face and the rock above the first ledge is referred to as the Lower Wall; the face above and right is the Upper Wall. Map, page 346.

2363 **SO HOLE LO 5.7 R/X** This is the short face route on the far left side, ending on a separate summit.

2364 **AGGARETE 5.10a R** Located to the right of **So Hole Lo,** on the left edge of the main part of the Green Wall. Climb thin cracks up to a ledge, then up to the top.

2365 **NORTH FACE 5.?** Face climb up a left-angling corner to a ledge. Start at the bottom of the right side of the main face, to the right of **Aggarête.**

2366 **DONUT HOLES 5.9+** A ledge system runs up and left across the main lower face. Start this route about halfway up this ledge, climbing discontinuous thin cracks.

2367 **HOLEACEOUS 5.10c** This is up on the ledge mentioned in **Donut Holes.** Start to the right and slightly lower than that route. Climb up very pocketed/huecoed face.

2368 **COHATOES 5.8** Start uphill and right of the start of the large ramp running across the lower main face. Climb large huecos up and right to another large ledge.

2369 **GUN SHY 5.10a** Start in the middle of the second (upper) ledge on the north face (the ledge separates the upper and lower main faces). Climb discontiuous flakes/cracks to face climbing.

2370 **BLOCK BUSTER 5.10a** This right-facing corner system goes up the center of the upper face, and starts at the right end of the ledge separating the upper and lower faces.

2371 **HOLEY COLD 5.10b** Located uphill from **Block Buster,** and at the right end of the upper face. Climb up flakes and holes, passing a pillar/flake of rock on the right halfway up.

WALT'S ROCKS

Walt's Rocks lie northwest of the summit of Queen Mountain. The approach is relatively straightforward. Follow the dirt road/trail from where you park the car to its very end (past the point at which you head off for the western area). Head eastward along a faint trail, angling up the hillside past a hidden gully/wash heading north. The band of cliffs seen along the eastern side of the gully (visible from where you park on the south side of Queen Mountain) is the Cirque of the Climbables. Continue up to the right of these rocks until it is possible to angle back left (northwest) above the top of these cliffs, and below the G-Spot and The Pearls. You'll reach a plateau from which you should head in a northeasterly direction. Soon, Walt's Rocks will appear to the northeast; head directly toward these formations. Map, page 346.

LOWER WALT'S ROCK

This is the lower of the two Walt's Rocks formations. It has a long southwesterly face. Map, page 346.

2372 **PURPLE PLACE 5.11** Located on the far left end on a separate block.

2373 **STEP FUNCTION 5.11b ★★★** This route face climbs past three bolts to a right-facing lieback.

2374 **K2R 5.9 ★** A hand crack in a right-facing corner leads to chimney climbing.

2375 **PERFECT FINGERS 5.10b ★★★★** A classic finger crack that jogs left into a left-facing corner.

2376 **COWBOY JUNKIE 5.11c ★★★★** 3 bolts, steep face to crack.

UPPER WALT'S ROCKS

This is the uppermost and smaller formation of the Walt's Rocks. Map, page 346.

2377 **ROUTE BEER 5.11a ★★★** Located on the northeastern corner of Upper Walt's Rocks. A thin seam leads to face climbing past two bolts, then to a thin crack diagonaling up and left. Finish up a small corner. Pro: Thin to 2 inches, two bolts.

2378 **GET WITH THE PLAN 5.10b ★★** Face climb up and slightly right to a crack/left-facing corner near the prow of the northwest corner of Upper Walt's Rock. Pro: To 2.5 inches.

2379 **HELLISH PLANET 5.10d ★★** Located near the middle of the southwest face. Climb a right-facing corner up and left, then on flakes up and right. Finish up the face to the top. Pro: To 3 inches.

2380 **AT YOUR PLEASURE 5.8 ★★★★** Climb the crack that starts out and right of a chimney with a large chockstone, and continue to a slot with bush at top. Located near the right end of the southwest face. Pro: To 3 inches.

2381 **WHITE RAIN 5.11a ★★★★★** This is the face route on the south end of the formation. Pro: To 2 inches, six bolts.

2382 **ENDORPHINE 5.10d ★** This is the face route just right of the arête. Pro: Thin, two bolts.

2383 **NO METAL WASTED 5.9+ X ★★★** This is the groove/face to the right of **Endorphine.**

2384 **CRACK QUEEN 5.11a ★★★** A steep fingers and hand crack. Pro: To 4 inches.

HUMPTY DUMPTY AREA

HUMPTY DUMPTY

This tower lies east of Walt's Rocks and is split by a 3- to 4-inch crack/flake. Routes are listed counter clockwise. Map, page 346.

2385 **FROG HAIR 5.10b ★★** Four bolts
2386 **HUMPTY DUMPTY 5.7 ★★** Climb a wide crack to a flake to a face.
2387 **STICK TO THE PLAN 5.10c R ★★★**
2388 **FALL LINE 5.10c ★★★** Three bolts, crosses **Humpty Dumpty.**
2389 **DRUGS BUT NO DRILLS 5.9 ★** This crosses **All Kings Men.**
2390 **ALL KINGS MEN 5.7** The flake opposite **Humpty Dumpty.**
2391 **I SAW STARS 5.10c ★★★★** Three bolts. This lies on the face opposite and to the east of **Humpty Dumpty.** Climb past two bolts to a thin crack that leads to a ledge. Continue off the ledge and up the face past one more bolt.

QUEEN MOUNTAIN FLATS

This is the area below (south) of Queen Mountain and about one mile east of the end of the trail/road used for the approach for the West and East Queen Mountain areas. Map, page 332.

THE WHITE CLIFFS

The White Cliffs are located approximately one mile east of the end of the trail/road were the approach up to Queen Mountain East begins (please refer to approach information for Queen Mountain on page 999). They appear as a light-colored cliff/dome across the desert floor. Good bouldering can be found on the approach. Plan on an hour's approach from the car.

The west side of the White Cliffs has several east-west corridors; there are two main corridors on the west side. These are referred to as the North Corridor and the South Corridor.

2392 **TRIAL SEPARATION 5.10d ★★★** This steep, four-bolt face climb is on the right wall of the south corridor.

THE SUN PROOF WALL

This is the north face of the North Corridor. It is hidden from the west. Approach this face from the top of the formation by climbing down into the corridor.

2393 **SUN PROOF 5.8+ ★★** Located at the left end of the face. Climb up and right past a bolt to a ramp, then up past a dike.

2394 **COOL CITY 5.10b ★★** Climb a crack to a bolt, then up face past horizontals, near the center of the wall.

2395 **GLOBAL WARMING 5.8 R** Located to the right of **Cool City** and to the left of a wide crack (**One of Two**). Climb a crack, then up a face past horizontals.

2396 **ONE OF TWO 5.6** This is the wide crack near the right end of the wall.

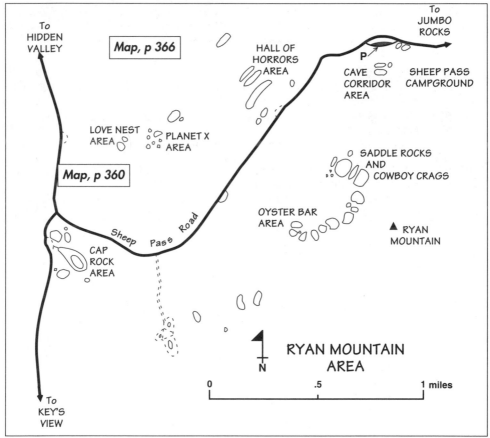

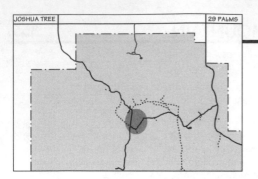

To
JUMBO
ROCKS

To
HIDDEN
VALLEY

Map, p 366

HALL OF
HORRORS
AREA

P

CAVE
CORRIDOR
AREA

SHEEP PASS
CAMPGROUND

LOVE NEST
AREA

PLANET X
AREA

Map, p 360

SADDLE ROCKS
AND
COWBOY CRAGS

OYSTER BAR
AREA

RYAN
MOUNTAIN

Sheep Pass Road

CAP
ROCK
AREA

RYAN MOUNTAIN
AREA

N

0   .5   1 miles

To
KEY'S
VIEW

RYAN AREA

The remainder of this part of the guide covers crags as they are encountered along the Quail Springs Road. From Hidden Valley Campground, head south for about two miles to a point where the Key's View Road branches off right. The Quail Springs Road curves east, then northeast, from here. From the point of its intersection with the Key's View Road, Quail Springs Road changes names (probably just to confuse people). For about the next 11 miles, the main road is called Sheep Pass Road.

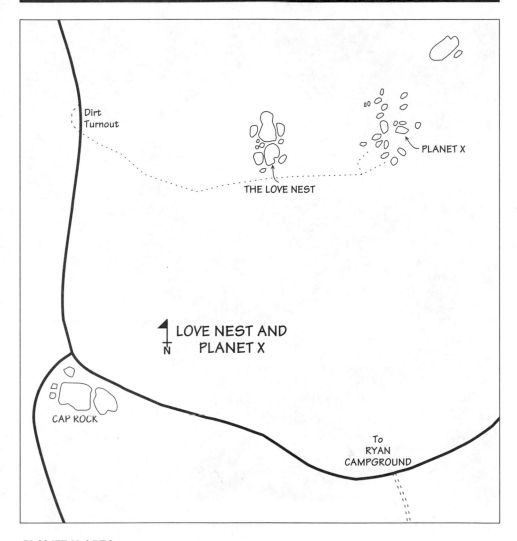

Dirt Turnout

PLANET X

THE LOVE NEST

LOVE NEST AND
PLANET X

N

CAP ROCK

To
RYAN
CAMPGROUND

PLANET X AREA

This area lies east of Quail Springs Road, and consists of two clumps of rocks/boulders called The Love Nest and Planet X. They are approached from the Quail Springs Road at a point onc-and-a-third miles south of Hidden Valley Campground and a third of a mile before you get to the Cap Rock/Key's View Road turnoff. The Love Nest is about .3 miles east of the road, Planet X is about .5 miles east of the road.

THE LOVE NEST

This is the first set of rocks encountered as you walk east from Quail Springs Road (about .3 mile). The established routes are located on the slightly-overhanging south face of the formation. Rattlesnakes are known to hibernate in large numbers under the formation. Watch your step in the spring and the fall! Maps, pages 356, 357.

2397   **WE DON'T NEED NO STINKING BADGES   5.11c ★★★**   Pro: Six bolts, bolt anchors.

2398   **BOYS DON'T CRY   5.12a ★★★**   Pro: Six bolts, bolt anchors.

2399   **SHAKIN LIKE MILK   5.11b ★★★**   Pro: Six bolts, bolt anchors.

PLANET X BOULDERS

A group of very large boulders lie further east and slightly north of The Love Nest (about .5 mile from the road). In the middle of this clump is a pinnacle scarred by several cracks. This is the Planet X Pinnacle. Six routes are known on this small formation. There is some good bouldering in this area. Maps, pages 356, 357.

2400 **PLANET CLAIRE** **5.10d** Climb the west arête then traverse onto the north face past five bolts.

2401 **PLANET Y** **5.10a** Pro: to 2".

2402 **SATURN SHEETS** **5.8** The direct variation is 5.10c.

2403 **PLANET X** **5.8+** Climb a crack past a fixed pin and bolt on the southeast face.

2404 **INEPT TUNE** **5.10b (TR)** Climb the face to right of **Planet X.** Start on **Planet Z** and climb up and left.

2405 **PLANET Z** **5.10d ★** Climb a crack (fixed rurp) to a face with two bolts on the east face.

2406 **SUBWAY TO VENUS** **5.11c/d ★★** Climb steep edges past four bolts on the north face.

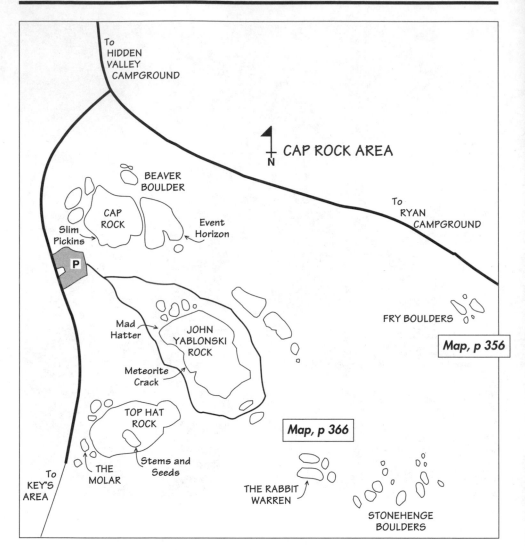

CAP ROCK

Cap Rock is situated at the southeast corner of the intersection of Quail Springs Road and Key's View Road. A large parking area is south of the main formation and is reached by driving south on Key's View Road for a short distance. Maps, above and page 356.

BEAVER BOULDER

Beaver Boulder is the very large boulder in front of Cap Rock's north side. It is quite obvious from Quail Springs Road. Several aid routes climb the boulder. Map, page 360.

2407 **RURP ROMP   A3** ★
2408 **LOST LID   A4 5.9** ★
2409 **BEAVER BOULDER FREE ROUTE   5.10d** ★   Pro: One bolt.
2410 **BOLT LADDER   A1**   This short bolt ladder is located on the east face of Beaver Boulder.

CAP ROCK – NORTHEAST AND NORTH FACES

See map on page 360.

2411　**EVENT HORIZON**　**5.10b R** ★★
2412　**RETIREMENT**　**5.10a**　Pro: Thin, two bolts.
2413　**NUTCRACKER**　**5.2**
2414　**SPACE ODYSSEY**　**5.10b R** ★
2415　**BUSH EVICTION**　**5.9**　The crack on the arête.
2416　**BUSH EVICTION DIRECT**　**5.10c**　Pro: One bolt.
2417　**FALSE LAYBACK**　**5.4**
2418　**FALSE PROPHET**　**5.9**
2419　**BLACK ICE**　**5.10b R**　Pro: One bolt.
2420　**LIL SQUIRT**　**5.9+**　Pro: Two bolts.
2421　**THE AYATOLLAH**　**5.11a (TR)** ★★★
2422　**HORROR-ZONTAL TERROR-VERSE**　**5.10b**　1Onebolt.
2423　**CIRCUS, CIRCUS**　**5.9**
2424　**CIRCUS**　**5.2** ★
2425　**ANNIVERSARY SPECIAL**　**5.8**　Two bolts.

CAP ROCK – SOUTH FACE

See map on page 360.

2426　**VISUAL NIGHTMARE**　**5.10a**
2427　**SLIM PICKINGS**　**5.10b**　The direct start is 5.10c.
2428　**SLIMMER PICKINS**　**5.10d** ★　Four bolts.
2429　**NOSE TO THE GRINDSTONE**　**5.11a** ★★　Pro: Very thin, two fixed pins.
2430　**ROBO COP**　**5.7+**　Four bolts.
2431　**THE TERMINATOR**　**5.9**　Five bolts.
2432　**DUNCE CAP**　**5.13a** ★★★　Five bolts.
2433　**HEY TAXI**　**5.11a**
2434　**CATCH A FALLING STAR**　**5.8** ★★
2435　**NOBODY WALKS IN LA**　**5.8+** ★
2436　**CATCH ME AT THE BAR**　**5.10a**　Pro: Two bolts.
2437　**CATCH A FALLING CAR**　**5.11a**　One bolt.
2438　**TUMBLING DICE**　**5.10a**　One bolt.

CAP ROCK — SOUTH FACE

2430

2431

2433

2426

DIRECT

← 2427 →

2429

2432

2428

2432

2433

2434

2435

2436

2437

2438

CAP ROCK — SOUTHEAST FACE

JOHN YABLONSKI ROCK

This is the large formation to the southeast of Cap Rock; the paved nature trail circumnavigates the entire formation. Map, page 360, 366.

2439　**HEARTBREAK RIDGE　5.8**　Climb past two bolts on the north side of the larger boulder.

2440　**HARTMAN　5.6**　The finger crack left of a low-angled face.

2441　**BARKHORN　5.8 (TR)**　Climb the low-angled face 10 feet right of above.

2442　**RAWL　5.5**　A finger crack to right of the low-angled face.

2443　**MAD HATTER　5.11c R**　This is the three-bolt route on the northwest corner of the rock.

2444　**METEORITE CRACK　5.10c**　This is a striking thin hands crack on the west face of Yablonski Rock. It is on your left as you take the righthand part of the loop trail.

2444a **TWEENER IN TROUBLE　5.8**　The chimney/offwidth between **Mereorite Crack** and **Tweeners Out for Glory.**

2445　**TWEENERS OUT FOR GLORY　5.6**　Two cracks lie to the right of the **Meteorite Crack**. This is the rightmost one.

THE RABBIT WARREN

This group of large boulders lies southeast of Yablonski Rock (southeast of the right-hand apex of the nature trail). Map, page 360, 366.

2446　**CARROT　5.8**　This is a finger crack just right of the preceding route.

2447　**MR. BUNNY MEETS THE EXPANDO FLAKE　5.10b (TR)**　This lieback up an expanding flake is on the back of this formation.

2448　**LITTLE BUNNY FU-FU　5.7**　Climb past two bolts on the southeast arête of the smaller, eastern boulder.

2449　**MR. BUNNY GOES ROLLERSKATING　5.9 (TR)**　This is the face right of Little Bunny Fu-Fu. Start with a hard mantel move.

2449a **STEMS AND SEEDS　5.11d**　Two bolts on east face of eastern boulder.

TOP HAT ROCK

This formation and associated boulders lie directly to the south of Cap Rock. Its west face lies adjacent to the Key's View Road. Map, page 360, 366.

2450　**TOO STRONG AND A TWEENER　5.11a**　A two-bolt route on the southeast corner/face of the formation.

2451　**TOP HAT　5.10d R**　Located on a boulder high up on the east side of Top Hat Rock. Pro: 3 bolts.

THE MOLAR

This is a large boulder on the west side of The Top Hat. It faces the road. Map, page 360, 366.

2452　**TOOTH DECAY　5.11c**　One bolt.

2453　**UP 40　5.11b R/X ★★**

2454　**THE SKIN OF THE TEETH　5.12d**　This 1 bolt route lies on the southwest corner/arête of The Molar.

WALLY WORLD

This crag is approached by driving towards Key's View from Cap Rock. Park at the first large turnout on the left, about one mile from the Cap Rock intersection. Wally World is the leftmost of several crags on the hillside about .25 mi. left (east) of the road. Four routes have been reported.

2455　**LARGE MARGE　5.7**　This is a straight-in crack on the left of the formation, facing the road.

2456　**HOTSEAT　5.7**　A crack/flake 10 feet right of **Large Marge.**

2457　**FACE　5.11a (TR)**　Climb the very short face above **Large Marge.**

2458　**DEVIL INSIDE　5.10c**　This two-bolt route goes up an overhanging knobby face around the corner to the right of **Large Marge.**

2459　**WALLY GEORGE　5.9**　This climbs a large dihedral on the right side of the formation. The route cuts left at the very top.

2454

2452

2453

THE MOLAR

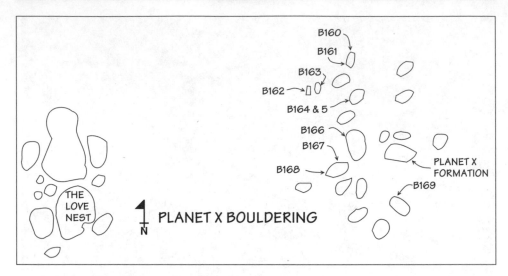

PLANET X BOULDERING

B160
B161
B163
B162
B164 & 5
B166
B167
B168
PLANET X
FORMATION
B169
THE
LOVE
NEST

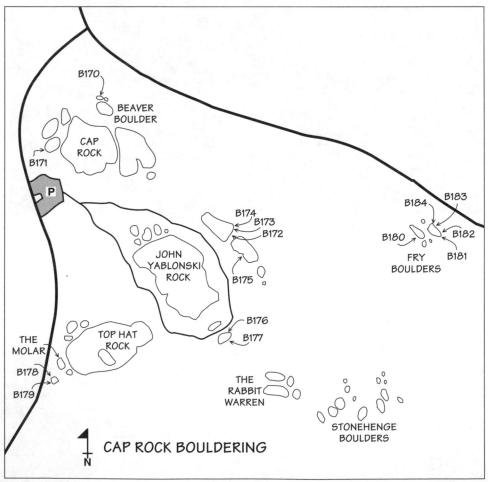

CAP ROCK BOULDERING

B170
BEAVER
BOULDER
CAP
ROCK
B171
P
B174
B173
B172
JOHN
YABLONSKI
ROCK
B175
B184   B183
B180   B182
B181
FRY
BOULDERS
B176
B177
THE
MOLAR
B178
B179
TOP HAT
ROCK
THE
RABBIT
WARREN
STONEHENGE
BOULDERS

PLANET X BOULDERING

Several excellent boulder problems can be found amoung the large boulders lying to the west and south of the actual Planet X Pinnacle. See the map on page 366.

B160 **PLANET X   B1 R**
B161 **PLANET CLAIRE   5.11+**
B162 **JERRY'S KIDS   B1 R**
B163 **NICE LADY   5.11**
B164 **SATELLITE BOULDER LEFT   5.11+**
B165 **SATELLITE BOULDER RIGHT   5.11+**
B166 **TERMINATOR   B1**
B167 **BOULDER CRACK   5.10+**
B168 **T1000   B1**
B169 **TURBOLATOR   B1**

CAP ROCK BOULDERING

The following boulder problems can be found in the Cap Rock area. Maps, pages 360, 366.

B170   **GRAHAM PARSONS MEMORIAL HAND TRAVERSE 5.9**   On small boulder in front of Beaver Boulder.
B171   **PARKING LOT CRANK 5.11+**   Steep thin crack faces parking lot.
B172   **ALL WASHED UP   B1**
B173   **SOAR EAGLE   B1+**
B174   **LUNGE FOR IT   5.11+**
B175   **UP 20   5.11 R**
B176   **LARGO DYNO   5.11+**
B177   **PUMPING MONZONITE   B1+**

THE STONEHENGE BOULDERS

These boulders lie east of The Rabbit Warren area and sport a number of good boulder problems from 5.9 to 5.11+. Maps, pages 360, 366.

B178 **POWELL CRANK   B1**
B179 **POWELL PINCH   5.11**

THE FRY BOULDERS

These boulders lie to the north east of the parking area for Cap Rock, roughly 1/3 the way towards Ryan Campground. Maps, pages 360, 366.

B180 **REACH FOR A PEACH   5.10**
B181 **FRYING PAN   5.10**
B182 **LEAP IN FAITH   5.10+**
B183 **FRY PROBLEM   5.11**
B184 **INTO THE FIRE   5.8**

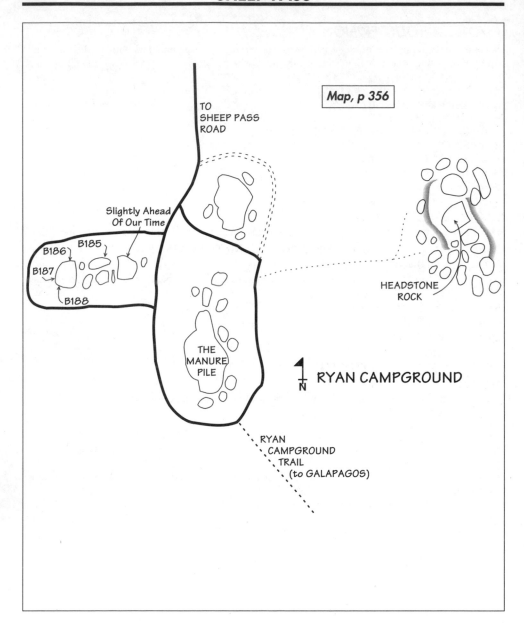

Map, p 356

TO
SHEEP PASS
ROAD

Slightly Ahead
Of Our Time

B186   B185

B187

B188

HEADSTONE
ROCK

THE
MANURE
PILE

RYAN CAMPGROUND

N

RYAN
CAMPGROUND
TRAIL
(to GALAPAGOS)

RYAN CAMPGROUND

Ryan Campground is located about .75 mile east of Cap Rock, along the Sheep Pass Loop Road. Take a dirt road about .25 mile south to the actual campground. A few routes are located in the campground, while the balanced pillar to the east (Headstone Rock) and other formations further east provide additional climbing. The grave of Frank James (discoverer of the Desert Queen Mine) is buried east of Headstone Rock, near the old Ryan Ranch Homestead (next to Lost Rocks). Map, page 368.

2460 **SLIGHTLY AHEAD OF OUR TIME   5.12a ★**   This is the bolt-ladder route on the large boulder behind campsite #27. This was the first 5.12 in the monument.

THE MANURE PILE

This formation lies near the center of Ryan Campground (behind campsite #16) and sports several routes on its west face. Map, page 368.

2461 **ALLEN STECK MEMORIAL ROUTE   5.8**   Pro: Two bolts.

2462 **MIGHTY HIGH   5.12a**   Pro: Thin cams, two boltss

2463 **TOM BOMBADIL   5.7**

2464 **BARELY CRANKIN'   5.5**

2465 **DECEPTION   5.10a**

2466 **BABY ROUTE   5.9**   This route lies behind campsite #19. A small roof is passed before a right-facing corner and crack lead to the summit.

2467 **CAMP WHORE   5.11a**   This route lies on the east face of The Manure Pile. Climb up 15 feet to a ledge, then 25 feet up slightly overhanging brown rock past a seam to a dike. Two bolts and pro.

HEADSTONE ROCK – SOUTH FACE

This pillar of rock sits on top of a jumble of rocks and boulders about 200 yards east of the campground. The first ascent of Headstone Rock was made in 1956 by Bob Boyle and Rod Smith. A rope, tossed over the summit, was climbed to reach the top. Map, page 368.

2468 **SW CORNER 5.6** ★★★
2469 **SOUTH FACE CENTER   5.9 (TR)** ★★
2470 **CRYPTIC 5.8** ★★★

HEADSTONE ROCK NORTH FACE

HEADSTONE ROCK – NORTH FACE

See map on page 368.
2471 **THE CUTTING EDGE   5.13b ★★**   Pro: Four bolts (some hard to clip).
2472 **HEADMASTER   5.12b (TR) ★★★**
2473 **HEADBANGERS' BALL   5.12c ★★**   Pro: Four bolts.

LOST ROCKS

These rocks lic east of Headstone Rock. The first and southernmost formation has two routes.
Map, page
2474 **M.F. DIRTY RAT 5.7** A small corridor is near the south side of this clum. Climb a clean
   hand crack on the left (north) side of this corridor.
2475 **DIRTY CAT 5.10c (TR)** This is a thin crack just right of **M.F. Dirty Rat.**
2476 **OFF RAMP 5.10d** This route is on a tall block (west-facing) at the north end of Lost
   Rocks. Pro: Four bolts.

RYAN CAMPGROUND BOULDERING

B185 **FLIGHT ATTENDANT   5.11+**
B186 **GIBB'S ARETE   5.10+**
B187 **GIBB'S FACE   5.10**
B188 **DREAMING OF THE MASTER   B2**
Several other good boulder problems lie on the boulders just west and south of Headstone Rock.

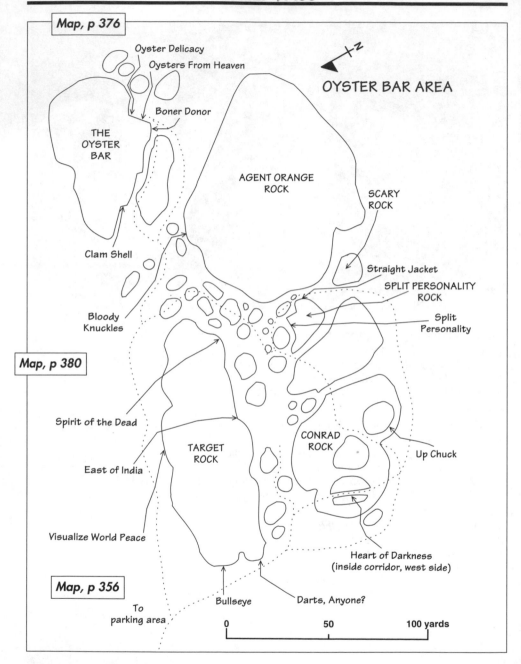

Map, p 376

Oyster Delicacy

Oysters From Heaven

OYSTER BAR AREA

Boner Donor

THE
OYSTER
BAR

AGENT ORANGE
ROCK

SCARY
ROCK

Clam Shell

Straight Jacket

SPLIT PERSONALITY
ROCK

Bloody
Knuckles

Split
Personality

Map, p 380

Spirit of the Dead

CONRAD
ROCK

TARGET
ROCK

Up Chuck

East of India

Visualize World Peace

Heart of Darkness
(inside corridor, west side)

Map, p 356

To
parking area

Bullseye

Darts, Anyone?

0   50   100 yards

OYSTER BAR AREA

This area essentially is the lowest portion of the Cowboy Crags, a band of cliffs that starts up and right (south) of Saddle Rocks and arches down the hillside to the south. The lowest formations are on the desert floor. These formations are referred to as the Oyster Bar Area. Map, page 356.

Park at a large turnout on the east side of the road about .5 mile south of the Hall of Horrors and Saddle Rocks parking area. The approach is a fairly level hike of about .3 mile. Map, page 380.

TARGET ROCK

This formation is closest to the road. It forms the northern part of a canyon; another large formation lies to the south. Map, page 372.

2477 **UNNAMED 5.9** The crack route 15 feet left of **Visualize World Peace.**

2478 **VISUALIZE WORLD PEACE 5.10c** This is a three-bolt face route near the middle of the north side of Target Rock. It climbs grey-colored rock.

2479 **ADULT GERBLES $1.59 5.7+** This is the crack route 15 feet right of Visualize World Peace.

2480 **ANCIENT FUTURE 5.9** Two bolt route on the left side of west face.

2481 **BETTER YOU THAN ME 5.10b** This is about 60 feet right of the above route, on the west face. Climb an arête past two bolts to easier climbing.

2482 **EAST OF INDIA 5.10a** This route lies on the south face of Target Rock (in the canyon), and starts in a short dihedral. Climb past one bolt to a loose crack.

2483 **SPIRIT OF THE DEAD 5.8 ★** This two-bolt face route lies on the southeast shoulder of Target Rock.

2484 **PEARLS BEFORE SWINE 5.8** This lies behind a tree on a 30-foot face near the southeast edge of Target Rock. Face climb to a horizontal traverse, then up a hand crack.

CONRAD ROCK

This formation lies just south of Target Rock and forms the southern part of the canyon between these two formations. A large split rock/boulder lies near the western end of Conrad Rock. **Heart of Darkness** lies in the narrow (north-south) corridor formed by this split rock. Map, page 372.

2485 **APOCALYPSE NOW 5.10b** This is the hand-and-fist crack on the western side of the corridor, to the right of **Heart of Darkness.** Pro: to 4 inches.

2486 **HEART OF DARKNESS 5.11c ★★★★** This is the excellent thin crack on the west side of the narrow corridor. Pro: Many thin to 1.5 inches.

2487 **UP CHUCK 5.7** A west-facing piece of rock is part-way up the south side of Conrad Rock. Climb the middle of the face (to the left of a crack) past two bolts.

2488 **COLON BLOW 5.7 R** Ascend the crack to the right of **Up Chuck.**

2489 **HEFFALUMP 5.5 R/X** This route is on the smooth, grainy corner that faces the road (west). Climb up a smooth corner to a small, flake-like bump, then to the top.

2490 **BOOM BOOM O'HARA 5.5** This is on the south face of the same rock as **Heffalump.** Climb a slanting gully to the top. (The entry move is the crux.)

SPLIT PERSONALITY ROCK

This is really a large boulder that sits atop the eastern end of Conrad Rock. It is distinguished by a flat, vertical face that faces to the northwest. It can be seen from the road and can be approached several different ways. The usual approach is to go around the east end of Target Rock, then scramble up boulders to the base. Map, page 372.

2490a **TOPPER 5.12a (TR)**

2491   **SPLIT PERSONALITY 5.11d ★★★**   This route climbs past five bolts on the arête of the vertical northwest face .

2492   **DISPOSITION CREVICE 5.11b ★★**   Climb the dihedral around and left of **Split Personality.** Pro: Thin nuts and a bolt.

2493   **STRAIGHT JACKET (AKA SHOCK THERAPY) 5.10c ★★**   Start down and around the corner (left) from **Split Personality.** Climb the overhanging face to a friction face above, passing three bolts.

2494   **5150 5.10b**   This four-bolt face route is around the back side of Split Personality Rock. It seems possible to avoid the first two bolts by climbing off boulders to the right. Pro: Some medium nuts.

SCARY ROCK

This 80-foot pinnacle is high on the southeastern side of Conrad Rock, and actually is southeast (through a corridor) from Split Personality Rock. It can be approached either by walking around the south side of Conrad Rock or from Split Personality Rock by walking southeast through the corridor east of that rock. The pinnacle is split by a crack. Descend by rapping off the backside, with the rope anchored to a tree on the front side! Map, page 372.

2495   **ECHO OF A SCREAM 5.10a ★**   This route climbs past no bolts on the face to the left of the crack splitting the pinnacle.

2496   **DON'T EVEN LOOK 5.9**   This is the crack splitting the pinnacle.

AGENT ORANGE ROCK

This large formation lies east and uphill from Conrad Rock, and Split Personality and Scary Rocks lie in the high break between it and Conrad Rock. It is easily recognized by the large orange area low on the northeast side. There are several large boulders in front of the orange area; **Pearls Before Swine** lies on one of these boulders.

2497 **THE IRON CURTAIN 5.11c ★★** This is 20 feet left of **Bloody Knuckles.** Four bolts, two on slab, two on headwall, two-bolt anchor.

2498 **BLOODY KNUCKLES 5.10b ★★** This route climbs up the orange face past three bolts, ending at a two-bolt rap anchor.

2499 **RUST IN PEACE 5.9 ★** Located to the right of the preceding route. Climb a flake/crack to a bolt, then continue to the same two-bolt anchor. Pro: Very thin to 1 inch.

THE OYSTER BAR

This formation lies to the northeast of Agent Orange Rock, Conrad Rock, etc. A wide gully separates it from Agent Orange Rock. Walk up this gully, then head east (left) to get to the steep face routes on the south side of the formation. A series of dihedrals are on the southwest face; the farthest left (north) is rated 5.9. Map, page 372.

THE OYSTER BAR

2503   2504

2500 **CLAM SHELL 5.9** Climb the farthest left dihedral on the southwest face passed one bolt.

2501 **BONOR DONOR 5.10a** This route lies left and around the corner from **Oysters From Heaven** (45 feet); 35 feet left of **Stress Puppet.** Pro: To 3.5 inches, two fixed pins, three bolts.

2502 **STRESS PUPPET 5.10a** This route is just around corner (left) from **Oysters From Heaven** (15 feet). Three bolts, fixed pin.

2503 **OYSTERS FROM HEAVEN 5.11c ★★★** This is the lefthand route on the south side of the formation. Pro: Six bolts, bolt anchor.

2504 **OYSTER DELACACY 5.11b ★★★** This is the six-bolt route on the right.

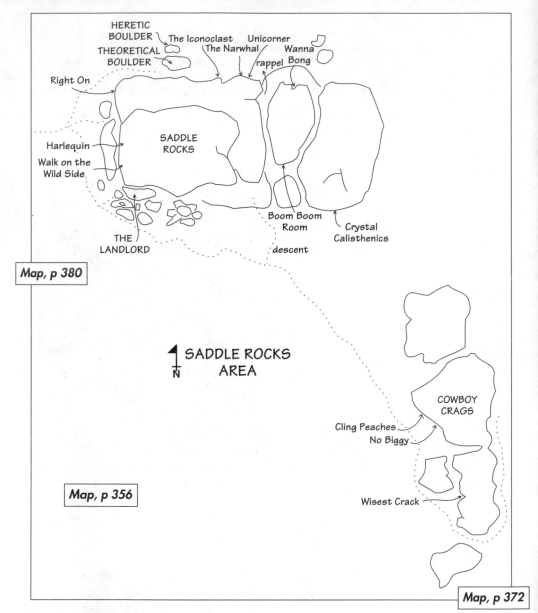

SADDLE ROCKS

This very large slab of rock lies about one mile northeast of Ryan Campground. A series of car pullouts on the right and left sides of Sheep Pass Loop Road leave about a .5 mile walk to the rock. The Hall of Horrors is on the west side of the road. Map, above.

HERETIC BOULDER
See map on page 376.
2505 **BRUSH YOUR TEETH WITH JESUS 5.10c** This is the rightmost route and climbs
thin cracks to a bolt. Above it, move left to a ramp/crack leading to the top.
2506 **BLIND MAN'S BLUFF 5.11c** This four-bolt climb is left of the previous route.

THEORETICAL BOULDER
This tall boulder is to the left (north) of Saddle Rocks. Map, page 376.
2507 **PRESBYTERIAN DENTAL FLOSS 5.10d**
2508 **EPISCOPALIAN TOOTHPICK 5.10c ★★**

Saddle Rocks has three distinct summits (lower, middle, upper). Foutes on Saddle Rocks will be
described left (north) to right (south) around the entire rock. **Wanna Bong** is the route furthest to
the right and lies on the north face.
2509 **WANNA BONG 5.9** This route climbs the obvious, wide crack-and-corner system on the
middle formation. It is the furthest left route.
2510 **I SMELL A RAT 5.10b** This is a five-bolt route face route left of **Unicorner.**
2511 **UNICORNER 5.8 ★★** This route climbs a giant, left-facing open book on the northeast
corner of the lower formation. This is just below the rappel route on the north end of the
lower formation.
2512 **THE NARWHAL 5.10b ★★** Start at the Unicorner, but follow a traversing crack that
heads up and right. It joins the top of **Orange Flake** after two pitches.
2513 **SPACE MOUNTAIN 5.10b ★★★** Start at **Unicorner,** but follow a traversing crack right
(**The Narwhal**) until you can climb straight up the steep face above past bolts. A little loose.
2514 **RAGING BULL DIKE 5.11d** This is down and right from the start of **The Narwhal.**
Climb up an overhanging dike with four bolts, then continue up a finger-and-hand crack to
the finish of **The Narwhal.**

2515 **THE ICONOCLAST 5.13a** ★★★★★ This route climbs the overhanging arête to the right of **Raging Bull Dike.**

2516 **KNOT AGAIN 5.9** This route is reported as starting 125 feet uphill from **R & R** in a left-leaning ramp system. It must go for at least two pitches, staying right of **Raging Bull Dike,** and ending at the point where **The Narwhal** meets **Orange Flake.**

2517 **R & R 5.8**

2518 **KID CALINGULA 5.10a** From the first bolt on **Orange Flake,** climb straight up past bolts to a belay in an undercling. The second pitch follows a thin crack up and right, then moves left to a bolt, then up to the upper ramp of **R & R.**

2519 **ORANGE FLAKE 5.8** ★★

2520 **RIGHT ON 5.5** ★★

2521 **BOSCH JOB 5.11d R** ★★ This is a bolted two-pitch climb between **Right On** and **High Cost of Living.**

2522 **THE HIGH COST OF LIVING 5.11a to 5.12a** (depending on height) ★★★★

2523 **A CHEAP WAY TO DIE 5.10d** ★★★

2524 **ROUGHRIDERS 5.11b** ★★★ Pro: 14 bolts

2525 **HARLEQUIN 5.10c R** ★★★

2526 **WALK ON THE WILD SIDE 5.7+** ★★★★

2526a **UNKNOWN 5.10b**

2527 **HAM SANDWICH 5.8**

The following three routes are on the detached slab right of **Walk on the Wild Side.**

2528 **THE KID 5.9** ★ Climb the left side of the slab past bolts.

2529 **THE LANDLORD 5.10d** ★★ This route up the center of the slab has many bolts.

2530 **THE RENTER 5.9** Climb the crack right of **The Landlord** and join that route for its last four bolts.

The following routes lie on the jumble of large rocks and boulders to the right of lower part of the main face of Saddle Rocks.

2531 **SHIT HAPPENS 5.9** Climb the steep face between **The Landlord** and **Money For Nothing.** Pro: Two bolts.

2532 **RED HOT FIRE BALLS 5.11c** Right of **Money For Nothing.**

2533 **MONEY FOR NOTHING 5.12a** Formerly known as **A2.**

2534 **CHICKS FOR FREE 5.12b** ★★★★ Climbs the left arête of the small, brown, blocky formation left of **Money For Nothing.** Three bolts.

2535 **WALK ON THE STEEP SIDE 5.10** This steep, 50-foot route with three bolts is to the right of **Money for Nothing.**

2536 **RAKER MOBILE 5.8**

SADDLE ROCKS – SOUTH FACE

SADDLE ROCKS – SOUTH FACE, LOWER SUMMIT

The lower formation has a gully/chimney (the descent route) splitting the upper south side. To the right (east) of this chimney is a low-angled face, which is the top of the lower formation. Map, page 376.

2537 **PRESTO IN C SHARP 5.7** This climbs a water streak on the low-angled face past two bolts.

2538 **SULLIVAN FROM COLORADO 5.9** This climbs up and right, past two horizontal cracks, from a chockstone in the corridor to the right (east) of **Presto in C Sharp.**

SADDLE ROCKS – SOUTH FACE, MIDDLE SUMMIT

See map on page 376.

2539 **PINNACLE AEROBICS TO PROMOTE BLOOD CIRCULATION 5.11b** Climb the left edge of the middle formation.

2540 **NUTS AND BOLTS 5.9** Climbs the west-facing arête to the left of **Boom Boom Room.**

2541 **BOOM BOOM ROOM 5.9** ★★ Named after a bar in Joshua Tree (which has changed names more often than can be counted), this route climbs past five bolts on the south face of the middle formation.

2542 **MORE HUSTLE THAN MUSCLE 5.8** This climbs a left-leaning, overhanging crack that is located about 90 feet right and around the corner from **Boom Boom Room.**

SADDLE ROCKS – SOUTH FACE, UPPER SUMMIT
See map on page 376.

2543 **FLAKES CAN COLLAPSE 5.8+** Climb a thin flake (just right of the crack/corner) up the ridge near the southwest corner of the upper summit. Pro: Thin nuts to 2 inches.

2544 **CRYSTAL CALISTHENICS 5.10a ★** Climb a crack left of a black streak and traverse right past a bolt to a dihedral and ledge. From the ledge, climb up and left along a crystal ridge and past a bolt to a shallow crack.

2545 **THE GOOD BOOK 5.9** This climbs up to the ledge mentioned in **Crystal Calisthenics,** then goes up a huge, left-leaning dihedral.

COWBOY CRAGS
These slabs lie up and right of Saddle Rocks. Map, page 376.

2546 **THE UNBEARABLE LIGHTNESS OF BEING 5.9** Climb a J-shaped crack on the buttress 100 feet left of **Cling Peaches,** eventually joining that route.

2547 **CLING PEACHES 5.9 R ★★** Start at a big pine tree. Climb up a flake to a bolt, then up and left past another bolt to an arching thin crack.

2548 **NO BIGGY 5.10b R/X ★** Climb straight up past the first bolt on **Cling Peaches.** One more bolt and poor nuts protect this long pitch.

2549 **IMMUNO REACTION 5.10a ★** This climbs a crack over a small roof 40 feet left of **Wisest Crack,** and continues up a dihedral to the top.

2550 **WISEST CRACK 5.7 ★★** This climbs a very clean crack in a dihedral to the top.

2551 **BABY FAE 5.11a ★** This climbs the face right of **Wisest Crack** past two bolts.

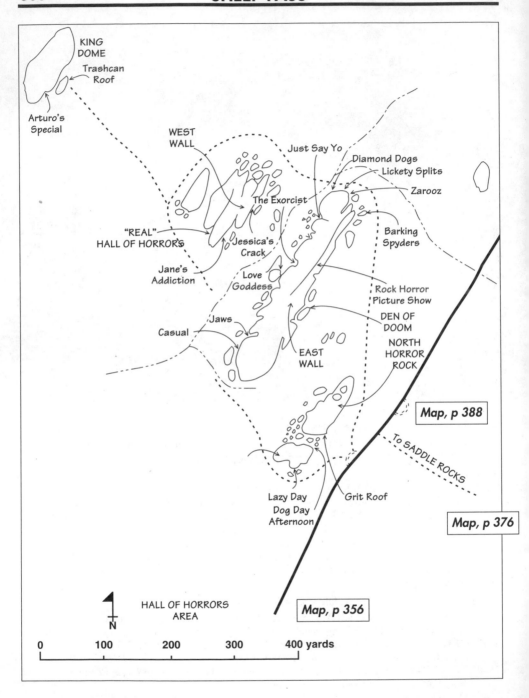

KING
DOME
Trashcan
Roof
Arturo's
Special
WEST
WALL
Just Say Yo
Diamond Dogs
Lickety Splits
Zarooz
The Exorcist
"REAL"
HALL OF HORRORS
Barking
Spyders
Jessica's
Crack
Jane's
Addiction
Love
Goddess
Rock Horror
Picture Show
Jaws
DEN OF
DOOM
Casual
NORTH
HORROR
ROCK
EAST
WALL
Map, p 388
To SADDLE ROCKS
Map, p 376
Lazy Day
Dog Day
Afternoon
Grit Roof
HALL OF HORRORS
AREA
N
Map, p 356

0	100	200	300	400 yards

HALL OF HORRORS

This fine area is located just west of the Sheep Pass Loop Road. Park for Saddle Rocks.   Map, page 380.

SOUTH HORROR ROCK

The southernmost rock, closest to the road.

2552 **GARDEN ANGEL   5.10a ★★**   Pro: Three bolts.

2553 **LAZY DAY   5.7 ★★**   Pro: To 2.5 inches.

2554 **PERHAPS   5.9**   Pro: To 2 inches. Start up **Lazy Day** but head up and right up a crack.

2555 **CACTUS FLOWER   5.11b ★★★**   Pro: Small camming units and bolts/bolt anchor.

2556 **THIS IS ONLY A TEST**   (Direct Start to **Cactus Flower**) **5.12a to d** (height dependant) One-bolt variation.

2557 **MY SENIOR PROJECT   5.9**

2558 **FLASH GORDON   5.7**

2559 **PULL MY FINGER BARBARA   5.11a**   Pro: Three bolts. An alternate finish for **Flash Gordon.**

2560 **FATHER OCEAN   5.12b (TR)**   Arête to left of **Dog Day Afternoon.**

2561 **DOG DAY AFTERNOON   5.10b ★★★**   This route lies opposite **Grit Roof,** on the Lazy Day rock. Five bolts protect good, steep face climbing.

2562 **OLD GUYS GONE NUTS, GO TO THE COPS   5.11c**   Face climb left of **Dog Day Afternoon.**

2563 **HOUSE OF GAMES   5.11b**   This is 50 feet right of **Dog Day Afternoon.** Three bolts.

NORTH HORROR ROCK

The northern rock, closest to the road. Map, page 380.

2564 **GRAPE NUTS, WHY NOT? 5.10a** Pro: Thin to 3 inches.

2565 **HOUSE OF THE HOMELESS 5.8+ ★★** Pro: Three bolts, bolt anchor.

2566 **GRIT ROOF 5.10c ★★**

2567 **GLUMPIES 5.9** Climb the crack in the corridor to the left of **Grit Roof.**

2568 **UNGAWAA 5.11a ★** Pro: Two bolts.

2568a **THE ICE EXPERIENCE 5.9**

2569 **ZARMOG THE DRAGON MAN 5.10a ★**

2570 **QUIVERING LIPS 5.8**

2571 **LIP SYNC 5.10c**

2572 **LIPPO SUCTION 5.10c** Climb the right side of the face past three bolts.

2573 **LIPPO LIPPY 5.9** Climb the center of the face to the left of **Lippo Suction.**

HALL OF HORRORS – EAST WALL (East Face)

The following routes lie on the east face/side of The East Wall of The Hall Of Horrors (facing the road). Map, page 380.

DEN OF DOOM

The Den of Doom is a small corridor on the east side of The East Wall, toward the southern end and behind rocks/boulders. The upper part of the brown, east-facing side of this corridor is visible from the trail. Map, page 380.

DEN OF DOOM – EAST FACE

2574 **DOOM DE DOOM DOOM 5.7 (TR)** Go up and left on the left side of the brown face.

2575 **FLAKES OF DOOM 5.6** Start as for the previous climb. Head straight up to knobby stuff.

2576 **DOOMED 5.6** Two bolts near the center of the face.

2577 **DOOMSDAY 5.9+** Four bolts on the right side of the face.

DEN OF DOOM – WEST FACE

Three toprope routes have been done on the west-facing side of the corridor. They are rated, from right to left: 5.6; 5.9; and 5.10a.

2578 **CREATURE FEATURE 5.11b** ★★ This route is on a small face on the east side (roughly the backside of **The Exorcist**). It is characterized by a giant white flake leaning against the face. Pro: Four bolts.

2579 **ROCKY HORROR PICTURE SHOW 5.11b/c** ★★★★ This is the obvious horizontal crack on the east face (backside of **The Exorcist**) that can be seen on the approach to **Zardoz**, et al., from the parking area. It has been climbed left to right. Pro: Many thin, medium to 3 inches.

2580 **GUARDIAN ANGELS 5.10a** This route is in a small alcove 100 feet southeast of **Zardoz**. Climb past four bolts on a steep face.

2581 **BONE ALONG 5.7** This is a one-bolt route to left of **Barking Spyders.**

2582 **BARKING SPYDERS 5.10a/b R** Marked by bolts and bashies on the right side of a small pillar left of **Zardoz.**

2583 **TEEN STEAM 5.10b** An overhanging wide crack in the gully left of **Zardoz.**

2584 **NO-DOZ 5.9+ R** The buttress right of Barking Spyders and left of **Zardoz.**

HALL OF HORRORS – EAST WALL (West Face)

The main "Hall" lies west of the formation that is next to the road. Most of the established routes lie within the canyon formed by two long domes. Map, page 380.

The following routes lie on the northeast end of main (center) Hall of Horrors formation. These routes share a bolt belay. Descent: A long rappel (100+ feet) or a class-3 walk-off (toward the top of formation, then around the east side to easier ground near **Nurn's Romp**).

2585 **ZARDOZ 5.8 R ★★** A few small nuts can be placed under the small roof near the bottom. The face above is runout.

2586 **BUNNIES 5.12a (TR) ★** This is the face between **Zardoz** and **Lickety Splits.** Consensus is that this route is not worth bolting.

2587 **LICKETY SPLITS 5.7 R ★★** Climb the thin crack/flake (small to medium pro). The unprotected face eases near top.

2588 **LICKEY DOGS (variation) 5.9+ R**

2589 **DIAMOND DOGS 5.10a ★★★** Pro: To 3 inches; bolts.

The following two routes lie on a rather insignificant lump of rock between the walk-off for the previous routes and **Nurn's Romp.** Descend left.

2590 **JUST SAY YO 5.9+ ★** Pro: To 2 inches, two bolts.

2591 **UNCERTAINTY PRINCIPAL 5.10a** Just right of **Just Say Yo.** Climb a crack and hand traverse right. Pro: To 3 inches.

The next several routes end on a interesting summit; the descent is somewhat tricky. The quickest (but most intimidating) way off is to walk to the left (northeast) until you must leap a deep fissure before easier scrambling leads you to the base. More popular is a circuitous and slightly grovelly descent to the right.

2592 **NURN'S ROMP 5.8 ★★** Pro: To 3 inches.

2593 **DOUBLE JEOPARDY 5.10c R ★** (leader **and** follower) If you feel compelled to do this route, cleverly volunteer to lead.

2594 **EXORCIST 5.10a ★★★** Somewhat of a Josh classic. Pro: Mostly thin nuts, one bolt; take 2 to 3 inches for belay.

2595 **IT 5.9** Pro: Thin to 3 inches.

2596 **ANTICHRIST 5.11a.** ★★ The hardest move is getting off the ground; most jump. Pro: Three bolts, 2 to 3 inches for belay.

2597 **THAT 5.10b** Climb either route ___ or ___ to reach base of this short, thin crack.

2598 **CAT ON A HOT TIN ROOF 5.10c**

2599 **WHAT 5.8** An easy crack, but not very classic.

2600 **LOVE GODDESS 5.12a ★★★** This is a four-bolt climb on the north side of the block of **La Cholla.**

2601 **MOONSHADOW 5.12c ★★★** Pro: Bolts up the arête.

2602 **LA CHOLLA 5.12d ★★★** Pro: Eight bolts.

2603 **AERO SPACE 5.10b** Pro: Mostly thin to 2 inches, belay bolts on top.

2603a **THIN AIR 5.9**

2604 **MILITARY INDUSTRIAL COMPLEX 5.10a** Pro: Two bolts; nuts for anchor.

2605 **BUENOS AIRES 5.10a ★**

2606 **JAWS 5.6 R ★★★**

2607 **CASUAL 5.9 ★**

2608 **DOIN' LIFE 5.10a ★** Pro: Three bolts, nuts for anchors.

2609 **SEARCH FOR KLINGONS 5.7** Pro: Two bolts, nuts for anchors.

2610 **HEMROIDIC TERROR 5.7 R ★**

2611 **THREE BOLTS CLOSER TO DIVORCE 5.10b** Pro: Three bolts, medium nuts.

2612 **RINGS AROUND URANUS 5.7** Climb a curving hand crack to a face with one bolt. This is right of **Hemroidic Terror.**

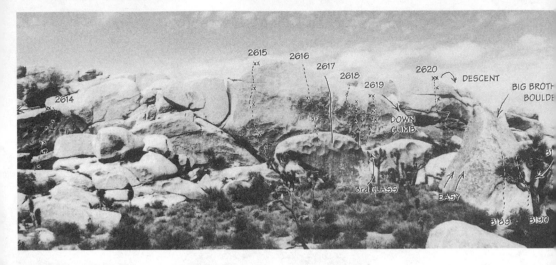

HALL OF HORRORS – WEST WALL (East Face)

A number of fine bolted face routes can be found on the West Wall in the Hall of Horrors. Map, page 380.

2613 **ALWAYS ON MY MIND   5.10c**   This route lies behind **Jane's Addiction** in an alcove. Pro: Small nuts, three bolts.

2614 **JANE'S ADDICTION   5.11b ★★★★**   Pro: Four bolts, fixed pin, bolt anchor.

2615 **AVANT CHAIN   5.12a ★★**   A reachy move up high may be the crux for shorter folk. Pro: Four bolts (chain hangers), bolt anchor.

2616 **SHAKING HANDS WITH THE UNEMPLOYED   5.10d**   Pro: Two bolts, nuts to 2.5 inches for belay.

2617 **JESSICA'S CRACK   5.6**

2618 **AVANT CAVE   5.11c ★★**   Pro: Small camming units, bolts, bolt anchor.

2619 **READ MY FLIPS   5.11a ★**   Pro: Three bolts.

2620 **READ MY LIPS   5.11a ★**   Pro: Small camming units to 2.5 inches; two bolts.

2621 **RAY'S CAFE   5.10a**   This loose crack lies about 20 feet right of **Read My Lips.** Climb up a loose hand crack, traverse left under a loose roof, and go up a finger crack to top. Pro: To 3 inches.

REAL HALL OF HORRORS

This is the narrow corridor behind **Jessica's Crack.** It is best entered through a narrow opening at the south end of the formation, about 200 feet left of Jessica's Crack.

2622 **STEMNGO   5.10c (TR)**   Walk about 25 feet past **First Eleven** (into the corridor); on the righthand side of the corridor you'll see some discontinuous seams. Stem up 10 feet, then move onto the wall and up an exit crack.

2623 **FIRST ELEVEN   5.11a**   This route is approached from the left of **Jessica's Crack.** Walking into the Real Hall of Horrors, it is the most obvious crack on the right wall, about 100 feet inside the corridor.

2624 **GOOD INVESTMENT   5.12a (TR)**   Climb a steep face to two overhanging cracks right of **First Eleven.** Variations exist.

2625 **NO OPTIONS   5.11b**   This three-bolt route is across the corridor from **Good Investment** The difficulty is belittled by the fact that one can chimney/bridge off the back wall during the crux. Done this way, the route warrants a 5.8/9 rating.

2626 **ROUTE RIGHT OF THE DUMBEST CLIMB IN THE MONUMENT   5.10**   This steep thin crack is right of **No Options** and across from **First Eleven.**

HALL OF HORRORS – WEST WALL (West Face)

This steep wall has two obvious horizontal cracks running across it and is full of large buckets. Map, page 380.

2627 **HOLDS TO HOLLYWOOD 5.4**
2628 **LEDGES TO LAUNDALE 5.10a ★**
2629 **BUCKETS TO BURBANK 5.8 ★**
2630 **PULLUPS TO PASADENA 5.10c**

HALL OF HORRORS BOULDERING

Several good boulder problems can be found on the two large boulders lying in the wash in the main "Hall". Other good problems are found in the vicinity of Kingdome. Photo, 386.

BIG BROTHER BOULDER

B189 **1984 IS TODAY 5.10+**
B190 **THE 4TH AMENDMENT 5.10-**
B191 **BIG BROTHER 5.11+**

SIDEKICK BOULDER

B192 **SIDEKICK 5.10**
B193 **SQUIRT 5.9**

LHMB (Lynn Hill Memorial Boulder)

This large boulder will be found just north-northwest of Kingdome. This boulder has several excellent problems from 5.11+ (north face) to B1 (LHMFP on the south center face).

KING DOME

This large rock lies about 250 yards northwest of the west wall of the Hall of Horrors. All known routes lie on the east face. Map, page 380.

2631   **AZTEC TWO-STEP** **5.7**   This route starts just left of the chimney system left of **Arturo's Special.** Climb up a crack for 30 feet and move right up another crack, exiting left where it fades at the top.

2632   **ARTURO'S SPECIAL** **5.8 ★**   This face route climbs the left margin of the main face of King Dome. Three bolts protect the climbing, which lies just right of a deep crack/chimney.

2633   **MISSION IMPOSSIBLE** **5.11b ★★★**   This improbable line climbs the center of the main face on knobs. The running start and jump to the first knob is the crux; its difficulty is probably dependent on the height of the climber.

2634   **TRASHMAN ROOF** **5.9 ★**   This is the short roof crack that lies at the base of the center of the main face of King Dome.

2635   **KEY TO THE KINGDOME** **5.9+**   Climb the stacked boulders 40 feet right of **Trashman Roof.** One bolt.

2636   **MAGIC KINGDOME** **5.8**   This is a one-bolt face climb about 50 feet right of **Trashman Roof.**

CAVE CORRIDOR

Cave Corridor is about .6 mile northeast of the Hall of Horrors/Saddle Rocks parking area. A large parking area on the right (south) side of Sheep Pass Loop Road is just next to the rocks. This parking area is a trailhead for the Ryan Mountain Trail. (Ryan Mountain is the large hill upon which Saddle Rocks lie.) Most of the climbing is on the two rocks that form a narrow canyon 120 yards south of the parking lot (Cave Corridor). Just at the eastern end (exit/entrance) of the parking area are several other smaller formations, these are Grotto and Cavern Rocks. The Junk Clump lies 150 yards southeast of the parking area (80 yards east of Cave Corridor).

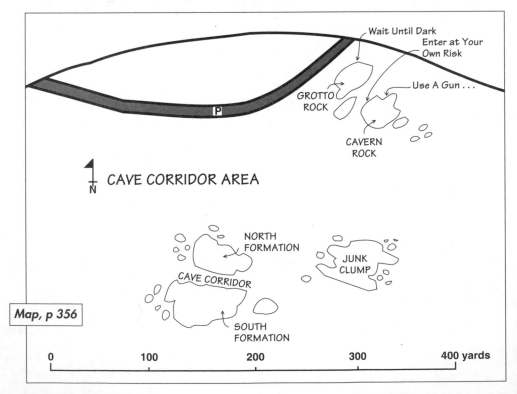

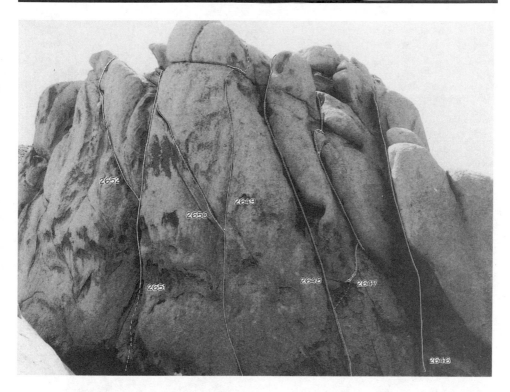

CAVE CORRIDOR – NORTH FORMATION

The following routes lie on the northernmost of the two formations that form the corridor. Map, page 388.

2637 **THE SOUND OF GRAINS SNAPPING 5.4** This is the wide dogleg crack on the north face. It is to the left of the following route.

2638 **THE SOUND OF RASHA'S EARS FLAPPING 5.10b** This four-bolt face route lies just left of the northwest corner of the north formation, facing the parking area.

2639 **PEANUT BRITTLE 5.8 (TR)** Start 20 feet left of **Omaha Beach** and climb a flake, then up the face to the top.

2640 **OMAHA BEACH 5.8** This is an old two-bolt climb on the west face of the North Formation (right and around the corner from **The Sound Of. . .**). It is to the right of an upside-down flake.

2641 **CARAMEL CRUNCH 5.10a**

2642 **BANANA SPLITS 5.10d ★★**

2643 **ROCKY ROAD 5.10d ★**

2644 **POX ON YOU 5.11d** Pro: Thin to 2-inch camming units, three bolts.

2645 **WHIPPED TOPPING 5.11b**

CAVE CORRIDOR

2651
2652
2653

CAVE CORRIDOR – SOUTH FORMATION

See map on page 388.

2646 **RESURRECTION 5.7**

2647 **UNWED MUDDLERS 5.7**

2648 **LUST WE FORGET 5.9**

2649 **Y KNOT 5.10b ★**

2650 **WORKOUT AT THE Y 5.9 ★**

2651 **REJUVENATION 5.6**

2652 **WHAT'S LEFT 5.9**

2653 **CHOCOLATE CHIPS 5.9** This route is on the west face, around and right of **Resurrection.** Two bolts.

2654 **SHAGGY DOG 5.9** This face climb is just left of the southwest corner and right of **Chocolate Chips.** Climb past five bolts to a two-bolt belay.

2655 **SHIFTING SANDS 5.11b** This is a two-bolt climb on the east face of a boulder facing **Chocolate Chips.** There is no belay on top; downclimb the backside and belay from a tree on the ground.

JUNK CLUMP

This clump of rocks lies southeast of Cave Corridor. Map, page 388.

2656 **SOMA 5.8** This two-bolt face route lies on the grainy southwest face of Junk Clump. Finish up a chimney.

2657 **BIG BROTHER 5.9** This is a short distance left of **Soma.** Follow a right-diagonalling groove past one bolt to the upper chimney on that route.

2658 **INTO THE BLACK 5.8** A right-slanting crack system left of **Big Brother.**

GROTTO ROCK

This is the small formation next to the road at the east end of the Cave Corridor parking lot. Map, page 388.

2659 **WAIT UNTIL DARK 5.10b** This route is on the northwest arête of the formation. Climb the corner past two bolts.

CAVERN ROCK

This formation lies just east of Grotto Rock, adjacent to the road. Map, page 388.

2660 **USE A GUN, GO TO JAIL 5.9+** This three-bolt face route lies on the northwest face of Cavern Rock, just left of a low-angled chimney.

2661 **ENTER AT YOUR OWN RISK 5.9** Another three-bolt face route on the west face of Cavern Rock, about 75 feet right of previous route.

SHEEP PASS CAMPGROUND

Sheep Pass Campground lies about .75 mile further east of Cave Corridor along the Sheep Pass Loop Road. This is a group campground. A road leads about .3 mile off the Sheep Pass Loop Road to the campground.

CAMPSITE NO. 4

The following route lies behind campsite #4.

2662 **WHERE SHEEP RAN SCARED 5.10c** This 25-foot route is the overhanging flake with a crack up its middle behind site #4.

TIMELESS VOID CLUMP

Just south of campsite #3 is a boulder with three problems on its west face. West of this boulder is a short wall with several problems. Left of this is an east-facing wall.

2663 **VAINO'S RENEGADE LEAD 5.10a** This is a right-facing corner. The crux is at a steep section. RPs are handy.

2664 **BULLOCKS FASHION CENTER 5.8** This route is on a wall left and behind **This Puppy.** Follow a lieback crack that is left of a block in the center of the face.

2665 **THIS PUPPY 5.6** Climb a crack/flake up and right to a steep thin crack with jugs.

WAILING SAX WALL

This wall is the backside (west face) of the Timeless Void Clump. It is approached by scrambling up the gully behind campsite #2. Going up this gully, one passes **Sanctify Yourself** on your right and **Ripples in Time** on your left. The Wailing Sax Wall is just over the notch at the top of the gully, on one's left. Photo, page 393.

2666 **HOLY CROSS 5.10a** This obvious short crack leads to a horizontal crack is the next crack right of **Jo Mama.** It is very thin over a tricky roof.

2667 **THE MORNING AFTER 5.8** This is the next crack right. It goes over the same roof as **Holy Cross.** It is also thin and zigzags.

2668 **TAKE FIVE 5.8** This is the main system on the wall. Follow thin to double cracks through a bulge.

2669 **IN A SILENT WAY 5.11c** This climb is right of **Take Five,** and passes five bolts.

2670 **MAIDEN VOYAGE 5.10a** Climb past four bolts into a crack down and right from **In A Silent Way.**

2671 **CAROLA'S HIP 5.7** This is a wide crack just right of **Maiden Voyage.**

2672 **MISHA'S MADNESS 5.9 (TR)** Climb the shallow crack immediately right of **Carola's Hip.**

2673 **FLAKEY PUFFS FROM HELL 5.10 (TR)** A short, steep corner leads to face climbing just right of **Misha's Madness.**

2674 **BIRDLAND 5.10c** This is a roof crack 40 feet right of **Flakey Puffs from Hell.**

2675 **SATCHMO 5.8** This climb ascends cracks on the face right of the corner next to **Birdland.**

To the right of the Wailing Sax Wall is a small tower with two toprope routes.

2676 **SMALL TOWN TASTE 5.10c (TR)** This route follows a left-facing corner to a crack.

2677 **ONE STORY TOWN 5.10 (TR)** Climb the face/arête right of the preceding route.

Three crackscross from the Wailing Sax Wall.

2678 **AULD LANG SYNE 5.8** This is a crack around the corner to the left of **New Year's Quickie.**

2679 **NEW YEAR'S QUICKIE 5.7** This is an obvious hand crack.

2680 **SKIN DEEP TOWN 5.6** This is a crack system on a pinnacle to the right of **New Year's Quickie.**

2681 **TIPPLES IN RIME 5.10a (TR)** This is 30 feet left of **Holy Cross,** on the extreme left end of the Wailing Sax Wall. It is just left of **Wailing Sax** (a route with a bolt). Climb an arête/face to a small roof; continue up face.

2682 **WAILING SAX 5.9** Climb discontinuous cracks over a roof and past one bolt 10 feet right of **Tipples in Rime.**

2683 **JO MAMA 5.8** This is the crack just right of **Wailing Sax.**

2684 **RIPPLES IN TIME 5.6** Climb up a face to a finger crack just left of the notch in the gully behind campsite #2.

2685 **SANCTIFY YOURSELF 5.9** This is a two-bolt face climb on the right side of the approach gully to the Wailing Sax Wall. It is about two-thirds of the way up the gully.

2686 **TURKEY TERROR 5.9 (TR)** Walk south from campsite #1 through a pass. A small buttress is southeast of the pass. This route climbs the south face of this buttress.

2687 **PUMPKIN PIE 5.8** This route climbs a thin crack 15 feet right of **Turkey Terror.**

TELEVISION WALL

From campsite #1, one can see a vertical arête about halfway between the pass to the south and the summit to the southwest (**Prime Time**). This formation is Television Wall.

2688 **YOUNG AND THE RESTLESS 5.7 R** This is the knife-edge arête left of **Prime Time.**

2689 **MTV 5.11b (TR)** This is a short crack-to-face climb on the left side of **Prime Time.**

2690 **PRIME TIME 5.10a (TR)** Climb directly up the arête mentioned above, past a partially detached knifeblade block near the top.

2691 **MR. ROGERS 5.5 ★** ·This is a crack/face system on the left side of Television Wall, but to the right of **Prime Time.**

2692 **NIGHTLINE 5.10c ★★** This face route lies right of **Mr. Rogers** (left of **Geraldo . . .**), and has one bolt. Pro: Thin to 2 inches.

2693 **GERALDO FOLLOWS OPHRY 5.0 ★★** This crack is located just right of **Nightline** and left of a chimney, and jogs left near its top.

2694 **TV TOWER 5.9** This route lies on the main face of the tower to the right of Televisoin Wall.

HOB NOB WALL

An obvious wall with several cracks in it is southwest of campsite #1, down and right of Television Wall.

2695 **EVENING WARM-DOWN 5.2** This is a crack left of **Hob Nob.**

2696 **HOB NOB 5.6** Climb the second crack from the right.

2697 **MARKING TIME 5.8 ★★** This is the face to the right of **Hob Nob.** Pro: Thin wires.

OTHER CAMPSITE NO. 1 AREA ROUTES

The following are located on different rocks behind (near) Campsite No. 1.

2698 **FOUR OF A KIND 5.9 (TR) ★** This is on the steep patina wall to the right and facing **Marking Time.** There are four different lines that can be taken from the same anchor: The right arête, the center face, the bulge to arête, and the left-stemming corner.

2699 **SOMETHING'S BURNING 5.11b ★★★** This is an overhanging patina face with three bolts on the north face of a leaning pillar up and left of the saddle behind Campsite #1. It faces Television Wall.

2700 **FIGUREHEAD 5.9 ★** This is the light-colored, "ship-bow looking," overhanging arête up and left behind Campsite #1. Start in a crack system on lower domed face.

SMALL WORLD AREA

This small area lies about 200 feet east on Sheep Pass Loop Road past the entrance to Sheep Pass Group Campground. It is to the north of the road.

PANORAMA PILLAR

This pillar lies on the north side of the main raod, is located high on the pass, and faces west.

2701 **SOUTH FACE 5.7 (TR)**

2702 **WEST FACE 5.10b (TR)**

2703 **NORTH FACE 5.10d (TR)**

SMALL WORLD CLIFF

This is a small, black, east-facing buttress.

2704 **MR. WIZARD 5.11d (TR)** This is the steep face route just left of **Pint-Size Planet.**

2705 **PINT-SIZE PLANET 5.10a** Climb over a roof into a left-facing corner. This is 30 feet left of **Small World.**

2706 **SMALL WORLD 5.8** This route climbs a finger-to-hand crack on the buttress.

2707 **DWARF STAR 5.10c (TR)** Climb the face 12 feet right of **Small World.**

2708 **TINY TERRA 5.10b (TR)** Go up the left-leaning ramp, then up the incipient crack. This is 20 feet right of **Small World.**

Bill Leventhal on the Skinhead Arete   Photo: John Mireles

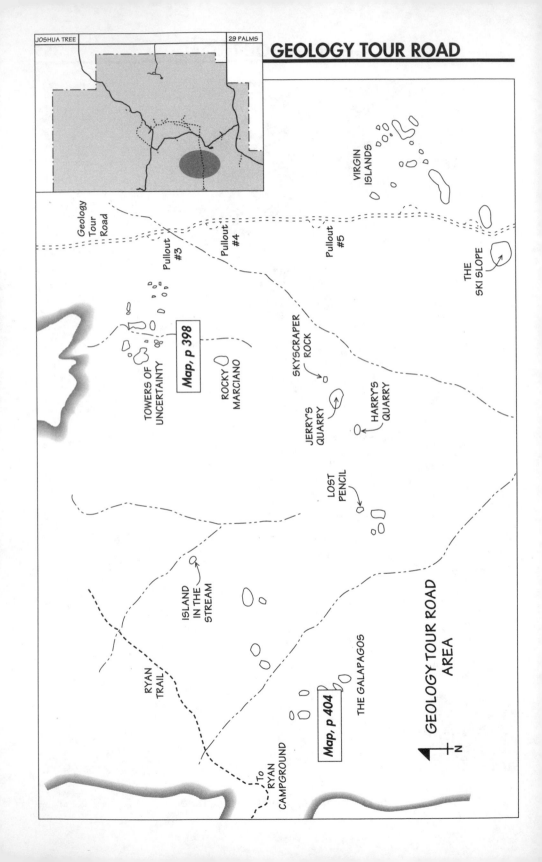

Geology
Tour
Road

Pullout #3

Pullout #4

Pullout #5

VIRGIN ISLANDS

THE SKI SLOPE

Map, p 398

TOWERS OF UNCERTAINTY

ROCKY MARCIANO

SKYSCRAPER ROCK

JERRY'S QUARRY

HARRY'S QUARRY

LOST PENCIL

ISLAND IN THE STREAM

RYAN TRAIL

To RYAN CAMPGROUND

THE GALAPAGOS

Map, p 404

GEOLOGY TOUR ROAD AREA

N

GEOLOGY TOUR ROAD

A dirt road heads south from Sheep Pass Loop Road approximately 2.5 miles east of Sheep Pass Campground. This is the Geology Tour Road, so named because of the self-guided geology tour that follows this road. Several climbing areas are located both east and west of this road. The "tour" has several marked stops, numbered sequentially; these marked stops have turnouts turn serve as approach parking for climbing areas. Reference to the marked stops is used to assist you in locating approach parking for specific areas. Map, page 396.

TOWERS OF UNCERTAINTY

This is the first area encountered on the Geology Tour Road. Park at tour marker #3 (2.8 miles down the road). The area lies to the west of the road about .3 mile; just south of a hill. As you approach the main rocks, you'll pass a number of smaller formations. The rock in this area is quite variable (poor to good).

This area has been popular with outward-bound classes and has seen a fair amount of route activity over the years. There are many other established routes that are not listed here; route information was not fully available at the time of publication. Maps, pages 396, 398.

TWO BOLT ROCK

This formation lies about 100 yards southwest of the southern part of the main rocks. The known routes lie on the east face. Map, page 398.

2709 **BRAIN FART 5.11c (TR)** A face climb by the thin seam just left of the center of the east face.

2710 **BENT OVER BACKWARDS 5.10c** This crack lies just right of the center of the east face, right of a very thin seam (**Brain Fart**).

2711 **DARRENS SCRAPE SCRAMBLE AND RAMBLE 5.6** This is the left diagonalling crack 20 feet right of **Bent Over Backwards,** and just left of a blank corner system.

2712 **FUSS RATTLE AND ROLL 5.7** This is the blank corner system about 25 feet right of **Bent Over Backwards.**

2713 **TWO BOLT WALL 5.9** Located further right of the previous climbs. Face climb past two horizontals, two bolts.

CROWS' NEST

This is the easternmost of the three northernmost rocks. The routes lie on the north face. Four easy cracks are found here, one on the northeast face and three on the north face. Map, page 398.

2714 **TRENCH CONNECTION 5.6** This is the left crack.

2715 **NO STRINGS ATTACHED 5.6** This is the next crack to the right.

2716 **CROW'S FEET 5.7** Second from the left.

2717 **EATING CROW 5.5** The rightmost crack.

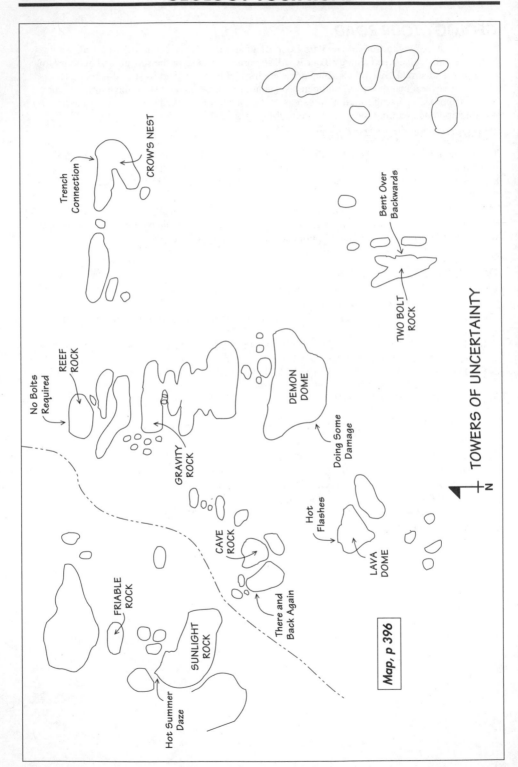

TOWERS OF UNCERTAINTY

N

CROW'S NEST

Trench Connection

Bent Over Backwards

TWO BOLT ROCK

REEF ROCK

No Bolts Required

DEMON DOME

GRAVITY ROCK

Doing Some Damage

Hot Flashes

CAVE ROCK

LAVA DOME

FRIABLE ROCK

There and Back Again

SUNLIGHT ROCK

Hot Summer Daze

Map, p 396

REEF ROCK

This formation is westmost of the three northern formations. It has several horizontal cracks. It is also the northern part of a series of formations separated by small canyons/gullys. Map, page 398.

2718 **I SHOULD BE DANCIN' 5.7**
2719 **CAT'S MEOW 5.9 ★**
2720 **NO BOLTS REQUIRED 5.10d R ★★**
2721 **TRAIL OF TIERS 5.10a ★★**

GRAVITY ROCK

This formation is one of the series of rocks that lies south of Reef Rock, separated by small canyons and gullys. The following routes are approached from the west side. The rock is distinguished by a wide chimney/gully with large boulders sitting atop it. Three seams are on the south face to the left of the chimney. Map, page 398.

2722 **LEFT OF CENTER　5.10b (TR)**　The left seam.

2723 **CENTER OF GRAVITY　5.10c (TR)**　The center seam.

2724 **RIGHT OF CENTER　5.11b (TR)**　The right seam.

2725 **CAVERNA MAGICA　5.10d R**　This is the face inside the chimney. Start below the first large chockstone and finish to its right.

DEMON DOME

This is the large formation at the southern end of the main north-south band of rocks; it is somewhat separated from the other formations to the north and has a patina north face with good route potential. The only known route is on the southwest face of the rock. Map, page 398.

2726 **DOIN' SOME DAMAGE　5.10c**　This is the left-leaning handcrack on the southwest side of Demon Dome. A horizontal crack down low gives access to the crack.

LAVA DOME

LAVA DOME

This is the dark-colored formation that lies southwest of Gravity Rock and west of the southernmost rock of the north-south series of rocks (with Reef Rock at its northern end). Map, page 398.

2727 **NOTHING TO FEAR 5.6**

2728 **BUT FEAR ITSELF 5.8**

2729 **HOT FLASHES 5.11c** Two bolts.

2730 **STANDING OVATION 5.10a** Climb up a face to a thin crack that is right and around the corner from the previous routes (on the west face).

2731 **THE RIGHT HAND OF LIGHT 5.10c (TR)** The steep face to the right of **Standing Ovation** on the west face.

CAVE ROCK
This small formation lies 120 feet almost directly north of Lava Dome (it is actually three separate small rocks). The west face has four cracks close together. The formation is named for the cave-like feature at the base of the north face. Map, page 398.

CAVE ROCK – WEST FACE
2732 **THERE AND BACK AGAIN 5.4 R ★**   This is the obvious protruding dike on the northwest corner.
2733 **FRESH GARLIC 5.9**   The first crack right of **There And Back Again.**
2734 **SEED OF IRONY 5.10a**   This climbs the parallel cracks to the right of **Fresh Garlic.**

CAVE ROCK – NORTH FACE
2735 **YOUNG SOLE REBEL 5.4**   Start left of the "cave," and follow the left crack above.
2736 **BROKEN NOSES 5.3**   The face/crack above and right of the "cave." The direct start is 5.8.

SUNLIGHT ROCK
This large formation is just northwest of Cave Rock, and is part of a series of rocks that form the westernmost part of the Towers of Uncertainty area. The known routes lie on the northwest sid of the rock. Map, page 398.

2737 **WONDERFUL WOBBLE 5.8**   These cracks lie just left of northwest arête, on the north face and to the left of **Hot Summer Daze.**
2738 **HOT SUMMER DAZE 5.10a**   This is the dihedral leading to a small roof on the northwest arête.
2739 **SIT UP AND THINK 5.9+**   This is to the right of **Hot Summer Daze.** Climb up a face past a horizonatl finger crack, then past a small roof.

FRIABLE ROCK
This is the small formation directly north of the northwest part of Sunlight Rock. Map, page 398.
2740 **RAP OR SNAP 5.7**   Climb a corner with jugs and buckets to a small roof on the southwest face of the rock.

ROCKY MARCIANO
This formation is located approximately .6 mile west of the Geology Tour Road. Park at Tour Marker #4 (3.1 mile south of Sheep Pass Loop Road). Map, page 396.
2741 **SIMPLE SIMON 5.11c ★**   The overhanging thin crack on the east face of Rocky Marciano.
2742 **DIGITIZER 5.11b ★★**   This is a clean, overhanging fingertip dihedral in the boulders at the southeast corner of the Rocky Marciano clump. FA: Alan Nelson and Tom Herbert, December 1986.

ISLAND IN THE STREAM
This formation is about 1 mile west of Rocky Marciano. The routes are on the north face. Map, page 396.
2743 **MESSAGE IN A BOTTLE 5.10c**   This is the leftmost line. The route has three bolts.
2744 **MIDDLE OF SOMEWHERE 5.12a**   This is the direct (left) finish to **Message in a Bottle.**
2745 **ADRIFT 5.11b**   The next bolted line to the right, with four bolts. It joins **Message in a Bottle** for its regular finish.
2746 **SHARKS IN THE WATER 5.10c**   This is a two-bolt climb right of **Adrift.**
2747 **WHISPER WHEN YOU SCREAM 5.9**   The farthest route right, this climb has three bolts.

ROCKY MARCIANO

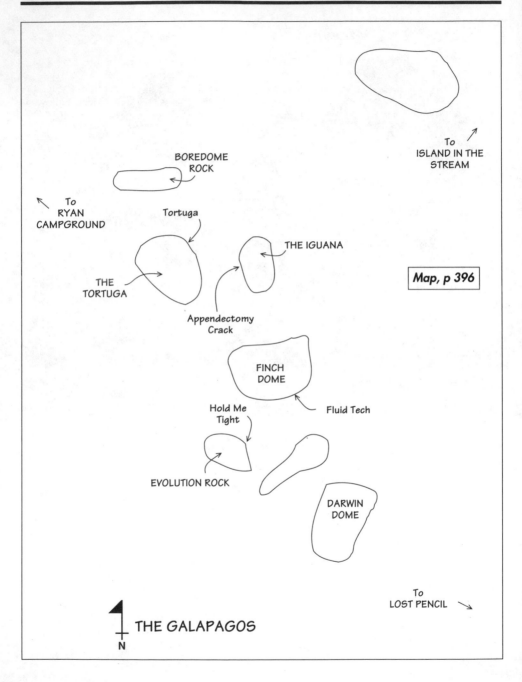

To
ISLAND IN THE
STREAM

BOREDOME
ROCK

To
RYAN
CAMPGROUND

Tortuga

THE IGUANA

Map, p 396

THE
TORTUGA

Appendectomy
Crack

FINCH
DOME

Hold Me
Tight

Fluid Tech

EVOLUTION ROCK

DARWIN
DOME

To
LOST PENCIL

THE GALAPAGOS

N

THE GALAPAGOS

This is one of the more remote climbing spots in the monument. These formations lie 1.7 miles west of Rocky Marciano and .8 mile southwest of Islands In the Stream. There are two possible approaches. The first is from Geology Tour Road near the Rocky Marciano or Jerry's Quarry parking areas (2.5 mile hike), and the second, probably the most easy approach, is from Ryan Campground. Hike approximately 2.5 miles along the Ryan Campground trail to Queen Valley, where the trail takes a sharp turn to the northeast. Head straight (southeast) for about .3 mile to the rocks. Maps, pages 396, 404.

BOREDOME ROCK

This small formation lies northwest of The Tortuga, closest to the Ryan Campground trail.

2748 **ENNUI 5.10b** This is a three-bolt face route in the northwest face of the rock.

THE TORTUGA

See map on page 404.

2749 **BARN BURNING 5.10b ★** This crack system, with one bolt, is on a large buttress on the west face of The Tortuga.

2750 **JABBERWOCKY 5.9** Face climb past one bolt toan obvious offwidth on the north face of the formation.

2751 **ELEMENTARY JAMMING 5.5 ★★** This is the clean hand crack left of **Jabberwocky.**

2752 **TORTUGA 5.11b ★★** A nice hand-and-finger crack on the east face of The Tortuga formation. It is the rightmost of three obvious crack systems on the east face.

2753 **GRIM ROPER 5.10c ★★** This is the leftmost of the three crack systems.

THE IGUANA

This formation is east of the The Tortuga. It is marked by two striking cracks on its west face. Map, page 404.

2754 **APPENDECTOMY CRACK 5.10d ★★★** The rightmost of the two cracks on the west face. It starts as an offwidth and exits with an overhanging hand crack.

2755 **MINE SHAFT 5.9 ★** This route lies 50 feet right of **Appendectomy Crack.** It is a finger crack in a right-facing corner leading to a chimney slot.

FINCH DOME

This formation lies south of The Iguana and southeast of The Tortuga. The southeast corner of the formation has an incredible thin hands crack. Map, page 404.

2756 **ONTOLOGY RECAPITULATES PHYLOGONY 5.11b A1 ★★★** This is the thin hands crack on the southeast corner of the formation. Climb the crack (5.11a) to a bolt belay. Aid off the anchor and face climb (5.11b) up past three bolts on face to the top.

EVOLUTION ROCK

This small formation is southwest of Finch Dome. It has one recorded route on the northeast corner. Map, page 404.

2757 **HOLD ME TIGHT 5.10d R ★★** This is the three-bolt face route on the northeast corner of Evolution Rock.

2758 **THE KLANSMAN 5.7** Two cracks forming an "X" are 30 feet to the right of **Hold Me Tight.** Climb the lower left past the upper right crack.

DARWIN DOME

This formation lies southeast of all the other formations listed above, and is distinguished by a smooth, low-angled face on the northwest side of the dome. The known routes are located on this low-angle slab. Map, page 404.

2759 **CONCEIVED IN IDAHO 5.8** This one-bolt face route passes several chickenheads on the left side of the smooth slab.

2760 **LUST IN THE LOVE DEN 5.6 ★★** This is the clean flake/crack in the middle of the northeast face.

2761 **CONSTRUCTION BLUES 5.6** This is the one-bolt face route on the righthand part of the northeast face.

JERRY'S QUARRY AND LOST PENCIL AREAS

To approach Jerry's Quarry and/or the Lost Pencil areas, park at tour marker #5 (3.7 mile south of Sheep Pass Road). Jerry's Quarry lies .75 mile west of the road, the Lost Pencil 1.3 mile west of the road. Map, page 396.

SKYSCRAPER ROCK

This small formation lies 80 yards northeast of Jerry's Quarry. Descent is by rappel. Map, page 396.

2762 **HOLIDAY IN DETROIT   5.10b**   This is the obvious left-leaning crack in a corner on the west side of the rock.

2763 **CROSS FIRE   5.12a R ★**   This three-bolt climb on the southwest face heads up and left next to a seam.

2764 **THE RUSTLER   5.11c ★★**   An undercling to the left leads to face climbing past one bolt. It is right of **Cross Fire,** on the south face.

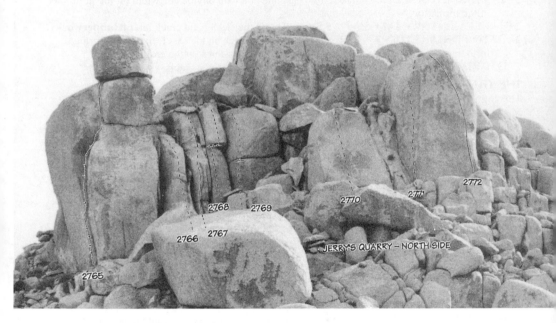

JERRY'S QUARRY

Jerry's Quarry is a complex set of boulders and rocks on sitting high off the desert floor about .75 mile west of the road. Map, page 396.

2765 **ALI SHUFFLE   5.10b ★**   Pro: To 4 inches.
2766 **TO HOLD AND TO HAVE   5.12c (TR) ★★**
2767 **ZEN AND THE ART OF PLACEMENT   5.11c ★★**
2768 **SPANK THE MONKEY   5.10b ★★**
2769 **IGOR'S FAILED ROAD TRIP   5.11a ★★**
2770 **TOFFIED EAR WAX   5.9**
2771 **ELEPHANT WALK   5.11d ★★★**   Five bolts.
2772 **EQUINOX   5.12c ★★★★★**
2773 **HUEVOS RANCHEROS   5.10b**   This hand-traversing face climb going up and right is on the first small group of rocks southeast of **Equinox.**

HARRY'S QUARRY

This formation lies about 300 yards southwest of Jerry's Quarry. The following routes are on the north side of the summit block, just left of a short summit dihedral. A two-bolt rap anchor is on top.

2774   **POKIN' A GOPHER**   **5.9+** ★   The center of the north face of the summit block. Pro: Four bolts.

2775   **DRAW THE LINE**   **5.10a (TR)**   Traverse left to a thin dike just left of **Pokin' A Gopher.**

2776   **MILK ARETE**   **5.10d** ★★★   This four-bolt arête lies on the southwest side of this formation.

LOST PENCIL

This balanced pillar of rock lies about 1.3 mile west of the road. The first ascent of the Lost Pencil was made in 1956 by Don Cornell and John Merriam, via a bolt ladder on the east side. Another bolt ladder is located on the north side. Other climbs have been done in the group of rocks near the Lost Pencil; no information was available at the time of this writing. Map, page 396.

2777   **INDIAN GIVER**   **5.11a** ★★   This route climbs the west face of the pillar.

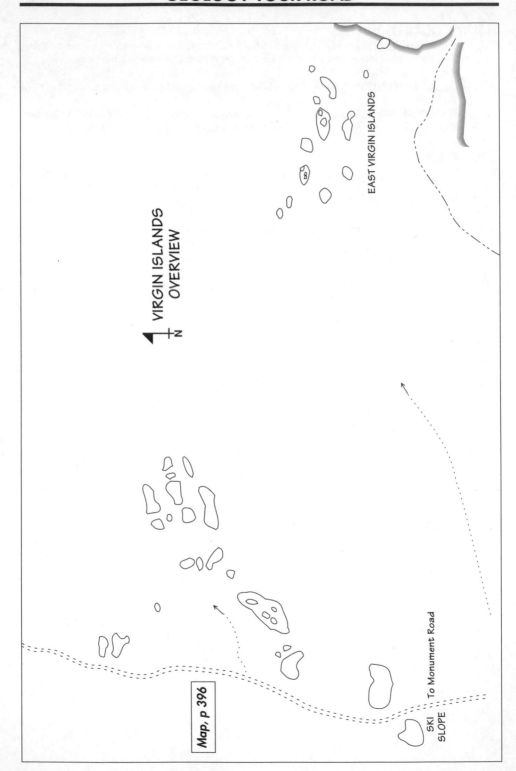

VIRGIN ISLANDS OVERVIEW

N

EAST VIRGIN ISLANDS

Map, p 396

To Monument Road

SKI SLOPE

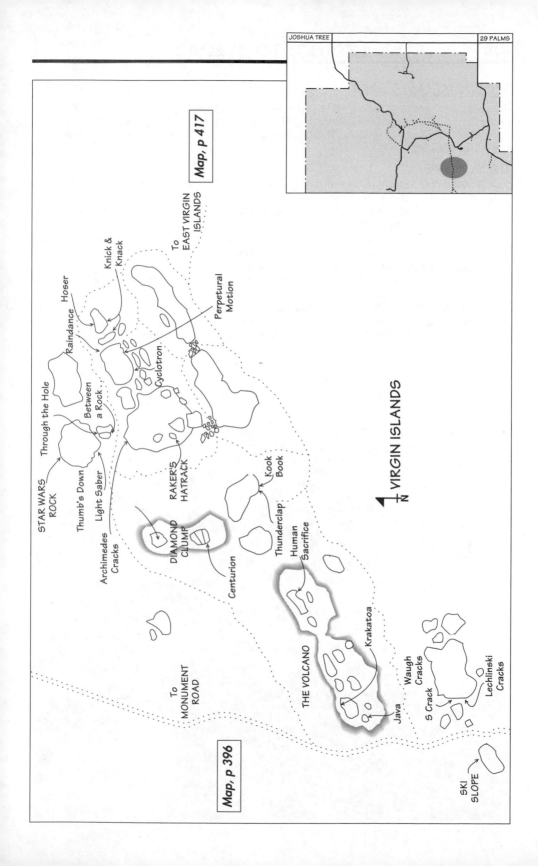

Map, p 417

VIRGIN ISLANDS

N

To EAST VIRGIN ISLANDS

Knick & Knack

Raindance   Hoser

Through the Hole

STAR WARS ROCK

Thumb's Down

Between a Rock

Light Saber

Archimedes Cracks

Perpetural Motion

Cyclotron

RAKER'S HATRACK

Kook Book

DIAMOND CLUMP

Centurion

Thunderclap

Human Sacrifice

To MONUMENT ROAD

THE VOLCANO

Krakatoa

Java

Waugh Cracks

S Crack

Lechlinski Cracks

SKI SLOPE

Map, p 396

VIRGIN ISLANDS AREA

Several piles of rock lie to the east of the parking spot for the Lost Pencil area (about .75 mile south on the Geology Tour Road from Lost Pencil parking and 4.5 miles south of the Sheep Pass Loop Road). These are the Virgin Islands. The East Virgin Islands are about 1.3 mile east of the road. Maps, pages 408, 409.

THE SKI SLOPE

This formation lies about 100 yards southwest of and across the Geology Tour Road from the **Lechlinski Cracks.** The known routes lie on the northwest side of the summit pillar and also on the slab facing northwest to the right of the summit block. The rap-off would be easier if bolts were installed. Maps, pages 396, 408.

2778 **EIGHT SIGNS OF A SHAKY MARRIAGE   5.10d** ★★ Climb the left side of the northwest face past three bolts. Pro: Thin to 2 inches.

2779 **MEET JOHN DOE   5.10c R** ★★ Start right and around the corner from the previous route. Face climb up and left onto the northwest face, then go straight up past two bolts. Pro: To 1 inch, three bolts.

2780 **RANDY THE RIVETER   5.8** This one-bolt route is on the center of the slab to the right and around the corner from the northwest face of the summit block.

2781 **RECONSTRUCTIVE SURGERY   5.10a** ★ This is a two-bolt route on the arête/slab to the right of the preceding climb.

VIRGIN ISLES

2784

2786 – 2789

2785

2783   2782

LECHLINSKI CRACK FORMATION

The formation furthest to the south has two parallel crack/flakes on the west face; these are the **Lechlinski Cracks.** Map, page 409.

2782 **LECHLINSKI CRACKS 5.9 ★** Start either side
2783 **WOODWARD CRACK 5.12a ★★** Pro: Thin to 2 inches, one bolt.
2784 **S CRACK 5.11a ★**
2785 **VOGEL CRACK 5.8**
2786 **WAUGH CRACK 5.10b ★★**
2787 **BLACK NIPPLE FETISH 5.11b ★★** Four bolts.
2788 **ELEVENFALL FACE 5.11d (TR)**
2789 **ROBERTS CRACK 5.9 ★** This climbs the lefthand thin crack.
2790 **KIDDIE CORNER 5.9** Climbs a nice 30-foot long dihedral hidden down low.

THE VOLCANO

This large rubble pile is northeast of the formation with **Lechlinski Cracks.** Map, page 409.

2791   **KRAKATOA   5.9**   This climbs a flake/crack/chimney system on the north side of the large summit block.

2792   **FRAT BOYS IN THE GYM   5.11b (TR)** ★   This climbs the overhanging south face of the formation containing **Krakatoa.**

2793   **JAVA   5.9+**   This is the chimney/slot just above the Volcano Boulder. It is just west of the large summit boulder.

VOLCANO BOULDER

2794   **HOT LAVA   5.11a** ★★★

2795   **OBSIDIAN   5.12b (TR)** ★★   Need small wires.

2796   **MAGMA   5.11d (TR)**

2797   **NO NUTS, NO HUEVOS   5.9**   This is on the south side of the formation and on the west side of the pass that splits The Volcano clump. It is a five-bolt face leading to a rappel bolt.

2798   **THE GO-GOS ON QUAALUDES   5.10c** ★★   This is directly north of **No Nuts, No Huevos.** It has five bolts and moves across an offwidth crack from left to right.

ROAD KILL ROCK

This is the large block just below **No Nuts, No Huevos** (north) and east of **The Go-Gos On Quaaludes.**

2799   **HAIR ON MY TREAD   5.11b** ★★   Climb the south face of the Road Kill Rock past three bolts.

2800   **SHARP DESIRE   5.8**   Another five-bolt route on an east-facing wall. This is on the southwest side of the pass that splits The Volcano.

HUMAN SACRIFICE BOULDER
This is the large, square boulder to the right (east) of Volcano Boulder. Map, page 409.

2801 **HUMAN SACRIFICE 5.11c** This climbs an overhanging hand and fist crack on the southeast face of the summit boulder, on the adjacent rubble pile.

2802 **DEFENDERS OF THE FARCE 5.10a** Climb the northwest face of the **Human Sacrifice** boulder past one bolt.

2803 **DICTATORS OF ANARCHY 5.12c ★★★★★** This route is located on the south arête of the **Human Sacrifice** boulder.

2804 **NEW WORLD ORDER 5.13b ★★★★★** Just right of **Dictators of Anarchy.** Pro: Six bolts; chain anchor.

The following two routes lie on the south end of a rubble pile north east of The Volcano. Map, page 409.

2805 **THUNDERCLAP 5.10a** The direct finish is 5.10d.

2806 **KOOK BOOK 5.10c**

A conglomeration of rubble piles lies east of The Volcano about 400 yards. A high, level valley rests in the midst of this group. There are two approaches into this valley (see photo). A pillar called Raker's Hatrack is on the northwest side of these rubble piles.

2807 **THE CAT IN THE HAT 5.10a** This is a steep three-bolt climb on a pillar 150 feet left of **Raker's Blaring Hat Rack.**

2808 **CHOLLA CRACK 5.10b** This is a short crack on the tier below **The Cat in the Hat.**

2809 **RAKER'S BLARING HAT RACK 5.10d ★★** This face climb acends the northwest side of the pillar, up a left-leaning dike system and past a black knob to the top. Rappel off with no anchors by stringing a rope over the top.

2810 **EDGE OF THE KNIFE 5.8 ★★** This climbs the northeast arête of the pillar, with no protection.

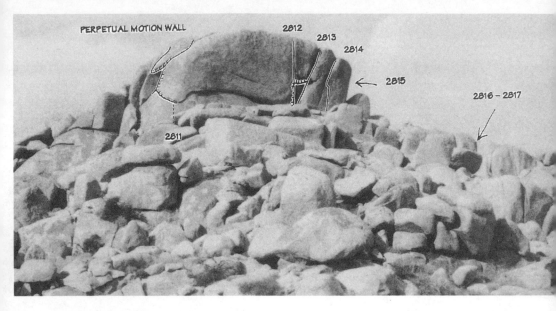

PERPETUAL MOTION WALL

This wall lies on the north side of the high valley mentioned previously. Map, page 409.

2811 **CYCLOTRON   5.8 to 5.10d**   The entry move is height dependent. Turn the roof on the left (5.10c), or to the right (5.7).

2812 **PERPETUAL MOTION   5.10d ★★★**

2813 **GROSS CHIMNEY   5.10a**

2814 **I EAT CANNIBALS   5.10d ★**

2815 **RAINDANCE   5.8**   Climb the overhanging corner to the top of the Perpetual Motion Wall.

The next two routes lie in the corridor about 75 feet east of the Perpetual Motion Wall.

2816 **KNICK   5.10a**   Climb a dihedral on the west (left) side of the corridor.

2817 **KNACK   5.10c ★★**   This is the finger crack on the right (east) side of the corridor.

Head north through the corridor to an open area. This forms the north side of the Perpetual Motion Rubble Pile.

2818 **LEAN TWO (left 5.8; right 5.10; both 5.9)**   These twin cracks lie east on the north side of the Perpetual Motion Piles.

2819 **HOSER   5.6**   This is a right-facing corner to the right of **Lean Two.**

2820 **GEORGIA O'KEEFE   5.10b**   A pillar lies against the face about 60 feet right of **Hoser.** This climbs the outer face of the pillar past three bolts.

2821 **LEFT ARCHIMEDES' CRACK   5.11a**   This route is the lefthand crack of two short cracks directly opposite (south) of **Hoser.** They lie on the western end of the north side of the Perpetual Motion Rubble Pile.

2822 **RIGHT ARCHIMEDES' CRACK   5.9**

STAR WARS ROCK

This rock lies north of the Perpetual Motion Rubble Pile and is easily distinguished by its overhanging south face and the presence of a large split boulder to its south. Map, page 409.

2823 **THUMBS DOWN LEFT 5.9** ★★

2824 **CEDRIC'S DEEP SEA FISH MARKET 5.10d** ★★ Pro: Many .75 to 1.5 inches.

2825 **LIGHT SABRE 5.10b** ★★★★

2826 **APOLLO 5.12c** ★★★

2827 **THE LEMMING 5.10d** This climbs the arête across from **Apollo** via a steep layback and finishes with a mantel.

2828 **THROUGH THE HOLE AND UP THE WALL 5.2**

2829 **BETWEEN A ROCK AND A HARD PLACE 5.10b**

2830 **TWO BLIND MICE 5.10** This route ascends a flared bombay chimney leading to a hand crack on the northeast face of the rock.

DIAMOND CLUMP

The Diamond Clump is the pile of rocks that lies west of Star Wars Rock and the Perpetual Motion Piles. Two large blocks sit atop the piles. The first (northern) block is the Diamond; the southern block is the Centurion. Map, page 409.

2831 **GEMSTONER 5.10a**   Climb the two-bolt face on the north face.

2832 **SPARKLE 5.8 (TR)**   Climb the arête to the right of **Gemstone.**

2833 **TEENAGE ENEMA 5.9 (TR)**

2834 **KILLER PUSSY 5.11a (TR)**

2835 **NURSES IN BONDAGE 5.9 (TR)**

2836 **JUST FOR THE THRILL OF IT 5.11a (TR)**   This climbs the face left of **Clearasil.**

2837 **CLEARASIL   left 5.8; center 5.7; right 5.2 (TR)**

2838 **CENTURION 5.10d**

2839 **RING OF FIRE 5.11b**   This route climbs a dike on a formation below **Centurion.** There are three bolts.

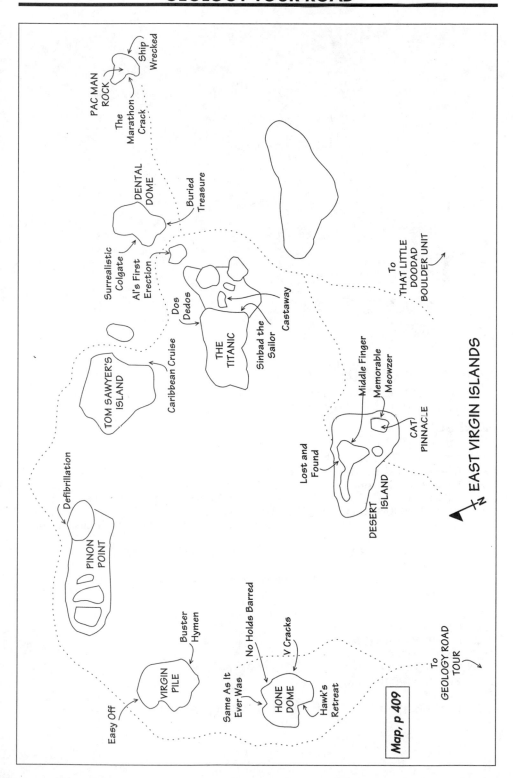

PAC MAN ROCK

Ship Wrecked

The Marathon Crack

DENTAL DOME

Buried Treasure

Surrealistic Colgate

Al's First Erection

Dos Dedos

THE TITANIC

Sinbad the Sailor

Castaway

TOM SAWYER'S ISLAND

Caribbean Cruise

Defibrillation

PINON POINT

Middle Finger

Memorable Meowzer

CAT PINNACLE

Lost and Found

DESERT ISLAND

Buster Hymen

VIRGIN PILE

Easy Off

Same As It Ever Was

No Holds Barred

V Cracks

HONE DOME

Hawk's Retreat

To THAT LITTLE DOODAD BOULDER UNIT

EAST VIRGIN ISLANDS

N

To GEOLOGY ROAD TOUR

Map, p 409

EAST VIRGIN ISLANDS

The East Virgin Islands lie almost directly east (and a little south) of the Virgin Islands. They lie about one mile east of the Geology Tour Road. Map, page 417.

HONE DOME

Map, page 417.

2840   **HAWKS RETREAT   5.10a**

2841   **DIAPER CHALLENGE   5.11c**   Five bolts.

2842   **V CRACKS   5.8 (both)**

2842A **GOOFY ARETE   5.10c**   This three-bolt face route is just right of **V Cracks.**

2843   **NO HOLDS BARRED   5.9+ (TR)**   This is a face climb 20 feet to the right of **V Cracks.**

2844   **KLEPTOMANIA   5.10a**   This face climb is on an arête just right of **No Holds Barred.** Three bolts.

2845   **SAME AS IT EVER WAS   5.9**   Start this crack in a corner around to the right of **Kleptomania.**

2846   **NO BOLD HARD   5.10d   This is the steep thin crack on the north face.**

VIRGIN PILE

Map, page 417.

2847   **ONE WAY UP   5.7**

2848   **GNARLY   5.10a (TR)**

2849   **RAD   5.9 (TR)**

2850   **TUBULAR   5.9 (TR)**

2851   **BITCHIN'   5.10b (TR)**

2852   **EASY OFF   5.6**

2853   **BUSTER HYMEN   5.9**   This route climbs the left-slanting crack that starts near a small roof.

PINON POINT

2854 **DEFIBRILLATION 5.10a** Climbs a short ugly crack on the back side of a boulder. Map, page 417.

TOM SAWYER'S ISLAND

2855 **CARIBBEAN CRUISE 5.11c ★★★** This is on the east face. Climb a shallow thin crack to a ledge, traverse left, then head up a crack that goes straight then slants right. Map, page 417.

2857

THE TITANIC

2856

THE TITANIC

Map, page 417.

2856 **SINBAD THE SAILOR 5.10c (TR)**

2857 **CASTAWAY 5.11c** Climb the roof crack formed by split boulders.

2858 **DOS DEDOS 5.4** Climb a low-angled crack above and to the right of **Castaway.**

2859 **SCOPE & HOPE 5.10b** Climbs a crack on the lower northeast side of Tom Sawyer's Island.

SNORKLE DOME
This formation lies in line with and halfway between Dental Dome and The Titanic. Map, page 417.

2860 **AL'S FIRST ERECTION 5.9** Located on the east side of Snorkle Dome. Climb up a crack to a horizontal break/headwall, then up the long buttress. Pro: To 2.5 inches, three bolts, two-bolt rap/belay anchor.

DENTAL DOME
Map, page 417.

2861 **SURREALISTIC COLGATE 5.10d R ★** Climbs the dihedral.

2862 **BURIED TREASURE 5.11c ★★** A very thin crack on the south face of Dental Dome.

PAC MAN ROCK
This small rock lies on the hillside about 150 yards east of Dental Dome. Map, page 417.

2863 **WIND SPRINT 5.9** Climb a leaning offwidth on the north side of the rock.

2864 **FLAKES OF GRASP 5.10c (TR)** Ascend the right-facing flakes just right of **Wind Sprint.**

2865 **SHIP WRECKED 5.12c** (boulder problem) This is the thin crack directly opposite **Marathon Crack** (which passes all the way through the formation).

2866 **THE MARATHON CRACK 5.12a** This is the thin crack on the southwest side of Pac Man Rock.

ORIENT ROCK
This formation is above and to the south of Pac Man Rock.

2867 **GIVEN UP FOR DEAD 5.10d** This is the slanting, overhanging crack on the north face of the rock.

2868 **MISSING IN ACTION 5.10d (TR)** This crack splits the east face.

DESERT ISLAND

Map, page 417.

2869 **LOST AND FOUND 5.7** This rather inobvious route climbs a thin crack just left of the chimney/gully system on the north side of Desert Island.

2870 **THE THUMB 5.6**

2871 **MIDDLE FINGER 5.7**

2872 **SPLIT MITTEN 5.6**

2873 **FUMBLERS BELOW THE ROOF 5.10c**

2874 **RUMBLERS BELOW THE FOOF 5.3** This climbs an easy crack left of **Fumblers Below the Roof.**

CAT PINNACLE

This is a large, flat-topped boulder just southeast of Desert Island. Map, page 417.

2875 **MEMORIAL MEOWZER 5.10c** Face climb past four bolts on the southeast face.

2876 **RONNIE AND CLYDE 5.11b (TR)** Climb the southwest arête left of **Memorial Meowzer.**

THAT LITTLE DOODAD BOULDER UNIT

This boulder lies on the hillside about 200 yard west of Pac Man Rock.

2877 **DIKE DA DOODAD 5.10c** Climb a dike past two bolts.

SQUAW TANK

Squaw Tank is approximately 1.25 mile south of the Virgin Islands on the east side of the Geology Tour Road. A small parking area is located here.

2878 **PICKPOCKET 5.6** A wall of giant solution pockets are on the left side looking east from the Squaw Tank parking area. Climb this wall with no protection..

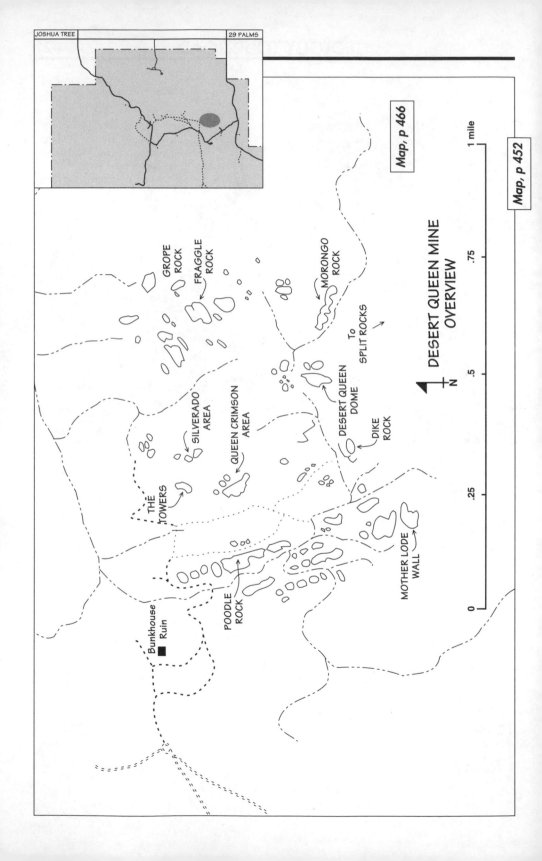

Map, p 466

Map, p 452

JOSHUA TREE

29 PALMS

GROPE ROCK

FRAGGLE ROCK

MORONGO ROCK

To SPLIT ROCKS

SILVERADO AREA

QUEEN CRIMSON AREA

DESERT QUEEN DOME

DIKE ROCK

THE TOWERS

MOTHER LODE WALL

POODLE ROCK

Bunkhouse Ruin

DESERT QUEEN MINE OVERVIEW

N

0   .25   .5   .75   1 mile

PINTO QUEEN AREA
DESERT QUEEN MINE AREA

The Desert Queen Mine was discovered in 1894 by Frank James, a mine worker at the Lost Horse Mine. Soon after the discovery, James was shot by Charles Martin, one of Jim McHaney's "Gang" members. McHaney took over the mining claim, until a bank foreclosed on it in 1896. McHaney reportedly paid Martin $4,700 to shoot James. The mine operated off and on in later years, ownership changing hands several times. Bill Keys aquired ownership several times, and the mine served as the focal point of greed and crime until the 1930s. A number of mine shafts (sealed with metal grating by the Park Service) and mining relics are found throughout this area. Trails and old roads crisscross the hills.

A dirt road heads to the north from the Sheep Pass Loop Road at the point where the Geology Tour Road heads south. Follow this road for approximately 3 miles to a parking area/trailhead. All routes in this area are approached from this point. However, the Fraggle Rock Area also may be approached from the Split Rocks/Loveland area.

From the parking area head east on a closed road/trail for about 300 yards. A small ruin of a stone bunkhouse below and to the right of the trail. Take an old road/trail south down the hillside here; it eventually meets up with a larger road that heads into the large wash (Gold Dust Gulch) below. Most descriptions for approaches will presume you are at Gold Dust Gulch.

The Fraggle Rock, Towers and Silverado areas are approached via a trail (the North Trail) that heads east from the point you enter Gold Dust Gulch. From Gold Dust Gulch, take the upper old road heading up (and north) on the east side of the canyon. Head up a steep gully just past some pump machinery and small cliffs; this leads to the northern portion of a high plateau above (east of) Gold Dust Gulch. Head east along the trail, over the ridges of the hillsides to the east. This trail also can be used to access Queen Crimson Dome and Deception Rocks.

To approach the remainder of the formations, head south along Gold Dust Gulch; directions are given accordingly. Maps, pages 422, 424.

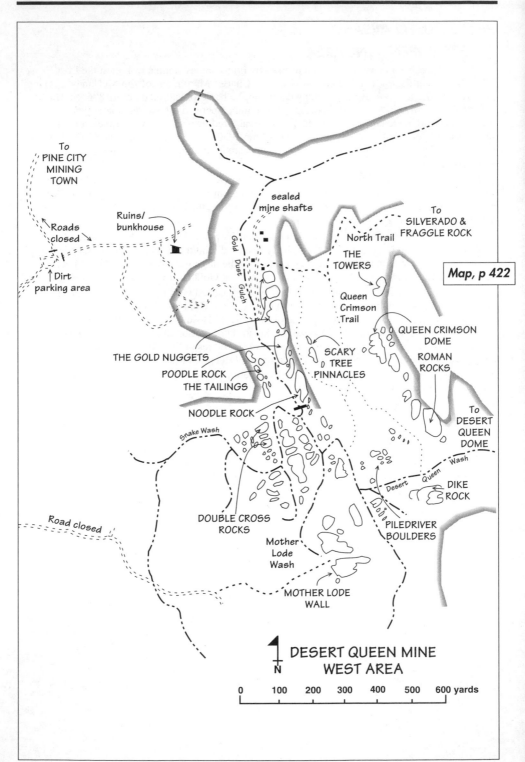

To
PINE CITY
MINING
TOWN

Roads
closed

Ruins/
bunkhouse

Dirt
parking area

sealed
mine shafts

To
SILVERADO &
FRAGGLE ROCK

North Trail

THE
TOWERS

Gold Dust Gulch

Queen
Crimson
Trail

QUEEN CRIMSON
DOME

ROMAN
ROCKS

THE GOLD NUGGETS

SCARY
TREE
PINNACLES

POODLE ROCK
THE TAILINGS

NOODLE ROCK

To
DESERT
QUEEN
DOME

Snake Wash

Desert Queen Wash

DIKE
ROCK

Road closed

DOUBLE CROSS
ROCKS

PILEDRIVER
BOULDERS

Mother
Lode
Wash

MOTHER LODE
WALL

DESERT QUEEN MINE
WEST AREA

N

0 100 200 300 400 500 600 yards

Map, p 422

GOLD DUST GULCH AREA

The following routes and formations lie along the eastern (west-facing) side of Gold Dust Gulch. They are described in the order in which they are encountered as you walk south in Gold Dust Gulch. Maps, pages 422, 424.

THE GOLD NUGGETS

These are the varied and broken formations that lie north of Poodle Rock (a dark formation dropping down into the wash 100 yards to the south). They are on the east side of the gulch. Map, page 424.

2879 **FREE FOR A FEE 5.10c**

2880 **FEAR OF MUSIC 5.11b** Pro: To 2 inches, nine bolts.

2881 **ONCE IN A LIFETIME 5.7** Located up and to the right of previous route. Start on an arête, the head up and right. Pro: Five bolts.

THE TAILINGS

This short cliff band lies on the west side of Gold Dust Gulch (facing east) and has numerous cracks and short face possibilities. It extends roughly opposite the southern part of The Gold Nuggets and Poodle Rock. Map, page 424.

2882 **TAUNTING FEAR 5.11d ★** This roof, which leads to a bolted face and bolt anchor, is on the right side of a narrow corridor near the northern end of The Tailings.

2883 **BULBISNESS 5.11b (TR) ★** This route lies opposite the southern part of Poodle Rock, and climbs a pocketed face to a roof with a crack. Bolt anchor.

POODLE ROCK

A large black face with several overhangs drops straight into the wash on the east side of Gold Dust Gulch, 100 yards south of where the trail/road enters the canyon. This is Poodle Rock. Maps, pages 422, 424.

2884 **SHOCK THE POODLE 5.9 ★** This route follows a large dike slanting up and right.

NOODLE ROCK

This formation is really a series of faces/cliffs on the east side of Gold Dust Gulch 125 yards south of Poodle Rock. The following routes are about 250 yards south of where the trail/road enters the canyon, and about 50 yards north of a stone dam across the wash. The face has several thin, vertical dike systems. Map, page 424.

2885   **HOUSES IN MOTION   5.10a ★**   This route goes up thin dikes on the left past four bolts to a roof. A two-bolt anchor/rap is below the roof.

2886   **LISTENING WIND   5.10c**   Located 15 feet right of above route. Climb past three bolts to ledge with two rap/anchor bolts.

DOUBLE CROSS ROCKS

These rocks lie on either side of the "S"-shaped wash that branches off Gold Dust Gulch just south of the dam. Map, page 424.

2887   **ROSE PARADE   5.8 ★**   This route lies on the east face of one of the first rocks encountered on the west side of the wash after making the "S"-turn. It is a bolted, bucketed face to a bolt anchor/rap.

MOTHER LODE WALL

From the parking area, continue up the road past a locked gate for about 1 mile. You'll see this wall off to the left, across a small valley. Map, page 424.

2888   **THIN IS IN   5.9**   Climb a vertical thin crack on a slab left of the main west face.

2889   **MY HUBBY IS CHUBBY   5.8+**   Climb the slab 100 feet left of **Thin is In** past a bolt into a corner.

2890   **LEAN AND SCREAM   5.11a R**   This is a vertical series of dikes on the left side of a large corridor. It is 50 feet left of **Thin is In.**

2891   **FAT IS WHERE IT'S AT   5.8**   Climb the crack just right of the chimney right of **Thin is In.**

2892   **MOTHER LODE   5.10b**   Climb a right-slanting dike to a bolt right of the previous routes, then up a steep crack.

2893   **AN UNRULY CAMEL   5.11a**   This is the four-bolt face right of **Mother Lode.** The move by the first bolt has not yet been freed; traversing in from the right to the second bolt avoids this A1 start.

MOTHER LODE WALL

SCARY TREE PINNACLES

These pinnacles/formations face west, and lie on the western edge of the plateau above and east of
Gold Dust Gulch and almost directly above Poodle Rock. It is best approached from either the
North Trail or the Queen Crimson Trail (to the south). It lies about 175 yards west of Queen
Crimson Dome. The known routes lie on two small "towers" that face west. Each tower has two-
bolt toprope anchors, although most routes can be lead. Map, page 424.

2894 **DUPLICITY 5.8 R**   Climb the north side of the lefthand (northern) "tower" up loose
flakes.

2895 **BLACK LIPSTICK 5.8 R**   Climb cracks and flakes up the west face of the north tower.

2896 **BLITZSTEEG 5.10b (TR)**   Climb the lefthand part of the west face of the southern
tower, staying left near the top.

2897 **DECEIT 5.7**   Start as for **Blitzsteeg,** but tend toward easier cracks on the right near the
top.

QUEEN CRIMSON DOME

This formation lies about 300 yards directly east of Poodle Rock, on the hillside forming the eastern edge of the plateau above and east of Gold Dust Gulch. It can be approached several ways. If you are near the road/trail leading down to Gold Dust Gulch, The North Trail (which leads to Fraggle Rock etc.) probably is the best approach. If you are coming from the south, take the Desert Queen Wash split to the east. From the point where the wash makes a sharp turn back south, hike north on the Queen Crimson Trail up to the plateau. Map, page 424.

2898 **WALT'S SOLO   5.8**   This is a fingercrack on the south face of a small dome above **Nerve Storm.**

2899 **DIG ME   5.11b (TR)**   Climb the face right of **Walt's Solo** into small dihedrals.

2900 **NERVE STORM   5.11c ★★★**   Pro: Thin to 3 inches, one bolt.

2901 **LIKE MY LUMP   5.10a ★**

2902 **SOFTWARE SLUTS   5.10d R ★**   Pro: Thin to 2 inches, fixed pin and two bolts.

2903 **MANWICH QUEEN   5.8 ★**   Pro: To 2 inches, three bolts.

2904 **DESERT PROFIT   5.11d ★★**   Pro: Eight bolts; bolt anchor.

2905 **HOLLOWED GROUND   5.11a ★★**   Five bolts, two-bolt chain anchor/rap.

2906 **QUEEN CRIMSON   5.10b**   Pro: To 2.5 inches.

ROMAN ROCKS

Roman Rocks are the small, west-facing formations that lie 250 yards south-southeast of Queen Crimson Dome and 150 yards north of Dike Rock. they can be reached easily by following the Gold Dust Gulch south until you can take the Desert Queen Wash split to the left (east), staying left (east) as the wash splits again. Pass The Piledriver Boulders to your left (north) and Dike Rock to the right (south). About 400 yards beyond the Gold Dust Gulch split, you will see some small crags against the hillside to the northeast. These are Roman Rocks. Map, page 424.

2907   **CAESAR 5.10b**   This is a two-bolt face route on west face of a wall several hundred yards right of Queen Crimson Dome.

2908   **BRUTUS 5.9+**   This short crack starting with a roof move is around and right from Caesar. Loose.

PILEDRIVER BOULDERS

This set of large boulders is about 50 yards north of Desert Queen Wash and 150 yards northwest of Dike Rock. Follow Gold Dust Gulch south, taking the Desert Queen Wash split to the left (east), and staying left (east) when the wash splits again. The Piledriver Boulders are on your left (north) about 250 yards after spliting off from Gold Dust Gulch. Map, page 424.

2909   **THE PILEDRIVER 5.11c**   This is an east-facing overhanging thin crack on the east face of the southern boulder in the boulder pile; it joins a large offwidth to the right. Pro: Thin to 1.5 inches, fixed stuff.

DIKE ROCK

This small, north-facing rock lies about 150 yards southeast of Piledriver Boulders and 30 yards south of Desert Queen Wash. Approach as for Piledriver Boulders, but continue 75 yards up (east) Desert Queen Wash. Dike Rock is the dark, blocky wall on your right, above some boulders. Map, page 424.

2910   **DIKE A RAMA 5.11a**   The leftmost vertical and left-slanting dike on the north face. Pro: Thin to 2 inches, two bolts on a vertical left-slanting dike.

2911   **CRACK 5.10d**   Obvious crack on formation.

2912   **UNKNOWN 5.10c**   A slab with two bolts 60 feet right of and off a ledge above Dike A Rama.

DESERT QUEEN DOME

This is the large formation high on the hillside at the top of Desert Queen Wash. Take the Desert Queen Wash from the split off Gold Dust Gulch for about 600 yards (to the east), until you reach a saddle. The formation is on your right. It is one of the highest summits in the area, and is easily seen from far away. Maps, pages 422, 424.

2913   **BIG DUMB AND UGLY 5.7**   This is the chimney system left of **Get The Balance Right.**

2914   **ONE POP, NO STOP 5.10c**   This is left of **Get The Balance Right.** Rap to the ledge 80 feet, on the left side, then climb the crack 60 feet into face. Three bolts, two-bolt anchor.

2915   **GET THE BALANCE RIGHT 5.10 ★★★**   Climbs the center of the west face past three bolts.

2916   **ALL-REET ARETE 5.8**   Climb an arête past two bolts down and right from **Get The Balance Right.**

2917   **DWEEB 5.7**   Climb the corner left of **Face Race.**

2918   **FACE RACE 5.10a (TR)**   Climb the face 15 feet left of **All-Reet Arête.**

2919   **RUSH HOUR 5.9**   Climb a thin crack/seam on the south face of Desert Queen Dome, just around the corner and right of **Face Race.**

THE TOWERS

These formations lie on the northwest corner of the hillside behind the Queen Crimson Plateau. There is a lower tier of rock with several "towers" that sit above. Routes are described right to left along the lower tier, then right to left on the towers. Map, page 424.

THE LOWER TIER

2920   **A BRIDGE TOO FAR   5.10a ★**   This is the obvious, clean finger crack that leads out of a chimney on the right side of the lower tier. Bolt anchor.

2921   **ABANDONED CLASSIC   5.12a (TR) ★★★**   This is to the left of **A Bridge Too Far** and near the northwest corner of the lower tier. Climb horizontal bands to a lieback that leads to a roof and face climbing above. Bolt anchor. An old bolt was found near the bottom.

2922   **BIG RED TRACTOR   5.11b (TR) ★★**   Climb horizontal bands to a left-leaning flake on the north end of the lower tier. Bolt anchors.

THE TOWERS

See map on page 424.

2923   **FUTURE BOY   5.12d (TR) ★★**   This route, which finishes on a slab above, is on a sharp northwest prow of the large boulder near the left end above the lower tier.

2924   **DEATH RIDES A PALE HORSE   5.8**   This is the hand crack around the corner and left of **Future Boy.**

2925   **XENALMORPH   5.10c ★★**   This bolted face route lies on the north side of a large boulder above the northwest corner of the lower tier. Bolt anchor/rap.

2926   **TIMES OF HOLYNESS   5.11c ★★★★**   This bolted face route lies on the north face of a boulder on the north east side of The Towers. Bolt anchors/rap.

2927   **UNDER A BLOOD RED SKY   5.12a (TR) ★★**   This is the thin face route to left and around on east side of same boulder containing **Times of Holyness.**

SILVERADO AREA

This area is best approached by following the North Trail from the mine shafts around the ridge (east) into the next wide valley/wash. (Incidently, Fraggle Rock will be easily seen to the southeast at this point.) The following routes lie on the west side of the wash (actually the back of the hillside containing Queen Crimson Dome), up on the hillside. Walk south and uphill to approach. Map, page 422.

2928 **SILVERADO 5.11b ★★** This is a lieback on the north face of several small formations on the west side of the wash.

2929 **HIGH PLAINS DRIFTER 5.10b ★★** Climb a shallow corner to a bolted face, crossing **Silverado.** Bolt anchor.

2930 **THE GOLDDIGGER 5.10c ★★** This is a hand crack left of Silverado, on the east face of the formation.

FRAGGLE ROCK

This is a large formation with a slightly overhanging north face on a hillside about .6 mile east of the Desert Queen Mine. There are some mine shafts and a fascinating miners' cabin among the boulders below its west side. Several approaches are possible. It can be approached via the North Trail by walking east until you are in the broad valley/wash containing Silverado. At this point, Fraggle Rock is easily visible to the southeast. From here, either continue east, drop down into the next canyon/wash, and head south (uphill) to Fraggle Rock, or head up the Silverado wash until a short hike over the hill to the east leads you the west face. It is also fairly easy to reach Fraggle Rock by hiking over the "pass" by Desert Queen Dome, then up a wash (east) until a gentle walk north takes you to the west face. Finally, Fraggle Rock may be approached by heading north from Split Rock, then up the hillside just right of **Morongo Man** (aim for the large formation at the top of the hill). From **Morongo Man,** the wash heading north ends at the east side of Desert Queen Dome. From the formation on the top of the hill (visible from Split Rocks), head straight north to Fraggle Rock. Map, page 422.

2931 **THE STILL 5.10c** ★ This route is on the left side of the east face, and climbs a seam to a face with three bolts.

2932 **POPPIN' AND BREAKIN' 5.10a** ★ This four-bolt route lies 15 feet right of **The Still,** on the right side of the east face.

2933 **PETRODYNAMICS 5.11a** ★★★ These overhanging double thin cracks in a corner are on the left side of the north face.

2934 **TIERS FOR FEARS 5.10d** ★★★★ This three-tiered hand crack is on the right side of the north face (100 feet right of **Petrodynamics**).

2935 **WUTHERING HEIGHTS 5.9** This three-bolt route is on the upper west side of the formation, 40 feet right of the upper corner of **Tiers For Fears.**

2936 **SCATTERED REMAINS 5.11b** ★★ This is the rightmost of double left-slanting cracks on the north-facing part of the west face of Fraggle Rock.

2937 **COSMIC TRIGGER 5.13a** ★★★★★ This is the leftmost overhanging face climb to a chain anchor on the southwest face.

2938 **I HAVE THE TOUCH 5.12d** ★★★★ This face climb is right of **Cosmic Trigger.**

2939 **JOLLY ROGER 5.10c** ★★ This face route is to the right and around the corner (facing south) of **I Have The Touch.**

The following route lies on the obvious huecoed face 100 feet south of Fraggle Rock.

2940 **SENSORY DEPRIVATION 5.12b** ★★★ This route is on the north side of the rock and is visible from the miners' cabin.

GROPE ROCK

This prominent tower of rock lies at the top of a wash just east of the wash leading to Fraggle Rock, and directly east of Fraggle Rock. It is best approached directly from the east face of Fraggle Rock. Map, page 422.

2941 **GROOP'O 5.11d (TR)** ★★ This route climbs a bucketed face to a left-slanting crack on the north face of Grope Rock. Bolt anchor.

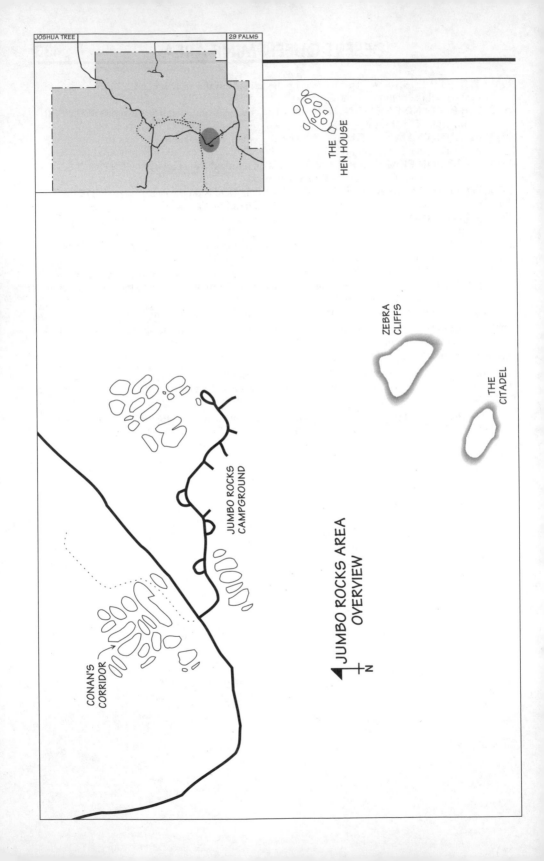

JOSHUA TREE | 29 PALMS

THE
HEN HOUSE

ZEBRA
CLIFFS

THE
CITADEL

CONAN'S
CORRIDOR

JUMBO ROCKS
CAMPGROUND

JUMBO ROCKS AREA
OVERVIEW

N

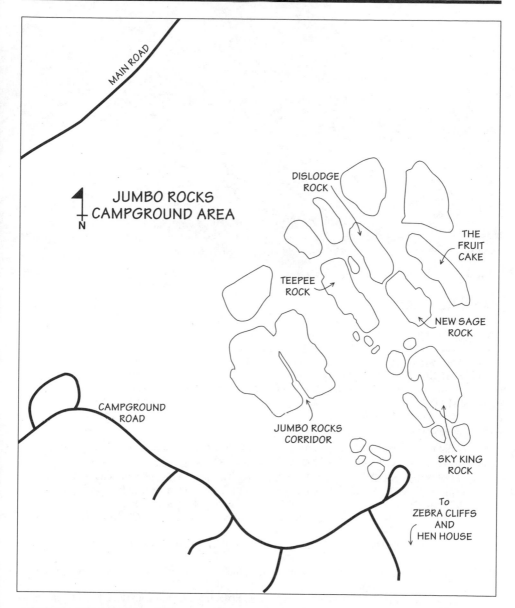

JUMBO ROCKS CAMPGROUND

Although Jumbo Rocks Campground has a fair amount of rock, most of it is very grainy and rough (even by Joshua Tree standards) and few worthwhile climbs have been done here. The entrance to the campground is approximately 1.3 miles further southeast from the Geology Tour Road turnoff along the Sheep Pass Loop Road. A very sharp turn in the road is encountered just before the campground. Maps, pages 343, 435.

Most of the recorded routes lie near the very end of the paved campground road (where a paved loop is found). This is the best place to park to approach the following climbs.

SKY KING ROCK
This formation is almost directly east of the end of the campground loop. Map, page 435.

2942 **CHANCE MEETING 5.6 A3** Pitons are necessary.

2943 **FLASHPOINT 5.11d** Pro: Thin to 2 inches.

2944 **THE FIRE GLOVE 5.10a** Climb a flare 15 feet left of **Flashpoint.**

2945 **DOUBLE DUTY 5.10c** These two cracks, which start in left-facing dihedrals, are on the north face of Sky King Rock about 30 feet apart. This is the left crack.

2946 **SHADY NOOK 5.5** This is the righthand crack. Start in the chimney mentioned in description to **Double Duty.**

TEEPEE ROCK
This formation lies about 150 yards north of Sky King Rock. The characteristic "teepee" shaped cracks on the west face form **Not A Hogan.** Map, page 435.

2947 **TORTOISE SKELETON CRACK 5.9+ ★** This left-facing dihedral leading to a handcrack (with a tortoise skeleton inside) on the north end of Teepee Rock.

2948 **RETIREMENT IS ALL THAT 5.7** This and the following route are at the far left (north) end of the west face; look for a cave 20 feet off the ground. Climb the crack out left of cave, then head straight up the easy face.

2949 **IT'S CRACKED UP TO BE 5.9** Start as for **Retirement . . .** but follow the crack to its end.

2950 **NOT A HOGAN 5.10a** This route climbs the teepee-shaped crack/cave system on the west face of the formation.

2951 **GRACIAS A DIOS 5.10d ★★** This is a right-facing dihedral with three bolts to the right of **Not A Hogan.** Above, go right around a roof, then up a crack to the face, climbing past two more bolts.

2952 **BUSY BEES 5.7** This is on the far right (north) end of the east face of Teepee Rock. Climb a chimney just past a huge, flat, sloping boulder.

2953 **SCORCHED EARTH 5.11c ★★★** This route lies about 100 feet right of **Busy Bees** and directly across the canyon from **Imtimidation Game.** Look for a diagonal crack about halfway up the face. The route is protected by three bolts and nuts to 2 inches.

DISLODGE ROCK

This is the formation directly east of Teepee Rock and north of New Sage Rock. The following routes are located on the west face, opposite **Busy Bees**. Map, page 435.

2954 **INTIMIDATION GAME 5.10d ★★** This is the middle of three cracks that lean left on the north (left) end of the west face (about 120 feet north and across the canyon from **Busy Bees**). Face moves lead to this finger crack.

2955 **DEHORNED UNICORN 5.9+** This is the rightmost of two cracks about 10 feet apart. It is directly across the canyon from **Busy Bees.**

2956 **PREPUBESCENT NARWHAL 5.6** This crack is 10 feet left of **Dehorned Unicorn.**

NEW SAGE ROCK

This is the large formation 100 yards northeast of Sky King Rock. Map, page 435.

2957 **AGAINST ALL TODDS 5.10c** This is on the south face, around and right from **Not a Hogan.** Climb a crack above a bucketed face.

2958 **JUMBO SHRIMP 5.6** This route climbs a crack leading to face climbing on the southeast arête of New Sage Rock, about 50 feet right of **Against All Todds.**

2959 **ZOAUVE DETENTE ??** Between **Jumbo Shrimp** and **The Wind Cries Mary.**

2960 **THE WIND CRIES MARY 5.7** This is an easy, right-leaning ramp leading to a finger crack above a small roof. It is 40 feet right of **Jumbo Shrimp.**

THE FRUIT CAKE

This is the wall/formation just east of New Sage Rock. Map, page 435.

2961 **GRAINY TRAIN 5.10c** An obvious, left-slanting crack leading to a roof is on the west side of the rock (the right side of the canyon between New Sage Rock and The Fruit Cake). Surmout the roof via a hand crack.

2962 **BEARDSLEY CABBAGE 5.7** Climb a chute that begins below some large boulders below the left (upper) end of the diagonal crack of **Grainy Train.**

JUMBO ROCKS CORRIDOR

A narrow corridor can be seen 100 yards to the northwest of the very end of the Jumbo Rocks Campground Loop. Many cracks lie on the left (west) side of the corridor. Map, page 435.

2963 **FINGERS OF FRENZY 5.12a (TR)** This is on the left side of the corridor, just before it severely narrows is a dihedral system. To the right of the dihedral is a right diagonalling thin crack. Climb this until another crack/ramp diagonalling left is reached. Follow this to a vertical hand crack and the top.

2964 **HANDSAW 5.10b** This route climbs the dihedral mentioned in the previous description. From the top of the dihedral, climb a hand crack to the top.

2965 **CARNAGE 5.10c** Walk into the narrow part of the corridor about 50-60 feet, passing several crack systems on the left wall. **Carnage** takes a hand crack that lies just left of **Mere Illusion.** It is loose at the bottom; a concave section about 25 feet up is the crux, and the rock improves above.

2966 **MERE ILLUSION 5.11a ★★** This route is near the deepest section of the corridor. Follow the steep face, climbing past three bolts until a move up and left gives access to a crack system. Climb the crack until you must exit left to reach the top.

ZEBRA CLIFFS – EAST FACE

ZEBRA CLIFFS

The Zebra Cliffs are a series of cliffs located around a large flat hill about .3 mile south of Jumbo Rocks Campground. Most of the routes lie on the eastern and northern exposures, although a few routes lie on the south and west sides.

Walk almost due south from the end of the campground, staying left (east) of a hill. The cliffs will soon be seen on a hillside to the south as a band of dark rock with distinctive horizontal streaks. Approaching the cliffs, you should come in at the northeast corner of the formation. There has been climbing activity at these cliffs for at least 15 years (mostly very easy routes), but no written information is available. See map, page 434.

ZEBRA CLIFFS – EAST FACE
The largest ("main") cliffs lie on the east face of the hillside. The routes are described left to right, starting at the far left end Map, page, 434.

2967 **CUT THIN TO WIN 5.10c ★★★** This is the leftmost route on the east face of a formation left of the main cliff. It is a distinct, right-slanting thin crack leading to a horizontal crack.

2968 **TOO WIDE TO TROT 5.10b** This crack with a wide start is right of the preceding route on a separate wall.

2969 **DREAMER 5.11a R ★★** This striking right-leaning crack is farther right, near the left side of the largest section of the cliff band.

2970 **UP AND DOWN 5.10a ★★** This is a three-bolt climb down and right from **Dreamer.**

2971 **SUCH A LINE (aka A Momentary Lapse of Reason) 5.10d** This difficult-looking crack, which splits and rejoins about halfway up, is right of Up and Down.

2972 **AROUND THE WORLD 5.10b ★★★★** This climb starts high in the gully right of **Such a Line,** and is best approached from above. Traverse left around a corner in a horizontal crack that curves upward after about 30 feet.

2973 **ICE CREAM FOR CROW 5.8** Climb the obvious dogleg crack between **Such A Line** and **Slip Sliding Away.**

2974 **GORILLA TACTICS 5.9+ ★** Start as for the **Ice Cream for Crow,** but traverse right and up an arête past two bolts. Can also be started directly (sans crack); 5.10c.

2975 **HORSE OF A DIFFERENT COLOR 5.10c/d** Climb the arête to the right of **Gorilla Tactics** past three bolts to a two-bolt anchor.

2976 **THE EDUKASHUN PRESIDENT 5.10c** Three bolts on a buttress between **Gorilla Tactics** and **Slip Slidin' Away.**

2977 **SLIP SLIDIN' AWAY 5.10c R** This four-bolt face climb that starts in very steep buckets is down and right of the previous routes.

2978 **BAD BRAINS 5.9** Two right-slanting cracks are about 100 feet right of **Slip Slidin' Away.** This is the lower of the two.

ZEBRA CLIFFS – NORTH FACE

ZEBRA CLIFFS
ZEBRA CLIFFS – NORTH FACE

The following routes are on the north side of the hill, and are described right to left from the northeast corner to the northwest corner of the formation. Map, page 434.

Corner n' Crack through **The Sand Truck** are on a short wall just right of the northeast corner of the formation.

2979 **CORNER N' CRACK** **5.10a** ★★ Start on the left edge of the wall. Climb up, then right to a thin crack.

2980 **SHORT CRACK 5.10a** Start in the obvious central crack, then traverse left on a dike to a thin crack just right of the upper crack of **Corner n' Crack.**

2981 **DAN CRUISE 5.6** Climb the obvious central crack/corner.

2982 **MRS. PAUL'S 5.9** Face climb up to a hand crack right of Dan Cruise.

2983 **FROZEN FISH FINGERS 5.9** This is another hand crack right of Mrs. Paul's. FA: Waugh, Mathews and Hershman, January 1987.

2984 **MORE FROZEN FOOD 5.10d** ★★★ Climb a face to a crack down and right from the previous routes, on the outer face of a block.

2985 **THE SAND TRUCK 5.11b/c** ★★ Climb the arête/face just to the right of **More Frozen Food.**

The following climbs lie further right along the formation's north side.

2986 **AGING HIPPIE CRACK 5.10b** This is about 100 yards right of **More Frozen Food.** Climb a straight-in crack on a block that doesn't quite reach the bottom or top.

2987 **JIM CRUISE 5.9** ★ This route climbs a bucketed wall to a crack about 100 yards right of **Aging Hippie Crack** (200 yards from **More Frozen Food**).

2988 **SHORT AND CRANK 5.10b R** ★ Climb a crack just right of Jim Cruise and continue up a face using a tied-off knob for protection.

2989 **ZEBRA DIHEDRAL (aka Ganjame) 5.10a** ★★★ This large, left-facing, curving dihedral is around and right from the previous routes.

ZEBRA CLIFFS – WEST SIDE

The west side of the formation has a few scattered rocks and boulders. To approach the following routes, walk west around the north face, then south. The first route is about 300 yards around and right (south) of **Zebra Dihedral,** on the northwest face of a large boulder. Other routes have been done in this area for which complete descriptions were not available at the time of this writing. Map, page 434.

2990 **SHAKING LIKE A LEAF 5.8 ★★** This is a two-bolt face route on northwest face of a 30-foot boulder.

2991 **CHIMPS AND CHEETAHS 5.9 ★** This is a three-bolt (35-foot) arête route found about 30 feet right of and higher up on the formation than **Shaking Like A Leaf.** Two-bolt anchor.

2992 **I EAT CANNIBAL 5.7** This is about 80 feet right of of **Shaking Like A Leaf.** Climb a small, 30-foot high, south-facing block with a horizontal crack. Pro: One bolt; small camming units to 2 inches.

2993 **FALLUN (ALL IN FUN) 5.7 ★** This is on a large, 35-foot high boulder 150 yards around and right of **Shaking Like A Leaf.** Climb up face to a crack that starts about one-third of the way up the boulder's south face.

ZEBRA CLIFFS – SOUTH SIDE

The following route (and the south point of the formation) are best approached by walking southwest (left) from the east face (**Cut Thin To Win**). Map, page 434.

2994 **DESERT SAFARI 5.11+ ★★★** This four-bolt face route is 125 yards around and left of **Cut Thin To Win.** Climb up to and past a shallow dihedral. Pro: Thin camming units to 2 inches for anchors.

HEN HOUSE FROM NORTH

3007
3008
2996 – 3005
3006

THE CITADEL

This formation/large hillside lies about .6 mile south of Jumbo Rock Campground. It lies .2 mile southwest of the Zebra Cliff formation. It can be approached by walking south from Jumbo Rocks around to the west (left) of the hill you pass (on the right) going to Zebra Cliffs. Alternatively, from the northeast corner of the Zebra Cliffs, you can walk to the right (west), then head slightly south. From this vantage, The Citadel appears as a large hillside. Several other routes have been done here, for which complete route information was lacking. Map, page 434.

2995　**NICE AND ICY　5.7**　This route lies on the west face of a dark brown rock near the southwest part of the formation. Climb the flared finger crack. Pro: Thin to 2 inches.

THE HEN HOUSE

The Hen House is a cluster of giant boulders about 3 mile east-northeast of the Zebra Cliffs. They can be approached from Jumbo Rocks Campground or from the Live Oak Picnic Area (Pope's Hat). It is about a mile approach, whichever way you go. See maps, pages 434, 443.

TAR AND FEATHERS BOULDER

This is the east-facing wall near the northeast corner of The Hen House. Map, page 443.

2996　**OUEF'S UP　5.10a R/X**　This is an unprotected face (solo or toprope) near the left side of the wall.

2997　**FOWL PLAY　5.11a**　Climb past a bolt into a thin crack right of **Ouef's Up.**

2998　**TAR　5.10d R ★★**　This two-bolt face climb is right of **Fowl Play.** From the second bolt, go left to the top.

2999　**FEATHERS　5.11b R ★★★**　From the second bolt of **Tar,** go straight up into a thin crack.

3000　**TALON SHOW　5.12c (TR) ★★★★**　Climb the arête right of **Tar** and **Feathers.**

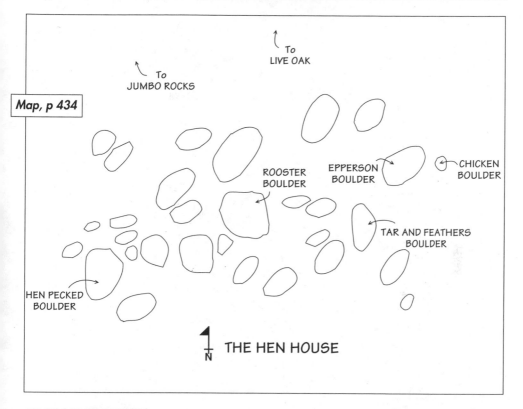

EPPERSON BOULDER
This is a large boulder northeast of Tar and Feathers Boulder. Map, above.

3001   **LITTLE RED ROOSTER   5.8**   This is a small right-facing corner/flake on the south face of Epperson Boulder. Pro: one fixed pin, one bolt.

3002   **FOGHORN LEGHORN   5.7 R**   This route is on the south face of Epperson Boulder. Climb an unprotected face right of a right-facing book (**Little Red Rooster**).

3003   **CHICKEN LITTLE   5.7+ (TR)**   This face/ramp is on the north side of Epperson Boulder and just left of Epperson's Footprints.

3004   **EPPERSON'S FOOTPRINTS   5.10a**   This three-bolt route is on the north side of Epperson Boulder.

CHICKEN BOULDER
This small boulder lies northeast of Tar and Feathers Boulder and just east of Epperson Boulder. Map, above.

3005   **EL POLLO LOCO   5.10c**   This five-bolt route is on the south face of the boulder.

ROOSTER BOULDER
This is the large, upper boulder on the north side of The Hen House. Map, above.

3006   **RUFFLED ROOSTER   5.9 ★**   This climb is on the northwest corner of Rooster Boulder. Climb past two bolts to a prominent horizontal crack. Continue up the easier, unprotected face.

HEN PECKED BOULDER
This is the large, west-facing boulder-pinnacle on the west side of The Hen House. Map, above.

3007   **PECKING ORDER   5.10c ★★**   This is the left route, with four bolts.

3008   **CHICKEN RUN   5.11d**   The right route, with two bolts.

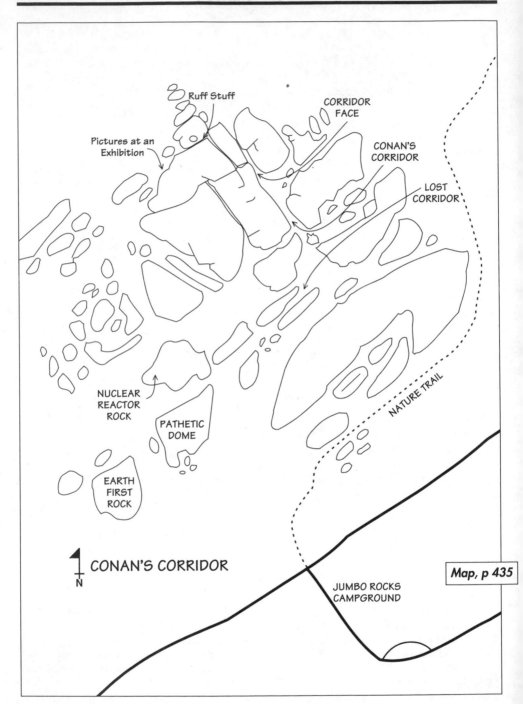

Ruff Stuff

CORRIDOR
FACE

Pictures at an
Exhibition

CONAN'S
CORRIDOR

LOST
CORRIDOR

NUCLEAR
REACTOR
ROCK

PATHETIC
DOME

NATURE TRAIL

EARTH
FIRST
ROCK

CONAN'S CORRIDOR

N

Map, p 435

JUMBO ROCKS
CAMPGROUND

CONAN'S CORRIDOR

This conglomeration of rocks lies almost directly acros the road (north) of the entrance to Jumbo Rocks Campground. Unlike Jumbo Rocks Campground, the rock tends to be quite good. Several excellent crack climbs are located on the east face of the Corridor Face. Map, page 444.

CORRIDOR FACE

Corridor Face is situated just north (and through) the corridor. From the parking area, walk northeast along a nature trail until you can take a left turn through a brush-filled valley. From the northwest end of the brush-filled valley, follow a narrow canyon north, through Conan's Corridor, until the widening valley reveals the Corridor Face. Map, page 444.

3009   **FOOL'S GOLD**   **5.8**   This is the leftmost route on the Corridor Face, and follows a prominent trough.

3010   **SONG OF THE SIREN**   **5.10c**   Start off a boulder right of **Fool's Gold.** Climb past a bolt to a horizontal crack, then up into a bottoming offwidth to the top.

3011   **SPIDERMAN**   **5.10a ★★★**   This route climbs the leftmost of two major crack systems on the left side of the Coridor Face. A short, overhanging section is encountered near the bottom. Protection is difficult above.

3012   **GREEN HORNET**   **5.10a (TR)**   Start up **Spiderman,** then move left into a left-leaning groove.

3013   **COLORADO CRACK**   **5.9 ★★★★**   This route climbs the crack just right of **Spiderman.** Excellent grey and black rock leads to a steep finger crack at the top.

3014   **TRUE DICE**   **5.10a R/X ★★★**   This serious lead climbs an unprotected face up to the center of three right-slanting cracks that lie right of **Colorado Crack,** and begin about halfway up the face.

3015   **GEM**   **5.8 ★★**   Climb an obvious hand crack to the right of **True Dice.**

3016   **WINTER WINE**   **5.10c ★★★**   This crack starts about 20 feet above the ground just to the right of Gem. Start at **Gem,** and face climb right to a short thin crack; climb this, then go right to the base of a crack that leads to the top. Pro: Very thin to 2 inches.

3017   **RUFF STUFF**   **5.10c**   This is on the north face of the Corridor Face formation. Climb a steep, incipient crack that turns to hand size as it goes through a bulge.

3018   **PICTURES AT AN EXHIBITION**   **5.10a**   This dike system lies on the north end of the formation just west of the Corridor Face formation and directly north of Nuclear Reactor Rock. Climb past three bolts to the top.

Two parallel cracks lie to the left of **Pictures at an Exhibition;** the left is 5.6 and the right is 5.8.

LOST CORRIDOR

This corridor lies about 100 yards to the south and slightly west of Corridor Face, and runs in an east-west direction (Conans Corridor runs north-south). It is reached while making the approach to Corridor Face. Map, page 444.

3019   **PISSING ON MYSELF**   **5.11b (TR)**   This route is on the south side of the Lost Corridor.

NUCLEAR REACTOR ROCK

This large rock lies almost straight north from near the beginning of the nature trail mentioned in the approach to Corridor Face. Map, page 444.

3020   **CUNNING LINGUIST**   **5.8**   This climbs a hand crack to a face with one bolt left of **We'll Get Them Little Pricks.**

3021   **WE'LL GET THEM LITTLE PRICKS**   **5.8**   Climb the southwest face of Nuclear Reactor Rock past one bolt.

3022   **STAN AND OLLIE**   **5.7**   This climbs a dike right of **We'll Get Them Little Pricks.** Starting the route directly is 5.9.

3023   **HELICOPTER MEMORY FARTS**   **5.9+**   Climb up past two bolts to an overhang to the right of **Stan & Ollie.**

3024   **NUKE THE WHALES**   **5.9**   This route lies on the left side of a corridor, on the east side of Nuclear Reactor Rock. Climb a finger-to-fist crack to the top.

PATHETIC DOME
This formation is south of Nuclear Reactor Rock and is the closest climbable formation to the road. Map, page 444.

3025 **PATHETIC DIKE** **5.8** Climb a dike on the right side, with one bolt.

3026 **PATHETIC CRACK** **5.6** An obvious hand crack is ten feet left of the dike.

3027 **PATHETIC FACE** **5.8** This unprotected face is ten feet left of the crack.

EARTH FIRST ROCK
This formation is just west of Pathetic Dome. Map, page 444.

3028 **LOOKS 5.0, SO LET'S SOLO** **5.5** This three-bolt face route is on the left end of the east face.

3029 **SO ANOTHER 5.3** **5.3** This is the wide crack/corner between **Looks 5.0, So Let's Solo** and **RyeNot.**

3030 **RYE NOT?** **5.9** A dike with one bolt is on the east face of the formation west of Pathetic Dome.

3031 **KNOT AGAIN** **5.6 R** This is the face 15 feet right of **Rye Not.**

THE WEDGE AREA
This large triangular rock is .8 miles past Jumbo Rocks Campground and about 350 yards north of the Sheep Pass Loop Road. A exhibit parking area on the north side of the road is the best approach to the following routes. Photo, below.

EXHIBIT ROCK
This is the formation just north of the road at the exhibit pullout, the west end on the formation is dark brown and has a scooped-out overhang at the bottom.

3032 **POINT OF INTEREST** **5.6** This is on the south face. Climb double cracks in a left-facing corner to a ledge, then up a steep wall using an obvious crack to a large ledge. Chimney to the top and downclimb off right.

3033 **EXHIBITIONIST** **5.10d (TR)** Located to the right of **Point of Interest.** Pull up to a shallow, left-leaning arch, lieback, and face climb to its end. Exit onto arch, then finish up **Point of Interest.**

THE WEDGE

This is the wedge ("V"-shaped block) sitting atop a large rock near the left (west) end of a large formation on the north side of the road. It is pretty obvious from the vicinity of the exhibit pullout.

3034 **WEDGE 5.4** This route climbs the chimney on the northwest side of The Wedge. The chimney ends on a ledge below the top, and a bolt protects face moves to the summit.

3035 **HEX 5.7** Climb a hand crack on the west face to the top.

3036 **WON'T GET FOOLED AGAIN 5.7** A "V"-shaped, low-angled face rises about 40 yards left of The Wedge. Pro: Two bolts, nuts for anchor.

FALSE MOOSEDOG TOWER

False Moosedog Tower is a steep formation with a straight-in hand-and-fist crack located about 60 yards to the left (west) of The Wedge (and about 60 left of the "V"-shaped face mentioned above). It is right of a dihedral capped by a roof.

3037 **WHO'S NEXT 5.8** This is the hand-and-fist crack right of the a left-facing dihedral capped by a roof.

3038 **WHO CAME FIRST 5.9** Start about 30 feet left of the fist crack of **Who's Next.** Traverse up and right along a dike past two bolts. From here, either continue straight up past three bolts to a bolt belay (var. 1); or traverse right to a left-facing dihedral and at a roof traverse back left to the belay (var. 2). Easy climbing leads past a bolt to the top.

3039 **QUADROPHENIA 5.7** This route lies about 50 feet left of **Who Came First.** Climb a left-facing crack to face climbing above, past one bolt to a two-bolt anchor/rap.

3040 **PURE AND EASY 5.6** Climb up a steep, pocketed face past one bolt to fractured varnish to the top. This is about 150 feet left of False Moosedog Tower.

3041 **LITTLE CEASAR 5.8** This is a three-bolt climb on a gritty, low-angled slab facing the road somewhere across from Skull Rock.

3042 **WHEN LIGHTNING STRIKES 5.10c** A rounded formation with two big horizontal cracks is about 200 yards east (right) of The Wedge. This is a four-bolt climb on the north face (away from the road).

3043 **BORN TO BE A COWBOY 5.10c** This face climb lies 15 feet left of **When Lightning Strikes.** Climb past two bolts to join that route at its third bolt.

3044 **CUNNING ROUTE 5.10a** This incipient crack with four bolts is across the canyon and a short distance right of the previous route (facing the road).

3045 **FISSURE MERDE 5.8** The left-leaning crack just right of the **Cunning Route.**

3046 **THE CHEESE GRATER 5.11a** This face roue lies on dark brown rock 100 yards east of the **Cunning Route.**

3047 **NEVER CRY LOUIE 5.7** Face route with one bolt left of **The Cheese Grater.**

3048 **THE GILA MONSTER 5.8+** This is the offwidth crack in brown rock to the right of **The Cheese Grater.**

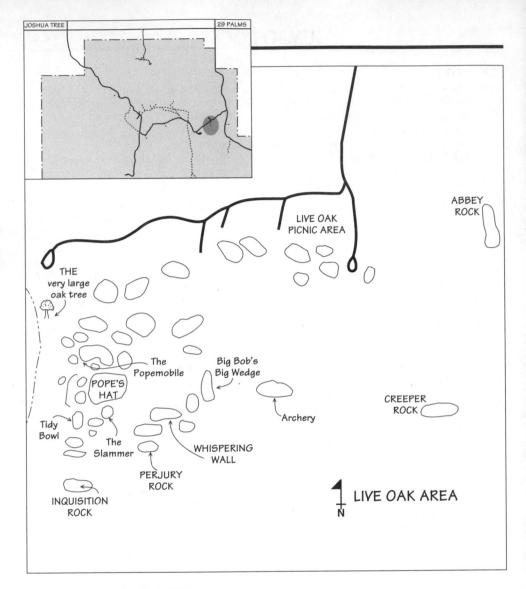

JOSHUA TREE

29 PALMS

ABBEY
ROCK

LIVE OAK
PICNIC AREA

THE
very large
oak tree

The
Popemobile

Big Bob's
Big Wedge

POPE'S
HAT

CREEPER
ROCK

Tidy
Bowl

Archery

The
Slammer

WHISPERING
WALL

PERJURY
ROCK

INQUISITION
ROCK

N

LIVE OAK AREA

LIVE OAK PICNIC AREA

The road that heads north to Split Rocks and south to Live Oak Picnic Area is approximately 1.2 miles northeast on the Sheep Pass Loop Road past Jumbo Rocks Campground. The road heading south curves to the southwest and gives access to the Pope's Hat. The Pope's Hat also can be reached easily from the Sheep Pass Loop Road, beginning from near a point 1mile past Jumbo Rocks Campground. It is about a 200-yard walk from the Sheep Pass Loop Road.

POPE'S HAT

This distinctive formation has the characteristic shape of a . . . It is located just south of the end of the western branch of the dirt road near a large oak tree. Map, page 444.

3049 **POPE'S HAT 5.9** Climb the short north face past three bolts.

3050 **NINCOMPOPE 5.11d ★★** Climbs the northwest face past five bolts.

3051 **POPE ON A ROPE 5.12d ★★★** This is an eight-bolt face route to the right of **Nincompope.**

3052 **DESERT STORM 5.10a ★** This four-bolt route lies just left of **Pope and Circumstance** on the south face of The Pope's Hat.

3053 **POPE AND CIRCUMSTANCE 5.9** Climb the south face of the Pope's Hat past three bolts. The second bolt is doubled and needs tie-offs or keyhole hangers.

3054 **IS THE POPE CATHOLIC? 5.6 (TR)** Climb the rappel line along the arête on The Pope's Hat.

POPE'S CAPE

This is the block/formation just north of the Pope's Hat. Map, page 448.

3055   **THE POPEMOBILE**   **5.10c ★★★**   This five-bolt face climb faces south and is directly north of **Pope's Hat** (across from **Nincompope**).

3056   **PAPAL SMEAR**   **5.10d ★**   Climb the crack to the right of **The Popemobile** past one bolt.

THE POPE BOULDERS

These are the large blocks/boulders just south of and around the Pope's Hat. Map, page 448.

3057   **THE SLAMMER**   **5.10b**   This two-bolt route traverses up and right on the south face of a block just south of The Pope's Hat.

3058   **TIDY BOWL**   **5.10d**   This route lies just below the southwest side of The Pope's Hat, and faces west on a bowl/scoop-shaped boulder. Pro: One fixed pin, four bolts.

3059   **PAPAL PLEASER**   **5.4**   From the large boulder at the base of the northeast face scramble up easy slabs to vertical cracks. Follow these cracks to the second horizontal crack. Head left, then up and right over a bulge to the top.

3060   **OH GOD!**   **5.2**   This is the south-facing slab on the large boulder 50 feet south of The Pope's Hat. It is in front of the rappel line, and there is a rappel bolt on top.

INQUISITION ROCK

This is the a large, low-angled, north-facing rock south of The Pope's Hat. Map, page 448.

3061   **WESTWARD HO!**   **5.2**   This is a wide crack 10 feet left of a right-slanting dike.

3062   **FUNKY GUNKIES**   **5.4**   Climb the aforementioned dike with no pro.

LIVE OAK PICNIC AREA ROUTES

The remaining routes in this section are scattered throughout the Live Oak area, mostly east of the Pope's Hat. Map, page 448.

ABBEY ROCK

3063   **DESERT SOLITAIRE**   **5.7**   This route is on the west face of a formation 175 feet east of the southern end of the entrance road to Live Oak. It climbs a partially hidden hand crack that widens up top, in a right-facing corner.

CREEPER ROCK

This is a north-facing rock about 200 yards southeast of **Desert Solitaire.** There are two obvious cracks. Map, page 448.

3064   **LEARNING TO CRAWL**   **5.6**   The left crack, an offwidth.

3065   **FINGER LOCKING GOOD**   **5.7**   The right crack, leaning fingers.

3066   **FINGERLOCKS OR CEDAR BOX**   **5.5**   Climb a short, varnished crack on a formation behind **Learning to Crawl.** Rappel.

3067   **ARCHERY**   **5.4**   A small natural arch is behind the rock west of The Pope's Hat. Climb a crack on the rock's left side, traverse right across the arch, and finish up a hand crack.

B179   **BIG BOB'S BIG WEDGE**   **5.11**   This boulder problem climbs a 30-foot roof crack on a rock just west of **Archery.** It is near the northeast side of the rock.

3068   **WASHOE CRACK**   **5.11a**   This is a diagonal thin crack above and right of **Big Bob's Big Wedge.** It slants from left to right and faces east.

3069   **BEAM ABOARD**   **5.9+ ★**   This is a three-bolt climb on a large boulder/face northwest of, and facing, **Big Bob's Big Wedge.** Rap slings are visible below the summit. This route is somewhat left of **Washoe Crack.**

3070   **HOBO CHANG BA**   **5.9**   This is at the top of the gully west of **Big Bob's Big Wedge,** on the right and about 200 feet up and left of **Beam Aboard.** Climb an RP crack to a horizontal, go left, then up past two bolts.

3071   **END OF THE LINE**   **5.9+**   Start as for **Hobo Chang Ba,** but after the initial crack, climb straight up past three bolts.

THE WHISPERING WALL

This is a large, south-facing wall east of the Pope's Hat. It is best approached from up the canyon southwest of Big Bob's Big Wedge in the canyon left of the one containing routes 3068 and 3069. It can be approached from the base of the Pope's Hat by heading east over several small summits to rap anchors on the top left side of the wall above **Jeepers Leepers** (two ropes needed). Six routes have been reported here. Map, page 448.

3072 **STEMSKI 5.6 ★★** Climb double cracks starting in an open book on the left side of the wall.

3073 **JEEPERS LEEPERS 5.9+ R** This is a two-bolt face climb right of **Stemski.**

3074 **MY 3 FRIENDS 5.7** Climb the first crack right of **Jeepers Leepers.**

3075 **INDIAN GARDEN 5.6** Climb the second crack right of **Jeepers Leepers,** with many bushes.

3076 **MORE CRAZY THAN LAZY 5.10b R** Climb a thin crack immediately right of Indian Garden, then go past two bolts to a ledge. Several variations from here lead to the true summit of the wall.

3077 **MOTHER BOARD BREAKDOWN 5.10c ★★★** Climb the face right of **More Crazy Than Lazy.** Pro: Thin cams, nine bolts.

3078 **CHARLOTTE'S WEB 5.11a ★★** Seven bolts.

PERJURY ROCK

This formation lies about 40 yards south of The Whispering Wall. The routes listed are on the south face. Map, page 448.

3079 **RAISE YOUR RIGHT HAND 5.10a** Climb past two bolts and horizontal cracks. This is about 15 feet left of the righthand arête.

3080 **REPEAT AFTER ME 5.10a** Climb the righthand arête past three bolts.

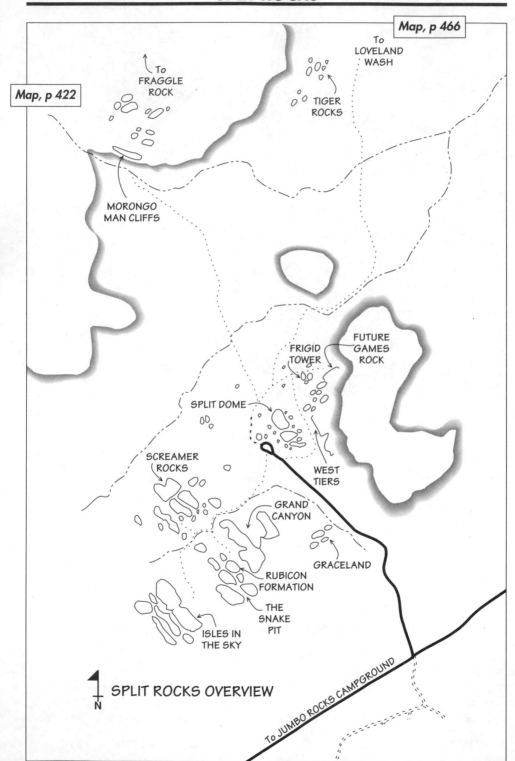

Map, p 466

Map, p 422

To LOVELAND WASH

To FRAGGLE ROCK

TIGER ROCKS

MORONGO MAN CLIFFS

FUTURE GAMES ROCK

FRIGID TOWER

SPLIT DOME

WEST TIERS

SCREAMER ROCKS

GRAND CANYON

GRACELAND

RUBICON FORMATION

THE SNAKE PIT

ISLES IN THE SKY

N

SPLIT ROCKS OVERVIEW

To JUMBO ROCKS CAMPGROUND

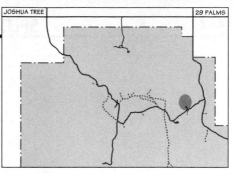

SPLIT ROCKS AREA

Take the marked road that heads north off the Sheep Pass Loop Road at a point 1.2 miles past Jumbo Rocks Campground. This road ends at the Split Rocks Parking Lot about 1 mile northwest of Sheep Pass Loop Road. Maps, pages 452, 454.

3081 **SHAVE YOUR BUMP 5.6** This route lies on the first climbable rock on the righthand (east) side of the road to Split Rocks. This is a one-bolt face route on a slab facing the road.

GRACELAND

This grouping of small rocks and boulders is about 300 yards south of the parking area and west of the road. The rocks are on your left as you drive toward the parking area. Map, page 452.

3082 **NOTHING BUT A GROUNDHOG 5.10b** Climb past one bolt to a finger crack on the north face of a large boulder low on the hill.

3083 **ELVIS IS EVERYWHERE 5.10c** This is a long face to the right (west) of **Nothing But A Groundhog.** Climb the dike past four bolts to two-bolt anchor.

3084 **PELVIC THRUST 5.10c** This three-bolt route is to the right of **Elvis Is Everywhere.**

3085 **BLUE SUEDE SHOES 5.7** This is to the right (west) of the main face. Climb the south side (inside face) of a large boulder past two bolts. Anchors are on top.

SPLIT ROCKS EAST PARKING AREA

The following routes lie generally east of the Split Rocks Parking Lot, but within the Split Rocks Area. Map, page 454.

SPLIT ROCK

Split Rock proper (the large boulder immediately north of the parking area) has been declared off limits to climbing activities by the monument. Please respect this closure. Map, page 454.

OVERBOLTED ROCK

This is the boulder just northeast of Split Rock. Map, page 454.

3086 **ANY BODY CAN BOLT 5.10a** Climb past three bolts on far left side of west face.

3087 **ARE YOU INEXPERIENCED 5.11c** Three bolts in middle of west face, right of prior route.

3088 **HIGH ENERGY 5.10a** This goes up past three bolts right of **Are You Inexperienced,** left of **Captain Safe.**

3089 **CAPTAIN SAFE 5.10b** This is right of the previous routes, near the arête of the boulder just northeast of Split Rock. It has two bolts.

3090 **BOULEVARD OF DREAMS 5.10b** The rightmost route, with three bolts.

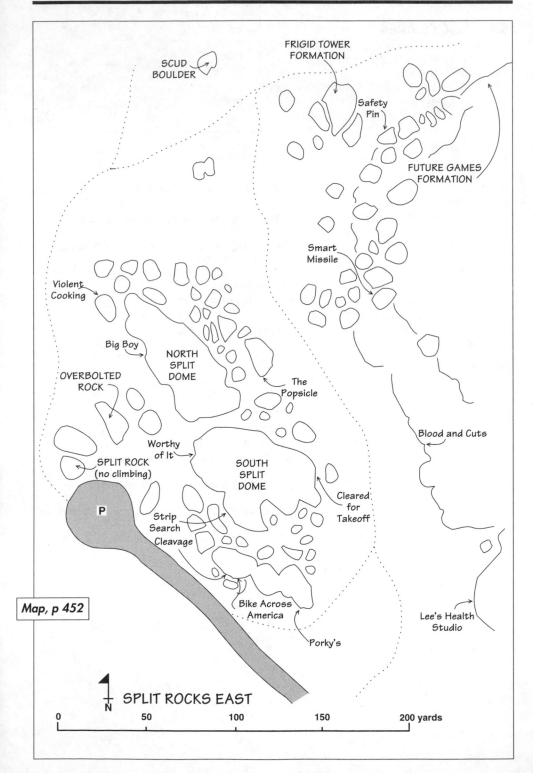

SCUD BOULDER

FRIGID TOWER FORMATION

Safety Pin

FUTURE GAMES FORMATION

Smart Missile

Violent Cooking

Big Boy

NORTH SPLIT DOME

The Popsicle

OVERBOLTED ROCK

Blood and Cuts

Worthy of It

SPLIT ROCK (no climbing)

SOUTH SPLIT DOME

P

Cleared for Takeoff

Strip Search Cleavage

Bike Across America

Lee's Health Studio

Porky's

Map, p 452

SPLIT ROCKS EAST

N

0   50   100   150   200 yards

SPLIT DOME – WEST FACE

SPLIT DOME

This large formation lies on the east side of the parking area. It has a "split" down the middle, directly east of the parking lot. Maps, pages 452, 454.

3091 **VIOLENT COOKING 5.10a** This route lies on the northwest corner of Split Dome. It is · about 150 feet north-northeast of Split Rock. Pro: two bolts, medium nuts.

3092 **IN AND OUT 5.9** This route is about 100 feet northeast of the parking lot in an A-shaped alcove left of a large block. Climb the offwidth crack on the left side of an alcove.

3093 **BIG BOY 5.9** This takes the hand crack on the right side of the alcove mentioned above.

3094 **WORTHY OF IT 5.8** This is to the right of the "split" in Split Dome and 100 feet right of **Big Boy/In And Out**, on the northwest corner of the formation. Follow a crack up to an obvious roof.

3095 **THE ENVIRONMENT-OIL PRESIDENT 5.10c** This route lies just right of **Worthy of It**. Pro: To 2.5 inches, three bolts.

The southern part of Split Dome is surrounded by many large boulders/faces. In fact, the portion of Split Dome facing the road south of the parking area is really a series of large boulders. Consult the map for exact locations.

3096 **STRIP SEARCH 5.10c** This left diagonalling seam is on the west face of the main Split Dome formation, 100 feet south (right) of **Worthy of It**, behind massive boulders. Descend to the northwest. Pro: Small to 2 inches, four bolts.

3097 **TURTLE VEIN 5.8** Climb the face 50 right of **Strip Search** on the south side of the formation. Pro: To 2.5 inches, two bolts.

The next routes are on the west faces of the boulders/rocks facing the road, on the southern part of Split Dome. They are on the right as one is driving into the Split Rocks Area.

3098 **CLEAVAGE 5.10c** Lieback an overhanging corner.

3099 **THE NIPPLE 5.10b** Start atop a boulder just right of **Cleavage.** Climb a series of left-curving cracks, then go up the face past a black chickenhead.

3100 **BIKE ACROSS AMERICA 5.10c** This climb is 20 feet right of **The Nipple**. Pro: Three bolts.

3101 **PORKY'S EXCELLENT ADVENTURE 5.8** Start 70 feet right of **The Nipple**. Pro: Two bolts.

SPLIT DOME – EAST FACE

SPLIT DOME – EAST FACE
The east face of the formation forms the left side of a small valley. Maps, pages 452, 454.

3102 **CLEARED FOR TAKEOFF 5.11b ★★** This is a prominent overhanging crack on the east face of Split Dome.

3103 **FLEA BITE 5.11d (TR)** Climb the arête/face just to the right of **Cleared For Takeoff**.

3104 **THE TORTOISE AND THE DOG 5.10b R ★** This is to the right of **Flea Bite**. Climb up and left to a bolt, then back up and right.

3105 **THE POPSICLE 5.11d ★★★**   This route is a short ways north of **Cleared for Takeoff**. The route climbs the southwest corner/arête of a very large boulder; it goes past three bolts.

WEST TIERS

The West Tiers are the rocks that form the eastern side of the small valley east of the Split Dome (they face Split Dome's east face and the road). Several "tiers" of rock characterize the northern part of this formation. This formation has many crack systems. Map, page 452.

3106 **LEE'S HEALTH STUDIO   5.11b/c ★★★**   This route lies on the southern part of West Tiers and is visible from the road. It lies about 75 yards southeast of the southern extremity of Split Dome (**Porky's Excellent Adventure**). A left-diagonalling dike marks the route. Pro: Three bolts, one fixed pin.

3107 **BLOOD AND CUTS   5.9**   This route is roughly opposite **Cleared For Takeoff**. Climb the hand crack 20 feet left of a left-facing corner.

3108 **HOT DOG IN A BUN   5.10d**   This route is in a waterchute to the left of Blood and Cuts. Pro: Four bolts, one fixed pin.

3109 **BLACK PANTHER   5.11c**   This west-facing black crack is to the left of **Blood and Cuts** (roughly opposite **The Popsicle**), on the first tier above the corridor. A large roof six feet off the ground makes this a challenging route.

The following routes are located at the left end of the tier above Blood and Cuts.

3110 **PREDATOR TIGRESS   5.11b ★★**   This route starts in a dark alcove on the back side of a large block (about 150 feet left and above **Blood And Cuts**). Undercling out left to an arête. Pro: Four bolts.

3111 **THE PATRIOT   5.10d ★★**   This route lies on the west-facing wall at the far left end of the tier. This is the left of two routes, and follows three bolts.

3112 **SMART MISSILE   5.10a R**   This route is two bolts to the right of **The Patriot**.

3113 **GAIA   5.11b**   This face route is on the north-facing wall to the right of the previous two routes. The route follows two bolts.

SCUD BOULDER

This is the rather large boulder on the approach to Future Games Rock and about 150 yards before Frigid Tower. The following routes are on the east face. Map, page 454.

3114 **THIS SCUD'S FOR YOU   5.11a ★**   This follows three bolts up the center of the SCUD boulder.

3115 **THIS SCUD'S A DUD   5.10d**   This route follows three bolts on the left side of the SCUD boulder.

3116 **DIKE FLIGHT   5.10+**   This route is on a large boulder that is about halfway between Split Rocks Parking Area and Future Games Rock. The climb is a two-bolt face climb that follows a dike slanting up and left.

FRIGID TOWER

This large boulder/rock lies directly on the trail from the Split Rock Parking Lot to Future Games Rock. It is split along its east-west axis by a chimney. Maps, pages 452, 454.

3117   **PUSS WUSS   5.10a** ★   This route lies on the left side of the north face of Frigid Tower. Climb a crack past a horizontal then go up face past two bolts to another crack. This crack leads to the summit.

3118   **THE SPUR OF THE MOMENT   5.12a** ★★★   This route is 40 feet to the right of **Puss Wuss** and right of a chimney. It is a four-bolt climb leading to a two-bolt anchor.

3119   **PRISONER OF INERTIA   5.10d** ★★   This climb is on the southwest face of Frigid Tower, near the center of the face (huge flake). Climb up past two bolts, then up left to the arête past two more bolts; two bolt anchor (same as for **The Spur of the Moment**).

3120   **FROZEN AT THE VOID   5.10c** ★★   Start to the right of **Prisoner of Inertia.** Climb past two bolts and a horizontal to the top of the flake; continue up the face above past one bolt.

3121   **SABRE   5.9**   This follows the crack to the right of a large chimney on the southwest face. Proceed up a left-facing corner to a roof, then up a wide crack at the top. Pro: To 3 inches.

FUTURE GAMES ROCK

This is the steep north-facing face that lies about 1 mile northeast of the parking lot. Map, page 452.

3122 **EXPLODING BROWN NODULES 5.11c**
3123 **ORNO-NECRO 5.11c ★** Pro: Thin to 2 inches.
3124 **THERAPEUTIC TYRANNY 5.11a R ★★** Pro: Thin to 4 inches.
3125 **THE BENDIX CLAWS 5.11a ★★★** Pro: Thin to 1.5 inches, one bolt.
3126 **HANG EM HIGH 5.12b ★★★** Pro: Thin to 1.5 inches, three bolts, one fixed pin.
3127 **CONTINUUM 5.8+ ★★★** Pro: To 3 inches.
3128 **GAMES WITHOUT FRONTIERS 5.13a/b ★★** Pro: Thin, three bolts.
3129 **INVISIBLE TOUCH 5.10b ★★** Pro: Thin to 2.5 inches.
3130 **INVISIBILITY LESSONS 5.9 ★★★★** Pro: To 2.5 inches.
3131 **DISAPPEARING ACT 5.10c ★★** Pro: Thin, four bolts.
3132 **SANDBLAST 5.7**

The next two routes are on the rock about 100 feet right of Future Games Rock.

3133 **CASUAL AFFAIR 5.10d ★★** This route ascends the left edge of the rock. Pro: Thin, one bolt.
3134 **SAFETY PIN 5.11c ★★** This route follows thin cracks up and left. It is just right of Casual Affair. Pro: Thin, one bolt, one fixed pin.

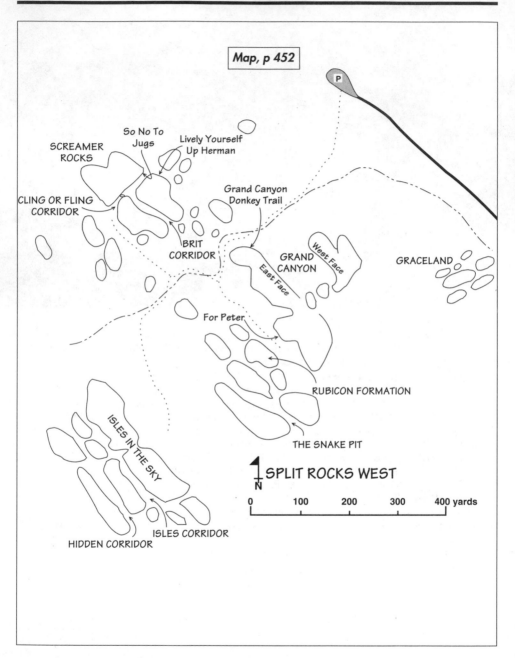

Map, p 452

SCREAMER
ROCKS

So No To
Jugs

Lively Yourself
Up Herman

CLING OR FLING
CORRIDOR

Grand Canyon
Donkey Trail

BRIT
CORRIDOR

GRAND
CANYON

West Face

East Face

GRACELAND

For Peter

RUBICON FORMATION

THE SNAKE PIT

ISLES IN THE SKY

SPLIT ROCKS WEST

N

| 0 | 100 | 200 | 300 | 400 yards |

ISLES CORRIDOR

HIDDEN CORRIDOR

GRAND CANYON – EAST FACE

SPLIT ROCKS – WEST PARKING AREA

The following routes lie to the west of the Split Rocks Parking Lot. Map, page 460.

GRAND CANYON

This is the first canyon to the south of the main wash heading southwest from the parking area. Routes lie on both sides of the canyon. Maps, pages 452, 460.

GRAND CANYON – WEST FACE

These routes lie on the smaller west face (east side) of Grand Canyon. The routes generally face **Grand Canyon Donkey Trail,** a route on the right (north) end of the east face (west side) of the canyon. Map, page 460.

3135 **SENDERO LUMINOSO 5.9** This route is directly opposite **Grand Canyon Donkey Trail** and climbs the west-southwest corner of a crag, passing three horizontal dikes and finishing with a hand crack. Two prominent chickenheads mark the route.

3136 **PUNISH THE MOSQUITO 5.10c** The leftmost (northern) route. Pro: Three bolts.

3137 **KOKOPELI 5.10d** The middle route. Pro: Three bolts.

3138 **BUNKING BRONCOS 5.10a** The right route. Pro: Three bolts, fixed RURP.

GRAND CANYON – EAST FACE

This is the steep east-facing wall that is visible from the parking lot. Map, page 460.

3139 **ELECTRIC BIRTHDAY PARTY 5.12b ★★★** This three-bolt line is the farthest left.

3140 **MIDNIGHT LUMBER 5.10d** Climb a left-facing dihedral that peters out into face climbing past a bolt. This is just right of the preceding route.

3141 **EVERY WHICH WAY BUT UP 5.12b R ★★** Climb Midnight Lumber to mid-height, then traverse right on a dike past four bolts to the upper section of **The Woodshed.**

3142 **THE WOODSHED 5.11d ★★★** This is the most obvious crack on the wall, about 40 feet left of **Grand Canyon Donkey Trail.**

3143 **GRAND CANYON DONKEY TRAIL 5.10a ★** This face climb is on the east face of a long wall about 250 yards southwest of the parking lot.

RUBICON FORMATION

This very large boulder/rock is to the west of Grand Canyon. It faces the backside of the west side of Grand Canyon. Maps, pages 452, 460.

3144 **FOR PETER 5.11c ★★★** This is directly across from the Rubicon Formation (on the west face of the west side of Grand Canyon). Climb up to and traverse a large dike.

3145 **TOTAL GENERIC PACKAGE 5.11c (TR) ★★★** Pro: Six bolts.

3146 **RUBICON 5.10d ★★★★** The direct start is 5.11+. Pro: Thin to 3 inches.

3147 **SEIZURE 5.12c ★★★** Pro: To 3 inches, five bolts.

THE SNAKE PIT

One of several areas in the monument that has recently been named "The Snake Pit" (just to confuse us). This particular area is a narrow north-south corridor just west of the Rubicon Formation. Maps, pages 452, 460.

3148 **COBRA CUNNING 5.9 R** The left slanting dike at north entrance to the corridor. Pro: Thin to 2.5 inches.

3149 **PIT VIPER 5.11b ★★** A nasty little dike climb on the east-facing (west) side of the corridor. Four bolts; two-bolt anchor/rap.

3150 **JUMPSTART 5.10a ★** Use two bolts to traverse left on the southern end of the east (west-facing) side of corridor.

3151 **THE EATING GORILLA COMES IN PEACE 5.10d** This route is across the corridor from **Pit Viper.** Climb up cracks/slot to a right-traversing crack under a roof; go right under roof to hanging belay at a corner. Continue traversing right to a ledge with rap anchors. Pro: Several fixed pins, thin to 2.5 inches.

ISLES IN THE SKY

This formation is about 1 mile southwest of the Split Rocks Parking Lot. Several obvious cracks are high on the east face. Easy scrambling leads up low angled slabs to a ledge system. Maps, pages 452, 460.

3152 **BEE GEES 5.10d**
3153 **NECTAR 5.4**
3154 **DEAD BEES 5.9 R ★**
3155 **DOLPHIN 5.7 ★★**
3156 **YOUNG GUNS 5.11d ★★★**
3157 **BIRD OF FIRE 5.10a ★★★★**
3158 **WINGS OF STEEL 5.11d ★★★**
3159 **RITES OF SPRING 5.9**

The next two routes are on a wall down and right from Isles in the Sky. The wall is characterized by large black flakes.

3160 **SAVE THE LAST STANCE FOR ME 5.9** Start right of a juniper tree and climb past four bolts.
3161 **SLAM DANCE 5.10c** This is right of the previous route. The climb has three bolts and passes a low-angled roof.
3162 **THE RAVEN 5.8** This is a three-bolt face route up solution pockets about 100 feet right of **Slam Dance.** Pro: To 3 inches.
3163 **WHITE MAMBA 5.12b ★★★** Traverse up and left along a long white dike on the wall 100 yards right of Isles In The Sky formation. Pro: Five bolts, two-bolt rap/anchor.

ISLES CORRIDOR – LEFT (West) SIDE

This narrow corridor has several good cracks on both sides of the corridor. Approach from the left (south) end of the ledge system on Isles In The Sky. Map, page 460.

3164 **DESCENT CRACK 5.2** This is the easy crack that can be used for a descent. It is the first crack on the left.

3165 **CRACK #2 5.6** The second crack on the left.

3166 **GROUNDER 5.9** The third crack from the left.

3167 **CRACK #4 5.10c** The fourth crack from the left.

3168 **CRACK #5 5.9+ ★★★** The fifth crack from the left.

3169 **METTLE DETECTOR 5.12b ★★★** This is a two-bolt climb between **Crack #5** and **Crack #6.**

3170 **CRACK #6 5.10a ★★★** The sixth crack from the left.

3171 **DREAMWORLD 5.10b** Climb the face to the right of **Crack #6** past one bolt. Near the top, either go straight up (5.10a) or to the right (5.8). Pro: Small to 2 inches.

3172 **HEAVY METTLE 5.11b** Start to the right of a wide crack. Climb a dike for a short distance (crux) then head up past a bolt to the top.

3173 **FREE ELECTRIC 5.11a** This is just right of **Heavy Mettle.** Start atop a boulder and face climb past two bolts along a dike.

ISLES CORRIDOR – RIGHT (East) SIDE

3174 **CRACK A 5.7+** The first crack on the right.

3175 **CRACK B 5.9** The second crack on the right.

3176 **MOUBIT 5.10a** Third crack from the right.

3177 **HOUR OF POWER 5.10a** Fourth crack from the right.

3178 **CRACK C 5.10c** Fifth crack from the right.

3179 **LIVING COLOR 5.12b (TR)** Climb the prominent overhanging face/arête up the center of a huge leaning pillar behind **Bird of Fire.** Belay bolts.

HIDDEN CORRIDOR

This corridor lies directly west of Isles Corridor, and is spanned by a giant chockstone at the south end. Map, page 460.

3180 **WEDLOCK 5.11a** Climb a thin crack up to a chockstone on the right (east) side, near the south end.

3181 **ROUTE 1202 5.10a** Climb a right-leaning crack system on the left side of the corridor.

SCREAMER ROCKS

The Screamer Rocks are the formations lying north and east of the open plain between Grand Canyon and Isles In The Sky. Maps, pages 452, 460.

CLING OR FLING CORRIDOR

3182 **BEAUTIFUL SCREAMER 5.11c ★★★** This is the leftmost route. Climb a crack past a bolt and three pins on the west face of the northernmost of two formations.

3183 **GULLYWOG 5.8 ★★** This route is to the right and around the corner from **Beautiful Screamer.** It is on the north side of a narrowing corridor that has a large chockstone wedged at its top.

3184 **LOST BOYS 5.10b** This is on the north side of the gully, directly opposite **Cling Or Fling.** Climb the face past two bolts, then go left to an easy crack.

3185 **ANGULAR MOMENTUM 5.9+ (TR)** This route lies on the north face (south side) of the corridor. Climb the face just right of a rotton crack (**Green Mansions**).

3186 **GREEN MANSIONS 5.8** Climb the "rotten crack" between **Angular Momentum** and **Cling or Fling.**

3187 **CLING OR FLING 5.11a ★★** This is a steep bolted face to the left of the **Green Mansions.**

3188 **PATANJALI'S SUTRA 5.11a (TR)** Start 20 feet left (east) of **Cling or Fling.**

3189 **CZECH COWS SAY BOO 5.9+** One bolt leads to a long crack in the back of the corridor on the south side (facing north).

BRIT CORRIDOR

This corridor runs roughly north-south and lies about 50 yards north of the Rubicon Formation. The north end of this corridor connects with the east end of the **Angular Momentum** corridor. Map, page 460.

3190 **BRITS IN DRAG** **5.10b ★★** Walk into the corridor until it narrows. At this point, two-pitch route lies on the east (left) face. Two bolts protect face climbing to a two-bolt belay. Follow a crack to the top.

The next four routes are on the wall opposite **Brits in Drag.**

3191 **PUNCTURE WOUND** **5.10c** This steep, widening crack is the farthest left route.

3192 **BATTERING RAM** **5.12c** This climbs past a bolt into a thin crack. This is the next route to the right.

3193 **LEAD BELLY** **5.10b ★** This and the previous route are most directly opposite **Brits in Drag.** Climb a steep face (no bolts) into a crack.

3194 **TWITTISH EMPIRE** **5.11b** The route is the farthest right. It is has one bolt and climbs the face leading into a crack.

The following routes are at the east end of the Cling or Fling corridor, and are best approached directly from the parking area by walking straight to the the east face of the rocks.

3195 **LIVELY YOURSELF UP HOMER** **5.10d ★★** This route lies on the east face, just south (left) of the entrance to the back of the corridor. It climbs a dike past four bolts.

3196 **SAY NO TO JUGS** **5.11a ★★** This route climbs past 4 bolts on the face 25 feet to the right of **Lively . . .,** It is on the righthand side of the corridor, .

MORONGO MAN CLIFFS

This cliff lies on the south side of the hills immediately north of Split Rocks parking area. This is, in actuality, very near Desert Queen Dome and Fraggle Rock (Desert Queen Mine Area). Hike north from the parking area, and you will see some cliffs on the southwest side of the drainage/wash that comes out of the hills to the north. A dihedral and roof are pretty obvious on these cliffs (**Morongo Man**). Map, page 452.

3197 **MORONGO MAN** **5.11c ★★★** This route climbs the dihedral to the roof, which is the obvious feature on the Morongo Man Cliffs.

3198 **MORONGO CHILD** **(var.) 5.10c** One can avoid the roof crack by traversing left along a horizontal crack.

3199 **FROM THE MOUTHS OF DOGS** **5.11b R ★★★** Climb an arête past three bolts to the left of Morongo Man. Pro: Medium to 2 inches for anchors.

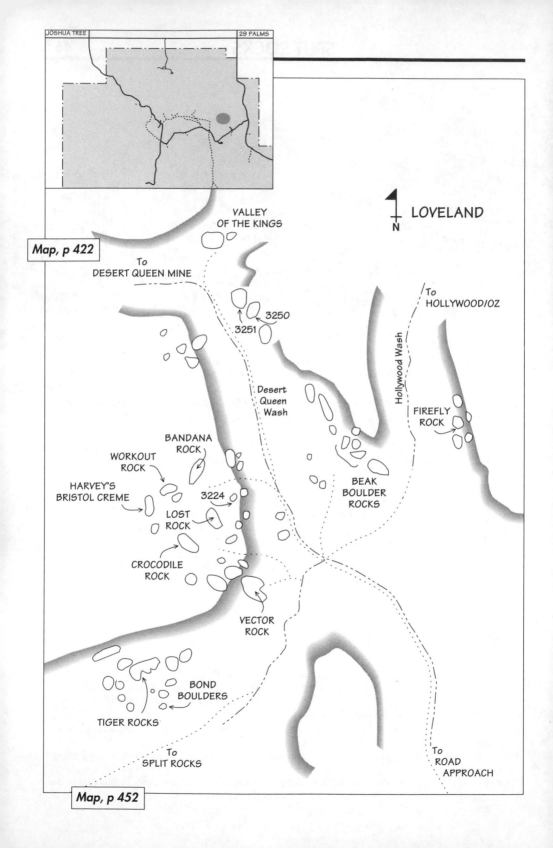

Map, p 422

Map, p 452

JOSHUA TREE

29 PALMS

LOVELAND
N

VALLEY
OF THE KINGS

To
DESERT QUEEN MINE

3250
3251

To
HOLLYWOOD/OZ

Desert
Queen
Wash

Hollywood Wash

FIREFLY
ROCK

BANDANA
ROCK

WORKOUT
ROCK

HARVEY'S
BRISTOL CREME

3224

LOST
ROCK

BEAK
BOULDER
ROCKS

CROCODILE
ROCK

VECTOR
ROCK

BOND
BOULDERS

TIGER ROCKS

To
SPLIT ROCKS

To
ROAD
APPROACH

LOVELAND

This loose conglomeration of large boulders and small formations lies north and northeast of the Split Rocks parking area. Map, page 452. A .75- to 1-mile walk northeast of the parking area will take you to Loveland. An alternate approach for some of the climbs is to drive about .75 mile past the Split Rocks turnoff along the Sheep Pass Loop Road to where a dirt mining road heads north. Hike about .75 mile along the mining road until the main wash is reached.

TIGER ROCKS

Tiger Rocks are the obvious south-facing rocks near the bottom of the southwestern "toe" of the hillside, northeast of Split Rocks. One walks below them and the Bond Boulders (see below) when approaching Loveland from Split Rocks. See map, page 466.

3200　**KON-TIKI 5.11c (TR)**　This is located on the west side of Kon-Tiki Boulder, a large boulder about 150 feet west of the Tiger Rocks.

3200a **BUSH BLOWS CHIPS 5.10c ★★★**　Pro: to 2.5 inches, 4 bolts, 2 bolt anchor/rap.

3201　**QUASAR 5.12a**　Pro: Thin to 2 inches.

3202　**ONE ARM GIANT 5.10d**

3203　**FLY AWAY 5.10d**

BOND BOULDERS

The Bond Boulders are two large boulders found below Tiger Rocks. Map, page 466.

3204　**ERCA 5.11a**　Three bolts.

3205　**MOONRAKER 5.10b**　This route is on the north face of the south boulder. Mantel, then climb past one bolt (may be missing).

3206　**DIAMONDS ARE FOREVER 5.10d**　Two bolts.

3207　**LIVE AND LET DIE 5.11a**　Three bolts.

3208　**DEEP, SHALLOW AND TWISTED 5.10c**　This is on a short, steep buttress of rock is west of the South Bond Boulder. Climb past three bolts on the left side of the south face.

VECTOR ROCK

This rock is easily seen upon entering the main Loveland wash. It appears as a large corner near the southeast end of the hillside facing east. Map, page 466.

3209 **VECTOR 5.11c ★★★★** This follows the thin, right-arching crack on the left wall of the Vector Rock dihedral.

3210 **ALL LOIN 5.10c** From the base of **Vector,** walk right around the corner and into a corridor. **All Loin** climbs the slightly overhanging finger crack on the left (south) wall.

Photo: Roger Linfield

CROCODILE ROCK

A small enclosed canyon lies up the hill and west of Vector Rock. Crocodile Rock is on the south side of this little canyon. Map, page 466.

3211 **I GET BY WITH A LITTLE HELP FROM MY FRIENDS 5.10a** ★★
3212 **B-MOVIE 5.10b** ★★★
3213 **CLAIM JUMPER 5.10d** ★★★ Pro: To 2 inches, three bolts.
3214 **HEAVY GOLD 5.10a** A dihedral with a gold-colored left wall is 100 feet right of **Claim Jumper.** Climb this dihedral, which starts on a ledge behind a tree.
3215 **HARVEY'S BRISTOL CREAM 5.10a** This double crack on the east face of a 50-foot rock is about 50 yards northwest of Crocodile Rock.

WORKOUT ROCK

This rock is about 30 yards northeast of **Harvey's Bristol Cream,** and about 70 yards north-northwest of Crocodile Rock. Map, page 466.

3217 **SPREAD & BUTTER 5.10b** This is the obvious right-facing dihedral that lies on the east face of Workout Rock.
3218 **LET'S GET PHYSICAL 5.10b** This is an offwidth/fist crack that starts 15 feet right of **Spread & Butter.**
3219 **ALMOST LIKE REAL CLIMBING 5.7** This lies between Vector Rock and the main Loveland wash, facing southeast. Climb an obvious finger-to-hand crack on a large boulder.
3220 **FISTING IN LOVELAND 5.9** This is a fist crack on a small buttress somewhere between Vector Rock and Bandana Rock. It faces northeast.

LOST ROCK

This is a large boulder/formation about 50 yards northeast of Crocodile Rock. Three routes ascend its northeast face. Map. page 466.

3221 **MISSING PERSONS 5.11c ★★★★** This is the leftmost of two bolted routes. There are seven bolts.

3222 **DESTINATION UNKNOWN 5.11d** The right route, with four bolts.

3223 **PEBBLE BEACH 5.7** Start right of **Destination Unknown.** Climb up and right past a "hole" and a flake to the top (no pro).

The next three routes are on large boulders east of Lost Rock. Map, page 466.

3224 **SHARP ARETE 5.10c ★★** This is the southeast arête of the westmost of the two boulders, and has three bolts.

3225 **SON OF OBSIDIAN 5.11c ★★** This is a two-bolt climb in the middle of the south face of the eastern boulder.

3226 **FORGOTTEN VENTURE 5.10b** This short, two-bolt route is right of **Son of Obsidian,** on the southeast corner of the boulder.

3228 **TRICKY MOVE 5.10a** This is a bolted route on the west face of another large boulder that lies south of the previous three routes.

BANDANA ROCK

This rock lies on the hillside about 200 yards north of the Vector Rock. Map, page 466.

3229 **MORE FOOL ME 5.9** This route climbs a hand crack that leads to the top of a pedestal. Follow a clean offwidth up the corner above.

3230 **SUZANNA'S BANDANA 5.7** This is to the right of **More Fool Me.** Climb up and left on a flake until you can climb a crack that leads up and right to the top.

3231 **DARK AGES 5.10a** To get to this route, walk up the main Loveland wash between Vector Rock and the Beak Boulders, then go left up the hillside past a large "Don Juan-type'" boulder. A formation with a crack splitting it called Medieval Highlands is another 70 yards west past the "Don Juan" boulder. This route climbs past three bolts on the face left of the crack.

THE BEAK BOULDER ROCKS

These rocks lie on the hillside to the east (right) of the main wash. The southern formation has a prominent beaked boulder near the southwest side. Map, page 466.

3232 **SOMETHING HEINOUS 5.9** A west facing wall with some left-slanting cracks is 100 yards left (north) and down from the Beak Boulder. This route climbs the leftmost cracks up to and over a roof before continuing to the top.

3233 **GOIN' DOWN THE ROAD FEELIN' BAD 5.10c** This clean, left-facing thin crack is 50 feet right of **Something Heinous.** Face climb or follow a crack on the right up to the leaning thin crack. Follow it to the top.

The next two routes are on a north-facing wall about 150 yards north of **Goin' Down the Road Feelin' Bad.**

3234 **I'M PREGNANT WITH SATAN'S BABY 5.11a** This is a face with four bolts left of an obvious arching finger crack.

3235 **STATUE OF ELVIS ON MARS 5.10a** This is the obvious, arching finger crack.

3236 **HEAVY SLANDER 5.10a (TR)** Climb a right leaning, slightly overhanging finger crack/lieback 50 feet right of **Something Heinous.**

The following three routes are on a boulder with sharp arêtes directly in front of the Beak Boulder.

3237 **SLEEK BEAK 5.10/11** This is on the east face, and passes three bolts.

3238 **SUPER BEAK OF THE DESERT 5.9** Climb the poorly-protected north arête of the boulder.

3239 **BEAK OF THE WEEK 5.7** This is the knife-edge south arête.

3240 **DESERT QUEEN 5.8** Climb the prominent hand crack on the wall below and to the right of the Beak Boulder.

3241 **FOR SURE 5.3** An interesting configuration of flakes and boulders is 100 yards right of the Beak Boulder This route climbs the chimney behind the flakes to the left.

3242 **TOTALLY TUBULAR 5.8** This totally enclosed, triangular shaped slot/chimney is behind the flakes and boulders comprising **For Sure.** Tunnel up the chimney/slot to the top.

3243 **SQUEEZE PLAY 5.10a** Climb the overhanging, converging and flared V-slot just outside and right of **Totally Tubular.**

On the backside (north and east) of the Beak Boulder Rocks are three prominent offwidth cracks.

3244 **THROBBING GRISTLE 5.12a (TR)** This is the leftmost of the three offwidth cracks on the backside of the Beak Boulder Rocks.

3245 **MODERN WARFARE 5.10a** Climb the middle of the three cracks, passing a bulge at the top.

3246 **KAMAKAZE 5.10c** Climb the offwidth in the corner 50 feet right of **Modern Warfare.**

LOVELAND NORTH

You'll find the following routes by continuing north-northwest up the main Loveland wash past all the previous formations. The identifying landmark is the point where the wash makes a distinct turn to the left (west). Map, page 466.

3247 **FOOL FOR A PRETTY FACE 5.10c** This is on the west face of a large boulder located a few hundred yards northwest of the Beak Boulders, at a point several hundred yards before the wash turns west. It is a three-bolt face climb just right of the northwest arête.

3248 **HEARTLESS 5.7** This prominent, 40-foot-long south-facing dihedral lies about 500 feet southeast of where the wash turns left (this is still well to the northwest of the Beak Boulder Rocks).

3249 **CRACK ADDICTION 5.10b** This is a right-slanting finger-and-hand crack is on the north side of the formation holding **Heartless.**

3250 **WHEN LOVE CAME TO TOWN 5.11c** This bolted face route lies north of the preceding routes on a west-facing, dark brown slab.

3251 **STRANGE KIND OF LOVE 5.11a** Climb a bolted face route on the southwest arête of a rock 100 yards north of **When Love Came To Town.**

3252 **IN THE NAME OF LOVE 5.11a** Start as for **Strange Kind of Love,** but climb up and right on the southwest face.

VALLEY OF THE KINGS

This area lies north and northeast of Loveland North, just west of the Hollywood/North Hollywood areas. Map, page 466.

3253 **HEART TRANSPLANT 5.10a** This is 100 yards north of where the main wash turns west. It is a hand crack right of a large roof on a southwest-facing formation.

3254 **REFLECTOR OVEN 5.10a** This is a thin face with two bolts on a formation about one mile north of the Beak Boulders. It faces southwest.

3255 **FIVE TWO-ISH 5.2** Climb a crack and left-leaning lieback just right of **Reflector Oven.**

3256 **YUPPIES DON'T DO OFFWIDTHS 5.9** An overhanging crack splitting the smooth east face of a large boulder is up the hillside to the west of **Reflector Oven.** A clean offwidth, which is the route, is around right and 100 feet up from this crack.

3257 **THE RAVEN 5.11b (TR)** This thin crack-to-steep face route lies on the south side of a large block up the hillside north of the point where the Loveland wash turns west. Bolt anchor.

FIREFLY ROCK

This rock lies on the hillside across a canyon/wash east of the Beak Boulder Rocks. It is about 150 yards north of an obvious rock with two dikes. Map, page 466.

3258 **FIREFLY 5.11b (TR)** Stem and lieback up a left-facing, bottomless corner to a roof about halfway up. Jam the crack above to the top.

The next two routes are on the alternate approach to Loveland (directly from the main road; not from Split Rocks), described on page___ .

3259 **WACKO PLACKO 5.10d** This route is on a formation just west of the road and parking area. Climb up and left to a crack on its west side. Go around a corner, then face climb past two bolts to the top.

3260 **TIDBIT 5.10a** This is on a small formation on the hillside to the left about halfway along the mining road on this alternate approach. Climb a fingercrack that lies on the right wall of a small dihedral on the formation's southeast face.

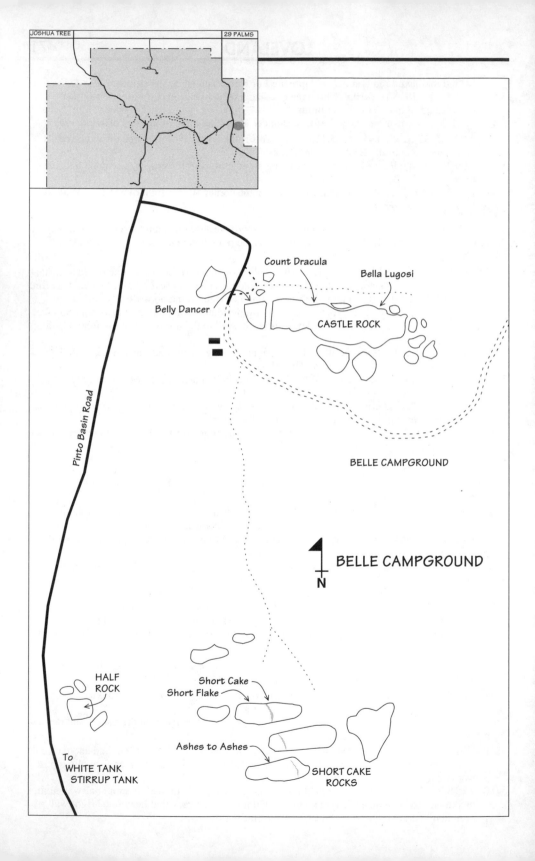

JOSHUA TREE   29 PALMS

Count Dracula

Bella Lugosi

Belly Dancer

CASTLE ROCK

Pinto Basin Road

BELLE CAMPGROUND

BELLE CAMPGROUND

N

HALF
ROCK

Short Cake
Short Flake

Ashes to Ashes

SHORT CAKE
ROCKS

To
WHITE TANK
STIRRUP TANK

BELLE CAMPGROUND

Sheep Pass Loop Road road takes a sharp turn left (north) and becoms Gold Park Road approximately 3.5 miles northeast of the Jumbo Rocks Campground. Gold Park Road descends, in about eight miles, to 29 Palms. At the point where the road changes names, another road splits off to the south; this is the Pinto Basin Road. A long and beautiful drive along the Pinto Basin Road eventually leads to U.S. Highway 10. Although the vast Pinto Basin and surrounding mountains are all part of the monument, little climbing potential exists.

Belle Campground is located about 1.25 miles south of the Pinto Basin Road from its junction with the Sheep Pass Loop Road. Most of the recorded climbs lie on the large, oblong formation in the middle of the campground, named Castle Rock. Map, page 472.

CASTLE ROCK – NORTH FACE

3261 **HALF CRACK 5.3**
3262 **ONE POINT CRACK 5.4**
3263 **TWO POINT CRACK 5.1**
3264 **MUSIC BOX 5.8**
3265 **BELLA LUGOSI 5.11c ★★**
3266 **THAT OLD SOFT SHOE 5.10d ★★**
3267 **BRIDE OF FRANKENSTEIN 5.12a (TR)** Climb the face between **That Old Soft Shoe** and **Transylvania Twist.**
3268 **TRANSYLVANIA TWIST 5.10d R ★★**
3269 **JUNCTION CHIMNEY 5.2**
3270 **RACKLESS ABANDON 5.10a X** The arête/right edge of **Junction Chimney.**
3271 **GROUND FINALE 5.10a**
3272 **CHIMNEY SWEEP 5.0**
3273 **COUNT DRACULA 5.10d ★★★**
3274 **DIAGNOSTICS 5.6 ★**
3275 **LOVE AT FIRST BITE 5.8 X**
3276 **DIABETICS 5.4**
3277 **BELLY DANCER 5.10d ★★★**
3278 **BELL-E-UP 5.11c ★★★** This route starts right of **Belly Dancer** and goes up and left around the corner, passing three bolts, to join **Belly Dancer** at its last bolt.
3279 **THE STRANGE ATTRACTER 5.12a ★** This grainy face climb starts to the right of **Bell-E-Up.** Head up and right, ending on south side.

CASTLE ROCK - SOUTH FACE

CASTLE ROCK – SOUTH FACE
See map on page 472.
3280 **TRUE GRIT 5.9**
3281 **YUCCA BOWL 5.6**
3282 **BONNY'S BOO-BOO 5.9**
3283 **BONNIE BRAE 5.7**
3284 **BUBBA'S TOURIST TRAP 5.9**
3285 **SAND IN MY SHOES 5.9 ★**

SHORT CAKE ROCKS
These formations lie about 200 yards south of Castle Rock and face north (toward Castle Rock). Short Cake Rocks are comprised of several large rocks with a prominent dike system running through the north and south faces. The three main rocks with established routes are referred to as Rock 1, Rock 2, and Rock 3. Map, page 472.

ROCK 1
This is the first formation south of Castle Rock, the dike runs up the center of this rock. Descend off back down dike (5.0). Map, page 472.
3286 **SHORT CAKE 5.10a ★** Climb the dike past two bolts.
3287 **SHORT FLAKE 5.6** Climb the flake and crack 25 feet right of **Short Cake.**

ROCK 2
This is the rock behind and left (southeast) of Rock 1. An unfinished three-bolt route lies to the left of the "dike." Map, page 472.
3288 **CAKE WALK 5.6** This route climbs the "dike" on the north side of Rock 2. One bolt, two-bolt belay/rap.

ROCK 3

This formation is behind (south) and slightly right (west) of Rock 1. It also is somewhat behind and more to the right (west) of Rock 2. There is a two-bolt rap anchor on top. Map, page 472.

3289 **ASHES TO ASHES** 5.10d ★ This steep three-bolt climb on the center of the north side of Rock 3.

3290 **BLUE SKY MINE** 5.10d (TR) Start as for **Ashes to Ashes** and traverse left, then up.

3291 **FOSSIL FIND** A2 This old aid climb follows thin cracks to the left of **Ashes to Ashes.**

3292 **BIG SANDY BOUND** 5.11a X ★★ This two-bolt face route lies on the south side of Rock 3. A "running" belay might help if you fell near the top.

HALF ROCK

This large boulder sits among several boulders almost directly west of Short Cake Rocks. All the routes are bolted and lie on the central, "pillar-like" boulder. Threre is a bolted rap anchor on top. Map, page 472.

3293 **VANISHING DESERT** 5.8 ★★ Start just left of the northeast arête and climb past three bolts up and left.

3294 **KINDLER AND GENTLER REAM JOB** 5.6 Climb up a flake on the northeast arête, then up the face past one bolt.

3295 **THE WETLANDS PRESIDENT** 5.10d ★ A two-bolt route on the left side of the south face.

3296 **GLOBAL WARMING** 5.11c ★★ A three-bolt route on south face to right of **The Wetlands President.**

VETO ROCK

This is the large split boulder that lies about 100 yards east of the campground.

3297 **RANGERS IN SPACE** 5.11a ★ Climb the bolted face route on the boulder's steepest side.

BECKY'S BUTTRESS AREA

This group of rocks is about 1 mile northeast of Belle Campground. They can be approached from the campground, but a slightly closer approach begins at a point midway along the road between the campground and the intersection of the Sheep Pass Loop Road with Pinto Basin Road. Becky's Buttress is the largest formation in the area; a west-facing rib leaning against a hillside.

3298 **BECKY'S BUTTRESS** 5.9 Climb the outer face of the buttress past four bolts.

3299 **ROAD DOGS** 5.7 This climbs a dihedral and overhanging thin crack on the right side of the steep north face of Becky's Buttress. It is left of the previous route.

3300 **GRAVITY PIRATES** 5.10 (TR) Climb overhanging buckets to a crack 25 feet left of **Road Dogs.**

3301 **GORBY GOES TO WASHINGTON** 5.8 This is a two-bolt climb on the north face of the clump of rocks 100 yards northeast of Becky's Buttress.

3302 **QUOTHE THE RAVEN** 5.7+ This route ascends the face to the right of

3303 **BOB** 5.10a This route ascends past three bolts on the dark east face of a rock 300 yards west of Becky's Buttress.

THE SATURN BOULDER

This aptly-named boulder is roughly halfway between Belle and White Tank Campgrounds, on the east side of the road.

3304 **THE SATURN BOULDER** 5.12b ★★★ Pro: Three bolts.

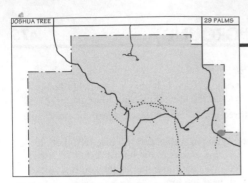

WHITE TANK CAMPGROUND

White Tank Campground lies about 1.25 miles south of Belle Campground, on the east side of the Pinto Basin Road. Lots of poor quality (some not-so-bad) rocks here, but not too many routes. (Not shown on a map.)

3306 **DESIDERIOUS DELIGHT 5.4** This route lies on the southeast corner of a pinnacle about 100 yards east of the campground and just west of a cement tank/dam.

3307 **QUAKING HAS-BEENS 5.9** This climbs the south face of the **Desiderious Delight** pinnacle. It has three bolts, but take some other pro along.

3308 **DOUBLE TROUBLE 5.11b (TR)** Climb double cracks on the north face of a formation southwest of **Desiderious Delight.** An old bolt is on top.

TIERRA INCOGNITO

3309

Photo: Rex Peiper

TIERRA INCOGNITO

This is the large, west-facing formation (perhaps the largest in White Tank Campground) that has dark rock on its left side and contains several right-diagonalling cracks.

3309 **TRICK OF THE TAIL 5.10a** Climb the most prominent right-diagonalling crack on Tierra Incognito.

3310 **JODY 5.10b** This steep finger crack is on the south face of a small boulder northeast of Tierra Incognito.

3311 **SHIT IT'S A BRIT 5.8** This route lies on the brown slab to the southeast of the main Tierra Incognito formation. Pro: Four bolts.

TORRE DEL SOL

This is a nice "tower" of rock just north of the old dam (actually "White Tank") that lies east-northeast of Tierra Incognito. It is best approached by walking east from the end of the campground loop along the nature trail leading to the dam. The following routes lie on the south face, a two-bolt anchor/rap is on summit.

3312 **WAITING FOR THE SUN 5.8** This is the crack on the left side of the south face.

3314 **COYOTE CRACK 5.7** This is the crack up the center of the south face.

3315 **NORTHERN LIGHTS 5.8+ ★★** Start as for **Coyote Crack,** but exit right and face climb past three bolts up and right.

BOVINE DOME

This small formation is 1.3 mile past White Tank Campground at the intersection of the Pinto Basin Road and the Stirrup Tank turnoff. There is a paved parking area here.

3316 **FOOTLOOSE 5.9** This is a short right-curving crack just right of the descent route on the face facing the main road (northeast face). It is 90 feet left of **Where Two Deserts Meet.**

3317 **UPEVIL 5.7** Climb obvious rotten cracks and flakes 30 feet left of **Where Two Deserts Meet.**

3318 **WHERE TWO DESERTS MEET 5.8 ★★** This is a right-curving thin crack on the north corner of the formation.

3319 **LOS TRES BOVINES 5.10c ★★** This three-bolt climb is just right of **Where Two Deserts Meet.** It starts by traversing right from the start of the above route.

3320 **WAITING FOR ALAN 5.4** Climb a crack right of a block on the southwest corner. Follow the crack right until it fades, then face climb to the top.

THE MAVERICK BOULDER

This isolated boulder lies across the road from Bovine Dome (about 200 yards).

3321 **DR GARLIC BREATH 5.10a** This one-bolt route faces away from the highway.

3322 **CLEARED FOR LANDING 5.8** Ascend rotten flake to a scoop on the west side of the Maverick Boulder.

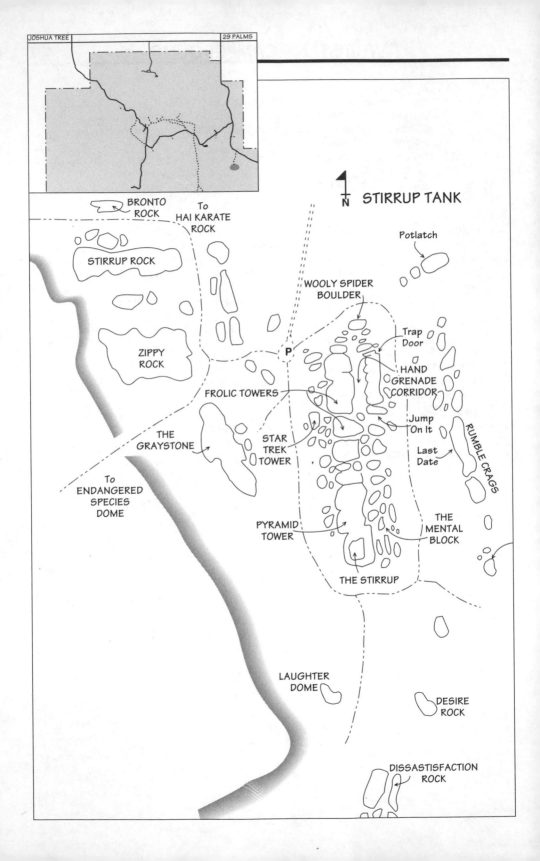

STIRRUP TANK

STIRRUP TANK AREA

Stirrup Tank is reached by way of a dirt road which is found about .3 mile south of White Tank Campground along the Pinto Basin Road. A paved parking area on the west side of the road marks the start of the dirt road. Follow this for about 1 1/4 miles to a parking area. Map, page 478.

3323 **CELTIC VATOR 5.10c** On a 45 foot tower just east of the road before getting to the parking area. A short brown dike can be seen about 15 feet from the top. Start at the right corner and diagonal up and left, eventually manteling the dike. No pro.

3324 **TRACTOR PULL 5.8** This is on a 40-foot boulder just south of **Celtic Vator.** Start below broken desert varnish below a short brown dike. Climb straight up, manteling the dike. No pro.

STIRRUP TOWERS

A north-south series of formations (The Stirrup Towers) lies on your left as you drive into the parking area. A large boulder with a wide crack on its right side is at the north end of The Strirup Towers; this is the Wooly Spider Boulder. At the extreme south end of Stirrup Towers is a prominent "perched" tower known as The Stirrup; it is the formation for which the entire Stirrup Tank area is named. Map, page 478.

WOOLY SPIDER BOULDER

A large boulder with a wide crack on the right side of its north face is at the north end of The Strirup Towers; this is the Wooly Spider Boulder. Map, page 478.

3325 **ARACHNIDS 5.5** Pro: One bolt.
3326 **TARANTULA 5.2**
3327 **WOOLY SPIDER 5.2**
3328 **NOT KING COLE 5.8**
3329 **BLACK WIDOW 5.10c** Pro: Two bolts.

STIRRUP TOWERS – WEST SIDE

There are number of climbs on both sides of (and in between) Stirrup Towers. The following routes either lie on the west side of Stirrup Towers or are best approached from that side. Please refer to both map and photographs for exact locations. Map, page 478.

STAR TREK TOWER

See map on page 478.

3330 **ROLLERSKATING WITH ALIENS 5.8** Pro: Two bolts.

3331 **BEAM ME UP SCOTTIE 5.10a ★** Pro: Three bolts.

3332 **THE ENTERPRISE 5.9 (TR)**

FROLIC TOWERS

See map on page 478.

3333 **FULL COUNT 5.8** This is a two-bolt face climb behind **Beam Me Up Scottie.** Two-bolt belay.

3334 **TOP-TOPIC 5.8** Pro: One bolt.

3335 **BUBLINKI 5.8** Pro: To 2.5 inches.

3336 **I SLEPT WITH L.K. 5.10a** This route climbs the thin crack 20 feet right of **Bublinki,** traversing right to a hand crack. Finish up the second pitch of **Space Metal** (5.9), or descend off to the north then head left out of the gap on the north side of the tower. Pro: To 2.5 inches.

3337 **SPACE METAL 5.10a ★** This is probably best approached from south end of the Hand Grenade corridor. Start down and right of **It Wasn't Very Good.** Climb up the arête past three bolts to ledge (5.10). The second pitch ascends east side of Frolic Tower past two bolts (5.9).

PYRAMID TOWER

Rap off the southeast corner of tower. Map, page 478.

3338 **GO ASK ALICE 5.10b ★** Climb up to the dike. Pro: To 2 inches, one fixed pin, three bolts.

3339 **FILET OF COLE 5.10b ★** Pro: Small to 3.5 inches, two bolts.

3340 **FRESH COMBINATION 5.6 ★** Pro: To 2 inches, one bolt.

THE STIRRUP

See map on page 478.

3341 **NOTCH ROUTE 5.6** Climb a hand crack out of the notch. This is on the north side of the tower.

3342 **EAST FACE 5.10a** Climb the steep, plated east face. Pro: Many small to 1 inches, no bolts.

STIRRUP TOWERS – EAST SIDE

The following routes generally lie on the eastern side of Stirrup Towers, and are best approached by walking around to the east of The Wooly Spider Boulder (the large boulder at the north end of Stirrup Towers). If you are in the vicinity of The Stirrup, just walk around the southern end of Stirrup Towers. Map, page 478.

HAND GRENADE CORRIDOR

A narrow corridor is on the northern end of the east side of Stirrup Towers, between Stirrup Towers and a north-south rock formation (Corridor Rock). This corridor runs along the east side of Grenade and Frolic Towers. On the north end of Corridor Rock, you will find **Trap Door** (5.6). Also, you can take a narrow passage at this point to enter the Hand Grenade Corridor. Map, page 478.

3343 **TRAP DOOR 5.4** This is a short, left-facing book formed by a white pillar leaning against a brown face. It is on the north end of Corridor Rock.

3344 **WINTERS MOON 5.11a** As you take the narrow passage past **Trap Door** to Hand Grenade Corridor, you will pass the south side of a large boulder. This route climbs past four bolts on the southwest side of this boulder.

3345 **HAND GRENADE 5.10a ★** This climbs the slanting hand crack on your right in the Hand Grenade Corridor. It leads to a ledge of sorts, then continues up a wide crack to the top of Hand Grenade Tower. Pro: To 4 inches.

3346 **HORSESHOE 5.11c ★★** This route lies 30 feet left of **Hand Grenade.** Face climb past four bolts to a crack. Pro: To 2 inches.

3347 **SUPREME COURT OR CONSERVATIVE RUBBER STAMP? 5.10b** This is a two-bolt face climb on the opposite side of Hand Grenade Corridor from **Hand Grenade** (on Corridor Rock).

3348 **JUMP ON IT 5.10b** This bolted face route lies on the south end of Corridor Rock on dark brown rock (not to be confused with **Space Metal** on the southeast arête of Frolic Tower).

THE MENTAL BLOCK

This large, "V"-shaped block is part of the jumble of boulders and rocks on the east side of Stirrup Towers, near its southern end. The Mental Block lies directly below the east side of Pyramid Tower. Map, page 478.

3349 **PARANOIA 5.11b ★★★** This is the righthand route on The V Block. Four bolts lead to rap anchors on the ledge above. Shares first bolt with the lefthand route.

3350 **MANIC DEPRESSION 5.11b ★★★** This is the lefthand route on The V Block; four bolts.

THE RUMBLE CRAGS

The Rumble Crags are just east of Stirrup Towers, and essentially parrallel the east side of Stirrup Towers. The routes are best approached by walking around the north end of Stirrup Towers (The Wooly Spider Boulder). Map, page 478.

3351 **POTLATCH 5.8** This is a straight-in finger crack on the northwest face of a large boulder about 150 yards northeast of Wooly Spider. It is easily seen on the drive in to the area.

3352 **ACCELERATOR 5.10b** This and the following route are on another large boulder right (southeast) of the previous route. This climbs the center of the north face past one bolt.

3353 **RUDY VALENTINE DAY 5.8** This is a poorly-protected climb 15 feet right of **Accelerator.**

The next two routes are on the west face of Rumble Rocks, east of the Stirrup Towers. Map, page 999.

3354 **LAST DATE 5.10b** This is a three-bolt climb on a short face.

3355 **WAR BABY 5.10a (TR)** Climb a very short smooth face 50 feet right of **Last Date.**

HERSHEY KISS

The Hershey Kiss is a small, pointed boulder/formation about 50 feet south of **War Baby.** There are two curving dikes on the north side. Map, page 478.

3356   **HERSHEY HIGHWAY   5.9 (TR)**   This is the left dike.

3357   **SPINAL TAP   5.9**   The right dike, with one bolt.

3358   **TRIAL BY FIRE   5.7**   This climbs a thin vertical dike on the east face of **Hershey Kiss.**

3359   **A NICE PAIR   5.9 ★★**   The face on the large boulder is about ready to slip off a very large south-facing ledge. This is a quarter-mile east of The Stirrup. Pro: Three bolts.

3360   **BRIGHT MOMENTS   5.9**   This is on a formation north of **A Nice Pair.** Go up a dike that splits into a V at the top. Two bolts.

DESIRE ROCK

This small formation lies about 100 yards southwest of **Hershey Kiss** and south of Stirrup Tower. Map, page 478.

3361   **PRIMAL URGE   5.9**   This climbs a brown open book on the east side of the formation.

DISSATISFACTION ROCK

Dissatisfaction Rcok is a large formation about 75 yards south-southwest of Desire Rock.

3362   **LESS THAN MEETS THE EYE   5.8**   This route is on the east face of Dissatisfaction Rock. It ascends a right-slanting system of discontinuous cracks to a large ledge. Pro: Thin to 2 inches.

LAUGHTER ROCK

This small formation is west of Desire Rock and north of Dissatisfaction Rock (southwest of Stirrup Tower).

3363   **CRACKUP   5.7**   This route climbs a short vertical crack on its southeast corner.

BIG ASS BOULDER

Head west from the vicinity of Desire Rock up the talus on the hillside. Big Ass Boulder is just that, up on the talus slope.

3364   **COOL MOVE, GRITTY ROCK, STANDARD PROCEDURE   5.10c**   Four bolts on the southeast face.

THE GRAYSTONE

This is the large rock southeast of Zippy Rock and opposite **Filet of Cole.** Map, page 478.

3365   **COWS IN THE SHADE   5.9**   Start in a short, right-slanting crack on the southeast side of the rock. Traverse left and go past two bolts to a bolt anchor on top.

3366   **CONVERGENCE CRACKS   Left, 5.9; Center, 5.8; Right, 5.10a R**

3367   **THE MICRO MILLENIUM   5.11d R ★★★**   Pro: Very tiny nuts.

3368   **THE MILLENIUM FALCON   5.11a (TR)**

3369   **THE EDGE   5.10b**   This two-bolt route lies on the left edge of the north side of a flake of rock 50 feet right of **The Micro Millenium.**

ZIPPY ROCK – EAST FACE

ZIPPY ROCK

This rock lies directly west of the parking area, and the following routes are on the east face. Map, page 478.

3370 **DON'T 5.10a** This big gritty face is left, around the corner and up a ways from Canalizo is . Pro 5 bolts.

3371 **CANALIZO 5.10c** This is a four-bolt climb just left of Gargoyle.

3372 **GARGOYLE 5.6**

3373 **THE MOUSTACHE 5.10a** Pro: Two bolts

3374 **FREE AS CAN BE 5.7**

3375 **DIE YOUNG 5.9**

3376 **JEDI MASTER 5.10c**

3377 **SHONGO PAVI 5.10c**

3378 **HANS SOLO 5.9**

3379 **J.B. GOES TO J.T. 5.8+ (TR)**

3380 **FLARING OFFWIDTH FROM HELL 5.10a** This is above **Hans Solo.** Hand traverse right, then up the offwidth. Tricky descent.

3381 **DOES ROYALTY GIVE HEAD 5.10c** This flake to the right of **Flaming Offwidth Form Hell,** joins with that route. Tricky descent.

3382 **WILD DREAM 5.10d** This is on the lower two-thirds of the face on the northwest side of Zippy Rock. It is a tilted block with brown patina rock/plates. Start at the left margin and diagonal right up the cracked plate to two bolts above near the skyline.

The next two routes are on the south face of a small rock between Zippy Rock and Stirrup Rock. Map page 478.

3383 **CAT PAWS 5.10b** The left route, with three bolts.

3384 **BLUE MOON 5.10b** The right climb, with two bolts.

STIRRUP ROCK – SOUTH FACE

This formation lies about 150 yards northwest of the parking area, and is easily distinguished by the very dark brown rock on the south face. Map, page 478.

3385 **DANCIN' DAZE 5.8** ★
3386 **PETER EASTER PUMPKIN EATER 5.10c** ★★
3387 **OVERPOWERED BY FUNK 5.12a** ★★

STIRRUP ROCK – NORTH FACE

See map on page 478.

3388 **CRACK KILLS 5.10c** This crack is about 50 feet to the left of **New Toy.**

3389 **SEEBOLT 5.11c** Start up **Crack Kills,** but exit right over a roof and climb the face above.

3390 **NEW TOY 5.6**

3391 **JUGULAR VEIN 5.8**

3392 **FRECKLE FACE 5.11a ★★★**

3393 **DO OR DIKE 5.9**

3394 **HOLD TIGHT TIL FOOTINGS RIGHT 5.11a (TR)** Climb a steep bucketed face about 25 right of **Do Or Dike.** The first moves are the crux.

3395 **FINGER BOWL 5.12a** This is approximately 100 feet to the right of **Do Or Dike.** Climb the right side of a very large boulder past four bolts.

BRONTO ROCK

This formation is just north of Stirrup Rock and is distinguished by the "X" formed by a crack and a dike on its south face. Map, page 478.

3396 **STEGASAURUS 5.9**
3397 **CRACK' N' UP 5.4**
3398 **TREMOR 5.10b (TR)**
3399 **FLASHFLOOD 5.11a (TR)**
3400 **STINGER 5.10a (TR)**
3401 **JUNKIE THRILL 5.6**
3402 **BUCKEYE 5.4** Climb an obvious dike left of center on the north face of the rock.

HAI KARATE ROCK

Walk west in a wash from Bronto Rock for 250-300 yards. This is a short brown wall up and left, facing north. Map, page 478.

3403 **FULL CONTACT KARATE   5.10b**   Climb an overhanging crack in a dark brown
     dihedral.

3404 **ZEN GOBLINS   5.10c**   This is the steep brown face with two bolts right of **Full Contact
     Karate.**

JERRY FALL WALL

This dark brown formation with several prominent cracks is east of Hai Karate Rock and slightly south. It can be found fairly easily when descending to the right from Hai Karate Rock.

3405 **DIABETIC SHOCK   5.10c**   This route lies on the approach to Endangered Species
     Dome, about halfway up the hill west-southwest of the parking area. From the vicinity of
     Star Trek Tower, the slab containing this route looks like a tooth with an overhang at the
     bottom. Pro: Three bolts.

ENDANGERED SPECIES DOME

This dome is about 1.3 mile west of the Stirrup Tank parking area. Walk west, passing along the south side of Zippy Rock. Continue up slabs and enter a hidden valley. This is the large east-facing rock at the end of the valley. There are two routes, both with bolts. Map, page 478.

3406 **REVENGE OF THE HERDS   5.8**   The leftmost bolted route.

3407 **THE RIGHT TO ARM BEARS   5.11b**   The rightmost bolted route.

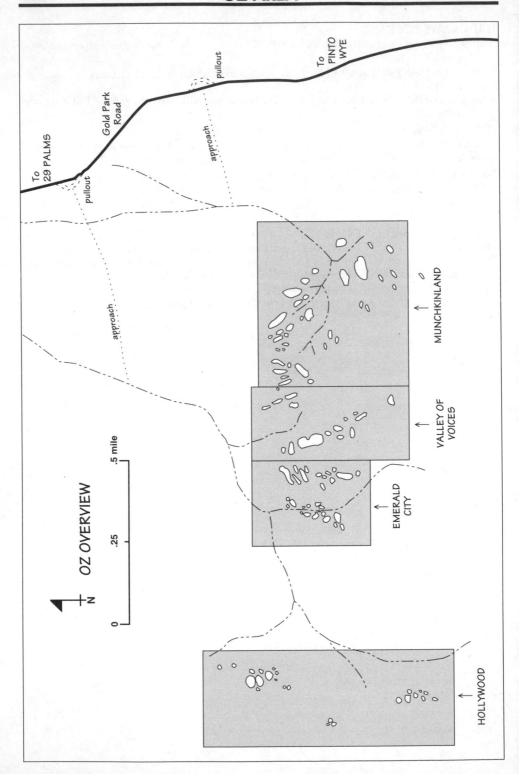

OZ

This complex and vast area of rocks covers an area about .5 mile west of Gold Park Road (the road to 29 Palms). It is just northeast of Loveland and just east of the Desert Queen Mine area. There are several distinct sub-areas within Oz: Munchkinland, The Valley of Voices, Emerald City and Hollywood. Map, page 488.

There are at least four different ways of approaching Oz, each approach depending on the specific area you wish to visit. However, the two main approaches are both from Gold Park Road (towards 29 Palms from the Sheep Pass Loop Road/Pinto Basin Road intersection).

Munchkinland is best approached from a dirt pullout on the east side of Gold Park Road, about 1.2 miles north of the Sheep Pass Loop Road/Pinto Basin Road intersection. Munchkinland appears as a cluster of dark rocks in a canyon to the southwest.

The Valley of Voices, Emerald City and Hollywood are best approached from a pullout (interpretive sign located here) on the west side of Gold Park Road about 1.4 miles north of the Sheep Pass Loop Road/Pinto Basin Road intersection .2 mile past the approach turnout for Munchkinland. A broad alluvial valley is to the west.

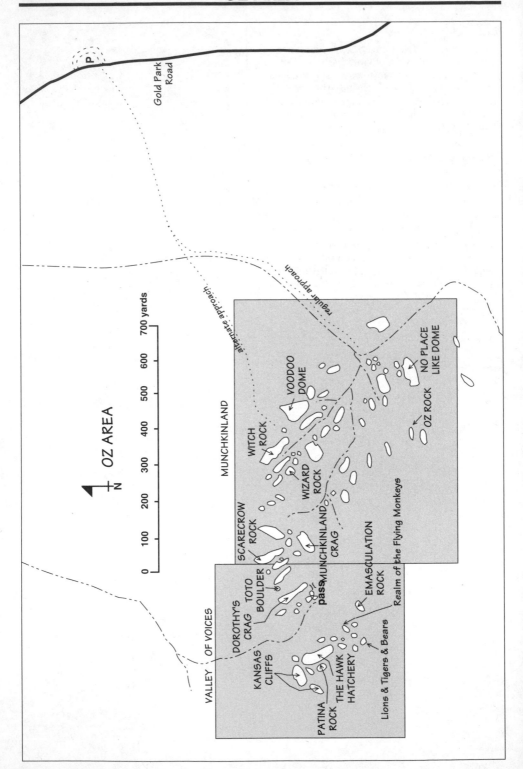

OZ AREA

N

0   100   200   300   400   500   600   700 yards

Gold Park Road

P

regular approach

alternative approach

MUNCHKINLAND

VALLEY OF VOICES

SCARECROW ROCK

WITCH ROCK

VOODOO DOME

WIZARD ROCK

OZ ROCK

NO PLACE LIKE DOME

MUNCHKINLAND CRAG

pass

DOROTHY'S CRAG

TOTO BOULDER

EMASCULATION ROCK

Realm of the Flying Monkeys

KANSAS CLIFFS

PATINA ROCK

THE HAWK HATCHERY

Lions & Tigers & Bears

MUNCHKINLAND

Munchkinland is best approached from a dirt pullout on the east side of Gold Park Road, about 1.2 miles north of the Sheep Pass Loop Road/Pinto Basin Road intersection. It appears as a cluster of dark rocks in a canyon to the southwest. Most of Munchkinland lies to the northwest of the dark rocks in the canyon, on the south-facing slopes of the hillside between the aforementioned canyon and the broad valley lying to the north (the approach to the other areas). Plan on 15 to 20 minutes for the initial approach. Maps, pages 490, 492.

NO PLACE LIKE DOME

As you enter the narrowing canyon, you will see a large dome to the southwest (ahead and left); it lies slightly behind and south of a formation with a roof on it. All known routes lie on the complex north face (facing toward the approach canyon). Map, page 492.

3408 **GLENDA CRACK   5.10d R ★★★**   Pro: Many small to 2 inches.
3409 **CLICK YOUR HEELS TWICE   5.10c ★★★**   Pro: Many small, two bolts.
3410 **THERE IS NO PLACE LIKE HOME   5.10c R**   Pro: To 2 inches, three bolts.
3411 **THE ANSWER   5.9 ★★**   Pro: To 3 inches.
3412 **HONEY   5.9 ★★★**   Pro: To 3 inches.
3413 **THE QUESTION   5.10b**   Pro: To 2.5 inches.
3414 **QUIVERS   5.5 ★★**   This is around on the right side of the formation. Traverse the lip of a roof past three bolts and ascend an arête.
3415 **(Variation) QUIVERS DIRECT   5.8 (TR)**   Climb straight up past the first bolt on **Quivers.**

OZ ROCK

This small dark tower lies to the west of No Place Like Dome, and is best approached by walking west in the initial streambed (on the north side of the formation just north of **No Place Like Dome**), then over a small rise to this rock, which is in a low wash. Map, page 492.

3416 **TOTO'S CANINE HOT LUNCH   5.8**   This routh lies on the south face of Oz Rock and climbs past two bolts.

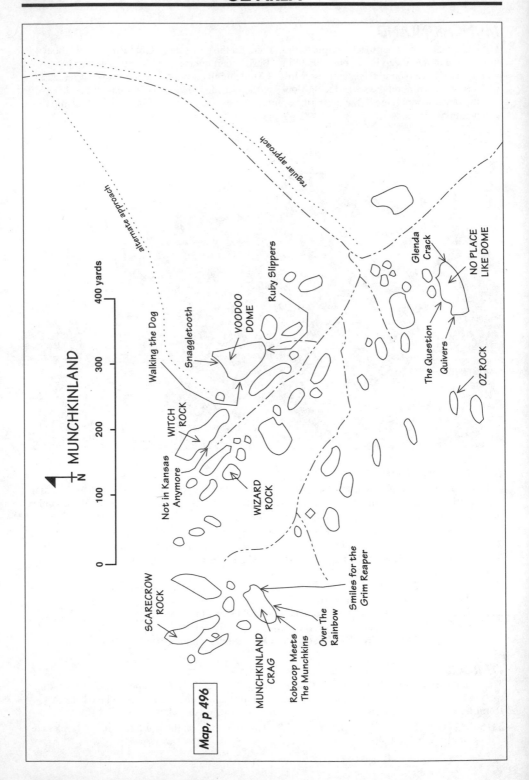

Map, p 496

N
MUNCHKINLAND

0   100   200   300   400 yards

alternate approach

regular approach

SCARECROW ROCK

MUNCHKINLAND CRAG

Robocop Meets The Munchkins

Over The Rainbow

Smiles for the Grim Reaper

Not in Kansas Anymore

WITCH ROCK

WIZARD ROCK

Walking the Dog

Snaggletooth

VOODOO DOME

Ruby Slippers

Glenda Crack

The Question

Quivers

NO PLACE LIKE DOME

OZ ROCK

VOODOO DOME

This formation lies about 325 yards north of No Place Like Dome. It is best approached by hiking to the right (following the streambed), then up the canyon roughly north for several hundred yards until the canyon opens up slightly. Ahead, the canyon narrows considerably (Witch Rock/**Not In Kansas Anymore** lies straight ahead on the right), and it is possible to walk east (right) again. After turning east (right), Voodoo Dome is straight ahead. Most routes lie on the west face, but a few are on the shorter northeast face (Wall of Voodoo) around to the left. Map, page 492.

3417 **RUBY SLIPPERS 5.11a** This route lies on the extreme righthand side of the formation, a clean, south-facing slab with three bolts and two-bolt rap anchor.

3418 **REJECT THE DOMINANT PARADIGM** Just right of **Walking The Dog.**

3419 **WALKING THE DOG 5.9** Start on jugs leading to a bolt, then traverse left and follow the arête past two more.

3420 **THE HOURGLASS 5.10c ★★** Pro: To 2 inches, three bolts.

3421 **MY LITTLE PRETTY 5.9+** Pro: Small to 2.5 inches, two bolts.

The following route lies on the Wall of Voodoo (the northeast face).

3422 **SNAGGLETOOTH 5.9 ★** Two "V" cracks lie on a large flake below a steep face. Climb the left crack straight up, then traverse left and up to another crack/flake to the top.

WITCH ROCK

Witch Rock lies about 100 yards northwest of Voodoo Dome and about 400 yards north of No Place Like Dome. From the vicinity of No Place Like Dome, it is best approached by hiking to the right (following the streambed), then head roughly north up the first canyon for several hundred yards until the canyon opens-up slightly. Ahead, the canyon narrows considerably. Witch Rock lies straight ahead on the right side of the narrow canyon. Maps, pages 490, 492.

3423 **NOT IN KANSAS ANYMORE 5.9+** This route is located approximately two-thirds of the way up the narrow canyon, on the righthand side. Climb an 80-foot torpedo-shaped buttress past three bolts.

WIZARD ROCK

This formation is part of the complex set of rocks that form the left side of the narrow canyon containing Witch Rock (which is the right side of the canyon). The only route, as well as the actual rock, both face west and are reached by taking the approach to Voodoo Dome and Witch Rock. at the point where you would go right to get to Voodoo Dome, go left (west) instead, heading over a small "pass." Head uphill along the western side of the rocks to your right. This formation may also be approached via another wash further west from the one taken to approach Voodoo Dome. Map, page 492.

3424 **GUARDIAN OF THE GATE 5.9+** This route lies about helfway up the west side of the rocks. Climb a steep face to a flake, then continue up face to the top. Pro: To 3 inches, three bolts.

MUNCHKINLAND CRAG

Approach this formation as you would Wizard Rock (either way suggested), but continue to the northwest for about 200 yards. The routes lie on the south face. Map, page 492.

3425 **ROBOCOP MEETS THE MUNCHKINS 5.10a ★★** Pro: One fixed pin, three bolts.

3426 **OVER THE RAINBOW 5.11a ★★** Pro: Three bolts.

3427 **SMILES FOR THE GRIM REAPER 5.10c ★★** Two pitches advised. Pro: To 3.5 inches.

SCARECROW ROCK

This formation is the righthand side of a small canyon that lies directly north (and behind) Munchkinland Crag. It also lies just east of the top of the Valley of Voices. It is probably equally easy to reach this formation via the Munchkinland approach as from the Valley of Voices approach. Map, page 492.

3428 **IF I ONLY HAD A BRAIN 5.10c** This is the leftmost of two obvious flake systems on a beautiful brown wall and has two bolts.

3429 **STRAW MAN 5.10c** This route with 3 bolts is just right of **If I Only Had A Brain.**

TOTO BOULDER

This large round boulder lies about 130 yards northwest of Munchkinland Crag, high on the hillside near the "pass" leading to the Valley of Voices. It lies about 80 yards west of Scarecrow Rock, above the west side of a a formation lying parrallel to Scarecrow Rock. It also is about 50 yards above and left of Dorothy's Crag. Map, page 492.

3430 **TOTO 5.10b** This is the two-bolt face route on the southwest corner/face of **Toto.** Two-anchor/rap bolts on top.

SCARECROW ROCK

3427

3426

3425

MUNCHKINLAND CRAG

Unfinished Route

APPROACH

MUNCHKINLAND CRAG

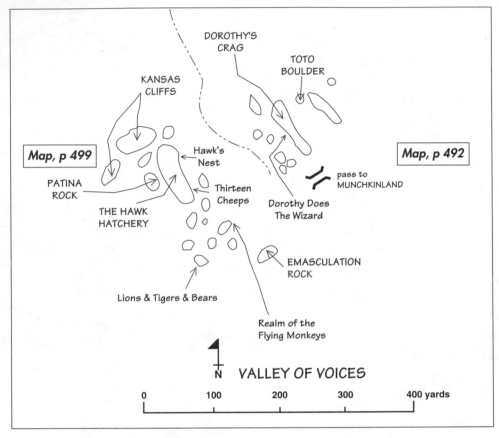

KANSAS
CLIFFS

DOROTHY'S
CRAG

TOTO
BOULDER

Map, p 499

Hawk's
Nest

Map, p 492

PATINA
ROCK

pass to
MUNCHKINLAND

Thirteen
Cheeps

THE HAWK
HATCHERY

Dorothy Does
The Wizard

EMASCULATION
ROCK

Lions & Tigers & Bears

Realm of the
Flying Monkeys

N VALLEY OF VOICES

0   100   200   300   400 yards

THE VALLEY OF VOICES

This small valley lies to the northwest of Munchkinland and is best approached (as are Emerald City and Hollywood) from a pullout (interpretive sign located here) on the west side of Gold Park Road about 1.4 miles north of the Sheep Pass Loop Road/Pinto Basin Road intersection (.2 mile past the approach turnout for Munchkinland). A broad alluvial valley is to the west. Walk up this valley approximately 1 mile until a small wash/valley appears to your left (south). This is the first valley/side wash encountered on the left (it is not very pronouced at the mouth, but rocks can be seen high up on the righthand side of the Valley of Voices from the main approach valley). Plan on 25-30 minutes to reach this point from the car. Map, page 490.

The Valley of Voices also can be reached via a small "pass" lying just to the northwest of Munchkinland Crag. Map, page 488.

EAST SIDE OF VALLEY OF VOICES

DOROTHY'S CRAG

This formation is high on the southern part of the east side of Valley of Voices. It is just north of the "pass" between Munchkinland and Valley of Voices. Map, page 490 and above.

3431 **DOROTHY DOES THE WIZARD 5.10b** This is the obvious central vertical crack.
   Pro: Thin to 3 inches.

WEST SIDE OF VALLEY OF VOICES

The west side of Valley of Voices has a multitude of crags and boulders that face east and, near the northern (lower) end of the valley, face north. The routes and formations are all described right to left (south to north). See map above.

EMASCULATION ROCK

This small formation is furthest south, and actually lies on the lower portion of a large hillside south of the hill containing the majority of the west-side formations. Map, page 496.

3432 **NO NUTS 5.10a** This route lies on the north face of Emasculation Rock. It is a crack that curves up and right near the center of the north face.

3433 **LIONS AND TIGERS AND BEARS 5.10a** This route lies on the south face of a formation up and right from Emasculation Rock, and essentially on the south side of a "pass" leading over the western ridge to Emerald City. It is a steep hand crack that leads to an arête with three bolts. Pro: To 3 inches.

3435 **REALM OF THE FLYING MONKEYS 5.11d ★★★★** This route lies on the overhanging and north-pointing arête/prow of a large boulder. Pro: Four bolts, two-bolt anchor/rap.

3436 **DOWN WHERE THE GOBLINS GO 5.10b** Follow the finger crack through a bulge to a slab finish. Pro: To 1.5 inches, two bolts.

THE HAWK HATCHERY

This broad and complex face lies in the middle of the western side of Valley of Voices. Map, page 496.

3437 **DANGLING DIGIT 5.8 ★** This is a hand crack that thins and jogs slightly right above bulge. Pro: To 3 inches.

3438 **THIRTEEN CHEEPS 5.10b ★** This very thin crack 30 feet right of Dangling Digit. The crack widens some at the top. Pro: Thin to 2 inches.

3439 **HAWKS NEST 5.7 ★★★** This is a steep, 120-foot hand crack with buckets.

PATINA ROCK

This formation lies about 50 yards above and behind (west of) The Hawk Hatchery. Map, page 496.

3440 **GRIPPED FOR PETINA 5.9 ★** Climb the crack in a right-facing corner to a bulge with a very wide crack, then follow an easier crack above. Pro: To 4 inches.

KANSAS CLIFFS

These various rocks lie on the north end of the west side of Valley of Voices, downhill and around the corner from The Hawk Hatchery. The rocks generally face to the north. Map, page 496.

3441 **UNTIE EM 5.8** Climb the steep face with jugs past three bolts.

3442 **WICKED WITCHCRAFT 5.11c ★★★** This route is about 100 yards up and right (west) of Untie Em. A large pine tree marks the crag. Climb a blunt arête past two horizontal seams. Pro: Five bolts, two-bolt anchor.

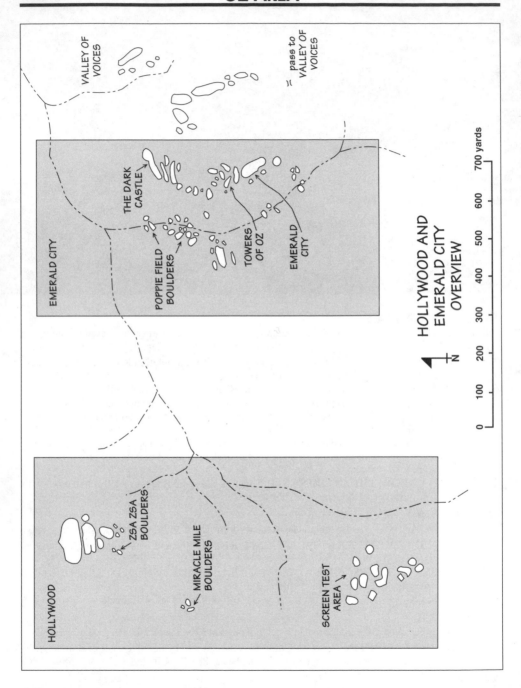

HOLLYWOOD AND
EMERALD CITY
OVERVIEW

N

0   100   200   300   400   500   600   700 yards

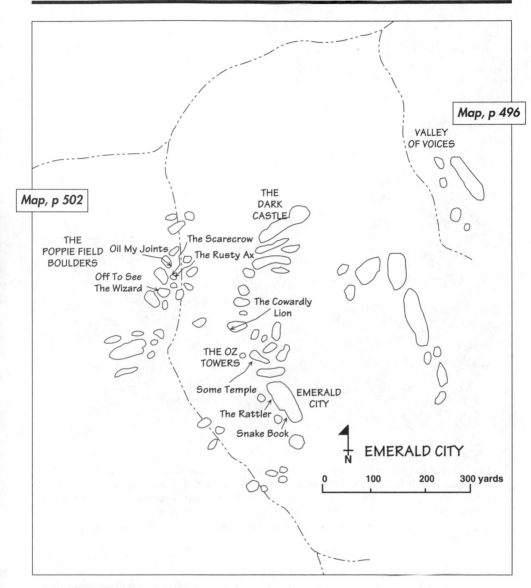

EMERALD CITY

This area is in the next valley west of Valley of Voices and is best approached (as are Valley of Voices and Hollywood) from a pullout (interpretive sign located here) on the west side of Gold Park Road about 1.4 miles north of the Sheep Pass Loop Road/Pinto Basin Road intersection (.2 mile past the approach turnout for Munchkinland). A broad alluvial valley is to the west. Walk up this valley for approximately 1.2 miles until a small wash/valley opens to your left (south); this is the Valley of Voices. Walk a little further and you will see a larger valley/wash heading up and south (on your left). It is easily recognized by the large number of huge boulders in the wash. Plan on 35-40 minutes to reach this point from the car. Map, page 488.

The Emerald City also could be reached via a small "pass" just to the southwest of the west side of Valley of Voices, and between Emasculation Rock and **Lions and Tigers and Bears.** This approach would only make sense if you were already either in Munchkinland or Valley of Voices. Map, page 488.

THE OZ TOWERS

3447

POPPY FIELD BOULDERS

3446

3445

3443

3444

THE POPPIE FIELD BOULDERS

These giant boulders fill the bottom half of the Emerald City canyon/wash. Several routes have been done on these boulders and much potential remains for short face and crack routes. The largest of the first set of boulders has an incredibly thin and overhanging crack on its north face. It has not gone free (at this time), but promises to be very difficult and good.

Another more numerous set of large boulders lies further up the wash (40-50 yards). Several routes have been done on these boulders.

The most obvious feature on these boulders is a hands-to-offwidth crack splitting the left side of a boulder facing north. (**The Rusty Ax**). Map, page 499.

3443   **THE RUSTY AX   5.6**   This is the obvious hands-to-offwidth crack splitting the left side of the north face of a large boulder near the center of the second set of boulders.

3444   **THE SCARECROW   5.10a**   This is a flaky two-bolt face route just right of **The Rusty Ax.**

3445   **OIL MY JOINTS   5.10c ★★**   This overhanging two-bolt route on the south end of the boulder just northwest of **The Rusty Ax.** Two-bolt anchor/rap.

3446   **OFF TO SEE THE WIZARD   5.10b ★★**   This two-bolt route lies on the west side of a large boulder 50 feet behind (southwest) of **The Rusty Ax.** Two-bolt anchor/rap.

THE OZ TOWERS

This set of large blocks has a prominent pinnacle set near the right-hand side.   Map, page 499.

3447 **THE COWARDLY LION   5.9+** Four bolts.

3449 **SONIC TEMPLE   5.11c ★★★★**   Five bolts. Two-bolt rap/anchor (toprope anchor for **Dave Ate The Cookie**).

3450 **DAVE ATE THE COOKIE   5.11d (TR) ★★★**   Start as for **Sonic Temple,** but climb up and right.

EMERALD CITY

This is the main formation facing west. It has some of the best routes in the entire Oz area. Map, page 499.

3451 **THE RATTLER   5.11a ★★★★**   Pro: To 4 inches, many 1 to 1.5 inches.

3452 **YELLOW BRICK ROAD   5.11a ★★★★**   Pro: Eight bolts; two-bolt anchor.

3453 **IN THE GREEN ROOM   5.9 ★**   Pro: To 4 inches.

3454 **IS THAT A MUNCHKIN IN YOUR POCKET   5.11b (TR) ★★★**

3455 **SNAKE BOOK   5.11b ★★★★**   The very attractive dihedral on right end of cliff. Pro: Many to 2 inches, two-bolt anchor/rap.

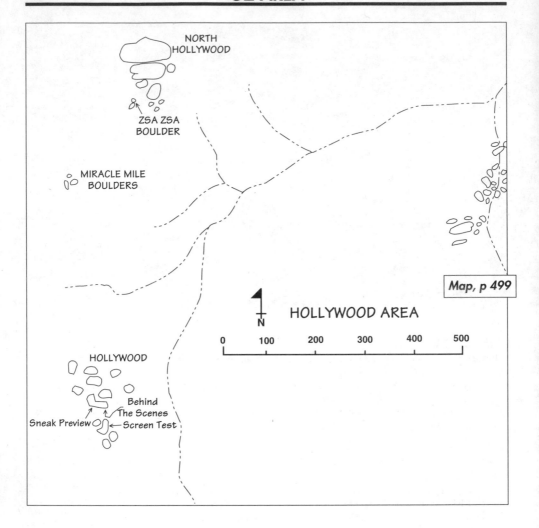

HOLLYWOOD

Hollywood is the next valley (which extends both north and south) beyond Emerald City. As with Valley of Voices and Emerald City, it is best approached from a pullout (interpretive sign located here) on the west side of Gold Park Road about 1.4 miles north of the Sheep Pass Loop Road/Pinto Basin Road intersection (.2 mile past the approach turnout for Munchkinland). Walk up a broad alluvial valley to the west for approximately 1.5 miles, past both Valley of Voices and Emerald City (two southern washes leading to high valleys). The main wash opens up considerably and continues straight west (eventually meeting up with Desert Quenn Mine) as well as extending both north and south. Plan on 45-55 minutes to reach this point from the car.   Map, page 488.

Hollywood is a vast area of boulders and formations that extends both north and south from the approach wash opens up and splits in three directions. Only a limited amount of activity has occured here. The wash extending to the north is called North Hollywood and the southern area is Hollywood proper. Hollywood lies just northeast of Loveland; in fact, it may be easier to approach Hollywood from Loveland, by walking east around the Beak Boulder and down into the canyon on the right.

NORTH HOLLYWOOD

As the name suggests, you must head north into the open side wash/flats where the wash opens up to reach North Hollywood. A large formation is about 350 yards to the north-northwest. There are no routes on this (yet) but several large boulders lie to the southwest of this formation. The Zsa Zsa Gabor Memorial Boulder is located here. Map, page 502.

ZSA ZSA GABOR MEMORIAL BOULDER

This triangular, clean-cut boulder is on the righthand side (north) of a large blocky boulder about 75 yards southwest of the large main formation described above. Map, page 502.

3456 **OPEN CONTAINER 5.8** Climb the face and edge on the northwest corner of the boulder. Pro: Two bolts; two-bolt anchor/rap.

3457 **LESBIAN LUST 5.9+ ★★★★** The southeast arête. Four bolts.

3458 **ASSAULT AND BATTERY 5.11a (TR)** Climb the center of north face.

MIRACLE MILE BOULDERS

These cleanly split boulders are somewhat similar to the Zsa Zsa Boulder, and lie with several other large boulders, higher on the ridge, about a quarter mile to the southwest of the Zsa Zsa Boulder. Map, page 502.

3459 **WALK OF FAME 5.10c ★★★** Ascend steep edges on the north face of the split boulder. Pro: Three bolts; two-bolt anchor/rap.

3460 **RIGHT DOUBLE FEATURE CRACK 5.8 ★★** This and the left crack are on the "other half" of the split boulder containing **Walk of Fame.** Pro: To 3 inches.

3461 **LEFT DOUBLE FEATURE CRACK 5.7 ★★★** Pro: To 3 inches.

HOLLYWOOD

This area lies to the south of the main wash where it splits/opens. This area could be perhaps more easily approached from Loveland (see approach information above). Map, page 502.

3462 **SCREEN TEST 5.11a** Pro: Five bolts; one-bolt belay.

3463 **SNEAK PREVIEW 5.9** This route is on the south face of the "s" boulder in the clump of towers in the center of the basin. Steep edges on right side of the face. Pro: Three bolts; two-bolt anchor/rap.

3464 **BEHIND THE SCENES 5.10a ★** Face climb 15 feet left of **Sneak Preview.** Pro: Three bolts.

MAGIC MOUNTAIN AREA

This is the small group of rocks on the west side of the road and just inside the monument from the 29 Palms entrance station. The first two routes are on a small dark tower 100 yards southwest of a parking area with a park information exhibit.

3465 **OATMEAL EATING AARDVARKS 5.7** Climb the north face of the tower above a bowl.

3466 **BLACK RHINO 5.9+** Two bolted face routes are to the right of **Oatmeal Eating Aardvarks.** This is the leftmost bolted route.

3467 **ENDANGERED SPECIES 5.10c** This is righthand bolted route to the right of **Oatmeal Eating Aardvarks.**

The following five routes are on the rocky hillside northwest of the dark tower.

3468 **ROARING RAPIDS 5.5** This is on a boulder with a large flake/crack on the left side of the hillside. Climb the face left of the flake/crack.

3469 **COLOSSUS 5.8** This climbs the aforementiond flake/crack.

3470 **DISPOSABLE HEROES 5.8** This is a two-bolt face climb about 150 feet right of the two previous routes.

The next two routes are on the largest face on the right side of the hillside.

3471 **FREE FALL 5.10a (TR)** Climb the left side of the face.

3472 **JET STREAM 5.8** Climb the right side of the face past two bolts.

INDIAN HEAD

INDIAN HEAD
FROM UTAH DOME

INDIAN HEAD

This large, south-facing formation lies high on the hillside west of Gold Park Road/Utah Trail (the main road from 29 Palms into the monument), at a point about 3 miles south of the 29 Palms Highway (Highway 62). A fairly long (1 mile) and uphill (about 1,000 ft.) hike leads to the base. Plan on about an hour for the approach.

3473 **OH GOD! 5.10c R ★★**   This two-pitch climb starts in a seam about 30 feet left of **Rude Awakening.**

3474 **RUDE AWAKENING 5.10c R ★★★★**   This two pitch face climb goes up the steep face left of **Goof Proof Roof.** Four bolts protect this route, together with a selection of nuts, lost arrows and knifeblades. There are some runout sections.

3475 **GOOF PROOF ROOF 5.8 A2+ ★★★**   Climb on aid past eight bolts to a sling belay just left of an obvious large roof. Nail out right along the lip of the roof, then up to another sling belay. Aid and free climb straight up to the top. A good selection of thin pins is needed.

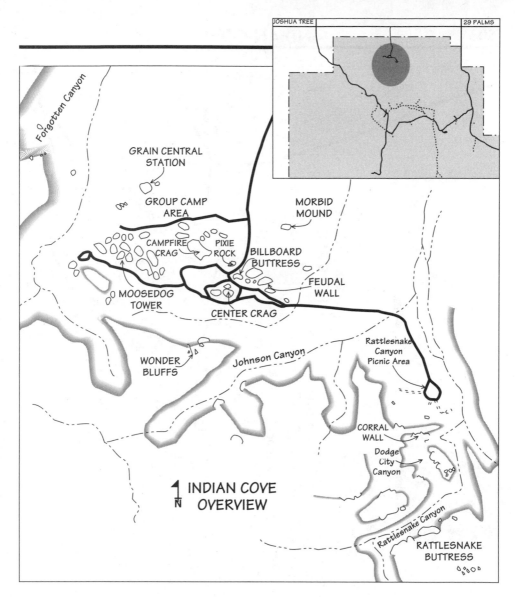

Forgotten Canyon

GRAIN CENTRAL
STATION

GROUP CAMP
AREA

MORBID
MOUND

CAMPFIRE
CRAG

PIXIE
ROCK

BILLBOARD
BUTTRESS

FEUDAL
WALL

MOOSEDOG
TOWER

CENTER CRAG

Rattlesnake
Canyon
Picnic Area

WONDER
BLUFFS

Johnson Canyon

CORRAL
WALL

Dodge
City
Canyon

INDIAN COVE
OVERVIEW

N

Rattlesnake Canyon

RATTLESNAKE
BUTTRESS

INDIAN COVE

This area is located along the northern edge of the Wonderland of Rocks, roughly 1000 feet lower in elevation than other parts of the monument (it's at 3000 feet; most of the monument is above 4000 feet). It is located just south of Highway 62 (29 Palms Highway), and is effectively isolated from all other climbing areas in the Monument. It is reached by driving east from the town of Joshua Tree about 9 miles. There, a small sign and some buildings point the way on the remaining three miles to Indian Cove Campground. Aside from being isolated from the other climbing areas of the monument, Indian Cove, due to a lower altitude, tends to have generally warmer temperatures and is less subject to the high winds that are the bane of winter climbing at Joshua Tree.

Because so many climbs start behind campsites, the monument's "Occupied Campsite Rule," particularly applies in Indian Cove. This "rule" states that the beginning or ending of a climb in an occupied campsite is only allowed when you have the permission of the person occupying the site (see Introduction about other park rules).

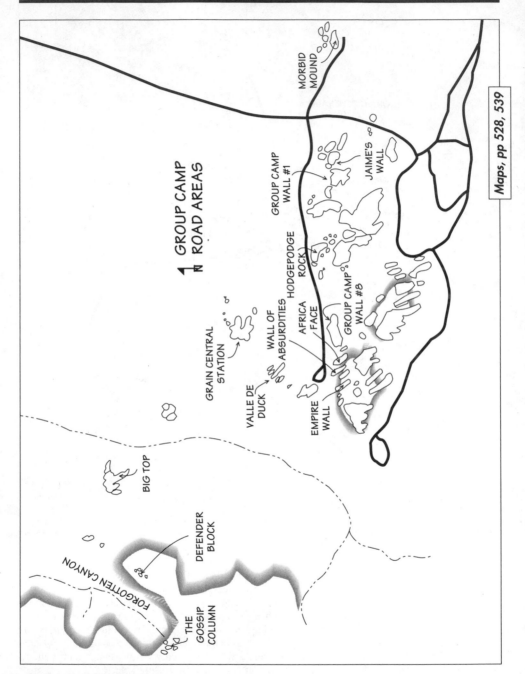

Maps, pp 528, 539

GROUP CAMP
ROAD AREAS

N

MORBID
MOUND

JAIME'S
WALL

GROUP CAMP
WALL #1

HODGEPODGE
ROCK

GROUP CAMP
WALL #8

WALL OF
ABSURDITIES

AFRICA
FACE

GRAIN CENTRAL
STATION

VALLE DE
DUCK

EMPIRE
WALL

BIG TOP

DEFENDER
BLOCK

FORGOTTEN CANYON

THE
GOSSIP
COLUMN

GROUP CAMP ROAD

A paved road plainly marked as the Group Campsites road heads off to the right (west) just as you get to Indian Cove, (about 200 yards before Billboard Buttress). The following climbs are found on cliffs behind the various group campsites, and are approached from various points along the Group Camp Road. See map above.

JAIME'S ROCK

This south-facing rock lies behind Campsite #1. Walk left and around the rock behind the campsite to reach the face. Map, page 506.

3476 **EASTER OVERFLOW 5.9**
3477 **JAIME CRACK 5.4 R**
3478 **STUD MUFFIN 5.10b**
3479 **JAIME'S BIG SHOW 5.7**
3480 **BIVVY KITTEN 5.9**
3481 **JUG-YUR-NOT 5.4** This route goes up discontinuous thin cracks on a dark slab about 110 feet right of **Jaime's Rock.**

GROUP CAMP #1 WALL

This is the north facing wall behind and to the right of the parking area for the campsite. Map, page 506.

3482 **KLETTERVERGNUGEN 5.9** Four bolts.

3483 **BLITZKRIEG 5.12a ★★★** Climb past five bolts to a two-bolt anchor left of **29 Bombs.**

3484 **29 BOMBS (AKA HITLER YOUTH) 5.11a ★★** Climb past three bolts to a two-bolt anchor.

HODGEPODGE ROCK – NORTH FACE

This bucketed face lies just south of the road between Campsites #3 and #4. Map, page 506.

3485 **MY WIFE IS AN ALIEN 5.12a R ★** There are no hangers on the five bolts.

3486 **HODGEPODGE 5.4 R** Climb the aforementioned bucketed face. Easy.

3487 **LIGAMENTOR SECONDS IN VANS 5.7 R**

3488 **MORNING STAR 5.9** One bolt.

3489 **HOT TUB HONEY 5.8 Three bolts.**

HODGEPODGE ROCK – SOUTHWEST FACE

This is just around the corner to the left of the north face.

3490 **HEDGEHOG 5.4**

3491 **HOGBACK 5.8** Three bolts.

3492 **TUMBLEWEED 5.6**

3493 **BAKERSFIELD BOMB 5.8** Two bolts.

3494 **BRIAR RABBIT 5.7**

3495 **SHORT CRACK 5.4**

3496 **BITTERSWEET 5.10a ★** Two bolts.

3497 **SEMISWEET 5.9 X**

HODGEPODGE ROCK

3487

3488

3489

3485

3486

HODGEPODGE ROCK
SOUTH FACE

3490

3493

3492

3495

3497

3496

3491

3494

90

GROUP CAMP 8 WALL

This steep face is directly behind Campsite #8. Map, page 506.

3498   **THE FAR SIDE**   ★   Begin at the left end of the face, climb up to a horizontal, traverse right then up and right in a finger crack.

3499   **PORTAL   5.9** ★   This is an obvious steep crack directly behind the campsite that widens higher.

3500   **MILK RUN   5.11a**   Start about 70 feet right of **Portal** and climb right past a bolt and over a roof to the top.

AFRICA FACE

This wall is to the left (east) of the end of the Group Campground Road (a loop). Map, page 506.

3501   **SIMBA   5.10d**   Three bolts.

3502   **GREYSTOKE   5.8 R**

WALL OF ABSURDITIES

This wall lies on the upper section of the formation. Scramble up the gully to the right (west) to approach. Map, page 506.

3503   **WHAT DOES THE INSIDE OF YOUR NOSE SMELL LIKE   5.4**

3504   **REAGAN DID A GOOD JOB   5.8 R**

3505   **KWIDGI-BO ON THE LOOSE   5.9 R**

3506   **BACK FROM RETIREMENT   5.7**   This climb is on the next formation to the right of The Wall of Absurdities, near the north "toe" of the formation. Climb to the left (above some bushes) to a crack that leads to a right-slanting crack above.

EMPIRE WALL

The easiest approach is to go up the rubble-filled gully to the right (west) of The Wall of Absurdities, then head right (west) to the base of this north-facing wall. The routes are of questionable quality. Map, page 506.

3507   **SUITE SISTER MARY   5.7 R**   Start at the left side of the face, climb up to a roof and head up and left along a crack until you can head straight up on the face, climbing past discontinuous cracks.

3508   **RAGING ORDER   5.8 R**   Begin as for **Suite Sister Mary,** but go right at the roof, then up the face and discontinuous cracks.

3509   **R.P. DELIGHTS   5.10a R**   This is 20 feet right of **Suite Sister Mary.** Head up and right atop a flake until you reach a left-leaning thin crack. Follow the crack until it widens up and eventually heads right to the top.

3510   **SCREAMING IN DIGITAL   5.6**   Start as for **R.P. Delights,** but continue up and right to a pillar of rock. Continue up a thin crack above.

3511   **NEUE REGAL   5.9**   This is 30 feet right of **R.P. Delights.** Climb up a low-angled face past the loose flake to a crack that goes through a small roof left of the rock pillar. Cross **R.P. Delights** and the face. Climb out left, then up.

3512   **FLAKE ROUTE   5.5**   This is to the right of the previous routes. Climb up 40 feet past loose rock to a continuous 150-foot, right-facing flake system.

3513   **TRUTH OR DARE   5.8 R**   This is the right-facing corner 15 feet right of **Flake Route** that leads to unprotected face climbing above.

BIG TOP

This formation is approximately 750 yards northwest of the end of the Group Campground "loop." Walk northwest about 350 yards to a large wash, continue about 400 yards to this formation in the desert plain. Map, page 506.

3514   **3 RING CIRCUS   5.10c** ★   This is a five-bolt face route on north side of formation.

3515   **WORKING WITHOUT A NET   5.9**   This is the short toprope route/high boulder problem on a boulder directly in front of **3 Ring Circus.**

3516   **MORE MY SPEED   5.3**   This is on the lefthand part of the south face. Ascend easy cracks up and right until a traverse up and left is possible.

3517   **LION TAMER   5.9** ★★   This is a two-bolt face route right of **More My Speed.**

3518   **SAWDUST AND PEANUT SHELLS**   **5.10a** ★★★   A five-bolt face route right of **Lion Tamer.**

3519   **GYPSY FORTUNE**   **5.10b (TR)**   This route up a dike lies far to the right of the main face.

3520   **ZELDA**   **5.5**   This is the 25-foot offwidth crack around and to the right of **Gypsy Fortune.**

FORGOTTEN CANYON

This "hidden" canyon lies about .6 mile northwest of the end of the Group Camp Road, just past and west of Big Top. A large wash is crossed about 350 yards northwest of the end of the road; Big Top is encountered 400 yards further. From Big Top head west about 300 yards then angle southwest into the canyon. The first formation on the left (south) is Defender Block; at the end of the canyon (350 yards further) is the Gossip Column, a brown formation with two pillars. Map, page 506.

DEFENDER BLOCK

This is the large, brown block on the righthand (left) side of Forgotten Canyon. The thin crack on the north face, with a dark streak running down the face, is **Defender.** There are two bolts on the summit. Map, page 506.

3521   **SHIATSU**   **5.10c (TR)**   This is the face left of **Defender.**

3522   **DEFENDER**   **5.11c (TR)** ★★★   This is the overhanging, flared finger crack on the right.

THE GOSSIP COLUMN

These are the brown "pillars" on the left side of the formation at the end of Forgotten Canyon; the righthand pillar/block is the higher of the two. Map, page 506.

3523   **RUBBERNECK BUSYBODY**   **5.11a** ★★   This five-bolt route lies on the south side of the lower lefthand block. Two-bolt anchor/rap.

3524   **RUMORS AND LIES**   **5.12a** ★★★★   Start near the right (southeast) corner of the higher block. Climb up past bolts and discontinuous thin cracks to a two-bolt anchor/rap. Pro: To 1.5 inches, six bolts.

3525   **NOTHING BUT HEARSAY**   **5.12a** ★★★★   Start as for **Rumors and Lies,** but traverse right after the fourth bolt to another crack leading to the top. Pro: To 2 inches, four bolts.

GROUP CAMP ROCKS

This area is comprised of several small rocks lying about 100 yards north of the end of the Group Camp Road. The southern face of the first rock encountered is referred to as the Group Camp Short Wall. The corridor formed by the northern two rocks is referred to as Valle De Duck. Map, page 506.

GROUP CAMP SHORT WALL

This flat, 40-foot face 100 yards north of the road's end has a number of cracks. The two thin cracks are 5.10d and 5.11a. There also are two nice 5.7 hand cracks.

VALLE DE DUCK

This is the east-west corridor lying between the two northernmost rocks of the Group Camp Rocks. Map, page 506.

3526   **YOUTH RUN WILD**   **5.8**   This crack leading to face climbing past two bolts is near the left end of the corridor. Two-bolt anchor/rap.

3527   **CHASE LOUNGE**   **5.11b**   This bolted face route is near the right end of the corridor, about 30 yards right of **Youth Run Wild** and 20 feet left **Gaston's Groove.**

3528   **GASTON'S GROOVE**   **5.11a** ★   This is the three-bolt route to the right of **Chase Lounge.**

GRAIN CENTRAL STATION

This large formation lies about 200 yards northeast of the road's end (directly north of Group Campsite 8) and 100 yards northeast of Group Camp Rocks. A smaller pillar/rock (The Grain Silo) lies just to the east of the main formation. Map, page 506.

3529 **STAIRCASE CRACK 5.4** This is a left-leaning crack in a corner at the left end of the northwest side.

3530 **B.M.T.C. LEADER 5.7** This ascends the right side of a large detached flake that leads to face climbing. It is on a buttress to the right of **Staircase Crack.**

3531 **SNOOPS 5.6** This is on the right side of a buttress of rock near the southwest corner of the formation, about 25 yards right of **BMTC Leader.** Climb the face past one bolt.

3532 **DANCING ON DIMES 5.7** Climb past three bolts on face just right of large chimney near southwest corner of formation. This is just right of **Snoops.**

3533 **GRAIN GANG 5.8** This crack lies in a recess near the right end of the southwest face of the formation. It starts with a small left-facing corner.

3534 **ZINGING IN THE GRAIN 5.8** This is a southeast-facing slab with one bolt 100 feet right of **Grain Gang.**

THE GRAIN SILO

This is the small rock just east of the main Grain Central Station formation.

3535 **MY GRAIN 5.11c** This is on the south face of **The Grain Silo.** Climb past two bolts to a flake, then climb an arête .

3536 **THE GREAT GRAIN ROBBERY 5.6** This is on the east face of The Grain Silo. Climb a finger crack to a grainy face leading up and right to a notch. Unprotected climbing leads to the top. The arête left of the grainy face has been toproped.

MORBID MOUND

This small rock is about 200 yards east of the entrance to the Group Camp Road; however, there is no parking on the main road at this point. Therefore, the approach is lengthened considerably. Either park near Billboard Buttress or near the right end of The Feudal Wall (Campsite 17) and hoof it north some 400 yards. Not really worth the hike. Map, page 506.

3537 **3RD CLASS IT 5.8** This is around the corner and left of **Bouncer.** Climb off a boulder to a bowl and follow two short cracks to the top.

3538 **DOA 5.8**

3539 **BOUNCER 5.8**

3540 **BRIMSTONE STAIRWAY 5.1**

3541 **DEADHEADS 5.4**

3542 **FLIES ON THE WOUND 5.7**

3543 **HILLSIDE STRANGLER 5.4**

3544 **FLY IN THE OINTMENT 5.11a (TR)**

3545 **DISAPPEARING BELAYER 5.7** Start at **Be Wary**, and afater 10 feet climb up and left to a large flake, then on to the top.

3546 **BE WARY 5.2** The right facing corner.

3547 **AMBULANCE DRIVER 5.1**

3548 **MYRMECOCYSTUS EWARTI 5.4**

3549 **MORITURI TE SALUTAMUS 5.9**

3550 **'TIL DEATH DO US FART 5.10d**

3551 **A LAST CIGARETTE SENOR? 5.9**

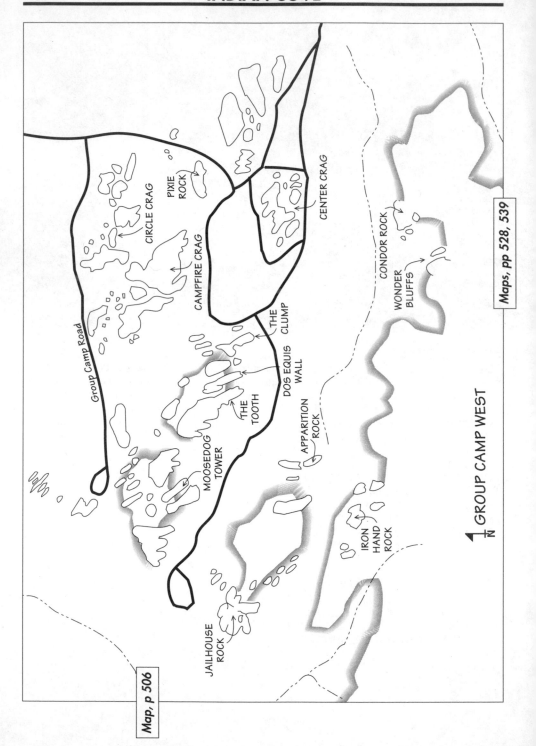

Map, p 506

Maps, pp 528, 539

GROUP CAMP WEST

N

Group Camp Road

CIRCLE CRAG

PIXIE ROCK

CAMPFIRE CRAG

CENTER CRAG

THE CLUMP

DOS EQUIS WALL

THE TOOTH

APPARITION ROCK

MOOSEDOG TOWER

CONDOR ROCK

WONDER BLUFFS

IRON HAND ROCK

JAILHOUSE ROCK

PIXIE ROCK

This popular rock lies just to your right (west) as you enter the campground. The righthand edge of the south face is an extremely steep, bucketed face. To the left is a lower-angled slab. Map, page 514.

3552 **LASCIVIOUS CONDUCT   5.11c ★★**
3553 **SCREAM CHUCK   5.7 R**
3554 **VAINO'S LOST IN POT (AKA THE SCAM)   5.7 R/X ★**
3555 **WHO'S FIRST   5.6 ★**
3556 **RHYTHM OF THE HEART   5.8 X ★**
3557 **SILENT SCREAM   5.10a ★★★**
3558 **SILENT BUT DEADLY   5.11b ★★★**
3559 **PIXIE STICK   5.10a (TR)**

CAMPFIRE CRAGS

This large formation is west of Pixie Rock. Its north face overlooks the ranger campfire area, where nature programs are conducted. The south face lies behind Campsites 46 through 50. Map, page 514.

CAMPFIRE CRAGS
NORTH FACE

CAMPFIRE CRAGS – NORTH FACE

Follow the trail toward the Campfire Circle area, the north face will be on your left. Several short cracks and faces lie below and right of the start of **Omega.** They range from 5.7 to 5.9.

3560 **OMEGA 5.7**
3561 **I HAD A DREAM 5.10b ★**
3562 **DATURA 5.12a R ★★**
3563 **KLINGON PIZZA 5.6 R**
3564 **BONFIRE 5.11b ★★★**
3565 **FAT MAN'S MISERY 5.6 R**
3566 **NO BETTER BIRTHS 5.10a**
3567 **NICKEL SLOTS 5.7 R**
3568 **OSTRICH SKIN 5.7 R**
3569 **AWFUL LOOSE 5.7 R**
3570 **PRESUPPOSITION 5.11d R ★★★**
3571 **PREJUDICIAL VIEWPOINT 5.11a R ★★**
3572 **CAMPFIRE GIRL 5.11d (TR)**
3573 **CRUMBLE CAKE 5.7**
3574 **AID ROUTE A3 R**
3575 **O'BULG 5.11a**
3576 **LITTLE BROWN EYE 5.8 ★** This route lies about 100 feet right (north) and somewhat in front of **O'Bulg,** on a separate small face. The route goes up thin cracks, past a brownish "scoop" located halfway up the route.

CIRCLE CRAG

This low wall lies directly behind seating area of the campfire circle, about 100 yards north of Campfire Crag. This is actually just to the left of Jaime's Rock and on the opposite side of the rocks from Group Campsite #1. Map, page 514.

3577 **SCOTCH WITH A TWIST 5.8 R** Climb the overhanging brown face and a bottoming crack on the left side of the face. The route is just left of **Scotch,** and joins that route near the top.

3578 **SCOTCH 5.6 R** Climb a pin-scarred crack and face up to a dark-colored "bowl." Follow cracks left and up, joining **Scotch With A Twist.**

3579 **GIN FIZZ 5.7 R** Start 10 feet right of **Scotch.** Climb an incipient crack to several mantel moves and the top.

3580 **WHISKEY 5.6** This is 20 feet right of **Scotch** and 10 feet right of **Gin Fizz.** Climb twin cracks that join into an easy gully.

3581 **AA 5.7** Climb a thin crack to a ledge, then up the hand crack. It is 80 feet right of **Whiskey.**

3582 **THE HABERDASHERY 5.8** This left-leaning crack is to the right of AA, at the right-end of Circle Crag, is .

3583 **JUGGURNOT 5.6** 150 feet right of AA (toward the entrance road) climb a south face on desert varnish.

CAMPFIRE CRAG – SOUTH FACE

3584 **ILLEGAL CAMPFIRE 5.7** This is a prominent left-slanting crack in brown rock on the upper portion on the left side of the southwest face.

3585 **ALPENTINE 5.9+ R** Face climb up to a flake, then up past a bolt to a left-facing corner behind Campsite # 49.

3586 **GENUINE COWHIDE 5.10a ★★** Pro: To 2 inches, one bolt

3587 **KALISHNAKOV KULTURE 5.12a ★★** Pro: Four bolts.

3588 **SPUD OVERHANG 5.10b R**

3589 **HEART SLAB 5.8** Five bolts

3590 **BANQUET 5.9**

3591 **C LUNCH 5.6 R**

3592 **KUNDALINI-LINGUINI-WEENIE 5.8 ★**

3593 **PICNIC 5.6**

3594 **FEAST 5.11**

3595 **FOOL'S RUBY 5.6 R**

THE CLUMP

A series of formations, which lie to the north of the road, run in an east-west direction along the campground road west of the Campfire Circle. The southeast end of these rocks is called The Clump. Routes are found on both the northeast and southwest faces. Map, page 514.

CLUMP CANYON

This small canyon is behind Campsite #60 (to the right of the northeast face of The Clump); the left wall is dark, brown-colored rock.

3596 **LITTLE JOE 5.11b (TR) ★★** This is on the lefthand overhanging wall of Clump Canyon. Climb a left-leaning crack until you can head up and right.

CLUMP CANYON – NORTHEAST FACE

3597 **D.B.'S TOPROPE 5.12b** This route lies directly behind Campsite #65. Climb a thin seam up overhanging rock.
3598 **FINALLY 5.4**
3599 **AT LAST 5.10a ★**
3600 **IT'S ABOUT TIME 5.9 R**
3601 **KINDA SORTA 5.9 R ★**
3602 **MAYBE 5.8**

CLUMP CANYON – SOUTHWEST FACE (AKA SPIDER WALL)

This is behind Campsite #71, on the right of a small "cove" of rock.

3603 **BORIS THE SPIDER** 5.9

3604 **SPIDER'S WEB** 5.8

3605 **POPPA SPIDER** 5.9 ★

3606 **MOMMA SPIDER** 5.9

3607 **CRACK 69** 5.5   This is the obvious, low-angled crack behind Campsite 69. It is about 70 feet right of **Momma Spider.**

PALMREADER WALL

This face with a hand crack up the center (**Palmreader**) is just left of the "cove" of rock forming the southwest face of The Clump (Spider Rock) and behind Campsites 74 & 75.

3608 **MYSTIC TEFLON 5.10c ★**   This follows three bolts left of **Palmreader.**
3609 **PALMREADER 5.8 ★★**   This is a short, perfect hand crack in the center of the face.
3610 **MADAME SALAMI 5.10a (TR)**   The face to the right of **Palmreader.**

DOS EQUIS AND CORONA WALLS

This steep, brown, west-facing wall lies above and behind campsite #80. The upper (lefthand) section of the wall is called the Dos Equis Wall. Map, page 514.

CORONA WALL

3611 **SECONDARY INSPECTION 5.9**   Climb the left-diagonalling crack starting near the center of the face.
3612 **BORDER PATROL 5.11c ★★**   Climb past six bolts, and join **The Ranger . . .**
3613 **THE RANGER IS WATCHING ME 5.10b**   Pro: To 2.5 inches, three bolts.

DOS EQUIS WALL

3614 **SKID ROW (AKA AIR PLAY) 5.10d R ★**
3615 **THE HIGHWAYMAN (AKA ROADRUNNER) 5.11b R ★★★**   Four bolts.
3616 **FLARE PLAY 5.10b ★**
3617 **SCARE WAY 5.10b ★★**
3618 **TRES EQUIS 5.8**
3619 **SOUTH BUTTRESS 5.7 ★★**

APPARITION ROCK

This rock is almost directly across the road from Dos Equis Wall. The three routes are on the north face and are visible from the road. Map, page 514.

3620 **APPARITION 5.10a ★★**
3621 **COSMOSIS 5.10a ★**
3622 **MOSAIC WALL 5.7**

IRON HAND ROCK

This is a brown formation about 200 yards behind Apparition Rock. Map, page 514.

3623 **DOGLEG RIGHT 5.10c**
3624 **IRON HAND 5.10a**
3625 **BROWN CAVE 5.2**

THE TOOTH

This is a prominent spire facing west about 50 yards west of Dos Equis Wall, and above Campsite #83. There are rappel bolts on top. Map, page 514.

3626 **WEST FACE 5.9** Start in a left-leaning crack and climb to a ledge (5.9). Above, either follow a crack around right onto the south face (5.7) or continue up and left to the north face (5.9).

3627 **MOUNTAINEERS' ROUTE Class 4 or 5** Climb the southeast side of The Tooth from the notch on the right.

3628 **CHARACTER FLAW 5.10c ★★** A four-bolt route on the face just right and behind the "tooth." Start out of the notch.

3629 **HANDCRACKER 5.8** This nice jam crack on brown rock is about 150 feet left of The Tooth and behind and right from Campsite #85. It faces the campground.

MOOSEDOG TOWER

This formation lies behind campsite #91. Rappel off the north side. Map, page 514.

3630 **HALF TIME 5.8** This is near the lefthand part of the west face of the formation. Climb up a left-slanting ramp until you can climb straight up to an obvious left-slanting crack.

3631 **LUCKY CHARMS 5.7 ★** Start as for **Half Time** (about 100 feet left and uphill from **Third Time's A Charm**). Climb a corner up and right to intersect **Third Time's A Charm.** Continue up and right to the ridge to join **Tranquility,** etc.

3632 **THIRD TIME'S A CHARM 5.10b ★★★**

3633 **BITCH IN HEAT 5.9 ★**

3634 **WANDERING WINNEBAGO 5.8+ R ★★**

3635 **DIRECT SOUTH FACE 5.9 ★★★**

3636 **TRANQUILITY 5.6 ★**

3637 **MOOSEDOG LIEBACK 5.?** Start on the lower, left end of the east face. Lieback up a right facing flake/corner.

3638 **HURRY UP AND WAIT 5.10a ★** This is on the east face, part way up the gully, about halfway up toward the start of **Quien Sabe?** Climb a vertical seam to a right-leaning crack. Take the crack up to the headwall, then traverse up to the finishing crack.

3639 **QUIEN SABE? 5.7 ★** Climb the right-angling ramp in the middle of the east face.

MISCELLANEOUS ROCKS

The Miscellaneous Rocks are the few remaining formations to the west of Moosedog Tower that are part of the same composite of rock running east-west from The Clump. The following routes lie among these otherwise unnamed rocks.

3640 **ROADSIDE SLAB 5.10b R ★** This brown slab with several discontinuous cracks is located 150 feet past Moosedog Tower along the road (behind campsite #93). It is hard to protect, but easily toproped.

3641 **TEARS 5.9** Walk up a small gully/canyon behind Campsite #96. Climb a crack on the right (eastern) wall until it is necessary to traverse left to another crack.

3642 **HUG DANCE 5.11b ★★** This six-bolt route is on a brown pillar of rock topped by a block. It is located about 175 feet north of the campground road, along a nature trail that begins about 100 yards west of Campsite #96.

JAILHOUSE ROCK

Jailhouse Rock is located at the extreme right (west) end of the campground. Drive to the end of the road and walk south to the rear of the large formation near the parking area. Map, page 514.

3643 **CELLBOUND 5.5 ★★** Climb the arête at the extreme right (southwest) end of Jailhouse Rock. Start in a short gully, then ascend the arête, using a dike and thin crack to get to a lieback corner that leads to the summit.

3644 **JAILBREAK 5.3** This route ascends the right-facing corner 30 feet left (west) of **Cellbound.**

3645 **A SNITCH IN TIME 5.8** Climb the crack through the overhang 15 feet left of **Jailbreak.**

CENTER CRAGS

The following formations all are located in the center of the campground and all are part of the same general mass of rock. The north side of Center Crags is called Center Crag, the south side is King Otto's Castle. Map, page 514.

CENTER CRAG

The north face of Center Crags is directly southwest of Billboard Buttress and faces the entrance to the campground. It is behind Campsite #28.

3646 **VERTICAL CORRECTOR 5.11a ★★** This route climbs the left side of the face up huecos past four bolts. It is almost directly behind Campsite #28.

3647 **OH GOD, ITS MY BOSS 5.8 ★** This three-bolt face route is on the upper center part of the north face of Center Crags, to the right and above **Vertical Corrector.**

3648 **AWESOME BETTY 5.10a** This one-bolt route is on the righthand part of the north face, about 75 feet right of **Oh God . . .**

KING OTTO'S CASTLE

KING OTTO'S CASTLE
This formation is the south side of Center Crags and lies generally behind Campsites #35 through #38. Map, page 514.

3649 **DON GENERO CRACK 5.10a** ★
3650 **UNKNOWN GRAIN 5.10a R**
3651 **THE BRIDGE 5.10d R**
3652 **GOODBYE MR. BOND 5.10c** ★★
3653 **QUIVERING SAVAGES 5.12a** ★★★
3654 **PANAMA RED 5.11c (TR)**
3655 **SWEAT BAND 5.10c** ★★
3656 **TARAWASSIE WIGGEL 5.10b** ★
3657 **PLAIN BUT GOOD HEARTED 5.6** ★
3658 **DATE QUEEN 5.8** Climb the offwidth crack right of **Plain but Good Hearted.**
3659 **SWEAT PANTS 5.11a**
3660 **DATE QUEEN CORRIDOR CRACK 5.11b R** ★★ This radically overhanging crack is in a corridor right of the preceding route.

CONDOR ROCK

This rock is about 200 yards south of King Otto's Castle and faces north. It sits near the bottom of the hillside and is obvious from King Otto's Castle. Map, page 514.

3661 **TOXIC AVENGER 5.10a** ★

3662 **TOXIC POODLE 5.10b** ★

3663 **THE FALCON 5.10b** ★★

3664 **THE CONDOR 5.11d** ★★★★ Climb the left-facing, left-leaning dihedral around the corner and to the right. Pro: Small to 2 inches, fixed pins.

WONDER BLUFFS

This crag lies southwest of Condor Rock (uphill and right) a couple hundred yards. It faces
northeast. Map, page 514.

3665 **GYPSY 5.10a** Climb the thin crack on the extreme left side of the Wonder Bluffs.

3666 **SLAM DUNK 5.8 ★** Climb the corner 25 feet right of **Gypsy.**

3667 **CONNIPTION 5.10b ★★★** This climbs up to the right side of the black triangular hole,
then up a nice hand crack to the top.

3668 **BLUEWIND 5.10b ★** Climb the straight crack right of **Conniption.**

3669 **NEGRO VORTEX 5.10a ★** Start up a left-facing corner 25 right of **Bluewind** (the start
of **Dry Rain**), then traverse sharply left and follow an awkward crack to face climbing that
leads to a thin crack and the summit.

3670 **GOMER PILE 5.9 ★** Start up **Dry Rain,** but head up and left to the middle of three
cracks.

3671 **DRY RAIN 5.7 ★** Climb a small, left-facing corner and continue up and right to the top.

3672 **PENCIL NECK GEEK 5.10b ★★** This takes the straight thin crack on the right side of
3the cliff.

3673 **BLOODY BUDDY 5.9** A large roof with a chimney splitting it rests high on the ridge
southwest of the Wonder Bluffs. This is a two-pitch route leading up to the roof. Start on a
dike with two bolts. Descend to the south.

Rico Miledi climbing Frontier Justice, 5.11c   Photo: Bill Freeman

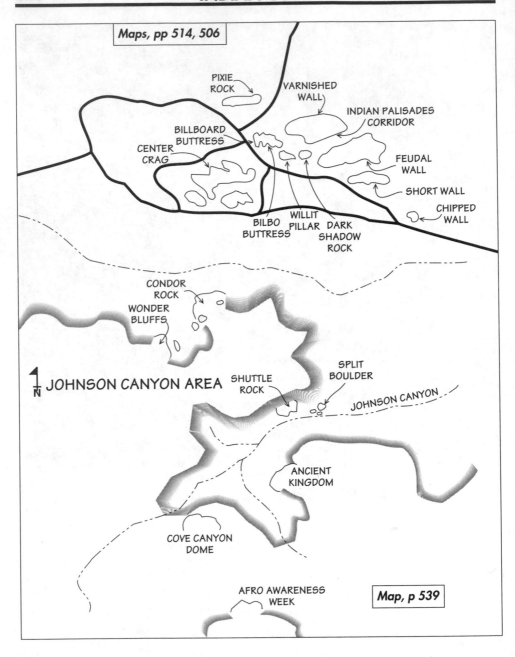

Maps, pp 514, 506

PIXIE ROCK

VARNISHED WALL

INDIAN PALISADES CORRIDOR

BILLBOARD BUTTRESS

CENTER CRAG

FEUDAL WALL

SHORT WALL

CHIPPED WALL

BILBO BUTTRESS

WILLIT PILLAR

DARK SHADOW ROCK

CONDOR ROCK

WONDER BLUFFS

N

JOHNSON CANYON AREA

SHUTTLE ROCK

SPLIT BOULDER

JOHNSON CANYON

ANCIENT KINGDOM

COVE CANYON DOME

AFRO AWARENESS WEEK

Map, p 539

VARNISHED WALL

This formation faces north and toward the entrance to the campground. It is to the left of the road as you drive into the campground. The wall lies to the northeast of Billboard Buttress and southeast of Pixie Rock, and is actually part iof the same formation that has Indian Palisades Corridor on its south side. Map, page 528.

3674 **EAST MEETS WEST 5.7 R**   Climb the face left of **With Malice and Forethought** past a bulge and a roof with a bolt.

3675 **WITH MALICE AND FORETHOUGHT   5.7 ★**   This route follows a right-slanting crack on the left side of the Varnished Wall. Climb over several roofs.

3676 **ABSENCE OF MALICE   5.11a (TR) ★★**

3677 **DOUBLE CRUX 5.8**

3678 **MOSAIC 5.8**

3679 **DISO SUCKS 5.6**

3680 **CRANK QUEENIE 5.8 ★**

BILLBOARD BUTTRESS

This small face lies just east of the split in the road as you enter the campground. A parking area and message board make this a stopping point for many climbers. The buttress is about 100 yards south of Pixie Rock, facing west. Map, page 528.

3681 **SHEET BENDS 5.8 ★** This is the left-facing corner around to the left of the main face.
3682 **CERAMIC BUS 5.11c R**
3683 **SQUAT ROCKETS 5.4 ★**
3684 **BILBO 5.9 ★**
3685 **WE DIVE AT DAWN 5.8 ★★**
3686 **GAIT OF POWER 5.10b ★**
3687 **THE REVEREND 5.8 ★★**
3688 **COOL WIND (AKA THE RABBI OR RED BECKEY) 5.10a ★**
3689 **DRIVING LIMITATIONS 5.8 ★★**
3690 **KNAUG AND HYDE 5.3 R ★**
3691 **THE FORGOTTEN CRACK 5.10a**

THE BILBO BUTTRESSES

These small walls and buttresses of rock lie immediately to the east of the east face of Billboard Buttress, and could really be considered part of that formation. Map, page 528.

3692 **WHITE TRASH 5.8**
3693 **VAL DE MELLO 5.10b ★★**
3694 **DEBBIE DOES DONUTS 5.6**

WILLIT PILLAR

This formation is near the road behind campsite #3 and about 75 yards right (east) of Billboard Buttress. Map, page 528.

3695 **FRAUD SQUAD 5.10d** Two bolts.

3696 **UNKNOWN HIGHWAY   A1**

3697 **HOLLYWOOD AND VAINO 5.10c R ★**

3698 **MAIN FACE (AKA CALL OF THE WEST) 5.9 ★★**

3699 **SOUTH FACE ROUTE 5.9**

3700 **THE FLARE 5.4 ★** Climb the right side of a huge chimney that is right of the **South Face Route** to easy face climbing.

3701 **WILLIT HOLD 5.8** This route lies to the right of **The Flare** (a large chimney). Climb past horizontals to a left-slanting seam.

INDIAN PALISADES CORRIDOR

This boulder filled canyon lies around to the right and behind Willit Pillar. All listed routes are on the left wall of the corridor. This is the backside of the Varnished Wall. Map, page 528.

3702 **TOE THE LINE 5.9 ★★** Climb up and right on a bolt-scarred seam, then head left to a finishing crack on the left side of the brown slab at the left end of formation. (This sits behind Willit Pillar.)

3703 **WILLIT SLAB 5.7** Climb the brown face past five bolts. This is 12 feet right of **Toe The Line.**

3704 **BITTER BREW 5.6 R** Begin about 15 feet right of **Willit Slab.** Climb up to a ledge, then continue up and right to a right-facing corner.

3705 **WHEAT CHEX 5.7** This is 20 feet left of a large roof in the center of the face, (about 30 yards right of **Bitter Brew**). Climb an arching crack to a hole, then follow a crack just right of the arch until face climbing leads to the top.

3706 **EYES OF AMBER 5.7** This route ascends the brown face 25 feet left of **Water Moccasin.**

3707 **CHIVALRY'S NOT DEAD 5.7 ★** This is a three-bolt route 15 feet right of **Eyes of Amber.**

3708 **SNAKES IN THE GRASS 5.9 (TR)** This is the face between **Chivalry's Not Dead** and **Water Moccasin.**

3709 **WATER MOCCASIN 5.4** Several bolts protect face climbing to a ledge on the right side of the face.

3710 **HARRELL-TURNER 5.10b** This three-bolt route lies 15 feet right of **Water Moccasin.**

3711 **SERPENT SCALES 5.6 ★** This three-bolt climb lies just right of **Harrell-Turner.**

3712 **COTTONMOUTH 5.6 X** Climb up patina plates to the bolt anchors to the right of **Serpent Scales.**

DARK SHADOWS ROCK

This formation lies about 40 yards east of Willit Pillar, directly behind Campsite #6. Map, page 528.

3713 **ANTI-GRAVITY ACROBATICS 5.11c R ★★** Three bolts.

3714 **FORGOTTEN GALAXY 5.11b R**

3715 **FORGOTTEN VARIATION 5.9+ R**

3716 **NAIL `N GRAVEL 5.10d R ★**

FEUDAL WALL EAST SIDE

THE FEUDAL WALL

A large formation lies above a small wash/canyon on the north of the road and to the right (east) of Billboard Buttress and Willit Pillar. This is the Feudal Wall. The low formation forming the south side of the wash/canyon is the Short Wall. Map, page 528.

3717   **ROUTE 1326**   **5.2**
3718   **COYOTE IN THE BUSHES**   **5.10a ★★**
3719   **SCARAMOUCH**   **5.2 ★**
3720   **SWISHBAH**   **5.7**
3721   **THE CHESSBOARD**   **5.8 R**
3722   **POCKET POOL**   **5.11d ★★★**   Five bolts.
3723   **LA REINA**   **5.9 ★★**
3724   **TEENAGE MUTANT NINJA BRITS (AKA THE BLOCK)**   **5.10a**
3725   **DUCHESS LEFT**   **5.4**
3726   **DUCHESS**   **5.6 ★★**
3727   **DUCHESS RIGHT**   **5.7**
3728   **MONACO**   **5.11b ★★★**
3729   **LANDSRAAD**   **5.10b**
3730   **THE CASTRUM**   **5.10a ★**
3731   **COURT JESTER**   **5.7**
3732   **MARCHESA**   **5.2 ★**
3733   **COCO-LOCO**   **5.10b ★**
3734   **NOT JUST ANOTHER PRETTY FACE**   **5.10d ★**
3735   **CROWN JEWELS**   **5.7 ★★**
3736   **DUM ROODLE**   **5.6**
3737   **CASTLES BURNING**   **5.12a ★★**

3738 **PRINCESS 5.7**
3739 **THE MIKADO 5.6 ★★**
3740 **SOCRATES SUCKS 5.10c (TR)**
3741 **CALIFORNIA CRACK 5.11a R ★★**
3742 **ARIZONA CRACK 5.11a R**
3743 **EL REY 5.10c R ★**
3744 **MINION 5.4**
3745 **CUBAN CONNECTION 5.8 R**
3746 **PET OR MEAT 5.10d ★★★**
3747 **TRAUTNER-FRY 5.10c R**
3748 **PANTHER CRACK 5.10d** This is an overhanging crack on the east end of the Feudal Wall, about 50 feet right of **Pet or Meat.** It doesn't quite reach the ground.
3749 **DRY LAKE 5.10b R** This route begins 25 feet right of **Panther Crack.** Go up a left-facing lieback to face climbing past two bolts and a fixed pin.
3750 **NORIEGA DOES PANAMA 5.10a** This three-bolt route is 30 feet right of **Dry Lake.**

SHORT WALL

This wall lies just south of the Feudal Wall. Most routes are on the south face; a few routes lie on the north face, facing the Feudal Wall. Map, page 528.

SHORT WALL – SOUTH FACE

3751 **STEP 'N OUT 5.10a** ★
3752 **DOUBLE TROUBLE 5.10a (TR)**
3753 **MAD RACE 5.4**
3754 **FLUFF BOY 5.8**
3755 **BELAY GIRL 5.10c** ★★
3756 **PFUNDT'S FOLLY 5.8**
3757 **RIFF RAFF ROOF 5.10a**
3758 **BOMBAY 5.8** ★
3759 **CALCUTTA 5.7+** ★
3760 **LEFT V CRACK 5.11b R** ★★
3761 **RIGHT V CRACK 5.10a** ★★★
3762 **FACE TO FACE 5.11c (TR)** ★

3763 **LINDA'S CRACK 5.2**
3764 **LINDA'S FACE 5.6 R**
3765 **CHOCKSTONE CHIMNEY 4th Class**
3766 **TIGHT SHOES 5.7 R**
3767 **DOUBLE CRACK 5.3 ★**
3768 **UP TO HEAVEN 5.8 R/X**
3769 **TOE JAM EXPRESS 5.3**
3770 **STEADY BREEZE 5.7 X**
3771 **S.O.B. 5.6**
3772 **MORNING WARM-UP 5.10a X**
3773 **AFTERNOON SHAKEDOWN 5.11a X**
3774 **GOTCHA BUSH 5.4 R/X**
3775 **RIGHT N UP 5.8 X**
3776 **DONNA T'S ROUTE 5.5** The crack near the right end of the south face.
3777 **BIG STEP 5.8 X** Climb the face just right of **Donna T's Route.**
3778 **OUT OF STEP 5.7 R** Follow a flake on the extreme right end of the face until it crosses **Big Step** and leads to **Donna T's Route.**

SHORT WALL – NORTH FACE
There are several toprope and solo-type routes (from 5.6 to 5.10a) on the north face of The Short Wall, about 50 feet right of **The Heart Route.**

3779 **THE HEART ROUTE 5.6** This climbs up to and past a "heart- shaped" depression on the north face.

CHIPPED WALL
This small formation lies about 50 yards southeast of The Short Wall. Map, page 528.

3780 **CHIPPED SUEY 5.7** This one-bolt face routeis directly behind Campsite #20.

JOHNSON CANYON (AKA COVE CANYON)

This is the first wash/canyon south of Indian Cove, behind the ridge containing the Wonder Bluffs. It is best approached from the Short Wall area by walking south to the start of the wash, which runs southwest. A large, split boulder is near the entrance of the canyon (but not immediately visible until one gets quite close to the canyon's mouth). Map, page 528.

CANYON ENTRANCE ROUTES

3781 **CUTE THE MOON** **5.6** ★★ This is a three-bolt face climb on the smooth inside of the split boulder.

3782 **EUHEDRAL** **5.7** This is a five-bolt route on a slab on the left at the start of the wash. It is directly above the split boulder, and has a tricky descent.

SHUTTLE ROCK

This brown face, which faces Ancient Kingdom, is on the northern (right) side of Johnson Canyon, about 400 yards west of the split boulder. Map, page 528.

3783 **GABBY'S SHUTTLE** **5.10c** Three bolts and a fixed pin protect the right-slanting seam.

ANCIENT KINGDOM

This wall is about 400 yards up the wash from the split boulder on the left (south) side of Johnson Canyon. It is a squarish 100-foot wall, with several cracks and corner systems, that faces north. Map, page 528.

3784 **SPANISH BAYONET** **5.9** ★★★ A bolt protects a traverse into this excellent thin crack on the left side of the formation.

3785 **CARMANIA** **5.7** ★★ This is the left-facing corner to the right of **Spanish Bayonet.**

3786 **BABYLONIA** **5.7**★ This route climbs the right-facing corner systems 25 feet right of **Carmania.**

3787 **THRASHER (AKA EL CAP)** **5.9** This is the obvious smooth, overhanging offwidth on the right end of the crag. Pro: to 6".

COVE CANYON DOME

This formation lies about 750 yards up Johnson Canyon, and about 300 yards past Ancient Kingdom, the large formation on the left (south). The known routes lie near the center of the formation. Map, page 528.

3788 **CRACKED ACTOR** **5.9** This is the leftmost obvious line on the dome and starts in a groove/trough that becomes a right-facing corner leading to a two-bolt belay. Continue up the crack to easier face climbing. A third junky pitch heads up a ramp to the right.

3789 **THE FLAKES** **5.9** The rightmost route starts immeadiately right of **Cracked Actor** in a steep left-facing book that leads to a thin flake system. Belay near two fixed pins. Continue up a left-facing corner, then take the crack to a ledge. Three pitches.

3790 **LET'S BOLT** **5.7** Start about 25 feet to the right of **Cracked Actor.** Climb a right-facing corner to the first belay of **Cracked Actor,** then follow that route to the top.

AFRO AWARENESS WEEK

This is the brown formation about 300 yards behind (south) of Cove Canyon Dome. It is reached by going up the side canyon between Ancient Kingdom and Cove Canyon Dome. Map, page 528.

3791 **TIED TO THE WHIPPING POST** **5.11a** This widening thin crack is on the right side of the rock, to the right of a chimney. A bolt is located near the bottom.

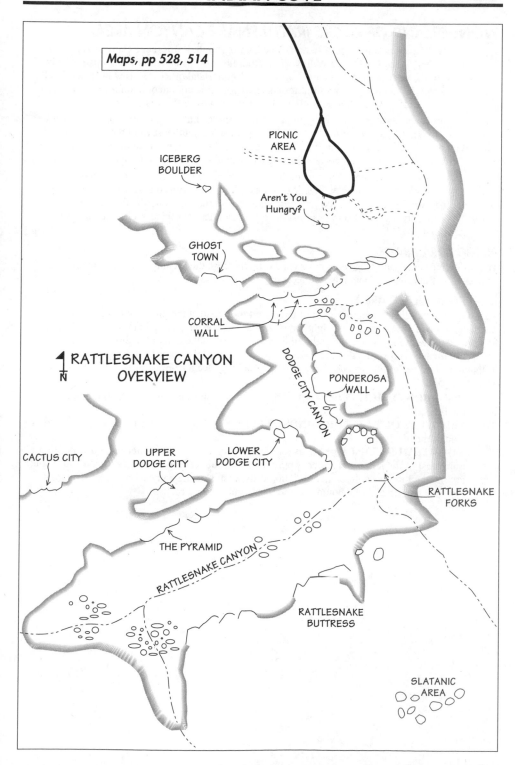

Maps, pp 528, 514

ICEBERG
BOULDER

PICNIC
AREA

Aren't You
Hungry?

GHOST
TOWN

CORRAL
WALL

DODGE CITY CANYON

PONDEROSA
WALL

RATTLESNAKE CANYON
OVERVIEW

N

CACTUS CITY

UPPER
DODGE CITY

LOWER
DODGE CITY

RATTLESNAKE
FORKS

THE PYRAMID

RATTLESNAKE CANYON

RATTLESNAKE
BUTTRESS

SLATANIC
AREA

WONDERLAND OF ROCKS (RATTLESNAKE CANYON AREA)

This beautiful canyon is southeast of Indian Cove Campground. Rattlesnake Canyon is part of the northern Wonderland of Rocks; the Willow Hole Area lies off this canyon further upstream. In fact, nearly all the washes in the northern half of the Wonderland of Rocks, as well as nearly all washes in Queen Mountain drain into Rattlesnake Canyon. It is not uncommon for running water (don't drink the stuff!) to be found in Rattlesnake Canyon most of the year.

The routes and areas described all are approached from the vicinity of a picnic area about 1 mile southeast of Indian Cove Campground. Take the road heading southeast from the vicinity of The Short Wall to the picnic area (parking). Some routes/areas lie adjacent to the picnic area and are but a short walk from the car; others are approached from the Rattlesnake Canyon wash proper.

Some of the areas that are approached from the Rattlesnake Canyon wash do not actually lie in Rattlesnake Canyon, but are located in side canyons. This guide tries to describe such areas in the order that they would be encountered (or approached) from the car along the Rattlesnake Canyon Wash. It is probably a good idea to examine the overview maps for this area before you start walking. Map, page 539.

PICNIC AREA CRAGS

The following routes and crags are approached directly from the vicinity of the picnic area. An approach up Rattlesnake Canyon **is not** necessary to reach them.

ICEBERG BOULDER AREA

This huge boulder lies to the northwest of the paved loop road at the picnic rea. As you drive into the paved loop, a dirt road on your right (west) heads in a westerly direction for a short distance. A few picnic tables are located at the end of this dirt road. From the end of the dirt road, walk west for approximately 100 yards, skirting some low rocks on the left (south). At this point, take a lefthand turn (to the south) around the low rocks. The huge Iceberg Boulder is obvious from here. Map, page 539.

3792 **BOURBON ON ICE 5.10d ★★★** This is a four-bolt route on left side of the north face of the boulder.

3793 **SLIGHTLY OUT OF OUR MINDS 5.11d ★★★** This is a three-bolt route on the right side of the north face.

3794 **BOORTEMUS 5.10d ★★★** This overhanging crack lies on another large boulder to the northwest of the Iceberg Boulder. Approach as for the Iceberg Boulder, but don't turn south around the low rocks. Instead, head 100 yards west, skirting some more rocks. This route lies on the north end of a boulder at the north end of these rocks.

GHOST TOWN

This crag faces north and is southwest of the paved loop at the picnic area. It can be seen easily from the intersection of a dirt road that heads west from the paved loop. From near this point, walk over a small saddle, down into a boulder-filled gully, then up to the base. Map, page 539.

3795 **HEADLESS HORSEMAN 5.11a ★★★**
3796 **DESPERADO 5.10b ★**
3797 **BRIDGE OF SIGHS 5.11b ★★★★**

END LOOP AREA

The following are approached directly from the end of the paved loop at the picnic area. Map, page 539.

3798 **AREN'T YOU HUNGRY 5.12c (TR) ★★** This is on the north side of the large boulder just south of the picnic area.
3798a **DON'T TOUCH THAT FRIEND 5.10a** This route starts in a left-facing dihedral on the rocks behind (south) and above **Aren't You Hungry.** Finish up a boulder/arête .

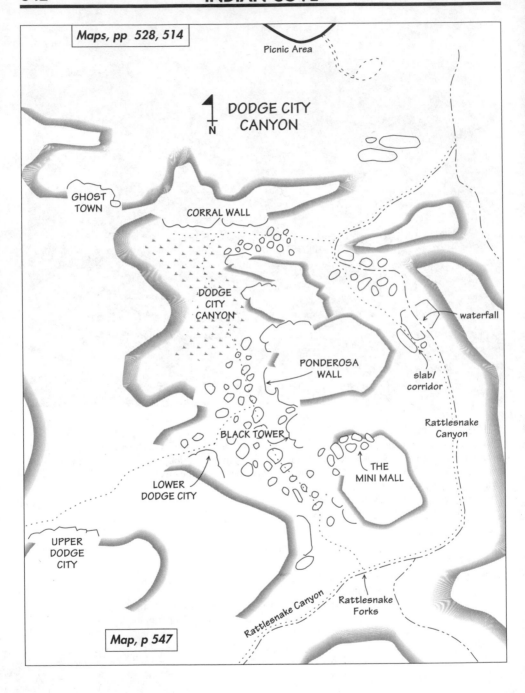

Maps, pp 528, 514

DODGE CITY CANYON

N

GHOST TOWN

CORRAL WALL

Picnic Area

DODGE CITY CANYON

PONDEROSA WALL

waterfall

slab/ corridor

Rattlesnake Canyon

BLACK TOWER

THE MINI MALL

LOWER DODGE CITY

UPPER DODGE CITY

Rattlesnake Canyon

Rattlesnake Forks

Map, p 547

Looking down Dodge City Canyon (north) at the Corral Wall

DODGE CITY CANYON AREAS

These various crags lie in what is essentially a side canyon off Rattlesnake Canyon. The approach to this canyon is in fact quite short from the picnic area parking; although the approaches to some of the crags in the "upper" reaches of Dodge City Canyon require considerable boulder hopping.

From the car, walk east to the Rattlesnake Canyon wash. Head south (up the canyon) for about 400 yards. At this point, the wash has turned to the southwest (right) and then makes an abrupt turn back east (left). The terrain becomes more jumbled past this point. When Rattlesnake Canyon turns sharply back east, head straight (southwest) up boulders through an obvious notch. Over the notch, the terrain levels (with lots of bushes and good trails). Immediately to your right (north) is the south-facing Corral Wall.

The other areas in Dodge City Canyon (Ponderosa Wall, Black Tower, Lower and Upper Dodge City and Cactus City) lie to the south and southwest and are further up the canyon. These other crags also can be approached from further up Rattlesnake Canyon, but the approached described above is probably the best way to get to them on the first visit, as the terrain can be confusing. Map, page 542.

CORRAL WALL

This formation faces south (it is one of Josh's warmer crags), is only about 15 minutes from the car, and has several good, moderately difficult climbs. It is a good choice on cold/windy days. Please use consideration about leaving this and **all** areas in and about Rattlesnake Canyon in **better** shape than you found them. This area can get heavy use, use established trails. Map, page 542.

3799 **CHUCK WAGON CRACK** **5.9** ★
3800 **RANCH HAND** **5.6**
3801 **ONLY OUTLAWS HAVE GUNS** **5.9+** Three bolts, two-bolt anchor/rap.
3802 **SIX-GUN BY MY SIDE** **5.10a** ★★ Five bolts, two-bolt anchor/rap.
3803 **PARTY IN THE DESERT** **5.10b** ★★★ Pro: To 2 inches, three bolts, two-bolt anchor/rap.
3804 **WILD WILD WEST** **5.10d** ★ Five bolts, two-bolt anchor/rap.
3805 **HIGH PLAINS DRIFTER** **5.9+** Pro: To 2 inches, two bolt anchor/rap.
3806 **HANG 'EM HIGH** **5.10a** ★★ Pro: To 2 inches, three bolts, two-bolt anchor/rap.
3807 **HIGH NOON** **5.10b R** ★ Pro: To 2 inches, two bolts, two-bolt rap.
3808 **RIDING SHOTGUN** **5.7** Pro: To 2 inches, two bolts. Two pitches.
3809 **EXFOLIATION CONFRONTATION** **5.9+** ★★ Four bolts, two-bolt anchor/rap.
3810 **WOODEN NICKLE** **5.5 R/X**
3811 **MARKED CARD** **5.9+ R**
3812 **TRIPLE BYPASS** **5.10b** ★

3813 **PONY EXPRESS 5.9** This is on the right end of Corral Wall, about 25 feet right of **Triple Bypass.** Climb up past two bolts, then take discontinuous cracks to a ledge. Two-bolt anchor/rap.

3814 **CZECH CRACK 5.10a** This crack is 15 feet right of **Pony Express,** and ends on the same ledge. Two-bolt anchor/rap.

3815 **BUCKET BRONCO 5.10a ★★** Start 25 feet right of **Czech Crack** (40 feet right of **Pony Express** and near the "notch" through which you enter into Doge City Canyon). Easy climbing leads to a ledge; above, three bolts protect the face to the top.

PONDEROSA WALL AND BLACK TOWER

Go over the notch into Dodge City Canyon and walk below the Corral Wall (on your right). Walk to near the middle of the Corral Wall, then head south up Dodge City Canyon. Stay on the left (east) side of the canyon, following a path that avoids the thick bushes. Above, boulder hopping brings you the base of The Ponderosa Wall, which is on your left (east) and faces west. The Black Tower is above and to the right (south), but part of the same series of cliffs. This area also can be approached from Rattlesnake Canyon from a point referred to as Rattlesnake Forks. If you are at Rattlesnake Forks, head over the notch (north) down into Dodge City Canyon; these formations will be on your right (east) after hopping down some boulders. The Mini Mall lies just southeast of here, on the top of the hill above and left of these crags. Map, page 542.

PONDEROSA WALL

3816 **HOP SING 5.8 ★★**
3817 **BONANZA 5.10b ★★** Pro: To 2 inches, three bolts.

BLACK TOWER

3818 **BLACK LIKE NIGHT 5.11d ★★★** Three bolts on the north face of the block.
3819 **COYOTE CRACK 5.9 ★** The right-slanting crack.
3820 **DOC HOLIDAY 5.10a ★**
3821 **BLAZING SADDLES 5.10a ★★**

LOWER DODGE CITY

This small crag has some excellent routes, and lies almost directly across (on the west side of) the canyon from Ponderosa Wall and Black Tower. Approach as for those crags, boulder hop up and right (west) to the base. This area also can be approached from Rattlesnake Canyon at a point referred to as Rattlesnake Forks. If you are at Rattlesnake Forks, head over the notch (north) down into Dodge City Canyon. Lower Dodge City is on your left (west) after hopping down some boulders. The Mini Mall lies just east of here, up on the top of the hill across the canyon (east) and up from these crags. Map, page 542.

3822 **THE HEALTH CARE PRESIDENT 5.6**
3823 **HANGMAN JURY 5.11c ★★★** Six bolts, two-bolt anchor/rap.
3824 **FRONTIER JUSTICE 5.11b ★★★★** Pro: To 2 inches, seven bolts, two-bolt anchor/rap.

UPPER DODGE CITY

This is not an easy place to approach. Just after going over the notch into Dodge City Canyon, walk below the Corral Wall (on your right). Walk to near the middle of the Corral wall, then head south up Dodge City Canyon. Stay on the left (east) side of the canyon, following a path to avoid the thick bushes. Above, boulder hopping brings you the base of The Ponderosa Wall, which is on your left (east). Lower Dodge City is on your right (east) across the canyon. From here, head west across the canyon, just below Lower Dodge City, up an indistinct side canyon running up and west from Lower Dodge City. This dark-colored face is found about 300 yards west of Lower Dodge City, facing north. The formation has several small roofs on it. Map, page 542.

3825 **STRING 'EM UP 5.11c ★★★** A five-bolt route just right of an arête at the left end of the formation. Two-bolt anchor/rap.

3826 **LYNCH MOB 5.11a ★★** This is a four-bolt route just right of **String 'Em Up.** Two-bolt anchor/rap.

3827 **SPAGHETTI WESTERN 5.11d ★★★★** This is an eight-bolt route up steep rock to the right of the previous climbs. Two-bolt anchor/rap.

CACTUS CITY

This south-facing crag lies about 400 yards directly west of Upper Dodge City (about 750 yards west of Lower Dodge City). In reality, it is not in Dodge City Canyon, but due to its proximity to Upper Dodge City, it is described here. It lies on the north side of a small side canyon that lies beyond a saddle at the end of Dodge City Canyon. This side canyon actually lies off Rattlesnake Canyon at a point several hundred yards west of The Pyramid.

If you are already near Upper Dodge City, continue west up the boulders and over a small saddle to reach the formation. However, if you are in Rattlesnake Canyon, it is easier to walk west up Rattlesnake Canyon past The Pyramid, then head uphill and north to reach Cactus City. Either way, this is a long walk for the two routes known. Map, page 547.

3828 **CACTUS PETE'S 5.10a R ★** Start about 60 feet right of a chimney, just right of the center of the formation. The first pitch goes up past 2 bolts to a 2 bolt belay. The 2nd pitch continues straight up crack systems to the top.

3829 **BURY ME WITH MY BOOTS ON 5.9 R ★★** Start as for **Cactus Pete's.** Do a short pitch up and right to a two-bolt belay. A long pitch past six bolts (up and right) leads to another two-bolt belay. An easy traverse right gets you off the climb.

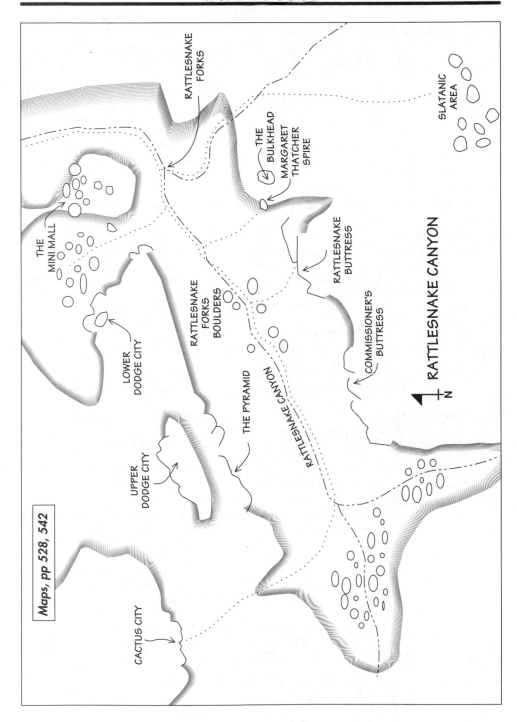

Maps, pp 528, 542

RATTLESNAKE FORKS

THE BULKHEAD

MARGARET THATCHER SPIRE

SLATANIC AREA

THE MINI MALL

RATTLESNAKE BUTTRESS

LOWER DODGE CITY

RATTLESNAKE FORKS BOULDERS

COMMISSIONER'S BUTTRESS

THE PYRAMID

RATTLESNAKE CANYON

RATTLESNAKE CANYON

N

UPPER DODGE CITY

CACTUS CITY

RATTLESNAKE CANYON AREA

The following formations and routes lie adjacent to or are approached from Rattlesnake Canyon. Most involve a bit of a hike from the car, but many routes are excellent and the remote setting is beautiful. The canyon is popular with hikers.

From the car, walk east to the Rattlesnake Canyon wash. Head south (up the canyon) for about 400 yards; at this point, the wash has turned to the southwest (right), and makes an abrupt turn back east (left). The terrain becomes more jumbled past this point, which also is the point from which you approach Dodge City Canyon. Just beyond this sharp lefthand turn in the canyon, the terrain becomes much rougher, and there are many large boulders. Stay on the righthand side of the wash/canyon, head up slabs to the right of the main wash. Go through a narrow "corridor," then drop back into the wash. This route avoids horrendous boulder hopping and a steep waterfall/watercourse through the rocks.

The streambed is somewhat rocky above this point, but turns right (west) and becomes quite level and sandy. Map, page 539, 547.

THE MINI MALL

Follow the canyon, as described above, to a point just before it levels off, turns west and becomes sandy. The Mini Mall lies on the top of the hillside on the right (northwest). It is really a conglomeration of large boulders/rocks that generally face north. The routes are about 30 to 40 feet in length. It is also possible to approach The Mini Mall from the vicinity of The Ponderosa Wall/Black Tower if you are in Dodge City Canyon. The main routes lie southeast of The Ponderosa Wall/Black Tower. One route on The Mini Mall (**Desert Whale**) actually faces into Dodge City Canyon above and right (south) of The Black Tower. Lastly, you could approach The Mini Mall by walking up Rattlesnake Canyon about 100 yards further to "Rattlesnake Forks," then head north through the notch into Dodge City Canyon. Map, page 547.

3830 **RETURN TO HELL 5.11b ★★** This three-bolt route lies near the left side of the Mini Mall, to the right and around the corner from a five-bolt "project." Climb a dark streaked face that steepens.

3831 **COOL THING 5.12b ★★★** This three-bolt route is about 50 feet right of **Return to Hell** up a steep north-facing block. Two-bolt anchor/rap.

3832 **WOMEN AND MONEY 5.12b (TR) ★★** This overhanging dark brown face lies about 40 feet right of **Cool Thing.** Two-bolt anchor.

3833 **DESERT WHALE 5.11c ★★★** This three-bolt overhanging face route faces west into Dodge City Canyon, and lies above and right of The Black Tower.

RATTLESNAKE FORKS

From the car, walk east to the Rattlesnake Canyon wash. Head south (up the canyon) for about 400 yards; at this point, the wash has turned southwest (right) and makes an abrupt turn back east (left). The terrain becomes more jumbled past this point (this also is the point from which you approach Dodge City Canyon). Just beyond this sharp lefthand turn in the canyon, the terrain becomes much rougher, and there are many large boulders. Stay on the righthand side of the wash/canyon at this point, and head up slabs to the right of the main wash. Go through a narrow "corridor," then drop back into the wash. This route avoids horrendous boulder hopping and a steep waterfall/watercourse through the rocks.

The streambed is somewhat rocky above this point, but turns right (west) and becomes quite level and sandy. About 120 yards further along the sandy wash, a "notch" or pass opens in the hillside to your right (north). This leads directly into Dodge City Canyon, near Lower Dodge City and the Ponderosa Wall/Black Tower. This point is known as "Rattlesnake Forks." The remaining formations will be described in relationship to this point. Map, page 547.

3834 **NITTY GRITTY 5.9** From Rattlesnake Forks, take the rough trail that heads north toward Dodge City Canyon. This route lies on the east-facing wall (on the left/west) just before you head through the "notch," and follows a discontinuous right-slanting crack.

MARGARET THATCHER SPIRE
This light-colored boulder/pillar lies about 250 feet uphill and south from Rattlesnake Forks. Map, page 547.

3835 **IRON LADY 5.8** This is a two-bolt face route on back (south) side of the formation. Poor anchor/rap.

THE BULKHEAD
This dark-colored pillar lies about 125 yards uphill and southeast of Rattlesnake Forks. Map, page 547.

3836 **EXILED IN SWEDEN 5.10d ★★★** This is a three-bolt face route on the north face.

3837 **BULKHEAD ARETE 5.10b R ★★★** Start on the north face, just right of **Exiled in Sweden.** Climb up and right to reach the northwest arête; climb up past a bolt, then head out right and up the west face. Pro: Thin to 2 inches.

SLATANIC AREA
This area lies high on the ridge south of Rattlesnake Canyon. The approach is lengthy, but the climbs excellent. Just before you get to Rattlesnake Forks (were the canyon levels and turns west), head uphill along a gully that lies just east of the ridge with The Bulkhead. Hike up the gully for about 275 yards, then cut west (right) to the ridge. Head up the ridge a short distance, then drop down into a narrow canyon/gully. Follow this up to the obvious north-facing arêtes. Map, page 547.

3838 **WITCH HUNT 5.10b ★★★★** Start in a thin crack on the left (the rightmost of two thin cracks) that leads to the lefthand arête protected by four bolts. Pro: Thin to 2 inches, four bolts, one-bolt anchor.

3839 **SOUTH OF HEAVEN 5.12d ★★★★★** This route starts down and right of **Witch Hunt.** Climb thin cracks up and right (two fixed pins) to the righthand arête. Two-bolt anchor, 80-foot rap. Pro: Thin , two fixed pins, six bolts.

RATTLESNAKE BUTTRESS

This obvious formation lies directly south and uphill from the Rattlesnake Forks area. The easiest approach is to walk west along the wash for about 125 yards past Rattlesnake Forks, then head uphill to the western toe of the formation. Map, page 547.

3840 **APPROACH PITCH   5.8+**   This can be used as an approach to **Taken For Granite, 200 Motels** or **Cactus Cooler.** Fourth-class face climbing leads to a ledge with trees. Follow a crack up and left as it peters out into face climbing. Pro: Thin to 2.5 inches.

3841 **TAKEN FOR GRANITE   5.8 ★★★**   Start in the rightmost of two chimneys, then head into the left crack. Pro: Thin to 3 inches.

3842 **200 MOTELS   5.8 ★★★**   Begin as for **Taken For Granite,** but head up and right into the righthand crack. Pro: Thin to 3 inches.

3843 **CACTUS COOLER   5.10b ★★**   This thin crack lies in a right-facing dihedral that goes up and left on discontinuous cracks and ramps to a ledge. Descend down to the right. Pro: Thin to 2 inches.

3844 **SCREAM OF THE BUTTERFLY   5.10b**   This is an unfinished route, but you can climb to third bolt and lower off.

3845 **ROY'S ROUTE   5.11b ★★★**   Eight bolts (the fifth is doubled), two-bolt anchor/160-foot rap.

3846 **TEST PILOT   5.10b ★**   Pro: To 4 inches.

RATTLESNAKE FORKS BOULDERS

You'll encounter several very large boulders along Rattlesnake Canyon to the west of Rattlesnake Forks. Map, page 547.

3847 **AROUND THE CORNER   5.8**   There are some large boulders on the left (south) a short distance up the wash past Rattlesnake Forks. This ascends the north arête/fin of a boulder past two bolts.

3848 **LOVE COMES IN SPURTS   5.10d ★★**   This route is on a large boulder lying directly in the wash about 250 yards past Rattlesnake Forks. Climb past three bolts on the boulder's north side.

COMMISSIONER'S BUTTRESS

This series of cliffs lies to the west of Rattlesnake Buttress. They begin about 150 yards west of Test Pilot/Rattlesnake Buttress and extend another 100 yards west, ending at a gap/talus field south of the Rattlesnake Canyon wash. This gap is actually Rattlesnake Canyon, and can be followed uphill to reach The Bullethead, The Duncecap, Lemon and Lime Domes and the rest of the Northern Wonderland of Rocks. With a car shuttle, you could head to Willow Hole and end up at the Willow Hole Parking Area nears Key's Corner.

3849 **GREAT COMMISSION 5.11a ★★** This short (50 foot), right-facing, left-leaning corner system lies near the middle of Commissioner Buttresses, in a brown section of rock. It is nearly opposite right (eastern) end of The Pyramid.

THE PYRAMID

This south facing formation lies on the north side of Rattlesnake Canyon about 400 yards past Rattlesnake Forks, and across and slightly west of Commissioners Buttress. Map, page 547.

3850 **PYRAMID POWER 5.9** Two pitches. Pro: To 3 inches.
3851 **SHAKE, RATTLE AND ROLL 5.11b R ★★** Two pitches. Pro: To 2 inches, eight bolts, two 2-bolt belays/rap stations.
3852 **HIGH TOPS 5.10a ★** Two pitches. Pro: To 3 inches. Rap off **Shake, Rattle and Roll.**
3853 **SNAKEYE PILLAR 5.7 ★★** Five bolts, two-bolt anchor/rap.
3854 **WRAP THAT RASCAL 5.10b ★**

5.0-5.1

- ☐ Chimney Sweep 5.0 (473)
- ☐ Geraldo Follows Ophry 5.0 ★★ (394)
- ☐ The Trough 5.0 (33)
- ☐ Trough, The 5.0 (242)
- ☐ Ambulance Driver 5.1 (513)
- ☐ B-1 5.1 ★ (33)
- ☐ Barney Rubble 5.1 (95)

- ☐ Bozo Buttress 5.1 (295)
- ☐ Brimstone Stairway 5.1 (513)
- ☐ Eye, The 5.1 ★★★ (205)
- ☐ Fissure of Men 5.1 (218)
- ☐ Simpatico 5.1 (33)
- ☐ Two Point Crack 5.1 (473)

5.2

- ☐ Be Wary (513)
- ☐ Beginner's Two (194)
- ☐ Brown Cave (521)
- ☐ Button Soup (224)
- ☐ Chute Up (233)
- ☐ Circus ★ (362)
- ☐ Decent Buckets (158)
- ☐ Descent Crack (464)
- ☐ Evening Warm-Down (394)
- ☐ Eyestrain (33)
- ☐ Five Two-ish (471)
- ☐ Helix (233)
- ☐ Junction Chimney (473)
- ☐ Linda's Crack (537)
- ☐ Marchesa ★ (534)

- ☐ Mastering (49)
- ☐ North Face, The X ★★ (306)
- ☐ Northwest Chimney (189)
- ☐ Nutcracker (362)
- ☐ Oh God! (450)
- ☐ Queen Mother's Route (339)
- ☐ Route 1326 (534)
- ☐ Rusty Pipes ★ (317)
- ☐ Scareamouch ★ (534)
- ☐ Tarantula (479)
- ☐ Three Swidgeteers (137)
- ☐ Through the Hole and Up the Wall (415)
- ☐ Westward Ho! (450)
- ☐ Wooly Spider (479)

5.3

- ☐ B-2 ★ (33)
- ☐ B-3 (33)
- ☐ Beginner's One (194)
- ☐ Beginner's Three (187)
- ☐ Broken Noses (402)
- ☐ Cary Granite (219)
- ☐ Double Crack ★ (537)
- ☐ Flake Hicky (254)
- ☐ For Sure (470)
- ☐ Half Crack (473)
- ☐ Jailbreak (523)

- ☐ Knaug and Hyde R ★ (530)
- ☐ More My Speed (510)
- ☐ Rumblers Below the Roof (421)
- ☐ Shardik (47)
- ☐ So Another 5.3 (446)
- ☐ Southeast Corner (184)
- ☐ Toe Jam Express (537)
- ☐ Turtle Soup (173)
- ☐ Upper Right Ski Track ★ (183)
- ☐ Wandering Tortoise (173)

5.4

- ☐ 39 Steps ★★ (283)
- ☐ Archery (450)
- ☐ Beatle Baily (109)
- ☐ Beatles, The (109)
- ☐ Belly Scraper (207)
- ☐ Bisk (173)
- ☐ Bivy at Gordon's (156)
- ☐ Blue Bayou (123)
- ☐ Bong, The ★★ (194)
- ☐ Borneo (107)
- ☐ Buckeye (486)
- ☐ Business Trip (205)
- ☐ Carolyn's Rump (204)
- ☐ Chicken Bones (254)
- ☐ Cornered (174)
- ☐ Custer Was Here (258)
- ☐ Deadheads (513)
- ☐ Desiderious Delight (476)
- ☐ Diabetics (473)
- ☐ Dos Dedos (419)
- ☐ Duchess Left (534)
- ☐ Easy Day (173)
- ☐ Eschar ★ (33)
- ☐ False Layback (362)
- ☐ Final Act (132)

- ☐ Finally (518)
- ☐ Fistfull of Bush (221)
- ☐ Flare, The ★ (532)
- ☐ Fright Night (52)
- ☐ Fun for the Whole Family (347)
- ☐ Funky Gunkies (450)
- ☐ Gotcha Bush R/X (537)
- ☐ Hedgehog (508)
- ☐ Hillside Strangler (513)
- ☐ Hodgepodge R (508)
- ☐ Holds to Hollywood (387)
- ☐ Hoopharkz (211)
- ☐ Jaime Crack R (507)
- ☐ Jug-Not (507)
- ☐ Mad Race (536)
- ☐ Minion (535)
- ☐ Mother Goose X (92)
- ☐ Myrmecocystus Ewarti (513)
- ☐ Nectar (463)
- ☐ Now We Know (58)
- ☐ Ohm on the Range (118)
- ☐ Once in a Blue Moon R (123)
- ☐ One Point Crack (473)
- ☐ Outhouse Flake (195)
- ☐ Pahrump (47)

5.4

- [ ] Paint and Body (267)
- [ ] Papal Pleaser (450)
- [ ] Penelope's Walk (206)
- [ ] Pet Project (84)
- [ ] Pokie's Big Change (310)
- [ ] Route 66 ★ (53)
- [ ] Short Crack (508)
- [ ] Skin and Bones R (27)
- [ ] Skinny Pin (212)
- [ ] Sound of Grains Snapping, The (389)
- [ ] Squat Rockets ★ (530)
- [ ] Staircase Crack (512)
- [ ] Tanning Salon (58)
- [ ] There and Back Again R ★ (402)
- [ ] Tubers in Space (206)
- [ ] Waiting for Alan (477)
- [ ] Walkway R (33)
- [ ] Wall of 10,000 Hold R (121)
- [ ] Water Moccasin (533)
- [ ] Wedge (447)
- [ ] What Does The Inside of Your Nose Smell Like (510)
- [ ] Yosemite Sam (104)
- [ ] Young Sole Rebel (402)

5.5

- [ ] 4U2DO2 5.5 X (120)
- [ ] Adams' Happy Acres (82)
- [ ] Arachnids (479)
- [ ] Bat Crack (186)
- [ ] Blistering (173)
- [ ] Blue Sky, Black Death (99)
- [ ] Boom Boom O'Hara (373)
- [ ] Bran New (209)
- [ ] Card Chimney (38)
- [ ] Cellbound ★★ (523)
- [ ] Climb of the Sentry (167)
- [ ] Crack 69 (519)
- [ ] Dial-a-Pile (130)
- [ ] Dilly Bar (131)
- [ ] Donna T's Route (537)
- [ ] Eating Crow (397)
- [ ] Elementary Jamming ★★ (405)
- [ ] Filch (32)
- [ ] Fingerlocks or Cedar Box (450)
- [ ] Flake Route (510)
- [ ] Fryer Flyers (94)
- [ ] Heffalump R/X (373)
- [ ] Jump Back Loretta (152)
- [ ] Kodiak (47)
- [ ] Lady in Waiting (337)
- [ ] Lizard Robbins (88)
- [ ] Lizard Taylor R (88)
- [ ] Looks 5.0, So Let's Solo (446)
- [ ] Matt Biondi Chimney (345)
- [ ] Maybe Baby (258)
- [ ] Men with Cow's Heads (105)
- [ ] Mr. Bunny's Tax Shelter (130)
- [ ] Mr. Rogers ★ (394)
- [ ] No Bones About It (27)
- [ ] Not Worth Your While (258)
- [ ] Patagucci (216)
- [ ] Quivers ★★ (491)
- [ ] Rawl (364)
- [ ] Richochet ★ (287)
- [ ] Right On ★★ (378)
- [ ] Roaring Rapids (503)
- [ ] Roboranger (118)
- [ ] Rocket Man (337)
- [ ] Secovar (184)
- [ ] Shady Nook (436)
- [ ] Spire Route ★ (59)
- [ ] Swain Lake R (120)
- [ ] Tang (165)
- [ ] The Chief ★★ (44)
- [ ] Too Silly to Climb (50)
- [ ] Wilson Regular Route ★ (101)
- [ ] Wooden Nickle R/X (543)
- [ ] Zelda (511)

5.6

- [ ] Aiguille de Joshua Tree X (108)
- [ ] Ain't Nothing But A J-Tree Thing (166)
- [ ] Air Crack (331)
- [ ] Angione Crack (329)
- [ ] Ashtray, The (240)
- [ ] Bitter Brew R (533)
- [ ] Black & Blue (123)
- [ ] Bloom County (83)
- [ ] Bookman Pitman (307)
- [ ] C Lunch R (517)
- [ ] Cake Walk (474)
- [ ] Carved Scoop (193)
- [ ] Cereal Killer (209)
- [ ] Chance Meeting A3 (436)
- [ ] Chapter 7 (285)
- [ ] Chili Dog (131)
- [ ] Chocolate Snake (133)
- [ ] Circe ★ (205)
- [ ] Construction Blues (405)
- [ ] Cottonmouth X (533)
- [ ] Cow Pie Corner (163)
- [ ] Crack #2 (464)
- [ ] Crack Worthy ★ (326)
- [ ] Curtain Call (132)
- [ ] Cute the Moon ★★ (538)
- [ ] D.E. Chimney, The ★★ (240)
- [ ] Damn Jam (199)
- [ ] Darrens Scrape Scramble and Ramble (397)
- [ ] Date Shake (131)
- [ ] Debbie Does Donuts (531)
- [ ] Deflowered ★★ (211)
- [ ] Diagnostics ★ (473)
- [ ] Diagonal Chimney (196)
- [ ] Diso Sucks (529)
- [ ] Doomed (382)
- [ ] Double Decker ★ (131)
- [ ] Double Dip ★★ (242)
- [ ] Dover Sole (39)
- [ ] Duchess ★★ (534)
- [ ] Dum Roodle (534)
- [ ] Easy Looker (272)
- [ ] Easy Off (418)
- [ ] Eff Four (242)
- [ ] Elusive Butterfly Arete (TR) (222)

5.6

- ☐ Elusive kButterfly ★★ (222)
- ☐ Fat Man's Misery R (516)
- ☐ Fields of Laughter X ★★ (307)
- ☐ Fifteen Minute Gap (264)
- ☐ Flakes of Doom (382)
- ☐ Fool's Ruby R (517)
- ☐ Fote Hog ★★ (167)
- ☐ Foul Fowl (204)
- ☐ Fresh Combination ★ (480)
- ☐ Gargoyle (483)
- ☐ Gaz Giz (184)
- ☐ Great Grain Robbery, The (512)
- ☐ Gut Reaction (267)
- ☐ Hartman (364)
- ☐ Health Care President, The (545)
- ☐ Heart Route, The (537)
- ☐ Hhecht (152)
- ☐ Hidden Taxes (130)
- ☐ Hob Nob (394)
- ☐ Homo Erectus (337)
- ☐ Hoser (414)
- ☐ Hush Puppies (294)
- ☐ Indian Garden (451)
- ☐ Is The Pope Catholic? (TR) (449)
- ☐ James Brown (46)
- ☐ Jaws R ★★★ (385)
- ☐ Jessica's Crack (386)
- ☐ Juggurnot (517)
- ☐ Jumbo Shrimp (437)
- ☐ Junkie Thrill (486)
- ☐ Karpkwitz (33)
- ☐ Kendall Mint Cake (254)
- ☐ Keystone Crack ★★ (279)
- ☐ Kindler and Gentler Ream Job (475)
- ☐ Klingon Pizza R (516)
- ☐ Knot Again R (446)
- ☐ Komodo Dragon R (88)
- ☐ Last Angry Arab (287)
- ☐ Last Minute Additions (110)
- ☐ Leaping Leana ★★ (152)
- ☐ Learning to Crawl (450)
- ☐ Linda's Face R (537)
- ☐ Lust in the Love Den ★★ (405)
- ☐ Mikado, The ★★ (535)
- ☐ Mike's Books ★★ (185)
- ☐ Mikita's Rescue (277)
- ☐ Moment's Notice R ★ (245)
- ☐ Moonwalk, The (296)
- ☐ Mr. Lizard Meets Flintstone (295)
- ☐ New Toy (485)
- ☐ No Strings Attached (397)
- ☐ Notch Route (480)
- ☐ Nothing to Fear (401)
- ☐ Nuts and Cherries (131)
- ☐ One of Two (355)
- ☐ One Small Step (296)
- ☐ Outer Limit A3 (187)
- ☐ Pathetic Crack (446)
- ☐ Pickpocket (421)

- ☐ Picnic (517)
- ☐ Plain But Good Hearted ★ (524)
- ☐ Point of Interest (446)
- ☐ Poodlesby (126)
- ☐ Prepubescent Narwhal (437)
- ☐ Pure and Easy (447)
- ☐ Queen Bee (337)
- ☐ Ranch Hand (543)
- ☐ Ranger J.B. (154)
- ☐ Ranger J.D. (154)
- ☐ Rejuvenation (391)
- ☐ Rip Off (40)
- ☐ Riples in Time (393)
- ☐ Roach Roof (109)
- ☐ Robaxol (118)
- ☐ Rotten Banana R (125)
- ☐ Rusty Ax, The (500)
- ☐ S.O.B. (537)
- ☐ Scotch R (517)
- ☐ Screaming in Digital (510)
- ☐ Self Abuse (105)
- ☐ Serpent Scales ★ (533)
- ☐ Shave Your Bump (453)
- ☐ Short Flake (474)
- ☐ Silkworm (95)
- ☐ Skin Deep Town (393)
- ☐ Snoops (512)
- ☐ Solar Technology (105)
- ☐ Split (156)
- ☐ Split Mitten (421)
- ☐ Splotch (156)
- ☐ Stemski ★★ (451)
- ☐ Student Unrest (216)
- ☐ Superfluous Bolt (327)
- ☐ Suzie's Cream Squeeze (222)
- ☐ SW Corner ★★★ (370)
- ☐ Swain in the Breeze ★★ (120)
- ☐ Swiss Cheese (99)
- ☐ Talus Phallus ★ (139)
- ☐ Taurus (105)
- ☐ The Chicken Ranch (47)
- ☐ The Gear Thief (29)
- ☐ This Puppy (392)
- ☐ Thumb, The (421)
- ☐ Tobin Bias (250)
- ☐ Transquility ★ (522)
- ☐ Trap Door (481)
- ☐ Trench Connection (397)
- ☐ Tulip R/X (33)
- ☐ Tumbleweed (508)
- ☐ Tweeners Out for Glory (364)
- ☐ Unwiped Butt (105)
- ☐ Upevil (476)
- ☐ Wasting Assets (285)
- ☐ West Chimney (187)
- ☐ Whiskey (517)
- ☐ Who's First ★ (515)
- ☐ Yucca Bowl (474)
- ☐ Zap #4 (305)

5.7

- AA (517)
- Able Was I Ere I Saw Ellsmere (52)
- Acuity (214)
- All Booked Up (179)
- All Kings Men (354)
- Almost Like Real Climbing (469)
- Almost Vertical (166)
- Andromeda Strain ★ (40)
- As The Crags Turn ★★ (321)
- As the Wind Blows (54)
- Awful Loose R (516)
- Aztec Two-Step (388)
- B.M.T.C. Leader (512)
- Baby Banana (124)
- Baby Face (52)
- Babylonia ★ (538)
- Back From Retirement (510)
- Ballbury (194)
- Barely Crankin' (369)
- Barrel Race ★ (350)
- Beak of the Week (470)
- Bear Necessities, The (85)
- Beardsley Cabbage (437)
- Beck's Bear (132)
- Betty Gravel (152)
- Big Dumb and Ugly (429)
- Bighorn Hand Crack (60)
- Bitch, Bitch (40)
- Bleed Proof (68)
- Blue Suede Shoes (453)
- Bone Along (383)
- Bonnie Brae (474)
- Bonzo Dog Band ★ (237)
- Boomerang (140)
- Boulder Face (40)
- Brain, The (298)
- Briar Rabbit (508)
- Bucket Brigade ★ (234)
- Buissonier ★★ (192)
- Bush Crack ★ (120)
- Busy Bees (436)
- Captain Kronos ★ (161)
- Carmania ★★ (538)
- Carola's Hip (392)
- Chatty Baby (344)
- Chile Willie (99)
- Chipped Suey (537)
- Chips Ahoy (237)
- Chivalry's Not Dead ★ (533)
- Chocolate Decadence (53)
- Classic Corner ★ (109)
- Colon Blow R (373)
- Commander Cody (130)
- Cough Up Phlem (161)
- Court Jester (534)
- Coyote Crack (477)
- Crackup (482)
- Creditor's Claim (285)
- Crow's Feet (397)
- Crown Jewels ★★ (534)
- Crumble Cake (516)
- Cuddlebone (285)
- Damm Dike (277)
- Dan Cruise (440)
- Dancing on Dimes (512)
- Deceit (427)

- Deceptive Corner ★★ (234)
- Desert Solitaire (450)
- Die-Hedral (271)
- Dimorphism (73)
- Disappearing Belayer (513)
- Dolphin ★★ (463)
- Doom De Doom Doom (TR) (382)
- Double Delight (131)
- Double Doglet ★★★ (98)
- Double Start (189)
- Dr. Seuss Vogel (118)
- Drawstring (186)
- Dreams of Red Rocks (58)
- Dry Rain ★ (526)
- Duchess Right (534)
- Dung Fu ★ (126)
- Dweeb (429)
- East Meets West R (529)
- Easy As PI (128)
- Eat What You Secrete (304)
- Edchada (263)
- Euhedral (538)
- Eyes of Amber (533)
- Fallun (All in Fun) ★ (441)
- False Smooth As Silk ★★ (95)
- Finger Locking Good (450)
- Flakey Flix (477)
- Flare (163)
- Flash Gordon (381)
- Flies on the Wound (513)
- Foghorn Leghorn R (443)
- Frankenwood (252)
- Frankie Lee (278)
- Free As Can Be (483)
- Freeway R (96)
- French Flies (1333)
- Frosty Cone ★★★ (131)
- Fuss Rattle and Roll (397)
- G-Wizz X (350)
- Geronimo ★★★ (188)
- Gin Fizz R (517)
- Goldilocks (206)
- Gorgasaurus (221)
- Grain for Russia (105)
- Grand Theft Avocado (210)
- Granny Goose (92)
- H & R Block ★ (130)
- Hawks Nest ★★★ (497)
- Heartless (471)
- Hemroidic Terror R ★ (385)
- Hex (447)
- Hex Marks The Poot ★★★ (289)
- Hoblett (194)
- Holden Back (164)
- Horn's A'Plenty R (348)
- Hot Cross Buns (82)
- Hotseat (364)
- Howard's Horror (200)
- Humpty Dumpty ★★ (354)
- I Eat Cannibal (441)
- I Should Be Dancin' (399)
- I'm So Embarrassed For You (132)
- Illegal Campfire (517)
- Illusion (73)
- Insider Information (141)
- Invasion On My Fantasy (308)

5.7

- [ ] Ironworks (144)
- [ ] It Satisfies (130)
- [ ] Jaime's Big Show (507)
- [ ] Jill and Jerry (279)
- [ ] Jumping Jehosaphat ★ (152)
- [ ] Jungle (184)
- [ ] Klansman, The (405)
- [ ] Knight Mare (283)
- [ ] Labyrinth, The (105)
- [ ] Large Marge (364)
- [ ] Lazy Day ★★ (381)
- [ ] Leap Year Flake (131)
- [ ] Left Double Feature Crack ★★★ (503)
- [ ] Left Overs (TR) (52)
- [ ] Let's Bolt (538)
- [ ] Lickety Splits R ★★ (384)
- [ ] Life's A Bitch and Then You Marry One ★★ (279)
- [ ] Ligamentor Seconds in Vans R (508)
- [ ] Little Bunny Fu-Fu (364)
- [ ] Little Rock Candy Crack (254)
- [ ] Lizard's Landing ★ (25)
- [ ] Look Mom, No Hands (49)
- [ ] Lost and Found (421)
- [ ] Lucky Charms ★ (522)
- [ ] Lumping Fat Jennie (152)
- [ ] M.F. Dirty Rat (371)
- [ ] Maggies Farm (125)
- [ ] Middle Finger (421)
- [ ] Minotaur ★ (105)
- [ ] Model T (83)
- [ ] Mom for the Road (49)
- [ ] Mosaic Wall (521)
- [ ] Mr Ranger Sir (85)
- [ ] Mr. Misty Kiss ★★★ (131)
- [ ] My 3 Friends (451)
- [ ] Nereltne ★★ (223)
- [ ] Never Cry Louie (447)
- [ ] New Decayed (287)
- [ ] New Year's Quickie (393)
- [ ] Nice and Icy (442)
- [ ] Nickel Slots R (516)
- [ ] Oatmeal Eating Aardvarks (503)
- [ ] Omega (516)
- [ ] Once in a Lifetime (425)
- [ ] One Way Up (418)
- [ ] Ostrich Skin R (516)
- [ ] Other Voces ★ (90)
- [ ] Out of Step R (537)
- [ ] Overhang Bypass ★★★ (187)
- [ ] Pacific Ave. Dorm ★ (94)
- [ ] Paint Me Gigi X (49)
- [ ] Palm-U-Granit (233)
- [ ] Pebble Beach (470)
- [ ] Pebbles and Bam Bam (273)
- [ ] Peglet (121)
- [ ] Phallus (201)
- [ ] Piddle Pug R (83)
- [ ] Pile, The (142)
- [ ] Pinnacle Stand (186)
- [ ] Poddle Lizard (88)
- [ ] Polar Bears in Bondage (47)
- [ ] Political Asylum (264)
- [ ] Pops Goes Hawaiian ★★ (44)
- [ ] Poultry Pilots (94)
- [ ] Power Line (248)

- [ ] Practice Rehearsal (132)
- [ ] Presto in C Sharp (378)
- [ ] Princess (535)
- [ ] Quadrophenia (447)
- [ ] Queen For A Day (337)
- [ ] Quien Sabe? ★ (522)
- [ ] Rainy Day Women (125)
- [ ] Ranger Rendezvous (120)
- [ ] Rap or Snap (402)
- [ ] Resurrection (391)
- [ ] Retirement Is All That (436)
- [ ] Return of Large Marge (345)
- [ ] Riding Shotgun (543)
- [ ] Right Between the Eyes ★★ (251)
- [ ] Rings Around Uranus (385)
- [ ] Ripples (173)
- [ ] Road Dogs (475)
- [ ] Roast Leg of Chair (251)
- [ ] Rock-A-Lot ★ (98)
- [ ] Rocky Horror (283)
- [ ] Ronnie's Rump (TR) (328)
- [ ] Roy's Solo (87)
- [ ] Sabretooth (237)
- [ ] Sandblast (459)
- [ ] Scream Chuck R (515)
- [ ] Scrumdillyishus ★ (131)
- [ ] Search for Klingons (385)
- [ ] She's So Unusual (84)
- [ ] Skinny Dip R ★★ (212)
- [ ] Slanta Claus, Left (164)
- [ ] Slipper When Wet (213)
- [ ] Smooth As Silk ★ (95)
- [ ] Snakeye Pillar ★★ (551)
- [ ] So Hole Lo R/X (351)
- [ ] Solo-Arium X (198)
- [ ] South Buttress ★★ (520)
- [ ] South Face (TR) (394)
- [ ] South Face Direct (310)
- [ ] Spaghetti & Chili (206)
- [ ] Spinner R (115)
- [ ] Spud Patrol (206)
- [ ] Stan and Ollie (445)
- [ ] Steady Breeze X (537)
- [ ] Stichter Quits ★★★ (242)
- [ ] Stucca By A Yucca (132)
- [ ] Sugar Daddy (140)
- [ ] Suite Sister Mary R (510)
- [ ] Suzanna's Bandana (470)
- [ ] Swift, The ★★ (101)
- [ ] Swishbah (534)
- [ ] Tender Flakes of Wrath ★ (44)
- [ ] Thrutcher (308)
- [ ] Tight Shoes R (537)
- [ ] Toe Jam ★★ (188)
- [ ] Tom Bombadil (369)
- [ ] Trial by Fire (482)
- [ ] Trivial Pursuit (327)
- [ ] Twins (140)
- [ ] Unknown (167)
- [ ] Unknown (272)
- [ ] Unnamed (149)
- [ ] Unwed Muddlers (391)
- [ ] Up Chuck (373)
- [ ] Vagmarken Buttress (29)
- [ ] Vaino's Lost in Pot R/X ★ (515)
- [ ] Velveeta Rabbit, The (112)

5.7

- [ ] West Face Overhang ★ (200)
- [ ] Wheat Chex (533)
- [ ] Where Janitors Dare (168)
- [ ] White Lightning ★★★ (126)
- [ ] White Powder (36)
- [ ] Willard ★ (287)
- [ ] Willit Slab (533)
- [ ] Wilma Rubble (95)

- [ ] Wind Cries Mary, The (437)
- [ ] Wisest Crack ★★ (379)
- [ ] With Malice and Forethought ★ (529)
- [ ] Won't Get Fooled Again (447)
- [ ] Yankee Poodle (233)
- [ ] Young and the Restless R (393)
- [ ] Zigzag (183)
- [ ] Zsa Zsa Goes to Jail R (40)

5.7+

- [ ] B Flat (82)
- [ ] B Sharp (82)
- [ ] Bib Bird (118)
- [ ] Calcutta ★ (536)
- [ ] Chicken Little (TR) (443)
- [ ] Coyote Bait (126)
- [ ] Crack A (464)
- [ ] Double Cross ★★★★ (189)

- [ ] Hip, Hip Belay R (117)
- [ ] Mental Physics ★★★★ (298)
- [ ] Quothe the Raven (475)
- [ ] Robo Cop (362)
- [ ] Sometimes We Crack Ourselves Up ★ (326)
- [ ] Three Musketeers, The (254)
- [ ] Tiptoe ★★ (33)
- [ ] Walk on the Wild Side ★★★★ (378)

5.8

- [ ] 200 Motels ★★★ (550)
- [ ] 3rd Class It (513)
- [ ] Acupuncture (148)
- [ ] Agony of Defeat R (56)
- [ ] All-Reet Arete (429)
- [ ] Allen Steck Memorial Route (369)
- [ ] Anniversary Special (362)
- [ ] Annointed Seagull (105)
- [ ] Ant Farm ★ (126)
- [ ] Aquino (129)
- [ ] Are We Ourselves (206)
- [ ] Arete (176)
- [ ] Around the Corner (550)
- [ ] Artificial Ingredients (309)
- [ ] Arturo's Special ★ (388)
- [ ] At Your Pleasure ★★★★ (353)
- [ ] Auld Lang Syne (393)
- [ ] Baby Roof ★★★ (52)
- [ ] Baby-Point-Five R/X (33)
- [ ] Bakersfield Bomb (508)
- [ ] Barkhorn (TR) (364)
- [ ] Beck's Bet ★ (98)
- [ ] Berkeley Dyke (194)
- [ ] Big Lie, The (264)
- [ ] Big Step X (537)
- [ ] Bivo Sham (328)
- [ ] Black Lipstick R (427)
- [ ] Blue Nun (123)
- [ ] Bolters Are Weak R (27)
- [ ] Bombay ★ (536)
- [ ] Bonecrusher Arete ★ (27)
- [ ] Boulder Crack (40)
- [ ] Bouncer (513)
- [ ] Brew 102 (92)
- [ ] Bryant Gumbel (92)
- [ ] Bublinki (480)
- [ ] Buckets to Burbank ★ (387)
- [ ] Bullocks Fashion Center (392)
- [ ] But Fear Itself (401)
- [ ] C.F.M.F. R/X (198)
- [ ] Carrot (364)
- [ ] Cashews Will Be Eaten (248)
- [ ] Catch a Falling Star ★★ (362)
- [ ] Cementary (298)
- [ ] Chaffe n' Up R (118)

- [ ] Chessboard, The R (534)
- [ ] Chimney (163)
- [ ] City H ★ (330)
- [ ] Cleared for Landing (477)
- [ ] Climb of the Cockroaches R (109)
- [ ] Cohatoes (351)
- [ ] Colossus (503)
- [ ] Commitments Are For Me (206)
- [ ] Conceived in Idaho (405)
- [ ] Conservative Policies (166)
- [ ] Courier's Tragedy, Act IV, Scene 8 (277)
- [ ] Crank Queenie ★ (529)
- [ ] Cranny ★★ (33)
- [ ] Cream Puff ★ (351)
- [ ] Cryptic ★★★ (370)
- [ ] Cuban Connection R (535)
- [ ] Cunning Linquist (445)
- [ ] Dancin' Daze ★ (484)
- [ ] Dangling Digit ★ (497)
- [ ] Dappled Mare ★★★ (101)
- [ ] Date Queen (524)
- [ ] Death Rides a Pale Horse (430)
- [ ] Deliver Us From Evil R ★ (294)
- [ ] Dental Hygiene (276)
- [ ] Desert Queen (470)
- [ ] Dinkey Doinks ★★ (97)
- [ ] Disposable Heroes (503)
- [ ] DOA (513)
- [ ] Dogleg ★★★ (189)
- [ ] Double Crux (529)
- [ ] Downpour ★ (113)
- [ ] Dream of White Poodles, A (242)
- [ ] Driving Limitations ★★ (530)
- [ ] Druids, The (351)
- [ ] Duplicity R (427)
- [ ] Edge of the Knife ★★ (413)
- [ ] Eff Eight (247)
- [ ] Fabulous T. Gordex Cracks, The (109)
- [ ] Face of Tammy Faye, The (166)
- [ ] False Tumbling Rainbow (150)
- [ ] Fantails (229)
- [ ] Fat Freddie's Escape (305)
- [ ] Fat Is Where It's At (426)
- [ ] Fat Man's Folly (276)
- [ ] Fatal Flaw ★ (97)

5.8

- [ ] Feltoneon Physics ★ (126)
- [ ] Filth R (32)
- [ ] Filthy Rich (272)
- [ ] Fingertip Traverse of Josh ★★ (135)
- [ ] First Steps (71)
- [ ] Fissure Merde (447)
- [ ] Five-Four-Plus (195)
- [ ] Flake and Bake (237)
- [ ] Flake, The ★★ (187)
- [ ] Flared Bear (168)
- [ ] Flat Tire (106)
- [ ] Flue, The ★★★ (201)
- [ ] Fluff Boy (536)
- [ ] Fool's Gold (445)
- [ ] Fooling Myself (256)
- [ ] Friend Eater (107)
- [ ] From Here to Infirmary (209)
- [ ] Full Count (480)
- [ ] Fun Stuff (233)
- [ ] Funky Dung (126)
- [ ] Funny Bone (252)
- [ ] Gem ★★ (445)
- [ ] Generic Route (116)
- [ ] Global Warming R (355)
- [ ] Go 'Gane (220)
- [ ] Go For Broke (247)
- [ ] Goof Proof Roof A2+ ★★★ (504)
- [ ] Gorby Goes to Washington (475)
- [ ] Grain Gang (512)
- [ ] Grain Surplus (105)
- [ ] Great Caesar's Ghost (350)
- [ ] Green Mansions (464)
- [ ] Greystoke R (510)
- [ ] Gullywog ★★ (464)
- [ ] Gumby Goes to Washington (310)
- [ ] H.R. Hardman ★ (264)
- [ ] Haberdashery, The (517)
- [ ] Half Time (522)
- [ ] Ham Sandwich (378)
- [ ] Handcracker (521)
- [ ] Hands Off ★★★ (197)
- [ ] Hang Ten (233)
- [ ] Hard Science ★ (273)
- [ ] Heart Slab (517)
- [ ] Heartbreak Ridge (364)
- [ ] Hit It Ethel ★ (53)
- [ ] Hogback (508)
- [ ] Holden Up (164)
- [ ] Hop Sing ★★ (544)
- [ ] Hope and Glory (136)
- [ ] Hot Tub Honey (508)
- [ ] Hot Tubs From Hell (209)
- [ ] I Am Not A Crook (264)
- [ ] I Can Believe It's A Sandbag (305)
- [ ] Ice Cream for Crow (439)
- [ ] In Search of Hush Puppies R/X (293)
- [ ] Into the Black (392)
- [ ] Into the Fire (367)
- [ ] Iron Lady (549)
- [ ] Jack the Ripper (271)
- [ ] Jane Pauley (92)
- [ ] Jet Stream (503)
- [ ] Jim Cruise ★ (44-
- [ ] Jo Mama (393)
- [ ] Jugular Vein (485)
- [ ] Kate's Bush (90)

- [ ] Kickoff (272)
- [ ] King of the Mountain (216)
- [ ] Kundalini-Linguini-Weenie ★ (517)
- [ ] Laid Back ★ (198)
- [ ] Leader's Fright R ★★★ (205)
- [ ] Left S Crack ★ (122)
- [ ] Less Than Meets the Eye (482)
- [ ] Little Brown Eye ★ (516)
- [ ] Little Ceasar (447)
- [ ] Little Red Rooster (443)
- [ ] Lizard Skin (88)
- [ ] Lost in Space ★★ (101)
- [ ] Love at First Bite X (473)
- [ ] Lucky Lady ★★ (178)
- [ ] Luminous Breast R (173)
- [ ] Lurch (131)
- [ ] Lurleen Quits (112)
- [ ] Lusting CLH (75)
- [ ] Mad Hatter, The (267)
- [ ] Magic Kingdome (388)
- [ ] Manwich Queen ★ (428)
- [ ] Marking Time ★★ (394)
- [ ] Maybe (518)
- [ ] Meanderthal (TR) (273)
- [ ] Misfortune Cookies (39)
- [ ] Mohave Green ★★ (329)
- [ ] Monkey Business ★★ (251)
- [ ] Monument Manor ★ (310)
- [ ] More Hustle Than Muscle (378)
- [ ] Morning After, The (392)
- [ ] Mosaic (529)
- [ ] Mr. Bunny vs. Six Unknown Agents (130)
- [ ] Mr. Michael Goes To Washington (99)
- [ ] Music Box (473)
- [ ] Neptune (105)
- [ ] No Rest for the Wicked R (27)
- [ ] Non-Decumbent Destiny (160)
- [ ] North Arete (192)
- [ ] North Face Center (190)
- [ ] Northwet Arete (176)
- [ ] Not King Cole (479)
- [ ] Nurn's Romp ★★ (384)
- [ ] Nuts Are For Men Without Balls (245)
- [ ] Oat Route, The (209)
- [ ] Oh God, It's My Boss ★ (523)
- [ ] Old Man and the Poodle, The (128)
- [ ] Omaha Beach (389)
- [ ] On the Air (267)
- [ ] Open Container (503)
- [ ] Orange Flake ★★ (378)
- [ ] Outward Bound Slab Route (49)
- [ ] Overdraft (TR) (285)
- [ ] Owatafooliam (120)
- [ ] Palmreader ★★ (520)
- [ ] Paranetieum (264)
- [ ] Parental Guidance Suggested ★ (276)
- [ ] Passing Zone R/X (96)
- [ ] Pathetic Dike (446)
- [ ] Pathetic Face (446)
- [ ] Peanut Brittle (TR) (389)
- [ ] Pearls Before Swine (373)
- [ ] Penny Lane (242)
- [ ] Perhaps the Surgeon General (130)
- [ ] Pfundt's Folly (536)
- [ ] Planetary Motion (95)
- [ ] Political Rehabilitation (264)

5.8

- [ ] Poodle in Shining Armor (127)
- [ ] Pop Tart (298)
- [ ] Porky's Excellent Adventure (455)
- [ ] Potlatch (481)
- [ ] Pumpkin Pie (393)
- [ ] Quivering Lips (382)
- [ ] Quivers Direct (TR) (491)
- [ ] R & R (378)
- [ ] R.M.L. ★★ (237)
- [ ] Raging Intensity (233)
- [ ] Raging Order R (510)
- [ ] Raindance (414)
- [ ] Raising Bran (209)
- [ ] Raker Mobile (378)
- [ ] Randy the Riveter (410)
- [ ] Ranger Danger (118)
- [ ] Rat Ledge ★ (277)
- [ ] Raven, The (463)
- [ ] Reagan Did A Good Job R (510)
- [ ] Red Line (295)
- [ ] Revenge of the Herds (487)
- [ ] Reverend, The ★★ (530)
- [ ] Rhythm of the Heart X ★ (515)
- [ ] Right 'n Up X (537)
- [ ] Right Double Feature Crack ★★ (503)
- [ ] Right Peyote Crack ★★ (224)
- [ ] Right Sawdust Crack ★★ (32)
- [ ] Roan Way ★★ (101)
- [ ] Robotics (122)
- [ ] Rollerskating with Aliens (480)
- [ ] Rose Parade ★ (426)
- [ ] Rudy Valentine Day (481)
- [ ] S'Nose of Winter (96)
- [ ] Safe Muffins R (305)
- [ ] Sail Away ★★★★ (156)
- [ ] Sakreteligious (298)
- [ ] Satchmo (393)
- [ ] Saturn Sheets (359)
- [ ] Savwafare 1st Everywhere (163)
- [ ] Scientific Americans R ★★ (38)
- [ ] Scotch with a Twist R (517)
- [ ] Season Opener ★★ (208)
- [ ] Sentinel Beach (167)
- [ ] Shaking Like A Leaf ★★ (441)
- [ ] Sharp Desire (412)
- [ ] Sheet Bends ★ (530)
- [ ] Sheltered (40)
- [ ] Shit It's A Brit (476)
- [ ] Slam Dunk ★ (526)
- [ ] Slanta Claus, Right (164)
- [ ] Small But Short (178)
- [ ] Small World (394)
- [ ] Snitch in Time, A (523)
- [ ] Snnfchtt (152)
- [ ] Solar Wind ★★ (314)
- [ ] Solo (151)
- [ ] Soma (392)
- [ ] Sound of One Shoe Tapping, The (233)
- [ ] South End of a Northbound Poodle (258)
- [ ] Southwest Passage (186)
- [ ] Space Walk ★ (128)
- [ ] Spaced Mountain (308)
- [ ] Spacely Sprockets (307)
- [ ] Span-nish Fly (207)
- [ ] Sparkle (TR) (416)
- [ ] Spider (188)

- [ ] Spider's Web (519)
- [ ] Spirit of the Dead ★ (373)
- [ ] Squeeze Play (309)
- [ ] Squirrel Roast (254)
- [ ] Steeped T (83)
- [ ] Stood Up (160)
- [ ] Stop Grumbling (95)
- [ ] Straight Flus (196)
- [ ] Supercollider (67)
- [ ] SW Face ★ (263)
- [ ] Swatchbuckler (121)
- [ ] Sweet Transvestite R (96)
- [ ] Tabby Litter (188)
- [ ] Take Five (392)
- [ ] Taken for Granite ★★★ (550)
- [ ] Tennis Shoe Crack ★ (210)
- [ ] The Awfulwidth R (41)
- [ ] Thin Spin (29)
- [ ] Three Amigos, The (319)
- [ ] Ticket to Nowhere (206)
- [ ] Tige (46)
- [ ] Too Bold To Bolt (242)
- [ ] Top-Topic (480)
- [ ] Totally Tubular (470)
- [ ] Toto's Canine Hot Lunch (491)
- [ ] Tractor Pull (479)
- [ ] Tragic Kingdom A1 (308)
- [ ] Treadmark Left (106)
- [ ] Treadmark Right (106)
- [ ] Tres Equis (520)
- [ ] Tri-Step (207)
- [ ] Troglodyte Crack (79)
- [ ] Truth or Dare R (510)
- [ ] Tucson Bound ★ (50)
- [ ] Tuna and Cheese (142)
- [ ] Turtle Days (74)
- [ ] Turtle Vein (455)
- [ ] Tweener in Trouble (364)
- [ ] Two Lost Soles (67)
- [ ] Ulysses's Bivouac (205)
- [ ] Undercling Bypass (58)
- [ ] Unicorner ★★ (377)
- [ ] Unknown (167)
- [ ] Unknown X (94)
- [ ] Untie em (497)
- [ ] Up to Heaven R/X (537)
- [ ] Urban Redevelopment ★ (139)
- [ ] Urine Trouble (263)
- [ ] V Cracks (418)
- [ ] Vagabonds R (29)
- [ ] Vanishing Desert ★★ (475)
- [ ] Vogel Crack (411)
- [ ] Volga Boat Men (41)
- [ ] Vulgar Boot Men (41)
- [ ] W.A.C. ★ (233)
- [ ] Waiting for the Sun (477)
- [ ] Wake Me When It's Over X (41)
- [ ] Wallaby Crack ★ (32)
- [ ] Walrus-Like and Wimpy R (141)
- [ ] Walt's Solo (428)
- [ ] We Dive at Dawn ★★ (530)
- [ ] We'll Get Them Little Pricks (445)
- [ ] Wet Pigeon ★ (105)
- [ ] Wha A Joke (326)
- [ ] What (385)
- [ ] When Two Become Three (121)

5.8

- [ ] Where Two Deserts Meet ★★ (477)
- [ ] Which Witch (40)
- [ ] White Collar Crime (264)
- [ ] White Trash (531)
- [ ] Who's Next (447)
- [ ] Whoville (139)
- [ ] Willit Hold (532)
- [ ] Without A Trace X (208)
- [ ] Wonderful Wobble (402)
- [ ] Worthy Of It (455)
- [ ] Youth Run Wild (511)
- [ ] Zardoz R ★★ (384)
- [ ] Zinging in the Grain (512)

5.8+

- [ ] Approach Pitch (550)
- [ ] Around the World ★★★★ (439)
- [ ] Bambi Meets Godzilla ★★ (246)
- [ ] Bighorn Bivvy ★ (25)
- [ ] Blonde Bombshell Babylon (82)
- [ ] Breakfast of Champions ★★ (290)
- [ ] Continuum ★★★ (459)
- [ ] Fidget With Swidgets (137)
- [ ] Flakes Can Collapse (379)
- [ ] Funny Money (256)
- [ ] Gila Monster, The (447)
- [ ] House of the Homeless ★★ (382)
- [ ] I Love Brian Piccolo ★ (90)
- [ ] J.B. Goes to J.T. (TR) (483)
- [ ] Josar Crack (121)
- [ ] Mush Puppies (82)
- [ ] My Hubby is Chubby (426)
- [ ] Night Gallery (117)
- [ ] Nobody Walks in LA ★ (362)
- [ ] Northern Lights ★★ (477)
- [ ] Planet X (359)
- [ ] Pleasure Pincipal (348)
- [ ] Press Conference, The ★ (349)
- [ ] Punked Out Porpoise ★★ (301)
- [ ] Roman Pretzel (90)
- [ ] Slap Prancing (26)
- [ ] Soup Rhymes With Poop (348)
- [ ] Such a Poodle (126)
- [ ] Sun Proff ★★ (355)
- [ ] Swaino Vista R (TR) (350)
- [ ] Test Tube Baby ★ (344)
- [ ] Wandering Winnebago R ★★ (522)
- [ ] Whale of a Time (53)

5.9

- [ ] Ace of Spades ★★★ (38)
- [ ] Addams Family ★ (131)
- [ ] Al's First Erection (420)
- [ ] Alice in Wonderjam ★★★ (263)
- [ ] All My Children (321)
- [ ] Alligator Lizard (88)
- [ ] Alligator Tears (154)
- [ ] Altitude Sickness (101)
- [ ] American Express ★ (129)
- [ ] An Eye to the West ★ (36)
- [ ] An Officer and a Poodle R (39)
- [ ] Ancient Future (373)
- [ ] Another Brick in the Wall (TR) (298)
- [ ] Answer, The ★★ (491)
- [ ] Ants in My Pants (339)
- [ ] Ass of Dog (237)
- [ ] Atomic Pile (130)
- [ ] Atrophy ★ (26)
- [ ] Autopia (309)
- [ ] Baby Route (369)
- [ ] Bacon Flake (237)
- [ ] Bad Boy Club R (110)
- [ ] Bad Brains (439)
- [ ] Bank Note Blues (50)
- [ ] Banquet (517)
- [ ] Barn Door, Left (TR) (99)
- [ ] Beauty and the Beach (167)
- [ ] Becky's Buttress (475)
- [ ] Beginner's Luck (194)
- [ ] Big Boy (455)
- [ ] Big Brother (392)
- [ ] Bilbo ★ (530)
- [ ] Biskering (172)
- [ ] Bitch in Heat ★ (522)
- [ ] Bivvy Kitten (507)
- [ ] Black Eye R (33)
- [ ] Blizzard (131)
- [ ] Bloddymir (33)
- [ ] Blood and Cuts (457)
- [ ] Bloody Buddy (526)
- [ ] Body Shaving For Competition (345)
- [ ] Bolivian Freeze Job ★ (99)
- [ ] Bonny's Boo-Boo (474)
- [ ] Boo Boo R (85)
- [ ] Boom Boom Boom ★★ (378)
- [ ] Boris the Spider (519)
- [ ] Boulder Dash ★★ (234)
- [ ] Break A Leg R (132)
- [ ] Bright Moments (482)
- [ ] Broken Bits ★★ (307)
- [ ] Bubba's Tourist Trap (474)
- [ ] Bury Me With My Boots On R ★★ (546)
- [ ] Bush Eviction (362)
- [ ] Buster Brown ★★ (46)
- [ ] Buster Hymen (418)
- [ ] Butterfingers Make Me Horny (166)
- [ ] Cactus Dog ★ (307)
- [ ] Cake Walk ★★★ (96)
- [ ] Calgary Stampede ★★ (50)
- [ ] Caligula (247)
- [ ] Campcraft (201)
- [ ] Casual ★ (385)
- [ ] Cat's Meow ★ (399)
- [ ] Charles Chips (139)
- [ ] Charles In Charge (139)
- [ ] Charlie Brown (261)
- [ ] Cherry Blossom (260)
- [ ] Chicken Mechanics ★ (94)
- [ ] Chicken Wing (270)
- [ ] Chimps and Cheetahs ★ (441)
- [ ] Chocolate Chips (391)
- [ ] Chuck Wagon Crack ★ (543)
- [ ] Circus, Circus (362)
- [ ] City Council (123)

5.9

- Clam Shell (375)
- Clamming at the Beach (50)
- Cling Peaches R ★★ (379)
- Cobra Cunning R (462)
- Cold Columbian (99)
- Cole-Lewis ★ (97)
- Colorado Crack ★★★★ (445)
- Controversial (258)
- Count on Your Fingers (166)
- Cows in the Shade (482)
- Coyote Crack ★ (544)
- Crack (233)
- Crack B (464)
- Cracked Actor (538)
- Credibility Gap (241)
- Creme Egg (TR) (254)
- Crystal Keyhole (168)
- Damper ★ (200)
- Date Rape ★ (97)
- Dave's Solo (242)
- Dazed and Confused ★★★ (298)
- Dead Bees R (463)
- Deep Throat (247)
- Defoliation ★ (322)
- Didn't Your Mama Ever Tell You About A Stranger's Bolts (295)
- Die Young (483)
- Direct South Face ★★★ (522)
- Dirty Surprise ★ (304)
- DMB, The ★★ (73)
- Do or Dike (485)
- Don't Even Look (374)
- Don't Look A Gift Frong in the Mouth (170)
- Don't Think Twice (125)
- Don't Touch That Flake (260)
- Drop a Frog ★ (79)
- Drop Your Drawers (79)
- Drugs But No Drills ★ (354)
- Duke, The A1 (288)
- Dummy's Delight ★★★ (178)
- Earn Quick or Die (160)
- East Face (190)
- Easter Overflow (507)
- Enchanted Stairway ★★ (308)
- Endless Summer (300)
- Enforcer, The ★ (214)
- Enter at Your Own Risk (392)
- Enter the Dragon (271)
- Enterprise, The (TR) (480)
- Euthyphro ★ (98)
- Excitable Boy (84)
- Exit Stage Right ★★ (274)
- Experiential Ed. (49)
- False Prophet (362)
- Farewell To Poodles, A (128)
- Fax Man (327)
- Feats Don't Fail Me Now R ★ (245)
- Fiendish Fists ★ (111)
- Fighting the Slime (132)
- Figurehead ★ (394)
- Fishing Trip (330)
- Fissure of Fish (304)
- Fisting in Loveland (469)
- Flakes, The (538)
- Flawless Fissure (107)
- Flintlock Dyno (228)
- Flower Power (248)
- Footloose (477)
- For A Few Swidgets More (137)
- For Whom the Poodle Tolls ★ (128)
- Four of a Kind (TR) ★ (394)
- Four-Car Garage (272)
- Fresh Garlic (402)
- Friendly Fists (58)
- Frozen Fish Fingers (440)
- Gail Winds ★ (52)
- Gardening At Night A1+ (282)
- General Hospital ★★ (321)
- Gentlemen Adventure X (250)
- Gentlemen Bumblies (250)
- Gila Monster (232)
- Gjoa (53)
- Glad Hander (339)
- Glumpies (382)
- Gnatty Dread (339)
- Gomer Pile ★ (526)
- Good Book, The (379)
- Graham Parsons Memorial Hand Traverse (367)
- Grain and Bear It (310)
- Grain Death (256)
- Gripped for Petina ★ (497)
- Grounder (464)
- GS-5 (TR) (112)
- Gut Full of Suds (246)
- Gypsy Queen (339)
- Hand Wobler Delight (298)
- Hans Solo (483)
- Head, Abdomen, Thorax A2 (331)
- Heat Wave (269)
- Herman (258)
- Hershey Highway (TR) (482)
- High Strung ★★ (286)
- Hit, The (214)
- Hobo Chang Ba (450)
- Honey ★★★ (491)
- Horny Corner (237)
- Hot Crystals ★ (105)
- Hot Fudge, A R ★ (131)
- Hunkloads to Hermosa (269)
- I Got It (296)
- Ice Experience, The (382)
- Immaculate Conception (136)
- In and Out (455)
- In The Green Room ★ (501)
- Infectious Smile (139)
- Innervisions (309)
- Intersection Mantel (185)
- Intruders, The A1 (338)
- Invisibility Lessons ★★★★ (459)
- Ironsides (82)
- Isotope ★★ (66)
- It (384)
- It's About Time R (518)
- It's Cracked Up To Be (436)
- Jabberwocky (405)
- Jack of Hearts ★ (38)
- Jewel of Denial, The (73)
- Joan Jetson ★ (307)
- Junkyard God (96)
- Just Another Crack From L.A. ★ (100)
- Just Another New Wave Route (116)
- Just Another Roadside Attraction ★ (87)

5.9

- ☐ K2R ★ (352)
- ☐ Keep the Ball Rolling (219)
- ☐ Kemosabe and Tonto (160)
- ☐ Kid, The ★ (378)
- ☐ Kiddie Corner (411)
- ☐ Kinda Sorta R ★ (518)
- ☐ Kippy Korner (172)
- ☐ Kiss Me Where I Pee (339)
- ☐ Klettervergnugen (508)
- ☐ Knot Again (378)
- ☐ Krakatoa (412)
- ☐ Kwidgi-Bo on the Loose R (510)
- ☐ La Reina ★★ (534)
- ☐ Largotot (228)
- ☐ Last Cigarette Senor?, A (513)
- ☐ Last Ticket to Obscuritiville ★ (24)
- ☐ Lead Us Not Into Temptation ★★★ (294)
- ☐ Leading Lady R (132)
- ☐ Lean Two (414)
- ☐ Lechlinski Cracks ★ (411)
- ☐ Legal Briefs (158)
- ☐ Letdown, The (67)
- ☐ Life in the Fat Lane (82)
- ☐ Life Without TV (140)
- ☐ Lion Tamer ★★ (510)
- ☐ Lippo Lippy (382)
- ☐ Little Big Man (337)
- ☐ Live From Tasmania ★ (112)
- ☐ Lone Ranger, The ★★ (112)
- ☐ Long-Necked Goose (181)
- ☐ Looney Tunes ★★★ (223)
- ☐ Lost Lid A4 ★ (361)
- ☐ Lov'in Kohler (211)
- ☐ Lovey ★ (54)
- ☐ Lunch Is For Wimps (141)
- ☐ Lust in the Wonderland ★ (307)
- ☐ Lust We Forget (391)
- ☐ M & M's Plain ★★ (254)
- ☐ Made in the Shade (52)
- ☐ Magic Touch, The (140)
- ☐ Main Face ★★ (532)
- ☐ Making Wind (TR) (180)
- ☐ Man's Best Friend (TR) (126)
- ☐ Manna From Heaven (218)
- ☐ Manny, Moe & Jack ★ (135)
- ☐ Mano Negra (93)
- ☐ Mare's Tail ★★ (101)
- ☐ McStumpy Sandwich (254)
- ☐ Mental Retread (106)
- ☐ Middle Peyote Crack ★★ (224)
- ☐ Midnight Dreamer (250)
- ☐ Midnight Rambler R (250)
- ☐ Mighty Mouse (285)
- ☐ Mine Shaft ★ (405)
- ☐ Misha's Madness (TR) (392)
- ☐ Momma Spider (519)
- ☐ Mommy Dearest (348)
- ☐ More Fool Me (470)
- ☐ Morituri Te Salutamus (513)
- ☐ Morning Star (508)
- ☐ Moveable Feast (100)
- ☐ Mr. Bunny Goes Rollerskating (TR) (364)
- ☐ Mr. Bunny's Petri Dish (287)
- ☐ Mr. Magoo (104)
- ☐ Mrs. Paul's (440)
- ☐ My Favorite Martian (351)

- ☐ My First First (156)
- ☐ My Laundry ★★★ (290)
- ☐ My Senior Project (381)
- ☐ Naptime for Meggles ★ (27)
- ☐ Negasaurus (221)
- ☐ Neue Regal (510)
- ☐ New Testament (218)
- ☐ Nice Pair, A ★★ (482)
- ☐ Ninny's Revenge (44)
- ☐ Nitty Gritty (548)
- ☐ No Nuts, No Huevos (412)
- ☐ Nobody Walks in L.A. ★★ (96)
- ☐ Nobody's Right Mind (216)
- ☐ North Overhang ★★★ (187)
- ☐ Northeast Arete (193)
- ☐ Norwegian Wood (252)
- ☐ Not in Kansas Anymore (494)
- ☐ Nuke the Whales (445)
- ☐ Nurses in Bondage (TR) (416)
- ☐ Nuts and Bolts (378)
- ☐ OK Korner (172)
- ☐ Ope's Crack ★★★ (245)
- ☐ Opus Dihedral ★ (83)
- ☐ Orphan ★★★ (189)
- ☐ Over the Hill (36)
- ☐ Overseer ★★★ (126)
- ☐ Owl ★ (315)
- ☐ Pachyderms to Paradise (159)
- ☐ Padded Handcuffs (47)
- ☐ Pagan Holiday (348)
- ☐ Pardon Me (264)
- ☐ Peabody's Peril ★★ (216)
- ☐ Penalty Runout R ★★ (111)
- ☐ Perhaps (381)
- ☐ Peruvian Power Layback (99)
- ☐ Perverts in Power (247)
- ☐ Pete's Handful ★★ (192)
- ☐ Pick-a-Nick Baskets R (85)
- ☐ Pig in Heat R (126)
- ☐ Pinhead ★ (222)
- ☐ Pitch Black ★ (94)
- ☐ Plantismal (301)
- ☐ Poetry in Motion ★ (118)
- ☐ Pom Pom Dancer (314)
- ☐ Pony Express (544)
- ☐ Poodle Jive (127)
- ☐ Pope and Circumstance (449)
- ☐ Pope's Hat (449)
- ☐ Poppa Spider ★ (519)
- ☐ Popular Mechanics ★★★ (38)
- ☐ Portal ★ (510)
- ☐ Primal Urge (482)
- ☐ Progressive Lizard ★ (88)
- ☐ Prom Queen (338)
- ☐ Psoriasis ★ (274)
- ☐ Psycho Groove (132)
- ☐ Pterodactydl Crack (139)
- ☐ Pyramid Power (551)
- ☐ Quaking Has-Beens (476)
- ☐ Quest for the Golden Hubris (278)
- ☐ Quit Doing Czech Grils (TR) (112)
- ☐ R.A.F. ★★ (233)
- ☐ Rad (TR) (418)
- ☐ Ravens Do Nasty Things To My Bottom (128)
- ☐ Reality Check (194)
- ☐ Red Eye (TR) (58)

5.9

☐ Rehab (173)
☐ Renter, The (378)
☐ Rich and Famous (272)
☐ Right Archimedes' Crack (414)
☐ Right Lizard Crack ★ (88)
☐ Right S Crack ★ (122)
☐ Rites of Spring (463)
☐ Roberts Crack ★ (411)
☐ Rock & Roll Gril (90)
☐ Rocky Candy ★★★ (98)
☐ Roller Coaster (67)
☐ Rolling Rock (TR) (95)
☐ Room to Shroom ★★★★ (278)
☐ Route 182 (128)
☐ Ruffled Rooster (443)
☐ Rush Hour (429)
☐ Rust in Peace ★ (375)
☐ Rye Not? (446)
☐ Sabre (458)
☐ Safety in Solitude (194)
☐ Same As It Ever Was (418)
☐ Sanctify Yourself (393)
☐ Sand in My Shoes ★ (474)
☐ Satin Finish (273)
☐ Save the Last Stance for Me (463)
☐ Schwee (326)
☐ Secondary Inspection (520)
☐ Semisweet X (508)
☐ Sendero Luminoso (461)
☐ Shaggy Dog (391)
☐ Shirley MaClaine Meets Edlinger (264)
☐ Shit Happens (378)
☐ Shit Sandwich (276)
☐ Shock the Poodle ★ (425)
☐ Short But Sweet ★★ (178)
☐ Silent But Deadly R (98)
☐ Sine Wave (62)
☐ Sitting Here in Limbo ★★ (237)
☐ Slab Happy ★★★ (345)
☐ Smithereens ★★★ (98)
☐ Smoke-a-Bowl ★ (126)
☐ Snaggletooth ★ (493)
☐ Snakes in the Grass (TR) (533)
☐ Sneak Preview (503)
☐ Snow Falls (272)
☐ Soft Core ★★ (273)
☐ Solar Flare ★ (38)
☐ Something Heinous (470)
☐ Soul Research (138)
☐ South Face Center (TR) ★★ (370)
☐ South Face Route (532)
☐ South Swell (322)
☐ Spanish Bayonet ★★★ (538)
☐ Sphincter Quits ★★ (154)
☐ Spinal Tap (482)
☐ Split Personality ★★★ (98)
☐ Spoodle ★ (127)
☐ Squirt (387)
☐ Stegasaurus (486)
☐ Stemulation R ★ (35)
☐ Stepping Out of Babylon (71)
☐ Stick To What ★★★ (242)
☐ Strawberry Jam ★★ (196)
☐ Sugar Daddy ★ (254)
☐ Sullivan from Colorado (378)
☐ Sunset Strip (153)

☐ Super Beak of the Desert (470)
☐ Super Roof ★★★ (210)
☐ Suzie's Lip Cheeze (222)
☐ Swidgeteria, The (137)
☐ T.S. Special R ★★★ (245)
☐ Take Two, They're Small (316)
☐ Tales of Brave Ulysses (170)
☐ Talking About My Variation (35)
☐ Tasgrainian Devel (112)
☐ Tears (523)
☐ Teddy ★★ (54)
☐ Teenage Enema (TR) (416)
☐ Teeter Totter (25)
☐ Tell Me I'm Not Dreaming (304)
☐ Terminator, The (362)
☐ Thin Air (385)
☐ Thin Flakes ★ (113)
☐ Thin Is In (426)
☐ Thin Man's Nightmare (276)
☐ Third World ★ (111)
☐ Thomson Roof ★ (44)
☐ Thrash or Crash (241)
☐ Thrasher (538)
☐ Throat Warbler Mangrove R (293)
☐ Thumbs Down Left ★★ (415)
☐ Tigers on Vaseline (309)
☐ Till Death Do Us Part (TR) ★★ (279)
☐ Toad Crack (274)
☐ Toe the Line ★★ (533)
☐ Toffied Ear Wax (406)
☐ Tofu the Dwarf (233)
☐ Top 40 to Middle Toilet (247)
☐ Totally Nuts R (96)
☐ Touch and Go ★★★★ (241)
☐ Touche Away ★ (174)
☐ Trashman Roof ★ (388)
☐ Trembling Toes ★ (304)
☐ Trivial Tower (327)
☐ Trowel and Error (298)
☐ True Democracy ★ (314)
☐ True Grit (474)
☐ Tubular (TR) (418)
☐ Tumbling Rainbow R ★★ (170)
☐ Turkey Terror (TR) (393)
☐ TV Tower (394)
☐ TVC15 R (248)
☐ Twisties R (229)
☐ Two Bolt Wall (397)
☐ Two Left Feet ★ (73)
☐ Two Our Surprise (40)
☐ Tyrannosaurus Rex (197)
☐ Unbearable Lightness of Being, The (379)
☐ Unconscious Obscenity (298)
☐ Unknown (272)
☐ Unnamed (373)
☐ Vivaldi Kazoo Concerts, Boyd Beaver, Soloist (277)
☐ Vorpal Sword ★ (105)
☐ Vulture's Roost (55)
☐ Wailing Sax (393)
☐ Walking the Dog (493)
☐ Wall Street (141)
☐ Wally George (364)
☐ Wanna Bong (377)
☐ Weathering Frights (35)
☐ West Arete (226)

5.9

- West Face (521)
- Western Saga ★ (167)
- What's Left (391)
- Where's Baldo? (327)
- Which Bitch ★ (40)
- Whips and Grains (316)
- Whisper When You Scream (402)
- White Line Fever (251)
- Who Came First (447)
- Why Do We Do This (329)
- Wild East R (237)
- Wild Gravity (102)
- Wild Wind ★★ (156)
- Wilted Flower Children (38)
- Wind Sprint (420)
- Wise Crack (196)
- Working Overtime ★★ (214)
- Working Without A Net (510)
- Workout at the Y ★ (391)
- Wuthering Heights (433)
- X-Rated Tits ★ (276)
- Year After Year (66)
- Yei-Bei-Chei Crack (208)
- Young Lust ★★★ (98)
- Yuppies Don't Do Offwidths (471)
- Zzzzz R ★★★ (248)

5.9+

- 976 R (127, 128)
- Alpentine R (517)
- Angular Momentum (TR) (464)
- Aqua Tarkus ★ (295)
- Beam Aboard ★ (450)
- Biological Clock ★ (131)
- Black Rhino (503)
- Brownie Points (46)
- Brutis (429)
- Canine Crack (25)
- Chalk Up Another One ★★ (199)
- Cheezels R (229)
- Chocolate Is Better Than Sex (166)
- Cowardly Lion, The (501)
- Crack #5 (464)
- Czech Cows Say Boo (464)
- Dehorned Unicorn (437)
- Don't Have A Cow (163)
- Donut Holes (351)
- Doomsday (382)
- Dungeon, The ★ (109)
- Early Bird ★★ (307)
- End of the Line (450)
- Exfoliation Confrontation ★★ (543)
- False Up 20 (146)
- Fingerstack or Plastic Sack (156)
- Flaming Arrow R ★ (272)
- Forgotten Variation R (533)
- Fun in the Sun (TR) (52)
- Go With The Floe` (52)
- Golden Years Variation ★ (126)
- Gorilla Tactics ★ (439)
- Guardian of the Gate (494)
- Helicopter Memory Farts (445)
- High Plains Drifter (543)
- Hour of Darkness (283)
- I Love Snakes (159)
- I'd Slap You But Shit Splatters (116)
- Ice Station Zebra (343)
- Java (412)
- Jeepers Leepers R (451)
- Jumar of Flesh (144)
- Just Say Yo ★ (384)
- Key to the Kingdome (388)
- Knuckle Cracker (184)
- Left Nixon Crack (193)
- Lesbian Lust ★★★★ (503)
- Lickey Dogs R (384)
- Lil Squirt (362)
- Loose Lady ★★★★ (178)
- Marked Card R (543)
- Mosar (121)
- My Little Pretty (493)
- No Holds Barred (TR) (418)
- No Metal Wasted X ★★★ (353)
- No-Doz R (383)
- Nuclear Waste (63)
- Only Outlaws Have Guns (543)
- Open Season (208)
- Pepason (233)
- Piss Crack (190)
- Pokin' A Gopher ★ (407)
- Primal Flake (289)
- Rich Bitch (272)
- Satchmo, The ★ (133)
- Separated At Mirth (140)
- Sit Up and Think (402)
- Stardust Memories (50)
- Texas Big Hair (285)
- Tootsie Pop ★★★ (351)
- Tortoise Skeleton Crack ★ (436)
- Use a Gun, Go to Jail (392)
- Zircon ★★★ (350)

5.10a

- 42N8 One (78)
- 4th Amendment, The (387)
- 7 (163)
- Ace of Dog ★ (237)
- Aftermath ★★★ (52)
- Against the Grain (TR) (170)
- Aggarete R (351)
- Aguility (272)
- Anty Matter (296)
- Anybody Can Bolt (453)
- Ape Man Hop ★ (53)
- Apparition ★★ (521)
- Arete #1 (TR) (71)
- Arraignment, The (277)
- Ash Gordon (282)
- At Last ★ (518)
- Awesome Betty (523)
- B Chili Dog ★ (131)
- Bad Lizards ★★ (277)
- Ball Bearing ★★ (167)
- Ball Monitor, The R ★★★ (344)
- Ballbearings Under Foot (274)

5.10a

- Ballet R/X ★ (200)
- Barley, Wheat ro Rey (It's All Grain) (116)
- Barn Door, Right (TR) (99)
- Beafcake (312)
- Beam Me Up Scottie ★ (480)
- Beef and Bean (142)
- Behind the Scenes ★ (503)
- Berserk ★ (118)
- Bimbo R/X (33)
- Bird of Fire ★★★ (463)
- Bird on a Wire ★★ (101)
- Birdman From Alcatraz (138)
- Biscuit Eater (214)
- Bittersweet ★ (508)
- Black Slacks (298)
- Blazing Saddles ★★ (544)
- Block Buster (351)
- Blue Nubian ★ (181)
- Blues Brothers ★★★ (123)
- Bob (475)
- Bold Is A Four Letter Word ★ (29)
- Bonglett, The (194)
- Bonor Donor (375)
- Boot Hill (330)
- Bottle in Front of Me ★★ (260)
- Bridge Too Far, A ★ (430)
- Broken Glass (151)
- Bucket Bronco ★★ (544)
- Buckwheat R (209)
- Buenos Aires ★ (385)
- Bunking Broncos (461)
- Burn Bush (287)
- Buyer Beware R (141)
- Cactus Pete's R ★ (546)
- Candelabra R ★ (210)
- Caramel Crunch (389)
- Castrum, The ★ (534)
- Cat in the Hat, The (413)
- Catch Me at the Bar (362)
- Cerebal Dysfunction ★ (260)
- Championship Wrestling ★ (155)
- Chestwig (90)
- Chicken (TR) (142)
- Closed on Mondays (246)
- Cole-Evans ★ (242)
- Cole-Lewis, The ★★ (68)
- Comic Book ★★★ (261)
- Coming Up Short (165)
- Control (244)
- Cool Wind ★ (530)
- Corner n' Crack ★★ (440)
- Cornerstone, The (241)
- Cosmic Debris ★ (296)
- Cosmosis ★ (521)
- Coyote in the Bushes ★★ (534)
- Crack #6 (464)
- Crimping Lessons ★★★★ (290)
- Crown Jewels (342)
- Cruelty to Animals (181)
- Crystal Calisthenics ★ (379)
- Cunning Route (447)
- Cyndie's Brain (209)
- Czech Crack (544)
- Dandelion ★★ (189)
- Dangling Woo Li Master ★★★★ (316)
- Dark Ages (470)
- Daze of Who (264)
- Death of A Decade (269)
- Death on the Nile ★ (234)
- Deception (369)
- Defenders of the Farce (413)
- Defibrillation (419)
- Deja Vu ★ (264)
- Desert Delirium ★★★ (323)
- Desert Storm ★ (449)
- Desperado (160)
- Deviate (188)
- Diamond Dogs ★★★ (384)
- Direct Start ★ (126)
- Dirty Dancing (200)
- Doc Holiday ★ (544)
- Dodo's Delight ★ (178)
- Doin' Life ★ (385)
- Don Genero Crack ★ (524)
- Don't (483)
- Don't Think Just Jump ★ (252)
- Don't Touch That Friend (541)
- Double Trouble (TR) (536)
- Dr. Garlic Breath (477)
- Dr. Scholl's Wild Ride (67)
- Drano ★★ (263)
- Draw the Line (TR) (407)
- East Face (480)
- East of India (373)
- Echo of a Scream ★ (374)
- Epperson's Footprints (443)
- Escape From The Planet Earth (274)
- Exhibit A (247)
- Exiled (129)
- Exorcist ★★★★ (384)
- Face It (TR) ★★ (224)
- Face Race (TR) (429)
- Fantasy of Light ★ (105)
- Feeling Groovy (247)
- Female Mud Massacre (TR) (211)
- Finger Food (246)
- Fire Glove, The (436)
- Fists of Fury (271)
- Flaring Offwidth from Hell (483)
- Forgotten Crack, The (530)
- Fortune Cookie (98)
- Free Climbing (213)
- Free Fall (TR) (503)
- Frontal Lobotomy ★★★ (261)
- Frontal Logranity (260)
- Frostline (195)
- Fruit Fly (343)
- Full Frontal Nudity ★★★ (261)
- Garden Angel ★★ (381)
- Garden Path (59)
- Gash, The (150)
- Gemstoner (416)
- Genuine Cowhide ★★ (517)
- Glue Rhymes With Poo (348)
- Gnarly (TR) (418)
- Gomez (TR) (131)
- Gone in 60 Seconds R ★ (242)
- Good to the Last Drop R ★★ (199)
- Good, Bad and Ugly, The (153)
- Gossamer Wings (101)
- Grand Canyon Donkey Trail ★ (461)
- Grape Nuts, Why Not? (382)

5.10a

- [ ] Green Hornet (TR) (445)
- [ ] Griffin, The R (98)
- [ ] Gripped Up The Hole ★ (175)
- [ ] Groove Avoidance System (TR) (250)
- [ ] Gross Chimney (414)
- [ ] Ground Finale (473)
- [ ] Guardian Angels (383)
- [ ] Gun for the Sun ★★ (54)
- [ ] Gun Shy (351)
- [ ] Gypsy (526)
- [ ] Hairline Fracture R ★★ (101)
- [ ] Half Track ★ (183)
- [ ] Halfway to Paradise R ★★★ (239)
- [ ] Hand Grenade ★ (481)
- [ ] Hand of the Bride A1 (328)
- [ ] Hands Away (150)
- [ ] Hang 'em High ★★ (543)
- [ ] Harder They Fall, The ★★ (111)
- [ ] Harvey's Bristol Cream (469)
- [ ] Hawks Retreat (418)
- [ ] Head Over Heals ★★★ (128)
- [ ] Heart and Sole ★★★★ (242)
- [ ] Heart Transplant (471)
- [ ] Heavy Gold (469)
- [ ] Heavy Slander (TR) (470)
- [ ] Heavy Water R (130)
- [ ] High Energy (453)
- [ ] High Tops ★ (551)
- [ ] Hobbit Hole Offwidth (228)
- [ ] Holden On (164)
- [ ] Holiday in the Sun R ★★ (94)
- [ ] Holy Cross (392)
- [ ] Holy Hand (298)
- [ ] Hot Summer Daze (402)
- [ ] Hot Tub of Death (209)
- [ ] Hour of Power (464)
- [ ] Houses in Motion ★ (426)
- [ ] Hurry Up and Wait ★ (522)
- [ ] I Can't Believe It's A girdle R ★★★★ (305)
- [ ] I Don't Know ★ (350)
- [ ] I Forgot (110)
- [ ] I Get By With A Little Help From My Friends (469)
- [ ] I Just Told You ★ (154)
- [ ] I Slept with L.K. (480)
- [ ] Ice Climbing (213)
- [ ] Imelda's New Shoes (129)
- [ ] Immuno Reaction ★ (379)
- [ ] In Elke's Absence ★ (322)
- [ ] In the Pit ★ (151)
- [ ] Iron Hand (521)
- [ ] Jack Grit (213)
- [ ] Jamburger (263)
- [ ] Jerry Brown ★★ (161)
- [ ] Jersey Girl (46)
- [ ] Jughead (240)
- [ ] Julius Seizure (76)
- [ ] Jumpstart ★ (462)
- [ ] Kachina (340)
- [ ] Kickin' Bach ★ (90)
- [ ] Kid Calingula (378)
- [ ] Killer Bees (118)
- [ ] Kleptomania (418)
- [ ] Knick (414)
- [ ] KP Corner (67)
- [ ] Labyrinth (348)

- [ ] Lean On Me ★ (90)
- [ ] Ledges to Laundale ★ (387)
- [ ] Left Route R ★ (92)
- [ ] Lemon Lemon ★ (70)
- [ ] Let's Eat Organ Meat (67)
- [ ] Like My Lump ★ (428)
- [ ] Lions and Tigers and Bears (497)
- [ ] Little Lieback (144)
- [ ] Lizard in Bondage R (88)
- [ ] Love Goat, The (317)
- [ ] M & M's Peanut (254)
- [ ] Mad Men, The ★ (267)
- [ ] Madame Salami (TR) (520)
- [ ] Maiden Voyage (392)
- [ ] Major Creative Effort (51)
- [ ] Mama Woolsey R ★ (192)
- [ ] Mantel (190)
- [ ] Marcos (129)
- [ ] Maxwell Grunster (24)
- [ ] Military Industrial Complex (385)
- [ ] Milk the Dog (314)
- [ ] Mind Over Splatter (128)
- [ ] Minor Detour (285)
- [ ] Modern Warfare (471)
- [ ] Monkey King (342)
- [ ] Monster Mash (139)
- [ ] More Funky Than Junky (126)
- [ ] Morning Warm-Up X (537)
- [ ] Mother Butler (310)
- [ ] Motor City Comix R (327)
- [ ] Moubit (464)
- [ ] Moustache, The (483)
- [ ] Mouthfull of Gank (221)
- [ ] Mr. Bunny Quits ★ (114)
- [ ] Mr. Bunny's Refund Check ★ (130)
- [ ] Mt Witness (196)
- [ ] Mud Dog (278)
- [ ] Muy Swaino R (350)
- [ ] Negro Vortex ★ (526)
- [ ] New Day Yesterday (79)
- [ ] Nip and Tuck (142)
- [ ] Nip in the Air (142)
- [ ] No Better Births (516)
- [ ] No Calculators Allowed ★★ (166)
- [ ] No Nuts (497)
- [ ] Nolina Crack ★ (38)
- [ ] Noriega Does Panama (535)
- [ ] North Face of the Eiger (164)
- [ ] Northwest Passage ★ (53)
- [ ] Not A Hogan (436)
- [ ] Not Forgotten ★ (156)
- [ ] Oh Pinyon Crack (49)
- [ ] Old Man Down the Road, The (76)
- [ ] One for the Road (49)
- [ ] Ooby Dooby (260)
- [ ] Orc, The ★★ (210)
- [ ] Ouef's Up R/X (442)
- [ ] Out To Grunge (234)
- [ ] Oversight (205)
- [ ] Pear-Grape Route (76)
- [ ] Penelope Street (TR) (233)
- [ ] Phineas P. Phart (211)
- [ ] Picking Up The Pieces (195)
- [ ] Pictures at an Exhibition (445)
- [ ] Pillar of Dawn (59)
- [ ] Pink Thing (330)

5.10a

- [ ] Pint-Size Planet (394)
- [ ] Pixie Stick (TR) (515)
- [ ] Planet Y (359)
- [ ] Playing Hookey ★★ (250)
- [ ] Pocket Veto (237)
- [ ] Polly Wants a Crack ★ (121)
- [ ] Poon (165)
- [ ] Poopdeck, The (217)
- [ ] Poppin' and Breakin' ★ (433)
- [ ] Prepackaged ★★★ (126)
- [ ] Pretty Gritty (96)
- [ ] Preying Mantels (333)
- [ ] Prime Time (TR) (393)
- [ ] Profundity (33)
- [ ] Puss Wuss ★ (458)
- [ ] Pyrannosaurus Next (197)
- [ ] Quarantine (240)
- [ ] Quarter Moon Crack (114)
- [ ] Quick Draw McGraw ★★ (242)
- [ ] R.D. Memorial (276)
- [ ] R.P. Delights R (510)
- [ ] Rackless Abandon X (473)
- [ ] Raise Your Right Hand (451)
- [ ] Rap Dancing (26)
- [ ] Raven's Reach (201)
- [ ] Ray's Cafe (386)
- [ ] Reconstructive Surgery (410)
- [ ] Red Obelisk, The ★ (307)
- [ ] Reflector Oven (471)
- [ ] Reggie on a Poodle (44)
- [ ] Remain in Light (348)
- [ ] Repeat After Me (451)
- [ ] Retirement (362)
- [ ] Ride A Wild Bago ★★ (154)
- [ ] Riders on the Storm (60)
- [ ] Riff Raff Roof (536)
- [ ] Right Arete (233)
- [ ] Right Baskerville Crack ★★★ (35)
- [ ] Right V Crack ★★★ (536)
- [ ] Roach Motel R (109)
- [ ] Roberts-Davis (232)
- [ ] Robocop Meets the Munchkins ★★ (494)
- [ ] Rock Lypso (71)
- [ ] Roof, The (245)
- [ ] Roofing Company ★★ (251)
- [ ] Route 1202 (464)
- [ ] Route 152 R (92)
- [ ] Run From Your Mother-In-Law (170)
- [ ] Sacred Cow (163)
- [ ] Safety in Numbers R (194)
- [ ] Sand Witch (40)
- [ ] Sawdust and Peanut Sheels ★★★ (511)
- [ ] Scarecrow, The (500)
- [ ] School Daze (283)
- [ ] Screaming Woman, The ★★ (51)
- [ ] Second Thoughts ★ (246)
- [ ] Seed of Irony (402)
- [ ] Shakin' the Shirts (222)
- [ ] Shooting Gallery Direct (117)
- [ ] Short Cake ★ (474)
- [ ] Short Crack (440)
- [ ] Short Stop (113)
- [ ] Shut Up and Climb (173)
- [ ] Silent Scream ★★★ (515)
- [ ] Sitting Around the Campfire Telling Fish Stories (TR) (216)
- [ ] Six-Gun By My Side ★★ (543)
- [ ] Slanta Claus, Center (164)
- [ ] Smart Missile R (457)
- [ ] Snatch, The ★ (240)
- [ ] Sole Food ★★ (139)
- [ ] Solid Gold ★★★★ (290)
- [ ] Space Metal ★ (480)
- [ ] Space Slot (251)
- [ ] Spiderman ★★ (445)
- [ ] Spitwad ★★ (98)
- [ ] Squeeze Play (471)
- [ ] Squid of My Desire (329)
- [ ] Stains of the Stars (87)
- [ ] Stand By Me (TR) (224)
- [ ] Standing Ovation (401)
- [ ] Start Trundling ★ (95)
- [ ] Step 'n Out ★ (536)
- [ ] Steppin' Out (340)
- [ ] Stinger (TR) (486)
- [ ] Stop Trundling (95)
- [ ] Stress Puppet (375)
- [ ] Strike It Rich ★ (289)
- [ ] Sublimination (76)
- [ ] Sudden Death ★ (111)
- [ ] Summer School (129)
- [ ] Tails of Poodles (124)
- [ ] Tax Man ★★★★ (130)
- [ ] Teenage Mutant Ninja Brits (534)
- [ ] Ten Conversations At Once (242)
- [ ] Terror in De Skies R (100)
- [ ] That's Powell Not Rowell (348)
- [ ] The Bone Club R ★★ (25)
- [ ] The Right Hand Dike (29)
- [ ] There Goes The Bride (329)
- [ ] Thing, The (130)
- [ ] Thumbs Up (79)
- [ ] Thunderclap (413)
- [ ] Tidbit (471)
- [ ] Time To Take The Garbage Out (317)
- [ ] Tipples in Rime (TR) (393)
- [ ] Top Flight (102)
- [ ] Tossed Green ★★★ (36)
- [ ] Tower of Godliness ★ (76)
- [ ] Toxic Avenger ★ (525)
- [ ] Trail of Tiers ★★ (399)
- [ ] Tres Fun (49)
- [ ] Trick of the Tail (476)
- [ ] Tricky Move (470)
- [ ] True Dice R ★★ (445)
- [ ] Truly Snooty Furniture (314)
- [ ] Try It, You'll like It (250)
- [ ] Tumbling Dice (362)
- [ ] Two Stage (170)
- [ ] Uh Cult, The (TR) (92)
- [ ] Uncertainty Principal (384)
- [ ] Underwear Bandit, The (310)
- [ ] Unknown (140)
- [ ] Unknown R (239)
- [ ] Unknown (298)
- [ ] Unknown Grain R (524)
- [ ] Unknown Route, The R ★★ (293)
- [ ] Up and Down ★★ (439)
- [ ] Upper Cow (163)
- [ ] Vanio's Renegade Lead (392)
- [ ] Violent Cooking (455)
- [ ] Visual Nightmare (362)

5.10a

- Vortex (73)
- Walker Spur (164)
- Wallflower (198)
- Wanton Soup (TR) (39)
- War Baby (TR) (481)
- War Crimes (82)
- War Games ★★ (283)
- Watanobe Wall ★★ (208)
- Way It Should Be, The ★★ (277)
- Weak Force, The ★ (310)
- Whales On Ice (308)
- What's Hannen (98)
- Where Brownies Dare (46)
- Where Ees De Santa Claus? (223)
- White Rabbit ★★ (263)
- Winning Time (277)
- Worthwhile Pile R (164)
- Yardy-Hoo and Away ★★★ (312)
- Yogi the Overbear (286)
- Zarmog the Dragon Man ★ (382)
- Zebra Dihedral ★★★ (440)
- Zondo's Perks ★ (244)

5.10b

- 1BRP ★ (333)
- 5150 (374)
- 80 Proof Roof ★★★ (263)
- Accelerator (481)
- Aero Space (385)
- Aging Hippie Crack (440)
- Ali Shuffle ★ (406)
- Aliens Ate My Buick (317)
- An Eye for An Eye and A Route for A Route ★★★ (276)
- Apocalypse Now (373)
- Appetite for Destruction (307)
- B For Beers R ★★ (26)
- B-Movie (469)
- B.L.T. (263)
- Baby Blue Eyes R (123)
- Bailey's Foster (75)
- Bald Women with Power Tools (41)
- Bandersnatch ★ (139)
- Barbara Bush ★ (120)
- Barking Spyders R (383)
- Barn Burning ★ (405)
- Barnie Rubble ★★ (273)
- Beaver Tail (350)
- Bedtime for Democracy ★ (50)
- Ben ★★ (287)
- Better You Than Me (373)
- Between a Rock and a Hard Place (415)
- Bighorn Dihedral ★ (71)
- Bitchen' (TR) (418)
- Black Hills Gold (TR) (258)
- Black Ice R (362)
- Blind Me With Science (118)
- Blitzsteeg (TR) (427)
- Bloody Knuckles ★★ (375)
- Bloody Tax Break ★ (130)
- Blue Monday ★ (123)
- Blue Moon (483)
- Bluewind ★ (526)
- Bonanza ★★ (544)
- Boogs' Route (78)
- Book of Changes ★★★★ (316)
- Boulevard of Dreams (453)
- Bounder, The (151)
- Brits in Drag ★★ (465)
- Broken China (34)
- Brown Squeeze (199)
- Bulkhead Arete R ★★★ (549)
- Burn Out ★ (158)
- Butt Buttress, The (168)
- C.S. Special ★★★ (237)
- Cactus Cooler ★★ (550)
- Caesar (429)
- Calling All Swidgets (137)
- Captain Safe (453)
- Cat Paws (483)
- Caught Inside on A Big Set ★★★★★ (316)
- Ceroots of the Gods (351)
- Chemical Warefare ★★★ (278)
- Chicken Lizard ★ (88)
- Cholla Crack (413)
- Clean Crack (56)
- Cliff Hanger R ★★ (111)
- Coco-Loco ★ (534)
- Cold War (349)
- Coliseum, The ★ (79)
- Come-N-Do-Me (208)
- Confessional R ★ (83)
- Conniption ★★★ (526)
- Cool City ★★ (355)
- Crack 'n' Up (TR) (486)
- Crack Addiction (471)
- Crack of Dark (309)
- Crash Course (247)
- Cripple Crack (181)
- Dead Man's Party R (103)
- Delightful Lady (TR) ★ (178)
- Desperado ★ (541)
- Dialing for Ducats (194)
- Dick Vandike (TR) (111)
- Direct Start (126)
- Dog Day Afternoon ★★★ (381)
- Don't Tred On Me (TR) ★ (106)
- Dorothy Does The Wizard (496)
- Down Where The Goblins Go (497)
- Dreamworld (464)
- Dry Lake R (535)
- Dyno in the Dark ★ (200)
- Echo Buttress (TR) (233)
- Eddie Hasel Takes Manhattan ★ (154)
- Edge, The (482)
- Effigy Too ★★★ (239)
- El Smear Or Land ★ (53)
- Elijah's Coming R (185)
- Ennui (405)
- Event Horizon R ★★ (362)
- Extra Chunky (256)
- Eyes Without A Face ★ (323)
- Falcon, The ★★ (525)
- Fantasia (308)
- Far Side of Crazy R (136)
- Feeding Frenzy (310)
- Figures on a Landscape ★★★★★ (293)
- Filet of Cole ★ (480)

5.10b

Filet of Rock Shark (216)
Finger Food (250)
Finger Stacks or Plastic Sacks (50)
Fire or Retire, Direct Finish R (141)
Fissure Todd (274)
Fisticuffs ★★★ (170)
Fitzroy Was Here ★★★ (263)
Flare Play ★ (520)
Flaring Rhoid ★ (180)
Flue Right R/X ★★ (201)
Forbidden Paradise ★★★ (242)
Forgotten Venture (470)
Formic Acidhead (164)
Foundation Crack (325)
Friendly Hands ★★★ (111)
Frisco Knight (TR) (194)
Frog Hair ★★★ (354)
Full Contact Karate (487)
Fusion Without Integrity (128)
Gait of Power ★ (530)
Ganado (76)
Garter Snake ★ (319)
Gem, The (342)
Georgia O'Keefe (414)
Get The Boot (317)
Get with the Plan ★★ (353)
Gettysburger, The ★★ (133)
Go Ask Alice ★ (480)
Goolabunga (221)
Grain Dance (TR) (152)
Grain Surgery R ★★★ (211)
Great Unknown, The ★★★ (68)
Gunks West (152)
Gypsy Fortune (TR) (511)
Ham & Swiss (263)
Handsaw (438)
Harrell-Turner (533)
Hesitation Blues ★ (100)
High Noon R ★ (543)
High Plains Drifter ★★ (431)
Hole In One (TR) (272)
Holey Cold (351)
Holiday in Detroit (406)
Horror-Zontal Terror-Verse (362)
Huevos Rancheros (406)
Hurricane Hugo (40)
I Forgot to Have Babies (TR) ★ (131)
I Had A Dream ★ (516)
I Smell A Rat (377)
If You Really Loved Me, You'd Buy Me A Turkey (289)
Iguana Masters ★★ (329)
Illusion Dweller ★★★★★ (169)
Inept Tune (TR) (359)
Invisible Touch ★★ (459)
Involvent ★★ (285)
Jacuzzi of No Return (209)
Jalapeno (TR) (142)
James Brown's Celebrity Hot Tub Party (29)
Jemiomagina ★★ (139)
Jet Stream (aka: Momentary Lapse of Reason) ★★ (25)
Jody (476)
Judas ★ (188)
Jump On It (481)
Jungle Cruise ★★★ (308)

Just Drive, She Said (338)
Just Stop It (29)
Keystone Arete (TR) ★★ (279)
Ladder Back R ★ (250)
Land of the Long White Cloug (213)
Landsraad (534)
Last Date (481)
Laura Scudders (276)
Lead Belly ★ (465)
Leap Erickson (TR) (131)
Left Baskerville Crack R (35)
Left Beetle Crack (109)
Left of Center (TR) (400)
Lemon Head, The ★ (70)
Let It All Hang Out (186)
Let's Get Physical (469)
Light Sabre ★★★ (415)
Lion's Share ★★★ (69)
Lips Like Sugar (254)
Little Criminals ★★ (25)
Living in a Fishbowl (67)
Lost Boys (464)
Love & Rockets (242)
Lower Band R ★★ (189)
Lower Life Forms (123)
Lower Right Ski Track ★★★ (183)
Mad Hatter, The (308)
Magnetic Woose (166)
Make Or Break Flake ★ (38)
Math (52)
Matt's Problem (224)
Mental Bankruptcy ★★ (308)
Mesopotamia ★★★ (287)
Ming Dallas, The (117)
Modern Jazz (90)
Moonraker (467)
Moonstruck (75)
More Crazy Than Lazy R (451)
Mortarfied (298)
Mother Lode (426)
Mr. Bunny Meets the Expando Flake (TR) (364)
Muffin Bandits ★★ (59)
My Favorite Things ★★ (325)
Naked Nancy (TR) (328)
Napkin of Shame ★ (114)
Narwhal, The ★★ (377)
New Hampshire, Naturally (76)
Nice and Steep and Elbow Deep (114)
Nipple, The (455)
No Biggy R/X ★ (379)
No Self Confidence ★★ (78)
None of Your Business R ★★ (154)
Not For Loan ★★ (168)
Nothing But A Groundhog (453)
Nuclear Waste (130)
Off to See the Wizard ★★ (500)
Offshoot (62)
On the Nob (126, 128)
Opportunist, The ★ (333)
Organ Grinder, The (339)
Orgasmatron, The (129)
Out On A Limb ★★★ (237)
Papa Woolsey ★★ (192)
Papillon (222)
Party in the Desert ★★★ (543)
Pencil Neck Geek ★★ (526)

5.10b

- ☐ Perfect Fingers ★★★★ (352)
- ☐ Perfect World ★★ (342)
- ☐ Peruvian Princess (123)
- ☐ Pinched Rib ★★★ (200)
- ☐ Pinyon Crack (133)
- ☐ Pirates of the Carabiner ★ (121)
- ☐ Podium, The ★★★ (316)
- ☐ Poodle Boy (330)
- ☐ Poodle Woof ★ (179)
- ☐ Poodle-oids from the Deep (127)
- ☐ Poodles Are People Too ★★★★ (126)
- ☐ Pop Rocks ★★ (98)
- ☐ Power Drop ★ (248)
- ☐ Power Lichen (248)
- ☐ Power Lunch (TR) (141)
- ☐ Power to the People (344)
- ☐ Pumping Ego ★★ (199)
- ☐ Queen Crimson (428)
- ☐ Question, The (491)
- ☐ Radio Free Utah (327)
- ☐ Ranger is Watching Me, The (520)
- ☐ Reach for a Peach (TR) (163)
- ☐ Red Crack, The ★ (347)
- ☐ Refrigerator — Left Side, The ★★★ (323)
- ☐ Rei Momo ★ (348)
- ☐ Rhythm & Blues ★★ (123)
- ☐ Rickets and Scurvy (50)
- ☐ Right Beetle Crack (109)
- ☐ Roadside Slab R ★ (523)
- ☐ Rollerball ★★★★ (219)
- ☐ Rope Drag (75)
- ☐ Run For Your Life ★★★★ (170)
- ☐ Sack in the Wash (79)
- ☐ Scare Way ★★ (520)
- ☐ Scaried Treasure ★★ (121)
- ☐ Schrodinger Equation, The R ★★★ (130)
- ☐ Scope & Hope (419)
- ☐ Scream of the Butterfly (550)
- ☐ Search for Chinese Morsels ★ (39)
- ☐ Shooting Gallery ★★ (117)
- ☐ Short and Crank ★ (440)
- ☐ Short But Slared (59)
- ☐ Shovling-Cole (186)
- ☐ Sidewinder ★★★★ (212)
- ☐ Sinner's Swing (TR) ★ (244)
- ☐ Sitting Bull ★★★ (68)
- ☐ Six-Pack Crack (144)
- ☐ Slammer, The (450)
- ☐ Slap and Tickle ★★ (348)
- ☐ Slim Pickings (362)
- ☐ Slushie ★ (131)
- ☐ Solosby (171)
- ☐ Sound Asleep (35)
- ☐ Sound of Rasha's Ears Flapping, The (389)
- ☐ Space Mountain ★★★ (377)
- ☐ Space Odyssey R ★ (362)
- ☐ Spank the Monkey ★★ (406)
- ☐ Spread & Butter (469)
- ☐ Spud Overhang R (517)
- ☐ Stainless Steel Rat (144)
- ☐ Stargazer ★★ (260)
- ☐ Statue of Elvis on Mars (470)
- ☐ Stepping Razor (71)
- ☐ Stinkbug, The (246)
- ☐ Stud Muffin (507)

- ☐ Suffering Catfish (283)
- ☐ Sunday Papers (179)
- ☐ Supreme Court or Conservative Rubber Stamp? (481)
- ☐ Surrealistic Pillar ★ (192)
- ☐ Swidgets Requierd (137)
- ☐ Swimming in a Sea of Deception (256)
- ☐ Sympathy to the Devil (186)
- ☐ Take A Seat (250)
- ☐ Tales of Powder ★ (104)
- ☐ Tar Face (TR) (337)
- ☐ Tarawassie Wiggel ★ (524)
- ☐ Team Scumbag (248)
- ☐ Team Slug (242)
- ☐ Teen Steam (383)
- ☐ Test Pilot ★ (550)
- ☐ That (385)
- ☐ The Falcon and the Snowman ★★ (242)
- ☐ The Podium of Indecision (29)
- ☐ Third Time's A Charm ★★★ (522)
- ☐ Thirteen Cheeps ★ (497)
- ☐ Thomson's Acne (TR) (44)
- ☐ Three Bolts Closer to Divorce (385)
- ☐ Three Burner Stove (160)
- ☐ Tinker Toys ★★ (97)
- ☐ Tiny Terra (TR) (394)
- ☐ TM's Terror (237)
- ☐ Toad Warrior ★ (76)
- ☐ Todd's Hardcover (TR) (179)
- ☐ Too Loose to Trek ★ (220)
- ☐ Too Old To Bolt (TR) (242)
- ☐ Tortoise and the Dog, The R ★ (456)
- ☐ Torturers Apprentice (247)
- ☐ Toto (494)
- ☐ Tower of Cleanliness ★★★ (76)
- ☐ Toxic Poodle ★ (525)
- ☐ Training for Patagonia R (99)
- ☐ Treinte Anos (TR) (189)
- ☐ Triple Bypass ★ (543)
- ☐ Tube, The (317)
- ☐ Tubular Balls ★ (261)
- ☐ Under a Raging Moon (59)
- ☐ Unknown (272)
- ☐ Unknown (327)
- ☐ Unknown (378)
- ☐ Unnamed (233)
- ☐ Val De Mello ★★ (531)
- ☐ Vice President R ★★★ (314)
- ☐ Vicki the Visitor (148)
- ☐ Wait Until Dark (392)
- ☐ Walt's Frozen Head (308)
- ☐ Watershute, The (185)
- ☐ Waugh Crack ★★ (411)
- ☐ Wayward Hayward (328)
- ☐ West Face (TR) (394)
- ☐ When You're Not A Jet (256)
- ☐ Whips and Grains (47)
- ☐ Why Does It Hurt When I Pee? ★ (98)
- ☐ Wired ★★ (83)
- ☐ Witch Hunt ★★★★ (549)
- ☐ Woof Woof (179)
- ☐ Worth Bagley Dihedral ★★ (329)
- ☐ Wrap That Rascal ★ (551)
- ☐ Y Knot ★ (391)

5.10

- [ ] Amoeba, The (123)
- [ ] Bedrock Arete (228)
- [ ] Black Todd (159)
- [ ] Blank, The (198)
- [ ] Bolt Heaven A1 (290)
- [ ] Chuckawalla (228)
- [ ] Corner (271)
- [ ] Dino's Egg (226)
- [ ] Face (193)
- [ ] Fiasco, The (67)
- [ ] Flakey Puffs from Hell (TR) (393)
- [ ] Frozen at the Void ★★ (458)
- [ ] Frying Pan (367)
- [ ] Get the Balance Right ★★★ (429)
- [ ] Gibb's Face (371)
- [ ] Gravity Pirates (TR) (475)
- [ ] Gripper Traverse (32)
- [ ] Intersection Boulder Left (185)
- [ ] Intersection Traverse (184)
- [ ] Left (176)
- [ ] Left Arete (233)
- [ ] Left Peyote Crack ★★ (224)
- [ ] Lollygobbleblissbombs R/X (229)
- [ ] Mustang Ranch (TR) (47)
- [ ] North Dakota Big Wall Problem (258)
- [ ] Northeast Face (192)
- [ ] Old Triangle Classic (190)
- [ ] One Story Town (TR) (393)
- [ ] Reach for a Peach (367)
- [ ] Right (176)
- [ ] Right Nixon Crack (193)
- [ ] Route Right of the Dumbest Climb in the Monument (386)
- [ ] Scoop Problem (193)
- [ ] Sidekick (387)
- [ ] South Face (190)
- [ ] Splatter Proof R (146)
- [ ] Surf's Up (270)
- [ ] Tomato Amnesia (321)
- [ ] Top of the Pops ★★★ (98)
- [ ] Two Blind Mice (415)
- [ ] Unknown (234)
- [ ] Unnamed (146)
- [ ] Unnamed (149)
- [ ] Unnamed (150)
- [ ] Unnamed (176)
- [ ] Unnamed (203)
- [ ] Unnamed (228)
- [ ] Walk on the Steep Side (378)
- [ ] What a Shame (67)

5.10c

- [ ] 3 Ring Circus ★ (510)
- [ ] Abolute Zero ★ (223)
- [ ] Against All Todds (437)
- [ ] Ahoy (165)
- [ ] Albatross, The (179)
- [ ] All Loin (468)
- [ ] Always on My Mind (386)
- [ ] Anacram ★★★ (96)
- [ ] April Fools R ★ (242)
- [ ] Astropoodle ★★ (128)
- [ ] Atari R ★★ (237)
- [ ] B.A.S.E. Arrest (75)
- [ ] Balance Due ★★★ (51)
- [ ] Band Saw ★★ (189)
- [ ] Bearded Cabbage ★★★ (188)
- [ ] Beaver Boulder Free Route (361)
- [ ] Beginner's Twenty-Six (194)
- [ ] Belay Girl ★★ (536)
- [ ] Bent Over Backwards (397)
- [ ] Beverly Drive (TR) (289)
- [ ] Bike Across America (455)
- [ ] Billabong ★★ (186)
- [ ] Birdland (393)
- [ ] Black Plastic Streetwalker R ★★★ (103)
- [ ] Black Widow (479)
- [ ] Blonde Eyebrow Fetish (75)
- [ ] Bongledesh (185)
- [ ] Born To Be A Cowboy (447)
- [ ] Brief Case (TR) (158)
- [ ] Broken Wing ★ (315)
- [ ] Brownian Motion (161)
- [ ] Bruiser, The ★★★ (214)
- [ ] Brush Your Teeth with Jesus (377)
- [ ] Bush Eviction Direct (362)
- [ ] C Sharp Roof (82)
- [ ] Canalizo (483)
- [ ] Carnage (438)
- [ ] Cat on a Hot Tin Roof (385)
- [ ] Celtic Vator (479)
- [ ] Center of Gravity (TR) (400)
- [ ] Ceremony ★ (105)
- [ ] Chamber of Commerce (123)
- [ ] Character Flaw ★★ (521)
- [ ] Cherry Bomb ★ (242)
- [ ] Chilly Willy A1 (111)
- [ ] Christmas Tree Arete ★★★ (347)
- [ ] Church Bazaar (188)
- [ ] Chute to Kill ★ (294)
- [ ] Circus Act (261)
- [ ] Clean and Jerk ★★★★ (155)
- [ ] Cleavage (455)
- [ ] Click Your Heels Twice ★★★ (491)
- [ ] Cole Salw (184)
- [ ] Cole-Gordon Offwidth (301)
- [ ] Common Law Marriage (73)
- [ ] Compassion of the Elephants, The ★★★ (247)
- [ ] Cool Move, Gritty Rock, Standard Procedure (482)
- [ ] Cosmic Book (265)
- [ ] Crack #4 (464)
- [ ] Crack C (464)
- [ ] Crack Kills (485)
- [ ] Cruising for Burgers ★ (261)
- [ ] Crystal Deva (79)
- [ ] Cut Thin to Win ★★★ (439)
- [ ] Cut to the Bone (317)
- [ ] Death by Misadventure X (186)
- [ ] Deep, Shallow and Twisted (467)
- [ ] Delusions (339)
- [ ] Desert Storm (308)
- [ ] Devil Inside (364)
- [ ] Diabetic Shock (487)
- [ ] Dike Da Doodad (421)
- [ ] Dike, The R ★★ (111)
- [ ] Dirty Cat (TR) (371)
- [ ] Disappearing Act ★★ (459)

5.10c

- [ ] Disco Sucks (192)
- [ ] Disobedience School (252)
- [ ] Distant Episode ★★ (260)
- [ ] Does Royalty Give Head (483)
- [ ] Dogleg Right (521)
- [ ] Doin' Some Damage (400)
- [ ] Don't Dick With Walt (199)
- [ ] Double Duty (436)
- [ ] Double Jeopardy R ★ (384)
- [ ] Dunce Cap, The ★★ (70)
- [ ] Dwarf Star (TR) (394)
- [ ] Dyno-Soar A1 (221)
- [ ] Edgar Rice Burros (101)
- [ ] Edge of Doom ★★★ (115)
- [ ] Edukashun President, The (439)
- [ ] El Pollo Loco (443)
- [ ] El Rey R ★ (535)
- [ ] Elvis Is Everywhere (453)
- [ ] Empty Street (75)
- [ ] Endangered Species (503)
- [ ] Environment-Oil President, The (455)
- [ ] Episcopalian Toothpick (377)
- [ ] Escape (Var.) (206)
- [ ] Evolutionary Thorwback (273)
- [ ] F.U.N. (TR) (237)
- [ ] Face of Mucis (TR) ★ (201)
- [ ] Fall From Grace ★ (242)
- [ ] Fall Line ★★★ (354)
- [ ] Fingertip Pleasure (TR) (161)
- [ ] Fire or Retire ★ (141)
- [ ] Fist Full of Crystals ★★ (211)
- [ ] Flakes of Grasp (TR) (420)
- [ ] Fool For A Pretty Face (471)
- [ ] Forsaken Mein-Key, The (277)
- [ ] Free For A Fee (425)
- [ ] Fumblers Below the Roof (421)
- [ ] Gabby's Shuttle (538)
- [ ] Gibberish (TR) (82)
- [ ] Go-Gos on Quaaludes, The ★★ (412)
- [ ] Goin' Down the Road Feelin' Bad (470)
- [ ] Golddigger, The ★★ (431)
- [ ] Good Dog Y'all (337)
- [ ] Good Grief (TR) (158)
- [ ] Goodbye Mr. Bond ★★ (524)
- [ ] Goofy Arete (418)
- [ ] Gordo Started It R/X (137)
- [ ] Graduate and Don't Look Back (277)
- [ ] Grainy Train (437)
- [ ] Grandpa Gander R ★ (92)
- [ ] Granulator, The (129)
- [ ] Greenhorn Dihedral ★★★ (317)
- [ ] Grim Roper ★★ (405)
- [ ] Grit Roof ★★ (382)
- [ ] Ground Ron (310)
- [ ] Halow Friction (275)
- [ ] Handlin' Snakeskin (159)
- [ ] Harlequin R ★★★ (378)
- [ ] Hawk Wind R ★★★ (314)
- [ ] Heaven Can Wait ★★★ (74)
- [ ] Heavy Handed (140)
- [ ] Hermanutic R ★★ (32)
- [ ] Hintertoiser Traverse, The (188)
- [ ] Holeaceous (351)
- [ ] Holly Device ★ (98)
- [ ] Hollywood and Vaino R ★ (532)
- [ ] Horn Dog ★ (126)

- [ ] Hourglass, The ★★ (493)
- [ ] I Fall Therefore I Am (26)
- [ ] I Saw Stars ★★★★ (354)
- [ ] Icon ★★★ (345)
- [ ] If I Only Had A Brain (494)
- [ ] Importance of Being Ernest, The R ★★★ (127)
- [ ] Iron Man Traverse (189)
- [ ] Iron Mantel R (118)
- [ ] It Seams Possible (295)
- [ ] Jah Loo (59)
- [ ] Jedi Master (483)
- [ ] Jolly Roger ★★ (433)
- [ ] Junior (192)
- [ ] Kamakaze (471)
- [ ] Knack ★★ (414)
- [ ] Kook Book (413)
- [ ] Laid Back and Doing It (300)
- [ ] Land of Wonder (339)
- [ ] Lazy Rhymer (TR) (118)
- [ ] Left Banana Crack ★★ (124)
- [ ] Left Mel Crack ★★ (90)
- [ ] Left Sawdust Crack ★ (32)
- [ ] Legolas (242)
- [ ] Lewd and Lascivious Conduct R ★ (98)
- [ ] Lip Sync (382)
- [ ] Lippo Suction (382)
- [ ] Listening Wind (426)
- [ ] Little Bit of Magic, A (58)
- [ ] Los Tres Bovines ★★ (477)
- [ ] Make That Move Or Six Foot Groove ★ (239)
- [ ] Marital Sin ★★★ (279)
- [ ] Martin Quits ★ (151)
- [ ] McDonld-Wilson R (40)
- [ ] Mechanic, The (TR) (214)
- [ ] Meet John Doe R ★★ (410)
- [ ] Memorial Meowzer (421)
- [ ] Mental Siege Tactics ★ (322)
- [ ] Message in a Bottle (402)
- [ ] Meteorite Crack (364)
- [ ] More Frozen Food ★★★ (440)
- [ ] Morongo Child (465)
- [ ] Mother Board Breakdown ★★★ (451)
- [ ] Move to the Groove (TR) (250)
- [ ] Moveable Feast ★ (127)
- [ ] Mystic Teflon ★ (520)
- [ ] Nestle Crunch ★ (254)
- [ ] Nightline ★★ (394)
- [ ] No Self Respect ★★★ (78)
- [ ] Nuts and Bolts of Climbing, The (60)
- [ ] O'Kelley's Crack ★★★★ (229)
- [ ] Oat Cuisine (209)
- [ ] Official Route of the 1984 Olympics, The ★★★ (206)
- [ ] Oh God! R ★★ (504)
- [ ] Oil My Joints ★★ (500)
- [ ] Omnia Exteres (49)
- [ ] One Move Leads To Another ★★ (321)
- [ ] One Pop, No Stop (429)
- [ ] Orc Sighs (210)
- [ ] Panty Shield, The (301)
- [ ] Pecking Order ★★★ (443)
- [ ] Pelvic Thrust (453)
- [ ] Personal Space (TR) ★★ (98)
- [ ] Peter Easter Pumpkin Eater ★★ (484)
- [ ] Piggle Pugg ★★★ (290)
- [ ] Pile in the Sky (174)

5.10c

- [ ] Pinch a Smelly Scrutinizer (215)
- [ ] Point of No Return ★ (251)
- [ ] Polytechnics ★★ (63)
- [ ] Popemobile, The ★★★ (450)
- [ ] Pretzel Logic (222)
- [ ] Prickly Pare ★★★ (350)
- [ ] Primal Scream (245)
- [ ] Pullups to Pasadena (387)
- [ ] Puncture Wound (465)
- [ ] Punish the Mosquito (461)
- [ ] Quantum Jump ★★★ (130)
- [ ] Rat Boy (181)
- [ ] Raving Skinhead (342)
- [ ] Red Sonja (342)
- [ ] Reggie's Pimple (TR) (44)
- [ ] Regular Route, The (263)
- [ ] Return of the Chuckwalla (250)
- [ ] Rhoid Warrior (148)
- [ ] Rice Cake Roof ★ (286)
- [ ] Right Hand of Light, The (TR) (401)
- [ ] Right Mel Crack ★★ (90)
- [ ] Right Route ★★ (92)
- [ ] Right Stuff, The (340)
- [ ] Roark (76)
- [ ] Rob'n the Cradle (56)
- [ ] Rude Awakening R ★★★★ (504)
- [ ] Ruff Stuff (445)
- [ ] Run From Your Wife (170)
- [ ] Russian Grain Crisis (260)
- [ ] S Cracker, The ★★★ (74)
- [ ] Sandbag (TR) (166)
- [ ] Sandworm R ★ (252)
- [ ] Scrambbled Leggs ★★ (133)
- [ ] Screaming Poodle, The (TR) ★★ (51)
- [ ] Sea Monkeys R (126)
- [ ] Secret of Mother Butler, The (310)
- [ ] Sen Blen ★ (38)
- [ ] Serious Fashion ★ (289)
- [ ] Shady Grove ★★ (250)
- [ ] Shame (163)
- [ ] Shark Fin, The ★★★ (344)
- [ ] Sharks in the Water (402)
- [ ] Sharp Arete (470)
- [ ] Shiatsu (TR) (511)
- [ ] Shin Bashers ★ (66)
- [ ] Shongo Pavi (483)
- [ ] Shower Scene (63)
- [ ] Sin City (244)
- [ ] Sinbad the Salor (TR) (419)
- [ ] Skeptic, The (123)
- [ ] Skinwalker (214)
- [ ] Skip Slidin' Away R (439)
- [ ] Slam Dance (463)
- [ ] Slip Skrig ★★★ (319)
- [ ] Small Town Taste (TR) (393)
- [ ] Smear Tactics (194)
- [ ] Smiles for the Grim Reaper ★★ (494)

- [ ] Socrates Sucks (TR) (535)
- [ ] Software Sluts R ★ (428)
- [ ] Solstice ★ (284)
- [ ] Song of the Siren (445)
- [ ] Spaghetti Sauce Sunset (40)
- [ ] Spiritworld (342)
- [ ] Stemngo (TR) (386)
- [ ] Steps Ahead A1 (71)
- [ ] Stick to the Plan R ★★★ (354)
- [ ] Still, The (433)
- [ ] Straight Jacket ★★ (374)
- [ ] Strain Gauge ★ (135)
- [ ] Straw Man (494)
- [ ] Strip Search (455)
- [ ] Studebaker Hawk ★★ (138)
- [ ] Sweat Band ★★★ (524)
- [ ] T-N-T (264)
- [ ] Take It For Granite ★★★ (261)
- [ ] Telegram for Mongo R ★★ (205)
- [ ] There Is No Place Like Home R (491)
- [ ] This Spud's For You (64)
- [ ] Three Best Friends You Ever Had, The ★★ (135)
- [ ] TKO ★ (138)
- [ ] Todd Couple, The ★ (83)
- [ ] Too Thin for Poodles (59)
- [ ] Too Wide to Trot (439)
- [ ] Trautner-Fry R (535)
- [ ] Trespassers Will Be Violated ★★★ (247)
- [ ] Trident ★ (105)
- [ ] Try Again ★★ (242)
- [ ] Tube Steak (163)
- [ ] Two Scoops Please R ★★ (197)
- [ ] Unknown (429)
- [ ] Unnamed ★★ (333)
- [ ] Use It Or Loose It (193)
- [ ] Vaino's Crack (144)
- [ ] Viper, The (307)
- [ ] Visualize World Peace (373)
- [ ] Walk of Fame ★★★ (503)
- [ ] Wee-Wee, The (207)
- [ ] Welcome to Joshua Tree ★★ (260)
- [ ] Wheer Sheep Ran Scared (392)
- [ ] When Ligthning Strikes (447)
- [ ] When Sheep Ran Scared ★★ (187)
- [ ] Wide World of Sports (56)
- [ ] Winds of Change (TR) (180)
- [ ] Winter Wine ★★★ (445)
- [ ] Wish You Were Here (250)
- [ ] Woman's Work Is Never Done ★★★ (214)
- [ ] Xenalmorph ★★ (430)
- [ ] Yabo Phone Home (135)
- [ ] Yogi (TR) (85)
- [ ] Zen Goblins (487)

5.10d

- [ ] Alexander's Salamander (59)
- [ ] Appendectomy Crack ★★★ (405)
- [ ] Ashes to Ashes ★ (475)
- [ ] Automatic Tiger (317)
- [ ] Bam Boozler ★★★ (219)
- [ ] Banana Splits ★★ (389)
- [ ] Barfing At Zeldas (125)
- [ ] Bark on Demand (178)
- [ ] Be Good Or Be Gone (167)
- [ ] Beadwagon (246)
- [ ] Bed of Nails (275)
- [ ] Bee Gees (463)
- [ ] Behind the Green Door (247)
- [ ] Belly Dancer ★★★ (473)
- [ ] Big Brown Eye ★★★ (314)
- [ ] Black Pearl ★★★★ (350)
- [ ] Blue Sky Mine (TR) (475)
- [ ] Boortemus ★★★ (540)
- [ ] Bourbon on Ice ★★★ (540)
- [ ] Bridge, The R (524)
- [ ] Bridge-It Bardot ★ (310)
- [ ] Brown 25 R ★★★ (161)
- [ ] Casual Affair ★★ (459)
- [ ] Caverna Magica R (400)
- [ ] Cedric's Deep Sea Fish Market ★★ (415)
- [ ] Centurion (416)
- [ ] Cheap Way to Die, A ★★★ (378)
- [ ] Cheez-It, The (250)
- [ ] Child's Play (TR) ★★ (166)
- [ ] Cinnamon Girl ★★ (74)
- [ ] Count Dracula ★★★ (473)
- [ ] Coyote Eggs (276)
- [ ] Crack (429)
- [ ] Cranking Skills or Hospital Bills ★ (141)
- [ ] Crescent Wrench ★★ (36)
- [ ] Crimp or Wimp (TR) (141)
- [ ] Crossroads ★ (239)
- [ ] Crystal Voyager ★ (331)
- [ ] Danny Gore (174)
- [ ] Decompensator of Lhasa, The ★★★ (211)
- [ ] Dhip (329)
- [ ] Diamondback ★ (212)
- [ ] Diamonds Are Forever (467)
- [ ] Digital Watch R ★★ (38)
- [ ] Doing That Scrapyard Thing ★★ (223)
- [ ] Dominatrix (316)
- [ ] Don't Be Nosey (TR) ★ (154)
- [ ] Don't Bosch Me Around ★★★★ (345)
- [ ] Don't Waltz With Dick (TR) (199)
- [ ] Dreamer ★★ (439)
- [ ] Eating Gorilla Comes in Peace, The (462)
- [ ] EBGB's ★★★★ (244)
- [ ] Eight Signs of a Shaky Marriage ★★ (410)
- [ ] Elbow Room (116)
- [ ] Endorphine ★ (353)
- [ ] Exhibitionist (TR) (446)
- [ ] Exiled in Sweden ★★★ (549)
- [ ] False TKO (139)
- [ ] Fatty Winds His Neck Out R (199)
- [ ] Fear of Flying (200)
- [ ] Flexible Hueys (TR) (329)
- [ ] Fly Away (467)
- [ ] Foreign Legion ★★★ (52)
- [ ] Fractured Fissure (TR) (205)
- [ ] Fraud Squad (532)
- [ ] Free Bubba John (141)
- [ ] Fugitive, The ★★ (74)
- [ ] Girdle Crossing ★★★ (305)
- [ ] Girls in the Mist ★★★ (26)
- [ ] Given Up For Dead (420)
- [ ] Glenda Crack R ★★★ (491)
- [ ] Godzilla Eats Human Sushi (275)
- [ ] Gordoba (339)
- [ ] Gracias A Dios ★★ (436)
- [ ] Grain of Truth ★ (112)
- [ ] Gravel Shower (TR) (103)
- [ ] Grungy (76)
- [ ] Gumby Saves Bambi (246)
- [ ] Gumshoe ★★★ (66)
- [ ] Hands Up (197)
- [ ] Hang and Swing ★★ (155)
- [ ] Hard Rock Cafe (317)
- [ ] Heavy Mettle ★★ (130)
- [ ] Hellish Planet ★★ (353)
- [ ] Henny Penny (256)
- [ ] Herbie's Hideaway (179)
- [ ] High Anxiety ★ (39)
- [ ] Higher Yield (49)
- [ ] Hobbit Roof ★★ (194)
- [ ] Hold Me Tight R ★★ (405)
- [ ] Horse of a Different Color (439)
- [ ] Hot Dog in a Bun (457)
- [ ] Hot Knife (233)
- [ ] How Spoilers Bleed (121)
- [ ] Hyperventilation (79)
- [ ] I Eat Cannibals ★ (414)
- [ ] Imaginary Voyage ★★★★ (103)
- [ ] Intimidation Game ★★ (437)
- [ ] Invisible Touch ★★ (212)
- [ ] It's Never Robot City (TR) (337)
- [ ] Jack in the Crack (317)
- [ ] Janus (73)
- [ ] Johnnie Come Lately (345)
- [ ] Jolly Rancher Firestix (254)
- [ ] Kidney Stone (TR) (206)
- [ ] Kiwi Route (213)
- [ ] Knight Shift (TR) (252)
- [ ] Kokopeli (461)
- [ ] Kool Aid A4 ★ (183)
- [ ] Laegar Domain ★★★ (137)
- [ ] Landlord, The ★★ (378)
- [ ] Lean and Scream (TR) (426)
- [ ] Left Lizard Crack R ★ (88)
- [ ] Lemming, The (415)
- [ ] Lieback and Lingerie R ★★ (173)
- [ ] Liquid Confidence (158)
- [ ] Liquid Rats (181)
- [ ] Lively Yourself Up Homer ★★ (465)
- [ ] Love Comes in Spurts ★★ (550)
- [ ] Man From Glad (339)
- [ ] Maneater, The (229)
- [ ] Maritimer, The (TR) (118)
- [ ] Micronesia (107)
- [ ] Middle Band R (189)
- [ ] Midnight Lumber (461)
- [ ] Milk Arete ★★★ (407)
- [ ] Minute Man (242)
- [ ] Missing in Action (TR) (420)
- [ ] Morning Thunder ★★★ (316)
- [ ] Munchkin Land (212)
- [ ] My Bride, My Hilti & My Shoulders (329)
- [ ] Nail 'n Gravel R ★ (533)

5.10d

- Navigator, The R (344)
- New Shoe Review, The (67)
- No Bolts Required R ★★ (399)
- No Falls (276)
- No Perch Is Necessary (141)
- No Shirt Needed ★★ (217)
- North Face (TR) (394)
- Not Just Another Pretty Face ★ (534)
- Oasis of Eden R ★★★ (277)
- Off Ramp (371)
- One Arm Giant (467)
- One Bolt Jolt (163)
- One Whole Chicken in A Can (304)
- Out For A Bite (TR) ★ (196)
- Out To Lunge (TR) ★ (234)
- Panther Crack (535)
- Papal Smear ★ (450)
- Patriot, The ★★ (457)
- Perpetual Motion ★★★ (414)
- Pet or Meat ★★★ (535)
- Pinky Lee ★ (233)
- Pit Bull Attach (151)
- Planet Claire (359)
- Planet Z ★ (359)
- Possessed By Elvis ★★ (237)
- Presbyterian Dental Floss (377)
- Prisoner of Inertia ★★ (458)
- Psycho (63)
- Pussy Galore ★ (158)
- Rain Dance R ★ (272)
- Raked Over The Coles ★★ (245)
- Raker's Blaring Hat Rack ★★ (413)
- Ratrace ★★ (113)
- Red Chile (TR) (142)
- Red Red (319)
- Red Tide R ★★★ (39)
- Restaurant at the End of the Universe ★ (87)
- Right Side (TR) (238)
- Roberts Crack (167)
- Rock Star R ★★ (283)
- Rocky Road ★ (389)
- RR Does It Again (TR) (107)
- Rubicon ★★★★ (462)
- Scared Bare (169)
- Semi Tough ★★★ (151)
- Sexy Sadye ★★★ (173)
- Shake the Monster (125)
- Shaking Hands with the Unemployed (386)
- Shibumi ★ (39)
- Sicker Than Jezouin (237)
- Simba (510)
- Sketches of Strain (469)
- Skid Row R ★ (520)
- Slimmer Pickins (362)
- Souvenir (181)
- Squatter's Right ★★ (130)
- Start Fumbling R (95)
- Stereo in B Flat (TR) (308)
- Stoli Driver (261)
- Such a Line (439)
- Surface Tension ★★★ (205)
- Surrealistic Colgate (TR) (420)
- Swain-Buckey ★★ (250)
- Talking Fish, The ★ (96)
- Taming of the Shoe, The R ★★★ (116)
- Tar (442)
- Tax Free R (130)
- Tchalk Is Cheap (59)
- Tequila (TR) (222)
- That Old Soft Shoe ★★ (473)
- This Scud's A Dud (457)
- Tidy Bowl (450)
- Tiers for Fears ★★★★ (433)
- Til Death Do Us Fart (513)
- Time and A Half (214)
- Tin God (247)
- To Air Is Human R ★★ (92)
- Too Secret to Find ★★★★ (51)
- Top Hat R (364)
- Tower of Babel (114)
- Toxic Avenger ★★ (44)
- Toxic Wasteland (256)
- Transylvania Twist R ★★ (473)
- Treasure of the Sierra Madre ★★★★★ (348)
- Trial Separation ★★★ (355)
- U.B. Kool (114)
- Uncle Fester ★ (92)
- Unknown A1 (338)
- Unknown (418)
- Unsolved Mystery (248)
- Wacko Placko (471)
- Wage and Price Ceiling (TR) ★ (251)
- Wet Rock Day (TR) ★ (217)
- Wetlands President, The ★ (475)
- What Is The Question? ★ (319)
- What's It To You ★★★ (154)
- Wild Dream (483)
- Wild Wild West ★ (543)
- Wolfman, The ★★ (148)
- Zion Train ★★ (293)
- Zola Budd (TR) (56)
- Zulu Dawn (192)

5.10+

- 1984 Is Today (387)
- Bam Bam (228)
- Betty Jo Yablonski R (149)
- Big Kahuna (TR) (270)
- Boulder Crack (367)
- Classic Curl (176)
- Dike Flight (457)
- Dynamo Hum (190)
- Gibb's Arete (371)
- Hensel Arete (193)
- Hooterville Trolley (67)
- How's Your Granny (228)
- Junior Varsity Problem (190)
- Leap in Fath (367)
- Liquid Wrench (270)
- McHaney Crack (TR) (270)
- Middle (176)
- Middle Arete/Face (233)
- Moonlight Crack (TR) (201)
- North Face (226)
- Northeas Arete (176)
- O.W. (83)
- Robbins Route, The (239)
- Southwest Problem (193)
- Stand Up For You Rights (149)
- Unzipper (TR) (242)
- Wonderful World of Art, The (192)

5.11a

- 29 Bombs ★★ (508)
- Absence of Malice (TR) ★★ (529)
- Abstract Roller Disco ★★★ (247)
- Acid Rock ★ (174)
- Adult Books ★★ (139)
- Afternoon Shakedown X (537)
- Alf's Arete ★★★★ (130)
- Alien Life Form Arete, The R (233)
- An Unruly Camel (426)
- Android Lust R ★★ (122)
- Animal Magnetism ★ (286)
- Antichrist ★★ (385)
- Are You Experienced? ★ (100)
- Arete #3 (TR) (71)
- Arete #4 (TR) (71)
- Arete Buster R ★ (83)
- Arizona Crack R (535)
- Assault and Battery (TR) (503)
- Ayatollah, The (TR) ★★★ (362)
- Baby Fae ★ (379)
- Bad Fun (215)
- Bald Ambition (327)
- Bebop Tango ★★★ (171)
- Beetle Corner (109)
- Bendix Claws, The ★★★ (459)
- Beta Zoid A2 (331)
- Big Moe R ★★★★ (234)
- Big Sandy Bound X ★★ (475)
- Black President ★★★★ (314)
- Blackout R ★ (94)
- Blue Ribbon R (325)
- Break Dancing (200)
- Breaking Away (TR) ★ (49)
- Breath of Death (269)
- British Airways R ★★ (245)
- Bronto's Or Us, The ★★ (111)
- Brothre from Another Planet R ★★ (131)
- Buford's House of Liver (286)
- Bullet Head (130)
- California Crack R ★★ (5353)
- Camp Whote (369)
- Cast Up A Highway (TR) (96)
- Catch a Falling Car (362)
- Cats Claws ★★ (83)
- Charlotte's Web ★★ (451)
- Cheap Thrills (TR) (87)
- Cheese (TR) (142)
- Cheese Grater, The (447)
- Chute to Kill ★★ (59)
- Claim Jumper (469)
- Cleared for Takeoff (456)
- Cleopatra ★★ (259)
- Cling or Fling ★★ (464)
- Coarse and Buggy ★★★★ (136)
- Colossus of Rhoids, The (148)
- Comic Relief ★ (158)
- Congratulations (TR) ★★ (166)
- Crack Queen ★★★ (353)
- Crazy Climber ★★★ (118)
- Cretin Bull Dancer ★★★ (100)
- Crime of the Century ★★★ (252)
- Daddy Long Legs ★ (140)
- Dance on Fire R ★★★ (26)
- Dike A Rama (429)
- Direct Wrench (TR) (36)
- Discoy Decoy ★★ (155)
- Dwindling Greenbacks R ★★ (82)
- Enos Mills Glacier R ★ (100)
- Erca (467)
- Evening At The Improv (326)
- Face (TR) (238)
- Face (TR) (364)
- Fascist Groove Thing (TR) (181)
- First Eleven (386)
- Flange, The (TR) (339)
- Flashflood (486)
- Fly in the Ointment (TR) (513)
- Fowl Play (442)
- Frank and Ernest (TR) (127)
- Freckle Face (485)
- Free Electric (464)
- Free Variation (111)
- Gaston's Groove ★ (511)
- Geometry ★★★ (52)
- Gilded Lump (241)
- Gold Hunk, The (TR) (241)
- Goldenbush Corner (184)
- Gravity Waves ★★★★★ (62)
- Great Commission ★★ (551)
- Green Chile (TR) (142)
- Hands To Yourself (TR) (197)
- Headless Horseman ★★★ (541)
- Here Comes The Bride ★★ (329)
- Hey Taxi (362)
- High Interest ★★ (49)
- History (TR) (33)
- Hold Tight Til Footings Right (TR) (485)
- Hollowed Ground ★★ (428)
- Honorable Hersheys (TR) (71)
- Hot Lava ★ (412)
- I'm Pregnant with Satan's Baby (470)
- Ignorant Photons From Pluto (TR) ★ (183)
- Igor's Failed Road Trip ★★ (406)
- Impulse Power ★ (140)
- In the Name of Love (471)
- Indian Giver ★★★ (407)
- Jamaican Bobsled ★★★ (345)
- Jumping Jack Crack ★★★ (212)
- Just for the Thrill of It (TR) (416)
- Keith's Work (TR) (166)
- Killer Pussy (TR) (416)
- Kilobyte (265)
- Last Unicorn, The ★★★★★ (68)
- Lay Back and Do It (TR) (150)
- Layaway Plan (TR) ★★ (129)
- Left Archimedes' Crack (414)
- Left Ski Track ★★★ (183)
- Leg Lifter, The ★ (41)
- Lemon Slicer, The ★★ (70)
- Let's Get Horizontal (TR) ★★ (210)
- Life in the Fast Lane ★★ (244)
- Lithophiliac ★★★ (73)
- Liturgy (298)
- Live and Let Die (467)
- Looking for Mercy (75)
- Loose Lips ★★★ (200)
- Lunar Lieback (198)
- Lynch Mob ★★ (546)
- Megabyte (TR) (265)
- Mercy Road (75)
- Mere Illusion ★★ (438)
- Milk Run (510)

5.11a

- [ ] **Millenium Falcon, The** (TR) (482)
- [ ] **Molten Mettle** (144)
- [ ] **Momento Mori** (181)
- [ ] **Naked Reagan** ★★★ (328)
- [ ] **Natural Selection** ★★★★ (76)
- [ ] **Need To Have A Word With Myself** ★ (326)
- [ ] **No San Francisco** (TR) (78)
- [ ] **North Side** (TR) ★★ (316)
- [ ] **Nose to the Grindstone** (362)
- [ ] **O'Bulg** (516)
- [ ] **Open Casket Funeral** (TR) (120)
- [ ] **Ordinary Route** R ★★ (250)
- [ ] **Out For Lunch** ★★ (234)
- [ ] **Outsiders, The** R ★ (114)
- [ ] **Over the Rainbow** ★★ (494)
- [ ] **Pale Rider** (330)
- [ ] **Patanjali's Sutra** (TR) (464)
- [ ] **Peanut Gallery, A** ★★★ (112)
- [ ] **Pearl Drops** ★★★★ (350)
- [ ] **Petrodynamics** ★★★ (433)
- [ ] **Pilgrim, The** (339)
- [ ] **Pinhead** (203)
- [ ] **Pocket Pussy** (TR) (105)
- [ ] **Poodle Smasher, The** ★★★ (322)
- [ ] **Popeye** ★★ (116)
- [ ] **Prejudicial Viewpoint** R (516)
- [ ] **Preparation H** (TR) (153)
- [ ] **Psychedelic Yupies** (TR) (224)
- [ ] **Pull My Finger Barbara** (381)
- [ ] **Pump Up The Volume** ★ (92)
- [ ] **Railroad** (250)
- [ ] **Rangers in Space** ★ (475)
- [ ] **Rattler, The** ★★★★ (501)
- [ ] **Read My Flips** ★ (386)
- [ ] **Read My Lips** ★ (386)
- [ ] **Red Headed Stranger** ★★ (284)
- [ ] **Red Hot Chili Peppers** (304)
- [ ] **Red Snapper** ★★★ (39)
- [ ] **Refrigerator — Right Side, The** (TR) (323)
- [ ] **Right Banana Crack** ★★★ (124)
- [ ] **Rites of Passage** (339)
- [ ] **Rock Shark** (256)
- [ ] **Rockwell 41C** ★ (213)
- [ ] **Romper Room** (44)
- [ ] **Rope Opera** (321)
- [ ] **Route Beer** ★★★ (353)
- [ ] **Rubberfat Syndrome, The** (TR) (169)
- [ ] **Rubberneck Busybody** ★★ (511)
- [ ] **Ruby Slippers** (493)
- [ ] **S Crack** ★ (411)
- [ ] **Sanctuary Much** (298)
- [ ] **Santa's Little Helpers** ★★ (233)
- [ ] **Say No To Jugs** ★★ (465)
- [ ] **Scar Wars** (301)
- [ ] **Schlong, The** (337)
- [ ] **Scoop Problem** (203)
- [ ] **Screen Test** (503)
- [ ] **Scud Missile** (308)
- [ ] **Ship of Fools** (217)
- [ ] **Shooting Star** ★★ (290)
- [ ] **Sigalert** (TR) (96)
- [ ] **Slow Mutants** ★★ (59)
- [ ] **Small Business** (123)
- [ ] **Smarter Than the Average Ranger** ★ (85)
- [ ] **Soft Cell** (269)
- [ ] **Soul Kitchen** (330)
- [ ] **Spam and Cheese** (TR) (142)
- [ ] **Spy Hole** (349)
- [ ] **Stop Making Sense** (95)
- [ ] **Strange Kind of Love** (471)
- [ ] **Such A Savage** ★★★★★ (290)
- [ ] **Sun City** (244)
- [ ] **Super Monster Killer** ★ (211)
- [ ] **Swain Song** ★★ (120)
- [ ] **Sweat Pants** (524)
- [ ] **Swept Away** ★★★★ (245)
- [ ] **Swift** ★ (116)
- [ ] **Symbolic of Life** ★ (153)
- [ ] **T. Gordon Liddy** (264)
- [ ] **Tap Dancing** R ★★★ (26)
- [ ] **Therapeutic Tyranny** ★★ (459)
- [ ] **Third Bolt from the Sun** ★ (109)
- [ ] **This Scud's For You** ★ (457)
- [ ] **Tied to the Whipping Post** (538)
- [ ] **Tights Camera Action** (TR) (197)
- [ ] **Todd Squad, The** (338)
- [ ] **Too Strong and a Tweener** (364)
- [ ] **Top Guns** ★ (301)
- [ ] **Traverse of No Return** (186)
- [ ] **Twisted Crystals** (200)
- [ ] **Two Flew the Coop** (TR) (252)
- [ ] **Ungawaa** ★ (382)
- [ ] **Unknown** ★ (144)
- [ ] **Unknown** (237)
- [ ] **Unknown** (272)
- [ ] **Unnamed** (TR) (343)
- [ ] **Venucian Fece** (TR) (212)
- [ ] **Vertical Corrector** ★★ (523)
- [ ] **Washoe Crack** (450)
- [ ] **Wedlock** (464)
- [ ] **Weekend Warrior** ★ (76)
- [ ] **Weenie Roast** (306)
- [ ] **Whatchasay Dude** (174)
- [ ] **White Rain** ★★★★★ (353)
- [ ] **Who Cares** ★★ (350)
- [ ] **Winds of Whoopee** ★★★ (180)
- [ ] **Winters Moon** (481)
- [ ] **Wren's Nest** (59)
- [ ] **Yellow Brick Road** ★★★★ (501)
- [ ] **Young Frankenstein** ★★ (104)
- [ ] **Zorba** R (317)
- [ ] **Zygote** (224)

5.11b

☐ Adrift (402)
☐ Air Voyager (295)
☐ Airy Scene ★★★ (131)
☐ Alpine Diversions ★★ (252)
☐ Animalitos ★★ (36)
☐ Arete #2 (TR) (71)
☐ Arms Are For Hugging ★★★ (52)
☐ Art of Deception (257)
☐ Atom Ant ★★ (66)
☐ Banana Peal ★★ (124)
☐ Big Red Tractor (TR) ★★ (430)
☐ Black Nipple Fetish ★★ (411)
☐ Bonfire ★★★ (516)
☐ Bridge of Sighs ★★★★ (541)
☐ Bulbisness (TR) ★ (425)
☐ Cactus Flower ★★★ (381)
☐ Catapult ★★★★ (76)
☐ Chaos (244)
☐ Chase Lounge (511)
☐ Chick Flakey ★ (254)
☐ Chongo Bolt Route (188)
☐ Compound W (TR) (153)
☐ Copperhead ★ (319)
☐ Creature Feature ★★ (383)
☐ Date Queen Corridor Crack R ★★ (524)
☐ Dead Man's Eyes (217)
☐ Death by Chocolate (252)
☐ Desert Song R ★★★ (169)
☐ Dig Me (TR) (428)
☐ Digitizer ★★ (402)
☐ Dimp For A Chimp (225)
☐ Disposition Cervice ★★ (374)
☐ Double Trouble (TR) (476)
☐ Electric Eye (250)
☐ Elmer Fudd (TR) (104)
☐ Erotic City ★★★ (41)
☐ Fang, The R (189)
☐ Fear of Music (425)
☐ Feathers ★★★ (442)
☐ Feeding the Rat (181)
☐ Fingers on a Landscape (222)
☐ Firefly (TR) (471)
☐ Forbidden Zone (338)
☐ Forgotten Galaxy R (533)
☐ Frat Boys in the Gym (TR) ★ (412)
☐ Friend Bender (206)
☐ From the Mouths of Dogs ★★★ (465)
☐ Frontier Justice ★★★★ (545)
☐ Garnet ★★ (350)
☐ Gia (457)
☐ Gomma Cocida ★ (93)
☐ Great TR, But Don't Bolt Me, A (TR) ★★ (35)
☐ Grip or Whip (TR) (141)
☐ Gunshy (247)
☐ Hair on My Tread ★★ (412)
☐ Hands Down (TR) (197)
☐ Happy Landings, Linda (100)
☐ Heavy Mettle (464)
☐ Highwayman, The R ★★★ (520)
☐ Ho Man! (284)
☐ House of Games (381)
☐ Hug Dance ★★ (523)
☐ I'm Not Afraid Anymore ★★★ (192)
☐ Inauguron, The ★★ (312)
☐ Is That A Munchkin in Your Pocket (TR) ★★★ (501)
☐ Jackalope (115)

☐ James Brown (TR) (161)
☐ Jane's Addiction ★★★★ (386)
☐ King Pin ★ (212)
☐ Knight in Shining Armor, The ★★★★ (79)
☐ Laserator (TR) (198)
☐ Latin Swing ★★ (171)
☐ Left V Crack R ★★ (536)
☐ Life Without Principle (308)
☐ Little Joe (TR) ★★ (518-519)
☐ Manic Depression ★★★ (481)
☐ Mark of Zorro ★★ (24)
☐ Meatlocker (339)
☐ Middle Age Crazy ★★★ (290)
☐ Misfits ★★ (239)
☐ Mission Impossible ★★★ (388)
☐ Monaco ★★★ (534)
☐ Morality Test ★★★ (312)
☐ Mortal Thoughts R ★ (154)
☐ MTV (TR) (393)
☐ Mulligan Stew (TR) (275)
☐ No Options (386)
☐ Ontology Recapitulates Phylogony A1 ★★★ (405)
☐ Overnight Sensation ★★ (204)
☐ Oyster Delacacy ★★★ (375)
☐ Papaya Crack ★★ (124)
☐ Paranoia ★★★ (481)
☐ Pat Adams Dihedral ★★★★ (131)
☐ Patricide (277)
☐ Pet Cemetery ★★★ (27)
☐ Pinnacle Aerobics to Promote Blood Circulation (378)
☐ Pissing on Myself (TR) (445)
☐ Pit Viper ★★ (462)
☐ Poaching Bighorn ★★★★ (317)
☐ Porky Pig (TR) ★ (233)
☐ Poseidon Adventure, The ★★ (301)
☐ Predator Tigress ★★ (457)
☐ Pretty in Pink (TR) ★★ (47)
☐ Private Idaho ★★★ (44)
☐ Psychokenesis ★★ (63)
☐ Psychotechnics ★★ (63)
☐ Puzzlin' Evidence (128)
☐ Quantum Mechanics ★★ (66)
☐ R.S. Chicken Choker ★★ (109)
☐ Rainy Day, Dream Away R ★★★ (170)
☐ Raven, The (TR) (471)
☐ Red Bull R ★★ (124)
☐ Return to Hell ★★ (548)
☐ Right of Center (TR) (400)
☐ Right to Arm Bears, The (487)
☐ Ring of Fire (416)
☐ Ronnie and Clyde (TR) (421)
☐ Roughriders ★★★ (378)
☐ Roundup, The (309)
☐ Route 499 (TR) ★★ (189)
☐ Roy's Route ★★★ (550)
☐ Scary Poodles ★★★ (127)
☐ Scattered Remains ★★ (433)
☐ Shake, Rattle and Roll R ★★ (551)
☐ Shakin Like Milk ★★★ (358)
☐ Shifting Sands (391)
☐ Silent But Deadly ★★★ (515)
☐ Silverado ★★ (431)
☐ Snake Book ★★★★ (501)
☐ Snicker Biscuit ★ (83)
☐ Solitary Confinement (240)
☐ Solo Dog ★★★ (239)

5.11b

- Something or Other (TR) (350)
- Something's Burning ★★★ (394)
- Sound of Waves, The (TR) (322)
- Speculum Scrapings (287)
- Spring or Fall (277)
- Step Function ★★★ (352)
- Stone Hinge (68)
- Svapada ★★ (314)
- Sweet Ginger ★★★ (256)
- Tail Gunner ★★★★ (58)
- Taraan (244)
- Time Avenger ★★ (307)
- Tortuga ★★ (405)
- Twittish Empire (465)

- Uncle Remus ★★★ (108)
- Unknown Soldier ★★★★ (293)
- Unnamed (TR) ★★ (55)
- Up 40 R/X ★★ (364)
- Vogels Are Poodles Too (TR) (122)
- Walking Pneumonia R/X ★ (290)
- Watasillywall (TR) (208)
- We Don't Need No Stinking Badges ★★★ (358)
- We Must, We Must, We Must Improve Our Bust ★★ (135)
- Wheel of Fortune ★★ (310)
- Whipped Topping (389)
- Wingtips (TR) (210)

5.11

- Arms for Hostages (TR) ★ (109)
- Augie Problem (184)
- Big Bob's Big Wedge (450)
- Black Pea (192)
- Cave Man (228)
- Classic Thin Crack (233)
- Comfortably Numb ★★ (210)
- Feast (517)
- Fruits of Labor (TR) (343)
- Fry Problem (367)
- Hensel Face (193)
- If It's Brown, Flush It (TR) ★ (161)
- Intersection Boulder Middle (185)
- Left (176)
- Mary Decker (TR) (56)
- Mr. DNA (TR) (206)
- Nice Lady (367)
- Old Wave (270)
- Orange Curtain (144)
- Pipper (32)
- Powell Face (228)
- Powell Pinch (367)

- Purple Place (352)
- Rats with Wings (201)
- Secret Sauce (115)
- Shindig (146)
- Sleek Beak (470)
- South Face R (176)
- Southwest Arete (176)
- Stable Girl (TR) (47)
- Undertow (203)
- Unnamed (176)
- Unnamed (176)
- Unnamed (192)
- Unnamed (203)
- Unnamed (203)
- Up 20 R (367)
- Varsity Crank Problem (190)
- Viva Las Vegas (TR) (47)
- Walk the Plank (217)
- Wally Gator (88)
- When You're A Sancho (TR) (273)
- Yardarm, The (217)

5.11c

- 30 Seconds Over Baghdad (343)
- 39 Slaps, The ★★ (114)
- 5.10 Who (TR) (139)
- Amazing Grace ★ (246)
- Anecdotes of Power (309)
- Animalargos R ★★★ (36)
- Anti-Gravity Acrobatics R ★★ (533)
- Anti-Gravity Boots R ★ (93)
- Are You Inexperienced (453)
- Avant Cave ★★ (386)
- Bat Cave, The ★★ (166)
- Beautiful Screamer ★★★ (464)
- Bell-E-Up ★★★ (473)
- Bella Lugosi ★ (473)
- Black Hole ★★ (140)
- Black Panther (457)
- Blind Man's Bluff (377)
- Boogie Woogie Blues, The (290)
- Bozo's Raindance (295)
- Brain Fart (TR) (397)
- Buried Treasure (420)
- Butterfly Crack ★★★ (32)
- Caribbean Cruise (419)
- Castaway (419)
- Cayenne (256)

- Ceramic Bus R (530)
- Charles Who? ★★ (139)
- Chicago Nipple Slump (TR) ★ (215)
- Combination Locks ★★ (263)
- Compact Physical ★ (71)
- Conceptual Continuity (TR) (181)
- Conundrum, The (338)
- Cowboy Junkie ★★★★ (352)
- Creamy Peanut Butter (TR) ★ (196)
- Cryogenics (250)
- Defender (TR) ★★★ (511)
- Desert Whale ★★★ (548)
- Diaper Challenge (418)
- Dick Enberg ★★ (155)
- Digitalis Destructi ★ (175)
- Electric Blue ★★★ (248)
- Euphrates ★★ (316)
- Exploding Brown Nudules (459)
- Face to Face (TR) ★ (536)
- Famous Potatoes ★ (64)
- Fly, The (335)
- For Peter ★★★ (462)
- Frigid Dare (TR) (211)
- G-Spot (350)
- Global Warming ★★ (475)

5.11c

- Grain Pile (245)
- Gravity Works ★★★ (62)
- Hands of Fire (TR) (79)
- Hangman Jury ★★★ (545)
- Headbangers' Ball ★★ (101)
- Heart of Darkness ★★★★ (373)
- Hercules ★★★ (120)
- Horseshoe ★★ (481)
- Hot Flashes (401)
- Hot Legs Contest (217)
- Hot Rocks ★★★★★ (223)
- Houdini Arete, The (TR) (52)
- Human Sacrifice (413)
- Hyperion ★★★★ (73)
- Igor Prince of Poodles (246)
- Illicit Operations (123)
- In a Silent Way (392)
- Into You Like a Train (TR) (88)
- Iron Curtain, The ★★ (375)
- It's Easy to be Distant When You're Brave ★★ (76)
- Jingus Con ★★ (122)
- Kodas Silence ★★★ (137)
- Kon-Tiki (TR) (467)
- Lascivisous Conduct ★★ (515)
- Lee's Health Studio ★★★ (457)
- Limp Wristed Faggot ★★ (136)
- Macho Combo, The ★★★ (348)
- Mad Hatter R (364)
- Magma (TR) (412)
- Middle S Crack R ★★★ (122)
- Midnight Oil (136)
- Missing Persons (470)
- More Monkey Thank Funky ★★★ (257)
- Morongo Man ★★★ (465)
- My Grain (512)
- My Life As A Dog ★★★ (344)
- Nerve Storm ★★★ (428)
- Nihilistic Pillar ★★ (300)
- Offroach, The (335)
- Old Guys Gone Nuts, Go to the Cops (381)
- Orno-Necro ★ (459)
- Oysters from Heaven ★★★ (375)
- Panama Red (TR) (524)
- Pearl Necklace ★★★★ (350)
- Piledriver, The (429)
- Pitball ★★ (150)
- Police & Thieves (248)
- Poodle Skirt (237)
- Puss n' Boots ★★ (178)
- Quest For Fire ★ (38)
- Red Hot Fire Balls (378)
- Revenge of the Chuckwalla ★ (250)
- Riddles in the Dark ★★ (229)

- Rock Dog Candy Leg (TR) ★★ (98)
- Rocky Horror Picture Show ★★★★ (383)
- Rocky vs. Rambo (272)
- Roller Coaster (TR) (219)
- Rule Britannia R ★★★ (245)
- Rustler, The ★ (406)
- Safety Pin ★★ (459)
- Sand Truck, The ★★ (440)
- Scar Is Born, A (272)
- Scorched Earth ★★★ (436)
- Secret Agent Man (TR) (174)
- Seebolt (485)
- Shamrock Shooter (90)
- Simple Simon ★★★ (402)
- Slip and Slide (TR) ★ (152)
- Snake Bite (339)
- Son of Obsidian (470)
- Sonic Temple ★★★★ (501)
- Sound of One Hand Slapping, The ★★ (305)
- Soviet Union ★★ (39)
- Spanking (TR) (67)
- Spider Line ★★★★ (188)
- Spontaneous Human Combustion ★ (97)
- Spy vs Spry ★★ (349)
- Street Sweeper ★★★ (245)
- String 'em Up ★★★ (546)
- Sweet Eternity R ★ (256)
- Times of Holyness ★★★★ (430)
- Tombstone, The ★★ (74)
- Tooth Decay (364)
- Toothpick, The (TR) (123)
- Total Generic Package (TR) ★★★ (462)
- Towering Inferno, The ★★ (301)
- Triathlon (TR) (155)
- Turd, The (244)
- Two Against Everest (aka: On the Back) ★ (24)
- Unknown (183)
- Unknown ★★ (210)
- Vector ★★★★ (468)
- Wangerbanger ★★★★ (229)
- Warp Factor R (140)
- Wet T-Shirt Night ★★★ (217)
- Wheat Beri-Beri R ★ (312)
- When Love Came to Town (471)
- When You're A Jet (TR) ★★★ (256)
- Whistling Sphincter (TR) ★ (92)
- White Bread Fever ★★★ (312)
- Who'da Thought (TR) ★ (97)
- Wicked Witchcraft ★★★ (497)
- Wokking the Dog (TR) ★ (39)
- Women in Cages (TR) ★ (47)
- Yet Another Cilley Toprope (TR) (56)
- Zen and the Art of Placement ★★ (406)

5.11d

- 29 Palms ★★★★ (114)
- Arms Control ★★★ (76)
- Avante Guard-Dog ★★ (75)
- Baby Huey Smokes Anti-Pipeload ★★ (93)
- Battle of the Bulge ★★ (242)
- Black Like Night ★★★ (544)
- Blue Velvet (TR) ★ (47)
- Border Patrol ★★ (520)
- Bosch Job R ★★ (378)

- Campfire Girl (TR) (516)
- Chicken Run (443)
- Condor, The ★★★★ (525)
- Cool But Concerned ★★★ (155)
- Dave Ate The Cookie (TR) ★★★ (501)
- Dawn Yawn ★★★ (73)
- Desert Profit ★★ (428)
- Destination Unknown (470)
- Dirty Tricks (264)

5.11d

- [ ] Dynamic Panic (188)
- [ ] Elephant Walk ★★★ (406)
- [ ] Elevenfall Face (TR) (411)
- [ ] Elvis Lives (345)
- [ ] Flashpoint (436)
- [ ] Flea Bite (TR) (456)
- [ ] Freeway Jam ★★ (139)
- [ ] Functional Analysis (TR) (248)
- [ ] Green Visitor ★★★ (109)
- [ ] Groop'o (TR) ★★ (433)
- [ ] Hidden Arch ★★★ (178)
- [ ] Iced Vo-Vo's (229)
- [ ] Iron Maiden ★★★ (256)
- [ ] Living Conjunction, The (TR) ★★ (221)
- [ ] Male Exotic Dancers ★★ (217)
- [ ] Master & Servant (TR) (252)
- [ ] Micro Millenium, The R ★★★ (482)
- [ ] Mike and Tom's Excellent Adventure R (349)
- [ ] Minor Threat (TR) (201)
- [ ] Monsey R (257)
- [ ] Mr. Wizard (TR) (394)
- [ ] Nincompope ★★ (449)
- [ ] Pocket Pool ★★★ (534)
- [ ] Popsicle ★★★ (456)
- [ ] Pox on You (389)
- [ ] Presupposition R ★★★ (516)
- [ ] Raging Bull Dike (377)
- [ ] Ramming Speed (136)
- [ ] Rattle and Hum ★ (212)
- [ ] Realm of the Flying Monkeys ★★★★ (497)
- [ ] Rockwork Orange ★★★ (272)
- [ ] Route of All Evil ★★ (27)
- [ ] Scary Monsters ★★★ (104)
- [ ] Skintight Mousehouse ★★ (319)
- [ ] Slightly Out of Our Minds ★★★ (540)
- [ ] Smoke and Mirrors ★★ (307)
- [ ] Snap on Demand ★ (178)
- [ ] Souls of Black (252)
- [ ] Sow Sickle ★★★ (136)
- [ ] Spaghetti Western ★★★★ (546)
- [ ] Speculator, The ★ (49)
- [ ] Split Personality ★★★ (374)
- [ ] Stems and Seeds (364)
- [ ] Stone Idol R ★★★ (290)
- [ ] Straight Out Of Compton (345)
- [ ] Subway to Venus ★★ (359)
- [ ] Super Spy (TR) ★ (174)
- [ ] Taunting Fear ★ (425)
- [ ] The Great Escape ★ (52)
- [ ] Trapeze ★★ (183)
- [ ] Unnamed ★★ (55)
- [ ] Up The Ante (TR) ★★ (108)
- [ ] Where Eagles Dare ★★ (168)
- [ ] Wings of Steel ★★★ (463)
- [ ] Woodshed, The ★★★ (461)
- [ ] Young Guns ★★★ (463)

5.11+

- [ ] Accomazzo Face (176)
- [ ] Bard's Ankle (193)
- [ ] Big Brother (387)
- [ ] Cole Arete (226)
- [ ] Cole Face (226)
- [ ] Copper Penny R (200)
- [ ] Crow's Nest, The (67)
- [ ] False Blockhead (146)
- [ ] Family Fued (228)
- [ ] Fist Full of Walnuts (176)
- [ ] Flight Attendant (371)
- [ ] Function, The R (193)
- [ ] Gunsmoke (271)
- [ ] Hensel Face (146)
- [ ] High Tension (39)
- [ ] How's Your Mama (228)
- [ ] Largo Dyno (367)
- [ ] Lechlinski's Corner (146)
- [ ] Lunge For It (367)
- [ ] Parking Lot Crank (367)
- [ ] Planet Claire (367)
- [ ] Satellite Boulder Left (367)
- [ ] Satellite Boulder Right (367)
- [ ] Sesert Safari ★★★ (441)
- [ ] Slam Dunk (190)
- [ ] Sorta High R (176)
- [ ] Stem Gem (190)
- [ ] Top Hat (TR) (298)
- [ ] Toprope Conversion (219)
- [ ] True Grit (146)
- [ ] Turnbuckle (176)
- [ ] Turtle Classic (176)
- [ ] Unnamed (176)
- [ ] Unnamed (176)
- [ ] Upsidedown Pineapple, The (201)
- [ ] Wheresabolt? (TR) (76)
- [ ] White Rastafarian R (228)
- [ ] Yabba-Dabba-Doo (228)
- [ ] Yabo Roof (146)

5.12a

- [ ] Abandoned Classic (TR) ★★★ (430)
- [ ] Apartheid ★★★ (225)
- [ ] Avant Chain ★★ (386)
- [ ] Bikini Whale ★★★ (170)
- [ ] Blitzkrieg ★★★ (508)
- [ ] Blood of Christ ★★★ (218)
- [ ] Bloodline, The ★★★★★ (345)
- [ ] Bombs Over Libya ★★★ (301)
- [ ] Boys Don't Cry ★★★ (358)
- [ ] Brain Damage (263)
- [ ] Brain Death ★★★ (263)
- [ ] Brass Monkey (308)
- [ ] Bride of Frankenstein (TR) (473)
- [ ] Bunnies (TR) ★ (384)
- [ ] Castles Burning ★★ (534)
- [ ] Chief Crazy Horse ★★★ (68)
- [ ] Cross Fire R ★ (406)
- [ ] Dances with Poodles (246)
- [ ] Datura R ★★ (516)
- [ ] Disrythmia ★★ (248)
- [ ] Electric Tree Gordon R ★★ (131)
- [ ] Emotional Rescue ★ (277)
- [ ] Fear Is Never Boring (330)
- [ ] Finger Bowl (485)
- [ ] Fingers of Frenzy (TR) (438)
- [ ] Gauntlet, The ★★ (140)

5.12a

- [ ] Glory Road (136)
- [ ] Good Investment (TR) (386)
- [ ] Gunslinger, The ★★★★ (293)
- [ ] Having Fun Yet X (203)
- [ ] High Ware (237)
- [ ] Hollow Dreams (TR) (123)
- [ ] Ionic Strength ★★★★ (66)
- [ ] It's Easy to be Brave from a Safe Distance ★★ (76)
- [ ] Kalishnakov Kulture ★★ (517)
- [ ] Leave It To Beaver ★★★★★ (155)
- [ ] Life's A Pitch ★★ (294)
- [ ] Linden-Frost Effect, The (53)
- [ ] Lobster, The (TR) ★★★ (155)
- [ ] Love Goddess ★★★ (385)
- [ ] Major Threat (TR) (201)
- [ ] Manly Dike, The ★★★★ (314)
- [ ] Marathon Crack, The (420)
- [ ] Middle of Somewhere (402)
- [ ] Mighty High (369)
- [ ] Money for Nothing (378)
- [ ] My Wife Is An Alien R ★ (508)
- [ ] Nothing But Hearsay ★★★★ (511)
- [ ] Nuclear Arms ★★★ (66)
- [ ] Official Rubber Tester (247)
- [ ] Over-Powered by Hootch (TR) (150)
- [ ] Overpowered by Funk ★★ (484)
- [ ] Pit Slut ★★ (150)
- [ ] Quasar (467)
- [ ] Quivering Savages ★★★ (524)
- [ ] Rap Bolters Are Weak ★★★ (154)
- [ ] Repo Man R ★★★ (293)
- [ ] Resurrection ★★★ (218)
- [ ] Riddler, The ★★ (237)
- [ ] Rumors and Lies ★★★★ (511)
- [ ] Sideburn ★★ (69)
- [ ] Slightly Ahead of Our Time ★ (369)
- [ ] Sole Fusion ★★★ (245)
- [ ] South Arete (TR) (238)
- [ ] Spur of the Moment, The ★★★ (458)
- [ ] Stairway to Heaven (TR) ★ (205)
- [ ] Stand and Deliver ★★★ (223)
- [ ] Strange Attracter, The ★ (473)
- [ ] Taxed to the Limit (49)
- [ ] Throbbing Gristle (TR) (471)
- [ ] Tic Tic Boom ★★★ (170)
- [ ] Topper (TR) (374)
- [ ] Toxic Waltz ★★★ (131)
- [ ] Transfusion ★★★ (73)
- [ ] Trapeze Center (183)
- [ ] Under a Blood Red Sky (TR) ★★ (430)
- [ ] Unknown ★★ (137)
- [ ] Waltzing Worm ★★★ (104)
- [ ] Wavecrest ★★★★ (322)
- [ ] When You're Erect ★★ (256)
- [ ] Woodward Crack ★★ (411)

5.12b

- [ ] 5 Crying Cowboys ★★★★ (79)
- [ ] Bates Motel, The ★★★ (62)
- [ ] Bikini Beach (TR) ★ (170)
- [ ] Black Diamond R ★★★★★ (345)
- [ ] Buffalo Soldier ★★ (225)
- [ ] Chameleon, The ★★★★ (169)
- [ ] Cheetah ★★ (244)
- [ ] Cool Thing ★★★ (548)
- [ ] D.B.'s Toprope (518)
- [ ] Electric Birthday Party ★★★ (461)
- [ ] Every Which Way But Up ★★★ (461)
- [ ] Father Ocean (TR) (381)
- [ ] Hang em High ★★★ (459)
- [ ] Headmaster (TR) ★★★ (371)
- [ ] Hicks for Free ★★★★ (378)
- [ ] It Don't Mean A Thing If It Ain't Got That Swing ★★★ (284)
- [ ] Jane's Getting Serious ★★★ (244)
- [ ] Kingsnake ★ (212)
- [ ] Living Color (TR) (464)
- [ ] Mettle Detector ★★★ (464)
- [ ] Potato Masher ★ (93)
- [ ] Real McCoy, The (TR) ★★ (239)
- [ ] Red Cross ★★★★ (345)
- [ ] Satanic Mechanic ★★★★ (172)
- [ ] Saturn Boulder, The ★★★ (475)
- [ ] Sensory Deprivation ★★★ (433)
- [ ] Slaves of Fashion ★ (301)
- [ ] Super Quickie (163)
- [ ] They Found Hitler's Brain ((113)
- [ ] Thin Red Line R ★★ (205)
- [ ] Three Men and A Baby (276)
- [ ] Toad Warriors R ★ (153)
- [ ] Vanishing Point (136)
- [ ] Warrior Eagle ★★★ (79)
- [ ] White Mamba ★★★ (463)
- [ ] White Mischief ★★ (248)
- [ ] Women and Money (TR) ★★ (548)
- [ ] Zen ★★★ (316)
- [ ] Zombie Woof ★★ (179)

5.12c

- [ ] Adder Dance ★★★ (319)
- [ ] Apollo ★★★ (415)
- [ ] Aren't You Hungry (TR) ★★ (541)
- [ ] Baby Apes ★★★ (225)
- [ ] Battering Ram (465)
- [ ] Brown Out (TR) (241)
- [ ] Camouflage (201)
- [ ] Cool But Not Too Concerned (TR) (155)
- [ ] Crash, The ★ (49)
- [ ] Dial Africa ★★★ (225)
- [ ] Dictators of Anarchy ★★★★★ (413)
- [ ] Equinox ★★★★★ (406)
- [ ] Flying Dutchman, The (217)
- [ ] Headbanger's Ball ★★ (371)
- [ ] Joker, The ★★ (166)
- [ ] Leper Messiah (TR) ★★★ (342)
- [ ] Medusa (218)
- [ ] Mind Body Problem (TR) (309)
- [ ] Mohawk, The ★★★ (68)
- [ ] Moonshadow ★★★ (385)
- [ ] No Self Control ★★★★ (78)
- [ ] Obsidian ★ (412)
- [ ] Outland (339)
- [ ] Question of Masculinity, A (TR) (186)

5.12c

- ☐ Quickstone R ★★★ (114)
- ☐ Railer ★ (170)
- ☐ Reefer Madness (TR) (150)
- ☐ Rots o' Rock (136)
- ☐ Seizure ★★★ (462)
- ☐ Ship Wrecked (420)
- ☐ Some Like It Hot ★★★★ (169)
- ☐ Steep Pulse . (144)
- ☐ Talon Show (TR) ★★★ (442)

- ☐ Talon, The ★★★ (315)
- ☐ Tarantula, The ★★★ (169)
- ☐ Thrill of Desire, The ★★★★ (75)
- ☐ To Hold and to Have (TR) ★★ (406)
- ☐ Trapeze Left (183)
- ☐ Unnamed (172)
- ☐ Walk on Water ★★★ (218)
- ☐ Warpath ★★★★★ (68)
- ☐ Watusi, The ★★ (225)

5.12d

- ☐ Acid Crack, The ★★★★ (116)
- ☐ Asteroid Crack (265)
- ☐ Book of Brilliant Things ★★★★★ (75)
- ☐ Desert Shield ★★★★ (172)
- ☐ Existential Decay R ★★ (300)
- ☐ Father Figure ★★★★ (277)
- ☐ Future Boy (TR) ★★ (430)
- ☐ I Have the Touch ★★★★ (433)

- ☐ Karma ★★★★ (316)
- ☐ La Cholla ★★★ (385)
- ☐ Mojave Green ★★★ (319)
- ☐ Pope on A Rope ★★★ (449)
- ☐ Skin of the Teeth, The (364)
- ☐ South of Heaven ★★★★★ (549)
- ☐ Tonic Boom ★★★ (170)

5.13a

- ☐ Cockroach, The (335)
- ☐ Cosmic Trigger ★★★★★ (433)
- ☐ Dihedralman ★★★ (75)
- ☐ Dunce Cap ★★★ (362)
- ☐ Hold Your Fire (148)
- ☐ Iconoclast, The ★★★★★ (378)
- ☐ Mamunia ★★★ (290)
- ☐ Mongoose ★★★★ (319)

- ☐ Moonbeam Crack, The ★★ (225)
- ☐ Nailed to the Cross (218)
- ☐ Persian Room, The (TR) (192)
- ☐ Powers That Be, The ★★★★★ (64)
- ☐ Puff Adder ★★★★ (319)
- ☐ Pumping Hate ★★★ (65)
- ☐ Red Rain ★★★ (319)
- ☐ Sun Bowl (257)

5.13b

- ☐ Automatic Venom Sprinkler ★★★ (319)
- ☐ Crowded Mental Hospital ★★★ (319)
- ☐ Cutting Edge, The ★★ (371)
- ☐ Games Without Frontiers ★★ (459)
- ☐ Hotpants ★★★★★ (319)
- ☐ Moondance (273)

- ☐ New World Order ★★★★★ (413)
- ☐ Pit Viper ★★★★ (319)
- ☐ Rastafarian (225)
- ☐ Scorpion, The ★★★ (169)
- ☐ Viper ★★★ (319)

5.13c

- ☐ Chain of Addiction ★★★★★ (64)
- ☐ Hydra ★★★★★ (69)

- ☐ Ocean of Doubt ★★★★★ (64)
- ☐ Rubber Boa ★★★ (319)

5.13d

- ☐ G String ★★★ (170)
- ☐ La Machine ★★★★ (64)

- ☐ New Deal ★ (248)
- ☐ Stingray (330)

1984 Is Today, 5.10+, 387
1BRP, 5.10b, 333
200 Motels, 5.8, 550
29 Bombs, 5.11a, 508
29 Palms, 5.11d, 114
3 Ring Circus, 5.10c, 510
30 Seconds Over Baghdad, 5.11c, 343
39 Slaps, The, 5.11c, 114
39 Steps, 5.4, 283
3rd Class It, 5.8, 513
41-MINUTE DOME, 342
42N8 ONE, 5.10a, 78
4th Amendment, The, 5.10-, 387
4U2DO2, 5.5 X, 120
5 Crying Cowboys, 5.12b, 79
5.10 Who, 5.11c (TR), 139
5150, 5.10b, 374
7, 5.10a, 163
80 Proof Roof, 5.10b, 263
976, 5.9+ R, 127, 128
AA, 5.7, 517
Abandoned Classic, 5.12a (TR), 430
ABBEY ROCK, 450
Able Was I Ere I Saw Ellsmere, 5.7, 52
Absolute Zero, 5.10c, 223
Absence of Malice, 5.11a (TR), 529
Abstract Roller Disco, 5.11a, 247
Accelerator, 5.10b, 481
Accomazzo Face, 5.11+, 176
Ace of Dog, 5.10a, 237
Ace of Spades, 5.9, 38
Acid Crack, The, 5.12d, 116
Acid Rock, 5.11a, 174
Acuity, 5.7, 214
Acupuncture, 5.8, 148
Adams' Happy Acres, 5.5, 82
Addams Family, 5.9, 131
Adder Dance, 5.12c, 319
Adrift, 5.11b, 402
Adult Books, 5.11a, 139
Adult Gerbles $1.59, 5.7+, 373
Aero Space, 5.10b, 385
AFPA ROCK, 40
AFRICA FACE, 510
AFRO AWARENESS WEEK, 538
AFRO BLUES WALL, 325
Aftermath, 5.10a, 52
Afternoon Shakedown, 5.11a X, 537
Against All Todds, 5.10c, 437
Against the Grain, 5.10a (TR), 170
AGENT ORANGE ROCK, 375
Aggarete, 5.10a R, 351
Aging Hippie Crack, 5.10b, 440
Agony of Defeat, 5.8 R, 56
Aguility, 5.10a, 272
Ahoy, 5.10c, 165
Aid Route, A2, 288
Aid Route, A3 R, 516
Aiguille de Joshua Tree, 5.6 X, 108
AIGUILLE DE JOSHUA TREE, 108
Ain't Nothing But A J-Tree Thing, 5.6, 166
Air Crack, 5.6, 331
Air Voyager, 5.11b, 295
Airy Scene, 5.11b, 131
Al's First Erection, 5.9, 420
Albatross, The, 5.10c, 179
Alexander's Salamander, 5.10d, 59
Alf's Arete, 5.11a, 130
Ali Shuffle, 5.10b, 406
Alice in Wonderjam, 5.9, 263
ALICE IN WONDERLAND AREA, 263
Alien Life Form Arete, The, 5.11a R, 233
Aliens Ate My Buick, 5.10b, 317

All Booked Up, 5.7, 179
All Kings Men, 5.7, 354
All Loin, 5.10c, 468
All My Children, 5.9, 321
All Washed Up, B1, 367
All Washed Up, B1, 367
All-Reet Arete, 5.8, 429
Allen Steck Memorial Route, 5.8, 369
Alligator Lizard, 5.9, 88
Alligator Tears, 5.9, 154
Almost Like Real Climbing, 5.7, 469
Almost Vertical, 5.7, 166
Alpentine, 5.9+ R, 517
Alpine Diversions, 5.11b, 252
ALPS ROCK, THE, 164
Altitude Sickness, 5.9, 101
Always on My Mind, 5.10c, 386
Amazing Grace, 5.11c, 246
Ambulance Driver, 5.1, 513
American Express, 5.9, 129
Amoeba, The, 5.10, 123
AMOEBA, THE, 123
An Eye for An Eye and A Route for A Route, 5.10b, 276
An Eye to the West, 5.9, 36
An Officer and a Poodle, 5.9 R, 39
An Unruly Camel, 5.11a, 426
Anacram, 5.10c, 96
Ancient Future, 5.9, 373
ANCIENT KINGDOM, 538
Android Lust, 5.11a R, 122
Andromeda Strain, 5.7, 40
Andecotes of Power, 5.11c, 309
Angione Crack, 5.6, 329
Anglo Saxophone, B1, 185
Angular Momentum, 5.9+ (TR), 464
Animal Magnetism, 5.11a, 286
Animal, The, B1—, 228
Animalargos, 5.11c R, 36
Animalitos, 5.11b, 36
Anniversary Special, 5.8, 362
Annointed Seagull, 5.8, 105
Another Brick in the Wall, 5.9 (TR), 298
Answer, The, 5.9, 491
Ant Farm, 5.8, 126
Anti-Gravity Acrobatics, 5.11c R, 533
Anti-Gravity Boots, 5.11c R, 93
Antichrist, 5.11a, 385
Ants in My Pants, 5.9, 339
Anty Matter, 5.10a, 296
Anybody Can Bolt, 5.10a, 453
Apartheid, 5.12a, 225
Ape Man Hop, 5.10a, 53
Apocalypse Now, 5.10b, 373
Apollo, 5.12c, 415
Apparition, 5.10a, 521
APPARITION ROCK, 521
Appendectomy Crack, 5.10d, 405
Appetite for Destruction, 5.10b, 307
Approach Pitch, 5.8+, 550
April Fools, 5.10c R, 242
Aqua Tarkus, 5.9+, 295
Aquino, 5.8, 129
Arachnids, 5.5, 479
Archery, 5.4, 450
Are We Ourselves, 5.8, 206
Are You Experienced?, 5.11a, 100
Are You Inexperienced, 5.11c, 453
Aren't You Hungry, 5.12c (TR), 541
Arete, 5.8, 176·
Arete #1, 5.10a (TR), 71
Arete #2, 5.11b (TR), 71
Arete #3, 5.11a (TR), 71
Arete #4, 5.11a (TR), 71

ARETE BOULDERS, THE, 233
Arete Buster, 5.11a R, 83
ARID PILES, 114-117
Arizona Crack, 5.11a R, 535
Arms Are For Hugging, 5.11b, 52
Arms Control, 5.11d, 76
Arms for Hostages, 5.11 (TR), 109
Around the Corner, 5.8, 550
Around the World, 5.8+, 439
Arraignment, The, 5.10a, 277
Art of Deception, 5.11b, 257
Artificial Ingredients, 5.8, 309
Arturo's Special, 5.8, 388
As The Crags Turn, 5.7, 321
As the Wind Blows, 5.7, 54
Ash Gordon, 5.10a, 282
ASH GORDON ROCK, 282
Ashes to Ashes, 5.10d, 475
Ashtray, The, 5.6, 240
Ass of Dog, 5.9, 237
Assault and Battery, 5.11a (TR), 503
ASTEROID BELT, 265
Asteroid Crack, 5.12d, 265
ASTRO DOMES, THE, 288
Astropoodle, 5.10c, 128
At Last, 5.10a, 518
At Your Pleasure, 5.8, 353
Atari, 5.10c R, 237
ATLANTIS AREA, 105
Atom Ant, 5.11b, 66
ATOM SMASHER BOULDERS, 66
Atomic Pile, 5.9, 130
Atrophy, 5.9, 26
Augie Problem, 5.11, 184
Auld Lang Syne, 5.8, 393
AUSSIE SNAKE FOODS, 229
Automatic Tiger, 5.10d, 317
Automatic Venom Sprinkler, 5.13b, 319
Autopia, 5.9, 309
Avant Cave, 5.11c, 386
Avant Chain, 5.122a, 386
Avante Guard-Dog, 5.11d, 75
AVIARY, THE, 138
Awesome Betty, 5.10a, 523
Awful Loose, 5.7 R, 516
Ayatollah, The, 5.11a (TR), 362
Aztec Two-Step, 5.7, 388
B Chili Dog, 5.10a, 131
B Flat, 5.7+, 82
B For Beers, 5.10b R, 26
B Sharp, 5.7+, 82
B-1, 5.1, 33
B-2, 5.3, 33
B-3, 5.3, 33
B-Movie, 5.10b, 469
B.A.S.E. Arrest, 5.10c, 75
B.L.T., 5.10b, 263
B.M.T.C. Leader, 5.7, 512
B52 ROCK, 44
Baby Apes, 5.12c, 225
Baby Banana, 5.7, 124
Baby Blue Eyes, 5.10b R, 123
Baby Face, 5.7, 52
Baby Fae, 5.11a, 379
Baby Huey Smokes Anti-Pipeload, 5.11d, 93
Baby Roof, 5.8, 52
Baby Route, 5.9, 369
Baby-Point-Five, 5.8 R/X, 33
Babylonia, 5.7, 538
Back From Retirement, 5.7, 510
BACK LOOP BOULDERING, 203
BACKSTREETS, THE, 49
Bacon Flake, 5.9, 237

Bad Boy Club, 5.9 R, 110
Bad Brains, 5.9, 439
Bad Fun, 5.11a, 215
Bad Lizards, 5.10a, 277
Bailey's Foster, 5.10b, 75
Bakersfield Bomb, 5.8, 508
Balance Due, 5.10c, 51
Bald Ambition, 5.11a, 327
Bald Women with Power Tools, 5.10b, 41
Ball Bearing, 5.10a, 167
Ball Monitor, The, 5.10a R, 344
Ballbearings Under Foot, 5.10a, 274
Ballbury, 5.7, 194
Ballet, 5.10a R?X, 200
Bam Bam, 5.10+, 228
Bam Boozler, 5.10d, 219
Bambi Meets Godzilla, 5.8+, 246
BANANA CRACKS, 124-125
Banana Peal, 5.11b, 124
Banana Splits, 5.10d, 389
Band Saw, 5.10c, 189
BANDANA ROCK, 470
Bandersnatch, 5.10b, 139
Bank Note Blues, 5.9, 50
BANKRUPT WALL, 285
Banquet, 5.9, 517
Barbara Bush, 5.10b, 120
Bard's Ankle, 5.11+, 193
Barely Crankin', 5.7, 369
Barfing At Zeldas, 5.10d, 125
Bark on Demand, 5.10d, 178
BARKER DAM, 276
BARKER DAM AREA, 267-278
Barkhorn, 5.8 (TR), 364
Barking Spyders, 5.10a/b R, 383
Barley, Wheat ro Rey (It's All Grain), 5.10a, 116
Barn Burning, 5.10b, 405
Barn Door, Left, 5.9 (TR), 99
Barn Door, Right, 5.10a (TR), 99
Barney Rubble, 5.1, 95
Barnie Rubble, 5.10b, 273
Barrel Race, 5.7, 350
BASKERVILLE ROCK, 35
Bat Cave, The, 5.11c, 166
Bat Crack, 5.5, 186
Bates Motel, The, 5.12b, 62
Battering Ram, 5.12c, 465
Battle of the Bulge, 5.11c/d, 242
BC BUTTRESS, 260
Be Good Or Be Gone, 5.10d, 167
Be Wary, 5.2, 513
Beadwagon, 5.10d, 246
Beafcake, 5.10a, 312
BEAK BOULDER ROCKS, THE, 470-471
Beak of the Week, 5.7, 470
Beam Aboard, 5.9+, 450
Beam Me Up Scottie, 5.10a, 480
BEAR ISLAND, 47
Bear Necessities, The, 5.7, 85
Bearded Cabbage, 5.10c, 188
Beardsley Cabbage, 5.7, 437
Beatle Baily, 5.4, 109
Beatles, The, 5.4, 109
Beautiful Screamer, 5.11c, 464
Beauty and the Beach, 5.9, 167
BEAVER BOULDER, 361
Beaver Boulder Free Route, 5.10c, 361
Beaver Tail, 5.10b, 350
Bebop Tango, 5.11a, 171
Beck's Bet, 5.8, 98
Beck's Bear, 5.7, 132
Becky's Buttress, 5.9, 475
BECKY'S BUTTRESS AREA, 475

Bed of Nails, 5.10d, 275
BED ROCK, 273
Bedrock Arete, 5.10, 228
BEDROCK BOULDER, 228
Bedtime for Democracy, 5.10b, 50
Bee Gees, 5.10d, 463
Beef and Bean, 5.10a, 142
BEETLE BUTTRESS, 109
Beetle Corner, 5.11a, 109
Beginner's Luck, 5.9, 194
Beginner's One, 5.3, 194
Beginner's Three, 5.3, 187
Beginner's Twenty-Six, 5.10c, 194
Beginner's Two, 5.2, 194
Behind the Green Door, 5.10d, 247
Behind the Scenes, 5.10a, 503
Belay Girl, 5.10c, 536
Bell-E-Up, 5.11c, 473
Bella Lugosi, 5.11c, 473
BELLE CAMPGROUND, 473
Belly Dancer, 5.10d, 473
Belly Scraper, 5.4, 207
Ben, 5.10b, 287
Bendix Claws, The, 5.11a, 459
Bent Over Backwards, 5.10c, 397
Berkeley Dyke, 5.8, 194
Berserk, 5.10a, 118
Beta Zoid, 5.11a A2, 331
Better You Than Me, 5.10b, 373
Betty Gravel, 5.7, 152
Betty Jo Yablonski, 5.10+ R, 149
Between a Rock and a Hard Place, 5.10b, 415
Beverly Drive, 5.10c (TR), 289
Bib Bird, 5.7+, 118
BIG ASS BOULDER, 482
Big Bob's Big Wedge, 5.11, 450
Big Boy, 5.9, 455
Big Brother, 5.11+, 387
Big Brother, 5.9, 392
BIG BROTHER BOULDER, 387
Big Brown Eye, 5.10d, 314
Big Dumb and Ugly, 5.7, 429
BIG HUNK, 250
Big Kahuna, 5.10+ (TR), 270
BIG LIE ROCK, THE, 349
Big Lie, The, 5.8, 264
Big Moe, 5.11a R, 234
Big Red Tractor, 5.11b (TR), 430
Big Sandy Bound, 5.11a X, 475
Big Step, 5.8 X, 537
BIG TOP, 510-511
Bighorn Bivvy, 5.8+, 25
Bighorn Dihedral, 5.10b, 71
BIGHORN DOME, 317
Bighorn Hand Crack, 5.7, 60
BIGHORN MATING GROTTO, 316
BIGHORN TERRACE, 316
Bike Across America, 5.10c, 455
Bikini Beach, 5.12b (TR), 170
Bikini Whale, 5.12a, 170
Bilbo, 5.9, 530
BILBO BUTTRESSES, THE, 531
Billabong, 5.10c, 186
BILLBOARD BUTTRESS, 530
Bimbo, 5.10a R/X, 33
Biological Clock, 5.9+, 131
Bird of Fire, 5.10a, 463
Bird on a Wire, 5.10a, 101
Birdland, 5.10c, 393
Birdman From Alcatraz, 5.10a, 138
Biscuit Eater, 5.10a, 214
Bisk, 5.4, 173
Biskering, 5.9, 172

Bitch in Heat, 5.9, 522
Bitch, Bitch, 5.7, 40
Bitchen', 5.10b (TR), 418
BITE ROCK, 148
Bitter Brew, 5.6 R, 533
Bittersweet, 5.10a, 508
Bivo Sham, 5.8, 328
Bivvy Kitten, 5.9, 507
Bivy at Gordon's, 5.4, 156
Black & Blue, 5.6, 123
Black Diamond, 5.2b R, 345
Black Eye, 5.9 R, 33
Black Hills Gold, 5.10b (TR), 258
Black Hole, 5.11c, 140
Black Ice, 5.10b R, 362
Black Like Night, 5.11d, 544
Black Lipstick, 5.8 R, 427
Black Nipple Fetish, 5.11b, 411
Black Panther, 5.11c, 457
Black Pea, 5.11, 192
Black Pearl, 5.10d, 350
Black Plastic Streetwalker, 5.10c R, 103
Black President, 5.11a, 314
Black Rhino, 5.9+, 503
BLACK ROCKS, THE, 333
Black Slacks, 5.10a, 298
Black Todd, 5.10, 159
BLACK TOWER, 544
Black Widow, 5.10c, 479
Blackout, 5.11a R, 94
Blank, The, 5.10, 198
Blazing Saddls, 5.10a, 544
Bleed Proof, 5.7, 68
Blind Man's Bluff, 5.11c, 377
Blind Me With Science, 5.10b, 118
Blistering, 5.5, 173
Blitzkrieg, 5.12a, 508
Blitzsteeg, 5.10b (TR), 427
Blizzard, 5.9, 131
BLOB AREA BOULDERING, 192-193
BLOB, THE, 192
BLOB, THE, 194
Block Buster, 5.10a, 351
Bloddymir, 5.9, 33
Blonde Bombshell Babylon, 5.8+, 82
Blonde Eyebrow Fetish, 5.10c, 75
Blood and Cuts, 5.9, 457
Blood of Christ, 5.11d/12a, 218
Bloodline, The, 5.12a, 345
Bloody Buddy, 5.9, 526
Bloody Knuckles, 5.10b, 375
Bloody Tax Break, 5.10b, 130
Bloom County, 5.6, 83
Blue Bayou, 5.4, 123
Blue Monday, 5.10b, 123
Blue Moon, 5.10b, 483
Blue Nubian, 5.10a, 181
BLUE NUBIAN WALL, 181
Blue Nun, 5.8, 123
Blue Ribbon, 5.11a R, 325
Blue Sky Mine, 5.10d (TR), 475
Blue Sky, Black Death, 5.5, 99
Blue Suede Shoes, 5.7, 453
Blue Velvet , 5.11d (TR), 47
Blues Brothers, 5.10a, 123
Bluewind, 5.10b, 526
Bob, 5.10a, 475
Body Shaving For Competition, 5.9, 345
Bold Is A Four Letter Word, 5.10a, 29
Bolivian Freeze Job, 5.9, 99
Bolt Heaven, 5.10 A1, 290
Bolt Ladder, A1, 361
Bolt, A Bashie and A Bold Mantel, A4 5.8, 223

Bolters Are Weak, 5.8 R, 27
Bombay, 5.8, 536
Bombs Over Libya, 5.12a, 301
Bonanza, 5.10b, 544
BOND BOULDERS, 467
Bone Along, 5.7, 383
Bonecrusher Arete, 5.8, 27
Bonfire, 5.11b, 516
Bong, The, 5.4, 194
Bongledesh, 5.10c, 185
Bonglett, The, 5.10a, 194
Bonnie Brae, 5.7, 474
Bonny's Boo-Boo, 5.9, 474
Bonor Donor, 5.10a, 375
Bonzo Dog Band, 5.7, 237
Boo Boo, 5.9 R, 85
Boogie Woogie Blues, The, 5.11c, 290
Boogs' Route, 5.10b, 78
Book of Brilliant Things, 5.12d, 75
Book of Changes, 5.10b, 316
Bookman Pitman, 5.6, 307
Boom Boom Boom, 5.9, 378
Boom Boom O'Hara, 5.5, 373
Boomerang, 5.7, 140
Boortemus, 5.10d, 540
Boot Hill, 5.10a, 330
Border Patrol, 5.11d , 520
BOREDOME ROCK, 405
Boris the Spider, 5.9, 519
Born To Be A Cowboy, 5.10c, 447
Borneo, 5.4, 107
Bosch Job, 5.11d R, 378
Bottle in Front of Me, 5.10a, 260
Boulder Crack, 5.10+, 367
Boulder Crack, 5.8, 40
Boulder Dash, 5.9, 234
Boulder Face, 5.7, 40
BOULDERING, 155
Boulevard of Dreams, 5.10b, 453
Bouncer, 5.8, 513
Bounder, The, 5.10b, 151
Bourbon on Ice, 5.10d, 540
BOVINE DOME, 477
Boys Don't Cry, 5.12a, 358
Bozo Buttress, 5.1, 295
Bozo's Raindance, 5.11c, 295
Brain Damage, 5.12a, 263
Brain Death, 5.12a, 263
Brain Fart, 5.11c (TR), 397
Brain, The, 5.7, 298
Bran New, 5.5, 209
Brass Monkey, 5.12a, 308
Break A Leg, 5.9 R, 132
Break Dancing, 5.11a, 200
Breakfast of Champions, 5.8+, 290
Breaking Away, 5.11a (TR), 49
BREAKING AWAY CLIFF, 49
Breath of Death, 5.11a, 269
Brew 102, 5.8, 92
Briar Rabbit, 5.7, 508
Bride of Frankenstein, 5.12a (TR), 473
Bridge of Sighs, 5.11b, 541
Bridge Too Far, A, 5.10a, 430
Bridge, The, 5.10d R, 524
Bridge-It Bardot, 5.10d, 310
Brief Case, 5.10c (TR), 158
Bright Moments, 5.9, 482
Brimstone Stairway, 5.1, 513
BRIT CORRIDOR, 465
British Airways, 5.11a R, 245
Brits in Drag, 5.10b, 465
Broken Bits, 5.9, 307
Broken China, 5.10b, 34

Broken Glass, 5.10a, 151
Broken Noses, 5.3, 402
Broken Wing, 5.10c, 315
BRONTO ROCK, 486
Bronto's Or Us, The, 5.11a, 111
Brothre from Another Planet, 5.11a R, 131
Brown 25, 5.10d R, 161
Brown Cave, 5.2, 521
Brown OUt, 5.12b/c (TR), 241
Brown Squeeze, 5.10b, 199
BROWN WALL, THE, 161
Brownian Motion, 5.10c, 161
Brownie Points, 5.9+, 46
Bruiser, The, 5.10c, 214
Brush Your Teeth with Jesus, 5.10c, 377
Brutus, 5.9+, 429
Bryant Gumbel, 5.8, 92
BUBBA ROCK, 44
Bubba's Tourist Trap, 5.9, 474
Bublinki, 5.8, 480
Bucket Brigade, 5.7, 234
Bucket Bronco, 5.10a, 544
Buckets to Burbank, 5.8, 387
Buckeye, 5.4, 486
Buckwheat, 5.10a R, 209
Buenos Aires, 5.10as, 385
Buffalo Soldier, 5.12b, 225
Buford's House of Liver, 5.11a, 286
Buissonier, 5.7, 192
Bulbisness, 5.11b (TR), 425
Bulkhead Arete, 5.10b R, 549
BULKHEAD, THE, 549
Bullet Head, 5.11a, 130
Bullocks Fashion Center, 5.8, 392
Bunking Broncos, 5.10a, 461
Bunnies, 5.12a (TR), 384
Buried Treasure, 5.11c, 420
Burn Bush, 5.10a, 287
Burn Out, 5.10b, 158
Burning Bush, 5.12c/13a, 218
Bury Me With My Boots On, 5.9 R, 546
Bush Crack, 5.7, 120
BUSH DOME, 90
Bush Eviction, 5.9, 362
Bush Eviction Direct, 5.10c, 362
Business Trip, 5.4, 205
Buster Brown, 5.9, 46
Buster Hymen, 5.9, 418
Busy Bees, 5.7, 436
But Fear Itself, 5.8, 401
BUTLER CORRIDOR, 310
Butt Buttress, The, 5.10b, 168
Butterfingers Make Me Horny, 5.8/9, 166
Butterfly Crack, 5.11c, 32
Button High, B1 R, 176
Button Soup, 5.2, 224
Buyer Beware, 5.10a R, 141
C Lunch, 5.6 R, 517
C Sharp Roof, 5.10c, 82
C.F.M.F., 5.8 R/X, 198
C.S. Special, 5.10b, 237
CACTUS CITY, 546
Cactus Cooler, 5.10b, 550
CACTUS COOLER ARETES, 71
Cactus Dog, 5.9, 307
Cactus Flower, 5.11b, 381
CACTUS FLOWER TOWERS, 339
Cactus Pete's , 5.10a R, 546
CACTUS SLUMP, THE, 350
Caesar, 5.10b, 429
Cake Walk, 5.6, 474
Cake Walk, 5.9, 96
Calcutta, 5.7+, 536

Calgary Stampede, 5.9, 50
California Crack, 5.11a R, 5353
Caligula, 5.9, 247
Calling All Swidgets, 5.10b, 137
Camouflage, 5.12c, 201
Camp Whote, 5.11a, 369
Campcraft, 5.9, 201
CAMPFIRE CRAG — SOUTH FACE, 517
CAMPFIRE CRAGS — NORTH FACE, 516
Campfire Girl, 5.11d (TR), 516
CAMPSITE NO. 4, 392
Canalizo, 5.10c, 483
Candelabra, 5.10a R, 210
CANDLESTEIN PASS, 123
CANDY BAR, THE, 246-256
Canine Crack, 5.9+, 25
CANYON ENTRANCE ROUTES, 538
CAP ROCK, 360
CAP ROCK, 362
CAP ROCK BOULDERING, 367
Captain Kronos, 5.7, 161
Captain Safe, 5.10b, 453
Caramel Crunch, 5.10a, 389
Card Chimney, 5.5, 38
Caribbean Cruie, 5.11c, 419
Carmania, 5.7, 538
Carnage, 5.10c, 438
Carola's Hip, 5.7, 392
Carolyn's Rump, 5.4, 204
Carrot, 5.8, 364
Carved Scoop, 5.6, 193
Cary Granite, 5.3, 219
Cashews Will Be Eaten, 5.8, 248
Cast Up A Highway, 5.11a (TR), 96
Castaway, 5.11c, 419
CASTLE ROCK, 473-474
CASTLE, THE, 79
Castles Burning, 5.12a, 534
Castrum, The, 5.10a, 534
Casual, 5.9, 385
Casual Affair, 5.10d, 459
Cat in the Hat, The, 5.10a, 413
Cat on a Hot Tin Roof, 5.10c, 385
Cat Paws, 5.10b, 483
CAT PINNACLE, 421
Cat's Meow, 5.9, 399
Catapult, 5.11b, 76
Catch a Falling Car, 5.11a, 362
Catch a Falling Star, 5.8, 362
Catch Me at the Bar, 5.10a, 362
Cats Claws, 5.11a, 83
Caught Inside on A Big Set, 5.10b, 316
CAVE CORRIDOR, 389
Cave Man, 5.11, 228
CAVE MAN CRAG, 139
CAVE ROCK, 402
Caveman, B2, 190
CAVEMAN BOULDER, 190
CAVERN ROCK, 392
Caverna Magica, 5.10d R, 400
Cayenne, 5.11c, 256
Cedric's Deep Sea Fish Market, 5.10d, 415
Cellbound, 5.5, 523
Celtic Vator, 5.10c, 479
Cementary, 5.8, 298
CENTER CRAG, 523
Center of Gravity, 5.10c (TR), 400
Central Scrutinizer, B1 X, 193
Centurion, 5.10d, 416
Ceramic Bus, 5.11c R, 530
Cereal Killer, 5.6, 209
CEREAL ROCK, 209
Cerebal Dysfunction, 5.10a, 260

Ceremony, 5.10c, 105
Ceroots of the Gods, 5.10b, 351
CERRO TORRE AREA, 263
CERRO TORRE TOWER, 263
Chaffe n' Up, 5.8 R, 118
Chain of Addiction, 5.13c, 64
CHAIR, THE, 250
Chalk Up Another One, 5.9+, 199
Chamber of Commerce, 5.10c, 123
Chameleon, The, 5.12b, 169
Championship Wrestling, 5.10a, 155
Chance Meeting, 5.6 A3, 436
Chaos, 5.11b, 244
Chapter 7, 5.6, 285
Character Flaw, 5.10c, 521
Charles Chips, 5.9, 139
Charles In Charge, 5.9, 139
Charles Who?, 5.11c, 139
Charlie Brown, 5.9, 261
Charlotte's Web, 5.11a, 451
Chase Lounge, 5.11b, 511
Chatty Baby, 5.7, 344
Cheap Thrills, 5.11a (TR), 87
Cheap Way to Die, A, 5.10d, 378
Cheese, 5.11a (TR), 142
Cheese Grater, B1, 190
Cheese Grater, The, 5.11a, 447
Cheetah, 5.12b, 244
Cheez-It, The, 5.10d, 250
Cheezels, 5.9+ R, 229
Chemical Warefare, 5.10b, 278
Cherry Blossom, 5.9, 260
Cherry Bomb, 5.10c, 242
Chessboard, The, 5.8 R, 534
Chestwig, 5.10a, 90
Chicago Nipple Slump, 5.11c (TR), 215
Chick Flakey, 5.11b, 254
Chicken, 5.10a (TR), 142
Chicken Bones, 5.4, 254
CHICKEN BOULDER, 443
Chicken Little, 5.7+ (TR), 443
Chicken Lizard, 5.10b, 88
Chicken Mechanics, 5.9, 94
Chicken Run, 5.11d, 443
Chicken Wing, 5.9, 270
Chief Crazy Horse, 5.12a, 68
Child's Play, 5.10d (TR), 166
Chile Willie, 5.7, 99
Chili Dog, 5.6, 131
Chilly Willy, 5.10c, A1, 111
Chimney, 5.8, 163
CHIMNEY ROCK, 200-201
Chimney Sweep, 5.0, 473
Chimps and Cheetahs, 5.9, 441
CHIPPED ROCK, 537
Chipped Suey, 5.7, 537
Chips Ahoy, 5.7, 237
Chivalry's Not Dead, 5.7, 533
Chockstone Chimney, 4th Class, 537
Chocolate Chips, 5.9, 391
Chocolate Decadence, 5.7, 53
Chocolate Is Better Than Sex, 5.9+, 166
Chocolate Snake, 5.6, 133
Cholla Crack, 5.10b, 413
Chongo Bolt Route, 5.11b, 188
CHONGO BOULDER, THE, 238
Christmas Tree Arete, 5.10c, 347
Chuck Wagon Crack, 5.9, 543
Chuckawalla, 5.10, 228
CHUCKAWALLA BOULDER, 228
Church Bazaar, 5.10c, 188
Chute to Kill, 5.10c, 294
Chute to Kill, 5.11a, 59

Chute Up, 5.2, 233
Cinnamon Girl, 5.10d, 74
Circe, 5.6, 205
CIRCLE CRAG, 517
Circus, 5.2, 362
Circus Act, 5.10c, 261
Circus, Circus, 5.9, 362
CIRQUE OF THE CLIMBABLES, 347
CITADEL, THE, 442
City Council, 5.9, 123
City H, 5.8, 330
Claim Jumper, 5.11a, 469
Clam Shell, 5.9, 375
Clamming at the Beach, 5.9, 50
Classic Corner, 5.7, 109
Classic Curl, 5.10+, 176
Classic Thin Crack, 5.11, 233
Clean and Jerk, 5.10c, 155
CLEAN CRACK, 5.10b, 56
CLEAN CRACK FORMATION, 56
Cleared for Landing, 5.8, 477
Cleared for Takeoff, 5.11a, 456
Cleavage, 5.10c, 455
Cleopatra, 5.11a, 259
Click Your Heels Twice, 5.10c, 491
Cliff Hanger, 5.10b R, 111
Climb of the Cockroaches, 5.8 R, 109
Climb of the Sentry, 5.5, 167
Cling or Fling, 5.11a, 464
CLING OR FLING CORRIDOR, 464
Cling Peaches, 5.9 R, 379
Closed on Mondays, 5.10a, 246
CLUMP CANYON, 518
CLUSTER, THE, 175
Coarse and Buggy, 5.11a, 136
Cobra Cunning, 5.9 R, 462
COCKROACH CRAG, 109
COCKROACH CRAGS, 335
Cockroach, The, 5.12d/13a, 335
Coco-Loco, 5.10b, 534
Cohatoes, 5.8, 351
COHN PROPERTY, THE, 133
Cold Columbian, 5.9, 99
Cold War, 5.10b, 349
Cole Arete, 5.11+, 226
COLE BOULDER, 226
Cole Face, 5.11+, 226
Cole Salw, 5.10c, 184
Cole-Evans, 5.10a, 242
Cole-Gordon Offwidth, 5.10c, 301
Cole-Lewis, 5.9, 97
Cole-Lewis, The, 5.10a, 68
Coliseum, The, 5.10b, 79
Colon Blow, 5.7 R, 373
Colorado Crack, 5.9, 445
Colossus, 5.8, 503
Colossus of Rhoids, The, 5.11a, 148
Combination Locks, 5.11c, 263
Come-N-Do-Me, 5.10b, 208
Comfortably Numb, 5.11, 210
Comic Book, 5.10a, 261
COMIC BOOK AREA, THE, 258-264
Comic Relief, 5.11a, 158
COMIC STRIP, THE, 261
Coming Up Short, 5.10a , 165
Commander Cody, 5.7, 130
COMMISSIONER BUTTRESSES, 551
Commitments Are kFor Me, 5.8, 206
Common Law Marriage, 5.10c, 73
Compact Physical, 5.11c, 71
Compassion of the Elephants, The, 5.10c, 247
Compound W, 5.11b (TR), 153
CONAN'S CORRIDOR, 445

Conceived in Idaho, 5.8, 405
Conceptual Continuity, 5.11c (TR), 181
CONDOR ROCK, 525
Condor, The, 5.11d, 525
Confessional, 5.10b R, 83
Congratulations, 5.11a (TR), 166
Conniption, 5.10b, 526
CONRAD ROCK, 373
Conservative Policies, 5.8, 166
CONSORT ROCK, 328
Construction Blues, 5.6, 405
Continuum, 5.8+, 459
Control, 5.10a, 244
Controversial, 5.9, 258
Conundrum, The, 5.11c, 338
Cool But Concerned, 5.11d, 155
Cool But Not Too Concerned, 5.12c (TR), 155
Cool City, 5.10b, 355
COOL DOME, 50
Cool Move, Gritty Rock, Standard Procedure, 5.10c, 482
Cool Thing, 5.12b, 548
Cool Wind, 5.10a, 530
COPENHAGEN WALL, 130
Copper Penny, 5.11+ R, 200
Copperhead, 5.11b, 319
Corner, 5.10, 271
Corner n' Crack, 5.10a, 440
Cornered, 5.4, 174
Cornerstone, The, 5.10a, 241
CORNERSTONE, THE, 321
CORONA WALL, 520
CORRAL WALL, 543-544
CORRIDOR FACE, 445
Cosmic Book, 5.10c, 265
Cosmic Debris, 5.10a, 296
Cosmic Trigger, 5.13a, 433
Cosmosis, 5.10a, 521
Cottonmouth, 5.6 X, 533
Cough Up Phlem, 5.7, 161
Count Dracula, 5.10d, 473
Count on Your Fingers, 5.9, 166
Courier's Tragedy, Act IV, Scene 8, 5.8, 277
Court Jester, 5.7, 534
COVE CANYON DOME, 538
Cow Pie Corner, 5.6, 163
Cowardly Lion, The, 5.9+, 501
COWBOY CRAGS, 379
Cowboy Junkie, 5.11c, 352
Cows in the Shade, 5.9, 482
Coyote Bait, 5.7+, 126
Coyote Crack, 5.7, 477
Coyote Crack, 5.9, 544
Coyote Eggs, 5.10d, 276
Coyote in the Bushes, 5.10a, 534
Crack, 5.10d, 429
Crack, 5.9, 233
Crack #2, 5.6, 464
Crack #4, 5.10c, 464
Crack #5, 5.9+, 464
Crack #6, 5.10a, 464
Crack 'n' Up, 5.10b (TR), 486
Crack 69, 5.5, 519
Crack A, 5.7+, 464
Crack Addiction, 5.10b, 471
Crack B, 5.9, 464
Crack C, 5.10c, 464
Crack Kills, 5.10c, 485
Crack of Dark, 5.10b, 309
Crack Queen, 5.11a, 353
Crack Worthy, 5.6, 326
Cracked Actor, 5.9, 538
Crackup, 5.7, 482
Crank City, B1 X, 176

Crank Queenie, 5.8, 529
Cranking Skills or Hospital Bills, 5.10d, 141
Cranny, 5.8, 33
Crash Course, 5.10b, 247
Crash, The, 5.12c, 49
Crazy Climber, 5.11a, 118
Cream Puff, 5.8, 351
Creamy Peanut Butter, 5.11c 9TRT), 196
Creature Feature, 5.11b, 383
Credibility Gap, 5.9, 241
Creditor's Claim, 5.7, 285
CREEPER ROCK, 450
Creme Egg, 5.9 (TR), 254
Crescent Wrench, 5.10d, 36
Cretin Bull Dancer, 5.11a, 100
Crime of the Century, 5.11a, 252
Crimp or Wimp, 5.10d (TR), 141
Crimping Lessons, 5.10a, 290
Cripple Crack, 5.10b, 181
CROCODILE ROCK, 469
Cross Fire, 5.12a R, 406
Crossroads, 5.10d, 239
Crow's Feet, 5.7, 397
Crow's Nest, The, 5.11+, 67
Crowded Mental Hospital, 5.13b, 319
Crown Jewels, 5.10a, 342
Crown Jewels, 5.7, 534
CROWS' NEST, 397
Cruelty to Animals, 5.10a, 181
Cruising for Burgers, 5.10c, 261
Crumble Cake, 5.7, 516
Cryogenics, 5.11c, 250
Cryptic, 5.8, 370
Crystal Calisthenics, 5.10a, 379
Crystal Deva, 5.10c, 79
Crystal Keyhole, 5.9, 168
CRYSTAL QUARRY, 79
Crystal Voyager, 5.10d, 331
Cuban Connection, 5.8 R, 535
Cuddlebone, 5.7, 285
CUDDLEBONE DOME, THE, 285
Cunning Linquist, 5.8, 445
Cunning Route, 5.10a, 447
Curtain Call, 5.6, 132
Custer Was Here, 5.4, 258
Cut Thin to Win, 5.10c, 439
Cut to the Bone, 5.10c, 317
Cute the Moon, 5.6, 538
Cutting Edge, The, 5.13b, 371
CYCLOPS BOULDERING, 203-206
CYCLOPS BOULDERS, THE, 203
CYCLOPS ROCK, 204-206
Cyclotron, 5.8 to 5.10d, 414
Cyndie's Brain, 5.10a, 209
Czech Cows Say Boo, 5.9+, 464
Czech Crack, 5.10a, 544
CZECH DOME, 165
D.B.'s Toprope, 5.12b, 518
D.E. Chimney, The, 5.6, 240
Daddy Long Legs, 5.11a, 140
DAIRY QUEEN WALL, 131
DAKOTA DOMES, THE, 258
Damm Dike, 5.7, 277
Damn Jam, 5.6, 199
Damper, 5.9, 200
Dan Cruise, 5.7, 440
Dance on Fire, 5.11a R, 26
Dances with Poodles, 5.12a, 246
Dancin' Daze, 5.8, 484
Dancing on Dimes, 5.7, 512
Dandelion, 5.10a, 189
Dangling Digit, 5.8, 497
Dangling Woo Li Master, 5.10a, 316

Danny Gore, 5.10d, 174
Dappled Mare, 5.8, 101
Dark Ages, 5.10a, 470
DARK SHADOWS ROCK, 533
Darrens Scrape Scramble and Ramble, 5.6, 397
DARWIN DOME, 405
Date Queen, 5.8, 524
Date Queen Corridor Crack, 5.11b R, 524
Date Rape, 5.9, 97
Date Shake, 5.6, 131
Datura, 5.12a R, 516
Dave Ate The Cookie, 5.11d (TR), 501
Dave's Solo, 5.9, 242
Dawn Yawn, 5.11d, 73
Daze of Who, 5.10a, 264
Dazed and Confused, 5.9, 298
Dead Bees, 5.9 R, 463
Dead Man's Eyes, 5.11b, 217
Dead Man's Party, 5.10b R, 103
Deadheads, 5.4, 513
Death by Chocolate, 5.11b, 252
Death by Misadventure, 5.10c X, 186
Death of A Decade, 5.10a, 269
Death on the Nile, 5.10a, 234
Death Rides a Pale Horse, 5.8, 430
Debbie Does Donuts, 5.6, 531
Deceit, 5.7, 427
Decent Buckets, 5.2, 158
Deception, 5.10a, 369
Deceptive Corner, 5.7, 234
Decompensator of Lhasa, The, 5.10d, 211
Deep Throat, 5.9, 247
Deep, Shallow and Twisted, 5.10c, 467
Defender, 5.11c (TR), 511
DEFENDER BLOCK, 511
Defenders of the Farce, 5.10a, 413
Defibrillation, 5.10a, 419
Deflowered, 5.6, 211
Defoliation, 5.9, 322
Dehorned Unicorn, 5.9+, 437
Deja Vu, 5.10a, 264
Delightful Lady, 5.10b (TR), 178
Deliver Us From Evil, 5.8 R, 294
Delusions, 5.10c, 339
DEMON DOME, 400
DEN OF DOOM, 382
DENTAL DOME, 420
Dental Hygiene, 5.8, 276
Descent, 5.5, 190
Descent Crack, 5.2, 464
Desert Delirium, 5.10a, 323
DESERT ISLAND, 421
Desert Profit, 5.11d, 428
Desert Queen, 5.8, 470
DESERT QUEEN DOME, 429
DESERT QUEEN MINE AREA, 423
Desert Shield, 5.12d, 172
Desert Solitaire, 5.7, 450
Desert Song, 5.11b R, 169
Desert Storm, 5.10a, 449
Desert Storm, 5.10c, 308
Desert Whale, 5.11c, 548
Desiderious Delight, 5.4, 476
DESIRE ROCK, 482
Desperado, 5.10a, 160
Desperado, 5.10b, 541
Destination Unknown, 5.11d, 470
Deviate, 5.10a, 188
Devil Inside, 5.10c, 364
Dhip, 5.10d, 329
Diabetic Shock, 5.10c, 487
Diabetics, 5.4, 473
Diagnostics, 5.6, 473

Diagonal Chimney, 5.6, 196
Dial Africa, 5.12c, 225
Dial-a-Pile, 5.5, 130
Dialing for Ducats, 5.10b, 194
DIAMOND CLUMP, 416
Diamond Dogs, 5.10a, 384
Diamondback, 5.10d, 212
Diamonds Are Forever, 5.10d, 467
Diaper Challenge, 5.11c, 418
DIARRHEA DOME, 314
Dick Enberg, 5.11c, 155
Dick Vandike, 5.10b (TR), 111
Dictators of Anarchy, 5.12c, 413
Didn't Your Mama Ever Tell You About A Stranger's Bolts,
5.9, 295
Die Young, 5.9, 483
Die-Hedral, 5.7, 271
Dig Me, 5.11b (TR), 428
Digital Watch, 5.10d R, 38
Digitalis Destructi, 5.11c, 175
Digitizer, 5.11b, 402
DIHEDRAL ROCK, 136
Dihedralman, 5.13a, 75
Dike A Rama, 5.11a, 429
Dike Da Doodad, 5.10c, 421
Dike Flight, 5.10+, 457
DIKE ROCK, 429
Dike, The, 5.10c R, 111
Dilly Bar, 5.5, 131
Dimorphism, 5.7, 73
Dimp For A Chimp, 5.11b, 225
Dinkey Doinks, 5.8, 97
Dino's Egg, 5.10, 226
DINO'S EGG BOULDER, 226
DINOSAUR ROCK, 220-221
DINOSAUR ROCK BOULDERINGHobbit Hole Offwidth,
5.10—, 228
Direct South Face, 5.9, 522
Direct Start, 5.10a, 126
Direct Start, 5.10b, 126
Direct Wrench, 5.11a (TR), 36
Dirty Cat, 5.10c (TR), 371
Dirty Dancing, 5.10a, 200
Dirty Surprise, 5.9, 304
Dirty Tricks, 5.11d, 264
Disappearing Act, 5.10c, 459
Disappearing Belayer, 5.7, 513
DISAPPOINTMENT DOME, 67
DISASTER DOME, 301
Disco Sucks, 5.10c, 192
Discoy Decoy, 5.11a, 155
DISLODGE ROCK, 437
DISNEYLAND DOME, 310
DISNEYLAND DOMES, 308-309
Diso Sucks, 5.6, 529
Disobedience School, 5.10c, 252
Disposable Heroes, 5.8, 503
Disposition Cervice, 5.11b, 374
Disrythmia, 5.12a, 248
DISSATISFACTION ROCK, 482
DISSOLUTION ROCK, 279
Distant Episode, 5.10c, 260
DMB, The, 5.9, 73
Do or Dike, 5.9, 485
DOA, 5.8, 513
Doc Holiday, 5.10a, 544
Dodo's Delight, 5.10a, 178
Does Royalty Give Head, 5.10c, 483
Dog Day Afternoon, 5.10b, 381
Dogleg, 5.8, 189
Dogleg Right, 5.10c, 521
Doin' Life, 5.10a, 385
Doin' Some Damage, 5.10c, 400

Doing That Scrapyard Thing, 5.10d, 223
Dolphin, 5.7, 463
Dominatrix, 5.10d, 316
DON GENERO CLIFFS, 319
Don Genero Crack, 5.10a, 524
DON JUAN BOULDER, 288
Don't, 5.10a, 483
Don't Be Nosey, 5.10d (TR), 154
Don't Bosch Me Around, 5.10d, 345
Don't Dick With Walt, 5.10c, 199
Don't Even Look, 5.9, 374
Don't Have A Cow, 5.9+, 163
Don't Look A Gift Frong in the Mouth, 5.9, 170
Don't Think Just Jump, 5.10a, 252
Don't Think Twice, 5.9, 125
Don't Touch That Flake, 5.9, 260
Don't Touch That Friend, 5.10a, 541
Don't Tred On Me, 5.10b (TR), 106
Don't Waltz With Dick, 5.10d (TR), 199
Donna T's Route, 5.5, 537
Donut Holes, 5.9+, 351
Doom De Doom Doom, 5.7 (TR), 382
Doomed, 5.6, 382
Doomsday, 5.9+, 382
Dorothy Does The Wizard, 5.10b, 496
DOROTHY'S CRAG, 496
Dos Dedos, 5.4, 419
DOS EQUIS WALL, 520
Double Crack, 5.3, 537
Double Cross, 5.7+, 189
DOUBLE CROSS ROCKS, 426
Double Crux, 5.8, 529
Double Decker, 5.6, 131
Double Delight, 5.7, 131
Double Dip, 5.6, 242
Double Doglet, 5.7, 98
Double Duty, 5.10c, 436
Double Jeoparty, 5.10c R, 384
Double Start, 5.7, 189
Double Trouble, 5.10a (TR), 536
Double Trouble, 5.11b (TR), 476
Dover Sole, 5.6, 39
Down Where The Goblins Go, 5.10b, 497
Downpour, 5.8, 113
Dr. Garlic Breath, 5.10a, 477
Dr. Scholl's Wild Ride, 5.10a, 67
Dr. Seuss Vogel, 5.7, 118
Drano, 5.10a, 263
Draw the Line, 5.10a (TR), 407
Drawstring, 5.7, 186
Dream of White Poodles, A, 5.8, 242
Dreamer, 5.10d, 439
Dreaming of the Master, B2, 371
Dreams of Red Rocks, 5.7, 58
DREAMSCAPE DOME, 342
Dreamworld, 5.10b, 464
Driving Limitations, 5.8, 530
Drop a Frog, 5.9, 79
Drop Your Drawers, 5.9, 79
Drugs But No Drills, 5.9, 354
Druids, The, 5.8, 351
Dry Lake, 5.10b R, 535
Dry Rain, 5.7, 526
Duchess, 5.6, 534
Duchess Left, 5.4, 534
Duchess Right, 5.7, 534
DUCKWADDLE DOMES, 309
Duke, The, 5.9 A1, 288
Dum Roodle, 5.6, 534
DUMB DOME, 310
Dummy's Delight, 5.9, 178
Dunce Cap, 5.13a, 362
Dunce Cap, The, 5.10c, 70

DUNCE CAP, THE, 70
Dung Fu, 5.7, 126
Dungeon, The, 5.9+, 109
Duplicity, 5.8 R, 427
DUTZI ROCK, 222
Dwarf Star, 5.10c (TR), 394
Dweeb, 5.7, 429
DWEEB SPIRE, 252
Dwindling Greenbacks, 5.11a R, 82
Dynamic Panic, 5.11d, 188
Dynamo Hum, 5.10+, 190
Dyno in the Dark, 5.10b, 200
Dyno-Soar, 5.10c A1, 221
Early Bird, 5.9+, 307
Earn Quick or Die, 5.9, 160
EARTH FIRST ROCK, 446
EAST COVE, 239
East Face, 5.10a, 480
East Face, 5.9, 190
EAST FACE, 327
EAST FACE, 439
EAST FACE, 461
East Meets West, 5.7 R, 529
East of India, 5.10a, 373
EAST VIRGIN ISLANDS, 418
Easter Overflow, 5.9, 507
Easy As PI, 5.7, 128
Easy Day, 5.4, 173
Easy JBMFP, B1, 146
Easy Looker, 5.6, 272
Easy Off, 5.6, 418
Eat What You Secrete, 5.7, 304
Eating Crow, 5.5, 397
Eating Gorilla Comes in Peace, The, 5.10d, 462
EBGB AREA, 244
EBGB's, 5.10d, 244
Echo Buttress, 5.10b (TR), 233
ECHO COVE, 233
ECHO COVE, 234
ECHO COVE BOULDERING, 233-237
ECHO COVE FORMATIONS, 240
Echo of a Scream, 5.10a, 374
ECHO ROCK, 242
ECHO ROCK, 235
ECHO ROCK AREA, 229
Edchada, 5.7, 263
Eddie Hasel Takes Manhattan, 5.10b, 154
Edgar Rice Burros, 5.10c, 101
Edge of Doom, 5.10c, 115
Edge of the Knife, 5.8, 413
Edge, The, 5.10b, 482
Edukashun President, The, 5.10c, 439
Eff Eight, 5.8, 247
Eff Four, 5.6, 242
Effigy Too, 5.10a/b, 239
Eight Signs of a Shaky Marriage, 5.10d, 410
EL DORADO, 56
El Pollo Loco, 5.10c, 443
El Rey, 5.10c R, 535
El Smear Or Land, 5.10b, 53
Elbow Room, 5.10d, 116
Electric Birthday Party, 5.12b, 461
Electric Blue, 5.11c, 248
Electric Eye, 5.11b, 250
Electric Tree Gordon, 5.12a R, 131
Elementary Jamming, 5.5, 405
ELEPHANT ARCHES, 314
ELEPHANT DOME, 159
Elephant Walk, 5.11d, 406
Elevenfall Face, 5.11d (TR), 411
Elijah's Coming, 5.10b R, 185
ELLSMERE ISLAND, 52
Elmer Fudd, 5.11b (TR), 104

Elusive Butterfly Arete, 5.6 (TR), 222
Elusive kButterfly, 5.6, 222
Elvis Is Everywhere, 5.10c, 453
Elvis Lives, 5.11d, 345
EMASCULATION ROCK, 497
EMERALD CITY, 499
EMERALD CITY, 501
Emotional Rescue, 5.12a, 277
EMPIRE WALL, 510
Empty Street, 5.10c, 75
Enchanted Stairway, 5.9, 308
END LOOP AREA, 541
End of the Line, 5.9+, 450
Endangered Species, 5.10c, 503
ENDANGERED SPECIES DOME, 487
Endless Summer, 5.9, 300
Endorphine, 5.10d, 353
Enforcer, The, 5.9, 214
Ennui, 5.10b, 405
Enos Mills Glacier, 5.11a R, 100
Enter at Your Own Risk, 5.9, 392
Enter the Dragon, 5.9, 271
Enterprise, The, 5.9 (TR), 480
ENTRANCE BOULDER, 149
Environment-Oil President, The, 5.10c, 455
Episcopalian Toothpick, 5.10c, 377
EPPERSON BOULDER, 443
Epperson's Footprints, 5.10a, 443
Equinox, 5.12c, 406
Erca, 5.11a, 467
Erotic City, 5.11b, 41
EROTIC DOME, 40-41
Escape (Var.), 5.10c, 206
Escape From The Planet Earth, 5.10a, 274
ESCAPE ROCK, 274
Eschar, 5.4, 33
Euhedral, 5.7, 538
Euphrates, 5.11c, 316
Euthyphro, 5.9, 98
Evening At The Improv, 5.11a, 326
Evening Warm-Down, 5.2, 394
Event Horizon, 5.10b R, 362
Every Which Way But Up, 5.12b, 461
Evoluntionary Thorwback, 5.10c, 273
EVOLUTION ROCK, 405
Excitable Boy, 5.9, 84
Exfoliation Confrontation, 5.9+, 543
Exhibit A, 5.10a, 247
EXHIBIT ROCK, 446
Exhibitionist, 5.10d (TR), 446
Exiled, 5.10a, 129
Exiled in Sweden, 5.10d, 549
Existential Decay, 5.12d R, 300
Exit Stage Right, 5.9, 274
Exorcist, 5.10a, 384
Experiential Ed., 5.9, 49
Exploding Brown Nudules, 5.11c, 459
Extra Chunky, 5.10b, 256
Eye, The, 5.1, 205
Eyes of Amber, 5.7, 533
Eyes Without A Face, 5.10b, 323
Eyestrain , 5.2, 33
F.U.N., 5.10c (TR), 237
Fabulous T. Gordex Cracks, The, 5.8, 109
Face, 5.10, 193
Face, 5.11a (TR), 238
Face, 5.11a (TR), 364
Face It, 5.10a (TR), 224
Face of Mucis, 5.10c (TR), 201
Face of Tammy Faye, The, 5.8, 166
Face Race, 5.10a (TR), 429
Face to Face, 5.11c (TR), 536
Falcon, The, 5.10b, 525

Fall From Grace, 5.10c, 242
Fall Line, 5.10c, 354
Fallun (All in Fun), 5.7, 441
False Blockhead, 5.11+, 146
False Layback, 5.4, 362
FALSE MOOSEDOG TOWER, 447
False Prophet, 5.9, 362
False Smooth As Silk, 5.7, 95
False TKO, 5.10d, 139
False Tumbling Rainbow, 5.8, 150
False Up 20, 5.9+, 146
FALSE UP 20 BOULDER, 146
Family Fued, 5.11+, 228
Family Rock How's Your Papa, B1, 228
Famous Potatoes, 5.11c, 64
Fang, The, 5.11b R, 189
Fantails, 5.8, 229
Fantasia, 5.10b, 308
Fantasy of Light, 5.10a, 105
Far Side of Crazy, 5.10b R, 136
Far Side, The, 5101
Farewell To Poodles, A, 5.9, 128
Fascist Groove Thing, 5.11a (TR), 181
FAT FREDDIE'S CAT, 306-307
Fat Freddie's Escape, 5.8, 305
Fat Is Where It's At, 5.8, 426
Fat Man's Folly, 5.8, 276
Fat Man's Misery, 5.6 R, 516
Fatal Flaw, 5.8, 97
Father Figure, 5.12d, 277
Father Ocean, 5.12b (TR), 381
Fatty Winds His Neck Out, 5.10d R, 199
Fax Man, 5.9, 327
Fear Is Never Boring, 5.12a, 330
Fear of Flying, 5.10d, 200
Fear of Music, 5.11b, 425
Feast, 5.11, 517
Feathers, 5.11b, 442
Feats Don't Fail Me Now, 5.9 R, 245
Feeding Frenzy, 5.10b, 310
Feeding the Rat, 5.11b, 181
Feeling Groovy, 5.10a, 247
Feltoneon Physics, 5.8, 126
Female Mud Massacre, 5.10a (TR), 211
FEUDAL WALL, THE, 534-535
Fiasco, The, 5.9/10, 67
Fidget With Swidgets, 5.8+, 137
Fields of Laughter, 5.6 X, 307
Fiendish Fists, 5.9, 111
Fifteen Minute Gap, 5.6, 264
Fighting the Slime, 5.9, 132
Figurehead, 5.9, 394
Figures on a Landscape, 5.10b, 293
Filch, 5.5, 32
Filet of Cole, 5.10b, 480
Filet of Rock Shark, 5.10b, 216
FILIPINO WALL, 129
Filth, 5.8 R, 32
Filthy Rich, 5.8, 272
Final Act, 5.4, 132
Finally, 5.4, 518
FINANCIAL WALL, 49
FINCH DOME, 405
Finger Bowl, 5.12a, 485
Finger Food, 5.10a, 246
Finger Food, 5.10b, 250
Finger Locking Good, 5.7, 450
Finger Stacks or Plastic Sacks, 5.10b, 50
Fingerlocks or Cedar Box, 5.5, 450
Fingers of Frenzy, 5.12a (TR), 438
Fingers on a Landscape, 5.11b, 222
Fingerstack or Plastic Sack, 5.9+, 156
Fingertip Pleasure, 5.10c (TR), 161

FINGERTIP ROCK, 161
Fingertip Traverse of Josh, 5.8, 135
Fire Glove, The, 5.10a, 436
FIRE ME A BURGER ROCK, 284
Fire or Retire, 5.10c, 141
Fire or Retire, Direct Finish, 5.10b R, 141
Fire'e or Retire'e, B1, 203
Firefly, 5.11b (TR), 471
FIREFLY ROCK, 471
First Eleven, 5.11a, 386
First Steps, 5.8, 71
FISH ROCK, 67
Fishing Trip, 5.9, 330
Fissure Merde, 5.8, 447
Fissure of Fish, 5.9, 304
Fissure of Men, 5.1, 218
Fissure Todd, 5.10b, 274
Fist Full of Crystals, 5.10c, 211
Fist Full of Walnuts, 5.11+, 176
Fistfull of Bush, 5.4, 221
Fisticuffs, 5.10b, 170
Fisting in Loveland, 5.9, 469
Fists of Fury, 5.10a, 271
Fitzroy Was Here, 5.10b, 263
Five Two-ish, 5.2, 471
Five-Four-Plus, 5.8, 195
Flake and Bake, 5.8, 237
Flake Hicky, 5.3, 254
Flake Route, 5.5, 510
Flake, The, 5.8, 187
Flakes Can Collapse, 5.8+, 379
Flakes of Doom, 5.6, 382
Flakes of Grasp, 5.10c (TR), 420
Flakes, The, 5.9, 538
Flakey Flix, 5.7, 477
Flakey Puffs from Hell, 5.10 (TR), 393
FLAKY BOULDER, 176
Flaming Arrow, 5.9+ R, 272
Flange, The, 5.11a (TR), 339
Flare, 5.7, 163
Flare Play, 5.10b, 520
Flare, The, 5.4, 532
Flared Bear, 5.8, 168
Flaring Offwidth from Hell, 5.10a, 483
Flaring Rhoid, 5.10b, 180
Flash Gordon, 5.7, 381
Flashflood, 5.11a (TR), 486
Flashpoint, 5.11d, 436
Flat Tire, 5.8, 106
Flawless Fissure, 5.9, 107
Flea Bite, 5.11d (TR), 456
Flexible Hueys, 5.10d (TR), 329
FLEXIBLE ROCK, 329
Flies on the Wound, 5.7, 513
Flight Attendant, 5.11+, 371
Flintlock Dyno, 5.9, 228
Flower Power, 5.9, 248
Flue Right, 5.10b R/X, 201
Flue, The, 5.8, 201
Fluff Boy, 5.8, 536
Fly Away, 5.10d, 467
Fly in the Ointment, 5.11a (TR), 513
Fly, The, 5.11c, 335
Flying Dutchman, The, 5.12, 217
FLYING FORTRESS, THE, 78
Foghorn Leghorn, 5.7 R, 443
Fool For A Pretty Face, 5.10c, 471
Fool's Gold, 5.8, 445
Fool's Ruby, 5.6 R, 517
Fooling Myself, 5.8, 256
FOOLPROOF TOWER, 286
FOOT, THE, 67
Footloose, 5.9, 477

For A Few Swidgets More, 5.9, 137
For Peter, 5.11c, 462
For Sure, 5.3, 470
For Whom the Poodle Tolls, 5.9, 128
Forbidden Paradise, 5.10b, 242
Forbidden Zone, 5.11b, 338
Foreign Legion, 5.10d, 52
Forgotten Crack, The, 5.10a, 530
Forgotten Galaxy, 5.11b R, 533
Forgotten Variation, 5.9+ R, 533
Forgotten Venture, 5.10b, 470
Formic Acidhead, 5.10b, 164
Forsaken Mein-Key, The, 5.10c, 277
FORTRESS AREA, THE, 75
FORTRESS, THE, 76
Fortune Cookie, 5.10a, 98
Fossil Find, A2, 475
Fote Hog, 5.6, 167
Foul Fowl, 5.6, 204
FOUND IN THE DUFFLE CRAG, 140
Foundation Crack, 5.10b, 325
FOUNDRY, THE, 144
Four of a Kind, 5.9 (TR), 394
Four-Car Garage, 5.9, 272
Fowl Play, 5.11a, 442
Fractured Fissure, 5.10d (TR), 205
FRAGGLE ROCK, 432
Frank and Ernest, 5.11a (TR), 127
Frankenwood, 5.7, 252
Frankie Lee, 5.7, 278
Frat Boys in the Gym, 5.11b (TR), 412
Fraud Squad, 5.10d, 532
FREAK BROTHERS DOMES, 305
Freckle Face, 5.11a, 485
Free As Can Be, 5.7, 483
Free Bubba John, 5.10d, 141
Free Climbing, 5.10a, 213
Free Electric, 5.11a, 464
Free Fall, 5.10a (TR), 503
Free For A Fee, 5.10c, 425
Free Variation, 5.11a, 111
Freeway, 5.7 R, 96
Freeway Jam, 5.1d, 139
FREEWAY WALL, THE, 95
French Flies, 5.7, 1333
Fresh Combination, 5.6, 480
Fresh Garlic, 5.9, 402
FRIABLE ROCK, 402
Friend Bender, 5.11b, 206
Friend Eater, 5.8, 107
Friendly Fists, 5.9, 58
Friendly Hands, 5.10b, 111
Fright Night, 5.4, 52
Frigid Dare, 5.11c (TR), 211
FRIGID TOWER, 458
Frisco Knight, 5.10b 9TR), 194
Frog Hair, 5.10B, 354
FROLIC TOWERS, 480
From Here to Infirmary, 5.8, 209
From the Mouths of Dogs, 5.11b, 465
Frontal Lobotomy, 5.10a, 261
Frontal Logranity, 5.10a, 260
Frontier Justice, 5.11b, 545
FRONTIER SPIRES, 337
FRONTIER WALL, 338-339
Frostline, 5.10a, 195
Frosty Cone, 5.7, 131
Frozen at the Void, 5.10, 458
Frozen Fish Fingers, 5.9, 440
FRUIT CAKE, THE, 437
Fruit Fly, 5.10a, 343
Fruits of Labor, 5.11 (TR), 343
FRY BOULDERS, THE, 367

Fry Problem, 5.11, 367
Fryer Flyers, 5.5, 94
Frying Pan, 5.10, 367
Fugitive, The, 5.10d, 74
Full Contact Karate, 5.10b, 487
Full Count, 5.8, 480
Full Frontal Nudity, 5.10a, 261
Fumblers Below the Roof, 5.10c, 421
Fun for the Whole Family, 5.4, 347
Fun in the Sun, 5.9+ (TR), 52
Fun Stuff, 5.8, 233
FUNCTION BOULDER, 193
Function, The, 5.11+ R, 193
Functional Analysis, 5.11d (TR), 248
Funky Dung, 5.8, 126
Funky Gunkies, 5.4, 450
Funny Bone, 5.8, 252
Funny Money, 5.8+, 256
Fusion Without Integrity, 5.10b, 128
Fuss Rattle and Roll, 5.7, 397
Future Boy, 5.12d (TR), 430
FUTURE GAMES ROCK, 459
G String, 5.13d, 170
G-Spot, 5.11c, 350
G-SPOT, 350
G-Wizz, 5.7 X, 350
Gabby's Shuttle, 5.10c, 538
GADGET DOME, 232
Gail Winds, 5.9, 52
Gait of Power, 5.10b, 530
GALAPAGOS, THE, 405
Games Without Frontiers, 5.13a/b, 459
Ganado, 5.10b, 76
Garden Angel, 5.10a, 381
Garden Path, 5.10a, 59
Gardening At Night, 5.9 A1+, 282
Gargoyle, 5.6, 483
Garnet, 5.11b, 350
Garter Snake, 5.10b, 319
Gash, The, 5.10a, 150
Gaston's Groove, 5.11a, 511
GATEWAY ROCK, 150-151
Gauntlet, The, 5.12a, 140
Gaz Giz, 5.6, 184
Gem, 5.8, 445
Gem, The, 5.10b, 342
Gemstoner, 5.10a, 416
General Hospital, 5.9, 321
Generic Route, 5.8, 116
Gentlemen Adventure, 5.9 X, 250
Gentlemen Bumblies, 5.9, 250
Genuine Cowhide, 5.10a , 517
Geometry, 5.11a, 52
Georgia O'Keefe, 5.10b, 414
Geraldo Follows Ophry, 5.0, 394
Geronimo, 5.7, 188
GET IT TOGETHER ROCK, 296
Get the Balance Right, 5.10, 429
Get The Boot, 5.10b, 317
Get with the Plan, 5.10b, 353
Gettysburger, The, 5.10b, 133
GHOST TOWN, 541
Gia, 5.11b, 457
Gibb's Arete, 5.10+, 371
Gibb's Face, 5.10, 371
Gibberish, 5.10c (TR), 82
Gila Monster, 5.9, 232
Gila Monster, The, 5.8+, 447
Gilded Lump, 5.11a, 241
GILLIGAN'S ISLAND, 54
Gin Fizz, 5.7 R, 517
Girdle Crossing, 5.10d, 305
Girls in the Mist, 5.10d, 26

Given Up For Dead, 5.10d, 420
Gjoa, 5.9, 53
Glad Hander, 5.9, 339
Glenda Crack, 5.10d R, 491
Global Warming, 5.11c, 475
Global Warming, 5.8 R, 355
GLORY DOME, 136
Glory Road, 5.12a, 136
Glue Rhymes With Poo, 5.10a, 348
Glumpies, 5.9, 382
Gnarly, 5.10a (TR), 418
Gnatty Dread, 5.9, 339
Go 'Gane, 5.8, 220
Go Ask Alice, 5.10b, 480
Go For Broke, 5.8, 247
Go With The Floe`, 5.9+, 52
Go-Gos on Quaaludes, The , 5.10c, 412
Godzilla Eats Human Sushi, 5.10d, 275
Goin' Down the Road Feelin' Bad, 5.10c, 470
GOLD DUST GULCH AREA, 425
Gold Hunk, The, 5.11a (TR), 241
GOLD NUGGETS, THE, 425
Golddigger, The, 5.10c, 431
Golden Years Variation, 5.9+, 126
Goldenbush Corner, 5.11a, 184
Goldilocks, 5.7, 206
Gomer Pile, 5.9, 526
Gomez, 5.10a (TR), 131
Gomma Cocida, 5.11b, 93
Gone in 60 Seconds, 5.10a R, 242
Good Book, The, 5.9, 379
Good Dog Y'all, 5.10c, 337
Good Grief, 5.10c (TR), 158
Good Investment, 5.12a (TR), 386
Good to the Last Drop, 5.10a R, 199
Good, Bad and Ugly, The, 5.10a, 153
Goodbye Mr. Bond, 5.10c, 524
Goof Proof Roof, 5.8 A2+, 504
Goofy Arete, 5.10c, 418
Goolabunga, 5.10b, 221
Gorby Goes to Washington , 5.8, 475
Gordo Started It, 5.10c R/X, 137
Gordoba, 5.10d, 339
Gorgasaurus, 5.7, 221
Gorilla Tactics, 5.9+, 439
Gossamer Wings, 5.10a, 101
GOSSIP COLUMN, THE, 511
Gotcha Bush, 5.4 R/X, 537
GRACELAND, 453
Gracias A Dios, 5.10d, 436
Graduate and Don't Look Back, 5.10c, 277
Graham Parsons Memorial Hand Traverse, 5.9, 367
Grain and Bear It, 5.9, 310
GRAIN CENTRAL STATION, 512
Grain Dance, 5.10b (TR), 152
Grain Death, 5.9, 256
Grain for Russia, 5.7, 105
Grain Gang, 5.8, 512
Grain of Truth, 5.10d, 112
Grain Pile, 5.11c, 245
GRAIN PILE ROCKS, 278
GRAIN SILO, THE, 512
Grain Surgery, 5.10b R, 211
Grain Surplus, 5.8, 105
Grainy Train, 5.10c, 437
GRAND CANYON, 461
Grand Canyon Donkey Trail, 5.10a, 461
Grand Theft Avocado, 5.7, 210
Grandpa Gander, 5.10c R, 92
Granny Goose, 5.7, 92
Granulator, The, 5.10c, 129
Grape Nuts, Why Not?, 5.10a, 382
Gravel Shower, 5.10d (TR), 103

Gravity Pirates, 5.10 (TR), 475
GRAVITY ROCK, 400
Gravity Waves, 5.11a, 62
Gravity Works, 5.11c, 62
GRAYSTONE, THE, 482
GREAT BURRITO, THE, 160
Great Caesar's Ghost, 5.8, 350
Great Commission, 5.11a, 551
Great Grain Robbery, The, 5.6, 512
Great TR, But Don't Bolt Me, A, 5.11b (TR), 35
Great Unknown, The, 5.10b, 68
Green Chile, 5.11a (TR), 142
Green Hornet, 5.10a (TR), 445
Green Mansions, 5.8, 464
GREEN ROOM, THE, 148
Green Visitor, 5.11d, 109
GREEN WALL, THE, 351
Greenhorn Dihedral, 5.10c, 317
GREY GIANT, 73
GREY GIANT, 79
Greystoke, 5.8 R, 510
Griffin, The, 5.10a R, 98
Grim Roper, 5.10c, 405
Grip or Whip, 5.11b (TR), 141
Gripped for Petina, 5.9, 497
Gripped Up The Hole, 5.10a, 175
Gripper Traverse, 5.10, 32
Grit Roof, 5.10c, 382
Groop'o, 5.11d (TR), 433
Groove Avoidance System, 5.10a (TR), 250
GROPE ROCK, 433
Gross Chimney, 5.10a, 414
GROTTO ROCK, 392
Ground Finale, 5.10a, 473
Ground Ron, 5.10c, 310
Grounder, 5.9, 464
GROUP CAMP #1 WALL, 508
GROUP CAMP 8 WALL, 510
GROUP CAMP ROCKS, 511
GROUP CAMP SHORT WALL, 511
Grungy, 5.10d, 76
GS-5, 5.9 (TR), 112
GUARDHOUSE, THE, 75
Guardian Angels, 5.10a, 383
Guardian of the Gate, 5.9+, 494
GULLY, THE, 240
Gullywog, 5.8, 464
GUMBY DOME, 310
Gumby Goes to Washington, 5.8, 310
Gumby Saves Bambi, 5.10d, 246
Gumshoe, 5.10d, 66
Gun for the Sun, 5.10a, 54
Gun Shy, 5.10a, 351
Gunks West, 5.10b, 152
Gunshy, 5.11b, 247
Gunslinger, The, 5.12a, 293
Gunsmoke, 5.11+, 271
GUNSMOKE AREA, 271
Gut Full of Suds, 5.9, 246
Gut Reaction, 5.6, 267
Gypsy, 5.10a, 526
Gypsy Fortune, 5.10b (TR), 511
Gypsy Queen, 5.9, 339
H & R Block, 5.7, 130
H.R. Hardman, 5.8, 264
Haberdashery, The, 5.8, 517
HAI KARATE ROCK, 487
Hair on My Tread, 5.11b, 412
Hairline Fracture, 5.10a R, 101
Half Crack, 5.3, 473
HALF ROCK, 475
Half Time, 5.8, 522
Half Track, 5.10a, 183

Halfway to Paradise, 5.10a R, 239
HALL OF HORRORS, 381
HALL OF HORRORS BOULDERING, 387
HALL OF HORRORS — EAST WALL , 384
HALL OF HORRORS — WEST WALL, 386
Halow Friction, 5.10c, 275
Ham & Swiss, 5.10b, 263
Ham Sandwich, 5.8, 378
Hand Grenade, 5.10a, 481
HAND GRENADE CORRIDOR, 481
Hand of the Bride, 5.10a, A1, 328
Hand Wobler Delight, 5.9, 298
Handcracker, 5.8, 521
Handlin' Snakeskin, 5.10c, 159
Hands Away, 5.10a, 150
Hands Down, 5.11b (TR), 197
Hands of Fire, 5.11c (TR), 79
Hands Off, 5.8, 197
Hands To Yourself, 5.11a 9TR), 197
Hands Up, 5.10d, 197
Handsaw, 5.10b, 438
Hang 'em High, 5.10a, 543
Hang and Swing, 5.10d, 155
Hang em High, 5.12b, 459
Hang Ten, 5.8, 233
Hangman Jury, 5.11c, 545
Hans Solo, 5.9, 483
HAPPY HUNTING ROUND, THE, 337
Happy Landings, Linda, 5.11b, 100
HARD ROCK, 314
Hard Rock Cafe, 5.10d, 317
Hard Science, 5.8, 273
Harder They Fall, The, 5.10a, 111
HARDLY ROCK, 276
Harlequin, 5.10c R, 378
Harrell-Turner, 5.10b, 533
HARRY QUARRY, 407
Hartman, 5.6, 364
Harvey's Bristol Cream, 5.10a, 469
Having Fun Yet, 5.12— X, 203
HAWK HATCHER, THE, 497
Hawk Wind, 5.10c R, 314
Hawks Nest, 5.7, 497
Hawks Retreat, 5.10a, 418
Head Over Heals, 5.10a, 128
Head, Abdomen, Thorax, 5.9 A2, 331
Headbanger's Ball, 5.12c, 371
Headbangers' Ball, 5.11c, 101
Headless Horseman, 5.11a, 541
Headmaster, 5.12b (TR), 371
HEADSTONE ROCK, 370
Health Care President, The, 5.6, 545
HEAP, THE, 215
Heart and Sole, 5.10a, 242
Heart of Darkness, 5.11c, 373
Heart Route, The, 5.6, 537
Heart Slab, 5.8, 517
Heart Transplant, 5.10a, 471
Heartbreak Ridge, 5.8, 364
Heartless, 5.7, 471
Heat Wave, 5.9, 269
Heaven Can Wait, 5.10c, 74
Heavy Gold, 5.10a, 469
Heavy Handed, 5.10c, 140
Heavy Mettle, 5.10d, 130
Heavy Mettle, 5.11b, 464
Heavy Slander, 5.10a (TR), 470
Heavy Water, 5.10a R, 130
Hedgehog, 5.4, 508
Heffalump, 5.5 R/X, 373
Helicopter Memory Farts, 5.9+, 445
Helix, 5.2, 233
HELL ROCK, 27

Hellish Planet, 5.10d, 353
HEMINGWAY BUTTRESS, 126-129
HEMINGWAY BUTTRESS, 129
Hemroidic Terror, 5.7 R, 385
HEN HOUSE, THE, 442
HEN PECKED BOULDER, 443
Henny Penny, 5.10d, 256
Hensel Arete, 5.10+, 193
HENSEL BOULDER, 193
Hensel Face, 5.11, 193
Hensel Face, 5.11+, 146
Herbie's Hideaway, 5.10d, 179
Hercules, 5.11c, 120
Here Comes The Bride, 5.11a, 329
HERETIC BOULDER, 377
Herman, 5.9, 258
HERMAN ROCKS, 258
Hermanutic, 5.10c R, 32
Hershey Highway, 5.9 (TR), 482
HERSHEY KISS, 482
Hesitation Blues, 5.10b, 100
Hex, 5.7, 447
Hex Marks The Poot, 5.7, 289
Hey Taxi, 5.11a, 362
Hhecht, 5.6, 152
Hicks for Free, 5.12b, 378
Hidden Arch, 5.11d, 178
HIDDEN CLIFF, THE, 170
HIDDEN CORRIDOR, 464
HIDDEN DOME, 50
Hidden Taxes, 5.6, 130
HIDDEN TOWER, 156
HIDDEN VALLEY CAMPGROUND, 183
HIDDEN WALL, 319
High Anxiety, 5.10d, 39
High Cost of Living, The, 5.11a to 5.12a, 378
High Energy, 5.10a, 453
High Interest, 5.11a, 49
High Noon, 5.10b R, 543
High Noon, B1 R, 271
HIGH PLAINS AREA, 39
High Plains Drifter, 5.10b, 431
High Plains Drifter, 5.9+, 543
High Strung, 5.9, 286
High Tension, 5.11+, 39
High Tops, 5.10a, 551
High Ware, 5.12a, 237
Higher Yield, 5.10d, 49
Highwayman, The, 5.11b R, 520
HILL STREET BLUES, 123
Hillside Strangler, 5.4, 513
HILLSIDE, THE, 49
Hintertoiser Traverse, The, 5.10c, 188
Hip, Hip Belay, 5.7+ R, 117
History, 5.11a (TR), 33
Hit It Ethel, 5.8, 53
HIT MAN ROCK, 214
Hit, The, 5.9, 214
Ho Man!, 5.11b, 284
Hob Nob, 5.6, 394
HOB NOB WALL, 394
Hobbit Roof, 5.10d, 194
Hoblett, 5.7, 194
Hobo Chang Ba, 5.9, 450
Hodgepodge, 5.4 R, 508
HODGEPODGE ROCK, 508
Hogback, 5.8, 508
Hold Me Tight, 5.10d R, 405
Hold Tight Til Footings Right, 5.11a (TR), 485
Hold Your Fire, 5.13a, 148
Holden Back, 5.7, 164
Holden On, 5.10a, 164
Holden Up, 5.8, 164

Holds to Hollywood, 5.4, 387
Hole In One, 5.10b (TR), 272
Holeaceous, 5.10c, 351
Holey Cold, 5.10b, 351
Holiday in Detroit, 5.10b, 406
Holiday in the Sun, 5.10a R, 94
Hollow Dreams, 5.11/12 (TR), 123
Hollowed Ground, 5.11a, 428
Holly Device, 5.10c, 98
HOLLYWOOD, 502-503
HOLLYWOOD, 503
Hollywood and Vaino, 5.10c R, 532
Holy Cross, 5.10a, 392
Holy Hand, 5.10a, 298
HOMESTEAD WALL, THE, 75
Homo Erectus, 5.6, 337
HONE DOME, 418
Honey, 5.9, 491
Honorable Hersheys, 5.11a (TR), 71
Hook and Ladder, 5.11a/5.12b, 330
HOOK AND LADDER AREA, 330
Hoopharkz, 5.4, 211
HOOTER ROCKS, 67
Hooterville Trolley, 5.10+, 67
Hop Sing, 5.8, 544
Hope and Glory, 5.8, 136
Horn Dog, 5.10c , 126
Horn's A'Plenty, 5.7 R, 348
Horny Corner, 5.9, 237
Horror-Zontal Terror-Verse, 5.10b, 362
Horse of a Different Color, 5.10c/d, 439
Horseshoe, 5.11c, 481
Hoser, 5.6, 414
Hot Cross Buns, 5.7, 82
Hot Crystals, 5.9, 105
Hot Dog in a Bun, 5.10d, 457
Hot Flashes, 5.11c, 401
Hot Fudge, A, 5.9 R, 131
Hot Knife, 5.10d, 233
Hot Lava, 5.11a, 412
Hot Legs Contest, 5.11c, 217
Hot Rocks, 5.11c, 223
Hot Summer Daze, 5.10a, 402
Hot Tub Honey, 5.8, 508
Hot Tub of Death, 5.10a, 209
HOT TUB, THE, 209
Hot Tubs From Hell, 5.8, 209
Hotpants, 5.13b, 319
Hotseat, 5.7, 364
Houdini Arete, The, 5.11c (TR), 52
HOUND ROCK, 36
HOUND ROCKS, 34
Hour of Darkness, 5.9+, 283
Hour of Power, 5.10a, 464
Hourglass, The, 5.10c, 493
House of Games, 5.11b, 381
House of the Homeless, 5.8+, 382
HOUSER BUTTRESS, 178-179
HOUSER BUTTRESS AREA, 178-181
Houses in Motion, 5.10a, 426
How Spoilers Bleed, 5.10d, 121
How's Your Granny, 5.10+, 228
How's Your Mama, 5.11+, 228
Howard's Horror, 5.7, 200
Huevos Rancheros, 5.10b, 406
Hug Dance, 5.11b, 523
Human Sacrifice, 5.11c, 413
HUMAN SACRIFICE BOULDER, 413
Humpty Dumpty, 5.7, 354
HUMPTY DUMPTY AREA, 354
HUNK ROCK EAST FACE, 269
HUNK ROCK WEST FACE, 267
Hunkloads to Hermosa, 5.9, 269

Hurricane Hugo, 5.10b, 40
Hurry Up and Wait, 5.10a, 522
Hush Puppies, 5.6, 294
HVCG BACK SIDE, 201
Hydra, 5.13c, 69
Hyperion, 5.11c, 73
Hyperventilation, 5.10d, 79
I Am Not A Crook, 5.8, 264
I Can Believe It's A Sandbag, 5.8, 305
I Can't Believe It's A girdle, 5.10a R, 305
I Don't Know, 5.10a, 350
I Eat Cannibal, 5.7, 441
I Eat Cannibals, 5.10d, 414
I Fall Therefore I Am, 5.10c, 26
I Forgot, 5.10a, 110
I Forgot to Have Babies, 5.10b (TR), 131
I Get By With A Little Help From My Friends, 5.10a, 469
I Got It, 5.9, 296
I Had A Dream, 5.10b, 516
I Have the Touch, 5.12d, 433
I Just Told You, 5.10a, 154
I Love Brian Piccolo, 5.8+, 90
I Love Snakes, 5.9+, 159
I Saw Stars, 5.10c, 354
I Should Be Dancin', 5.7, 399
I Slept with L.K., 5.10a, 480
I Smell A Rat, 5.10b, 377
I'd Slap You But Shit Splatters, 5.9+, 116
I'm Not Afraid Anymore, 5.11b, 192
I'm Pregnant with Satan's Baby, 5.11a, 470
I'm So Embarrassed For Your, 5.7, 132
Ice Climbing, 5.10a, 213
Ice Cream for Crow, 5.8, 439
Ice Experience, The, 5.9, 382
Ice Station Zebra, 5.9+, 343
ICEBERG BOULDER AREA, 540
Iced Vo-Vo's , 5.11d, 229
Icon, 5.10c, 345
Iconoclast, The, 5.13a, 378
If I Only Had A Brain, 5.10c, 494
If It's Brown, Flush It, 5.11 (TR), 161
If You Really Loved Me, You'd Buy Me A Turkey, 5.10b, 289
Ignorant Photons From Pluto, 5.11a (TR), 183
Igor Prince of Poodles, 5.11c, 246
Igor's Failed Road Trip, 5.11a, 406 .
IGUANA DOME, 329
Iguana Masters, 5.10b, 329
IGUANA, THE, 405
Illegal Campfire, 5.7, 517
Illicit Operations, 5.11c, 123
Illusion, 5.7, 73
Illusion Dweller, 5.10b, 169
Imaginary Voyage, 5.10d, 103
IMAGINARY VOYAGE FORMATION, 103
Imelda's New Shoes, 5.10a, 129
Immaculate Conception, 5.9, 136
Immuno Reaction, 5.10a, 379
Importance of Being Ernest, The, 5.10c R, 127
Impulse Power, 5.11a, 140
In a Silent Way, 5.11c, 392
In and Out, 5.9, 455
In Elke's Absence, 5.10a, 322
In Search of Hush Puppies, 5.8 R/X, 293
In The Green Room, 5.9 , 501
In the Name of Love, 5.11a, 471
In the Pit, 5.10a, 151
INAUGURON DOME, 312
Inauguron, The, 5.11b, 312
INDIAN CAVE BOULDER, 146
Indian Garden, 5.6, 451
Indian Giver, 5.11a, 407
INDIAN HEAD, 504

INDIAN PALISADES CORRIDOR, 533
INDIAN WAVE BOULDERS, 270
Inept Tune, 5.10b (TR), 359
Infectious Smile, 5.9, 139
Innervisions, 5.9, 309
INQUISITION ROCK, 450
Insider Information, 5.7, 141
Intersection Boulder Left, 5.10, 185
Intersection Boulder Middle, 5.11, 185
Intersection Boulder Right, B1, 185
Intersection Mantel, 5.9, 185
INTERSECTION ROCK, 183-187
INTERSECTION ROCK BOULDERING, 184-187
Intersection Traverse, 5.10, 184
INTERSTATE CRAG, 139
Intimidation Game, 5.10d, 437
INTIMIDATOR ROCKS, THE, 29
Into the Black, 5.8, 392
Into the Fire, 5.8, 367
Into You Like a Train, 5.11c (TR), 88
Intruders, The, 5.9 A1, 338
Invasion On My Fantasy, 5.7, 308
Invisibility Lessons, 5.9, 459
Invisible Touch, 5.10b, 459
Invisible Touch, 5.10d, 212
Involvent, 5.10b, 285
Ionic Strength, 5.12a, 66
Iron Curtain, The, 5.11c, 375
IRON DOOR CAVE BOULDER, 228
IRON DOOR CAVE BOULDERS, 226
Iron Hand, 5.10a, 521
IRON HAND ROCK, 521
Iron Lady, 5.8, 549
Iron Maiden, 5.11d, 256
Iron Man Traverse, 5.10c, 189
Iron Mantel, 5.10c R, 118
Ironsides, 5.9, 82
Ironworks, 5.7, 144
IRS WALL, THE, 130
Is That A Munchkin in Your Pocket, 5.11b (TR), 501
Is The Pope Catholic?, 5.6 (TR), 449
ISLAND IN THE STREAM, 402
ISLES IN THE SKY, 463
Isotope, 5.9, 66
It, 5.9, 384
It Don't Mean A Thing If It Ain't Got That Swing, 5.12b, 284
It Satisfies, 5.7, 130
It Seams Possible, 5.10c, 295
It's About Time, 5.9 R, 518
It's Cracked Up To Be, 5.9, 436
It's Easy to be Brave from a Safe Distance, 5.12a, 76
It's Easy to be Distant When You're Brave, 5.11c, 76
It's Never Robot City, 5.10d (TR), 337
IVORY TOWER, THE, 64
J.B. Goes to J.T., 5.8+ (TR), 483
Jabberwocky, 5.9, 405
Jack Grit, 5.10a, 213
Jack in the Crack, 5.10d, 317
Jack of Hearts, 5.9, 38
Jack the Ripper, 5.8, 271
Jackalope, 5.11b, 115
Jacuzzi of No Return, 5.10b, 209
Jah Loo, 5.10c, 59
Jailbreak, 5.3, 523
JAILHOUSE ROCK, 523
Jaime Crack, 5.4 R, 507
Jaime's Big Show, 5.7, 507
JAIME'S ROCK, 507
Jalapeno, 5.10b (TR), 142
JAM OR SLAM ROCK, 141
Jamaican Bobsled, 5.11a, 345
Jamburger, 5.10a, 263

James Brown, 5.11b (TR), 161
James Brown, 5.6, 46
James Brown's Celebrity Hot Tub Party, 5.10b, 29
Jane Pauley, 5.8, 92
Jane's Addiction, 5.11b, 386
Jane's Getting Serious, 5.12b, 244
Janus, 5.10d, 73
Java, 5.9+, 412
Jaws, 5.6 R, 385
JB's Variation, (TR), 237
JBMF BOULDER, 146
JBMF BOULDERS, 144-146
JBMFP, B1+, 146
Jedi Master, 5.10c, 483
Jeepers Leepers, 5.9+ R, 451
JELLYSTONE, 85
Jemiomagina, 5.10b, 139
Jerry Brown, 5.10a, 161
JERRY FALL WALL, 487
Jerry's Kids, B1 R, 367
JERRY'S QUARRY, 406
JERRY'S QUARRY AND LOST PENCIL AREAS, 406
Jersey Girl, 5.10a, 46
Jessica's Crack, 5.6, 386
Jet Stream, 5.8, 503
Jet Stream (aka: Momentary Lapse of Reason), 5.10b, 25
Jewel of Denial, The, 5.9, 73
Jill and Jerry, 5.7, 279
Jim Cruise, 5.8, 44-
JIMMY CLIFF AREA, 110-113
Jingus Con, 5.11c, 122
Jo Mama, 5.8, 393
Joan Jetson, 5.9, 307
Jody, 5.10b, 476
JOHN YABLONSKI ROCK, 364
Johnnie Come Lately, 5.10d, 345
Joint Effort, A4, 188
Joker, The, 5.12c, 166
Jolly Rancher Firestix, 5.10d, 254
Jolly Roger, 5.10c, 433
Josar Crack, 5.8+, 121
Judas, 5.10b, 188
Jug-Yur-Not, 5.4, 507
Juggurnot, 5.6, 517
Jughead, 5.10a, 240
Jugular Vein, 5.8, 485
Julius Seizure, 5.10a, 76
Jumar of Flesh, 5.9+, 144
JUMBO ROCKS CAMPGROUND, 435
JUMBO ROCKS CORRIDOR, 438
Jumbo Shrimp, 5.6, 437
Jump Back Loretta, 5.5, 152
Jump Chump, B1, 176
Jump On It, 5.10b, 481
Jumping Jack Crack, 5.11a, 212
Jumping Jehosaphat, 5.7, 152
Jumpstart, 5.10a, 462
Junction Chimney, 5.2, 473
Jungle, 5.7, 184
Jungle Cruise, 5.10b, 308
Junior, 5.10c, 192
Junior Varsity Problem, 5.10+, 190
JUNK CLUMP, 392
Junkie Thrill, 5.6, 486
Junkyard God, 5.9, 96
Just Another Crack From L.A., 5.9, 100
Just Another New Wave Route, 5.9, 116
Just Another Roadside Attraction, 5.9, 87
Just Drive, She Said, 5.10b, 338
Just for the Thrill of It, 5.11a (TR), 416
Just Say Yo, 5.9+, 384
Just Stop It, 5.10b, 29
K2R, 5.9, 352

Kachina, 5.10a, 340
KACHINA WALLS, 340
Kalishnakov Kulture, 5.12a, 517
Kamakaze, 5.10c, 471
KANSAS CLIFFS, 497
Karma, 5.12d, 316
Karpkwitz, 5.6, 33
Kate's Bush, 5.8, 90
KATE'S CRAG, 337
Keep the Ball Rolling, 5.9, 219
Keith's Work, 5.11a (TR), 166
Kemosabe and Tonto, 5.9, 160
KEN BLACK MEMORIAL DOME, 94
Kendall Mint Cake, 5.6, 254
Key to the Kingdome, 5.9+, 388
KEYS RANCH, 232
Keystone Arete, 5.10b (TR), 279
KEYSTONE BLOCK, 279
Keystone Crack, 5.6, 279
Kickin' Bach, 5.10a, 90
Kickoff, 5.8, 272
Kid Calingula, 5.10a, 378
Kid, The, 5.9, 378
Kiddie Corner, 5.9, 411
Kidney Stone, 5.10d (TR), 206
Killer Bees, 5.10a, 118
KILLER CRACKS, THE, 271
Killer Pussy, 5.11a (TR), 416
Kilobyte, 5.11a, 265
Kinda Sorta, 5.9 R, 518
Kindler and Gentler Ream Job, 5.6, 475
KING DOME, 388
King of the Mountain, 5.8, 216
KING OTTO'S CASTLE, 524
King Pin, 5.11b, 212
Kingsnake, 5.12b, 212
Kippy Korner, 5.9, 172
Kirkatron, B1, 155
Kiss Me Where I Pee, 5.9, 339
Kiwi Route, 5.10d, 213
Klansman, The, 5.7, 405
Kleptomania, 5.10a, 418
Klettervergnugen, 5.9, 508
Klingon Pizza, 5.6 R, 516
Knack, 5.10c, 414
Knaug and Hyde, 5.3 R, 530
Knick, 5.10a, 414
Knight in Shining Armor, The, 5.11b, 79
Knight Mare, 5.7, 283
Knight Shift, 5.10d (TR), 252
KNOCKOUT ROCK, 138
Knot Again, 5.6 R, 446
Knot Again, 5.9, 378
Knuckle Cracker, 5.9+, 184
Kodas Silence, 5.11c, 137
Kodiak, 5.5, 47
Kokopeli, 5.10d, 461
Komodo Dragon, 5.6 R, 88
Kon-Tiki, 5.11c (TR), 467
Kook Book, 5.10c, 413
Kool Aid, 5.10d A4, 183
KP Corner, 5.10a, 67
Krakatoa, 5.9, 412
Kundalini-Linguini-Weenie, 5.8, 517
Kwidgi-Bo on the Loose, 5.9 R, 510
La Cholla, 5.12d, 385
La Machine, 5.13d, 64
La Reina, 5.9, 534
LABOR DOME, 214
Labyrinth, 5.10a, 348
Labyrinth, The, 5.7, 105
Ladder Back, 5.10b R, 250
Lady in Waiting, 5.5, 337
Laegar Domain, 5.10d, 137
Laid Back, 5.8, 198
Laid Back and Doing It, 5.10c, 300
LAKESIDE ROCK, 276
Land of the Long White Cloug, 5.10b, 213
Land of Wonder, 5.10c, 339
LAND THAT TIME FORGOT, THE, 162
Landlord, The, 5.10d, 378
Landsraad, 5.10b, 534
Large Marge, 5.7, 364
LARGO BOULDER, 176
Largo Dyno, 5.11+, 367
Largo Dyno, B1, 228
Largonaut, B1—, 190
Largotot, 5.9, 228
Lascivisous Conduct, 5.11c, 515
Laserator, 5.11b (TR), 198
Last Angry Arab, 5.6, 287
Last Cigarette Senor?, A, 5.9, 513
Last Date, 5.10b, 481
Last Minute Additions, 5.6, 110
Last Ticket to Obscuritiville, 5.9, 24
Last Unicorn, The, 5.11a, 68
Latin Swing, 5.11b, 171
LAUGH ROCK, 326
LAUGHTER ROCK, 482
Laura Scudders, 5.10b, 276
LAVA DOME, 401
Lay Back and Do It, 5.11a (TR), 150
Layaway Plan, 5.11a (TR), 129
Lazy Day, 5.7, 381
LAZY DOME, 73
Lazy Rhymer, 5.10c (TR), 118
Lead Belly, 5.10b, 465
Lead Us Not Into Temptation, 5.9, 294
Leader's Fright, 5.8 R, 205
Leading Lady, 5.9 R, 132
Lean and Scream, 5.10d (TR), 426
Lean On Me, 5.10a, 90
Lean Two, 5.9, 414
Leap Erickson, 5.10b (TR), 131
Leap in Fath, 5.10+, 367
Leap Year Flake, 5.7, 131
Leaping Leana, 5.6, 152
Learning to Crawl, 5.6, 450
Leave It To Beaver, 5.12a, 155
LECHLINSKI CRACK FORMATION, 411
Lechlinski Cracks, 5.9, 411
Lechlinski's Corner, 5.11+, 146
Ledges to Laundale, 5.10a, 387
Lee's Health Studio, 5.11b/c, 457
Left, 5.10, 176
Left, 5.11, 176
Left Archimedes' Crack, 5.11a, 414
Left Arete, 5.10, 233
Left Banana Crack, 5.10c, 124
Left Baskerville Crack, 5.10b R, 35
Left Beetle Crack, 5.10b, 109
Left Double Feature Crack, 5.7, 503
LEFT HAND OF DARKNESS, 92-93
Left Lizard Crack, 5.10d R, 88
Left Mel Crack, 5.10c, 90
Left Nixon Crack, 5.9+, 193
Left of Center, 5.10b (TR), 400
Left Overs, 5.7 (TR), 52
Left Peyote Crack, 5.10, 224
Left Route, 5.10a R, 92
Left S Crack, 5.8, 122
Left Sawdust Crack, 5.10c, 32
Left Ski Track, 5.11a, 183
Left V Crack, 5.11b R, 536
Leg Lifter, The, 5.11a, 41
Legal Briefs, 5.9, 158

Legolas, 5.10c, 242
Lemming, The, 5.10d, 415
LEMON DOME, 70
Lemon Head, The, 5.10b, 70
Lemon Lemon, 5.10a, 70
Lemon Slicer, The, 5.11a, 70
LENTICULAR DOME, 298
Leper Messiah, 5.12c (TR), 342
Lesbian Lust, 5.9+, 503
Less Than Meets the Eye, 5.8, 482
Let It All Hang Out, 5.10b, 186
Let's Bolt, 5.7, 538
Let's Eat Organ Meat, 5.10a, 67
Let's Get Horizontal, 5.11a (TR), 210
Let's Get Physical, 5.10b, 469
Letdown, The, 5.9, 67
Lewd and Lascivious Conduct, 5.10c R, 98
LHMB, 387
Lickety Splits, 5.7 R, 384
Lickey Dogs, 5.9+ R, 384
Lieback and Lingerie, 5.10d R, 173
Life in the Fast Lane, 5.11a, 244
Life in the Fat Lane, 5.9, 82
Life Without Principle, 5.11b, 308
Life Without TV, 5.9, 140
Life's A Bitch and Then You Marry One, 5.7, 279
Life's A Pitch, 5.12a, 294
Ligamentor Seconds in Vans, 5.7 R, 508
Light Sabre, 5.10b, 415
Like My Lump, 5.10a, 428
Lil Squirt, 5.9+, 362
LIME DOME, 70
Limp Wristed Faggot, 5.11c, 136
Linda's Crack, 5.2, 537
Linda's Face, 5.6 R, 537
Linden-Frost Effect, The, 5.12a, 53
Lion Tamer, 5.9, 510
Lion's Share, 5.10b, 69
Lions and Tigers and Bears, 5.10a, 497
Lip Sync, 5.10c, 382
Lippo Lippy, 5.9, 382
Lippo Suction, 5.10c, 382
Lips Like Sugar, 5.10b, 254
Liquid Confidence, 5.10d, 158
Liquid Rats, 5.10d, 181
Liquid Wrench, 5.10+, 270
Listening Wind, 5.10c, 426
Lithophiliac, 5.11a, 73
Little Big Man, 5.9, 337
Little Bit of Magic, A, 5.10c, 58
Little Brown Eye, 5.8, 516
Little Bunny Fu-Fu, 5.7, 364
Little Ceasar, 5.8, 447
Little Criminals, 5.10b, 25
LITTLE HUNK, 247
LITTLE HUNK, 250
LITTLE HUNK,
Little Joe, 5.11b (TR), 518-519
Little Lieback, 5.10a, 144
Little Red Rooster, 5.8, 443
Little Rock Candy Crack, 5.7, 254
LITTLE ROCK CANDY MOUNTAIN, 254
LITTLE STUFF CRAGS, 178
Liturgy, 5.11a, 298
Live and Let Die, 5.11a, 467
Live From Tasgrainia, 112
Live From Tasmania, 5.9, 112
LIVE OAK PICNIC AREA ROUTES, 450
Lively Yourself Up Homer, 5.10d, 465
Living Color, 5.12b (TR), 464
Living Conjunction, the, 5.11d (TR), 221
Living in a Fishbowl, 5.10b, 67
Lizard in Bondage, 5.10a R, 88

Lizard Robbins, 5.5, 88
Lizard Skin, 5.8, 88
Lizard Taylor, 5.5 R, 88
LIZARD'S HANGOUT, 88
Lizard's Landing, 5.7, 25
LIZARD'S LANDING, 23-25
LLOYD'S ROCK, 107
Lobster, The, 5.12a (TR), 155
LOCOMOTION ROCK, 152
Lollygobbleblissbombs, 5.10d R/X, 229
Lone Ranger, The, 5.9, 112
Long-Necked Goose, 5.9, 181
Look Mom, No Hands, 5.7, 49
Looking for Mercy, 5.11a, 75
Looks 5.0, So Let's Solo, 5.5, 446
Looney Tunes, 5.9, 223
Loose Lady, 5.9+, 178
Loose Lips, 5.11a, 200
Los Tres Bovines, 5.10c, 477
Lost and Found, 5.7, 421
Lost Boys, 5.10b, 464
LOST CORRIDOR, 445
LOST HORSE RANGER STATION WALL, 120-121
LOST HORSE WALL, 100-101
Lost in Space, 5.8, 101
LOST IN THE SHUFFLE CRAG, 140
LOST IN THE WONDERLAND SLAB, 323
Lost Lid, 5.9 A4, 361
LOST PENCIL, 407
LOST ROCK, 67
LOST ROCK, 470
LOST ROCKS, 371
Lov'in Kohler, 5.9, 211
Love & Rockets , 5.10b, 242
Love at First Bite, 5.8 X, 473
Love Comes in Spurts, 5.10d, 550
Love Goat, The, 5.10a, 317
Love Goddess, 5.12a, 385
LOVE NEST, THE, 358
LOVELAND, 467
LOVELAND NORTH, 471
Lovey, 5.9, 54
LOW MOTIVATION DOME, 331
Lower Band, 5.10b R, 189
LOWER COW ROCK, 163
LOWER DODGE CITY, 545
Lower Life Forms, 5.10b, 123
Lower Right Ski Track, 5.10b, 183
LOWER TIER, THE, 430
Lucky Charms, 5.7, 522
Lucky Lady, 5.8, 178
Luminous Breast, 5.8 R, 173
Lumping Fat Jennie, 5.7, 152
Lunar Lieback, 5.11—, 198
Lunch Is For Wimps, 5.9, 141
Lunge For It, 5.11+, 367
Lurch, 5.8, 131
Lurleen Quits, 5.8, 112
Lust in the Love Den, 5.6, 405
Lust in the Wonderland, 5.9, 307
Lust We Forget, 5.9, 391
Lusting CLH, 5.8, 75
Lynch Mob, 5.11a, 546
M & M's Peanut, 5.10a, 254
M & M's Plain, 5.9, 254
M.F. Dirty Rat, 5.7, 371
Macho Combo, The, 5.11c, 348
Mad Hatter, 5.11c R, 364
Mad Hatter, The, 5.10b, 308
Mad Hatter, The, 5.8, 267
Mad Men, The, 5.10a, 267
Mad Race, 5.4, 536
Madame Salami, 5.10a (TR), 520

Made in the Shade, 5.9, 52
Maggies Farm, 5.7, 125
Magic Kingdome, 5.8, 388
MAGIC MOUNTAIN AREA, 503
Magic Touch, The, 5.9, 140
Magma, 5.11c (TR), 412
Magnetic Woose, 5.10b, 166
Maiden Voyage, 5.10a, 392
Main Face, 5.9, 532
Major Creative Effort, 5.10a, 51
Major Threat, 5.12a (TR), 201
Make Or Break Flake, 5.10b, 38
Make That Move Or Six Foot Groove, 5.10c, 239
Making Wind, 5.9 (TR), 180
Male Exotic Dancers, 5.11d, 217
Mama Woolsey, 5.10a R, 192
Mamunia, 5.13a, 290
Man From Glad, 5.10d, 339
Man's Best Friend, 5.9 (TR), 126
Maneater, The, 5.10d, 229
Manic Depression, 5.11b, 481
Manly Dike, The, 5.12a, 314
Manna From Heaven, 5.9, 218
Manny, Moe & Jack, 5.9, 135
Mano Negra, 5.9, 93
Mantel, 5.10—, 190
MANURE PILE, THE, 369
Manwich Queen, 5.8, 428
Marathon Crack, The, 5.12a, 420
Marchesa, 5.2, 534
Marcos, 5.10a, 129
Mare's Tail, 5.9, 101
MARGARET THATCHER SPIRE, 549
Marital Sin, 5.10c, 279
Maritimer, The, 5.10d (TR), 118
Mark of Zorro, 5.11b, 24
Marked Card, 5.9+ R, 543
Marking Time, 5.8, 394
Martin Quits, 5.10c, 151
Mary Decker, 5.11 (TR), 56
MARY WORTH BUTTRESS, THE, 260
Master & Servant, 5.11d (TR), 252
Mastering, 5.2, 49
Math, 5.10b, 52
Matt Biondi Chimney, 5.5, 345
Matt's Problem, 5.10b, 224
MAVERICK BOULDER, THE, 477
Maxwell Grunster, 5.10a, 24
Maybe, 5.8, 518
Maybe Baby, 5.5, 258
McDonld-Wilson, 5.10c R, 40
McHaney Crack, 5.10+ (TR), 270
McStumpy Sandwich, 5.9, 254
Meanderthal, 5.8 (TR), 273
Meatlocker, 5.11b, 339
Mechanic, The, 5.10c (TR), 214
Mediterranean Sundance, B1+, 185
Medusa, 5.12c, 218
Meet John Doe, 5.10c R, 410
Megabyte, 5.11a (TR), 265
MEL'S DINER, 90
MELON, THE, 343
Memblews Mumblephone, B1, 190
Memorial Meowzer, 5.10c, 421
Men with Cow's Heads, 5.5, 105
Mental Bankruptcy, 5.10b, 308
MENTAL BLOCK, THE, 481
Mental Physics, 5.7+, 298
Mental Retread, 5.9, 106
Mental Siege Tactics, 5.10c, 322
Mercy Road, 5.11a, 75
Mere Illusion, 5.11a, 438
Mesopotamia, 5.10b, 287

MESOPOTAMIA DOME, 287
Message in a Bottle, 5.10c, 402
Meteorite Crack, 5.10c, 364
Mettle Detector, 5.12b, 464
MICRO CRAG, 83
Micro Millenium, The, 5.11d R, 482
Micronesia, 5.10d, 107
Middle, 5.10+, 176
Middle Age Crazy, 5.11b, 290
Middle Arete/Face, 5.10+, 233
Middle Band, 5.10d R, 189
Middle Finger, 5.7, 421
MIDDLE KINGDOM, THE, 55
Middle of Somewhere, 5.12a, 402
Middle Peyote Crack, 5.9, 224
Middle S Crack, 5.11c R, 122
Midnight Dreamer, 5.9, 250
Midnight Lumber, 5.10d, 461
Midnight Oil, 5.11c, 136
Midnight Rambler, 5.9 R, 250
Mighty High, 5.12a, 369
Mighty Mouse, 5.9, 285
MIGHTY MOUSE ROCK, 285
Mikado, The, 5.6, 535
Mike and Tom's Excellent Adventure, 5.11d R, 349
Mike's Books, 5.6, 185
Mikita's Rescue, 5.6, 277
MILEPOST, THE, 133
MILES OF PILES ROCK, 180-181
Military Industrial Complex, 5.10a, 385
Milk Arete, 5.10d, 407
Milk Run, 5.11a, 510
Milk the Dog, 5.10a, 314
MILL AREA, THE, 327
Millenium Falcon, The, 5.11a (TR), 482
Mind Body Problem, 5.12c (TR), 309
MIND BODY ROCK, 309
Mind Over Splatter, 5.10a, 128
MINDLESS MOUND, 125
Mine Shaft, 5.9, 405
Ming Dallas, The, 5.10b, 117
MINI CRAG, 83
MINI MALL, THE, 548
Minion, 5.4, 535
Minor Detour, 5.10a, 285
Minor Threat, 5.11d (TR), 201
Minotaur, 5.7, 105
Minute Man, 5.10d, 242
MIRACLE MILE BOULDERS, 503
MIRAGE ROCK, 304
MISCELLANEOUS ROCKS, 523
Misfits, 5.11b, 239
Misfortune Cookies, 5.8, 39
Misha's Madness, 5.9 (TR), 392
Missing in Action, 5.10d (TR), 420
Missing Persons, 5.11c, 470
Mission Impossible, 5.11b, 388
Model T, 5.7, 83
Modern Jazz, 5.10b, 90
Modern Warfare, 5.10a, 471
Mohave Green, 5.8, 329
Mohawk, The, 5.2c, 68
Mojave Green, 5.12d, 319
MOLAR, THE, 364
Molten Mettle, 5.11a, 144
Mom for the Road, 5.7, 49
Moment's Notice, 5.6 R, 245
Momento Mori, 5.11a, 181
Momma Spider, 5.9, 519
Mommy Dearest, 5.9, 348
Monaco, 5.11b, 534
Money for Nothing, 5.12a, 378
Mongoose, 5.13a, 319

Monkey Business, 5.8, 251
Monkey King, 5.10a, 342
Monsey, 5.11d R, 257
Monster Mash, 5.10a, 139
Monument Manor, 5.8, 310
Moonbeam Crack, The, 5.13qa, 225
Moondance, 5.13a/b, 273
Moonlight Crack, 5.10+ (TR), 201
Moonraker, 5.10b, 467
Moonshadow, 5.12c, 385
MOONSTONE, THE, 296
Moonstruck, 5.10b, 75
Moonwalk, The, 5.6, 296
Moosedog Lieback, 5.?, 522
MOOSEDOG TOWER, 522
Morality Test, 5.11b, 312
MORBID MOUND, 513
More Crazy Than Lazy, 5.10b R, 451
More Fool Me, 5.9, 470
More Frozen Food, 5.10c, 440
More Funky Than Junky, 5.10a, 126
MORE FUNKY THAN MONKEY, 257
More Hustle Than Muscle, 5.8, 378
More Monkey Thank Funky, 5.11c, 257
More My Speed, 5.3, 510
Morituri Te Salutamus, 5.9, 513
Morning After, The, 5.8, 392
Morning Star, 5.9, 508
Morning Thunder, 5.10d, 316
Morning Warm-Up, 5.10a X, 537
Morongo Child, 5.10c, 465
Morongo Man, 5.11c, 465
MORONGO MAN CLIFFS, 465
Mortal Thoughts, 5.11b R, 154
Mortarfied, 5.10b, 298
Mosaic, 5.8, 529
Mosaic Wall, 5.7, 521
Mosar, 5.9+, 121
Mother Board Breakdown, 5.10c, 451
Mother Butler, 5.10a, 310
Mother Goose, 5.4 X, 92
Mother Lode, 5.10b, 426
MOTHER LODE WALL, 426
Motor City Comix, 5.10a R, 327
Moubit, 5.10a, 464
MOUNDS, 247
Mountaineers's Route, Class 4 or 5, 521
Moustache, The, 5.10a, 483
Mouthfull of Gank, 5.10a, 221
Move to the Groove, 5.10c (TR), 250
Moveable Feast, 5.10c, 127
Moveable Feast, 5.9, 100
Mr Ranger Sir, 5.7, 85
Mr. Bunny Goes Rollerskating, 5.9 (TR), 364
Mr. Bunny Meets the Expando Flake, 5.10b (TR), 364
Mr. Bunny Quits, 5.10a, 114
Mr. Bunny vs. Six Unknown Agents, 5.8, 130
Mr. Bunny's Petri Dish, 5.9, 287
Mr. Bunny's Refund Check, 5.10a, 130
Mr. Bunny's Tax Shelter, 5.5, 130
Mr. DNA, 5.11 (TR), 206
Mr. Lizard Meets Flintstone, 5.6, 295
Mr. Magoo, 5.9, 104
Mr. Michael Goes To Washington, 5.8, 99
Mr. Misty Kiss, 5.7, 131
Mr. Rogers, 5.5, 394
Mr. Wizard, 5.11d (TR), 394
Mrs. Paul's, 5.9, 440
Mt Witness, 5.10a, 196
MT. GROSSVOGEL, 118
MTV, 5.11b (TR), 393
Mud Dog, 5.10a, 278
Muffin Bandits, 5.10b, 59

Mulligan Stew, 5.11b (TR), 275
Munchkin Land, 5.10d, 212
MUNCHKINLAND, 491
MUNCHKINLAND CRAG, 494
Mush Puppies, 5.8+, 82
Music Box, 5.8, 473
Mustang Ranch, 5.10 (TR), 47
MUSTANG RANCH, 47
Muy Swaino, 5.10a R, 350
My 3 Friends, 5.7, 451
My Bride, My Hilti & My Shoulders, 5.10d, 329
My Favorite Martian, 5.9, 351
My Favorite Things, 5.10b, 325
My First First, 5.9, 156
My Grain, 5.11c, 512
My Hubby is Chubby, 5.8+, 426
My Laundry, 5.9, 290
My Life As A Dog, 5.11c, 344
My Little Pretty, 5.9+, 493
My Senior Project, 5.9, 381
My Wife Is An Alien, 5.12a R, 508
Myrmecocystus Ewarti, 5.4, 513
MYSTIC COVE, 316
Mystic Teflon, 5.10c, 520
Nail 'n Gravel, 5.10d R, 533
Nailed to the Cross, 5.13a, 218
Naked Nancy, 5.10b (TR), 328
Naked Reagan, 5.11a, 328
Nameless, A3, 169
NANCY REAGAN'S FACE, 328
Napkin of Shame, 5.10b, 114
Naptime for Meggles, 5.9, 27
Narwhal, The, 5.10b, 377
Natural Selection, 5.11a, 76
Navigator, The, 5.10d R, 344
Nectar, 5.4, 463
Need To Have A Word With Myself, 5.11a, 326
Negasaurus, 5.9, 221
Negro Vortex, 5.10a, 526
NEGROPOLIS, THE, 26
Neptune, 5.8, 105
Nereltne, 5.7, 223
Nerve Storm, 5.11c, 428
Nestle Crunch, 5.10c, 254
Neue Regal, 5.9, 510
Never Cry Louie, 5.7, 447
New Day Yesterday, 5.10a, 79
New Deal, 5.13d, 248
New Decayed, 5.7, 287
New Hampshire, Naturally, 5.10b, 76
NEW JERSEY DOME, 46
NEW SAGE ROCK, 437
NEW SHOE REVIEW, THE, 5.10d, 67
New Testament, 5.9, 218
New Toy, 5.6, 485
New Wave, B1, 270
New World Order, 5.13b, 413
New Year's Quickie, 5.7, 393
Nice and Icy, 5.7, 442
Nice and Steep and Elbow Deep, 5.10b, 114
Nice Lady, 5.11, 367
Nice Pair, A, 5.9, 482
Nickel Slots, 5.7 R, 516
Night Gallery, 5.8+, 117
Nightline, 5.10c, 394
Nihilistic Pillar, 5.11c, 300
Nincompoe, 5.11d, 449
Ninny's Revenge, 5.9, 44
Nip and Tuck, 5.10a, 142
Nip in the Air, 5.10a, 142
Nipple, The, 5.10b, 455
Nitty Gritty, 5.9, 548
NIXON CRACKS, 193

No Better Births, 5.10a, 516
No Biggy, 5.10b R/X, 379
No Bolts Required, 5.10d R, 399
No Bones About It, 5.5, 27
No Calculators Allowed, 5.10a, 166
No Falls, 5.10d, 276
No Holds Barred, 5.9+ (TR), 418
No Metal Wasted, 5.9+ X, 353
No Mistake Or Big Pancake, 5.10d-5.11b, 239
No Nuts, 5.10a, 497
No Nuts, No Huevos, 5.9, 412
No Options, 5.11b, 386
No Perch Is Necessary, 5.10d, 141
NO PLACE LIKE DOME, 491
No Rest for the Wicked, 5.8 R, 27
No San Francisco, 5.11a (TR), 78
No Self Confidence, 5.10b, 78
No Self Control, 5.12c, 78
No Self Respect, 5.10c, 78
No Shirt Needed, 5.10d, 217
No Strings Attached, 5.6, 397
No-Doz, 5.9+ R, 383
Nobody Walks in L.A., 5.9, 96
Nobody Walks in LA, 5.8+, 362
Nobody's Right Mind, 5.9, 216
Nolina Crack, 5.10a, 38
NOMAD DOME, 287
Non-Decumbent Destiny, 5.8, 160
None of Your Business, 5.10b R, 154
NOODLE ROCK, 426
Noriega Does Panama, 5.10a, 535
North Arete, 5.8, 192
NORTH ASTRO DOME, 293
North Dakota Big Wall Problem, 5.10, 258
NORTH DAKOTA DOME, 258
North Face, 5.10+, 226
North Face, 5.10d (TR), 394
North Face, 5.4, 176
North Face, 5.?, 351
NORTH FACE, 440
North Face Center, 5.8, 190
North Face of the Eiger, 5.10a, 164
North Face, The, 5.2 X, 306
NORTH HOLLYWOOD, 503
North Overhang, 5.9, 187
North Side, 5.11a (TR), 316
NORTH TOWER, 316
Northeas Arete, 5.10+, 176
Northeast Arete, 5.9, 193
Northeast Corner, 5.6, 190
Northeast Face, 5.10, 192
NORTHEAST FACE, 328
Northern Lights, 5.8+, 477
Northwest Chimney, 5.2, 189
Northwest Chimney, 5.4, 195
Northwest Passage, 5.10a, 53
Northwet Arete, 5.8, 176
Norwegian Wood, 5.9, 252
Nose to the Grindstone, 5.11a, 362
Not A Hogan, 5.10a, 436
Not For Loan, 5.10b, 168
Not Forgotten, 5.10a, 156
Not in Kansas Anymore, 5.9, 494
Not Just Another Pretty Face, 5.10d, 534
Not King Cole, 5.8, 479
NOT SO COOL DOME, 50
Not Worth Your While, 5.5, 258
Notch Route, 5.6, 480
Nothing But A Groundhog, 5.10b, 453
Nothing But Hearsay, 5.12a, 511
Nothing to Fear, 5.6, 401
Now We Know, 5.4, 58
Nuclear Arms, 5.12a, 66

NUCLEAR REACTOR ROCK, 445
Nuclear Waste, 5.10b, 130
Nuclear Waste, 5.9+, 63
Nuke the Whales, 5.9, 445
Nurn's Romp, 5.8, 384
Nurses in Bondage, 5.9 (TR), 416
Nutcracker, 5.2, 362
Nuts and Bolts, 5.9, 378
Nuts and Bolts of Climbing, The, 5.10c, 60
Nuts and Cherries, 5.6, 131
Nuts Are For Men Without Balls, 5.8, 245
O'Bulg , 5.11a, 516
O'Kelley's Crack, 5.10c, 229
O.W., 5.10+, 83
Oasis of Eden, 5.10d R, 277
Oat Cuisine, 5.10c, 209
Oat Route, The, 5.8, 209
Oatmeal Eating Aardvarks, 5.7, 503
OB/GYN DOME, 287
Obsidian, 5.12, 412
Ocean of Doubt, 5.13b/cq, 64
Off Camber, B1—, 203
Off Ramp, 5.10d, 371
Off to See the Wizard, 5.10b, 500
Official Route of the 1984 Olympics, The, 5.10c, 206
Official Rubber Tester, 5.12a, 247
Offroach, The, 5.11c, 335
Offshoot, 5.10b, 62
Oh God!, 5.10c R, 504
Oh God!, 5.2, 450
Oh God, It's My Boss, 5.8, 523
Oh Pinyon Crack, 5.10a, 49
Ohm on the Range, 5.4, 118
Oil My Joints, 5.10c, 500
OK Korner, 5.9, 172
OLD A HOTIE ROCK, 300
Old Guys Gone Nuts, Go to the Cops, 5.11c, 381
Old Man and the Poodle, The, 5.8, 128
Old Man Down the Road, The, 5.10a, 76
Old Triangle Classic, 5.10, 190
Old Wave, 5.11, 270
OLD WOMAN BOULDERING, 190-192
OLD WOMAN, THE, 188-190
OLYMPIC DOME, 345
Omaha Beach, 5.8, 389
Omega, 5.7, 516
Omnia Exteres, 5.10c, 49
On the Air, 5.8, 267
On the Nob, 5.10b, 126, 128
Once in a Blue Moon, 54 R, 123
Once in a Lifetime, 5.7, 425
One Arm Giant, 5.10d, 467
One Bolt Jolt, 5.10d, 163
One for the Road, 5.10a, 49
One Move Leads To Another, 5.10c, 321
One of Two, 5.6, 355
One Point Crack, 5.4, 473
One Pop, No Stop, 5.10c, 429
One Small Step, 5.6, 296
One Story Town, 5.10 (TR), 393
One Way Up, 5.7, 418
One Whole Chicken in A Can, 5.10d, 304
Only Outlaws Have Guns, 5.9+, 543
Ontology Recapitulates Phylogony, 5.11b A1, 405
Ooby Dooby, 5.10a, 260
Ope's Crack, 5.9, 245
Open Casket Funeral, 5.11a (TR), 120
Open Container, 5.8, 503
Open Season, 5.9+, 208
Opportunist, The, 5.10b, 333
Opus Dihedral, 5.9, 83
Orange Curtain, 5.11, 144
Orange Flake, 5.8, 378

Orange Julius, B1+, 203
Orc Sighs, 5.10c, 210
Orc, The, 5.10a, 210
Ordinary Route, 5.11a R, 250
Organ Grinder, The, 5.10b, 339
Orgasmatron, 5?, 41
Orgasmatron, The, 5.10b, 129
ORIENT ROCK, 420
Orno-Necro, 5.11c, 459
ORPHAN, 5.9, 189
Ostrich Skin, 5.7 R, 516
OTHER CAMPSITE NO. 1 AREA ROUTES, 394
Other Voces, 5.7, 90
OTTER CLIFFS, THE, 167
Ouef's Up, 5.10a R/X, 442
Out For A Bite, 5.10d (TR), 196
Out For Lunch, 5.11a, 234
Out of Step, 5.7 R, 537
Out On A Limb, 5.10b, 237
Out To Grunge, 5.10a, 234
Out To Lunge, 5.10d (TR), 234
OUTBACK BOULDERING, THE, 226-228
Outer Limit, 5.6 A3, 187
Outhouse Flake, 5.4, 195
OUTHOUSE ROCK, 195-196
Outland, 5.12, 339
OUTSIDE, 208
Outsiders, The, 5.11a R, 114
OUTWARD BOUND SLAB, 49
Outward Bound Slab Route, 5.8, 49
Over the Hill, 5.9, 36
Over the Rainbow, 5.11a, 494
Over-Powered by Hootch, 5.12a (TR), 150
OVERBOLTED ROCK, 453
Overdraft, 5.8 (TR), 285
Overhang Bypass, 5.7, 187
Overnight Sensation, 5.11b, 204
Overpowered by Funk, 5.12a, 484
Overseer, 5.9, 126
Oversight, 5.10a, 205
Owatafooliam, 5.8, 120
Owl, 5.9, 315
OWL PINNACLE, 315
OYSTER BAR AREA, 372
OYSTER BAR, THE, 375
Oyster Delacacy, 5.11b, 375
Oysters from Heaven, 5.11c, 375
OZ, 489
OZ ROCK, 491
OZ TOWERS, THE, 501
PAC MAN ROCK, 420
Pachyderms to Paradise, 5.9, 159
Pacific Ave. Dorm, 5.7, 94
Padded Handcuffs, 5.9, 47
Pagan Holiday, 5.9, 348
Pahrump, 5.4, 47
Paint and Body, 5.4, 267
Paint Me Gigi, 5.7 X, 49
Pale Rider, 5.11a, 330
Palm-U-Granit, 5.7, 233
Palmreader, 5.8, 520
PALMREADER WALL, 520
Panama Red, 5.11c (TR), 524
PANORAMA PILLAR, 394
Panther Crack, 5.10d, 535
Panty Shield, The, 5.10c, 301
Papa Woolsey, 5.10b, 192
Papal Pleaser, 5.4, 450
Papal Smear, 5.10d, 450
Papaya Crack, 5.11b, 124
Papillon, 5.10b, 222
Paranetieum, 5.8, 264
Paranoia, 5.11b, 481

Pardon Me, 5.9, 264
Parental Guidance Suggested, 5.8, 276
PARKING AREA BOULDER, 150
Parking Lot Crank, 5.11+, 367
PARKING LOT ROCKS, 43-44
Party in the Desert, 5.10b, 543
Passing Zone, 5.8 R/X, 96
PASTRY PILE, THE, 351
Pat Adams Dihedral, 5.11b, 131
PATAGONIA PILE, 216-217
Patagucci, 5.5, 216
Patanjali's Sutra, 5.11a (TR), 464
Pathetic Crack, 5.6, 446
Pathetic Dike, 5.8, 446
PATHETIC DOME, 446
Pathetic Face, 5.8, 446
PATINA ROCK, 497
Patricide, 5.11b, 277
Patriot, The, 5.10d, 457
PEA BRAIN, 307
Peabody's Peril, 5.9, 216
Peanut Brittle, 5.8 (TR), 389
Peanut Gallery, A, 5.11a, 112
Pear-Grape Route, 5.10a, 76
Pearl Drops, 5.11a, 350
Pearl Necklace, 5.11c, 350
Pearls Before Swine, 5.8, 373
PEARLS, THE, 350
Pebble Beach, 5.7, 470
Pebbles and Bam Bam, 5.7, 273
Pecking Order, 5.10c, 443
PEEWEE ROCK, 207
Peglet, 5.7, 121
Pelvic Thrust, 5.10c, 453
Penalty Runout, 5.9 R, 111
Pencil Neck Geek, 5.10b, 526
Penelope Street, 5.10a (TR), 233
Penelope's Walk, 5.4, 206
Penny Lane, 5.8, 242
PEP BOYS CRAG, THE, 135
Pepason, 5.9+, 233
Perfect Fingers, 5.10b, 352
Perfect World, 5.10b, 342
Perfidious, A4 5.6, 192
Perhaps, 5.9, 381
Perhaps the Surgeon General, 5.8, 130
PERJURY ROCK, 451
PERNICIOUS DOME, 58
Perpetual Motion, 5.10d, 414
PERPETUAL MOTION WALL, 414
PERRY MASONARY, 298
Persian Room, The, 5.13a 9TR), 192
Personal Space, 5.10c (TR), 98
Peruvian Power Layback, 5.9, 99
Peruvian Princess, 5.10b, 123
Perverts in Power, 5.9, 247
Pet Cemetery, 5.11b, 27
PET CEMETERY, THE, 27
Pet or Meat, 5.10d, 535
Pet Project, 5.4, 84
PET ROCK, 84
Pete's Handful, 5.9, 192
Peter Easter Pumpkin Eater, 5.10c, 484
Petrodynamics, 5.11a, 433
PEYOTE CRACKS, 224-225
Pfundt's Folly, 5.8, 536
Phallus, 5.7, 201
Phineas P. Phart, 5.10a, 211
Pick-a-Nick Baskets, 5.9 R, 85
Picking Up The Pieces, 5.10a, 195
Pickpocket, 5.6, 421
Picnic, 5.6, 517
Pictures at an Exhibition, 5.10a, 445

Piddle Pug, 5.7 R, 83
Pig in Heat, 5.9 R, 126
Pig Pen, B1, 203
Piggle Pugg, 5.10c, 290
Pile in the Sky, 5.10c, 174
Pile, The, 5.7, 142
PILEDRIVER BOULDERS, 429
Piledriver, The, 5.11c, 429
Pilgrim, The, 5.11a, 339
Pillar of Dawn, 5.10a, 59
PILLARS OF PAIN, THE, 174
Pinch a Smelly Scrutinizer, 5.10c, 215
Pinched Rib, 5.10b, 200
Pinhead, 5.11—, 203
Pinhead, 5.9, 222
Pink Thing, 5.10a, 330
Pinky Lee, 5.10d, 233
Pinnacle Aerobics to Promote Blood Circulation, 5.11b, 378
Pinnacle Stand, 5.7, 186
PINON POINT, 419
Pint-Size Planet, 5.10a, 394
PINTO QUEEN AREA, 423
Pinyon Crack, 5.10b, 133
PINYON CRAG, 133
Pipper, 5.11, 32
Pirates of the Carabiner, 5.10b, 121
Piss Crack, 5.9+, 190
Pissing on Myself, 5.11b (TR), 445
Pit Bull Attach, 5.10d, 151
Pit Slut, 5.12a, 150
Pit Viper, 5.11b, 462
Pit Viper, 5.13b, 319
Pitball, 5.11c, 150
Pitch Black, 5.9, 94
PITTED ROCK, 150
PITTED ROCK, 151
PIXIE ROCK, 515
Pixie Stick, 5.10a (TR), 515
Plain But Good Hearted, 5.6, 524
Planet Claire, 5.10d, 359
Planet Claire, 5.11+, 367
Planet X, 5.8+, 359
Planet X, B1 R, 367
PLANET X AREA, 357
PLANET X BOULDERING, 367
PLANET X BOULDERS, 359
Planet Y, 5.10a, 359
Planet Z, 5.10d, 359
Planetary Motion, 5.8, 95
Plantismal, 5.9, 301
PLAYHOUSE ROCK, 132
Playing Hookey, 5.10a, 250
Pleasure Pincipal, 5.8+, 348
PLYMOUTH ROCK, 263
Poaching Bighorn, 5.11b, 317
Pocket Pool, 5.11d, 534
Pocket Pussy, 5.11a (TR), 105
Pocket Veto, 5.10a, 237
Poddle Lizard, 5.7, 88
Podium, The, 5.10b, 316
Poetry in Motion, 5.9, 118
POETRY ROCK, 118
Point of Interest, 5.6, 446
Point of No Return, 5.10c, 251
Pokie's Big Change, 5.4, 310
Pokin' A Gopher, 5.9+, 407
Polar Bears in Bondage, 5.7, 47
Police & Thieves, 5.11c, 248
Political Asylum, 5.7, 264
Political Rehabilitation, 5.8, 264
Polly Wants a Crack, 5.10a, 121
Polytechnics, 5.10c, 63
Pom Pom Dancer, 5.9, 314

PONDEROSA WALL, 544
Pony Express, 5.9, 544
Poodle Boy, 5.10B, 330
Poodle in Shining Armor, 5.8, 127
Poodle Jive, 5.9, 127
POODLE ROCK, 425
Poodle Skirt, 5.11c, 237
POODLE SMASHER AREA, 322
Poodle Smasher, The, 5.11a, 322
Poodle Woof, 5.10b, 179
Poodle-oids from the Deep, 5.10b, 127
Poodles Are People Too, 5.10b, 126
Poodlesby, 5.6, 126
Poon, 5.10a, 165
POON TANG ROCK, 165
Poopdeck, The, 5.10a, 217
Pop Rocks, 5.10b, 98
Pop Tart, 5.8, 298
Pope and Circumstance, 5.9, 449
POPE BOULDERS, THE, 450
Pope on A Rope, 5.12d, 449
POPE'S CAPE, 450
Pope's Hat, 5.9, 449
POPE'S HAT, 449
Popemobile, The, 5.10c, 450
Popeye, 5.11a, 116
Poppa Spider, 5.9, 519
POPPIE FIELD BOULDERS, THE, 500
Poppin' and Breakin', 5.10a, 433
Pops Goes Hawaiian, 5.7, 44
Popsicle, 5.11d, 456
Popular Mechanics, 5.9, 38
Porky Pig, 5.11b (TR), 233
Porky's Excellent Adventure, 5.8, 455
Portal, 5.9, 510
Poseidon Adventure, The, 5.11b, 301
Possessed By Elvis, 5.10d, 237
POTATO HEAD, THE, 206
Potato Masher, 5.12b, 93
Potlatch, 5.8, 481
Poultry Pilots, 5.7, 94
POWELL BOULDER, 228
Powell Crank, B1, 367
Powell Face, 5.11, 228
Powell Pinch, 5.11, 367
Power Drop, 5.10b, 248
Power Lichen, 5.10b, 248
Power Line, 5.7, 248
Power Lunch, 5.10b (TR), 141
Power to the People, 5.10b, 344
Powers That Be, The, 5.13a, 64
Pox on You, 5.11d, 389
Practice Rehearsal, 5.7, 132
Predator Tigress, 5.11b, 457
Prejudicial Viewpoint, 5.11a R, 516
Prepackaged, 5.10a, 126
Preparation H, 5.11a (TR), 153
Prepubescent Narwhal, 5.6, 437
Presbyterian Dental Floss, 5.10d, 377
Press Conference, The, 5.8+, 349
Presto in C Sharp, 5.7, 378
Presupposition, 5.11d R, 516
Pretty Gritty, 5.10a, 96
Pretty in Pink, 5.11b (TR), 47
Pretzel Logic, 5.10c, 222
PREVIOUSLY UNRELEASED MATERIAL, 283
Preying Mantels, 5.10a, 333
Prickly Pare, 5.10c, 350
Primal Flake, 5.9+, 289
Primal Scream, 5.10c, 245
Primal Urge, 5.9, 482
Prime Time, 5.10a (TR), 393
PRIME TIME CRAG, 117

Princess, 5.7, 535
PRINGLE ROCK, 309
Prisoner of Inertia, 5.10d, 458
Private Idaho, 5.11b, 44
Profundity, 5.10a (or 5.10c), 33
Progressive Lizard, 5.9, 88
Prom Queen, 5.9, 338
PROTOZOAN, THE, 123
Psoriasis, 5.9, 274
Psychedelic Yupies, 5.11a (TR), 224
Psycho, 5.10d, 63
Psycho Groove, 5.9, 132
Psychokenesis, 5.11b, 63
Psychotechnics, 5.11b, 63
Pterodactydl Crack, 5.9, 139
Puff Adder, 5.13a, 319
Pull My Finger Barbara, 5.11a, 381
Pullups to Pasadena, 5.10c, 387
Pump Up The Volume, 5.11a, 92
Pumping Ego, 5.10b, 199
Pumping Hate, 5.13a, 65
Pumping Monzonite, B1+, 367
Pumpkin Pie, 5.8, 393
Puncture Wound, 5.10c, 465
Punish the Mosquito, 5.10c, 461
PUNK ROCK, 301
Punked Out Porpoise, 5.8+, 301
Pure and Easy, 5.6, 447
Purple Place, 5.11, 352
Puss n' Boots, 5.11c, 178
Puss Wuss, 5.10a, 458
Pussy Galore, 5.10d, 158
Puzzlin' Evidence, 5.11b, 128
Pyramid Power, 5.9, 551
PYRAMID TOWER, 480
PYRAMID, THE, 551
Pyrannosaurus Next, 5.10a, 197
Quadrophenia, 5.7, 447
Quaking Has-Beens, 5.9, 476
Quantum Jump, 5.10c, 130
Quantum Mechanics, 5.11b, 66
Quarantine, 5.10a, 240
Quarter Moon Crack, 5.10a, 114
Quasar, 5.12a, 467
Queen Bee, 5.6, 337
Queen Crimson, 5.10b, 428
QUEEN CRIMSON DOME, 428
Queen For A Day, 5.7, 337
Queen Mother's Route, 5.2, 339
QUEEN MOUNTAIN AREA, 333
Quest For Fire, 5.11c, 38
Quest for the Golden Hubris, 5.9, 278
Question of Masculinity, A, 5.12c (TR), 186
Question, The, 5.10b, 491
Quick Draw McGraw, 5.10a, 242
Quickstone, 5.12c R, 114
Quien Sabe?, 5.7, 522
Quit Doing Czech Grils, 5.9 (TR), 112
Quivering Lips, 5.8, 382
Quivering Savages, 5.12a, 524
Quivers, 5.5, 491
Quivers Direct, 5.8 (TR), 491
Quothe the Raven, 5.7+, 475
R & R, 5.8, 378
R.A.F., 5.9, 233
R.D. Memorial, 5.10a, 276
R.M.L., 5.8, 237
R.P. Delights, 5.10a R, 510
R.S. Chicken Choker, 5.11b, 109
RABBIT WARREN, THE, 364
Rackless Abandon, 5.10a X, 473
Rad, 5.9 (TR), 418
Radio Free Utah, 5.10b, 327

Raging Bull Dike, 5.11d, 377
Raging Intensity, 5.8, 233
Raging Order, 5.8 R, 510
Railer, 5.12c, 170
Railroad, 5.11a, 250
Rain Dance, 5.10d R, 272
Raindance, 5.8, 414
Rainy Day Women, 5.7, 125
Rainy Day, Dream Away, 5.11b R, 170
Raise Your Right Hand, 5.10a, 451
Raising Bran, 5.8, 209
Raked Over The Coles, 5.10d, 245
Raker Mobile, 5.8, 378
Raker's Blaring Hat Rack, 5.10d, 413
Ramming Speed, 5.11d, 136
Ranch Hand, 5.6, 543
Randy the Riveter, 5.8, 410
Ranger Danger, 5.8, 118
Ranger is Watching Me, The, 5.10b, 520
Ranger J.B., 5.6, 154
Ranger J.D., 5.6, 154
Ranger Rendezvous, 5.7, 120
Rangers in Space, 5.11a, 475
Rap Bolters Are Weak, 5.12a, 154
Rap Dancing, 5.10a or c, 26
Rap or Snap, 5.7, 402
Rastafarian, 5.13b, 225
Rat Boy, 5.10c, 181
Rat Ledge, 5.8, 277
RAT ROCK, 277
Ratrace, 5.10d, 113
Rats with Wings, 5.11, 201
Rattle and Hum, 5.11d, 212
Rattler, The, 5.11a, 501
RATTLESNAKE BUTTRESS, 550
RATTLESNAKE FORKS, 548
RATTLESNAKE FORKS BOULDERS, 550
Raven's Reach, 5.10a, 201
Raven, The, 5.11b (TR), 471
Raven, The, 5.8, 463
Ravens Do Nasty Things To My Bottom, 5.9, 128
Raving Skinhead, 5.10c, 342
Rawl, 5.5, 364
Ray's Cafe, 5.10a, 386
Reach for a Peach, 5.10, 367
Reach for a Peach, 5.10b (TR), 163
Read My Flips, 5.11a, 386
Read My Lips, 5.11a, 386
Reagan Did A Good Job, 5.8 R, 510
REAL HALL OF HORRORS, 386
REAL HIDDEN VALLEY AREA, THE, 148
Real McCoy, The, 5.12b (TR), 239
Reality Check, 5.9, 194
Realm of the Flying Monkeys, 5.11d, 497
Reconstructive Surgery, 5.10a, 410
RED BLUFFS, 319
Red Bull, 5.11b R, 124
RED BURRITO, THE, 142
Red Chile, 5.10d (TR), 142
Red Crack, The, 5.10b, 347
Red Cross, 5.12a/b, 345
Red Eye, 5.9 (TR), 58
Red Headed Stranger, 5.11a, 284
Red Hot Chili Peppers, 5.11a, 304
Red Hot Fire Balls, 5.11c, 378
Red Line, 5.8, 295
Red Obelisk, The, 5.10a, 307
RED OBELISK, THE, 307
Red Rain, 5.13a, 319
Red Red, 5.10d, 319
Red Snapper, 5.11a, 39
Red Sonja, 5.10c, 342
Red Tide, 5.10d R, 39

REEF ROCK, 399
Reefer Madness, 5.12c var. (TR), 150
Reflector Oven, 5.10a, 471
Refrigerator — Left Side, The, 5.10b, 323
Refrigerator — Right Side, The, 5.11a (TR), 323
REFRIGERATOR, THE, 323
REGGIE DOME, 44
Reggie on a Poodle, 5.10a, 44
Reggie's Pimple, 5.10c (TR), 44
Regular Route, The, 5.10c, 263
Rehab, 5.9, 173
Rei Momo, 5.10b, 348
Reject the Dominant Paradigm, 493
Rejuvenation, 5.6, 391
Remain in Light, 5.10a, 348
Renter, The, 5.9, 378
Repeat After Me, 5.10a, 451
Repo Man, 5.12a R, 293
Restaurant at the End of the Universe, 5.10d, 87
Resurrection, 5.11d/12a, 218
Resurrection, 5.7, 391
Retirement, 5.10a, 362
Retirement Is All That, 5.7, 436
Return of Large Marge, 5.7, 345
Return of the Chuckwalla, 5.10c, 250
Return to Hell, 5.11b, 548
Revenge of the Chuckwalla, 5.11c, 250
Revenge of the Herds, 5.8, 487
Reverend, The, 5.8, 530
Rhoid Warrior, 5.10c, 148
Rhythm & Blues, 5.10b, 123
Rhythm of the Heart, 5.8 X, 515
Rice Cake Roof, 5.10c, 286
Rich and Famous, 5.9, 272
RICH AND FAMOUS CLIFF, 272
Rich Bitch, 5.9+, 272
Richochet, 5.5, 287
Rickets and Scurvy, 5.10b, 50
Riddler, The, 5.12a, 237
Riddles in the Dark, 5.11c, 229
Ride A Wild Bago, 5.10a, 154
Riders on the Storm, 5.10a, 60
Riding Shotgun, 5.7, 543
Rieder Problem, B1, 184
Riff Raff Roof, 5.10a, 536
Right, 5.10, 176
Right 'n Up, 5.8 X, 537
Right Archimedes' Crack, 5.9, 414
Right Arete, 5.10—, 233
Right Banana Crack, 5.11a, 124
Right Baskerville Crack, 5.10a, 35
Right Beetle Crack, 5.10b, 109
Right Between the Eyes, 5.7, 251
Right Double Feature Crack, 5.8, 503
Right Hand of Light, The, 5.10c (TR), 401
Right Lizard Crack, 5.9, 88
Right Mel Crack, 5.10c, 90
Right Nixon Crack, 5.10, 193
Right of Center, 5.11b (TR), 400
Right On, 5.5, 378
Right Peyote Crack, 5.8, 224
Right Route, 5.10c, 92
Right S Crack, 5.9, 122
Right Sawdust Crack, 5.8, 32
Right Side, 5.10d (TR), 238
Right Stuff, The, 5.10c, 340
Right to Arm Bears, The, 5.11b, 487
Right V Crack, 5.10a, 536
RIM ROCK, 343
Ring of Fire, 5.11b, 416
Rings Around Uranus, 5.7, 385
Rip Off, 5.6, 40
Riples in Time, 5.6, 393

Ripples, 5.7, 173
Rites of Passage, 5.11a, 339
Rites of Spring, 5.9, 463
Roach Motel, 5.10a R, 109
Roach Roof, 5.6, 109
Road Dogs, 5.7, 475
ROAD KILL ROCK, 412
ROADSIDE ROCK, 87
Roadside Slab, 5.10b R, 523
Roan Way, 5.8, 101
Roaring Rapids, 5.5, 503
Roark, 5.10c, 76
Roast Leg of Chair, 5.7, 251
Rob'n the Cradle, 5.10c, 56
Robaxol, 5.6, 118
Robbins Route, The, 5.10+, 239
Roberts Crack, 5.10d, 167
Roberts Crack, 5.9, 411
Roberts-Davis, 5.10a, 232
Robo Cop, 5.7+, 362
Robocop Meets the Munchkins, 5.10a, 494
Roboranger, 5.5, 118
Robotics, 5.8, 122
Rock & Roll Gril, 5.9, 90
ROCK 1, 474
ROCK 2, 474
ROCK 3, 475
Rock Dog Candy Leg, 5.11c (TR), 98
ROCK GARDEN VALLEY, 98
ROCK HUDSON, 223
ROCK HUDSON BOULDERING, 228
Rock Lypso, 5.10a, 71
ROCK OF AGES, 275
Rock Shark, 5.11a, 256
Rock Star, 5.10d R, 283
Rock-A-Lot, 5.7, 98
Rocket Man, 5.5, 337
Rockwell 41C, 5.11a, 213
Rockwork Orange, 5.11d, 272
ROCKWORK ROCK, 272
Rocky Candy, 5.9, 98
Rocky Horror, 5.7, 283
Rocky Horror Picture Show, 5.11b/c, 383
ROCKY MARCIANO, 402
Rocky Road, 5.10d, 389
Rocky vs. Rambo, 5.11c, 272
RODEO ROCK, 289
Roller Coaster, 5.11c (TR), 219
Roller Coaster, 5.9, 67
Rollerball, 5.10b, 219
ROLLERBALL FORMATION, 219
Rollerskating with Aliens, 5.8, 480
Rolling Rock, 5.9 (TR), 95
Roman Pretzel, 5.8+, 90
ROMAN ROCKS, 429
Romper Room, 5.11a, 44
Ronnie and Clyde, 5.11b (TR), 421
Ronnie's Rump, 5.7 (TR), 328
ROOF ROCK, 221
Roof, The, 5.10a, 245
Roofing Company, 5.10a, 251
Room to Shroom, 5.9, 278
ROOM TO SHROOM, 278
ROOSTER BOULDER, 443
Rope Drag, 5.10b, 75
Rope Opera, 5.11a, 321
Rose Parade, 5.8, 426
Rots o' Rock, 5.12c, 136
Rotten Banana, 5.6 R, 125
Roughriders, 5.11b, 378
Roundup, The, 5.11b, 309
Route 1202, 5.10a, 464
Route 1326, 5.2, 534

Route 152, 5.10a R, 92
Route 182, 5.9, 128
Route 499, 5.11b (TR), 189
Route 66, 5.4, 53
Route kBeer, 5.11a, 353
Route of All Evil, 5.11d, 27
Route Right of the Dumbest Climb in the Monument, 5.10, 386
Roy's Route, 5.11b, 550
Roy's Solo, 5.7, 87
RR Does It Again, 5.10d (TR), 107
Rubber Boa, 5.13c, 319
Rubberfat Syndrome, The, 5.11a (TR), 169
Rubberneck Busybody, 5.11a, 511
RUBBLE ROCKS, 219
Rubicon, 5.10d, 462
RUBICON FORMATION, 462
Ruby Slippers, 5.11a, 493
Rude Awakening, 5.10c R, 504
Rudy Valentine Day, 5.8, 481
Ruff Stuff, 5.10c, 445
Ruffled Rooster, 5.9, 443
Rule Britannia, 5.11c R, 245
RUMBLE CRAGS, THE, 481
Rumblers Below the Roof, 5.3, 421
Rumors and Lies, 5.12a, 511
Run For Your Life, 5.10b, 170
Run From Your Mother-In-Law, 5.10a, 170
Run From Your Wife, 5.10c, 170
Rurp Romp, A3, 361
Rurp Seam, B1, 190
Rush Hour, 5.9, 429
Russian Grain Crisis, 5.10c, 260
Rust in Peace, 5.9, 375
Rustler, The, 5.11c, 406
Rusty Ax, The, 5.6, 500
Rusty Pipes, 5.2, 317
RUSTY WALL, 229
RYAN AREA, 356
RYAN CAMPGROUN, 369
RYAN CAMPGROUND BOULDERING, 371
Rye Not?, 5.9, 446
S Crack, 5.11a, 411
S CRACK FORMATION, 122
S Cracker, The, 5.10c, 74
S'Nose of Winter, 5.8, 96
S.O.B., 5.6, 537
SAAVY DOME, 163
Sabre, 5.9, 458
Sabretooth, 5.7, 237
Sack in the Wash, 5.10b, 79
Sacred Cow, 5.10a, 163
SADDLE ROCK, 376
SADDLE ROCKS, 378
Safe Muffins, 5.8 R, 305
Safety in Numbers, 5.10a R, 194
Safety in Solitude, 5.9, 194
Safety Pin, 5.11c, 459
Sail Away, 5.8, 156
Sakreteligious, 5.8, 298
Same As It Ever Was, 5.9, 418
Sanctify Yourself, 5.9, 393
SANCTUARY, THE, 298
Sancturary Much, 5.11a, 298
SAND CASTLE, THE, 156
Sand in My Shoes, 5.9, 474
Sand Truck, The, 5.11b/c, 440
Sand Witch, 5.10a, 40
Sandbag, 5.10c (TR), 166
Sandblast, 5.7, 459
Sandworm, 5.10c R, 252
SANDWORM ROCK, 252
Santa's Little Helpers, 5.11a, 233

Satanic Mechanic, 5.12b, 172
Satchmo, 5.8, 393
Satchmo, The, 5.9+, 133
Satellite Boulder Left, 5.11+, 367
Satellite Boulder Right, 5.11+, 367
Satin Finish, 5.9, 273
Saturday Night Live, B1, 150
Saturn Boulder, The, 5.12b, 475
SATURN BOULDER, THE, 475
Saturn Sheets, 5.8, 359
Save the Last Stance for Me, 5.9, 463
Savwafare 1st Everywhere, 5.8, 163
Sawdust and Peanut Sheels, 5.10a, 511
Say No To Jugs, 5.11a, 465
Scar Is Born, A, 5.11c, 272
Scar Wars, 5.11a, 301
Scare Way, 5.10b, 520
Scareamouch, 5.2, 534
SCARECROW ROCK, 494
Scarecrow, The, 5.10a, 500
Scared Bare, 5.10d, 169
Scaried Treasure, 5.10b, 121
Scary Monsters, 5.11d, 104
Scary Poodles, 5.11b, 127
SCARY ROCK, 374
SCARY TREE PINNACLES, 427
Scatterbrain, B1+, 193
SCATTERBRAIN BOULDER, 193
Scattered Remains, 5.11b, 433
Schlong, The, 5.11a, 337
SCHOOL BOULDER, 190
School Daze, 5.10a, 283
Schrodinger Equation, The, 5.10b R, 130
Schwee, 5.9, 326
Scientific Americans, 5.8 R, 38
Scoop Problem, 5.10, 193
Scoop Problem, 5.11—, 203
Scope & Hope, 5.10b, 419
Scorched Earth, 5.11c, 436
Scorpion, The, 5.13b, 169
Scotch, 5.6 R, 517
Scotch with a Twist, 5.8 R, 517
Scrambbled Leggs, 5.10c, 133
Scream Chuck, 5.7 R, 515
Scream of the Butterfly, 5.10b, 550
SCREAMER ROCKS, 464
Screaming in Digital, 5.6, 510
Screaming Poodle, The, 5.10c (TR), 51
Screaming Woman, The, 5.10a, 51
Screen Test, 5.11a, 503
Scrumdillyishus, 5.7, 131
SCUD BOULDER, 457
Scud Missile, 5.11a, 308
Sea Monkeys, 5.10c R, 126
Search for Chinese Morsels, 5.10b, 39
Search for Klingons, 5.7, 385
Season Opener, 5.8, 208
Second Thoughts, 5.10a, 246
Secondary Inspection, 5.9, 520
Secovar, 5.5, 184
Secret Agent Man, 5.11c (TR), 174
Secret of Mother Butler, The, 5.10c, 310
Secret Sauce, 5.11, 115
SECRET VALLEY, 312
Seebolt, 5.11c, 485
Seed of Irony, 5.10a, 402
Seizure, 5.12c, 462
Self Abuse, 5.6, 105
Semi Tough, 5.10d, 151
Semisweet, 5.9 X, 508
Sen Blen, 5.10c, 38
Sendero Luminoso, 5.9, 461
SENILE CANYON, 328

SENILE DOME, 328
Sensory Deprivation, 5.12b, 433
Sentinel Beach, 5.8, 167
SENTINEL, THE, 167-169
Separated At Mirth, 5.9+, 140
SERGEANT ROCK, 283
Serious Fashion, 5.10c, 289
Serpent Scales, 5.6, 533
Sesert Safari, 5.11+, 441
Sexy Sadye, 5.10d, 173
Shady Grove, 5.10c, 250
Shady Nook, 5.5, 436
SHADY SPOT, THE, 55
Shaggy Dog, 5.9, 391
Shake the Monster, 5.10d, 125
Shake, Rattle and Roll, 5.11b R, 551
Shakin Like Milk, 5.11b, 358
Shakin' the Shirts, 5.10a, 222
Shaking Hands with the Unemployed, 5.10d, 386
Shaking Like A Leaf, 5.8, 441
Shame, 5.10c, 163
Shamrock Shooter, 5.11c, 90
Shardik, 5.3, 47
Shark Fin, The, 5.10c, 344
SHARK FIN, THE, 344
Sharks in the Water, 5.10c, 402
Sharp Arete, 5.10c, 470
Sharp Desire, 5.8, 412
Shave Your Bump, 5.6, 453
She's So Unusual, 5.7, 84
SHEEP PASS CAMPGROUND, 392
Sheet Bends, 5.8, 530
Sheltered, 5.8, 40
Shiatsu, 5.10c (TR), 511
Shibumi, 5.10d, 39
Shifting Sands, 5.11b, 391
Shin Bashers, 5.10c, 66
Shindig, 5.11, 146
Ship of Fools, 5.11a, 217
Ship Wrecked, 5.12c, 420
Shipwrech, B1 R, 176
SHIPWRECK BOULDER, 176
Shirley MaClaine Meets Edlinger, 5.9, 264
Shit Happens, 5.9, 378
Shit It's A Brit, 5.8, 476
Shit Sandwich, 5.9, 276
Shock the Poodle, 5.9, 425
Shongo Pavi, 5.10c, 483
Shooting Gallery, 5.10b, 117
Shooting Gallery Direct, 5.10a, 117
Shooting Star, 5.11a, 290
Short and Crank, 5.10b, 440
Short But Slared, 5.10b, 59
Short But Sweet, 5.9, 178
Short Cake, 5.10a, 474
SHORT CAKE ROCKS, 474
Short Crack, 5.10a, 440
Short Crack, 5.4, 508
Short Flake, 5.6, 474
SHORT ROCK, 165
Short Stop, 5.10a, 113
SHORT WALL, 536-537
SHORTER WALL, 98-99
Shovling-Cole, 5.10b, 186
Shower Scene, 5.10c, 63
Shut Up and Climb, 5.10a, 173
SHUTTLE ROCK, 538
Sicker Than Jezouin, 5.10d, 237
Sideburn, 5.12a, 69
Sidekick, 5.10, 387
SIDEKICK BOULDER, 387
Sidewinder, 5.10b, 212
Sigalert, 5.11a (TR), 96

Silent But Deadly, 5.11b, 515
Silent But Deadly, 5.9 R, 98
Silent Scream, 5.10a, 515
Silkworm, 5.6, 95
Silverado, 5.11b, 431
SILVERADO AREA, 431
Simba, 5.10d, 510
Simpatico, 5.1, 33
Simple Simon, 5.11c, 402
Sin City, 5.10c, 244
Sinbad the Salor, 5.10c (TR), 419
Sine Wave, 5.9, 62
Sinner's Swing, 5.10b (TR), 244
Sit Up and Think, 5.9+, 402
Sitting Around the Campfire Telling Fish Stories, 5.10a (TR), 216
Sitting Bull, 5.10b, 68
Sitting Here in Limbo, 5.9, 237
Six-Gun By My Side, 5.10a, 543
Six-Pack Crack, 5.10b, 144
Skeptic, The, 5.10c, 123
Sketches of Strain, 5.10d, 469
SKI SLOPE, THE, 410
Skid Row, 5.10d R, 520
Skin and Bones, 5.4 R, 27
Skin Deep Town, 5.6, 393
SKIN GRAFT, THE, 58
Skin of the Teeth, The, 5.12d, 364
Skinny Dip, 5.7 R, 212
Skinny Pin, 5.4, 212
Skintight Mousehouse, 5.11d, 319
Skinwalker, 5.10c, 214
Skip Slidin' Away, 5.10c R, 439
SKY KING ROCK, 436
SKYSCRAPER ROCK, 406
SLAB CANYON, 325
SLAB DOME, 345
Slab Happy, 5.9, 345
Slam Dance, 5.10c, 463
Slam Dunk, 5.11+, 190
Slam Dunk, 5.8, 526
Slammer, The, 5.10b, 450
SLANTA CLAUS ROCK, 164
Slanta Claus, Center, 5.10a, 164
Slanta Claus, Left, 5.7, 164
Slanta Claus, Right, 5.8, 164
Slap and Tickle, 5.10b, 348
Slap Prancing, 5.8+, 26
SLATANIC AREA, 549
Slaves of Fashion, 5.12b, 301
Sleek Beak, 5.10/11, 470
Slightly Ahead of Our Time, 5.12a, 369
Slightly Out of Our Minds, 5.11d, 540
Slim Pickings, 5.10b, 362
Slimmer Pickins, 5.10d, 362
Slip and Slide, 5.11c (TR), 152
Slip Skrig, 5.10c, 319
Slipper When Wet, 5.7, 213
Slow Mutants, 5.11a, 59
SLUMP ROCK, 142
Slushie, 5.10b, 131
Small Business, 5.11a, 123
Small But Short, 5.8, 178
Small Town Taste, 5.10c (TR), 393
Small World, 5.8, 394
SMALL WORLD AREA, 394
SMALL WORLD CLIFF, 394
Smart Missile, 5.10a R, 457
Smarter Than the Average Ranger, 5.11a, 85
Smear Tactics, 5.10c, 194
Smiles for the Grim Reaper, 5.10c, 494
SMITH ROCK, 60
Smithereens, 5.9, 98

Smoke and Mirrors, 5.11d, 307
Smoke-a-Bowl, 5.9, 126
Smooth As Silk, 5.7, 95
Snaggletooth, 5.9, 493
Snake Bite, 5.11c, 339
Snake Book, 5.11b, 501
SNAKE DOME, 159
SNAKE PIT, THE, 307
SNAKE PIT, THE, 462
Snakes in the Grass, 5.9 (TR), 533
Snakeye Pillar, 5.7, 551
Snap on Demand, 5.11d, 178
Snatch, The, 5.10a, 240
Sneak Preview, 5.9, 503
Snicker Biscuit, 5.11b, 83
SNICKERS, 252
SNICKERS, 256-257
Snitch in Time, A, 5.8, 523
Snnfchtt, 5.8, 152
Snoops, 5.6, 512
SNOOZE ROCK, 27
SNORKLE DOME, 420
Snow Falls, 5.9, 272
So Another 5.3, 5.3, 446
So High, B1 X, 176
SO HIGH BOULDER, 176
So Hole Lo, 5.7 R/X, 351
Soar Eagle, B1+, 367
Socrates Sucks, 5.10c (TR), 535
Soft Cell, 5.11a, 269
Soft Core, 5.9, 273
Software Sluts, 5.10c R, 428
Solar Flare, 5.9, 38
Solar Technology, 5.6, 105
Solar Wind, 5.8, 314
Sole Food, 5.10a, 139
Sole Fusion, 5.12a, 245
Solid Gold, 5.10a, 290
Solitary Confinement, 5.11b, 240
Solo, 5.8, 151
Solo Dog, 5.11b, 239
Solo-Arium, 5.7 X, 198
Solosby, 5.10b, 171
SOLOSBY FACE, 171
Solstice, 5.10c, 284
Soma, 5.8, 392
Some Like It Hot, 5.12c, 169
Something Heinous, 5.9, 470
Something or Other, 5.11b (TR), 350
Something's Burning, 5.11b, 394
Sometimes We Crack Ourselves Up, 5.7+, 326
Son of Obsidian, 5.11c, 470
Song of the Siren, 5.10c, 445
Sonic Temple, 5.11c, 501
Sorta High, 5.11+ R, 176
Soul Kitchen, 5.11a, 330
Soul Research, 5.9, 138
Souls of Black, 5.11d, 252
Sound Asleep, 5.10b, 35
Sound of Grains Snapping, The, 5.4, 389
Sound of One Hand Slapping, The, 5.11c, 305
Sound of One Shoe Tapping, The, 5.8, 233
Sound of Rasha's Ears Flapping, The, 5.10b, 389
Sound of Waves, The, 5.11b (TR), 322
Soup Rhymes With Poop, 5.8+, 348
South Arete, 5.12a (TR), 238
SOUTH ASTRO DOME, 289
SOUTH ASTRO DOME, 295
South Buttress, 5.7, 520
SOUTH DAKOTA DOME, 258
South End of a Northbound Poodle, 5.8, 258
South Face, 5.10, 190
South Face, 5.11 R, 176

South Face, 5.7 (TR), 394
South Face Center, 5.9 (TR), 370
South Face Direct, 5.7, 310
South Face Route, 5.9, 532
South of Heaven, 5.12d, 549
SOUTH SIDE, 441
South Swell, 5.9, 322
SOUTH TOWER, 316
Southeast Corner, 5.3, 184
Southwest Arete, 5.11, 176
Southwest of Nowhere, 5.4 or 5.8, 327
Southwest Passage, 5.8, 186
Southwest Problem, 5.10+, 193
Souvenir, 5.10d, 181
SOUVENIR ROCK, 181
Soviet Union, 5.11c, 39
Sow Sickle, 5.11d, 136
Space Metal, 5.10a, 480
Space Mountain, 5.10b, 377
Space Odyssey, 5.10b R, 362
Space Slot, 5.10a, 251
Space Walk, 5.8, 128
Spaced Mountain, 5.8, 308
Spacely Sprockets, 5.8, 307
Spaghetti & Chili, 5.7, 206
Spaghetti Sauce Sunset, 5.10c, 40
Spaghetti Western , 5.11d, 546
Spam and Cheese, 5.11a (TR), 142
Span-nish Fly, 5.8, 207
Spanish Bayonet, 5.9, 538
Spank the Monkey, 5.10b, 406
Spanking, 5.11c (TR), 67
Sparkle, 5.8 (TR), 416
Speculator, The, 5.11d, 49
Speculum Scrapings, 5.11b, 287
Sphincter Quits, 5.9, 154
SPHINX, THE, 259
Spider, 5.8, 188
Spider Line, 5.11c, 188
Spider's Web, 5.8, 519
Spiderman, 5.10a, 445
Spinal Tap, 5.9, 482
Spinner, 5.7 R, 115
Spire Route, 5.5, 59
Spirit of the Dead, 5.8, 373
Spiritworld, 5.10c, 342
Spitwad, 5.10a, 98
Splatter Proof, 5.10 R, 146
Split, 5.6, 156
SPLIT DOME, 455
Split Mitten, 5.6, 421
Split Personality, 5.11d, 374
Split Personality, 5.9, 98
SPLIT PERSONALITY ROCK, 374
SPLIT ROCK, 453
SPLIT ROCKS AREA, 453
Splotch, 5.6, 156
Spontaneous Human Combustion, 5.11c, 97
Spoodle, 5.9, 127
SPORTS CHALLENGE ROCK, 154-155
Spread & Butter, 5.10b, 469
Spring or Fall, 5.11b, 277
Spud Overhang, 5.10b R, 517
Spud Patrol, 5.7, 206
Spur of the Moment, The, 5.12a, 458
Spy Hole, 5.11a, 349
SPY TOWER, 349
Spy vs Spry, 5.11c, 349
Squat Rockets, 5.4, 530
Squatter's Right, 5.10d, 130
SQUAW TANK, 421
Squeeze Play, 5.10a, 471
Squeeze Play, 5.8, 309

Squid of My Desire, 5.10a, 329
Squirrel Roast, 5.8, 254
Squirt, 5.9, 387
Stable Girl, 5.11 (TR), 47
Stainless Steel Rat, 5.10b, 144
Stains of the Stars, 5.10a, 87
Staircase Crack, 5.4, 512
Stairway to Heaven, 5.12a (TR), 205
Stan and Ollie, 5.7, 445
Stand and Deliver, 5.12a, 223
Stand By Me, 5.10a (TR), 224
Stand Up For You Rights, 5.10+, 149
Standing Ovation, 5.10a, 401
STAR TREK TOWER, 480
STAR WARS ROCK, 415
Stardust Memories, 5.9+, 50
Stargazer, 5.10b, 260
Start Fumbling, 5.10d R, 95
Start Trundling, 5.10a, 95
Statue of Elvis on Mars, 5.10b, 470
Steady Breeze, 5.7 X, 537
Steep Pulse, 5.12 (TR), 144
Steeped T, 5.8, 83
Stegasaurus, 5.9, 486
Stem Gem, 5.11+, 190
STEM GEM BOULDER, 190
Stem Gem Mantel, B1, 190
Stemngo, 5.10c (TR), 386
Stems and Seeds, 5.1d, 364
Stemski, 5.6, 451
Stemulation, 5.9 R, 35
Step 'n Out, 5.10a, 536
Step Function, 5.11b, 352
Steppin' Out, 5.10a, 340
Stepping Out of Babylon, 5.9, 71
Stepping Razor, 5.10b, 71
STEPPING STONES, THE, 71
Steps Ahead, 5.10c, A1, 71
Stereo in B Flat, 5.10d (TR), 308
STEVE CANYON, 208-213
Stichter Quits, 5.7, 242
Stick to the Plan, 5.10c R, 354
Stick To What, 5.9, 242
Still, The, 5.10c, 433
Stinger, 5.10a (TR), 486
Stingray, 5.13d, 330
Stinkbug, The, 5.10b, 246
STIRRUP ROCK — NORTH FACE, 485
STIRRUP ROCK — SOUTH FACE, 484
STIRRUP TANK AREA, 479
STIRRUP TOWERS, 479
STIRRUP, THE, 480
Stoli Driver, 5.10d, 261
Stone Hinge, 5.11b, 68
Stone Idol, 5.11d R, 290
STONEHENGE BOULDERS, THE, 367
Stood Up, 5.8, 160
Stop Grumbling, 5.8, 95
Stop Making Sense, 5.11a, 95
Stop Trundling, 5.10a, 95
Straight Flus, 5.8, 196
Straight Jacket, 5.10c, 374
Straight Out Of Compton, 5.11d, 345
Strain Gauge, 5.10c, 135
Strange Attracter, The, 5.12a, 473
Strange Kind of Love, 5.11a, 471
Straw Man, 5.10c, 494
Strawberry Jam, 5.9, 196
Street Sweeper, 5.11c, 245
Streetcar Named Desire, B1+, 271
Stress Puppet, 5.10a, 375
Strike It Rich, 5.10a, 289
String 'em Up, 5.11c, 546

Strip Search, 5.10c, 455
Stucca By A Yucca, 5.7, 132
Stud Muffin, 5.10b, 507
Studebaker Hawk, 5.10c, 138
Student Unrest, 5.6, 216
Sublimination, 5.10a, 76
Subway to Venus, 5.11c/d, 359
Such a Line, 5.10d, 439
Such a Poodle, 5.8+, 126
Such A Savage, 5.11a, 290
Sudden Death, 5.10a, 111
Suffering Catfish, 5.10b, 283
Sugar Daddy, 5.7, 140
Sugar Daddy, 5.9, 254
SUICIDE HORN ROCK, 71
Suite Sister Mary, 5.7 R, 510
Sullivan from Colorado, 5.9, 378
Summer School, 5.10a, 129
SUMMIT OR PLUMMET ROCK, 137
Sun Bowl, 5.13a, 257
Sun City, 5.11a, 244
Sun Proff, 5.8+, 355
SUN PROFF WALL, THE, 355
Sunday Papers, 5.10b, 179
SUNLIGHT ROCK, 402
SUNSET ROCK, 153
Sunset Strip, 5.9, 153
Super Beak of the Desert, 5.9, 470
SUPER BLOCK, THE, 69
SUPER CREEPS WALL, 104
SUPER DOME, THE, 68
SUPER HEROS WALL, 104
Super Monster Killer, 5.11a, 211
Super Quickie, 5.12b, 163
Super Roof, 5.9, 210
Super Spy, 5.11d (TR), 174
Supercollider, 5.8, 67
SUPERCOLLIDER ROCK, 67
Superfluous Bolt, 5.6, 327
Supreme Court or Conservative Rubber Stamp?, 5.10b, 481
Surf's Up, 5.10, 270
Surface Tension, 5.10d, 205
SURPRISE ROCK, 304
Surrealistic Colgate, 5.10d (TR), 420
Surrealistic Pillar, 5.10b, 192
Suzanna's Bandana, 5.7, 470
Suzie's Cream Squeeze, 5.6, 222
Suzie's Lip Cheeze, 5.9, 222
Svapada, 5.11b, 314
SW Corner, 5.6, 370
SW Face, 5.8, 263
Swain in the Breeze, 5.6, 120
Swain Lake, 5.5 R, 120
Swain Song, 5.11a, 120
Swain-Buckey, 5.10d, 250
Swaino Vista, 5.8+ R (TR), 350
Swatchbuckler, 5.8, 121
Sweat Band, 5.10c, 524
Sweat Pants, 5.11a, 524
Sweet Eternity, 5.11c R, 256
Sweet Ginger, 5.11b, 256
Sweet Transvestite, 5.8 R, 96
Sweetspot, B1, 185
Swept Away, 5.11a, 245
Swidgeteria, The, 5.9, 137
SWIDGETERIA, THE, 137
Swidgets Requierd, 5.10b, 137
Swift, 5.11a, 116
Swift, The, 5.7, 101
Swimming in a Sea of Deception, 5.10b, 256
Swishbah, 5.7, 534
Swiss Cheese, 5.6, 99
Symbolic of Life, 5.11a, 153

Sympathy to the Devil, 5.10b, 186
T-N-T, 5.10c, 264
T. Gordon Liddy, 5.11a, 264
T.S. Special, 5.9 R, 245
T1000, B1, 367
Tabby Litter, 5.8, 188
Tail Gunner, 5.11b, 58
TAILINGS, THE, 425
Tails of Poodles, 5.10a, 124
Take A seat , 5.10b, 250
Take Five, 5.8, 392
Take It For Granite, 5.10c, 261
Take Two, They're Small, 5.9, 316
Taken for Granite, 5.8, 550
Tales of Brave Ulysses, 5.9, 170
Tales of Powder, 5.10b, 104
Talking About My Variation, 5.9, 35
Talking Fish, The, 5.10d, 96
Talon Show, 5.12c (TR), 442
Talon, The, 5.12c, 315
Talus Phallus, 5.6, 139
Taming of the Shoe, The, 5.10d R, 116
Tang, 5.5, 165
Tanning Salon, 5.4, 58
Tap Dancing, 5.11a R, 26
Tar, 5.10d, 442
TAR AND FEATHERS BOULDER, 442
Tar Face, 5.10b (TR), 337
Taraan, 5.11b, 244
Tarantula, 5.2, 479
Tarantula, The, 5.12c, 169
Tarawassie Wiggel, 5.10b, 524
TARGET ROCK, 373
Tasgrainian Devel, 5.9, 112
Taunting Fear, 5.11d, 425
Taurus, 5.6, 105
Tax Free, 5.10d R, 130
Tax Man, 5.10a, 130
Taxed to the Limit, 5.12a, 49
Tchalk Is Cheap, 5.10d, 59
Team Scumbag, 5.10b, 248
Team Slug, 5.10b, 242
Tears, 5.9, 523
TECHULATOR, THE, 59
Teddy, 5.9, 54
Teen Steam, 5.10b, 383
Teenage Enema, 5.9 (TR), 416
Teenage Mutant Ninja Brits, 5.10a, 534
TEEPEE ROCK, 436
Teeter Totter , 5.9, 25
Telegram for Mongo, 5.10c R, 205
Telekinesis, 5.11c or 5.10a, 64
TELEVISION WALL, 393-394
Tell Me I'm Not Dreaming, 5.9, 304
Ten Conversations At Once, 5.10a, 242
Tender Flakes of Wrath, 5.7, 44
Tennis Shoe Crack, 5.8, 210
Tequila, 5.10d (TR), 222
Terminator, B1, 367
TERMINATOR BOULDER, 144
Terminator, The, 5.9, 362
Terminator, The, B1, 144
Terror in De Skies, 5.10a R, 100
Test Pilot, 5.10b, 550
Test Tube Baby, 5.8+, 344
Texas Big Hair, 5.9+, 285
That, 5.10b, 385
THAT LITTLE DOODAD BOULDER UNIT, 421
That Old Soft Shoe, 5.10d, 473
That's Powell Not Rowell, 5.10a, 348
The Awfulwidth, 5.8 R, 41
The Bone Club, 5.10a R, 25
THE BROWNIE GIRL DOME, 46

The Chicken Ranch, 5.6, 47
The Chief, 5.5, 44
The Falcon and the Snowman, 5.10b, 242
The Gear Thief, 5.6, 29
The Great Escape, 5.11d, 52
The Podium of Indecision, 5.10b, 29
The Right Hand Dike, 5.10a, 29
The Trough, 5.0, 33
THE WART WEST FACE, 153
THEORETICAL BOULDER, 377
Therapeutic Tyranny, 5.11a, 459
There and Back Again, 5.4 R, 402
There Goes The Bride, 5.10a, 329
There Is No Place Like Home, 5.10c R, 491
They Found Hitler's Brain, 5.12b, (, 113
Thin Air, 5.9, 385
Thin Flakes, 5.9, 113
Thin Is In, 5.9, 426
Thin Man's Nightmare, 5.9, 276
Thin Red Line, 5.12b R, 205
Thin Spin, 5.8, 29
THIN WALL, THE, 166
Thing, The, 5.10a, 130
Third Bolt from the Sun, 5.11a, 109
Third Time's A Charm, 5.10b, 522
Third World, 5.9, 111
Thirteen Cheeps, 5.10b, 497
This Is Only A Test, 5.12a to d, 381
This Puppy, 5.6, 392
This Scud's A Dud, 5.10d, 457
This Scud's For You, 5.11a, 457
This Spud's For You, 5.10c, 64
Thomson Roof, 5.9, 44
Thomson's Acne, 5.10b (TR), 44
Thrash or Crash, 5.9, 241
Thrasher, 5.9, 538
Three Amigos, The, 5.8, 319
Three Best Friends You Ever Had, The, 5.10c, 135
Three Bolts Closer to Divorce, 5.10b, 385
Three Burner Stove, 5.10b, 160
Three Men and A Baby, 5.12b, 276
Three Musketeers, The, 5.7+, 254
THREE PILE ISLAND, 148
Three Swidgeteers, 5.2, 137
Thrill of Desire, The, 5.12c, 75
Throat Warbler Mangrove, 5.9 R, 293
Throbbing Gristle, 5.12a (TR), 471
THRONE OF THE MATRIARCH, 342
THRONE OF THE MONKEY KING, 342
Through the Hole and Up the Wall, 5.2, 415
Thrutcher, 5.7, 308
THRUTCHER DOME, 308
THRUTCHER DOME, 310
Thumb, The, 5.6, 421
Thumbs Down Left, 5.9, 415
Thumbs Up, 5.10a, 79
Thunderclap, 5.10a, 413
Tic Tic Boom, 5.12a, 170
Ticket to Nowhere, 5.8, 206
Tidal Wave, B1+, 228
Tidbit, 5.10a, 471
Tidy Bowl, 5.10d, 450
Tied to the Whipping Post, 5.11a, 538
TIERRA INCOGNITO, 476
Tiers for Fears, 5.10d, 433
Tige, 5.8, 46
TIGER ROCKS, 467
Tigers on Vaseline, 5.9, 309
Tight Shoes, 5.7 R, 537
Tights Camera Action, 5.11a 9TR), 197
Til Death Do Us Fart, 5.10d, 513
Till Death Do Us Part, 5.9 (TR), 279
TIMBUKTU TOWERS, 62

Time and A Half, 5.10d, 214
Time Avenger, 5.11b, 307
Time To Take The Garbage Out, 5.10a, 317
TIMELESS VOID CLUMP, 392
Times of Holyness, 5.11c, 430
Tin God, 5.10d, 247
Tinker Toys, 5.10b, 97
Tiny Terra, 5.10b (TR), 394
TINY TOTS ROCK, 97
Tipples in Rime, 5.10a (TR), 393
Tiptoe, 5.7+, 33
TIRE TREAD WALL, 106
TITANIC, THE, 419
TKO, 5.10c, 138
TM's Terror, 5.10b, 237
To Air Is Human, 5.10d R, 92
To Hold and to Have, 5.12c (TR), 406
Toad Crack, 5.9, 274
TOAD ROCK,
Toad Warrior, 5.10b (Var.), 76
Toad Warriors, 5.12b R, 153
Tobin Bias, 5.6, 250
Todd Couple, The, 5.10c, 83
Todd Squad, The, 5.11a, 338
Todd's Hardcover, 5.10b (TR), 179
Toe Jam, 5.7, 188
Toe Jam Express, 5.3, 537
Toe the Line, 5.9, 533
Toffied Ear Wax, 5.9, 406
Tofu the Dwarf, 5.9, 233
Tom Bombadil, 5.7, 369
TOM SAWYER'S ISLAND, 419
Tomato Amnesia, 5.10, 321
Tombstone, The, 5.11c, 74
TOMBSTONE, THE, 74
Tonic Boom, 5.12d, 170
Tons of Junk, A3, 136
Too Bold To Bolt, 5.8, 242
Too Loose to Trek, 5.10b, 220
Too Old To Bolt, 5.10b (TR), 242
Too Secret to Find, 5.10d, 51
Too Silly to Climb, 5.5, 50
Too Strong and a Tweener, 5.11a, 364
Too Thin for Poodles, 5.10c, 59
Too Wide to Trot, 5.10c, 439
Tooth Decay, 5.11c, 364
TOOTH, THE, 521
Toothpick, The, 5.11c (TR), 123
Tootsie Pop, 5.9+, 351
Top 40 to Middle Toile, 5.9, 247
TOP BLOCK, THE, 351
Top Flight, 5.10a, 102
Top Guns, 5.11a, 301
Top Hat, 5.10d R, 364
Top Hat, 5.11+ (TR), 298
TOP HAT ROCK, 364
Top of the Pops, 5.10, 98
Top-Topic, 5.8, 480
Topper, 5.12a (TR), 374
Toprope Conversion, 5.11+, 219
TORRE DEL SOL, 477
Tortoise and the Dog, The, 5.10b R, 456
Tortoise Skeleton Crack, 5.9+, 436
Tortuga, 5.11b, 405
TORTUGA, THE, 405
Torturers Apprentice, 5.10b, 247
Tossed Green, 5.10a, 36
Total Generic Package, 5.11c (TR), 462
Totally Nuts, 5.9 R, 96
Totally Tubular, 5.8, 470
Toto, 5.10b, 494
TOTO BOULDER, 494
Toto's Canine Hot Lunch, 5.8, 491

Touch and Go, 5.9, 241
TOUCH AND GO FACE, 241
Touche Away, 5.9, 174
TOWER 1, 174
TOWER 2, 174
TOWER 3, 174
Tower of Babel, 5.10d, 114
Tower of Cleanliness, 5.10b, 76
Tower of Godliness, 5.10a, 76
TOWER OF POWER, 344
TOWER ROCKS, 345
Towering Inferno, The, 5.11c, 301
TOWERS OF UNCERTAINTY, 397
TOWERS, THE, 430
TOWERS, THE, 430
Toxic Avenger, 5.10a, 525
Toxic Avenger, 5.10d, 44
Toxic Poodle, 5.10b, 525
Toxic Waltz, 5.12a, 131
Toxic Wasteland, 5.10d, 256
Tractor Pull, 5.8, 479
Tragic Kingdom, 5.8 A1, 308
Trail of Tiers, 5.10a, 399
Training for Patagonia, 5.10b R, 99
TRAINING GROUND, THE, 310
Transfusion, 5.12a, 73
Transquility, 5.6, 522
Transylvania Twist, 5.10d R, 473
Trap Door, 5.6, 481
Trapeze, 5.11d, 183
Trapeze Center, 5.12a, 183
Trapeze Left, 5.12c, 183
TRASHCAN ROCK, 31-33
Trashman Roof, 5.9, 388
Trautner-Fry, 5.10c R, 535
Traverse of No Return, 5.11a, 186
Treadmark Left, 5.8, 106
Treadmark Right, 5.8, 106
Treasure of the Sierra Madre, 5.10d, 348
TREINTE ANOS, 5.10B (TR), 189
Trembling Toes, 5.9, 304
Trench Connection, 5.6, 397
TRES AMIGOS CLIFF, 319
Tres Equis, 5.8, 520
Tres Fun, 5.10a, 49
Trespassers Will Be Violated, 5.10c, 247
Tri-Step, 5.8, 207
Trial by Fire, 5.7, 482
Trial Separation, 5.10d, 355
TRIANGLE BOULDER, 190
Triathlon, 5.11c (TR), 155
Trick of the Tail, 5.10a, 476
Tricky Move, 5.10a, 470
Trident, 5.10c, 105
TRIFLING ROCK, 327
Triple Bypass`, 5.10b, 543
Trivial Pursuit, 5.7, 327
Trivial Tower, 5.9, 327
Troglodyte Crack, 5.8, 79
Trough, The, 5.0, 242
Trowel and Error, 5.9, 298
True Democracy, 5.9, 314
True Dice, 5.10a R, 445
True Grit, 5.11+, 146
True Grit, 5.9, 474
Truly Snooty Furniture, 5.10a, 314
Truth or Dare, 5.8 R, 510
Try Agan, 5.10c, 242
Try It, You'll like It, 5.10a, 250
Tube Steak, 5.10c, 163
Tube, The, 5.10b, 317
Tubers in Space, 5.4, 206
Tubular, 5.9 (TR), 418

Tubular Balls, 5.10b, 261
Tucson Bound, 5.8, 50
Tulip, 5.6 R/X, 33
Tumbleweed, 5.6, 508
Tumbling Dice, 5.10a, 362
Tumbling Rainbow, 5.9 R, 170
TUMBLING RAINBOW FORMATION, 170
Tuna and Cheese, 5.8, 142
Turbolator, B1, 367
Turd, The, 5.11c, 244
Turkey Terror, 5.9 (TR), 393
Turnbuckle, 5.11+, 176
TURNBUCKLE BOULDER, 176
Turtle Classic, 5.11+, 176
Turtle Days, 5.8, 74
Turtle Know, B1, 176
TURTLE ROCK, 172
TURTLE ROCK BOULDERING, 176
Turtle Soup, 5.3, 173
Turtle Vein, 5.8, 455
TV Tower, 5.9, 394
TVC15, 5.9 R, 248
Tweener in Trouble, 5.8, 364
Tweeners Out for Glory, 5.6, 364
Twins, 5.7, 140
Twisted Crystals, 5.11a, 200
Twisties, 5.9 R, 229
Twittish Empire, 5.11b, 465
Two Against Everest (aka: On the Back), 5.11c, 24
Two Blind Mice, 5.10, 415
TWO BOLT ROCK, 397
Two Bolt Wall, 5.9, 397
Two Flew the Coop, 5.11a (TR), 252
Two Left Feet, 5.9, 73
Two Lost Soles, 5.8, 67
Two Our Surprise, 5.9, 40
Two Point Crack, 5.1, 473
Two Scoops Please, 5.10c R, 197
Two Stage, 5.10a, 170
Tyrannosaurus Rex, 5.9, 197
U.B. Kool, 5.10d, 114
Uh Cult, The, 5.10a (TR), 92
Ulysses's Bivouac, 5.8, 205
Unbearable Lightness of Being, The, 5.9, 379
Uncertainty Principal, 5.10a, 384
Uncle Fester, 5.10d, 92
Uncle Remus, 5.11b, 108
UNCLE REMUS, 108
Unconscious Obscenity, 5.9, 298
Under 6'2", Don't Know What You'll Do, 5.11a to 5.12a (TR), 156
Under a Blood Red Sky, 5.12a (TR), 430
Under a Raging Moon, 5.10b, 59
Undercling Bypass, 5.8, 58
Undertow, 5.11, 203
Underwear Bandit, The, 5.10a, 310
UNFORSEEN DOME, 304
Ungawaa, 5.11a, 382
Unicorner, 5.8, 377
Unknown Grain, 5.10a R, 524
Unknown Highway, A1, 532
Unknown Route, The, 5.10a R, 293
Unknown Soldier, 5.11b, 293
Unsolved Mystery, 5.10d, 248
Untie em, 5.8, 497
Unwed Muddlers, 5.7, 391
Unwiped Butt, 5.6, 105
Unzipper, 5.10+ (TR), 242
Up 20, 5.11 R, 367
Up 40, 5.11b R/X, 364
Up and Down, 5.10a, 439
Up Chuck, 5.7, 373
Up The Ante, 5.11d (TR), 108

Up to Heaven, 5.8 R/X, 537
Upevil, 5.6, 476
Upper Cow, 5.10a, 163
UPPER COW ROCK, 163
UPPER DODGE CITY, 546
Upper Right Ski Track, 5.3, 183
Upsidedown Pineapple, The, 5.11+, 201
Urban Redevelopment, 5.8, 139
Urine Trouble, 5.8, 263
Use a Gun, Go to Jail, 5.9+, 392
Use It Or Loose It, 5.10c, 193
V Cracks, 5.8, 418
Vagabonds, 5.8 R, 29
Vagmarken Buttress, 5.7, 29
VAGMARKEN HILL, 28-30
Vaino's Crack, 5.10c, 144
Vaino's Lost in Pot, 5.7 R.X, 515
Val De Mello, 5.10b, 531
VALLE DE DUCK, 511
VALLEY OF THE DOLLS, 344
VALLEY OF THE KINGS, 471
VALLEY OF VOICES, THE, 496
Vanio's Renegade Lead, 5.10a, 392
Vanishing Desert, 5.8, 475
Vanishing Point, 5.12b, 136
VARNISHED WALL, 529
Varsity Crank Problem, 5.11, 190
Vector, 5.11c, 468
VECTOR ROCK, 468
Velveeta Rabbit, The, 5.7, 112
Venucian Fece, 5.11a (TR), 212
Vertical Corrector, 5.11a, 523
VETO ROCK, 475
Vice President, 5.10b R, 314
Vicki the Visitor, 5.10b, 148
Violent Cooking, 5.10a, 455
Viper, 5.13b, 319
Viper, The, 5.10c, 307
VIRGIN ISLANDS AREA, 410
VIRGIN PILE, 418
Visual Nightmare, 5.10a, 362
Visualize World Peace, 5.10c, 373
Viva Las Vegas, 5.11 (TR), 47
Vivaldi Kazoo Concerts, Boyd Beaver, Soloist, 5.9, 277
Vogel Crack, 5.8, 411
Vogels Are Poodles Too, 5.11b (TR), 122
VOICE'S CRAG, 82
VOLANCO BOULDER, 412
VOLCANO, THE, 412
Volga Boat Men, 5.8, 41
VOODOO DOME, 493
Vorpal Sword, 5.9, 105
Vortex, 5.10a, 73
Vulgar Boot Men, 5.8, 41
Vulture's Roost, 5.9, 55
VULTURE'S ROOST, 55
W.A.C., 5.8, 233
Wacko Placko, 5.10d, 471
Wage and Price Ceiling, 5.10d (TR), 251
Wailing Sax, 5.9, 393
WAILING SAX WALL, 392
WAILING WALL, THE, 158
Wait Until Dark, 5.10b, 392
Waiting for Alan, 5.4, 477
Waiting for the Sun, 5.8, 477
Wake Me When It's Over, 5.8 X, 41
Walk of Fame, 5.10c, 503
Walk on the Steep Side, 5.10, 378
Walk on the Wild Side, 5.7+, 378
Walk on Water, 5.12b/c, 218
Walk the Plank, 5.11, 217
Walker Spur, 5.10a, 164
Walking Pneumonia, 5.11b R/X, 290

Walking the Dog, 5.9, 493
Walkway, 5.4 R, 33
WALL AREA BOULDERING, THE, 198-199
Wall of 10,000 Hold, 5.4 R, 121
WALL OF ABSURDITIES, 510
WALL OF BIBLICAL FALLACIES, 218
Wall Street, 5.9, 141
WALL STREET, 141
WALL, THE, 197-198
Wallaby Crack, 5.8, 32
Wallflower, 5.10a, 198
Wally Gator, 5.11, 88
Wally George, 5.9, 364
WALLY WORLD, 364
Walrus-Like and Wimpy, 5.8 R, 141
Walt's Frozen Head, 5.10b, 308
WALT's ROCKS, 352
Walt's Solo, 5.8, 428
Waltzing Worm, 5.12a, 104
Wandering Tortoise, 5.3, 173
Wandering Winnebago, 5.8+ R, 522
WANE'S WALL, 58
Wangerbanger, 5.11c, 229
Wanna Bong, 5.9, 377
Wanton Soup, 5.10a (TR), 39
War Baby, 5.10a (TR), 481
War Crimes, 5.10a, 82
War Games, 5.10a, 283
Warp Factor, 5.11c R, 140
Warpath, 5.12c, 68
Warrior Eagle, 5.12B, 79
Washoe Crack, 5.11a, 450
Wasting Assets, 5.6, 285
Watanobe Wall, 5.10a, 208
Watasillywall, 5.11b (TR), 208
WATCHA CALL IT PILLAR, 350
Water Moccasin, 5.4, 533
WATERGATE ROCK, 264
Watershute, The, 5.10b, 185
WATTS TOWERS, 139
Watusi, The, 5.12c, 225
Waugh Crack, 5.10b, 411
WAVE BOULDER, 176
Wavecrest, 5.12a, 322
WAVECREST ROCK, 322
WAY GONE DOME, 331
Way It Should Be, The, 5.10a, 277
Wayward Hayward, 5.10b, 328
We Dive at Dawn, 5.8, 530
We Don't Need No Stinking Badges, 5.11b, 358
We Must, We Must, We Must Improve Our Bust, 5.11b, 135
We'll Get Them Little Pricks, 5.8, 445
Weak Force, The, 5.10a, 310
Weathering Frights, 5.9, 35
WEDDING BLOCK, THE, 329
Wedge, 5.4, 447
WEDGE AREA, THE, 446
WEDGE BOULDER, 176
WEDGE, THE, 447
Wedlock, 5.11a, 464
Wee-Wee, The, 5.10c, 207
Weekend Warrior, 5.11a, 76
Weenie Roast, 5.11a, 306
WEENIE, THE, 306
Welcome to Joshua Tree, 5.10c, 260
West Arete, 5.9, 226
West Chimney, 5.6, 187
West Face, 5.10b (TR), 394
West Face, 5.9, 521
WEST FACE, 327
WEST FACE, 461
West Face Center, B1, 190
West Face Overhang, 5.7, 200

WEST SIDE, 441
WEST TIERS, 457
WEST WORLD, 330
Western Saga, 5.9, 167
Westward Ho!, 5.2, 450
Wet Pigeon, 5.8, 105
Wet Pigeon, 5.8, 105
Wet Rock Day, 5.10d (TR), 217
Wet T-Shirt Night, 5.11c, 217
Wetlands President, The, 5.10d, 475
Wha A Joke, 5.8, 326
Whale of a Time, 5.8+, 53
Whales On Ice, 5.10a, 308
What, 5.8, 385
What a Shame, 5.9/10, 67
What Does The Inside of Your Nose Smell Like, 5.4, 510
What Is The Question?, 5.10d, 319
What's Hannen, 5.10a, 98
What's It To You, 5.10d, 154
What's Left, 5.9, 391
Whatchasay Dude, 5.11a, 174
Wheat Beri-Beri, 5.11c R, 312
Wheat Chex, 5.7, 533
Wheel of Fortune, 5.11b, 310
Wheer Sheep Ran Scared, 5.10c, 392
When Ligthning Strikes, 5.10c, 447
When Love Came to Town, 5.11c, 471
When Sheep Ran Scared, 5.10c, 187
When Two Become Three, 5.8, 121
When You're A Jet, 5.11c (TR), 256
When You're A Sancho, 5.11 (TR), 273
When You're Erect, 5.12a, 256
When You're Not A Jet, 5.10b, 256
Where Brownies Dare, 5.10a, 46
Where Eagles Dare, 5.11d, 168
Where Ees De Santa Claus?, 5.10a, 223
Where Janitors Dare, 5.7, 168
Where Two Deserts Meet, 5.8, 477
Where's Baldo?, 5.9, 327
Wheresabolt?, 5.11+ (TR), 76
Which Bitch, 5.9, 40
Which Witch, 5.8, 40
Whipped Topping, 5.11b, 389
Whips and Grains, 5.10b, 47
Whips and Grains, 5.9, 316
Whiskey, 5.6, 517
Whisper When You Scream, 5.9, 402
WHISPERING WALL, THE, 451
Whistling Sphincter, 5.11c (TR), 92
White Bread Fever, 5.11c, 312
WHITE CLIFFS OF DOVER, 38
WHITE CLIFFS, THE, 355
White Collar Crime, 5.8, 264
White Lightning, 5.7, 126
White Line Fever, 5.9, 251
White Mamba, 5.12b, 463
White Mischief, 5.12b, 248
White Powder, 5.7, 36
White Rabbit, 5.10a, 263
White Rain, 5.11a, 353
White Rastafarian, 5.11+ R, 228
WHITE RASTAFARIAN BOULDER, 228
WHITE TANK CAMPGROUND, 476
White Trash, 5.8, 531
Who Came First, 5.9, 447
Who Cares, 5.11a, 350
Who'da Thought, 5.11c (TR), 97
Who's First, 5.6, 515
Who's Next, 5.8, 447
Whoville, 5.8, 139
Why Do We Do This, 5.9, 329
Why Does It Hurt When I Pee?, 5.10b, 98
Wicked Witchcraft, 5.11c, 497

Wide World of Sports, 5.10c, 56
Wild Dream, 5.10d, 483
Wild East, 5.9 R, 237
Wild Gravity, 5.9, 102
WILD GRAVITY FORMATION, 102
Wild Wild West, 5.10d, 543
Wild Wind, 5.9, 156
Willard, 5.7, 287
Willit Hold, 5.8, 532
WILLIT PILLAR, 532
Willit Slab, 5.7, 533
Wilma Rubble, 5.7, 95
Wilson Regular Route, 5.5, 101
Wilted Flower Children, 5.9, 38
WIMP TOWER, THE, 166
Wind Cries Mary, The, 5.7, 437
Wind Sprint, 5.9, 420
Winds of Change, 5.10c (TR), 180
Winds of Whoopee, 5.11a, 180
Wings of Steel, 5.11d, 463
Wingtips, 5.11b (TR), 210
Winning Time, 5.10a, 277
Winter Wine, 5.10c, 445
Winters Moon, 5.11a, 481
Wired, 5.10b, 83
Wise Crack, 5.9, 196
Wisest Crack, 5.7, 379
Wish You Were Here, 5.10c, 250
Witch Hunt, 5.10b, 549
WITCH ROCK, 494
With Malice and Forethought, 5.7, 529
Without A Trace, 5.8 X, 208
WIZARD ROCK, 494
WIZZ SITE, 350
Wokking the Dog, 5.11c (TR), 39
Wolfman, The, 5.10d, 148
Woman's Work Is Never Done, 5.10c, 214
Women and Money, 5.12b (TR), 548
Women in Cages, 5.11c (TR), 47
Won't Get Fooled Again, 5.7, 447
WONDER BLUFFS, 526
Wonderful Wobble, 5.8, 402
Wonderful World of Art, The, 5.10+, 192
WONDERLAND OF ROCKS, 279-331
WONDERLAND VALLEY AREAS, 282
Wooden Nickle, 5.5 R/X, 543
Woodshed, The, 5.11d, 461
Woodward Crack, 5.12a, 411
Woof Woof, 5.10b, 179
Wooly Spider, 5.2, 479
WOOLY SPIDER BOULDER, 479
Working Overtime, 5.9, 214
Working Without A Net, 5.9, 510
Workout at the Y, 5.9, 391
WORKOUT ROCK, 469
Worth Bagley Dihedral, 5.10b, 329
WORTH BAGLEY MEMORIAL DOME, 329
Worthwhile Pile, 5.10a R, 164
WORTHWHILE PILE, 164

Worthy Of It, 5.8, 455
Wrap That Rascal, 5.10b, 551
Wren's Nest, 5.11a, 59
Wuthering Heights, 5.9, 433
X FACTOR DOME, 139
X-Rated Tits, 5.9, 276
Xenalmorph, 5.10c, 430
Y Knot, 5.10b, 391
Yabba-Dabba-Doo, 5.11+, 228
YABLONSKI BOULDER, 149
YABO BOULDERS, 146
Yabo Phone Home, 5.10c, 135
Yabo Roof, 5.11+, 146
Yankee Poodle, 5.7, 233
Yardarm, The, 5.11, 217
Yardy-Hoo and Away, 5.10a, 312
Year After Year, 5.9, 66
YEARLY ROCK, 66
Yei-Bei-Chei Crack, 5.9, 208
Yellow Brick Road, 5.11a, 501
Yet Another Cilley Toprope, 5.11c (TR), 56
Yogi, 5.10c (TR), 85
Yogi the Overbear, 5.10a, 286
Yosemite Sam, 5.4, 104
Young and the Restless, 5.7 R, 393
Young Frankenstein, 5.11a, 104
Young Guns, 5.11d, 463
Young Lust, 5.9, 98
Young Sole Rebel, 5.4, 402
Youth Run Wild, 5.8, 511
Yucca Bowl, 5.6, 474
Yuppies Don't Do Offwidths, 5.9, 471
Zap #4, 5.6, 305
Zardoz, 5.8 R, 384
Zarmog the Dragon Man, 5.10a, 382
ZEBRA CLIFFS, 439
ZEBRA CLIFFS, 440
Zebra Dihedral, 5.10a, 440
Zelda, 5.5, 511
Zen, 5.12b, 316
Zen and the Art of Placement, 5.11c, 406
Zen Goblins, 5.10c, 487
Zigzag, 5.7, 183
Zinging in the Grain, 5.8, 512
Zion Train, 5.10d, 293
ZIPPY ROCK, 483
Zircon, 5.9+, 350
Zoauve Detente, ??, 437
Zola Budd, 5.10d (TR), 56
Zombie Woof, 5.12b, 179
ZOMBIE WOOF ROCK, 179
Zondo's Perks, 5.10a, 244
Zorba, 5.11a R, 317
ZSA ZSA GABOR MEMORIAL BOULDER, 503
Zsa Zsa Goes to Jail, 5.7 R, 40
Zulu Dawn, 5.10d, 192
Zygote, 5.11a, 224
ZZZZZ, 5.9 R, 248